9196

D0753313

THE
COWBOY
ENCYCLOPEDIA

THE
COWBOY
ENCYCLOPEDIA

Richard W. Slatta

ABC-CLIO

Santa Barbara, California
Denver, Colorado
Oxford, England

Copyright © 1994 by Richard W. Slatta and ABC-CLIO

All rights reserved. No part of this publication may be reproduced, stored in a retrieval system, or transmitted, in any form or by any means, electronic, mechanical, photocopying, recording, or otherwise, except for the inclusion of brief quotations in a review, without prior permission in writing from the publishers.

Library of Congress Cataloging-in-Publication Data

Slatta, Richard W., 1947–
      The cowboy encyclopedia / Richard W. Slatta.
         p.   cm.
      Includes bibliographical references and index.
      1. Cowboys—America—Encyclopedias.   2. Cowboys—West (U.S.)—Encyclopedias.
   3. Frontier and pioneer life—America—Encyclopedias.   4. Frontier and pioneer life—
   West (U.S.)—Encyclopedias.   5. America—Social life and customs—Encyclopedias.
   6. West (U.S.)—Social life and customs—Encyclopedias.   I. Title.
   E20.S56   1994   978'.003—dc20   94-19824

ISBN 0-87436-738-7

00 99 98 97 96 95   10 9 8 7 6 5 4 3 2

Cover illustration: Bronco Buster *(ca. 1905) by William H. Dunton. The Rockwell Museum, gift of William C. Whitridge.*

ABC-CLIO, Inc.
130 Cremona Drive, P.O. Box 1911
Santa Barbara, California 93116-1911

This book is printed on acid-free paper ⊗.
Manufactured in the United States of America

978
SLA
1994

For Zoya Maxine Atkinson
and Jerome David Slatta,
my favorite saddle pals

Preface, ix
Acknowledgments, xiii

The Cowboy Encyclopedia, 1

Appendix A: Film and Videotape Sources, 413
Appendix B: Museums, 415
Appendix C: Periodicals, 419
Appendix D: Western Cultural Happenings, 425
Bibliography, 427
Illustration Credits, 455
Index, 457

PREFACE

One of the goals of this book is to refute generations of pundits who have been declaring the cowboy dead, dying, or disappeared for more than a century. Charles Moreau Harger, writing in *Scribner's Magazine* (June 1892), pronounced one of many such epitaphs: "The cow-boy, with his white, wide-rimmed hat, his long leathern cattle whip, his lariat, and his clanking spur is a thing of the past."

Some aspects of cowboy life have certainly changed. This encyclopedia reminds us, however, that cowboys and their culture are alive and well in the United States, Canada, and Latin America. Just visit any of the hundreds of cowboy songfests, poetry gatherings, chuck wagon cookoffs, ranch rodeos, collectibles shows, and other western happenings. You'll find plenty of living cowboy culture.

This book is the first and only major reference work to focus on the essentials of cowboy history, culture, and myth for both North and South America. I hope the book entertains and enlightens readers. I've tried to include something for students of cowboy life and lore, fanciers and collectors of western Americana, rodeo buffs, and armchair cowpokes. If you enjoy rodeoing, dude ranching, real ranching, or visiting places such as the National Cowboy Hall of Fame in Oklahoma City, the Buffalo Bill Historical Center in Cody, Wyoming, and other cowboy sites, this book is for you. It's written for a general audience, but I won't mind if other historians and frontier scholars take a look too.

A word about this book's organization and approach. I have tried to integrate rather than

fragment information. I chose to present information in longer, topical entries rather than to break the book into short, disparate bits and pieces. For example, saddles are covered in a single essay. The entry traces Spanish influence on the western stock saddle and also covers the *recado,* the saddle of the Argentine gaucho. If you look up the term *recado,* you find instructions to "See Saddle." These longer entries have subtopical headings to speed the locating of specific information.

This integrated approach often places Latin American material less familiar to most readers within a comparative North American context. About two-thirds of the text focuses on the American West. The remaining one-third covers Canada and Latin America. I mean no slight to our neighbors north or south of the border. The proportions simply reflect my estimate of the interests of readers and the relative size of the different reading markets.

Interests in cowboy history and culture are as varied as old ranch hands. I cover cowboy equipment and dress, work and play, cultural imagery in pulps and other fictional literature, films, western music and singers, historians who have studied the cowboy, Native-American and African-American cowboys, women, rodeo (stampedes in Canada, *charreada* in Mexico), the cowboy's environment (plains, pampas, llanos), and locations such as museums, dude ranches, and historic sites.

This is not a general encyclopedia of the West or the frontier. The focused coverage is what makes this book unique. Vardis Fisher, for example, is certainly an important western literary figure, but his work did not focus on the cowboy, so he is not included.

I do not include entries on famous or infamous lawmen, gunfighters, or outlaws; military history, forts, and battles; farming and sheep raising; natural history; non-equestrian Indian cultures; cities, other than cow towns; mining; the fur trade; mountain men; or the oil industry. Frontier religion gets little attention for the simple reason that most nineteenth-century cowboys had little time or use for organized religion or church-going.

SMELLY FISH AND ENCYCLOPEDIA WRITING

To help you understand and appreciate this book's lineage, I would like to share some behind-the-scenes comments about how I conceived and wrote it. To criticize the Eisenhower administration's lack of aid to Latin America, Colombian President Carlos Lleras Restrepo told a story about a fish seller. A man opened a fish stand and put up a sign that read: "Fresh Fish Sold Here." A friend came along and said, "Your sign is too long. Obviously no one sells rotten fish. Your sign should read: 'Fish Sold Here.'" A second helpful compadre stopped by and opined, "It's obvious *where* you are selling fish. Why not just put up a sign that reads: 'Fish Sold.'?" A third friend observed: "Obviously no one would give away fish." The man shortened his sign to read simply: "Fish." Finally a fourth friend happened by and pointed out that anyone could tell by the smell what he was selling. "You need no sign at all." "That's the way it is with U.S. aid," said Lleras Restrepo. "After all the discussion we have had here, all that is left is the smell."

What do smelly fish have to do with the *Cowboy Encyclopedia?* Like the fish seller, I, too, strive to be concise. I try to convey a maximum of information with a minimum of words. I want to be accurate. I do not wish to oversimplify. I do not, however, have space sufficient to cover every nuance, every detail. In this push for conciseness, I hope I avoided the fish monger's fate of leaving only smell and no substance.

I am certainly not the first writer to face the quandary of cramming complexity into a short space. Samuel Johnson, who had something to say about most everything, accepted the burden of limits as an occupational hazard. "In all printed sentences," he wrote in 1787, "some degree of accuracy must be sacrificed to conciseness."

Shakespeare, of course, left us his much-quoted but seldom observed epigram in *Hamlet:* "Brevity is the soul of wit." We might do well to remember Samuel Taylor Coleridge's definition of an epigram, which echoes Shakespeare: "What is an Epigram? a dwarfish whole, Its body brevity, and wit its soul."

The problem of brevity is especially acute when writing about things I have spent nearly two decades researching. How do I condense so much research into short entries of a few hundred words?

In each entry, no matter how short, I tried to cover the traditional five W's of journalism: who, what, where, when, and why. After providing a basic definition, I tried to explain the historical and cultural significance of the subject. Why was the topic, person, or event important in its own time? What is the longer term historical and cultural significance? For each entry, I tried to provide at least a bare-bones historical context.

I consider it especially important to establish an appropriate context and significance for biographical entries. I strive to show the transcendental importance of people whose lives I've reduced to a few hundred words. In exploring the Zen of biography, we might ponder the words of Alan Watts: "Every individual is an expression of the whole realm of nature, a unique action of the total universe." Even if we do not wish to push quite that far into the Zen of things, we give our individual subject a meaningful context, even if it is somewhat less than the total universe.

Recognizing the limitations of a single entry, I have appended a lengthy topical bibliography to point readers toward greater depth and breadth of inquiry. A seemingly minor element of an entry, cross-referencing, is actually very important. You can follow cross references (indicated with boldface type or by "see" or "see also") to find comparable topics and additional related information. By reading several related entries, you can build up a more complete understanding of a topic. By riding the trails blazed by cross references, you can assemble a reasonably varied and comprehensive interpretation of most topics of cowboy life and history. You have the burden of assimilating and synthesizing varied bits and pieces of information, but such synthesis is a fundamental part of the challenge and joy of any historical inquiry.

In selecting topics for inclusion, I have taken into account the relative significance of cattle-raising regions in a nation's economy and culture. I do not describe riders of Peru, the Gran Chaco (Paraguay), western Patagonia, and south-central Bolivia because of the small scale of their operations and their lack of national cultural significance. I mention only in passing the cowpens of the colonial Carolinas and the small ranching operations of Spanish Florida. For the United States, I give greatest attention to Texas and the Great Plains, with a few words about the Pacific Northwest. In Canada, Alberta gets most of the attention.

Historians and other writers have always labored under constraints of language and space. I, too, have been necessarily selective, but I hope you find plenty to interest you. Perhaps a more honest title for this encyclopedia would be "An Ambitious Compilation of a Whole Lot of Stuff, with Necessary and Acknowledged Omissions and Abridgments, about Many Interesting Things and People Who Rode Horses and Chased Cattle around the Americas."

If I omitted a favorite topic, please consult the many reference works listed in the acknowledgments and throughout the book. You are welcome to drop me a line with suggested additions, corrections, and queries. Remember, too, that "an encouraging word" or two won't swell my hat size.

You can reach me at the History Department, North Carolina State University, Raleigh, North Carolina, 27695-8108. Please enclose a business-sized SASE (self-addressed, stamped envelope) if you would like a reply.

ACKNOWLEDGMENTS

This encyclopedia grew out of prior research for *Cowboys of the Americas,* published in 1990 by Yale University Press. That book found a receptive audience among aficionados of the American West. The National Cowboy Hall of Fame honored the book with its 1991 Western Heritage Wrangler Award for nonfiction.

I would like to thank Yale University Press for permission to adapt material from *Cowboys of the Americas* for use in *The Cowboy Encyclopedia.*

ARCHIVAL SOURCES

I conducted archival research in several countries to gather the information presented here. I have drawn upon university libraries around the country as well as manuscript, newspaper, and other collections at the following repositories:

Archivo de la Nación, Caracas, Venezuela
Archivo General de la Nación, Buenos Aires, Argentina
Archivo Histórico de la Provincia de Buenos Aires "Ricardo Levene," La Plata, Argentina
Biblioteca Nacional, Caracas, Venezuela
Biblioteca Nacional, Buenos Aires, Argentina
Fundación John Boulton Library, Caracas, Venezuela
Glenbow Archives, Calgary, Alberta, Canada
Hispanic Division, Library of Congress, Washington, D.C.
Library of Congress, Washington, D.C.
Nettie Lee Benson Latin American Collection, University of Texas, Austin
Prints and Photographs Division, Library of Congress, Washington, D.C.
Universidad Nacional de la Provincia de Buenos Aires Library, La Plata, Argentina
University of Calgary Library, Alberta, Canada
Western Range Cattle Industry Study, Colorado Heritage Center, Denver

ELECTRONIC SOURCES

By using electronic sources, both online via modem and distributed on CD-ROM, I could consult references that are generally more up-to-date than printed versions. For basic fact-checking, I consulted several electronic encyclopedias, including *The Academic American Encyclopedia,* Online Edition (Grolier Electronic Publishing, Danbury, Connecticut, 1993). This electronic encyclopedia includes 33,000 articles and ten million words and is updated quarterly. I access the online text-only version via modem on CompuServe, an electronic information utility based in Columbus, Ohio.

Another electronic service, America Online, provided access to *Compton's Encyclopedia, Online Edition.* Grolier also markets a CD-ROM version of the same information as the Software Toolworks *Multimedia Encyclopedia.* The CD-ROM version supplements text with full-motion video, sound, and color and black-and-white illustrations. I also used the 1994 edition of *Encarta,* another encyclopedia distributed on CD-ROM and copyrighted by Microsoft Corporation and Funk & Wagnall's Corporation. It includes elaborate search options, a historical timeline, and a special section devoted to history.

CompuServe's Electronic News Service, a computerized clipping service, helped me locate contemporary news items about modern cowboy culture. The service provides keyword searches of stories from selected news organizations, such as United Press International and Reuters, as well as national and international newspapers.

I found the reference volumes of ABC-CLIO's Electronic Library on CD-ROM very helpful for bibliographical research. *Bibliography of Native North Americans on Disc* includes nearly 60,000 citations covering 200 ethnic groups on a single CD-ROM. I was quickly able to locate 79 articles, books, and reviews dealing with Native Americans and horses. Equally helpful is the CD-ROM version of *America: History and Life.* The Fall 1993 disc includes 6,082 references to Native Americans, 212 citations for Ranch, 221 for Cowboy, 485 for Cattle, and 308 for Horse. *Historical Abstracts on Disc* covers broad ranges of historical journals.

PRINTED SECONDARY SOURCES

I have relied upon many commendable printed reference works. Several ABC- CLIO books were consulted, including Barry Klein's *Reference Encyclopedia of the American Indian,* Ronald Fritze's *Legend and Lore of the New World before 1492,* and *Dictionary of Native American Mythology,* by Sam D. Gill and Irene Sullivan. Many of the firsthand descriptions that I quote come from Clifford P. Westermeier's wonderful collection, *Trailing the Cowboy: His Life and Lore as Told by Frontier Journalists* (Caxton Printers, 1955). *The Reader's Encyclopedia of the American West* (Harper and Row, 1977), compiled by Howard Lamar, remains an important reference work. As helpful as it is, the book is misnamed. It should really be titled an "encyclopedia of the frontier." It strikes me as odd to find listings for Rhode Island and New York in a book supposedly about the "American West."

Despite some errors and omissions, Denis McLoughlin's *Wild and Woolly* (Doubleday,

1975) is also useful. For helpful definitions and concise information, nothing is more essential than *Western Words* by Ramon F. Adams (University of Oklahoma Press, 1968).

Two more recent dictionaries depend heavily on Adams. *A Dictionary of the Old West* by Peter Watts (Knopf, 1977) is very derivative of Adams but adds some new material. *Dictionary of the American West,* by Winfred Blevins (Facts on File, 1993), includes "5,000 terms and expressions from 'a-going and a-coming' to Zuni." Blevins again relies heavily on Adams for cowboy and ranching terms. The latter book also covers Native Americans as well as logging, mining, and mountain man terminology. Unfortunately, in casting such a big loop, Blevins leaves out some terms we need to know, like *buckle bunny.* His bibliography is brief.

Dictionaries focus narrowly on words. Real people get left out. Dan L. Thrapp's four-volume *Encyclopedia of Frontier Biography* (University of Nebraska Press, 1988) is *the* essential source for western biographical entries. It covers historical figures well but does not include important figures in today's cowboy culture.

Some of the entries mention additional sources within the text or at the end of the entry. The Historiography of the Cowboy entry will put you on the trail of helpful studies by other historians and scholars. The Periodicals entry describes the best popular magazines that cover cowboy history and culture.

Something must be left out of any book. I decided to cover only major fictional writers and literary topics in order to leave more space for historical topics. Readers interested in cowboy fiction should consult the *Encyclopedia of Frontier and Western Fiction* (1983), edited by Jon Tuska and Vicki Piekarski.

I have included major topics for Latin America and Canada, but my primary focus is the American West. Readers should consult Charles Scribner's massive four-volume *Encyclopedia of Latin American History* (1995) for additional details of history south of the border.

PEOPLE WHO HELPED

This book has been a joy to research and write. I have lots of good folks around the country to thank. Suzanne Chance at ABC-CLIO invited me to undertake this project. I thank her for getting the ball rolling and taking a chance on me. Gracias to ABC-CLIO's Elizabeth Neel for providing me with the Electronic Library.

Several history graduate assistants at North Carolina State University helped me. Corinne Frist Glover, Nils E. Mikkelsen, Janine Cairo, Stephen Keadey, and Mark Mayer researched and wrote some of the entries; their bylines appear under a number of essays. Sarah Minor did bibliographical research on cowboys.

Some material appeared in a different form in *Western Styles* and *Cowboys & Indians* magazines. Thanks to editors Sue Copeland and Charlotte Berney for permission to use material that appeared in their respective publications.

Thanks to Ray White for sharing his expertise and enthusiasm for B-western movies. June Bowles of the history department staff transcribed taped interviews. Janice Mitchell kept the faxes and other communications coming and going. A hearty thanks, also, to the hundreds of scholars and observers whose contributions I recognize in my bibliography.

Settle into your favorite armchair and flip open any page in this encyclopedia. I'm confident you'll quickly immerse yourself in the vitality and excitement of cowboy culture today and yesterday. Saddle up, move 'em out, and enjoy the ride!

Cary, North Carolina
October 1994

ABBEY, EDWARD
(1927–1989)

Born in Home, Pennsylvania, writer and environmentalist Ed Abbey grew up on a farm in the Allegheny Mountains. He spent most of his adult life in the Southwest. He hitchhiked to the Pacific Coast at age 17. He went into the army and was released in 1947, after which he moved to the Southwest. He attended the University of New Mexico in Albuquerque and in 1951 received a Bachelor's degree. He tried his hand at further education and work in the East, but soon gave up on urban, industrial society in favor of the Southwest.

Beginning in the mid-1950s, Abbey became one of the Southwest's most acute observers and eloquent spokesmen. "I'd always been strongly drawn by the Western landscape," noted Abbey, "mostly because of movies."

Abbey wrote a wide range of fiction and nonfiction. His writings reflect two fundamental passions: a concern for preserving the natural environment and a belief in the rights and responsibilities of the individual. These values emerge in delightful variations, which reveal Abbey to be an anarchist, cynic, naturalist, humorist, and preservationist. The zany cast of characters in *The Monkey Wrench Gang* (1975), a novel about guerrilla ecologists, is perhaps the best manifestation of Abbey's humor, individualism, and dedication to preserving the environment.

Abbey filled his work with striking images of western landscapes, mostly the stark beauty of the desert Southwest. Cowboys often appeared in his writing. For Abbey, the cowboy represented the clear-eyed simplicity, honesty, freedom, and rugged individualism of bygone days. The cowboy is ever threatened with extinction by the juggernaut of encroaching modern industrial society. Modernity threatens and often destroys the cowboy, along with the wild, beautiful natural landscape that gives the West its special character and meaning. Abbey's cowboys fight to preserve the traditional West, a land filled with "things which are free, decent, sane, clean and true."

In 1956 Abbey published his second novel, *The Brave Cowboy.* The tragic cowboy hero in this novel is Jack Burns, who has a no-nonsense, uncomplicated world view. When police demand identification, Burns replies, "Don't have none. Don't need none. I already know who I am."

The Brave Cowboy captures the conflict between the cowboy's anarchism and the restrictions of modernizing, urbanizing, industrializing society. Abbey explored this theme again and again in his writings. Unlike traditional formula cowboy novels, *The Brave Cowboy* does not triumph in the end. In an ending laden with homely but powerful imagery, Burns and his faithful mare Whisky end up smashed and broken, struck down by a truck filled with toilets. The novel became a powerful **film,** *Lonely Are the Brave* (Universal, 1962), starring Kirk Douglas.

In 1962 Abbey published *Fire on the Mountain.* Once again another tough, old westerner, John Vogelin, comes into conflict with modernity, this time represented by the United States Air Force. Abbey based the main character on a real New Mexican cattleman, John Prather. In the novel, the military, needing more land for a missile range, tries to force Vogelin off his ranch. Ranch people can readily identify with the old rancher's reverential feelings for the land. Like Jack Burns, John Vogelin ends his life in tragedy, but true to his principles. The old rancher, however, passes along the fire of his faith to his 12-year-old grandson, Billy Star.

Perhaps Abbey's most unusual work is *Good News* (1980), a science-fiction cowboy novel. Abbey set the novel in a horrific future, where his greatest fear was realized. The greed of industrialists and the excesses of capitalism brought massive pollution and nuclear destruction to the earth. Now people in cities and in the countryside fight to survive. A cowboy, again named Jack Burns, along with his Hopi companion Sam Banyaca, preserve the old cowboy and Indian ways; in so doing they are able to survive.

Burns and Banyaca befriend Arthur Dekker, a young boy whose rancher father has just been killed in a gunfight with rustlers. They go to the city, which is ruled by the Chief, an evil military dictator. While searching for his long-lost son Charlie, Burns joins up with a student underground fighting against the dictatorship. Once again, Abbey pits traditional cowboy values, such as individualism, in a battle against the evils and excesses of modernity.

Cowboys even appear in one of Abbey's brilliantly descriptive and evocative nonfiction works—his 1968 memoir, *Desert Solitaire: A Season in the Wilderness,* in which a section is entitled "Cowboys and Indians." Abbey's vignette of Viviano Jacquez, a Basque cowhand, aptly describes the twentieth-century cowboy: "He knows the basic skills of the trade: can shoe a horse, rope and brand and castrate a calf, fix a flat tire, stretch barbed wire, dynamite a beaver dam or lay out an irrigation ditch."

Abbey obviously loved and venerated the West. His memorable cowboy characters serve as powerful literary reminders that, despite change, cowboy tradition endures. (Ronald 1982; Tuska and Piekarski 1983)

ABBOTT, EDWARD C.
(1860–1939)
Cowboy and writer known as Teddy Blue. See Autobiographies by Cowboys.

ABERDEEN ANGUS
Term once used for Angus cattle. See Cattle Breeds.

ABILENE
City in Kansas. See Cow Towns.

ACCIÓN
Royal license required to hunt wild cattle during the Spanish colonial era in the Río de la Plata. See *Vaquería.*

ACIÓN
Stirrup leather.

ADAMS, CLIFTON
(1919–)
Novelist who writes formula westerns under various names.

ADAMS, ANDY
(1859–1935)
Cowboy and writer. See Autobiographies by Cowboys.

ADAMS, RAMON FREDERICK
(1889–1976)
For decades, bibliographer and lexicographer Ramon Adams was a "bur under the saddle" for historians of the American West who did not get all their facts right. His early training as a concert violinist gave little hint of his future as a student of western history, especially outlaws. After a poorly set broken arm ended his musical career, Adams built a profitable business making candy. He published most of his books after retiring from business in the mid-1950s. Thereafter, he devoted himself to his true passion, western Americana.

Born in Moscow, Texas, Adams developed a deep fascination with bandits and outlaws in Texas and New Mexico. Working outside the canons of academic life gave Adams freedom to explore and look at things his own way. This latitude and freedom, however, also meant that he expended some of his considerable energies on trivial pursuits, which limited his contributions to the field of history. Adams had no patience for sloppy or inaccurate research, and many writers flinched under his stinging criticism. "Just as burs under the saddle irritate a horse," he wrote, "so the constant writing of inaccurate history irritates the historian."

Adams contributed most significantly to the history of the cowboy in two major areas. First, he compiled impressive working bibliographies of books and other publications about the cowboy. *The Rampaging Herd: A Bibliography of Books and Pamphlets on Men and Events of the Cattle Industry* (1959) is his most important bibliographical contribution.

Adams also showed great skill as a lexicographer. He published his first book, *Cowboy Lingo,* in 1936. Eight years later he published *Western Words,* which appeared in an expanded edition in 1968. This superb dictionary of cowboy terminology emphasizes ranching terms from the borderlands. *Western Words* illustrates as well as any book available the tremendous debt owed by the western range cattle industry to vaqueros and Mexican ranching. Both of these books remain indispensable to anyone who specializes in cowboy and western history.

Anyone interested in the cowboy will revel in two other books by Adams: *The Old-Time Cowhand* (1961) and *Come an' Get it: The Story of the Old Cowboy Cook* (1952). *The Old-Time Cowhand* contains a wealth of information on cowboy material culture. Much of the information is the same as that found in *Western Words,* but the topical organization provides for wonderfully engaging chapters on everything from chaps, slickers, and bedrolls to cowboy humor and **religion.** Written in the colloquial idiom of the cowboy, the book conveys both the flavor and information of cowboy life. In *Come an' Get it: The Story of the Old Cowboy Cook,* Adams used the vehicle of material culture, this time **food,** to convey a great deal about the **humor** and life of the cowboy.

With 24 books in all, Adams left an impressive corpus of material relating to the cowboy. (Thrapp 1988)

AFRICAN-AMERICAN COWBOYS

Black slaves tended cattle, usually on foot, in the colonial Old South. Black jockeys, trainers, and grooms handled expensive quarter horses that were raised and raced by the southern gentry. During the early days of ranching (the 1830s and 1840s) on the south Texas coast, Anglo slaveholders brought their slaves to Texas from other southern states, and by 1845, Texas had an estimated 100,000 whites and 35,000 slaves. By 1861 the state had 430,000 whites and 182,000 slaves.

While slavery still existed, some odd reverse discrimination occurred. Because of their value as property, slaves were sometimes treated differently. Rancher Abel "Shanghai" Pierce recalled breaking horses in Texas in 1853, with several slaves assisting (Durham and Jones 1983). A superior ordered Pierce to break the most dangerous mounts; the slaveholder did not want to risk injuring slaves, because "those Negroes are worth a thousand dollars a piece."

Conditions worsened for southern blacks when Reconstruction ended in 1877. Tens of thousands of ex-slaves migrated from southern states to Kansas from late 1877 through 1879. Unfortunately, they found bleak prospects, a harsh climate, and barren land. Only an estimated one-third of the "exodusters" stayed.

After the Civil War, ranches east of the Trinity River often had all-black crews, while west of the Nueces River, ranchers employed **vaqueros** more often than black cowboys. Far fewer blacks populated the northern ranges: for instance, Montana censuses counted only 183 African Americans in 1870 and 346 in 1880.

Frontier regions lack the extensive documentation typical of cities, and this makes it difficult to accurately compute the number of cowboys or their ethnicity. According to the highest estimate, the trail drives north out of Texas from 1866 to 1895 employed about 63 percent white, 25 percent black, and 12 percent Mexican or Mexican-American cowboys. Unfortunately, most African-American and Hispanic cowboys faced social and economic discrimination in the West as they did elsewhere in the country.

Famous African-American Cowboys
Several black cowboys gained some notoriety. Few people would have known about Bose Ikard had it not been for the **television** movie, *Lonesome Dove.* Ikard was born a slave in Mississippi in 1847. Five years later his master brought him to Texas. As a youth, he learned the cowboy trade on a ranch near Weatherford. Freed by the Civil War, Ikard went to work for Charles **Goodnight** and Oliver Loving, and in

1866 he helped them blaze the Goodnight-Loving Trail. Goodnight had many words of praise for his trusted hand. "He surpassed any man I had in endurance and stamina." Ikard and Goodnight both died in 1929.

The life of Isom Dart (born Ned Huddleston) took a very different direction from Ikard's. He was born a slave in Arkansas in 1849. After emancipation, he went west to Texas. Huddleston soon began stealing Mexican horses and swimming them across the Rio Grande for sale in Texas. He moved to northwest Colorado and became involved in gambling and fighting. After brushes with the law, he took work as a **bronc buster.** Although he was a great horseman, Huddleston could not keep to the straight and narrow; he joined a gang of rustlers in 1875. A rancher and his cowboys ambushed and killed the entire gang, except for Huddleston. At that point, Huddleston changed his name to Isom Dart and again tried to go straight. After additional brushes with the law, Dart turned to hunting and breaking wild horses. He then bought his own ranch. Tom **Horn,** the bounty hunter, did not accept Dart's turn to lawful life. Horn shot and killed Dart, who died at age 51.

A mass of myth and legend surrounds many westerners. The character of Deadwood Dick is yet another example of art influencing life. Edward L. Wheeler's first **pulp novel** starring Deadwood Dick appeared in 1877, and Wheeler wrote more than 30 more of these novels before his death in 1885. Many men, including Nat Love, claimed to be the real Deadwood Dick. (Love was born a slave in Tennessee in 1854; some sources give the birthplace as Ohio.) In 1907 Love published *The Life and Adventures of Nat Love, Better Known in the Cattle Country as "Deadwood Dick."* Love relates his supposed adventures in typical western tall-tale fashion. His life story reads much like a pulp novel, with brave, heroic deeds at every turn. He claimed to have acquired his nickname by winning a roping contest in 1876 in Deadwood, Arizona. Exactly where fact left off and fancy took over will never be known, but Love certainly became one of the

most successful self-promoting cowboys of his day. (We have somewhat sounder historical data on Bill **Pickett,** the Texas-born African-American cowboy credited with the invention of steer wrestling.)

Like other cowboys, African-American cowboys are still very much alive. The National Black Cowboys Association claims more than 20,000 members, most of whom compete in amateur **rodeo** or otherwise enjoy life on horseback. The Black West Museum in Denver offers a glimpse at the regional history and culture of African Americans. (Durham and Jones 1965; Katz 1971, 1977)

See also African-American Cowboys in Film; Discrimination on the American Frontier.

AFRICAN-AMERICAN COWBOYS IN FILM

African-American western films have been few and far between. Most have been independently produced on limited budgets. The first appears to be *Trooper K,* a 1916 film about the Tenth Cavalry Regiment. In the 1930s, talented singer and performer Herb Jeffries decided that African Americans should have their own westerns. He was billed as Herbert Jeffrey on movie posters, "Black America's first singing cowboy in the movies." Jeffries starred in *Harlem on the Prairie, Harlem Rides the Range, Bronze Buckaroo,* and *Two-Gun Man from Harlem.* He had a fine singing voice and his films well mimicked all the elements of then-popular white **B westerns.** He reappeared in 1993 in a **film documentary,** *The Black West,* part of a three-episode TBS television series entitled "The Untold West." At age 82, he retained his strong, melodious voice and bubbling personality.

Hollywood did not follow the trail blazed by the pioneering Jeffries. African Americans remained relatively rare in westerns and rarer still in starring roles. During the 1970s, however, heightened racial awareness ushered in a renewed interest in black culture. In *Buck and the Preacher* (1972), a black version of the classic wagon train story, Sidney Poitier made his directing debut and starred as Buck. Harry Belafonte costarred as

Isom Dart, born a slave, became a cowboy in every sense of the word. He rustled horses, was a bronc buster, and owned his own ranch.

the fast-talking, gun-toting preacher. Together they wipe out a racist gang headed by Cameron Mitchell.

Probably the most famous cowboy film with a black star was the hilarious *Blazing Saddles* (1974). This bawdy satire, directed by Mel Brooks, included parodies of just about everything. Cleavon Little starred as the hip, black sheriff. Bad taste and farce abound, but the film is funny. Gene Wilder plays the Waco Kid, a gunslinger. Madeline Kahn's heroine is a wonderful caricature of Marlene Dietrich *(Destry Rides Again)*.

A few westerns figured in the "blaxploitation" (black exploitation) movies of the early 1970s. Excessive violence, stilted dialogue, R ratings, and macho heroes characterized this genre. *Soul Soldier* (1972) provides a violent, coarse depiction of the Tenth Cavalry Regiment, the topic of the first African-American film. Ex-pro-football player Fred Williamson starred in several such films. A larger-and-tougher-than-life black gunslinger looms in *The Legend of Nigger Charley* (1972). In *Boss Nigger* (1974), a bounty hunter terrorizes townspeople. Williamson carried the role to its absurd extreme in *Joshua* (1976), even smoking the evil little cigars used by Clint **Eastwood** in his spaghetti westerns. Williamson lightened up a bit in *Adios, Amigo* (1976), in which he and Richard Pryor provide some humorous moments as slapstick con men.

More African-American westerns appeared in the late 1980s and early 1990s. Unfortunately, many suffered from quality defects not unlike the earlier blaxploitation films. *Silverado* (1985), with Danny Glover and Kevin Costner, turned out to be an expensive box office flop. Although a commercial failure, it is a very enjoyable, lively **film.** Glover's character possesses strength and believability. (Glover narrated the 1993 TBS documentary, *The Black West*.)

The very bloody *Posse* (1993) is a black spaghetti western. Mario Van Peebles directs and stars in this tale of revenge. Jesse Lee (Pebbles) embarks on a vendetta to kill the Klansmen who murdered his father. Veteran African-American actor Woody Strode, who appeared in John Ford's *Sergeant Rutledge,* is the film's narrator. Along the way, Pebbles and his crew take on more Klansmen who are armed with a Gatling gun. As in *The Wild Bunch,* this kind of heavy hardware lends itself to massive bloodshed. Despite their shortcomings, both *Silverado* and *Posse* hold out hope for more authentic, multiracial depictions of cowboy life in the future.

Two 1993 cowboy film events delivered on that promise and provided starring opportunities for black actors. The films are distinguished by far better scripts and roles than has usually been the case for African-American actors playing cowboys.

Morgan Freedman played an important role as Ned Logan in Clint Eastwood's Academy Award winner, *Unforgiven.* Freedman's character has competence lacking in either Eastwood's William Munny or Jaimz Woolvett's Schofield Kid. Munny, long out of the saddle, keeps falling down as he tries to mount his horse. The Schofield Kid, an aspiring young gunfighter, is so near-sighted he can't hit anything. Logan is still a crack shot, keeps his head, and exudes strength and dignity.

The 1993 **television** film, *Return to Lonesome Dove,* provided a major role for Louis Gossett, Jr. He plays a fictional character named Isom Picket. "The character," according to Gossett, "is based on two real men. One was Isom Dart, a con man in the old West. The other was [Willie M.] Bill **Pickett,** a real cowboy and trail boss." Gossett enjoyed the role and took it to heart. "I'm a full-fledged cowboy now," said the actor, "and I'm thinking about buying one of the horses because I've got a couple of Western films coming up." (Garfield 1982; Null 1990)

AFTOSA

Hoof-and-mouth or foot-and-mouth disease, an affliction suffered by cattle. Fearing the spread of *aftosa,* the United States restricted live cattle imports from Argentina and other nations. The disease can attack any cloven-hoofed animal. It

Nat Love, who relished telling tales of his adventures, claimed to be the original Deadwood Dick, having earned the nickname by winning a roping contest in Deadwood, Arizona. He is shown here in his "fighting clothes."

affects cattle with running sores in the mouth and on the hooves. *(Encarta* 1994)

AGUARDIENTE

Rum-like alcoholic beverage distilled from sugarcane. The liquor is consumed throughout Latin America.

AIRIN' THE LUNGS

Colloquial term for swearing or vulgarity.

AIRIN' THE PAUNCH

Colloquial term for vomiting.

AIRTIGHTS

Colloquial term for canned goods, such as canned beans, milk, or fruit.

ALBERTA

See Cowboys of Canada; Beef Cattle Industry.

ALFALFA DESPERADO

One of many humorous cowboy terms for a farmer.

ALKALI GRASS

Also wheat grass—grass that grows in alkaline soils of the Rocky Mountains area.

ALLEN, HENRY WILSON
(1912–1991)

Novelist who wrote formula westerns under various names.

ALLEN, REX

Actor, singer. See Films, Cowboy.

ALLEN, REX, JR.

Singer. See Music.

ALPARGATAS

Crude, homemade leather sandals worn by gauchos of Argentina and *huasos* of Chile.

ALVIN AND THE CHIPMUNKS

Cartoon characters. See Hat Acts.

AMANSADOR

Horse tamer. See Bronc Buster.

AMERICAN COWBOY CULTURE ASSOCIATION

The revival of cowboy culture in the 1980s and 1990s has spawned many new organizations. On 12 October 1990, devotees of western culture met at the Lincoln Country Cowboy Symposium in Lubbock, Texas. They founded the American Cowboy Culture Association. "Its purpose is to promote all areas of cowboy culture and to allow all individuals, groups and organizations who are involved in these various areas to band together to promote cowboy culture as a whole."

The group has a distinguished set of officers, including Stella Hughes (historian), B. Byron Price, executive director of the **National Cowboy Hall of Fame** (first vice-president), and singer and poet Red Steagall (second vice-president). Alvin G. Davis of Lubbock, Texas, serves as president. The Executive Committee includes historian Jim Hoy, singer and folklorist Hal Cannon, actor Richard Farnsworth, cowboy poet Waddie **Mitchell,** musicologist Jim Bob Tinsley, and **rodeo** star Larry Mahan.

The association sponsors the annual National Cowboy Symposium and Celebration in Lubbock, Texas. The group works in conjunction with the Ranching Heritage Association at Texas Tech University. Events include **poetry,** singing, story-telling, cutting, team roping and penning, and more. Artisans and performers demonstrate trick riding and roping; saddle, tack, hat, spur, and boot making; and other skills.

For information on the American Cowboy Culture Association or the Ranching Heritage Association, write to P.O. Box 4040, Lubbock, TX 79409; tel. 806-742-2498.

AMERICAN QUARTER HORSE ASSOCIATION

See Quarter Horse.

ANDERSON, BRONCHO BILLY

Stage name of actor Max **Aronson.** See Films, Cowboy.

ANGORAS

Hair-covered, goat-hide chaps, good for cold weather. See Chaps.

ANGUS

See Cattle Breeds.

APACHE

See Indians as Cowboys.

APPALOOSA

See Horses.

APPLE

Colloquial term for saddle horn, from the Spanish term *manzana,* meaning apple.

ARONSON, MAX
(1882–1971)

Film actor also known as Broncho Billy Anderson and Gilbert M. Anderson. See Films, Cowboy.

ARAPAHO

Like the **Cheyenne,** the Arapaho are an Algonquin-speaking North American Indian tribe. Little is know of their early history and migrations. The late eighteenth century, however, found them in the Red River Valley of Minnesota. They migrated slowly south and west until, by 1790, they were on the central Great Plains.

The Arapaho first acquired horses from the Comanche. The horse's arrival radically altered their culture. The Arapaho abandoned permanent settlements and became buffalo nomads because the animals supplied food, clothing, housing, bedding, and other necessities.

The Arapaho split into northern and southern branches in the 1830s, about the same time as the Cheyenne tribe split. The northern Arapaho preferred the cooler climate of the Big Horn and Powder rivers. The southern tribe gravitated toward the warmer region south of the Platte River. The southern Arapaho carried on extensive trade with whites and other Native Americans, and they served as intermediaries between northern and southern plains tribes.

The southern Arapaho and Cheyenne developed a special relationship. In 1840 increasing white migration prompted them to make a lasting peace with other plains tribes. Disease and hardship took a toll on the southern Arapaho, however, and by 1846 they numbered only about 10,000 people.

Trouble with the United States government started around 1846 when some Arapaho and Comanche warriors attacked wagon trains along the Santa Fe Trail. In September 1851 Plains Indians signed their first treaty with the U.S. government. Washington recognized that Native Americans had rights to the land; in exchange Indians allowed whites to build roads and move people through their lands.

The declining number of bison made the Arapaho more and more dependent on government rationing and annuities. In the mid-1850s, southern Arapaho chiefs discussed adopting an agricultural economy. In 1858, at the initiation of the Arapaho, the Plains Indian chiefs told the Indian agent they wanted a new treaty. They wished to live on certain lands and farm, in exchange for protection from the army and tools for farming. With the Fort Wise Treaty of 1861, the southern Arapaho and southern Cheyenne ceded most of their land in exchange for a triangle of territory skirting the Arkansas River. They would also received $450,000 in annuities over 15 years. The Indians repudiated this treaty shortly afterwards, however, feeling they had been cheated. Relations between the southern Arapaho and whites worsened. In 1864, after whites fired on Chief Left Hand, the Arapaho and Cheyenne began raiding stage stations and wagon trains.

While the two tribes negotiated a treaty with the government, they camped along Sand Creek in southeastern Colorado. Volunteers, led by Colonel John M. Chivington, attacked the Indian village on 29 November 1864, resulting in a massacre that rekindled warfare between Plains Indians and the army. The southern Arapaho as a tribe did not take an active part, but a few of their warriors rode north to fight alongside other Indian tribes.

In 1867 the southern Arapaho and southern Cheyenne were assigned a reservation between the Arkansas and Cimarron rivers in New Indian Territory (now Oklahoma). The northern Arapaho settled on a reservation in Wyoming. The southern Arapaho were expected to supplement their government rations by farming. They proved slightly more successful at agriculture than the Cheyenne, but they did not wish to relinquish their plains culture. The near extinction of the buffalo, however, ended any hope of returning to the old way of life.

In the early 1880s the Arapaho and Cheyenne leased grazing rights on some of their land to cattlemen. Both tribes had complaints about this arrangement, and in 1885 President Cleveland ordered the cattlemen to remove their herds from Arapaho-Cheyenne land.

The Arapaho and Cheyenne sold their "surplus lands" to the U.S. government for $1.5 million in 1891, and the ensuing Oklahoma Land Rush attracted a huge influx of white settlers. The Arapaho and Cheyenne, who once roamed widely across the Great Plains, were reduced to a sedentary life on the reservation. (Coel 1981; Kroeber 1983)

—*Janine M. Cairo*

ARBUCKLE'S BRAND
See Coffee.

AREPA
Corn cake, often filled with meat, eaten in Venezuela and other parts of South America.

ARMAS
Spanish forerunner of **chaps**. Riders fastened two large pieces of cowhide to the sides of the **saddle**. These coverings protected a rider's legs from thorns

and brush. Riders in brushy regions of northeastern Brazil, northern Argentina, and northern Mexico used *armas*. (Foster-Harris 1955)

ARMITAS
See Chaps.

ARMY MODEL
See Firearms.

ARNESS, JAMES
Actor who played Matt Dillon on "Gunsmoke." See Television.

ARNOLD, EDDIE
(1918–1990)
Singer. See Music.

ART OF THE COWBOY
Origins of Western American Art
Cowboy art has been popular for more than a century, and interest shows no signs of abating. About all that has changed is the variety of the art works themselves. Traditionally, cowboy art, whether painting or sculpture, aspired to represent authentic moments in ranch life. True, many artists added a dash of romance or heightened drama, but artists strived to accurately depict **horses,** landscapes, **tack,** clothing, and other subjects.

As art historian Royal B. Hassrick points out, the cowboy loomed large among subjects painted by nineteenth-century artists in the American West. Initially, however, artists who traveled to the West focused on the color and exotic drama of Native American life. George Catlin (1796–1872), for example, recorded the power and beauty of *Keokuk on Horseback* (1835). His *Buffalo Chase* (1832–1833) strikingly communicates the power and importance of the horse to the Indian buffalo hunt.

Karl Bodmer (1809–1893) also recorded vivid images of Indian life. The Swiss-born draftsman accompanied Prince Maximilian of Wied Neuwied on a journey through the western plains in 1833. Thanks to Bodmer's paintings of Indians, particularly Sioux, the mounted warrior, resplendent in war paint and feathers, became an image known to most Americans by the late nineteenth century.

Western landscapes provided a second major artistic subject. The so-called Rocky Mountain School—Thomas Hill (1829–1913), Albert Bierstadt (1830–1902), and Thomas Moran (1837–1926)—recorded romanticized visions of the grandeur of Yosemite, Yellowstone, and other majestic western sites. They were not above rearranging the huge mountains and waterfalls of their landscapes to enhance their art.

Alfred Jacob Miller (1810–1874) painted memorable Indian scenes and landscapes. In 1837 he traveled the Oregon Trail at the invitation of Scottish sportsman Sir William Drummond Stewart. Based on this single visit to the West, he painted a large number of canvases documenting Indian and fur trade life of the time. Several of his works, including *Hunting Buffalo* and *Shoshone Caressing His Horse* well illustrate aspects of Native American equestrian life.

Greater numbers of whites pushed westward in the years following the Civil War, and the ensuing conflicts between cavalry soldiers and Indians became a third major theme in western painting. Frederic **Remington** provided many

memorable, romanticized images of battling cavalrymen and dangerous Indians. The shock of the Sioux defeat of Custer's Seventh Cavalry in 1876 rocked the nation and provided a central moment immortalized by many, many painters. As with much western painting, ideology, supposition, and romance strongly colored the canvases.

Nineteenth-Century Cowboy Art

Post–Civil War **trail drives** northward from Texas brought the cowboy to the attention of artists and the rest of the American people. Artists soon tried to capture the danger and drama of the long drives. They also depicted cowboys as wild ruffians who painted a town red at the end of a drive. Paintings of cowboys, like the growing mountain of **pulp novels,** helped to shape perceptions of the cowboy and his character.

Charles Marion **Russell** and Frederic Remington probably did more than any other artists to create enduring images of nineteenth-century cowboy life. Because he cowboyed in the West, especially Montana, Russell brought firsthand knowledge of ranch life to his works.

Thomas Moran managed to capture the natural grandeur of the American West in his paintings. Here he has painted the Grand Canyon of the Yellowstone (1872).

He accurately detailed horses, **cattle,** tack, people, and places, but his special genius was a flair for **humor,** action, and story-telling. *The Strenuous Life* (1901) well portrays several of these elements. The center of the action is a cowboy and his horse downed by a charging **longhorn.** A taut lariat ties the bull's horn in the foreground to another cowboy trying to help his pard from the background. Two other cowboys give aid; one with a lasso, the other with his six-gun. One can almost hear the horse's cry and the longhorn's snort. Russell loved the old-time cowboy life he saw slipping away, and his paintings celebrate and memorialize the era.

Frederic Remington, Russell's contemporary, provided equally powerful images of cowboy life. While Russell focused his work on the cowboy, Remington produced a broader corpus of paintings and drawings. He painted dramatic cavalry scenes and Indians in a wide variety of poses, including attacking wagon trains and cowboys. He also crafted exciting bronzes. Like Russell, Remington felt nostalgia for the quickly vanishing Old West. Together, their paintings captured that nostalgia and communicated it to huge audiences who viewed their works in original form and in reproductions.

What Royal Hassrick terms the "retrospective spirit of Remington and Russell" lives on in many twentieth-century artists, such as N. C. Wyeth, Harold Von Schmidt, Newman Myrah, Don Spaulding and John Clymer (see below).

Many other painters also contributed important visual documents to the modern cowboy archive. English-born James Walker (1819–1889) is best known for his sweeping battle scenes. Caught in Mexico City at the outbreak of the Mexican War, he fled to American lines. He knew Mexican life firsthand and produced richly detailed paintings of **vaquero** life in California. He captured colorful horses, tack, and the vaquero's wonderfully ornate clothing. His *California Vaqueros* (1876–1877), for example, is an excellent document for social history.

Like Remington, Charles Schreyvogel (1861–1912) included cavalry attacks, Indians, and cowboys among his subjects. Born in New York, he worked hard and secured patronage to study art in Europe. Motivated by poor health, he went west to Colorado and Arizona in 1893. Winning a major art award for a cavalry painting *(My Bunkie)* in 1900 catapulted Schreyvogel from anonymity to fame. During the last dozen years of his life he acquired great fame and respect for his western works. Theodore **Roosevelt** figured among his admirers. Remington, in fact, grew quite envious of Schreyvogel's popularity, whose skill certainly rivaled his own. Blood poisoning ended the talented artist's life shortly before his fiftieth birthday.

Twentieth-Century Artists

After the turn of the century, the cowboy lost none of his artistic appeal. Iowa-born Frank Tenney Johnson (1874–1939) carried on in the tradition of Remington. After studying art in Wisconsin and New York, in 1904 he returned to Colorado and the Southwest as an illustrator for *Field and Stream* and other magazines. He also illustrated many Zane **Grey** novels. He later moved to California, where he turned from illustration to painting. Johnson showed particular skill at the subtle shadings of night scenes and in rendering horses accurately.

Johnson's contemporary, William Herbert Dunton (1874–1939), also left a fine corpus of paintings of cowboy life. He grew up in the decidedly non-cowboy country of Maine. Beginning about 1896, however, he took summer trips to the West, first to Montana. Work as a ranch hand interspersed with artistic study provided him with a happy blend of experience and technical training. His realistic illustrations became well known and popular in *Harper's, Scribner's,* and other publications. He became part of the vibrant Taos art community in 1912. Nine years later he abandoned New York permanently and moved to Taos.

After studying art in San Francisco, Maynard Dixon (1875–1946) actually worked as a cowboy in the Southwest. Like most of his contemporaries, he painted stylized, nostalgic cowboy scenes with convincing touches of authenticity. He illustrated for magazines and also painted murals. Canadian-born Will **James** also made his mark as an illustrator and writer during the 1920s and 1930s.

Another German-born painter, W. H. D. ("Big Bill") Koerner (1879–1938) also worked in the retrospective mode of his nineteenth-century predecessors. Koerner, already an artist in grammar school, did not live in the West until the last dozen years of his life. Despite his lack of firsthand observation, he realistically and epically depicted cowboy life in paintings such as *Moving the Herd* (1923) and *Trail Herd to Wyoming* (1923). Later he traveled to Montana, California, and the Southwest. He continued doing illustrations for the *Saturday Evening Post* and documenting cowboy life. For example, he painted *Reata* (1931) for the *Post*. It shows colorful vaqueros hard at work on the range. He also illustrated books for a galaxy of western authors, including Eugene Manlove **Rhodes**, Henry H. Knibbs, Bernard DeVoto, Zane Grey, and Emerson **Hough**. Illness forced him to end his career in 1935, but he left a legacy of more than 2,400 illustrations, about one-fourth of which capture western scenes. His New Jersey studio has been reconstructed at the **Buffalo Bill Historical Center** in Cody, Wyoming.

Large-circulation magazines like the *Saturday Evening Post* played an important role in the careers of many western illustrators, including N. C. (Newell Convers) Wyeth (1882–1935). The Massachusetts-born artist sold his first painting, *Bronco Buster,* in 1903. It adorned the cover of the *Saturday Evening Post*. After several trips to the West, Wyeth settled in Pennsylvania. In great demand as an illustrator, he also drew admiration for his dramatic depiction of cowboys, usually rugged, heroic, and often in danger. Wyeth, Harold Von Schmidt, and Olaf Wieghorst (1899–1988), a native of Denmark, exhibit similar blends of drama and nostalgia for bygone days of cowboys and Indians. *Letter from Home* (n.d.) is a nostalgic scene of a cowboy enjoying a letter. *The Roper* (n.d.) shows a cowboy chasing down a cow.

Many of the western painters and illustrators knew and studied with one another. Wyeth,

along with Harvey Dunn, Maynard Dixon, W. H. D. Koerner, Frank Schoonover, and others, studied with master illustrator Howard Pyle. Dunn taught many other illustrators, including Harold Von Schmidt.

California-born Harold Von Schmidt (1893–1982) became a leading illustrator for national magazines during the 1930s and 1940s. He also worked as a cowhand. "I had a chance to be with Indians, to take part in trail drives and to get to know cattle and horses as a working cowboy," he recalled. He painted in a rugged, epic style, an heir to Remington and his mentors. "Our job," he said, "is to tell the truth as we know it—beautifully and yet forcefully." He put that philosophy to work in his many paintings and illustrations. He showed cowboys hard at work in *Gully Washer* (1949) and *Cold Riding* (1954), and at play in *Home Sweet Home* and *Evening Courtship* (1932).

It would have been great if someone could have taken full-color photographs during the nineteenth-century heyday of the cowboy. Viewing a John Clymer (1907–1989) painting is about the next best thing—or maybe even better. Born in the central Washington town of Ellensburg, Clymer studied widely. N. C. Wyeth was among his teachers. His photorealism and minute attention to detail are immediately identifiable, as demonstrated in *The Gold Train* (1970).

Illinois-born Tom Ryan (1922–) paints similar cowboy scenes with the clarity and detail of photorealism. *Sharing an Apple* (1969) manages to mix authenticity and sentimentality. Harry Jackson and Newman Myrah, both born in 1921, are other important representatives of the retrospective spirit. Jackson, like Remington before him, creates works in both paint and bronze.

Given the drama and likelihood of the event, many western painters have depicted stampedes. Jackson's *Stampede* (1963), for example, shows a fallen cowboy with his foot caught in the stirrup and about to be overtaken by the herd. As a youngster, Jackson had worked on Wyoming's Pitchfork Ranch, and appropriately enough, his work resides at the Whitney Gallery of Western Art at the Buffalo Bill Historical Center in Cody,

Wyoming. Nick Eggenhofer (1897–?) has also rendered a dramatic treatment of the stampede.

El Paso–born Tom Lea (1907–) has provided a variety of powerful images of western life. Many of his oil paintings, such as *Cattle on an Early Mexican Hacienda,* offer compelling glimpses of history. He has also painted "portraits" of **longhorns** and other **cattle breeds.** Lea wrote, painted, and illustrated his own books as well as those of others. Several of folklorist James Frank **Dobie**'s books feature Lea illustrations. Lea also illustrated his own historical work, *King Ranch* (1957). In addition, he wrote a fine novel of the Texas-Mexican border, *The Wonderful Country* (1952).

Gary Morton and Willie Matthews paint ranch scenes in the photorealist tradition. Morton gathers material for his paintings firsthand on the range: "I loved those cowboy days so much that I had to paint 'em for others to enjoy." Distinctive watercolors by Matthews adorned the covers of Warner Western albums released in the early 1990s.

Thanks to this galaxy of painters, illustrators, and sculptors, we have a variety of entertaining and informative artwork depicting cowboy life, past and present. Like western fiction and history, "cowboy" painting long suffered slings and arrows from the eastern cultural elite. Today museums around the country and the world display a wide range of western art, representational and other types.

Traditional though the medium may be, western art is not without contemporary controversy. In 1991 an exhibit titled "The West as America" opened at the Smithsonian's National Museum of American Art. The stridently revisionist interpretations given to traditional western paintings elicited howls of outrage. Historian and former Librarian of Congress Daniel Boorstein termed the exhibit "perverse, historically inaccurate, destructive." Many viewers judged the exhibit curators guilty of anachronism and an excess dose of postmodernism. The entire controversy reminds us, however, that the cowboy and the West remain highly charged cultural icons.

Of course, just as you can't believe everything you read, you can't believe everything you see in pictures, but many painters memorializing the cowboy have taken pains to be accurate. Even if they don't always totally succeed, we can still admire the effort and enjoy the view. (Ainsworth 1968; Hassrick 1987; San Diego Museum of Art 1981; *Southwest Art* magazine; Taft 1982)

See also Cowboy Artists of America Museum; Appendix B.

ASADO

Meat, usually beef, roasted over an open fire. Huge herds of wild cattle roamed much of the **pampas** in Argentina through the mid-nineteenth century. Given its great abundance, **gauchos** developed a fondness for beef, and they preferred it cooked *asado* style. The cook skewered the meat—sometimes lamb or goat, but often a side of beef ribs—on an *asador,* a metal frame. Charcoal from a slow-burning fire gradually roasted the spitted meat. Gauchos favored cooking with the wood of the *quebracho* tree because it produced very little smoke. The technique is used today and still produces delicious meat. (Slatta 1992)

ASSOCIATION SADDLE

Also called Committee saddle or contest saddle. See Rodeo.

AUTOBIOGRAPHIES BY COWBOYS

Cowboy autobiographies can make wonderfully entertaining reading. The best of the genre offers unique glimpses into everyday cowboy life. These writings serve as valuable primary sources. The heyday of open-range western ranching slipped by so fast (lasting roughly from 1866 to 1886) that many elements escaped thorough historical documentation. Autobiographies by working cowboys and other ranch folk help to flesh out the particulars of that ephemeral time.

In 1885 Charles Angelo **Siringo** published the first cowboy autobiography. The reading public loved his book. He gave it a wonderfully descriptive title: *A Texas Cow Boy or Fifteen Years* *on the Hurricane Deck of a Spanish Pony Taken from the Real Life of Charles A. Siringo, an Old Stove Up Cowpuncher Who Has Spent Nearly a Life Time on the Great Western Cattle Ranges.* His tales of cowboy life charmed an eastern audience already enthralled with tales of the Wild West. In the text, he ventured a humorous opinion about the future of cowboying:

Cattle are becoming so tame from being bred up with short horns that it requires but very little skill and knowledge to be a Cow-boy. I believe the day is not far distant when cow-boys will be armed with prod-poles to punch the cattle out of their way—instead of **firearms.** Messrs Colt and Winchester will have to go out of business or else emigrate to Arkansas and open up prod-pole factories.

Siringo continued writing and put much of his life, real and imagined, in print. His five later autobiographical volumes reveal a western penchant for tall tales. In his first effort, however, Siringo provides some insights into real cowboy life of the 1870s and 1880s. Of Siringo, folklorist James Frank **Dobie** said, "No other cowboy ever talked about himself so much in print; few had so much to talk about." Siringo's pioneering literary effort quickly spawned a host of imitators.

Theodore **Roosevelt** reveled in his few years in the Dakota Badlands. His observations and memoirs helped bring respectability to cowboy literature. His *Ranch Life and the Hunting Trail* (1888) is a good read. Roosevelt penned detailed descriptions, tinged with a bit of romance, of "bully" life on the range. He drew this portrait of the cowboy:

They are smaller and less muscular than the wielders of ax and pick; but they are as hardy and self-reliant as any men who ever breathed—with bronzed, set faces, and keen eyes that look all the world straight in the face without flinching as they flash out from under the broad-brimmed hats.

Peril and hardship, and years of long toil broken by weeks of brutal dissipation, draw haggard lines across their eager faces, but never dim their reckless eyes nor break their bearing of defiant self-confidence.

Montana rancher and politician Granville Stuart adds another look from the big house in his posthumously published memoir, *Forty Years on the Frontier* (1925).

W. S. James published another early autobiography, *Cowboy Life in Texas,* in 1893. J. Frank Dobie described James as "a genuine cowboy who became a genuine preacher and wrote a book of validity. This is the best of several books of reminiscences by cowboy preachers, some of whom are as lacking in the real thing as certain cowboy artists."

W. S. James should not be confused with William Roderick ("Will") **James.** The latter illustrated and wrote many books. He titled his autobiographical volume *Lone Cowboy* (1930). Like many writers looking back over their own past, James took liberties with the truth. To remake himself into a bona fide westerner, for example, James changed his birthplace from Quebec to Montana. He also abandoned his given name, Ernest Dufault. Thanks to his experience as a cowhand, **rodeo** rider, and stunt rider, however, James developed an impressive firsthand knowledge of **ranch work.** His folksy western prose, humorous sketches, and authentic recollections combined to make his writings very popular.

Bogus and sensationalized **pulp novels** often have threatened to bury the writings of real working cowboys. Ever since *Buck Taylor, King of the Cowboys* (1887), by Prentiss Ingraham, pulp novels have enjoyed a huge, appreciative audience. Ned **Buntline,** Zane **Grey,** Max **Brand,** and countless nameless purveyors of pulp conditioned readers to expect blazing gunfights and larger-than-life heroes on every other page. Pulp publishers had a strong vested interest in increased sales and circulation but little interest in historical accuracy or authenticity.

Many fiction writers jumped aboard the cowboy memoir bandwagon. In *Guide to Life and Literature of the Southwest* (1942), Dobie blasted several pseudo-autobiographies: "A blatant farrango of lies" is his curt description of Frank Harris's *My Reminiscences as a Cowboy* (1930). Dobie found "equally worthless ... the debilitated and puerile lying" of the *Autobiography of Frank Tarbeaux* (1930), as told to Donald H. Clark. Dobie dismissed the *Memoirs of Bryant B. Brooks* (1939) as a book "printed to satisfy the senescent vanity of a property-worshiping, cliché-parroting reactionary."

One must likewise approach the *Life of "Billy" Dixon* (1914) with great caution. Beginning in January 1913, Dixon recounted events from his life to his wife Olive King Dixon. He died several months later, after which she wrote up the memoirs of his life in the Texas Panhandle. The book is a classic case of too many cooks. Dixon's story first filtered through his wife. Frederick S. Barde then edited her lengthy notes (taking great literary license) into a published volume. The result should be read more as a Texan's tall tale than as a historical document.

According to Dixon, he rode a mule four miles in pursuit of a buffalo. "The buffalo fell dead at the first shot. The explosion scared the mule into hysteria, but his was no worse than mine. I had not only killed a buffalo, but had killed, unaided, the first buffalo I ever saw." Similar heroics appear elsewhere in the book.

Amid the bogus and forgettable, however, appeared many reliable, authentic firsthand accounts. Andy Adams left us a lively novelized account of a cattle drive, *The Log of a Cowboy* (1903). Like many others of the horseback literati, the Indiana-born Adams took some license with the literal truth. His descriptions, however, rang true and appealed to readers who demanded realism. Adams offered an unvarnished portrait of cowboy life that stood in welcome contrast to the silliness and romanticism of the pulps. As Dobie noted, Adams left "a just and authentic conception of trail men, trail work, range cattle, cowboy horses, and the cow country in general."

Trail drives could be very rough. Adams recounted the difficulties of controlling a trail herd, feverish with thirst:

We threw our ropes in their faces, and when this failed, we resorted to shooting; but in defiance of the fusillade and the smoke they walked sullenly through the line of horsemen across their front. Six-shooters were discharged so close to the leaders' faces as to singe their hair.... In a number of instances wild steers deliberately walked against our horses, and then for the first time a fact dawned on us that chilled the marrow in our bones,—the herd was going blind.

The cowboys let the thirsty herd backtrack to some lakes on the Old Western Trail in Texas. It took the cattle 24 hours or more to reach the lakes. "Contrary to our expectation, they drank very little at first, but stood in the water for hours. After coming out, they would lie down and rest for hours longer, and then drink again before attempting to graze, their thirst overpowering hunger." After a few days of rest, water, and grass, "the herd had recovered its normal condition."

The Roaring Twenties brought rapid social changes, urbanization, and the proliferation of automobiles and other mechanical gadgets. As the country rushed into an uncertain future, many people longed for the simplicity of bygone frontier days. George W. Saunders founded the Old Time Trail Drivers Association in 1915. He got hundreds of ranchmen and cowboys to write autobiographical sketches. J. Marvin Hunter of Bandera, Texas, compiled these sketches into two volumes, *The Trail Drivers of Texas* (1920, 1923). Unfortunately, Hunter, who later published *Frontier Times,* cleaned up the language in the memoirs in order to make it more proper and grammatical. As with all memoirs, we must take into consideration dimming memories and the propensity to romanticize and spin tall tales, but nevertheless, the collected memoirs remain an important source of firsthand impressions of trail and ranch life.

George Saunders wrote an entry in which he recalled herding cattle from Texas to Mexico as a ten-year-old.

That night shortly after dark something scared the beeves and they made a run. I had never heard anything like the rumbling noise they made, but I put spurs to my horse and followed the noise. We ran those cattle all night and at daybreak we found we had not lost a beef, but we had five or six bunches four or five miles apart, and two or three men or boys with each bunch.

Trail boss and ranch manager Jack Potter, born in 1864, provided a lively sketch titled "Coming Down the Trail." His writing blends **humor** with authentic, sometimes salty, language. Potter later published other articles about his experiences on the cattle frontier.

Fifty Years on the Old Frontier, by James Henry Cook, also appeared in 1923. Cook had many, varied western experiences. He trailed cattle north, served as an army scout, and rode with the Texas Rangers. His memoir gave readers a real taste of cowboy life from the south Texas brush country to the northern cattle trails. Cook's treatment of Billy the Kid was as inaccurate as most, but he was more reliable on his own life. He also took pains to document and defend vanishing traditional Indian life.

Baylis John Fletcher also wrote a realistic trail drive narrative in *Up the Trail in '79.* The manuscript remained unpublished at the time of his death in 1912, but the University of Oklahoma Press finally printed it in 1968. Fletcher had helped herd longhorns from Texas to Wyoming in 1879, and in his account he reported on a near-disaster as the herd passed through Victoria, Texas:

A lady, fearful that the cattle would break down her fence and ruin her roses, ran out of the pickets and, waving her bonnet

frantically at the cattle, stampeded those in front. With a dull roar, they charged back upon the rear of the herd, and but for the discreet management of boss Arnett, heavy damage to city property would have resulted.

Writers who might bamboozle drugstore cowboys from Manhattan could not fool a real old-time hand. Many cowboys could read and write, so cowboy writings got intense scrutiny from knowledgeable critics. Some cowboys had a flair for writing, but many did not, so collaborators sometimes helped move a cowboy's memories from under his hat to the printed page. Lewis F. Crawford of the North Dakota Historical Society, for example, aided Ben Arnold in producing *Rekindling Camp Fires* (1926).

Perhaps the most famous collaboration in cowboy literature came during the late 1930s. Edward Charles ("Teddy Blue") **Abbott** tried for years to interest someone in his memories of range life. Part of the difficulty was his unwillingness to sensationalize it by adding phony gunfights and other contrivances popular in the shoot-'em-up market. Until he was in his late seventies, Abbott had little success in publishing. In 1937, however, he met a young New York writer named Helena Huntington Smith at his ranch near Lewiston, Montana. They collaborated on writing his memoirs, and their effort, the memorable *We Pointed Them North,* appeared in 1939. The book "is all Teddy Blue," claimed Smith modestly. "My part was to keep out of the way and not mess it by being literary."

Unlike many cowboy authors, Abbott did not shy away from talking about frontier **prostitution.** "As Mag Burns used to say, the cowpunchers treated them sporting women better than some men treat their wives." He once became angry with the owner of a "parlor house" in Miles City, Montana. He rode his horse right into the house. The madam locked the door and called for the police. "But there was a big window in the room that was low to

ALBUQUERQUE ACADEMY
LIBRARY

the ground, and Billy [his horse] and me went through it and got away."

"Cowboy Annie lived at Mag Burns' house. She was the N Bar outfit's girl. They were all stuck on her except the bookkeeper, the cook, and me. Her pal was my sweetheart. But Cowboy Annie surely had the rest of them on her string." Abbott also recalled another famous "chippie" in Miles City, Connie the Cowboy Queen. "Connie had a $250 dress embroidered with all the different brands—they said there wasn't an outfit in the Yellowstone down to the Platte, and over in the Dakotas, too, that couldn't find its brand on that dress."

In Miles City, Abbott said, "we'd go in town and marry a girl for a week, take her to breakfast and dinner and supper, be with her all the time. You couldn't do that in other places.... Lincoln [Nebraska] had a very religious mayor and was fast getting civilized. You couldn't walk around with those girls in the daytime like you could in Miles City."

The women's perspective on ranch life is far from absent. Clarice E. Richards, in *A Tenderfoot Bride* (1920), recounts Colorado ranch life. Mary Kidder Rak provided a look at Arizona ranch life in *A Cowman's Wife* (1934). She poses a fundamental question that has likely occurred to many ranch **women:**

> I cannot imagine that the clergyman be-
> lieves that every man should be able to
> deliver a sermon, or that the hardware
> merchant expects everyone to know the
> price of nails. Then why should a cowman
> judge the rest of humanity upon the basis
> of a familiarity with the cattle industry? I
> find that my husband is by no means alone
> in doing so.

In 1941 Agnes Morley Cleaveland published her memoirs of New Mexico ranch life. Folklorist J. Frank Dobie calls her *No Life for a Lady* the "best book on range life from a woman's point of view ever published." Laura V. Hamner offered a glimpse of ranch life in the Texas Panhandle in *Short Grass and Longhorns* (1943). Monica

Hopkins provided a glimpse at the Alberta range in *Letters from a Lady Rancher* (1981).

Working cowboys have continued to record their memories in print. Many retired cowboys feel as though they are the last of the breed. Daniel G. Moore *(Log of a Twentieth Century Cowboy,* 1965) felt that way: "I find myself one of only a small remnant of the old boys I knew." Ike Blasingame *(Dakota Cowboy,* 1958) lamented that "many of those I knew and worked with on the old cattle ranges of the north have gone to the Happy Hunting Grounds." A Texas cowboy, Blasingame worked in South Dakota on lands leased by the Matador Land and Cattle Company. (The original Matador Ranch began in 1879 in the Texas Panhandle. By the 1920s, the ranch had expanded to include 1.5 million acres, owned or leased.)

Contrary to their impressions, Moore and Blasingame were not the last cowboys. Glen R. ("Slim") Ellison, who worked in north central Arizona, left two volumes of reminiscences written in cowboy lingo: *Cowboys under the Mogollon Rim* (1968) and *More Tales from Slim Ellison* (1981).

Winona Johnson Holloway has published two volumes of memoirs of life in eastern Oregon and western Nevada. *Moving On* details life in Wallowa County, Oregon, from 1920 to 1945. Of greater interest because of its details on ranch life is *Moving Out* (1992). This volume covers the lives of Merritt and Winona Holloway and their three sons from 1946 until 1950. Ranching in the desert and mountain country of western Nevada was not for the faint of heart. *Moving Out* offers an intimate glimpse at cowboy life there in the late forties. It also offers memorable portraits of Jim Daniels and other Nevada cow people. In the book, Holloway recorded a concise, accurate description of a buckaroo's meager belongings:

> A bedroll served as a closet and a dresser,
> a bank and a lock box and might weigh as
> much as one hundred pounds. No one else
> messed with a man's bedroll, because it
> held all his "possibles" and personal be-

longings; comb, towel, clean clothes, medicine, extra tobacco, writing material, extra money, and in one case I know of, a rosary.

In the 1980s, Margot Liberty and Barry Head teamed up with Ray Holmes to bring his memoirs to print. They began documenting his life with a 1981 film, *On the Cowboy Trail* (see Films, Documentary). The result of hundreds of hours of transcribed audiotapes, *Working Cowboy* appeared in 1994. Liberty is Helena Huntington Smith's daughter. The book recalls ranch life in early twentieth-century Wyoming. It also includes practical advice about cowboying and ranch work.

So far neither cowboys nor cowboying has passed forever. True, much has changed, but compare Charlie Siringo's century-old memoir, Teddy Blue's of a half-century ago, and recent thoughts of Ray Holmes. You'll find the same grit and spirit that have always characterized cowboys. We owe a debt of thanks to all the cowboy autobiographers for the pleasure and instruction they've provided. (Branch 1961; Dobie 1952)

AUTRY, GENE
(1907–)

Unlike many western movie stars, singer Gene Autry had authentic western roots. He was born in Tioga, Texas, and his father was a cattle dealer and horse trader. Autry, influenced by his paternal grandfather, a Baptist minister, sang in the church choir and bought his first guitar at age 12. He attended high school in Texas, and then his family moved to Oklahoma. Some of Autry's early jobs and experiences, such as working as a telegraph operator and traveling with a medicine show, later showed up in his **films.** Autry credits Will Rogers with encouraging him with his singing career while he was still a railroad telegraph operator.

After a faltering start in New York show business in 1928, Autry returned to Oklahoma to sing on a Tulsa **radio** station, KVOO. In 1930 he recorded his first hit, "That Silver-Haired

Daddy of Mine" (written with Jimmy Long). A move to Chicago's WLS introduced him to Smiley Burnette, who became his comic Hollywood sidekick.

Appropriately, Autry and Burnette first sang in a film starring the screen's first singing cowboy, Ken Maynard. *In Old Santa Fe* (1934) marked the beginning of Autry's long cinema singing career. The film also boosted the career of another soon-to-be-famous sidekick, George ("Gabby") Hayes. His credits eventually included his popular "Melody Ranch" radio program, more than 90 films, an equal number of **television** episodes, and more than 300 recorded songs.

Autry often played himself in his films, which probably increased the audience's identification with him. He understood the charm of the **B-western** movie and how to deliver it to an audience. In his autobiography *(Back in the Saddle,* 1978), Autry listed his recipe: a good story and good **music,** a dash of comedy and romance, and fights and chases played out under vast western skies. He added his own special touches—lots of singing, his wonder horse Champion, and bits of modernity, with telephones, automobiles, and other twentieth-century gadgetry. Frog Milhouse, Smiley Burnette's sidekick character, became a model for the genre. Later another first-class comic sidekick, Pat Buttram, also worked with Autry.

Autry used his popularity to preach basic values, mandated, he says, by Herb Yates at Republic Studios. The "Ten Commandments of the Cowboy," aimed at admiring youth, summed up the values that Autry and other film good guys communicated through their characters: The good cowboy never takes unfair advantage; never betrays a trust; keeps his word; tells the truth; is kind to children, the elderly, and animals; is tolerant; helps those in distress; works hard; respects women, his parents, and the law; is clean in his thought, speech, and habits; and is patriotic.

Autry also had a hand in shaping the American **rodeo** industry. As a rodeo producer during the 1940s, he altered the nature of modern rodeo. First he marginalized the contestants in general and **women** in particular. Autry helped reduce women, who once starred and competed against men, to secondary roles as barrel racers and rodeo queens. He also spiced rodeos with his own singing performances. The introduction of singers and other entertainers shifted the focus away from the rodeo contestants toward Autry and other celebrities.

Autry enlisted in the Army Air Corps in 1942. "Every movie cowboy ought to devote time to the Army winning or to helping win until the war is won—the same as any other American citizen," he said. Autry made a sincere patriotic sacrifice. His annual salary of $600,000 in 1941 fell to little more than $100 per month in the army. In his absence, a singing newcomer named Roy **Rogers** lay claim to the title "King of the Cowboys."

The war years and changes in the movie industry set Autry to thinking more seriously about his financial future. He skillfully invested and crafted an economic empire that made him a multimillionaire. In 1960 he put Champion out to graze and hung up his spurs. His business interests in the electronic media, the California Angels baseball team, hotels, and ranches kept him busy. The Country Music Hall of Fame inducted Autry as a member in 1969. He still had time for old friends, however. He gave money to a destitute, alcoholic old Ken Maynard right up to the actor's death in 1973. Autry's longtime first wife, Ina Mae Spivey, died in 1980. In 1982 he married his second wife, Jackie Elam, and quit drinking.

The Gene Autry Western Heritage Museum in Los Angeles perpetuates the mythical and movie West that he helped to shape. On Autry's 85th birthday on 29 September 1992, 100 schoolchildren gathered at the museum to serenade him with "Happy Birthday." A decorative cowboy riding a galloping steed topped his birthday cake, big enough to feed far more than a hundred hungry children. Autry observed that "kids have always supported me. I've always had a great following of kids." Outfitted with his usual white cowboy hat, Autry expressed a special birthday wish: "My wish is that everybody's dream would come true."

Autry's hit theme song, "Back in the Saddle Again," enjoyed a revival in 1993 on the soundtrack for the film *Sleepless in Seattle.* The soundtrack stayed on *Billboard Magazine's* charts for more than a dozen weeks, selling more than two million copies. Autry and Ray Whitley wrote the song, first recorded in 1939. Like Autry himself, his music keeps coming back. (Autry 1978; LeCompte 1993; McDonald 1987)

AXLE GREASE

Humorous term for butter.

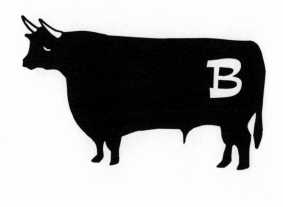

B WESTERNS

Western films changed over time and still continue to change. Film critic Brian Garfield points out that the B westerns "were filmed with great vigor, good production values and magnificent action sequences." The action appealed to audiences, especially youngsters.

The plots of many oaters (B westerns) came straight from **pulp novels,** whose predictable plots and heroes translated well to the screen. The predictability of formula westerns also provided part of their fascination. Classic B westerns had a timelessness built around the characteristics detailed in the following paragraphs.

Despite their lack of imaginative plot, dialogue, character development, and depth, B westerns captivated audiences. They especially appealed to youngsters, particularly little boys. The Bs featured lots of action, usually in the form of ritualized violence. They ended predictably: right prevailed over wrong. B-western cowboys proved to be a laconic, almost tongue-tied lot. Simple plots and uncomplicated characters (straight shooters) gave audiences a clear picture of the good and bad guys. Sidekicks added humorous touches. Once in a great while, a more daring director might add a hint of chaste love.

Westerns were star-centered and action-packed. Stars developed strong, loyal followings among their fans. Indeed, the B westerns celebrated the rugged individualism of the frontier. The hero was always the focus of action, and action was what the western genre was all about. Most B-western fans picked out and cheered for one special hero: Fred Thomson, Randolph Scott, Tom Tyler, Audie Murphey, Hoot Gibson, Allan ("Rocky") Lane, Buck Jones, Charles Starrett ("the Durango Kid"),

Actor William S. Hart in a still from a 1917 B-western film, The Narrow Trail, *an action-packed thriller based on pulp fiction.*

Johnny Mack Brown, Wild Bill Elliott, or any one of a host of others. The star's presence (along with his horse) was far more important than plot, dialogue, or any other **film** element.

Right always won over wrong, often against great odds. The hero often undertook and succeeded at super heroic tasks. One variant, known as the Bob Steele plot after the actor who played the role, pitted a young man against outlaws who had murdered some family member, usually his father. He faced many setbacks along the way, but his righteous vengeance was fulfilled in the end. Small but scrappy Bob Steele (born Robert North Bradbury, Jr., 1906–1988) often undertook such missions of vengeance in his oaters. In many ways, Superman became the modern successor to the cowboy hero.

Heroes needed villains to fight. A number of character actors became stock villains in the Bs. Fans knew to boo the bad guys—Forrest Tucker, Jack Elam, Jack Palance, Ted De Corsia, and others—the minute they appeared on screen.

Comic relief often came in the form of a faithful, zany sidekick. Smiley Burnette, Al ("Fuzzy") St. John, John Forest ("Fuzzy") Knight, George ("Gabby") Hayes, Pat Buttram, and other funny sidekicks became stars in their own right. Buttram appeared in some 40 films and as a regular on Gene **Autry**'s **television** program from 1950 to 1956. Buttram died in January 1994 at age 78. Autry lauded his old sidekick: "He was great, off the film and on the film. If I was … doing a stage show he would be sitting back there. If I needed a good one-liner right quick, he would give me a good routine."

Like the sidekick, the hero's horse might inject a note of **humor** now and then. The horse might give the hero, ever bashful with women, a nudge in the back that pushes him into the heroine's arms. Some B-western cowboy stars even gave equal billing to their horses. A brave, intelligent horse often saved his rider—and the day. Children love animal stories, so the heroic **horses of the movies** had great audience appeal.

We cannot imagine the Lone Ranger without Silver or Tonto without Scout. William S. Hart

rode Fritz, and Fred Thomson ran down the bad guys astride Silver King. Tom Mix's Tony and Ken Maynard's Tarzan had nearly as many fans as their masters.

Serials or cliffhangers often played with feature westerns. The serials distilled and exaggerated the B-western formula. Action scenes were even more action-packed, heroes more heroic, villains more villainous. The serials provided an excellent means of seeing the essence of the Bs.

The ravages of time and nitric-based films have destroyed many of the old Bs. A wide selection is still available, however, immortalized on videotape. Fans of all ages continue to seek out the old stars just for "the thrill of it all." (Etulain 1981, 1983; Everson 1992; Garfield 1982; Lenihan 1980; McDonald 1987; Rollins 1983; Tuska 1976, 1985, 1990)

"BACK IN THE SADDLE AGAIN"

Song (1938) and also a film. See Autry, Gene.

BAGUAL

Gaucho term for a wild horse.

BAILE

Spanish term for dance, also used by Anglos in the Southwest.

BAKE

To overheat a horse by riding too fast, long, or hard.

BALLARD, TODHUNTER
(1903–1980)

Novelist who wrote formula westerns under various names.

BANDANNA

General purpose cloth used by cowboys as a wash cloth, water filter, dust mask, etc.

BANGTAIL

Colloquial term for wild horse (mustang).

BAQUERO

Variant of **vaquero** or buckaroo, meaning cowboy.

BAQUIANO

Specialties were developed by some gauchos of Argentina and Uruguay, and one such specialist was the *baquiano* (also *baqueano)*, a **gaucho** guide and scout. On the trackless **pampas,** which was nearly devoid of landmarks, guides served very important roles. Military expeditions, wagon trains, ranchers, and foreigners traversing vast stretches of open plains all depended upon the scout's knowledge of the terrain. Baquianos used the stars to navigate, and they knew subtle landmarks and signs that escaped the eye of most travelers.

Domingo F. **Sarmiento,** in *Life in the Argentine Republic in the Days of the Tyrants* (1846, 1971), recorded the specialized knowledge of the pampas acquired by guides:

If he finds himself upon the pampa in impenetrable darkness, he pulls up herbs from different places, smells their roots and the earth about them, chews their foliage, and by often repeating this proceeding, assures himself of the neighborhood of some lake or stream, either of salt or freshwater, of which he avails himself, upon finding it, to set himself exactly right. It is said that General [Juan Manuel de] Rosas knows the pasturage of every estate in the south of Buenos Ayres by the taste.

Unique knowledge of foliage, terrain, trails, and water sources earned guides better wages than the average gaucho ranch hand. Scouts also played important roles in the many civil and Indian wars that plagued Argentina through the late nineteenth century. Sarmiento described the scout sensing the approach of enemy forces:

He also detects the direction in which they are approaching by means of the movements of the ostriches, deer, and guanacos, which fly in certain directions. At shorter distances he notices the clouds of dust, and estimates the number of the hostile force by their density.

(Sarmiento 1971; Slatta 1992)

BAR BIT

See Bit.

BAR DOG

Colloquial term for bartender.

BARBED WIRE

Also barb wire. See Fencing.

BAREBACK RIDING

See Rodeo.

BARKER, SQUIRE OMAR
(1894–1985)

Western author of poetry, fiction, and nonfiction.

BASE BURNER

Colloquial term for a drink of whiskey.

BAT WINGS

See Chaps.

BAXTER, GEORGE OWEN

One of many pseudonyms used by pulp novelist Frederick Schiller **Faust,** who also wrote under the name Max Brand. (Nolan 1985; Tuska and Pietarski 1983)

BAXTER SPRINGS, KANSAS

See Cow Towns.

BAYETÓN

Large poncho used by the **llanero** of Venezuela.

BEADLE, ERASTUS
(1821–1894)

See Pulp Novels.

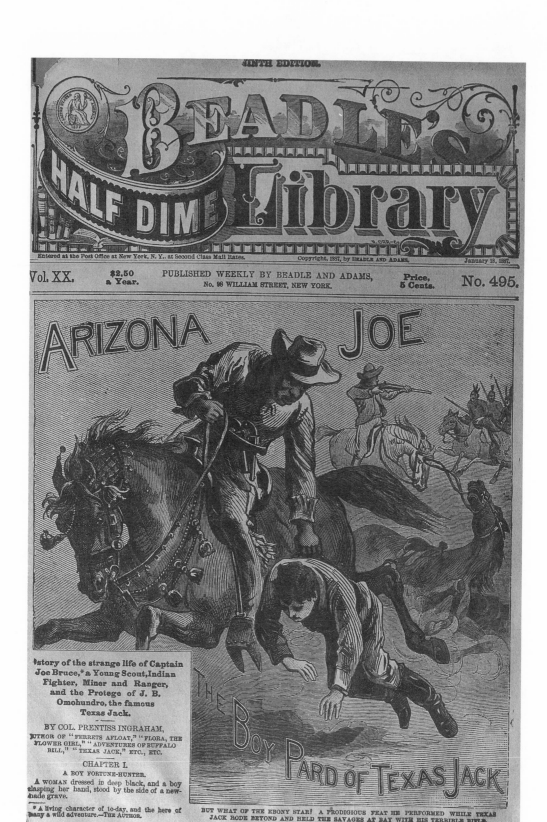

NINTH EDITION.

BEADLE'S HALF DIME Library

Entered at the Post Office at New York, N. Y., at Second Class Mail Rates. Copyright, 1887, by BEADLE AND ADAMS. January 18, 1887.

Vol. XX. $2.50 a Year. PUBLISHED WEEKLY BY BEADLE AND ADAMS, No. 98 WILLIAM STREET, NEW YORK. Price, 5 Cents. No. 495.

ARIZONA JOE

THE Boy Pard of Texas Jack

story of the strange life of Captain Joe Bruce,* a Young Scout, Indian Fighter, Miner and Ranger, and the Protege of J. B. Omohundro, the famous Texas Jack.

BY COL. PRENTISS INGRAHAM,

AUTHOR OF "FERRETS AFLOAT," "FLORA, THE FLOWER GIRL," "ADVENTURES OF BUFFALO BILL," "TEXAS JACK," ETC., ETC.

CHAPTER I.

A BOY FORTUNE-HUNTER.

A WOMAN dressed in deep black, and a boy clasping her hand, stood by the side of a new-made grave.

* A living character of to-day, and the hero of many a wild adventure.—THE AUTHOR.

BUT WHAT OF THE EBONY STAR? A PRODIGIOUS FEAT HE PERFORMED WHILE TEXAS JACK RODE BEYOND AND HELD THE SAVAGES AT BAY WITH HIS TERRIBLE RIFLE.

Erastus Beadle started this weekly pulp magazine to thrill readers with wild adventures of heroic cowboy figures such as Texas Jack and his protégé, Captain Joe Bruce.

BEADLE AND ADAMS

See Pulp Novels.

BEADLE'S HALF-DIME LIBRARY

Pulp magazine started by Erastus Beadle in the late nineteenth century. See Pulp Novels.

BEAN EATER

Colloquial and derogatory term for Mexican.

BEAN MASTER

Colloquial term for cook.

BEEF

See Food.

BEEF CATTLE INDUSTRY

When we boil it all down, a cowboy is the frontline employee of the beef cattle industry. His fast rise to fame (and employment) came with the great **trail drives** north from Texas. The purpose of those drives remains the core of the beef industry. Workers get cattle from where they are bred to where they are fed to where they are processed into beef with the best profit margin. Raising, feeding, and moving cattle is what cowboy life is all about.

In almost half the states in the nation, the cattle industry ranks as a major source of rural income. In 1984, for example, U.S. income from the sale of cattle and calves reached $30.6 billion, more than 20 percent of all cash farm income.

Much has changed in the beef cattle industry, but one thing remains the same: The number of cattle as well as prices can vary widely from year to year. The costs of animals, grazing land, feed, and fertilizers, along with export demand, can change suddenly. In some years, ranchers must sell cattle for less than the cost of raising them. Many years at least some ranchers face bankruptcy.

Early Ranching

The cattle frontier usually followed the trappers and traders and preceded the farmers. Settlers in colonial Massachusetts raised cattle in the Charles River valley and later in upper New York and the Mohawk Valley. For a short time, cattlemen raised stock among the cane brakes and marshes of the tidewater region before retreating into the piedmont and mountain valleys. Once beyond the Appalachians, cattle, sheep, and swine production became increasingly important all the way west to the Mississippi River.

Like many historical errors, misinformation about the origins of northern plains ranching goes back a long way. Joseph Nimmo *(Harper's New Monthly Magazine,* November 1886) erroneously recorded the beginning date of northern plains ranching as December 1866. According to Nimmo, a government trader, caught in a blinding snowstorm on the Laramie plains of Wyoming, set his herd loose. Some of the animals wintered over, thereby proving that cattle could be grazed.

"Road ranching" actually preceded Nimmo's dating by more than two decades. During the 1840s, livestock traders along western trails exchanged stock with emigrants bound for Oregon or California. Among them was Richard Grant, who traded animals with western emigrants at Fort Hall, Idaho, as early as 1843. He and other early road ranchers learned that cattle could survive northern winters.

Lancaster P. Lupton in Colorado and Granville Stuart in western Montana traded cattle in the early 1860s. These beef industry pioneers were originally cattle traders, not ranchers. Stuart, however, did go on to become, among other things, a prominent rancher and vigilante leader.

The cavalry's removal of the Indian threat during the 1870s eliminated the last major barrier to northern plains ranching. Destruction of the bison removed the only major grazing competitor to cattle. Indian reservations and military forts also generated demand for beef, which ranchers gladly filled.

On the southern plains during the late 1840s and later, a series of incidents spurred minor livestock booms. Provisioning troops in New Mexico, beginning in 1846, spurred livestock production. Ranchers also traded stock with emigrants heading west during the 1850s. The Gadsden Purchase of 1853 stimulated growth in the Southwest, and the Colorado gold rush of 1859, an Arizona mining boom in 1862, and the coming of the railroad in 1883 created other markets. By the early 1890s, however, a combination of drought and falling livestock prices effectively ended open-range ranching and the heyday of the **vaquero** in Arizona.

The Spanish brought hardy creole cattle to what is today the American Southwest. The original animals, related to the Andalusian fighting bulls, kept the **ringy** temperament of their ancestors. As Fay Ward notes in *The Cowboy at Work,* "They are among the sturdiest of all the **cattle breeds;** they can go farther to water and grass, and still thrive, than any other type of cattle to be found on the North American continent."

In the early seventeenth century, English shorthorn cattle were imported by colonists on the East Coast of the United States. These were dual- and triple-purpose cattle for producing meat, milk, and the tallow and hides that were important colonial export items. Settlers who moved westward took their cattle with them, especially the oxen that pulled the wagons and later supplied the power to break the tough prairie sod. By 1860 the cattle industry of the Corn Belt states was highly developed; that of the Great Plains and the Mountain States was not fully stocked until the 1880s, however.

It was, of course, the great trail drives northward from Texas, beginning in 1866, that turned the northern Great Plains into cowboy country. Cowboys drove millions of Texas longhorns from overstocked ranges in the southern part of the state to railheads in Kansas. From there the brutes traveled by rail car to midwestern feedlots and packing plants. Some cows were driven to the Northwest, where they became foundation stock for present-day herds.

Great Britain made important contributions to western ranching with three important cattle breeds: shorthorns, Angus, and Herefords.

Angus, once called Aberdeen Angus, is a cattle breed imported from Scotland. The animals are hornless, black in color, and they fatten quickly and smoothly. Scottish herders developed the breed in the shires of Aberdeen and Angus during the mid-1700s, and importers introduced them to the United States in 1873.

Nineteenth-century ranchers crossed hardy longhorns with Durhams or Herefords. The resulting stock proved to be good **rustlers** (capable of feeding on marginal range). Early crossbreeders used shorthorns, but Herefords and Angus became favored later. Capital from Scottish and British investors also helped fuel the great ranching boom of the 1870s and 1880s.

Nineteenth-century ranches varied widely in size, styles, and profits. Many ranchers scratched out a meager living with small herds and lived in crude accommodations, but many huge ranches developed from Texas northward. By the end of the nineteenth century, Richard King had accumulated some 1.27 million acres in his south Texas ranch. The **King Ranch** employed 300 vaqueros who worked 65,000 cattle and 10,000 horses. John **Chisum**'s well-named Rancho Grande straddled the border between west Texas and New Mexico. In a single season before Chisum died in 1884, his cowboys branded 18,000 calves. Charles **Goodnight**'s XIT outfit in the Texas Panhandle covered some 700,000 acres in 1883.

Large outfits also developed on the northern plains. In 1884 in Montana, ten companies owned 90 percent of the livestock in the area of Fort Benton. The Swan Land and Cattle Company owned or controlled 600,000 acres in Nebraska and Wyoming. Illegal **fencing** of public lands offered another means of extending one's holdings. Up to 95 percent of the final titles filed under the Desert Land Act of 1877 probably were fraudulent. As usual, unscrupulous speculators, not family ranchers and farmers, profited.

From the Open Range to Feedlots
By the mid-1880s the range had become overstocked, and barbed-wire fences and

railroads crisscrossed the Great Plains. By this time, homesteaders were winning the battle with ranchers for dominance of the public domain, and ranching was changing from a frontier industry to a corporate enterprise. Then came the severe winters of 1885–86 and 1886–87, which destroyed more than three-fourths of the herds on the northern plains.

During the 1890s, fenced pasture and farms replaced most open range, and the great era of roundups and trail drives ended. Today legend has transformed the cowboy of this period into the epitome of the frontier hero.

During the nineteenth century, ranchers generally fed their animals on grass. Beginning with George W. Dole's packing house in 1832, Chicago became the premier cattle market in the country. After the Civil War, railroads tied together the vast supply of western range cattle and the Chicago market. By 1890 stockyards in the city slaughtered more than 2 million head of livestock annually.

Dividing the industry into breeding and feeding components came as an offshoot of the cottonseed oil industry. During the 1890s, mills in Texas, Oklahoma, and New Mexico began using their byproducts, meal and hulls, to feed cattle. Cattlemen rented pens in feed yards adjacent to the mills and fattened their animals with the byproducts. One Oklahoma cattleman recalled that "our rations were simple—meal and hulls, corn and molasses, which were fed by hand from mule-drawn wagons." This mill feeding served as a prototype for modern custom feed yards.

Cattlemen faced a problem, however, in the form of "meal evil." Some steers went blind on a ration of meal and hulls. By trial and error, ranchers learned to supplement with alfalfa, which corrected the dietary deficiency. (Modern feeders supplement with carotene and vitamin A to prevent eyesight problems in animals.) By the 1960s, researchers had eradicated another livestock problem, screwworms.

Cowboying and ranching continued to change substantially in the twentieth century. Specialization affected the beef cattle industry, as it did all businesses. The key to the cattle business is holding down costs and making the best possible market connection. Recognizing the need for cooperation in the face of rapid changes, ranchers formed the American National Cattlemen's Association in 1898. Like the earlier state and regional **stockmen's association**, this group lobbied government on behalf of the beef industry.

During the early twentieth century, silage became a popular cattle feed. Silos sprang up all over the West. In September 1929 Paul Vickers and others founded the Texas Breeder-Feeder Association to promote cooperation between farmers producing silage and ranchers fattening cattle. The Depression took its toll on cattle feeding, but ranchers and farmers persisted as well as they could.

Feedlots cluster in several parts of the country. One focus is the western high plains (Texas, Oklahoma, Kansas, Colorado, Nebraska). Another is the Corn Belt (Iowa, Illinois, Indiana, Ohio). California also has a significant feedlot industry.

Since the early 1960s, the area comprised of the Texas/Oklahoma Panhandle and eastern New Mexico has become the nation's feedlot center. Like the economy in general, the feedlot boom went bust in the 1970s. During the 1980s, however, the region's feedlots rebounded to fatten from four million to nearly six million cattle annually.

The feedlot provides high-concentrate or high-energy rations, supplemented with protein, vitamins, and minerals. The yearlings feed in the confinement of a feedlot for three to five months. Feedlot owners try to put on about two pounds per day on an animal. This weight gain will bring the cattle to slaughter weight of 1,100 pounds by the age of 18 to 24 months.

North American Beef Industry Today
In its simplest form, production of beef cattle for slaughter consists of three steps. Beef cows nurse their calves for the first six to eight months on the range. Animals graze on pasture or range in summer. Ranchers might add a bit of protein

concentrate and roughage in winter, but generally they supply very little additional feed.

At weaning time calves weigh about 450 pounds. The rancher generally sells his animals to a feedlot operator. Over the next six to twelve months, the feedlot operator feeds the cattle on high-quality roughage or pasture. The yearlings, weighing about 650 pounds, are now ready for serious fattening.

For the past century, public health concerns have led to increased regulation of the meat-packing industry. The federal government began meat inspections as early as the 1890s. Progressive-era legislation in 1906 required more rigorous inspection of all livestock destined for interstate or foreign markets. The Packers and Stockyards Act of 1921 added further controls. A 1967 act finally forced all meat packers to abide by federal inspection requirements.

Humanitarian concerns have forced some changes in processing techniques. The Humane Methods Slaughter Act of 1978 requires that cattle (and other animals) be rendered insensible before they are killed. Many meat packers use a captive bolt (stun gun) on cattle and sheep.

Once stunned, cattle are chained by one leg and hoisted onto an efficient, overhead pulley that moves along a continuous rail system. Gravity helps drain the blood quickly from the slaughtered carcasses. As the carcasses move along the rail, they are skinned, disemboweled, beheaded, and split down the backbone into two sides. After refrigeration, sides of beef are shipped out for further processing into various beef cuts.

Despite changing diet and health concerns, beef remains big business. Annual beef consumption (excluding veal) in the United States fell from 94.4 pounds per capita in 1977 to a shade under 80 pounds per person a decade later. In 1986, however, the beef industry still slaughtered nearly 38 million head for beef and another 3.5 million for veal. Beef's average retail

This late nineteenth-century ranch—Upper Walrond—is on the vast plains of Alberta, the great open-range ranching area in Canada.

price per pound rose from $.82 in 1966 to $1.55 in 1976 and $2.40 in 1986.

Texas, Iowa, Nebraska, Kansas, Illinois, California, Minnesota, Missouri, South Dakota, Oklahoma, Wisconsin, Colorado, Montana, and Indiana are the chief beef-producing states. About two million American ranchers and farmers raise animals for meat. By-products such as hides, tallow, and bone meal account for about 15 percent of an animal's value. About 62 percent of beef is sold cut. About 25 percent is ground into hamburger, and 14 percent goes to processed meats, such as bologna.

Ranching has always been risky business. The rancher faces threats on all sides. Adverse weather, the cost of feed, government policies, and changing consumer attitudes can all depress the beef market. In the past decade consumer health concerns gradually tilted the beef market away from the traditional, heavily marbled corn-fed beef toward leaner cuts. Despite changing tastes, many consumers still agree with the Beef Council: "Beef is real food for real people."

Beef Cattle in Canada

Cattle made an appearance in western Canada well before cowboys. By the early eighteenth century, fur trading posts throughout the Canadian Northwest maintained small herds of livestock. Spanish explorers carried livestock during the early 1790s from the Pacific Coast of Mexico and California to their remote outpost at Nootka Sound, abandoning the post and their northwest claims soon thereafter. By the War of 1812, cattle could be found along the Red River and, by the 1840s, at Fort Edmonton.

Oregonians also trailed animals northward into British Columbia. Between 1859 and 1870, some 22,000 Oregon cattle entered Canada, mostly along the Okanagan Trail that ran through the Okanagan country of eastern Washington to the port of entry at Osoyoos. Some of the American drovers settled in British Columbia. Cattle multiplied during the 1850s and 1860s in the areas of Lytton, Lillovet, Caribou, Quesnel, and Williams Lake. As in Mexico, Brazil, and the American Southwest, a

mining boom, this one along the Fraser River, fueled demand for livestock.

Americans continued to trail herds up the Okanagan Trail from Oregon as long as the mining boom lasted, but ranching declined in the late 1860s along with the mining. The building of the Canadian Pacific Railway in 1883 and the Klondike gold strike of 1898 fueled two more short-lived livestock booms. Ranching in British Columbia, as in many other northern ranges, suffered from overstocking, overgrazing, and losses due to harsh winter weather.

Ranching came relatively late and very briefly to the prairies of Saskatchewan. Charles Reid established a ranch in 1886, but there were few other ranches or cowboys in the region until the mid-1890s. A report in 1899 by a North West Mounted Police officer provided a glowing description of the Swift Current-Maple Creek region: "The district is in the most prosperous condition, and the livestock industry, in which almost the entire population may be said to be engaged, to a greater or a lesser extent, is bringing large sums of money into the county."

Ranching enjoyed an ephemeral heyday during the first years of the twentieth century. Ranch hands, about half from Canada and half from the United States, found good, steady work. By 1905, however, farming rapidly swept aside cattle on the western Canadian prairies. Cowpunchers faced unemployment or "sod busting" (farming) as their unpalatable alternatives.

The foothills and plains east of the Rockies in Alberta became the great open-range ranching area of Canada, and Alberta developed a flourishing cowboy culture. As in the United States, the first phase of Alberta ranching depended on access to free grass on the open range. From about 1874 to 1881, cattle slowly supplanted bison on the range. Local markets—the Canadian Mounted Police and reservation Indians—stimulated early ranching. As on the American Great Plains, the bison disappeared, Indians were reduced to reservation life, and the rich grasses were left to the cattleman.

Calgary became the economic and social center of cowboy life, not unlike Fort Worth or Cheyenne. The ranching boom began in about 1881 and peaked between 1885 and 1895. As in Saskatchewan, ranching lost its preeminence to agriculture during the first decade of the twentieth century.

Ranchers held the first **roundup** in southern Alberta during the summer of 1879 in the Macleod district. Sixteen cowboys gathered some 500 to 600 head. Disappointed with the number of cattle, some ranchers moved their herds south across the border to Montana. Many believed that despite government grants of beef to reservations, Indian depredations continued to take a toll on Alberta livestock.

F. W. Ings *(Canadian Cattlemen,* December 1938) recalled roundups of the 1880s:

> We adopted pretty much the same system as was carried on across the border. Our roundups were community affairs, the different ranches in the district sending representatives called "reps" to ride with wagons of that part, hence I rode with the Bar-U representing our OH brand.
>
> These reps took six to eight horses of their own, their saddles and bed rolls. Each man had a good slicker as he had to be out in all sorts of weather. Some of us had tents and most had waterproof tarpaulins in which to roll our blankets, and to spread under and over us at night.
>
> Most of our best riders came from the States and they taught us all we knew of cattle lore. Over there, cattle and roundup were an old story, to us they were a new game. We were young and we learned quickly; we had to, it was essential that we knew these things.

A leasing system, established in December 1881, permitted leases of up to 100,000 acres—a provision that aided big ranchers at the expense of small stockmen (just as public policy did in Latin America). The leases obligated ranchers to establish one head per ten acres within three years' time.

The *Fort Macleod Gazette* (1 July 1882) filed an upbeat report on that year's summer roundup at Pincher Creek:

> There is an immense number of stock in this section now and these thoroughly organized round-up parties are a matter of necessity. We are informed that the Pincher Creek cattle are in splendid condition, and we can easily believe this, as that country can hold its own with any of these parts, all of which are hard to beat.

As in earlier decades, Oregon supplied some cattle to the Alberta ranges. Bert Huffman *(Canadian Cattlemen,* March 1939) recounted one such transaction. "In the spring of 1884 J. Q. Shirley, a pioneer cattleman of Oregon and Idaho, received an order for 2500 head of young cattle from some new cattle company starting up a ranch in the Calgary district" [probably the Cochrane Ranche]. Young Bert accompanied his father, William, who helped gather cattle for the Shirley drive.

> I remember that we paid around $30 each for three year old steers and $20 to $25 for heifers. Many of theirs were "dogies," from milk cows, raised around barns and settlers homes and were miserable animals to drive in a bunch.

Ten cowboys drove the herd the 650 miles to the Calgary range. Young Bert did not get to make the drive, but his older friend Tom Lloyd went along as a **wrangler.**

> My chum, Tom Lloyd, sat up with me night after night, telling me of that wonderful 650 mile drive, of fording and swimming rivers, of bucking bronchos and herds of antelope encountered on the way, of the most wonderful town of "Calgarry," which was so different from our frontier Oregon towns, of the great prai-

ries, "larger than all of Oregon," where the cattle were counted, classified, branded and delivered to their new owners.

Alberta ranchers occupied the foothills on the eastern slope of the Canadian Rockies from the Montana border 240 miles north to the Red Deer River. Mary Ella Inderwick, a rancher's wife, described the countryside near the North Fork Ranch in a letter written in 1884: "We are in the foothills—no plains here—but the most glorious ranges of hills and rolling prairie— which all seems so near that one starts to ride to a certain land mark but finds oneself still no nearer at the end of an hour." She reported being able to see rooftops 22 miles away.

Ranching boomed during the 1880s. Historian David Breen reports that nearly 110,000 cattle grazed western Canadian ranges by 1889. Fifty-seven large ranches accounted for 89 percent of the total production. England provided the main market for Alberta beef, and exports more than doubled from about 62,000 animals in 1882 to 143,000 in 1885. In 1898 total exports peaked at 213,000 animals. Under assault from farmers, the ranching industry declined quickly thereafter. Alberta alone exported 75,000 cattle in 1906. Five years later the total for Alberta fell to only 12,000 head.

Despite its rich grasses and fortuitous Chinook winds, the Canadian prairie was no paradise. Riding along the Montana-Alberta border in 1881, Duncan McEachran, a cattleman, reported a number of natural hazards. Gopher holes pocked the **plains** and downed many a horse and rider. McEachran judged the holes "very dangerous to horses unaccustomed to them." Prairie-bred mounts learned to avoid the holes. He also complained of attacks from ravenous "bulldog-flies" and mosquitoes. The bulldog-fly, bigger than a bee, "makes a large hole in the skin, and the blood flows freely from it. These flies are very pertinacious, and the poor horses become frantic under their torment." Such pests plagued riders in all plains areas, particularly during the hot summer months.

Potentially violent rancher-farmer altercations occurred in Albert as they did in the United States. Sam Livingston, a farmer, settled on land near Fish Creek, Alberta, in 1875. In 1885 hands from the large Cochrane Ranche began driving his livestock from lands claimed by the ranch. "For the present," responded Livingston, "I defend my claim as my neighbours do, behind my Winchester." Elected chairman of a farmers' group in April 1885, he proclaimed that farmers "must either fight for our rights or leave the country."

The Canadian frontier, however, proved much less violent than its counterpart to the south. Disputes generally ended through the judicial process, not in gunplay. Many ranchmen, however, found little to admire in the wave of agricultural immigrants that engulfed them. In 1910 Mounted Police Superintendent Richard Burton Deane received a complaint of horse theft. The victim, an immigrant Mormon farmer from the United States named Roueche, lost two animals to men who worked for him for a few days. The superintendent complained that farmers, "having been too careless and too indolent to take reasonable care of their horses," now showed that "they were too careless and too indolent to make a reasonable attempt to recover their property. The Western prairie is swarming with useless settlers of this calibre."

The boom of the 1880s stimulated a healthy demand for cowboys. Alberta's cowboys initially came from a variety of sources. Early ranchers in the 1870s hired Indians and former Mounties. In *Canadian Cattlemen* (March 1941), cattleman Frank G. Roe recalled that in those early days "a large percentage of the labor employed on the ranches was either half-breed or Indian." Canadians often used the term *half-breed* to mean the *métis*—mestizo trappers, hunters, and subsistence farmers of mixed Indian and French parentage. In Latin America most cowboys were Indians, mestizos, or otherwise of mixed blood, but in Canada, the métis, a large mixed-blood population, seldom worked on cattle ranches.

Captain John Stewart developed a substantial cattle ranching operation and raised horses for sale to his ex-colleagues of the Mounted Police. The Mounted Police thus provided both market and manpower to the incipient ranch industry. Cowboys also rode up from the United States to work the Alberta range. By the late 1880s, Canadian and British hands had replaced most of the earlier cowboys, although ranchers still added American hands during **trail drives** and roundups.

Ranchers on the sparsely populated Alberta frontier did experience occasional shortages of skilled cowboys. In the early days of ranching in the 1870s, few men could be found with the necessary horsemanship and knowledge of animals, grasses, and weather. In 1883 John R. Craig, a rancher, complained that "first-class experienced cowboys are not plentiful." On the other hand, he found "imitations" in great abundance.

The early small ranches employed one or two men per 100 cattle. Mrs. Duthie, a Pincher Creek ranch wife, recalled that their bunkhouse usually held about five hands and a cook. Big outfits hired fewer men in proportion to the number of cattle; a large ranch needed only one hand per thousand head.

Montana cowboys quickly filled the bill, and by the mid-1880s Alberta ranchers had more hands. Rancher John D. Higinbotham recalled that from 1884 to 1887 herds were trailed from as far south as Texas up to Alberta. Released at the end of the drive, the cowboys found themselves out of work. "For a time the country was overrun with unemployed punchers and broncho-busters," Higinbotham explained. Alberta ranchers generally found sufficient manpower to keep pace with the expanding livestock industry.

The Canadian frontier was also home to **remittance men,** who came from England to make their fortunes in the West, bringing along money sent by their families in Great Britain for their maintenance. Few remittance men experienced any great success on the frontier. As open-range ranching declined in the United States, cowboys pushed north looking for work. Not until World War I did Canadian ranchers again face labor shortages, and most British hands did not return to Alberta after the war. The Alberta ranges became increasingly populated by hands from the United States, but the livestock industry was already in decline.

Some Canadian cowboys enjoyed upward mobility. George Lane, for example, worked his way up from cowboy to ranch foreman. He purchased two Alberta ranches, the Flying E in 1892 and the YT spread on the Little Bow River a few years later. Expanding his operations through a partnership, he controlled some 30,000 head of cattle by the early twentieth century. Other provident cowboys—such as John Ware and Herb Miller, who became ranchers near Macleod—achieved similar success. As with most success stories of the Henry Ford and Andrew Carnegie genre, however, these are exceptions that prove the rule of infrequent upward mobility.

According to a Miss Shaw, quoted in the London *Times* (21 October 1898), the Canadian West offered ample opportunity:

> Any man having earned enough money to buy a cow may turn her loose upon the public range. Upon branding her calf in the following spring, he will be the possessor of two animals instead of one, and may continue while he works for wages to add to the number of his herd, until such time as he sees a chance of making profit enough to justify the establishment of a separate homestead.

Miss Shaw's optimism caused her to overlook a few unavoidable facts. Without a bull in addition to one cow, offspring were unlikely. In addition, the land lease laws of Canada promoted large operations at the expense of small ranchers. Finally, the seasonal work and generally low wages of ranch work made it unlikely that many cowboys could save enough to make the considerable investment needed to start a ranch. The most a cowboy could hope for was a position as a ranch foreman or manager, at double to triple the wages earned by the average hand.

Canadian ranchers organized to cooperate in solving common, far-flung range problems and to voice a political agenda. Eleven ranchers around Macleod organized in 1883 into an association. In 1890 ranchers formed a province-wide organization, the Alberta Stock Growers' Association, which became the Western Stock Grower's Association two years later. Issues ranging from combating **rustling** and wolves to lobbying about import and export policies came before such groups.

Canadian ranchers enjoyed several practical advantages over their counterparts to the south. Indian "pacification" preceded the cattle frontier in Canada. Canadian ranchers did not have to mount private armies of their own cowboys, as did ranchers in the United States and Latin America. The Mounted Police had largely established the rule of law and subdued the Indian population before livestock raising reached Alberta. "Flying patrols" of Mounties watched for strangers on the range, persecuted rustlers, and visited ranches regularly.

The South-Western Stock Association, headquartered at Macleod, offered rewards to assist the Mounted Police with frontier law enforcement. The **stockmen's association** announced in 1883 that it would pay $100 for information leading to the conviction of anyone who killed cattle, stole **horses,** or set fire to the range.

In 1884, ten companies controlled two-thirds of the stocked land in southwest Alberta. Four—the Cochrane, Walrond, Oxley, and North-West Cattle Company ranches—controlled almost half the land. The Cochrane Ranche leased 189,000 acres, the Oxley and Walrond 180,000 acres each. As in the United States, speculators profited from the leasing arrangement. Their activities further reduced opportunities for small operators.

Unlike the many self-made men of the ranching frontier in the United States, Canada's ranchers were ready-made gentlemen. Most came from eastern Canada or England, complete with upper-class tastes and conservative politics to match. As one observer noted in 1911, Canada's ranchers "are hardly of the traditional bronco-busting, raw-punching sort. They are Englishmen of the country class." The ranching elite mixed and married with the urban upper crust at the Ranchman's Club in Calgary, founded in 1891.

Until the tide of national politics turned against them, the conservative ranching elite of Alberta boasted an impressive record of successful lobbying. Land leases, particularly choice, well-watered range, went to large ranching companies, and tariffs favored beef exporters. The stock raisers succeeded for about 20 years in keeping out competition from ranchers and farmers in the United States. The threat of sheepmen was met by requiring special grazing permits granted through the Ministry of the Interior. The Canadian ranching frontier offered the cowboy a measure of civility and comfort, but few cowhands could aspire to gather a herd and obtain leases themselves.

Natural and political phenomena combined in the early years of the twentieth century to push farming onto the western Canadian ranges. The region experienced higher-than-average summer rainfall from 1900 through 1905, fueling confidence in the potential of dryland farming. The Liberal government of Canada promoted western settlement. Farmers, many of them emigrants from the United States, pushed confidently into the Canadian West. Most hopes became quickly dashed, however, as rainfall levels returned to normal. A harsh winter in 1906–1907 further dampened farmers' dreams for making it big in the "Last Best West."

Buoyed by strong international markets, Alberta ranchers withstood the agricultural onslaught and expanded their herds, but the harsh winter struck livestock as hard as it did the farmers. In early December 1906 the temperature in Alberta fell to -30°F. By February the mercury fell to -40°, and the bitter cold lasted through March. The diary of rancher H. M. Hatfield recorded the effects of the winter on his place near Macleod. "This wind is warranted to

bite anything living or dead," he wrote
on 30 December 1906. "Cold a terror"
(30 December 1906). "This is the worst winter
I have ever seen" (17 January 1907). "I wonder
if the blamed snow ever will melt" (18 March).
"The winter lasted over *26 weeks*" (15 May).
Some large ranches lost 80 percent of their herds,
but small outfits suffered less.

Despite the harsh winter, Alberta's spring
roundup in 1907 was one of the province's
biggest. Cowboys collected some 130,000 head.
Alberta livestock fared reasonably well in cold
weather, because most ranchers had been putting
up hay since the 1880s. Some ranchers cut only
enough hay for saddle horses; cattle rustled for
themselves. Most ranchers, however, made
provision for heavy snows. Canadian cowboys
worked on hay rigs well before it became
common for hands in the United States.

Wesley F. Orr, a Calgary rancher, wrote a letter
on 20 December 1891 to John Stephenson in
Denver. Orr reveals a cautious approach toward
winter dangers. "We do occasionally have pretty
cold weather but very seldom have much heavy
wind when it is very cold so that cattle and horses
do well on the ranges all the year. . . . All stock
men put up some hay against a storm. Last
winter the loss of stock was not over 4 percent."

The heyday of the cattleman and cowboy was
drawing to a close in Alberta, however, as it had
two decades earlier in the United States. In both
cases, weather, agricultural immigration, and
public policy combined to shake the livestock
industry. Senator Daniel E. Riley recalled the fast
changes that came with farming (*Canadian
Cattlemen,* June 1938):

> This tremendous influx of settlers was
> most disastrous to the cattlemen as it
> drove their herds from their summer graz-
> ing grounds, the well-grassed plains and
> prairies, to the rough lands of the foothills
> and the poorer parts East where the grass,
> though luxuriant, had not the fattening
> qualities of the gramma or as it is known,
> the buffalo grass. It meant the removal of
> entire herds and the curtailment of others.

Vast lands, once leased for grazing, were sold to
farmers by the government and by the Canadian
Pacific Railway. Dryland farming likewise went
into decline, but irrigation technology later
revived agriculture on the Canadian prairies. Still
later, in the 1970s, oil gave rise to yet another
Texas-style boom and bust in the region.

Not all cowboys accepted the passing of the
cattle frontier gracefully. A mock will, penned in
1919 by a Saskatchewan cowboy, reveals a
bitterness against "sodbusters." The cowboy
wished to "create a fund, to be ultimately used
for the extermination of that class of vermin,
commonly known as farmers." He added a
clause three years later: "I leave to each and every
Mossback my perpetual curse as some reward to
them for their labors in destroying the *Open
Range,* by means of that most pernicious of all
implements, the plow."

Beef Cattle in Argentina

The beef industry in the Río de la Plata extends
all the way back to the mid-sixteenth century.
Wild cattle and horses escaped from the
Spanish. Soon millions of cattle grazed the rich
grasses of the **pampas.** The Río de la Plata
lacked rich mineral deposits, but it became a
wealth-producing region thanks to its huge herds
of wild cattle and horses. **Gauchos** engaged in
licensed wild-cattle hunts *(vaquerías)* by
obtaining a special permit *(acción).* Often,
however gauchos hunted without permission.
Merchants exported the gathered hides, tallow,
and by-products.

The growth of cities in Latin America also
generated markets for livestock for local
consumption. The founding of Santa Fe in 1573
and Juan de Garay's refounding of Buenos Aires
in 1580 spurred hinterland development insofar
as hostile Indians permitted. Cattle appeared in
the Mesopotamian provinces of Corrientes and
Entre Ríos by 1583.

Hides sold in both internal and external
markets, but exports to Europe boomed during
the eighteenth century. Buenos Aires exported
about 185,000 hides from 1726 to 1738. City
officials, concerned over the diminishing herds,

took sterner measures to limit unsanctioned hunting by Indians and gauchos.

By the mid-1700s, wealthier ranchers (*estancieros*) began laying claim to well-watered sections of the pampas and to the animals that grazed there. Gauchos began taming wild cattle instead of merely hunting them. Ranchers continued to use the tough, rangy creole cattle for hide and salted meat exports.

Some ranchers also bred mules, the sterile offspring of jackasses and mares. In mountainous regions such as Salta, mules served as mounts. In many areas, including mining centers like Potosí in Upper Peru (now Bolivia), mules worked in the mines and as pack animals. Muleteers (*arrieros*) drove long pack trains of more than 80 mules each from Potosí and Chile to cities in the Río de la Plata. During the colonial period, the pampas around Córdoba became an important mule-breeding center.

Ranchers also raised oxen (castrated cattle). These important draft animals pulled high-wheeled carts across the pampas and up trails to the mining regions of Upper Peru. Some ranches included *mataderos* or slaughterhouses to produce beef for local consumption.

Buenos Aires exported more than half a million cattle hides during the decade of the 1810s, a figure that rose to 2.3 million during the decade of the 1840s. Hides accounted for 65 percent of the city's total exports in 1822. By the 1890s, however, the amount fell to 26 percent. Chilled beef, wool, wheat, and other cereals marginalized the hides industry. Argentina, however, remains a leading producer of leather clothing and shoes.

Dried Beef Exports

During much of the colonial era, gauchos slaughtered wild cattle on the pampa simply for their hides and tallow. During the eighteenth century, dried meat or *charqui*, exported to feed Cuban and Brazilian slaves, became another important product. During the late eighteenth and early nineteenth century, the slaughter and meat-drying operation moved from the **estancia** to the *saladero* (meat-salting plant). Quick,

substantial profits attracted many to invest, including young rancher and future dictator Juan Manuel de Rosas.

Bourbon trade liberalization during the 1780s boosted the *charqui* trade from Buenos Aires, Montevideo, and other port cities. Salted meat exports from Buenos Aires rose tenfold from about 984 tons in the 1810s to 9,860 tons in the 1830s. Exports more than doubled again during the 1840s.

The primitive saladeros were definitely low-tech. Discarded meat, bones, and blood drew scavengers, raised a stench, and created health hazards, including water pollution. Despite their primitive methods, saladeros south of Buenos Aires were processing some 250,000 cattle per year by about 1850. In Uruguay and Rio Grande do Sul, traditional saladeros remained economic mainstays until the twentieth century.

The Sheep Boom

Sheep, of the genus *Ovis*, have long been raised for their wool and meat. Beginning in the 1820s British ranchers began importing sheep and grazing them in cooler areas of the Argentine pampas. Despite resistance from traditional cattle ranchers, the sheep population grew gradually.

Initially ranchers raised merino sheep and exported wool to French and British textile mills. Both men and women earned relatively high wages during the busy shearing season. During the 1860s thicker-fleeced Rambouillet sheep replaced the merinos. With the development of chilled meat technology, ranchers imported Lincoln and Romney Marsh sheep, breeds that provided good mutton, and Argentina's sheep population jumped to 61 million in 1880. Sheep and farming pushed cattle farther out onto more remote areas of the pampa. By 1895 Argentina's sheep population numbered nearly 75 million head.

Chilled Beef Exports

By the 1880s ranchers began raising hybrid cattle for the European chilled beef trade. Cereals and chilled beef eclipsed both the traditional hides and salted beef trade in importance. In 1895, 5,500 Argentines labored in 39 saladeros, but salted meat accounted for only about 2 percent of total national exports.

Mataderos (slaughterhouses) supplied beef to local markets. Thanks to refrigeration technology, during the 1880s *frigoríficos* (meat-packing plants) began replacing saladeros and mataderos. At the plants, workers butchered animals and packed the chilled meat for transport in refrigerator ships to Europe.

Frigoríficos required higher quality meat, so ranchers introduced blooded bulls from Europe and planted alfalfa for feed to improve their stock. The British controlled most meat-packing houses during the first decade of the twentieth century. By 1914, however, the North American meat-packing industry had taken control of one-half to two-thirds of Argentina's production. Fearing *aftosa* (foot-and-mouth disease), the United States restricted live cattle imports from Argentina. Despite stiff competition and trade barriers, Argentina remains among the world's top ten sheep and cattle producers and consumers. (Atheron 1961; Ball 1993; Brado 1984; Breen 1983; Dale 1960; Evans 1976; Holden 1970; Jordan 1993; Lamar 1977; Sáenz Quesada 1980; Slatta 1990, 1992; Solberg 1987; Ward 1958)

See also Cattle Breeds.

BEERY, NOAH, JR.
(1913–1994)
Actor. See Films, Cowboy.

BELLY WASH
Colloquial term for weak **coffee**.

BIBLE
Colloquial term for a small packet of papers used to roll cigarettes.

BICKHAM, JACK MILES
(1930–)
Novelist who has written formula westerns under various names.

BIERSTADT, ALBERT
(1830–1902)
Artist. See Art of the Cowboy.

BIG AUGUR
Also big sugar. Colloquial terms for ranch owner.

BIG FOUR HAT
See Hat.

BIG HOUSE
Colloquial term for the owner's ranch house.

BIG LOOP
See Rustling.

THE BIG TRAIL
Film (1930). See Wayne, John ("Duke").

BILL SHOW
Colloquial term for a Wild West show, probably derived from the names of the two leading show promoters. See Cody, William Frederick ("Buffalo Bill"); Lillie, Gordon William ("Pawnee Bill").

BISCUIT
Colloquial term for **saddle** horn.

BISCUIT ROLLER
Also biscuit shooter. Colloquial terms for cook. See Food.

BIT
This part of a bridle fits around and in the horse's mouth. A bit consists of several parts, including two cheek pieces that connect to the reins, a mouthpiece (a straight or curved metal piece that fits into the horse's mouth), and a bottom bar. A rider can pull on the reins and exert pressure on the bit to guide a horse.

Most cowboys prefer to break a horse using a hackamore rather than a bridle, because the bit can injure a horse's mouth. According to Fay Ward, "Next to cutting his wind off, the use of a bit in breaking a bronc has caused more horses to fight back, cold-jaw, and stampede than any other procedure. A cold-jawed horse is one that keeps his jaw closed and is likely to get the bit in his teeth and run with it."

Bits come in a wide variety of types and shapes. The Spanish conquistadors used a snaffle bit, which is split in the middle. Mexican bits often feature extra chains that jingle and add decorative touches. A bar bit, as the term indicates, consists of a single, solid metal bar. Spade and ring bits can injure a horse's mouth if the rider pulls very sharply on the reins. (Foster-Harris 1955; Ward 1958)

See also Tack.

BIT HOUSE

Colloquial term for cheap saloon.

BLACK, BAXTER
(1945–)

The 1980s marked a wonderful renaissance of an oldtime cowboy pastime, **poetry.** Today hundreds of cowboy (and cowgirl) poets gather throughout the West to recite old favorites and to present new material. Baxter Black has emerged as the nation's leading humorous cowboy poet. Raised in New Mexico, Black now lives at his ranch near Brighton, Colorado. Before becoming a full-time poet and performer, Black worked as a large animal veterinarian. In 1983 Black married folklorist Guy Logsdon's daughter, Cindy Lou.

Black wrote his first poem, "The Cowboy and His Dog," around 1980. A decade later he had published a half-dozen poetry books, including two volumes of *Croutons on a Cow Pie.*

His quizzical expressions and large, drooping mustache are instantly recognizable and have become familiar to people across the country. "The Oyster" may be his most famous poem. The plot involves an eastern woman (innocent of western ways), her cowboy suitor, and a misunderstanding about mountain oysters.

Appearances on "The Johnny Carson Show," often with fellow poet Waddie **Mitchell,** and spots on National Public Radio extended Black's range of fans far beyond the West. He also displays his zany **humor** around the nation via newspaper columns, public appearances, and videotapes.

The multi-talented Black writes songs, plays the guitar, and tells humorous stories and tall tales. While humor is the staple of his writing and performances, Black can also tackle more serious topics. His 1986 poem, "Legacy of the Rodeo Man," is a fine, moving tribute to **rodeo** cowboys:

> And while they pose like statues in that
>   flicker of an eye
> There's somethin' almost sacred, you
>   can see it if you try.
> It's guts and love and glory—one
>   mortal's chance at fame
> His legacy is rodeo and cowboy is his
>   name.

Black's books include *Coyote Cowboy Poetry* and *Croutons on a Cow Pie.* His audio cassettes include *Generic Cowboy Poetry, The Buckskin Mare, Baxter Black Live, Live at the Grange,* and *Live Uptown.* His poems and stories are available in books, audiocassettes, and videotapes from the Ranch House Library, P.O. Box 520982, Tulsa, Oklahoma 74152; tel. (918) 743-2171. (Black 1986; *Cowboy Poet* magazine; Martin 1992)

BLACK, CLINT
(1962–)

Singer. See Hat Acts.

BLACK COWBOYS

See African-American Cowboys.

BLACK JACK

Horse ridden by B-western film star Allan ("Rocky") Lane.

BLACK-EYED SUSAN

Colloquial term for a six-gun. See Firearms.

BLACKFOOT

See Indians as Cowboys.

BLACKSMITHING

Colloquial term for pimping. See Prostitution.

BLANDENGUE

Indians of the **pampas** held their own against white encroachment from the sixteenth century until the 1880s. They waged particularly fierce attacks near Buenos Aires during the 1740s. Neither Spanish troops nor ragtag militia **gaucho** units had been able to deter them. During this period the Buenos Aires *cabildo* (town council) instructed Governor José de Andonaegui to build new forts and create new military units. These companies of *blandengues,* irregular gaucho cavalry units, would patrol the countryside. The first three blandengue units, formed in 1752, served at Mercedes (Luján), Salto, and Magdalena, sites in what is now Buenos Aires Province. Each unit consisted of 50 men plus officers.

Once formed, however, the blandengue units languished for lack of dependable personnel and supplies. During the next decade, most of the units ceased to function. Governor Francisco de Paula Bucareli, who served from 1766 to 1770, reconstituted three blandengue units. He attracted soldiers by paying back wages, some overdue for 20 months. He strengthened frontier forts and mounted an offensive against hostile Indians of the plains. Then a terrible drought decimated wild and Indian herds, prompting some Indians to sue for peace.

During the viceregal period beginning in 1776, Bourbon strategists paid greater attention to the Río de la Plata region. Increased trade (legal and contraband) in the region had given it greater economic significance. In 1778 Juan José de Vértiz y Salcedo became the region's second viceroy. He hoped to improve and regularize frontier forts. In 1779 he tried to provide uniforms for at least some blandengue troops. The soldiers usually wore traditional gaucho dress—homemade boots *(botas de potro)* baggy diaper-like pants *(bombachas),* and ragged coats. Most units often lacked **firearms.** They relied instead on the traditional gaucho weapons—the **bolas,** lance, and knife.

Vértiz gave instructions to beef up all *comandancias* (substantial frontier forts). The strengthened forts were to include a rectangular corral protected by a spiked wall and ditch, bulwarks for artillery, a drawbridge, and a portcullis (iron grating to reinforce the gate). Like many Spanish directives, these went largely unimplemented. Most frontier forts remained primitive, and the blandengues remained poorly armed. Frontier units often faced shortages of pasture and water during the dry season.

In 1779 the ring of fortifications protecting Buenos Aires included six forts manned by blandengues. Unsalaried militias, serving for rations alone, manned five other *fortines* (small, crude forts).

The effectiveness of blandengue cavalry and other frontier troops suffered because of the class conflict of rural society. The rich and powerful made repressive demands on the poor gauchos, who saw little reason to give up their self-sufficient life as wild-cattle hunters and itinerant ranch hands. The government often resorted to conscription to force gauchos to endure the constraints and privations of military life. Protecting property rights (a concept alien to gauchos) of those who denied them access to wild livestock probably made little sense to gauchos.

Blandengues and other gaucho frontier troops faced harsh treatment, abysmal conditions, and late or nonexistent pay. These bad conditions motivated many recruits to desert. Profiteering frontier commanders forced soldiers to tend their own livestock and perform other labor (they made more money by selling overpriced goods to their troops). Some commanders treated low-ranking troops like servants.

Race and class placed a wide gulf between officers and enlisted men. Some commanders failed to report post vacancies so they could keep the wages of missing soldiers. Unscrupulous frontier merchants charged high prices and kept poor soldiers and their families in debt.

After gaining independence in 1816, the new Argentine Republic made another failed attempt to resurrect blandengue units. As in colonial times, the military used forced recruitment to dragoon unwilling gauchos. Military patrols scoured the countryside for recruits. If they could, gauchos quickly mounted up and fled from the recruiters.

Blandengues, or at least the term, disappeared in the nineteenth century, but the long-term problems and shortcomings of frontier defense remained. A century after the original blandengue units had been formed, conditions for gauchos in the frontier military remained abysmal. (Slatta 1989; 1992)

BLAZING SADDLES
See African-American Cowboys in Film.

BLOCKER LOOP
See Rope.

BLOW A STIRRUP
Losing a stirrup while riding a horse. A rider is disqualified from **rodeo** riding events if his foot slips out of the stirrup.

BLOWOUT
Colloquial term for a celebration, such as the "Old Glory Blowout" (4 July 1882) organized by Buffalo Bill **Cody** in North Platte, Nebraska.

BLUE LIGHTNIN'
Colloquial term for six-gun. See Firearms.

BLUE ROAN
Dark mahogany-colored **horse**, immortalized in Bruce Kiskaddon's poem, "That Little Blue Roan."

BLUE STEM
Bluish-green grass that grows on the Great Plains. Also called gumbo grass, it makes good feed for cattle. See Plains.

BOB WIRE
Colloquial rendering of barbed wire. See Fencing.

BOBTAIL GUARD
The first cowboy guarding the cattle at night.

BODEGA
Spanish term for a cheap saloon.

BODMER, KARL
Artist. See Art of the Cowboy.

BOG RIDER
See Ranch Work.

BOGGY TOP
Colloquial for a pie baked without a top crust.

BOLAS
Bolas (or *boleadoras*) are weapons that hail from Argentina. They consist of two or three rawhide thongs tied together at one end. The other end of each thong is tipped with leather-covered rocks or metal balls. The Indian or **gaucho** first whirls the bola around his head to build momentum. He then flings the weapon to entangle the feet of a fleeing rhea (ostrich), guanaco, horse, cow, or bull. With its legs snared by the rawhide thongs, the animal crashes to the ground.

There is ample evidence of Indian influences in the material culture and language of the Río de la Plata region. Indians developed the bolas long before the Spanish arrived. Gauchos subsequently adopted the dangerous weapon, which they called *las tres Marías* (the three Marys).

Another variant, called *la bola perdida*, consisted of a single stone tied to a single thong. Again whirled around the head, this instrument became a dangerous weapon. It could be used by someone mounted or afoot to strike an enemy in the head.

Scottish writer Robert Bontine Cunninghame **Graham** left many excellent descriptions of gaucho life. In "La Pampa" (published in *Rodeo*, 1936), he described a gaucho hunting a rhea or **pampas** ostrich with the bolas:

Letting the *bolas* go, so easily, it seemed as if his will and not his hand directed them, they hurtled through the air, revolving on their own axis sixty or seventy yards, and, when the *sogas* (ropes) met the ostrich's neck, the centrifugal force being averted, the balls fell down and, wrapping tightly round the legs, soon threw the giant bird upon its side.

The gaucho might then use the smaller single stone of the *bola perdida* to crack the animal's skull.

Using the bolas takes considerable practice. During his visit to the pampas in the early 1830s, young scientist Charles Darwin tried his hand at using the weapon. He recorded the unfortunate outcome in his *Journal* (1839). Darwin's timing and skill left much to be desired. When he threw the bolas, one hung in a bush and another wrapped around his own horse's leg. Scientist and horse crashed to the ground. "The Gauchos roared with laughter," he wrote. "They cried they had seen every sort of animal caught, but had never before seen a man caught by himself." (Graham 1936, 1978; Slatta 1992)

See also Boleada.

BOLEADA

A gaucho hunt using the *bolas* is called a *boleada*. Hunting provided **gauchos** with entertainment, food, and income. Gauchos stalked wild cattle and horses for their hides. They also hunted rheas (ostriches of the **pampa**) for their feathers, prized in European fashion markets.

Gauchos developed different bolas to use against different sized prey. Large animals like cattle needed longer, stronger bolas. They hunted ostriches and small mammals with much lighter weight bolas.

U.S. naval officer Thomas Jefferson Page *(La Plata, the Argentine Confederation, and Paraguay,* 1859) described the different types of hunting bolas that gauchos used:

The bolas are of two kinds: that used for catching cattle consists of three wooden balls, or stones, about three inches in diameter, covered with raw hide, each joined to the other in a common centre by a thong of the same of about three feet in length. The other is of two balls, smaller, and is used to catch ostriches. The gaucho holds the smallest ball in his right hand, and, giving the other two a rapidly whirling movement, throws them with great velocity and unerring aim at the legs of the animal; and the more he struggles to extricate himself, the more he becomes entangled.

William MacCann *(Two Thousand Miles' Ride Through the Argentine Provinces,* 1853) described the gaucho's tactics during an ostrich hunt:

Hunting ostriches is a favourite sport. When a hunting-party is formed, it is customary to move in a circular form, gradually closing in upon the birds until they become alarmed, and seek safety in flight; the hunters then give chase, and when within proper distance throw the bolas at their legs, and so bring them to the ground.

Boleadas had considerable economic importance, because gauchos could sell ostrich feathers for export to the merchant at the local **pulpería.** But beyond that, the hunt became a festive occasion. Dozens of riders might gather from miles around to participate. Gauchos sometimes set range fires to drive the ostriches out of brushy areas into the open where the bolas could do their work. Naturally, this practice did nothing to endear them to ranchers who lost livestock and grazing lands to the fires.

The Argentine ranching elite and their political representatives wanted to deprive the gaucho of his ability to subsist independently. Hunting provided income that helped the gaucho maintain his economic independence. The ranching elite, often faced with labor shortages, wished to coerce gauchos into working as subservient peons on the large **estancias** of the pampa. Argentine officials, at the request of the landed elite, repeatedly forbade boleadas and other gaucho pastimes. By the late nineteenth century, the government had successfully eliminated the gaucho's major means of remaining self-sufficient, including hunting on the pampas.   (Graham 1936, 1978; Slatta 1992)

BOMBACHAS
See Gaucho.

BOMBILLA
Metal straw used to sip gaucho tea *(mate)*. See Coffee.

"BONANZA"
See Television.

BONE ORCHARD
Also bone yard. Colloquial terms for cemetery.

BONZAL
Also bosal, *bozal*. See Tack.

BOOGERED UP
Also stove up. Colloquialism for crippled or badly injured.

BOONE, RICHARD
(1917–1981)
Actor. See Television.

BOOT HILL
Generic colloquialism for cemetery.

BOOTS
Along with his wide-brimmed **hat,** a cowboy's boots are the most identifiable part of his dress. Like the remainder of his clothing, boots were designed and crafted to help the cowboy ride. The narrow, pointed toes slipped quickly into the stirrup. The high heels hugged the stirrups and prevented the cowboy's feet from sliding through. The uppers were high enough to protect legs from brush and thorns. Boots fit tightly, however, making them uncomfortable for walking. A cowboy would sooner die than walk, though, so walking comfort played no role in boot design or selection.

Cowboys in Texas and the Southwest, of course, saw examples of boots and **spurs** used by Mexican **vaqueros** and **charros;** long skilled in leather work, Hispanic horsemen had developed wonderful tooled clothing and tack. Boot lore credits "Big Daddy" Joe Justin with making the first Anglo boots at Spanish Fort, Texas. His family became so successful that **Justins** became a western synonym for boots just as Stetson meant hat. Today the bootmaking company that bears his name produces 3.5 million pairs a year.

Working from Hispanic and British models, Anglo cowboys put their own special stamp on things. In *The Cowboy Boot Book* (1992), an entertaining and delightfully illustrated study, Tyler Beard summarizes the boot's evolution:

> Cowboys originally wore every type of shoe and boot known to man. It was these cattle drives after the Civil War that made them realize what sort of boot they needed. When they reached Kansas, with its small boot and shoe shops, the cowboy and the bootmaker slowly created the various types of boots suitable for cowboy work and attractive to cowboy vanity.

The Coffeyville boot became popular just after the Civil War. Made in the Kansas town of the same name, the boot drew its inspiration from the English Wellington and U.S. Cavalry footwear. Large mule-ear bootstraps aided a man in pulling them on. The term *mule-ear* aptly describes the shape of these leather pull straps stitched to the outside tops of the boots.

Cowboy fashion changes, albeit slowly and modestly. During the 1870s, new taller styles appeared (14 to 17 inches high). Cowboys and ranchers wore what were called cattleman, stovepipe, and drover styles. Heels got higher, reaching as high as four inches or so. Toes might be square-box or round-coin. Most cowboys favored the latter, because the sharp edges on box-toed boots wore out more quickly.

David Dary *(Cowboy Culture)* describes the impact of Texas trail drivers on the Kansas boot industry of the 1870s:

> Many cowboys bought new clothes when they reached the end of the trail. Many

also purchased new boots. The Texans seem to have preferred custom-made boots. In Abilene, Tom C. McInerney employed as many as twenty men in his boot shop during the summer months to meet the demand. His boots were high-heeled, red-topped, with tooled Lone Stars and crescent moons. They sold for $12 to $20 a pair.

If he could afford it, a cowboy would save up to purchase custom-mades—boots fitted and constructed exactly to his feet. A bootmaker would take the necessary measurements and construct the "shop-mades." During the 1880s less expensive ready-mades became available by mail order. A hand would really have to be down on his luck to wear stogies (cheap, secondhand boots). It's hard to say which would be more painful, the humiliation or the blisters from boots shaped to someone else's foot.

Despite increased ornament and decoration, boot style remains functional. Take the "wrinkles," for example, the fancy stitching across the vamp of a boot. This stitching makes the vamp (the part covering the top of the foot) more flexible and comfortable than solid, stiff leather. Because the leather flexes with the wrinkles, it does not become creased and bumpy.

In the twentieth century, movie and **rodeo** cowboys raised the boot from the mundane to the exotic. Silent film star Tom Mix wore intricately tooled boots. He tucked his pants inside the boots to show off the artwork better. Singing cowboy Gene **Autry** emulated the style as he rose to fame in the 1930s and 1940s. Celebrity demand for unique and artistic boots created a market for high-end bootmakers for the stars.

One would be hard-pressed to find a shoe store that does not stock cowboy boots these days. Heel height today generally ranges from a conservative 1-inch walking heel to a 2-inch high heel. Brands range from no-names to Justin, Tony Lama, Hyer, Acme (which also includes Dan Post, Lucchese, and Dingo), Nocona, Rocketbuster, and many more. As for styles,

color, stitching, and material, anything is possible. Custom bootmakers can fashion wonderfully individualized boots, perfectly appropriate for the symbol of American individualism, the cowboy. (Beard 1992; Dary 1981; Ward 1958)

See also Bota de Potro.

BOREIN, EDWARD
(1872–1945)
Artist. See Art of the Cowboy.

BOTA DE POTRO
Living in a rural, preindustrial culture, **gauchos** of the Río de la Plata had to make much of their own weapons, **tack,** and clothing. Not surprisingly, they relied upon readily available sources of raw materials—the vast herds of wild cattle and horses that roamed the **pampas.** The homemade *bota de potro,* a soft, open-toed riding boot, was fashioned from the hide of a colt's back legs. Gauchos simply killed a colt, stripped off the leg skins, and pulled them over their feet. The supple boot covered the foot up to the knee.

The gaucho learned to make these boots from the Indians of the pampa. The thin-skinned boots wore out after only a few months, and the gaucho would then kill another colt to make new boots. Such was the bounty of wild horses; no one gave any thought to killing a young animal simply to make footwear.

During the nineteenth century, however, ranchers demanded that the homemade boots be outlawed. Wild horses became more scarce, and ranchers believed that vagabond gauchos rustled their colts just to make boots. By the late nineteenth century, merchants began importing machine-made boots from Europe. Today the traditional bota de potro is found mostly in folklore museums. (Nichols 1968; Slatta 1992)

BOWER, BERTHA MUZZY
(1871–1940)
Novelist who wrote formula westerns, especially ranch romances.

BOYD, WILLIAM
(1895–1972)

Actor. See Television; Films, Cowboy.

BRAHMA CATTLE

See Cattle Breeds.

BRAIN TABLET

Colloquial term for cigarette.

BRANCH, E. DOUGLAS
(1905–1945)

Writer. See Historiography of the Cowboy.

BRAND, MAX

Pen name for Frederick Schiller **Faust**.

BRAND

Distinctive mark burned into the hide of cattle
and horses to indicate ownership. See Roundup.

BRAND ARTIST

Colloquial term for a **rustler** who alters brands
with a running iron.

BRANDING

See Roundup.

THE BRAVE COWBOY

Novel. See Abbey, Edward.

BRAVE MAKER

Colloquial term for whiskey.

BREEDS, CATTLE

See Cattle Breeds.

BRIDLE

See Bit; Tack.

BRIGHAM YOUNG COCKTAIL

Colloquial term for strong whiskey.

BRITISH COLUMBIA

See Beef Cattle Industry; Cowboys of Canada.

BRONC

Also bronco or broncho. See Horses.

BRONC BUSTER

A cowboy who could tame wild horses, also
called bronc peeler, bronc breaker, or wild horse
breaker.

Contrary to myth, not all cowboys could ride
any horse alive. Experienced hands could ride a
mount broken reasonably well, but the bronc
buster who could tame wild horses was a breed
apart. His special skill and horse sense earned
him the esteem of his peers and better wages.

Gaucho Bronc Busters

A **gaucho** bronc buster first roped a wild horse,
sometimes tightening the lasso to cut off the
animal's breath. The weakened animal fell to the
ground. He was blindfolded, and a bridle and bit
were forced onto him. The tamer then snubbed,
or tied, the animal with a short rope to a post and
mounted. Turned loose, the horse bucked until
he tired and submitted to his rider.

Most gaucho mounts remained only
half-broken by the standards of most horsemen.
Gauchos could control half-wild mounts, so they
wasted little time in "overtaming." They marked
horses that had been ridden by trimming their
manes and tails. In *Don Segundo Sombra,* the
famous gaucho novel by Ricardo **Güiraldes**, the
lead character enjoys great prestige and respect
because he is a *domador* (bronc buster).

Old gaucho technique broke animals to the
saddle quickly and, by today's standards, brutally.
If a horse suffered injuries or death during the
process, it mattered little, since horses were so
cheap and plentiful. If a horse died, someone
simply salvaged the horsehide.

By the late nineteenth century, however,
large feral herds disappeared in Argentina, and
ranchers imported more expensive blooded
stock from Europe. Breaking techniques had to
become gentler, since riders could not tame these
expensive mounts with the same harsh treatment
given to the old creole horses.

This rugged bronc rider, Joe De Moarsh, is clad in angoras, or goatskin chaps, with the hair left on.

Llanero Bronc Busters

Llaneros of Colombia and Venezuela employed horsebreaking methods similar to those of the gaucho. Like cowboys everywhere, they loved to put a new hand to the test by giving him a wild horse to ride. If thrown, the newcomer lost face. If successful, however, he proved his mettle and earned respect. As on the **pampas,** tamers relied more on crude strength and brutality than on finesse.

Despite their strenuous, seemingly brutal taming practices, llaneros apparently gave their broken mounts better care than did gauchos.

Sir Edward R. Sullivan *(Rambles and Scrambles in North and South America,* 1853) described a novel llanero bronco busting session. The practice, which resembled tailing bulls, was anything but gentle:

An active man and a good horseman will jump on a wild horse without bridle or saddle, armed with nothing but his spurs, and gallop across the plain kicking the poor beast until he begins to flag, when he slips off, and catching hold of the tail gives the horse a heavy fall. A few falls of this kind will tame the wildest horse, and convince him that the thing upon his back is his master.

Vaquero Bronc Busters

Vaqueros developed a number of horse taming techniques, none very gentle to the animals. David Woodman, Jr. *(Guide to Texas Emigrants,* 1835, 1974) recounted the method used on **mustangs** by Texas vaqueros in the 1830s: "By starving, preventing them from taking any repose, and continually keeping them moving, they make them gentle by degrees, and finally break them to submit to the **saddle** and bridle."

As in Argentina, the relative abundance of horses in California influenced their treatment. In 1842 Edward Vischer, a German visitor, expressed shock at the indifferent and brutal treatment that vaqueros gave their mounts: "The barbarous Californians look upon the horse as a useful commodity which is of little value and

easily replaced." Europeans, accustomed to scarce, expensive horses, often expressed shock at the cavalier treatment accorded to mounts in the Americas.

Like other Latin American horsemen, vaqueros preferred to avoid breaking and riding mares. They considered it unmanly to ride a mare. Stallions would be tied, haltered, blindfolded, and saddled, as in Argentina. Gauchos might consider the horse sufficiently broken after a day's work. In contrast, the vaquero spent several days taming a mount.

A horse tamer *(amansador)* let the horse fight and tire himself at the end of a long rope for an hour or so. He then blindfolded the animal and mounted him. Removing the blindfold, the tamer, sometimes tied to the saddle, would ride for a couple of hours. He might continue using the blindfold when mounting and dismounting to avoid being kicked. The initial taming sessions continued for five or six days.

Mexican and *Californio* bronc busters earned top wages, as did their counterparts elsewhere. In the late nineteenth century, a good hand in California might earn $12 a month. The tamer could command $20 a month. Itinerant pairs of men would ride a circuit of ranches each year. Good work meant an invitation to return to work with the next year's crop of colts.

Horse breakers continued to draw higher wages in the twentieth century. According to folklorist J. Frank **Dobie,** vaqueros in Texas earned $25 to $30 a month plus food in 1931. Special skills, such as taming or cooking, brought a premium of at least $5 per month, but ranchers usually paid Anglo hands $10 a month more than they paid vaqueros, regardless of skills.

Bronc Busters in the American West

Bronco busting took its toll on riders as well as on horses. In the American West, men who "snapped broncs" did not have long careers. Smart "peelers" (bronc busters) developed their own special techniques. William Henry Sears rode for the Moore and Powers Ranch, 20 miles east of Las Animas, Colorado, in the 1870s. He told how the hands there used a novel and wily method of horse taming: "I had my share of breaking wild bronchos while on this ranch. Always we took the wild horses to a large sand bar opposite old Fort Wise and there these bronchos were broken. It did not take long for they were soon worn out from bucking in the deep sand."

Ross Santee's description of bronco busting in *Cowboy* (1928) adds further evidence of the Anglo cowboy's indebtedness to the vaquero: "Each bronc was roped, an' after he choked down, a hackamore [from the Spanish *jáquima*] was put on his head. Then he was tied outside with a long rope, so's he could move around a lot. An' most of them, after they'd fought the ropes an' throwed themselves a time or so, would begin to quiet down. Specially, as soon as their noses got sore from pullin' on the ropes."

In *Scribner's Magazine* (July 1907), L. A. Huffman watched a tamer at work in 1907. The rider used "just a plain, ordinary, single-rigged cow-saddle, bridle, and lariat, spurs, quirt, and some short pieces of grass rope for the cross-hobbling." Once snubbed and hobbled, the horse felt the weight of the 40-pound saddle for the first time. The rider twisted the horse's ear to distract him as he mounted for the first time. Several bucking sessions were required to bring the horse under the man's power.

Canadian Bronc Busters

In the *Canadian Cattlemen* (December 1938) cowman Fred Ings describes horse breaking in Alberta in the 1880s. Like Ross Santee, he shows that vaquero methods traveled a long way north of Mexico. Tamers would catch the horses "by the front foot with the rope and by a twist throw them, and while they were down put on the hackamore and blindfold them, then let them up. A blinded horse will usually stand when held without too much fuss till the saddle is on. One rides with a hackamore which is a braided rawhide halter with the headstall fairly closely fitting and the nosepiece adjustable so that pulling on the shanks smothers a horse down, cutting off his wind and making him possible to control."

Bert Sheppard, a cattleman from Longview, Alberta, took pains to point up the difference between snapping broncs on a working ranch and bronc riding in a rodeo (*Canadian Cattlemen,* March 1949).

According to traditional unwritten ranch code, a horse should not be beaten over the head or spurred in the shoulder. In contrast, a rodeo rider receives extra points for spurring in the shoulders. Everything in front of the cinch was supposed to belong to the horse. Horse breaking consists of encouraging a horse to do the right thing and discouraging him from doing the wrong. When a horse decided to buck he was discouraged while bucking by whipping him with a shot loaded quirt. A top rider would whip him every jump until he quit and then either pet him or leave him alone. The easier he rode his horse and the more rein he gave him the better rider he was considered.

Without a doubt, bronco busting had its ups and downs. Oklahoma cowboy Raisins Rhoads worked at the Chapman-Barnard Ranch in the 1940s. The ranch foreman (Ben Johnson, Sr.) ordered him to break some horses in a very rocky corral. "Ben," asked Rhoads, "what about all them rocks? He said when I turn this son-of-a-bitch loose, you're gonna try and ride him. You're not gonna want to fall down there on them rocks!"

Most old-time cowboys are long on nostalgia. Not everyone, however, holds fond memories of bronco busting. Another Oklahoma cowboy, Dink Talley, had no regrets at leaving bronco busting behind: "Ridin' them old bronc horses was about the worst."

Some women could hold their own among the bronc peelers. Oklahoman June Cotton Martin Finn grew up with ranch work. By her early teens, she was sure she could do almost anything a cowboy could. She didn't let being small and female keep her out of the bronco busting business. "I even talked Ben into letting me break horses," she recalled. "And one of the horses I broke was one of the first ones they sent out there" [for Hollywood movies].

"We had a lot of old hammerhead horses that wasn't worth a dime," June Finn conceded, "but we had some that really were good work horses." A good horse is "one that's not lazy, one that will step on out. One that can turn real fast, because when you're headin' cattle, them cattle can turn right around." And that's what a good peeler produced—first-rate cow ponies. (Dary 1981; Denhardt 1975; Dobie 1931; Slatta 1990; Ward 1958)

BRONCO BILLY
1980 film. See Eastwood, Clint.

BROOKS, GARTH
(1956–)
Singer. See Hat Acts.

BROOKS AND DUNN
Singers. See Hat Acts.

BROOMTAIL
Also broomie—colloquialisms for long, bushy-tailed range mare, probably unbroken.

BROWN, JOHNNY MACK
(1904–1974)
Actor. See Films, Cowboy.

BROWN GARGLE
Colloquial term for coffee.

BRUSH COUNTRY
See Brush Popper.

BRUSH POPPER
Cowboys must cope with a wide range of terrain and climate. Montana hands might face cruel, freezing blizzards. Colombian llaneros must drive cattle through swollen, tropical rivers infested with electric eels. The brush country of southwest Texas, however, surely ranks among the more difficult terrain faced by working cowboys.

In brush country *(brasada),* man and beast face dense groves of thorny mesquite and other low-growing shrubs and squat trees. Spanish dagger, prickly pear, and other cacti of varying sizes also inflict pain. A cowhand working cattle in such difficult terrain was called a brush popper (also brush hand or brush buster).

Western authority Ramon **Adams** *(Western Words)* provides one possible origin for the term. "The brush popper knows he will never catch a cow by looking for a soft entrance into the brush; therefore, he hits the thicket center, hits it flat, hits it on the run, and tears a hole in it." Because they could hide in brush country, many cattle remained wild there, well after feral animals had become rarities elsewhere.

Cotton clothing would not stand up to the rigors of brush country thorns. Brush poppers took to wearing close-fitting garments that would not snag in the brush. A tight canvas jacket protected the torso. Snug leather **chaps** and large taps *(tapaderos)* hanging from the **saddle** protected legs and feet.

Ranch expert Jo Mora *(Trail Dust and Saddle Leather)* nominated the brush popper as the very best cowboy:

> Apart from fighting the fierce thorns, just the physical straining effort of forcing a way through that all-enveloping tangle at full speed, when the sun is sizzling at the top rung, kills plenty of fine horses. What the thorns can't do, the sun can; and many and many a pony gets wind-broken or sun-struck.

With visibility severely limited by thickets, a brush hand faced surprise charges from longhorn bulls. Folklorist J. Frank **Dobie** provided the classic description of these tough men and their land in *Vaquero of the Brush Country* (1929). Later, in *The Longhorns* (1941), Dobie quoted cowboy Rocky Reagan on the dangers and difficulties of working cattle in the brush:

> I got close enough to throw my rope and caught him [an old, roan longhorn bull]

by only one horn. At the feel of the rope, instead of breaking loose, as he could have done very easily, he wheeled like a cutting horse and rammed one of his sharp horns into the breast of my mount. The horn went in six or eight inches. The horse stood there trembling. Maybe I was trembling too. For what seemed a good while the steer remained in his tracks, working—gouging—his horn deeper into the horse. Then he gave a jerk, turned, and left. I was helpless, without any sort of gun. The horse died.

"Winter is the best time to run wild cattle in," says Reagan. "The leaves are then shedding so that a man can see farther through the brush; horses can run longer in the cool weather without becoming windbroken, and cattle are not so likely to die from getting overheated."

The thick brush and close quarters prevented cowboys from shaking out a large loop for roping; thus the brush popper also became known as a small-loop man because the terrain didn't permit anything larger. (Adams 1968; Dobie 1929, 1941; Mora 1973)

BUCK REIN
See Rodeo.

BUCKAROO
Another term for cowboy, anglicized from **vaquero.** Hands in Oregon, Washington, Idaho, and Nevada seemed particularly fond of the term. It likely reached them via California. Vaqueros from California, for example, worked on ranches in eastern Oregon. (Adams 1968; Blevins 1993; Bramlett 1987)

BUCKET OF BLOOD
Colloquial term for violence-prone frontier **saloon.**

BUCKING STRAP
See Rodeo.

BUCKLE BUNNIES
Female groupies who follow and befriend **rodeo** riders.

BUFFALO BILL
See Cody, William Frederick ("Buffalo Bill").

BUFFALO BILL HISTORICAL CENTER
The Buffalo Bill Historical Center in Cody, Wyoming, is among the nation's foremost repositories of western culture. The large complex includes several fascinating units. The Buffalo Bill Museum commemorates and documents the life of William Frederick ("Buffalo Bill") **Cody** as a military scout, Pony Express rider, buffalo hunter, and Wild West showman. Artifacts include costumes and personal items used by Cody and Annie **Oakley.** The Deadwood Stage (restored to its nineteenth-century glory) sits just inside the main entrance. The center consists of several museums and a library.

The Whitney Gallery of Western Art includes wonderful works depicting traditional plains and mountain life, with works by most of the leading western artists of the nineteenth and twentieth centuries. Visitors enjoy depictions of Native Americans by George Catlin and Alfred Miller. The collection includes landscapes by Albert Bierstadt and Thomas Moran. The Charles M. **Russell** wing, along with paintings and sculptures by Frederic **Remington,** illustrate cowboy life. Twentieth-century artists are also represented, including James Bama, Harry Jackson, and others.

The Cody Firearms Museum includes hundreds of weapons illustrating the history of **firearms** from the early sixteenth century through the twentieth century. The Winchester Arms Collection, donated to the center in 1988, forms the heart of the museum. Visitors can learn about firearms technology and the artistry that has gone into decorating many weapons.

The Plains Indian Museum includes more than 5,000 ethnographic items. The Sioux, **Cheyenne,** Shoshone, Crow, **Arapaho,** Blackfeet, and Gros Ventre cultures are represented. Exhibits include clothing, tools, riding **tack,** and a recreated Sioux camp from 1890. Visually stunning displays illustrate the importance of the **horse** and the buffalo in Plains Indian cultures.

The center sponsors many programs of interest to specialists and the general public. The Harold McCracken Research Library includes an important collection of books and manuscripts, and the research staff is excellent. The center sponsors a cowboy songfest each April, a frontier festival and powwow in June, and a Plains Indian seminar in September. A summer institute in western studies runs annually from mid-June through early July. The center publishes and distributes books, videotapes, audiotapes, posters, art reproductions, and other materials pertaining to western culture and history.

Address: 720 Sheridan Avenue, P.O. Box 1000, Cody, WY 82414; tel. 307-587-4771.

BUFFALO BILL MEMORIAL MUSEUM AND BUFFALO BILL'S GRAVE

William Frederick ("Buffalo Bill") **Cody** is buried atop Lookout Mountain, off Interstate 70 west of Denver, Colorado. The small museum, founded in 1921, features a self-guided tour that traces Cody's extraordinary life and career. The displays consist mostly of memorabilia collected by Cody's close friend and fellow performer, Johnny Baker. On his deathbed, Cody said, "I wish Johnny would come," but the friend arrived after Cody died on 10 January 1917.

An estimated 25,000 mourners paid their respects in 1917 when Cody was buried. The burial stirred some controversy at the time. Cody's written will indicated his desire to be interred on Cedar Mountain, Wyoming. His wife Louisa claimed that Cody changed his mind and asked for burial at Lookout Mountain. "You can look down into four states from there. It's pretty up there," Cody said, according to Louisa. Cynics charge that Harry H. Tammen's payment of $10,000 to Louisa strongly influenced her burial decision. Tammen, an unscrupulous

Denver financier and promoter, was certainly not above trying to turn a profit on Cody's death.

Since 1954 the grave site and museum have been administered by the City and County of Denver's Parks and Recreation Department. The museum commemorates Cody's burial and hosts special activities throughout the year. The museum includes a large collection of paintings by western artist Robert O. Lindneux, plus Cody posters, pulp literature, photographs, and a small exhibit entitled "Native Americans of the West."

Address: Lookout Mt. Road, Rt. 5 Box 950, Golden, CO 80401; tel. 303-526-0747. (Rosa and May 1989; Russell 1960; Sell and Weybright 1955)

BUFFALO GRASS
See Plains.

BUFFALO SOLDIER
An African-American cavalryman. See African-American Cowboys.

BUFORD
Colloquial term for a small, weak, easily thrown **rodeo** steer or calf.

BUG JUICE
Colloquial term for whiskey.

BUILD A LOOP
The act of shaking out a coil of **rope** in preparation for roping.

BULL DURHAM
See Food.

BULL HIDES
Heavy leather **chaps.**

BULL RIDING
See Rodeo.

BULL RIGGING
See Rodeo.

BULL TAILING

See *Charro*.

BULL WHIP

See Quirt.

BULLDOGGING

Steer wrestling. See Rodeo; Pickett, Willie M. (Bill).

BUMBLEBEE WHISKEY

Colloquial term for liquor strong enough to "sting."

BUNKHOUSE

The bunkhouse served as lodging, usually primitive, for cowhands working on the ranch. Often a single, large room, the bunkhouse included few amenities. Bunks might be simple metal-frame cots or even more primitive, with rawhide thongs stretched across a wooden frame. A table and a few chairs for card-playing and reading provided the only other furniture. A few pegs or nails in the wall served to hold tack and a jacket. A cowboy's "war bag," stowed under his bunk, held "dofunnies" (meager personal belongings).

An iron stove of some type warmed the bunkhouse in winter. A **coffee** pot more than likely sat atop the stove. On the southern plains, hands often slept out under the stars rather than in a hot, stuffy bunkhouse during the summer. Better accommodations meant a wood floor and maybe even real glass windows.

Cowboys managed to come up with colorful, often sarcastic, terms for most things in their lives. According to Ramon **Adams** *(Western Words)*, a bunkhouse might be labeled a dice house (applied to anywhere that permitted gambling), doghouse, dump, ram pasture, shack, or, if especially humble, a dive (also applied to low-life **saloons**). However crude, the bunkhouse offered more comfort than the dugouts and one-man line shacks that dotted outlying areas of a ranch. (Adams 1968; Forbis 1978)

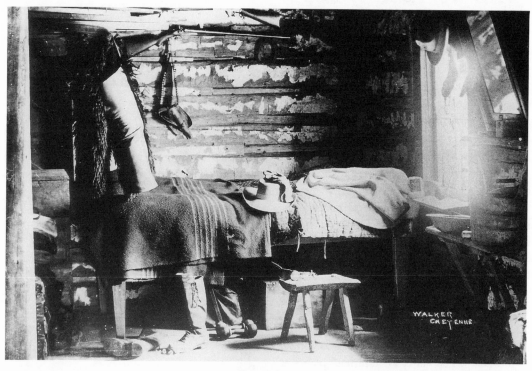

Makeshift bunkhouses were set up to house a cowhand's bed, equipment, and what little belongings he owned.

BUNTLINE, NED
(1823–1886)

Ned Buntline, born Edward Zane Carroll Judson, led an exciting, vagabond life. He ran away from home to work as a cabin boy just 13 years after his birth in Stamford, New York, leaving a solid, respectable, middle-class family. The details of his life are difficult to verify, because he applied what became his literary trademark—exaggeration—to stories of his own life. He even gave three different birthdates for himself. His work at sea continued until the early 1840s. He also married his first wife at that time, the first of at least five.

In May 1844 the world first heard the name by which Judson would become famous. In Philadelphia, he published two issues of *Ned Buntline's Magazine*. During the next 25 years, he wrote, started several short-lived magazines, earned extra money as a bounty hunter, incited a New York riot, and survived hanging by a mob. His seemingly endless string of dime novels finally began earning him a comfortable income, reputedly $20,000 per year.

In 1869 a fateful meeting occurred at Fort McPherson, Nebraska, between Buntline and Buffalo Bill **Cody,** then an army scout. Buntline, at age 46, made 23-year-old Cody the hero of four dime novels and a play. Eager, thrill-seeking readers snapped up *Buffalo Bill, the King of the Bordermen, Buffalo Bill's Best Shot, or the Heart of Spotted Tail, Buffalo Bill's Last Victory, Dove Eye the Lodge Queen,* and *Hazel Eye, the Girl Trapper.* Indifferent to truth, Buntline depicted Cody as a temperance crusader, among other things, while the real-life Buffalo Bill thoroughly enjoyed prodigious drinking binges.

Buntline's play with Cody, *The Scouts of the Prairie, or Red Deviltry as It Is,* opened in Chicago on 18 December 1872. In the hastily written play, the egomaniacal Buntline even included a slot for himself delivering a temperance lecture.

With Chicago street people as Pawnee chiefs and Italian dancer Giuseppina Morlacchi as the Indian maiden Dove Eye, the production had Buntline's trademark unreality about it.

Even a terrible script and production could not dull Cody's luster. Crowds loved him, and a western star was born. Buntline had also enlisted Virginia-born John Burwell **Omohundro, Jr.,** to play Texas Jack. Omohundro had experience as a cowboy and scout and showed his skill with the lasso onstage.

Countless other pulp writers picked up on the topic and made Cody a living legend to fans of the penny dreadfuls, or pulp novels. As Cody's fame grew, Buntline also enjoyed greater attention by having his name linked to that of the great Buffalo Bill. Buntline and other pulp writers also added Texas Jack to the pantheon of dime novel mythical heroes.

Buntline, an attractive rogue, became the leading western pulp writer of his day. According to historian Don Russell, he wrote a total of 557 dime novels. His mixed character and checkered past prompted writer Jay Monaghan to title his biography *The Great Rascal* (1953). (Milton 1980; Tuska and Piekarski 1983, 1984)

See also Pulp Novels.

BUNTLINE SPECIAL
See Firearms.

BUSTER
One of many terms for **bronc buster.**

BUTTERMILK
Horse belonging to singer/actress Dale Evans.

BUTTON
Colloquial term for a young boy.

BUZZARD WINGS
See Chaps.

CABALLADA

See Wrangler.

CABEROS

Also *cabestro.* See Rope.

CABEZA DEL FUSTE

Spanish term for the head of the saddle-tree; anglicized to fustry or fuste. See Saddle.

CACTUS

Movie horse of Sunset Carson, B-western actor.

CALABOOSE

Colloquial term for jail, from the Spanish *calabozo.*

CALAMITY JANE
(ca. 1852–1903)

Martha Jane **Canary**; also a gambling term for the queen of spades. See Women.

CALF FRIES

Fried calves' testicles, also called mountain oysters or prairie oysters—a cowboy delicacy. See Food.

CALF ROPING

See Rodeo.

CALF SLOBBERS

Colloquial term for meringue, as on pie.

CALGARY EXHIBITION AND STAMPEDE

The Canadian ranching frontier exhibited little of the wild violence and disorder that characterized other cowboy haunts of the Americas. On the Canadian frontier, civilization preceded settlement. The Royal Canadian Mounted Police maintained a level of law and order uncommon in other frontier regions.

For fun-loving, sporting cowboys, a little law could chafe mightily. Canadian cowboy fun quickly came under legal regulation. During the 1880s, long, five-mile races had become very popular. Police at Fort Calgary in Alberta prohibited Sunday horse races in September 1883. Races could be held on other days, though, and afternoon horse races would draw riders from all over the province. Contests on July 1 (Dominion Day) were particularly popular.

In addition to horse races, Albertans enjoyed ranch rodeos and "cowboy tournaments." In 1893 Calgary had its first cowboy tournament in which contestants received prizes. Winners of the 600-yard horse race and of the roping competition received $75 saddles. George Lane, a rancher from High River, arranged the contests at the Calgary midsummer fair.

In 1912 Calgary commenced its famous Stampede, one of the world's great **rodeo** extravaganzas. Promoter Guy Weadick pushed the idea of a rodeo to commemorate the good old days. Four leading stockmen—George Lane, Pat Burns, A. E. Cross, and Archie J. McLean—put up the necessary investment of $100,000 (Canadian). The Stampede was a hit from the very beginning. Mexican **vaqueros** and cowboys from the United States participated along with Canadians.

The ranching movement in western Canada began a couple decades later than in the United States. During the early twentieth century, wheat farming quickly began pushing back the ranching frontier, and many realized the heyday of ranching and the cowboy had already passed. As one journalist noted, the Stampede symbolized "the final wave of the hat in token of farewell."

Like the Pendleton Roundup, the Calgary Stampede mixed historical and mythical images of bygone days. Indians in full regalia, including Sarcees, Blackfeet, and Stoneys, mixed with cowboys, chuck wagons, Mounted Police, and marching bands. In 1938 Kenneth Coppock exhorted fans to dress for the occasion and add to the atmosphere. "An effort is being made to have a larger proportion of Stampede patrons wear big **hats** during the show to help keep up the spirit of the old West."

Nearly every year since 1912, rodeo fans and tourists have flocked to Calgary in July for a taste of Canada's mythical Wild West. Other rodeos, professional and amateur, also remain popular. Ranchers' roundups for amateurs have been held in Alberta since at least 1916. By the 1930s Alberta enjoyed some 30 rodeos per year.

The Stampede, however, remains the big event. Its famous Rangeland Derby determines the World Championship for Chuckwagon Racing, in which four-horse teams pull each of the wagons. The Stampede includes, of course, the standard rodeo events—saddle bronc, bareback, bull riding, calf roping and steer wrestling.

Address: P.O. Box 1860, Calgary, Alberta, Canada T2P 2M7; tel. 800-661-1260; 403-261-0101. (Dempsey 1955; Kelly 1965; Slatta 1990)

CALIFORNIA DRAG ROWELS

Spurs used by **vaqueros** and other riders in Spanish California. The rowels are low enough to drag on the ground.

CALIFORNIA PANTS

Sturdy, heavy wool pants commonly worn on the range; often patterned with checks or stripes.

CALIFORNIA PRAYER BOOK

Gambling term for a deck of cards.

CALIFORNIA RIG

Also California saddle. See Saddle.

CALIFORNIO

See Vaquero.

CAMPANYERO

Southwest cowboy term for friend or companion, from the Spanish *compañero*.

CAN OPENERS

Colloquial term for spurs.

CAÑA

Type of rum; sugarcane liquor. See Saloons.

CANADA, PLAINS FRONTIER IMAGERY

Many nineteenth-century Canadians considered their western provinces a vast wasteland or desert. Expeditions led by Henry Youle Hind and John Palliser in 1857 fostered the negative, desert images. Hind first applied the name Great American Desert to the Canadian prairies, and Palliser's reports reinforced the image. Owing to lack of rainfall, conventional wisdom held that the prairies of southern Saskatchewan and Alberta never could be farmed.

A huge area called Palliser's Triangle was thought to be unsuitable for settlement. The region was bounded on the east by the Souris River in the Turtle Mountains, marked on the south by the 49th parallel, and it extended westward to Calgary and north to Saskatoon. Ironically, both men also stressed the fertility of large areas, but it was the desert imagery that stuck.

In an 1882 report *(Manitoba and the Great North West),* John Macoun flatly asserted that the Cypress Hills region was unsuitable for agriculture. Ranchers with large holdings used the same argument to fend off the subdivision of their lands for farming. Only the great fear of American expansionism from the south pushed the Canadian government to survey its uninviting plains territories.

Not everyone accepted the views of Hind, Palliser, and Macoun. Garden myths accompanied the desert imagery. The boosterism, optimism, and expansionism that pervaded the American West also invaded western Canada. A glowing counter myth to Palliser's Triangle developed. Utopian poetry and prose lauded the richness and opportunity that awaited immigrants to the region.

An 1883 pamphlet described the "nice prairie, covered with beautiful grass, and dotted here and there with little poplar forests which gives the whole a very romantic appearance." The settlers, continued the pamphlet, "look forward to a very happy and contented future." Such idealized descriptions convinced many people. In the first decade of the twentieth century, thousands of

American dryland farmers turned their ambitions and energies northward to the "Last Best West"—the Canadian prairies.

Unfortunately for the optimistic new settlers, prairie reality fell far short of their utopian dreams. Beset by the harsh, chilling winters and inconstant rainfall, prairie farmers quickly faced ruin. By World War I, the decade-long dryland farming boom was bust. Thousands of disillusioned homesteaders returned to the United States. Palliser's desert seemed to have gained its revenge. Not until the later development of suitable irrigation technology was the desert finally overcome, in myth and reality. Today wheat farming is big business on the Canadian prairies.

Many observers considered cattle regions as representing backwardness, violence, obstacles to progress, and the antithesis of civilization. Simultaneously, however, frontiers represented hope and the potential for future greatness. Cattle frontiers served as boundary or transitional regions where different nations or cultures fought and shared.

In *Wolf Willow,* Wallace **Stegner** captured the essence of frontier regions:

Frontiers are lines where one body of law stops and another body of law begins. Partly by reason of that difference of basic law, and from the moment the boundary is drawn, they also become lines of cultural division as real for many kinds of human activity as the ecological boundaries between woods and plains, plains and mountains, or mountains and deserts. Likewise they have their inevitable corollaries. They create their own varieties of lawbreakers, smugglers particularly, and they provide for the guilty and the hunted the institution of sanctuary.

(Breen 1983; Francis 1989; Slatta 1990)

CANADA, VIOLENCE

Unlike the situation on other frontiers, law and order, in the form of the Royal Canadian Mounted Police, predated the cattle industry in Alberta. Gunplay—indeed guns in general—played a smaller role than in the American West. In *An Emigrant in the Canadian Northwest* (1929), Herbert Church recalled that by the late 1880s "it was the regular custom to leave your gun at the livery stable with your horses and saddle outfit. Guns were seldom carried on the range."

Historian J. W. Grant MacEwan recognized that pulp writers and Hollywood filmmakers created most of the violence on the Canadian cattle frontier. The Canadian cowhand might be a bit unpolished,

… but he didn't go around shooting holes in people or barroom chandeliers. Those who concocted the biggest lies about his shooting and courting evidently overlooked the fact that he was a working man. His devotion to duty and his skills in handling cattle would have made truer and better reading. Cowboys who remained with the herd through a bad blizzard knew the meaning of duty and service.

Gunplay, however, was not entirely absent from Alberta. In Lethbridge in 1912, a young cowpuncher named Richard Christian shot and seriously wounded a former city detective named Pat Egan. The cowboy confessed and remained unrepentant. As he told police,

Egan had ordered me out of town on several different occasions and at one time was instrumental in having me sent up for stealing a watch. When he passed me on the street he applied a vile name to me and I promptly pulled my gun and shot. I am not sorry that I shot him, and would do it again under the circumstances, as I will not take the name he called me under any circumstances from anyone, and if I was to swing for it tomorrow I would still be glad that I committed the deed.

The Mounted Police established the rule of law (and a monopoly over **firearms**) before significant numbers of settlers reached the western prairies in the late nineteenth century. Indians were, for the most part, secured on reservations, so that "cowboy and Indian" battles, popularized in American movies and **television**, did not occur in Canada. As Pierre Berton well documents in *Hollywood's Canada,* **films** included many distorted elements grafted from the mythology and folklore of the American Old West. The reality, as usual, was far different from the cinematic images. (Berton 1975; MacEwan 1975)

CANARY, MARTHA JANE

Calamity Jane's given name. See Women.

CANNED COW

Colloquial term for canned milk.

CANNON, HAL
(1948–)

Singer and poetry gathering organizer. See Poetry.

CANTINA

Spanish for tavern or **saloon.**

CANTLE

Raised back on a **saddle.**

CAPATAZ

Ranch foreman who works under the manager or *mayordomo.*

CAPORAL

Term adopted from the Spanish for ranch foreman or roundup boss.

CARBINE

See Firearms.

CAREY, HARRY
(1878–1947)

Western film actor. See Films, Cowboy.

CARNE SECO

Spanish term for dried beef.

CARTWRIGHT, BEN

Patriarch of the Ponderosa Ranch on "Bonanza." The character was played by Lorne Greene. See Television.

CASSIDY, HOPALONG

Fictional character created by author Clarence Mumford and made famous by actor William Boyd.

CAT WAGON

Wagon that carried **prostitutes** along cattle trails.

CATCH PEN

Fenced area for holding rough stock or cattle.

CATGUT

Colloquial term for rawhide **rope.**

CATLIN, GEORGE
(1796–1872)

Artist. See Art of the Cowboy.

CATTLE ASSOCIATION

See Stockmen's Association.

CATTLE BREEDS

People in southeastern Europe domesticated wild cattle *(Bovidae primigenius)* at least 8,500 years ago. Herders in southern Asia domesticated *B. indicus* (zebu or Brahma cattle) about the same time. Since then, humankind has taken advantage of the wide range of useful products that cattle provide: meat, leather, milk, power, and tallow.

Ranchers have developed a wide range of cattle breeds over the centuries, depending on the purpose they see for the animals. The Angus, Hereford, and shorthorn breeds continue to make up a large part of the beef cattle population.

Shorthorns first came to the United States from England in 1783. By the mid-nineteenth century, several shorthorn breeders' associations had been formed. The animals range in color from solid red to solid white. They may also be spotted or roan. (Polled shorthorns, a branch of the same breed, have no horns.) Since 1935 the American Shorthorn Breeders' Association has set breed standards for the country.

Another English breed, the Hereford or whiteface, originated in the mid-1700s in Herefordshire, England, from a cross between English and Dutch stock. The red animals have a white face and a white strip running along the top of the neck. They eat voraciously and gain weight quickly. Political leader Henry Clay imported Herefords as early as 1817. In 1882 breeders formed the American Hereford Association. Since then the breeding of polled Herefords has led to the formation of the American Polled Hereford Association.

Yet another import, the Brahma or zebu, comes from India. These animals tolerate heat and resist disease and insect attacks better than most breeds. Their distinctive hump of cartilage and fat above the neck and withers gives the large zebu a somewhat menacing look. Colors range from various shades of gray to red. Unlike most breeds, Brahmas can tolerate the hot, humid Gulf Coast. Indeed, the **King Ranch** in Texas crossed Brahmas and shorthorns to produce a new breed, the Santa Gertrudis. Breeders have also experimented with a Brahma-Hereford cross (the Braford) and a Brahma-Angus cross, the Brangus.

A relative newcomer to the United States is the Charolais, native to France. The first animals arrived here in 1934 via Mexico. Beef producers initially thought very little of this large, muscular all-white breed, but its fast growth and heavier weight at a younger age soon attracted adherents.

Ranchers increasingly produce hybrid cattle to improve the animals in some way. In recent decades, ranchers and farmers have sought to increase the return on their investments. Some breeds, such as the red poll and milking shorthorn from Great Britain and the Simmental, Chianina, and Limousin from continental Europe, produce both milk and beef. The brown Swiss, Jersey, Guernsey, and Ayrshire breeds are strictly milk producers tended by dairy farmers, not cowboys. Some 90 percent of American dairy cows are the distinctively colored black-and-white holsteins (called Friesians in Europe). The Purebred Dairy Cattle Association, founded in 1940, maintains a "score card" to evaluate dairy cow conformation.

Ranchers have also turned to artificial insemination to shore up profits. By using this practice, ranchers can inseminate thousands of heifers with semen from genetically superior bulls. Biotechnicians have added another capability to improve herds—embryo transfers. Top pedigreed cows may now be injected with a hormone that causes multiple ovulation. The eggs are then artificially inseminated, and the resulting embryos are withdrawn from the cow and each implanted in the uterus of another cow, which carries the calf to term.

Specialized markets have opened new opportunities to ranchers. The venerable Corriente breed, for example, is much in demand for team roping competition. Members of the North American Corriente Association, located in Casper, Wyoming, breed animals to fill that niche market. Organized in 1982, the group has grown to nearly 400 members raising 4,000 registered animals.

The Corriente breed developed in colonial Mexico from cattle imported from Spain. Like its cousin, the **longhorn,** the hardy Corriente is a tough survivor. Members of the Texas Longhorn Breeders Association dedicate themselves to perpetuating that historic breed.

The long arm of technology has introduced many changes into cattle breeds. Not even the venerable Texas longhorn is safe from change. Thanks to genetics researchers at Texas A&M University, the breeders of the future may produce a longhorn without horns. Was this another A&M attempt to take revenge on their archrivals in Austin, the University of Texas Longhorns? No, it wasn't. In 1993 a team of scientists isolated the horn gene in cattle. Using this genetic information, breeders will be able to produce longhorns and other cattle without horns. As any cowboy can attest, horns can do plenty of damage, so with this advance, stockmen can save money because of fewer animal injuries. Cattle without horns will not cause as much meat and hide damage to other animals, thereby improving the rancher's profit margin.

By the late 1980s, the world's cattle population numbered about 1.3 billion. The United States, with an estimated 34 million beef cattle and about 10 million dairy cattle, ranked behind India, Brazil, and the former Soviet Union in total numbers. (Friend 1978; Rouse 1970)

See also Beef Cattle Industry.

CATTLE DETECTIVE
See Horn, Tom.

CATTLE DRIVE
Also cattle trail. See Trail Drive.

CATTLE GUARD
See Fencing.

CATTLE KATE
See Women.

CATTLE TOWNS
See Cow Towns.

CAVALLARD
Term taken from the Spanish *caballada,* meaning a band of saddle **horses.** Cowboys corrupted the Spanish word into many English variations, including cavvyard and cavvy. The cowboy who herded the horses was known as a cavvy-man or **wrangler.** The word *remuda* is a synonym for *caballada.* (Blevins 1993)

CENTER-FIRE RIG
See Saddle.

CEPO
Wooden stocks used by civil and military authorities in Argentina to punish **gauchos.**

CHAIN BIT
See Bit.

CHAMPION
Horse of film and singing star Gene **Autry.**

CHANGADOR
A Spanish term for **rustler** used in Argentina.

CHAPS
Cowboys pronounce this word "shaps," thereby mimicking the sound of the original Spanish terms *chaparejos* or *chaparreras.* All the terms refer to leather leggings worn to protect a working cowboy. Chaps generally cover the front and sides of the legs and fasten with thongs or buckles behind the legs.

Often working among brush, thorns, and cacti, cowboys in all parts of the Americas quickly learned to protect their exposed thighs and shins. Some hands, like the Texas **brush popper,** worked in very hostile environments, making chaps indispensable. Chaps also provided protection against cold, snow, or rain and the bite of an angry animal.

As with other elements of clothing and equipment, cowboys adapted chaps to their own special needs and environments. Mexican **vaqueros** fashioned chaps called *chivarras* out of goatskin. *(Chiva* is the Spanish word for goat.) Angoras were another type of chaps made from goatskin, but with the hair left on for extra warmth. Unfortunately, angoras did not fair well in the rain. When wet they would soak up water and leave the rider smelling like a soggy goat.

Another Mexican variation was *armitas* or *chigaderos,* which Anglo cowboys shortened to "chinks." Unlike regular chaps, this shortened model extended just below the knee. Chinks gained favor in warmer climates, because they were not as hot to wear as long chaps.

Anglo cowboys developed other variations on the theme. Shotgun or Texas leg chaps offered the most protection because they encased the legs entirely. A cowboy had to slip them up over the feet like a pair of pants, which meant first having to take off **spurs.** Bat wings (chaps shaped like bat wings when laid flat), were made of heavy cowhide and held onto the legs with snaps,

Leather chaps were used and continue to be used today as a form of protection against the elements and rough terrain, but function does not completely overshadow form. These chaps are decorated with white leather appliqués and silver studs.

making them quicker and easier to take on and off.

Winged chaps or Texas wing chaps appeared in the 1890s. Amply cut on the outer edge, they buckled at the thigh and calf, but not at the knee. This arrangement gave greater freedom of movement to the leg. In some cases, cowboys buckled the chaps only at the thigh and let the lower portion hang free. Wyoming cowboys developed a trimmer model with narrow "wings" called the Cheyenne cut or Cheyenne leg. By cutting away a bit of leather covering the lower, inside leg, cowboys prevented the chaps from catching on the stirrups.

Cowboys applied their creativity with language to chaps. There were many cowboy terms for chaps, including bull hides, buzzard wings, grizzlies, hair pants, riding aprons, and twelve-hour leggin's. In addition, we find specialized variations such as parade chaps, dude chaps, and **rodeo** chaps. Again taking cues from the vaquero, some cowboys liked decorative silver **conchas** on their chaps. (Adams 1968; Foster-Harris 1955; Ward 1958; Watts 1977)

CHARANGO

Small ukelele-like instrument played by **gauchos** in the Río de la Plata. The sound box is made from an armadillo shell.

CHARQUE

Dried or jerked beef.

CHARREADA

Mexican **rodeo,** also known as *charrería. See Charro.*

CHARRO

The *charro,* an upper-class horseman, represents one of two equestrian traditions that developed in New Spain (colonial Mexico). The charro tradition perpetuates the upper-class equestrian heritage of the Spanish gentleman rider or *caballero,* a Spanish term literally meaning horseman. This linguistic evidence shows the high status associated with equestrian life in Spanish culture. A parallel working cowboy tradition developed among the mostly Indian **vaqueros** who actually tended the cattle herds of New Spain.

The first charros were the Spanish elite who were rewarded with *encomiendas,* royal grants of Indian labor bestowed upon the conquistadors and court favorites. These hacendados or gentlemen ranchers became New Spain's landed elite. The charro tradition retained *jinetea,* a short-stirrup riding style earlier adopted by Spanish riders from the Moors. The style evolved as a military tactic. By riding with short stirrups, cavalrymen could stand high above an enemy and slash downward with sword or lance. This riding style joined the earlier *la brida* school of long stirrups and stiff posture. (Heavily armored knights developed la brida during the medieval era.)

Riding exhibitions in Mexico began during the early days of the conquistadors. To impress their indigenous subjects and hone cavalry skills, Spanish gentlemen were required to gather periodically for mounted drills called *alardes.* The riding style used was the jinetea, with short stirrups and neck reining to control mounts. Gradually these military parades evolved into pleasure rides and exhibitions. Spaniards performed a number of riding feats during the sixteenth century, including the popular ring race *(sortija)* and jousts with cane poles *(juegos de cañas).* Over time some of the vaquero's work-related skills from **roundup** and branding worked their way into these upper-class riding contests.

Richly dressed and well mounted, the caballeros (gentlemen) of New Spain would ride out and survey their estates. They might offer a few words of instruction to the ranch manager, but most preferred urban life to daily ranch chores. Their stylized riding evolved over time into the distinctively Mexican mounted exhibitions called *charrería.* During the 1880s Mexico City hosted the nation's first public exhibition of charro riding. In 1894, charros exhibited their riding and roping skills to audiences in the United States. The group, led by Vicente Oropeza, performed with Buffalo Bill's Wild West Show in New York.

In the early twentieth century, charro dress underwent refinement and enrichment. Riders donned expensive fabrics, highlighted with gold and silver. More than ever, the dress reflected the wealth and upper-class status of the wearer.

The great social and political upheavals of the Mexican Revolution (1910–1920) threatened the charro with extinction. Faced with revolutionary violence and the commandeering of their livestock, many ranchers fled their estates. Some sought refuge in cities, while others fled across the border to the United States. The destruction and demands of the revolutionary armies greatly depleted the stock of **horses** and **cattle** in Mexico. Amidst the violence and devastation, however, charro imagery did not disappear. Emiliano Zapata, leader of the agrarian rebels from the state of Morelos, wore charro dress. Indeed, as a teenager, Zapata became a skilled charro competitor. He thus claimed the traditionally conservative charro imagery on behalf of the revolution.

Relative peace returned with the administration of Alvaro Obregón in 1920. A new revolutionary elite, its power base in the north of Mexico, took command of the revolution and the nation.

Charrería (Charreada)

After the Mexican Revolution, riding exhibitions retained popularity, particularly on the large haciendas of northern Mexico. Nostalgic landowners and many city dwellers reinvigorated the charreada after the upheaval. In 1921 Ramón Cosío González, a Tamaulipas lawyer, organized the National Association of Charros. He and like-minded Mexicans reinstated the centuries-old dress and riding exhibitions of the charro. Not even the great Mexican Revolution could sweep away the charro tradition.

By the 1960s some 365 charro clubs existed in Mexico. Unlike **rodeo** in the United States, charro riding remains amateur and the province of those who can afford to participate for fun, not profit. The National Federation of Charros sponsors events around the country.

In her fine study, *Charrería Mexicana*, Kathleen Mullen Sands contrasts American and Mexican rodeo:

Concerned primarily with style rather than speed, as in U.S. rodeo, the events of the charreada are based on the dominance of man over animal and have evolved from occupational skills required for the management of cattle on large ranches. Some charreada events appear quite similar to rodeo—there is bronc riding, bull riding, and team roping. But the distinctions become obvious in the clothing of the competitors, in the minutes taken instead of seconds to perform an event, in rope flourishes and pivotal spins on horseback, and in several events not found in American rodeo—tailing bulls, leaping from a galloping horse to a wild mare and riding her to a standstill, reining competitions, and roping wild mares.

Like American and Chilean rodeos and Canadian stampedes, charreadas have a fixed schedule of events for participants. The festivities open with a parade *(desfile)* of richly dressed riders (men and **women**) into the keyhole-shaped competition arena or *lienzo*. The traditional charro costume is form-fitting, elegant, and conservatively colored. It features tight chaps over richly embroidered pants, a short waist-length jacket, and a broad-brimmed sombrero. Silver **spurs** often hang from the short, flat-heeled charro **boots. Saddles** and **tack** likewise reflect the wealth and respect for tradition that typify charros. A traditional textile overgarment, the serape, is rolled behind each rider's saddle.

A band plays the spirited "March of Zacatecas," the charro anthem. In the *cala de caballo,* the first event, riders perform a complex set of maneuvers. Mounts must spin, back up, turn, sprint, and stop quickly on command. Charros then rope on horseback and on foot. Competitors **rope** mares by their hind feet *(concuros de peales* or *piales en el lienzo)* and front feet *(manganas a caballo* and *manganas a pie).* Unfortunately, mares sometimes suffer broken legs in these horse-tripping events.

In team roping *(terna),* virtually identical with American rodeo, one rider lassoes an animal's head and the other lassoes the hind legs. A team has eight minutes to complete its throws. Competitors exhibit great skill and flourish; they are truly artists with their ropes.

Charros also ride bulls and mares bareback. The charro bull rider holds on with two hands. He must, however, ride the bull to a standstill! One event that did not pass over to American rodeo is the *cola,* or bull tailing. As was traditionally done, the rider anchors the tail under his right leg for leverage. Riders have only 60 meters to tail a bull and do so within about three to five seconds. As a special event, a mounted charro might evade and chase a bull. The startling thing about this feat *(rejonear)* is that the rider controls his mount without using the reins.

The famous *paso de la muerte* (ride of death) concludes the competition. A rider leaps from his mount onto the back of a wild mare and rides the animal bareback to a standstill. Miscalculation can be costly. A rider might fall beneath the mare's feet or be trampled by several hazers, who ride behind to keep the mare running. Following this display of courage, strength, and timing, the charreada is over. Judges tally team scores, and winners take their bows. There is no prize money.

Charros must be rich enough to finance their hobby without earning anything from the competitions. Fans, officials, and contestants linger to chat and perhaps enjoy a drink and some food.

Women continue to play a relatively minor role in Mexican charreada. A few women participate as *escaramuzas,* in which teams of eight perform precision maneuvers riding side-saddle. The very ladylike drills emphasize grace, not speed or apparent athleticism. Women are also featured in the *jarabe tapatio,* typical dances performed as a break in the riding action. They wear a typical outfit called the *china poblana* and remain on the sidelines during the main events contested by the men. (LeCompte 1985; Norman 1969; Sands 1993)

CHESTNUTT, MARK
(1963–)
Singer. See Hat Acts.

CHEYENNE

The Cheyenne were an Algonquin-speaking North American Indian tribe. They moved westward from northeastern Minnesota in the late seventeenth century and settled near the Red River, which flows along the border between Minnesota and the Dakotas. The Cheyenne supported themselves as farmers and lived in earth lodge villages.

The arrival of the **horse** in the eighteenth century changed the Cheyenne way of life. Horses initially appeared in Spanish settlements in the Southwest, reaching the northern plains around 1650. The Cheyenne were using horses by 1760. By 1772 horses were common among the tribes north and east of the Missouri River. It is believed the Cheyenne first got horses from either the **Arapaho,** Kiowa, or Crow in the Black Hills or that they captured wild horses.

In later years the Cheyenne would get horses by capturing them from their enemies. The Cheyenne became famous as mounted hunters and warriors. They had always been hunters, but the horse allowed them to follow the migratory

buffalo and other big game. They could kill enough food in one day to last for months.

The adoption of a migratory plains culture gradually brought broad changes to the Cheyenne. They abandoned their permanent earth lodge homes for buffalo-hide tipis and gave up farming for buffalo hunting and trading. They served as middlemen between fur traders and their Native American allies. They also bartered British and American goods to southern nations, such as the Arapaho and Kiowa, for horses and Spanish goods.

The Cheyenne rode only their best horses in battle. On a raid, the warrior rode out on an ordinary horse and led his fighting horse. A warrior's fighting horse was one of his most prized possessions. Warriors asked a shaman to dedicate it to ensure success. He promised not to ride the horse for several months after battle. Breaking the promise killed the horse and brought the owner bad luck. In preparation for battle, a warrior stood his horse in water and rubbed dirt on its shoulders and head.

The Cheyenne also developed a horse worship ceremony. They believed that animals, including the mighty horse, had supernatural powers. According to John Stands in Timber, the Cheyenne had adopted the ceremony from the Arapaho. The men met in a tipi to eat and sing horse medicine songs.

In 1832 the Cheyenne split into two branches. The northern Cheyenne lived in western Montana and the southern Cheyenne lived along the Arkansas River, which runs through southern Kansas and southeastern Colorado. It is not known for sure why the tribe split. According to southern Cheyenne folklore, their group journeyed south in search of wild horses.

The Cheyenne had numerous allies, but they developed a special relationship with the Arapaho. The two tribes had known each other since they had been neighbors on the Sheyenne River near what is now the Minnesota-North Dakota border. The Arapaho, like the Cheyenne, shifted westward to the Missouri River and the Black Hills. They aided each other and hunted together.

It is not known exactly when the Cheyenne first encountered whites. In 1806 the Lewis and

Clark expedition met them in the Black Hills of Dakota on their return voyage down the Missouri River. (An expedition journal describes the Cheyenne as "rich in horses and dogs.") White in-migration during the nineteenth century poisoned relations with virtually all plains peoples, leading to armed warfare. The northern Cheyenne played an important role in the defeat of General Custer and the Seventh Cavalry at the Battle of the Little Bighorn in 1876.

The southern Cheyenne established friendly relations with the Bent family, who opened a trading post on the Arkansas River in 1832. The peace between the Cheyenne and the whites ended when the U.S. Army attacked peaceful Cheyenne camps at Ash Hollow in 1855 and again at Sand Creek in 1864. For the next several years the Cheyenne fought constant battles against the army and white settlers.

By 1875 the southern Cheyenne and southern Arapaho were restricted to a reservation in western Indian territory, present-day Oklahoma. They suffered horrible living conditions, and many died from hunger and disease. In 1877–78 the army destroyed the northern Cheyenne camps of Dull Knife and Two Moons, and survivors were sent south to join the southern Cheyenne in Oklahoma. They too suffered from disease, malnutrition, and the harsh climate.

In the summer of 1878, Dull Knife fled the reservation and led 300 northern Cheyenne north on a march homeward. The northern Cheyenne settled on a reservation on the Tongue River in Montana, where they remain to this day.

The southern Cheyenne and Arapaho had a difficult time becoming self-sufficient on the reservation. They did not want to return to a life of farming. They tenaciously fought to maintain their equestrian, plains culture. The virtual extinction of the buffalo finally forced the Cheyenne to return to farming.

Lack of success in agriculture led them to lease some of their land for grazing to cattle ranchers. This relationship ended because some Cheyenne felt the cattle interfered with their use of the land.

Indians began raiding the white-owned herds for their own use. In 1885 President Grover Cleveland ordered the cattlemen to remove their herds from Cheyenne-Arapaho territory.

In 1891 the Cheyenne and Arapaho ceded all their surplus lands to the U.S. government for $1.5 million. At noon, 19 April 1892, some 30,000 settlers raced to claim the unassigned Indian lands. Within hours, the Cheyenne and Arapahos became a minority in their former territory. (Berthrong 1963, 1976; Hoebel 1960; Roe 1955; Stands in Timber 1967)

—*Janine M. Cairo*

CHEYENNE CUT

Also Cheyenne leg. See Chaps.

CHEYENNE ROLL

Cowboys wanted their **saddles** as comfortable and functional as possible. Ramon Adams *(Western Words)* describes a saddle innovation called the Cheyenne roll:

A saddle devised by Frank Meanea, a saddlemaker in Cheyenne, to create something different from the saddles of his day. The saddle was made with a leather flange extending over, to the rear, of the cantle board. The saddle was brought out about 1870 and became very popular throughout the seventies and eighties, especially east of the Rockies.

(Adams 1968; Beatie 1982)

CHICKEN PULL

See Equestrian Games.

CHICKEN SADDLE

Humorous term for a very small **saddle**, such as an English-style saddle.

CHIFLE

Hollowed horn used to carry liquids.

CHIHUAHUAS

See Spurs.

CHINKS

A type of **chaps**, anglicized from *chigaderos*.

CHIPMUNKS

Cartoon characters. See Hat Acts.

CHIRIPÁ

Traditional, baggy, diaper-like **gaucho** pants.

CHISHOLM, JESSE

(1805–1868)

Trader. See Trail Drives.

CHISHOLM TRAIL

See Trail Drives.

CHISUM, JOHN SIMPSON

(1824–1884)

Well-known cattleman John Chisum was born in Madison County in western Tennessee and moved to Texas with his family in 1837. Chisum worked as a building contractor and served as clerk of Lamar County for eight years. In 1854 he became involved with the cattle business, which would dominate the remainder of his life.

The Civil War provided the impetus for the early growth of Chisum's cattle industry. Initially he supplied beef to the Confederate department of the Trans-Mississippi. The fall of Vicksburg to General Ulysses S. Grant in 1863, however, forced Chisum to shift his focus toward the western frontier. By late 1866 he was supplying cattle to New Mexico and Arizona. In 1867 he formed a partnership with Charles **Goodnight;** five years later he settled along the Pecos River near Bosque Grande, New Mexico.

In New Mexico Chisum established his ranch's reputation as the largest in the West, if not the world. By 1875 more than 100 cowboys tended 80,000 head of cattle that grazed on his ranch at South Spring, near the confluence of the Hondo and Pecos rivers. He reputedly controlled grasslands for 150 miles along the Pecos. To protect his vast herds, Chisum developed the distinctive Long Rail brand and the jinglebob earmark.

Chisum kept a well-armed crew of at least 50 cowboys, who not only maintained the cattle but served as a defense against the lawlessness and competition in Lincoln County, New Mexico. Like many others of his time, Chisum would resort to violence to protect and promote his interests. Prior to the famous Lincoln County War, small ranchers near Seven Rivers united against Chisum in the Pecos War (1877). Chisum and his ranch crew reacted to the threat with **violence** of their own.

Contrary to popular opinion at the time, Chisum took no active part in the violence of the Lincoln County War (1878–81). He left behind few personal records, making it difficult to recreate his views or precise role in the affairs of his time. He had friendly relations with ranchers Alexander McSween and John Tunstall and was a rival of the faction led by Lawrence G. Murphy and James J. Dolan. Many people in New Mexico believed that Chisum was somehow indirectly involved in the violence; Governor Lew Wallace held the prominent cattleman to be its root cause.

Chisum revealed the extent of his power after the war. At his instigation officials appointed Pat Garrett as sheriff of Lincoln County, giving him the formidable mission of bringing William H. ("Billy the Kid") Bonney to justice and restoring law and order to the county.

In the wake of the Lincoln County War, Chisum faced the beginning of the end of both his cattle business and open-range ranching. Unwise and questionable business dealings left virtually all of his property at South Springs in bond to another company. In 1879 he returned to his smaller ranch on the Pecos River. In 1884 Chisum died at Eureka Springs, Arkansas, after treatment for a neck tumor. He was buried at Paris, Texas, his first town of residence in the West. He left an estate worth $500,000 to his relatives.

Chisum never married. When questioned why, he responded that no woman had courted him hard enough. He was noted for his generosity to his friends and his distaste for extravagance.

Because of his name and involvement with ranching, Chisum is sometimes erroneously linked to the Chisholm Trail. That famous trail followed an earlier trade route blazed after the Civil War by Jesse Chisholm. (Hinton 1956, 1957; Thrapp 1988)

—*Nils E. Mikkelsen*

CHISUM
Film (1970). See Wayne, John.

CHIVARRAS
See Chaps.

CHOKE THE HORN
To grab the **saddle** horn, something no cowboy wants to be seen doing.

CHOPPER
Hand who cuts out cattle during **roundup.**

CHOW
Colloquial term for **food.**

CHUCK
Also chow, grub—colloquial terms for **food.**

CHUCK WAGON
See Food.

CHUCK WAGON CHICKEN
Humorous term for fried bacon.

CHUCK-LINE RIDER
Also grub-line rider. Unemployed hand who rode from ranch to ranch, exchanging a bit of news and gossip for a meal.

CHURN TWISTER
Derogatory term for farmer.

CIELO
Argentine folkdance enjoyed by **gauchos.**

CINCH
A wide strap extending underneath a horse's belly and holding the **saddle** in place. The word comes from the Spanish *cincha*. **Vaqueros** used cinches made of braided horsehair. In the more industrialized United States, cinches might be made of hair, cotton, canvas, or leather. Rings at each end provide a means of tightening or loosening the cinch. (Beatie 1982; Ward 1958)

CINCHADA
Horseback tug-of-war. See Equestrian Games.

CIRCLE RIDER
See Roundup.

CLARK, (CHARLES) BADGER, JR.
(1883–1957)
The original cowboy poet "lariat," Badger Clark is the most revered name in cowboy **poetry.** He was born in Iowa, but he grew up in South Dakota. Like so many others, Clark migrated to the Southwest for health reasons. He cowboyed at an Arizona ranch and began sending his family letters in verse. Clark learned that he could sell and perform his poetry, so he traded the saddle for the pen. He authored many venerable poems, with "The Cowboy's Prayer" perhaps his most recited work. He published his first book in 1915, *Sun and Saddle Leather*. In later life he returned to South Dakota, a state that named him poet laureate in 1937. (Thrapp 1988)

CLARK, WALTER VAN TILBURG
(1909–1971)
Novelist, author of *The Ox-Bow Incident* (1940). See Literature.

CLAW LEATHER
See Choke the Horn.

CLOTHESLINE
Colloquial term for rope.

CLOTHING

See Boots; Chaps; Hat; Spurs.

CLYMER, JOHN
(1907–1989)

Artist. See Art of the Cowboy.

COBIJA

Llanero poncho.

COBURN, WALT
(1889–1971)

Pulp novelist.

COCINERO

Camp cook, anglicized to coosie, cusie, and other variants.

CODY, WILLIAM FREDERICK
(1846–1917)

William F. Cody, a frontiersman, scout, buffalo hunter, and entertainer, has become one of the central icons of America's frontier heritage. Cody, more widely known as Buffalo Bill, lived the reality of frontier life. In his role as Wild West showman, however, he shaped the mythology of the frontier more strongly than any other person.

Cody was born on 26 February 1846 in LeClair, Scott County, Iowa Territory. His family moved to Kansas in 1854, and there Cody's varied life on the frontier began. His father died in 1857, leaving young William to provide for the family. At the age of 14 he rode as a mounted messenger for Majors & Russell and then for the Pony Express. He reputedly took a record-setting ride covering 322 miles with 21 horses. He served in the Civil War with irregular militia units and with the Seventh Kansas Volunteer Cavalry. His wartime duties included scouting and spying.

Cody met Louisa Frederici while serving in the military and married her in 1866. Theirs was not a happy marriage. They ran an inn in Kansas after the war, but Cody could not abide a sedentary life. He rode farther west, hiring on as a scout and guide. In 1867–68 he earned his

nickname, Buffalo Bill, shooting thousands of buffalo to supply meat for workers building the Kansas Pacific Railroad. He even gave his government issue gun a name, the Lucretia Borgia.

Cody served for a decade in the cavalry beginning in 1868 and fought in several campaigns against the Indians. General Philip Sheridan named him chief of scouts for the Fifth U.S. Cavalry. Cody impressed him with a 60-hour, 350-mile ride to deliver dispatches. In one campaign, Cody killed a Sioux chief named Tall Bull and later bestowed that name on a prize horse. His most famous Indian encounter occurred on 17 July 1876 while scouting for General Wesley Merritt. He killed and scalped a Cheyenne chief named Yellow Hand (or Yellow Hair). Cody later would reenact this action countless times in his Wild West show.

Dime novelist Ned **Buntline** played a major role in Cody's transformation from scout and buffalo hunter to frontier hero. The two met in 1869. A popular and prolific writer, Buntline made Cody the hero of four novels and a play.

By the early 1870s, Cody had become famed as a frontiersman. The year 1872 proved especially eventful. During that year he guided a buffalo hunting expedition for Grande Duke Alexis of Russia. Nebraskans elected him to the State Legislature, but he soon resigned. He also got into theater, appearing as himself at the Chicago opening of Buntline's *Scouts of the Prairie* on 16 December. While artistically appalling, Cody's persona and the excitement of screaming Indians and blasting six-guns entertained audiences. Cody broke with Buntline after a year but never lost his zest for performing.

Buffalo Bill became very popular among the seemingly insatiable eastern readers of the penny dreadfuls. In addition to Buntline's four novels about Cody, the prolific Prentiss Ingraham added another 121 titles. All told, over a thousand pulp publications made Cody their hero.

Cody used his notoriety to begin a theatrical career. He toured for 11 years, acting in melodramas depicting life and death on the frontier. In 1879 Cody took a personal hand in creating his own mythology, publishing his not-always-reliable autobiography, *The Life of Hon. William F. Cody, Known as Buffalo Bill.*

His flair for showmanship and organization came to the fore in 1882. He organized a Fourth of July celebration, the Old Glory Blowout, for his hometown of North Platte, Nebraska. Events included **rodeo** competition and horseback exhibitions that provided the germ for his world-famous show.

Buffalo Bill Cody perpetuated the mythology of the Wild West. He is pictured here with Sitting Bull.

The following summer, Cody began touring with his Wild West, an exhibition of Indian fights, roundups, stage robberies, and buffalo hunts that opened at the Omaha Fairgrounds on 19 May 1883. Gordon William ("Pawnee Bill") **Lillie** worked for Cody as an interpreter. The show's stars included Johnny Baker ("the Cowboy Kid") and Buck **Taylor** ("King of the Cowboys"). Taylor, like Cody, became immortalized in pulp literature. It was Prentiss Ingraham's 1887 potboiler about Taylor that began his rise as a literary legend.

Annie **Oakley** (Phoebe Anne Mozee or Little Sure Shot) joined the show for the 1884–85 season and became a leading attraction. Her superb marksmanship amazed audiences everywhere. Cody's partner, Nate Salsbury, deserves much credit for keeping things running. Cody, overly fond of alcohol, sometimes incapacitated himself with drink. Salsbury contributed a steadying influence and shrewd business sense.

In 1887 Cody and Salsbury packed up their 200 actors and 300 head of livestock and sailed to England to perform for Queen Victoria's Golden Jubilee. Fascinated, the queen requested an encore performance. The troupe performed at Earl's Court for 30,000 to 40,000 people each day from May through October. They returned for a several-year tour of the Continent in 1889. Back in the U.S., an estimated six million people saw Cody's appearances at the 1893 Chicago World's Fair. Promoters of Cheyenne Frontier Days, first held in 1897, invited Cody's troupe to perform there the following year.

Cody considered his show an educational endeavor. He strived hard to give audiences an authentic look at real frontier events. Granted, he gave events a theatrical flair, but he recruited real old-time cowboys, bona fide Indians (including Sitting Bull for a season), and an international cast.

Like **pulp novels** and later **B westerns,** Buffalo Bill promoted the simple formulas of good versus evil, of civilization against frontier savagery. He understood the need for action and excitement. His Wild West promised audiences "the grandest, most realistic and overwhelmingly thrilling war-spectacle ever seen."

Cody broadened his Wild West by internationalizing the cast. He hired two Hispanic cowboys from San Antonio, Texas. Champion vaquero rider Antonio Esquivel performed off and on from 1883 to 1905. Another **vaquero,** José ("Mexican Joe") Berrara, amazed audiences with his rope tricks. Cody also included Argentine **gauchos** and Russian cossacks. He renamed the expanded operation Buffalo Bill's Wild West and Congress of Rough Riders of the World.

Cody spent his money lavishly, foolishly, and generously. Much of his wealth went into his 4,000-acre Scout's Rest Ranch in western Nebraska. His Wyoming investments included 400,000 acres in the Big Horn Basin and the founding of Cody, Wyoming, complete with the Irma Hotel and a newspaper, *The Cody Enterprise.* He also lost half a million dollars in a mining scam. His conflict-ridden marriage to Louisa ("Lulu") ended in divorce. Cody claimed she tried to poison him at Christmas in 1900 and sued for divorce. The stormy, sensational proceedings came to a head in 1905. Cody lost his suit and had to pay Lulu's $318 in court costs. The two reconciled five years later.

Beset by financial woes, Cody briefly joined his show with that of a rival from 1911 to 1913. Major Gordon W. ("Pawnee Bill") Lillie had organized his Far East show in 1888. He recognized the appeal of exotic costumes, such as those worn by Mexican *charros.* He also emphasized the special skills of foreign riders that made them great hits with North American audiences. Like Cody, Lillie toured widely throughout the United States and Europe.

Production and travel costs had become too great, and in 1913 both Cody and Lillie were forced into bankruptcy. Cody continued scheming for ways to make money for a few more years. He appeared with the 101 Ranch Wild West in a rather unsuccessful 1916 season. Cody's health declined along with his finances, and he died in Denver on 10 January 1917.

Controversial in life, Cody was also the center of a controversy after his death. He had long spoken of being buried in Cody, Wyoming, the town he created. His wife, however, said that he changed his mind shortly before dying. She said he now favored Lookout Mountain, west of Denver. The fact that Harry Tammen and the *Denver Post* agreed to finance the funeral probably played a role in the change of venue.

Cody's importance to cowboy culture persists long after his death. Cowboy singer Michael Martin **Murphey** often performs in a long buckskin coat reminiscent of Cody's dress. Some original film of Cody survives, and countless B westerns have perpetuated his mythology.

Cody's life and legend are commemorated at several locations. The most impressive memorial is a vast museum complex, the **Buffalo Bill Historical Center,** at Cody, Wyoming. Exhibits of posters, paintings, photographs, and artifacts document Cody's life as well as the Wild West show. The center also includes the Cody Firearms Museum, Plains Indian Museum, Whitney Gallery of Western Art, and the McCracken Library. The **Buffalo Bill Memorial Museum** sits adjacent to his grave on Lookout Mountain, Colorado. His Scout's Rest Ranch, near North Platte, Nebraska, also draws visits from Cody's many fans. (Rosa and May 1989; Russell 1960; Thrapp 1988)

—*Janine Cairo and Richard W. Slatta*

COE, DAVID ALLAN
(1939–)
Singer. See Hat Acts.

COFFEE
Cowboys in both North and South America demanded a strong, hot drink loaded with caffeine; in the United States they expected hot, strong "brown gargle" (coffee) with every meal. Woe to the cook who turned out a pot of "belly wash." The **llaneros** of northern South America also favored strong coffee, mixed with some semirefined sugar, if available. Canadian hands might drink tea instead of coffee. **Gauchos** of South America used *mate,* a strongly caffeinic tea in use for hundreds if not thousands of years.

In the American West, cowhands drank copious quantities of strong black coffee, brewed in three-to five-gallon pots, with every meal. Hands might compliment the camp cook by calling his brew "six-shooter coffee," strong and thick enough to float a six-gun.

Arbuckle's Means Coffee
Before 1865, westerners had to buy green coffee and roast the beans as best they could. Canadian ranchers did the same. Many a skillet of roasting beans got burned, and the chore was tedious and time-consuming. In 1865, John and Charles Arbuckle, grocers in Pittsburgh, developed a special roasting and coating technique that kept beans tasty for long periods. The special egg and sugar glaze that sealed flavor in the beans made Arbuckle's Ariosa Coffee ideal for cow camps and ranch houses. The brand also became immensely popular among the Navajo. John Arbuckle moved to New York in the 1870s while Charles maintained the Pittsburgh business. They quickly made believers of skeptical coffee trade experts who ridiculed the notion that people would buy coffee in "little paper bags, like peanuts."

A sound product, plus a bit of creative marketing, such as merchandise coupons and a sugar candy stick in each one-pound package, made Arbuckle's synonymous with coffee throughout the West. Customers could redeem coupons for aprons, window curtains, watches, and even a .32-caliber revolver. The firm's logo, a flying angel, became a well-known icon on the range. *Arbuckle's* also served as a derisive term for a greenhorn hand, who the boss supposedly got by trading stamps given away with coffee.

In *Western Words,* Ramon Adams repeats the "secret recipe" for good camp coffee: Wet down a couple pounds of Arbuckle's. Boil it for two hours. Toss in a horse shoe. If the shoe sinks, it ain't ready to drink.

In their *Cowboy Poetry Cookbook* (1992), Cyd McMullen and Anne Wallace McMullen offer a more realistic recipe for "Buckaroo Coffee." You need a big enamel pot, well blackened by many campfires. Fill the pot with clear, cold water and toss in two large handfuls of coffee. Set the pot in a fire. As the coffee begins to boil and you smell that fine aroma, drop an egg into the pot. This will settle the grounds. Keep the pot on the edge of the fire, ready for anyone who might ride up.

Coffee in Latin America

It shouldn't surprise us that many Latin American cowboys also relished good, strong coffee, since the region has long been the world's leading coffee producer. In 1987, for example, Latin America produced 62 percent of the world's coffee beans. **Llaneros** in Venezuela and Colombia (the region's second-largest coffee producer after Brazil) and **vaqueros** in Mexico enjoyed their coffee as much as their Anglo-American cousins. Cautioned one student of the llanero, "Give the llanero bad liquor, bad tobacco, or bad food, but never bad coffee." (Ovalles 1905) In town, llaneros might splurge and take their coffee with milk *(café con leche)*. Llaneros and Mexican **vaqueros** preferred their coffee sweetened with raw sugar.

Mate

While cowboys of northern South America, Mexico, and points north drank lots of hot black coffee, **gauchos** and *huasos* in southern South America consumed *mate*. This highly caffeinic tea is produced from the leaves of *Ilis paraguariensis,* a plant related to holly. Grown in Paraguay and the rest of the Paraná River basin, mate has long been a favorite beverage of the region's Indian population. The Spanish adopted the drink, and its popularity continues. Chileans sometimes take their mate with a bit of sugar in the morning; Argentines tend to favor it straight.

For huasos and gauchos, however, mate represents far more than an invigorating beverage. Ritual and proper equipment are tied inextricably to the consumption of the tea. Mate is sipped through a metal tube *(bombilla),* sometimes embellished with ornate silver and gold work. The tube has a strainer at one end that is inserted into a small, hollowed-out gourd (also called a *mate)* filled with tea leaves and hot water. The liquid is replenished with more hot water as the gourd empties. Fresh leaves are added as needed. Mate is consumed communally if at all possible. Gauchos and huasos imbibe a few sips and pass the gourd to the next person. This sharing and the use of a communal straw symbolizes friendship and trust among those who are drinking the mate.

Because of its importance, mate made its way into gaucho folklore. According to a traditional poem, you could convey different messages by serving the beverage in various ways.

> Bitter mate shows indifference.
> Sweet mate, friendship.
> Mate with balm-mint, displeasure.
> Mate with cinnamon, "you're on my mind."
> Mate with brown sugar, congeniality.
> Mate with orange peel, "come and look for me."
> Mate with bee balm, "your sadness pains me."
> Mate with milk, respect.
> Mate with coffee, offense pardoned.

During the late nineteenth century, mate even became the focus of a public health debate. Critics of the gaucho and his lifestyle attacked mate drinking as unhygienic and a waste of time. Defenders of the drink countered by linking it to the Argentine way of life and national character. Such polemics changed few minds. Mate remains widely used in rural and urban society throughout the Southern Cone.

Milk, Anyone?

Despite being surrounded by cows, cowboys seldom consumed fresh milk in their coffee or any other way. Canned condensed milk might be used for cooking in North America but never for drinking. A number of practical considerations militated against milk. First, cowboys hated any footwork, including milking cows. Second, storage, transportation, and spoilage presented major problems, especially in warmer climates. Third, it was no easy feat to milk wild cattle, and much stock during the days of open-range ranching was anything but tame.

In *Cattle Trade* (1874), Joseph G. **McCoy** noted that "in camp, on the trail, on the ranch in Texas, with their countless thousands of cattle, milk and butter are almost unknown, not even milk or cream for the coffee is had." With his usual rich man's condescension toward ranch hands, he attributed the lack of milk to "pure shiftlessness and the lack of energy." Theodore **Roosevelt** also remarked the absence of milk: "Most ranchmen [in the early 1880s] never had milk. I knew more than one ranch with ten thousand head of cattle where there was not a cow that could be milked."

Similar problems and prejudices concerning milk arose in Latin America. The wealthy and city dwellers might dilute their coffee with milk, but poor working cowboys took it black. On his visit to the Venezuelan llanos in 1876 and 1877, German traveler Karl Sachs to his dismay found no milk for his coffee. Ranchers did produce and sell cheese *(queso de mano),* but not butter. Venezuelan writer Ramón Páez likewise complained in his *Wild Scenes* (1863) about having to take his coffee black. The typical llanos ranch house reminded him of

> … a bee-hive of vast proportions, natu-rally suggesting the idea of a "land of milk and honey." Unfortunately neither of these could be obtained either for love or money, although the woods and pastures of the estate abounded in both the crea-tures that produced them. So we were compelled to resort to our reserved stock of *papelón* [raw sugar] to sweeten our cof-fee, and to its own delicious natural aroma in the place of milk.

(Adams 1952; Slatta 1990, 1992)

COFFEE GRINDING
See Rope.

COFFIN VARNISH
Colloquial term for whiskey. See Saloons.

COGBURN, ROOSTER
Character in the 1969 movie *True Grit.* See Wayne, John.

COIL
Another term for a **rope.**

COLEAR
To grab a running bull by the tail. See *Charro; Equestrian Games.*

COLT, SAMUEL
(1814–1862)
See Colt Firearms.

COLT FIREARMS
"God didn't make men equal; Sam Colt did," goes the old western adage. Without question, Connecticut-born Samuel Colt had a great impact on western history and cowboy life. During his relatively short life (1814–1862), Colt revolutionized the **firearms** industry.

Colt established his first factory in Paterson, New Jersey, in 1836. Although his name became synonymous with revolvers, Colt's early rifles and carbines received more attention than his pistol designs. One of his early models was the Paterson pistol, a five-shooter produced in 1839. In the West, however, Colt would become best known for the immense popularity of his revolvers, pistols with a revolving cylinder that held six shells. Colt offered belt, **holster,** and pocket pistols, choices that he continued to produce later.

Texans liked his handguns, but Colt was unable to interest the U.S. Army. Unfortunately for Colt, weak demand brought his company to bankruptcy in 1842. History came to his rescue, however, in the form of the Mexican War. Military demands for weaponry spurred renewed interest in his products, and he resumed business in 1846. The Colt Dragoon or Army model (so-called because U.S. mounted infantry used them) became a popular seller, especially to the government. These big .44 caliber six-shooters, weighing four pounds and two ounces, rolled off Colt's assembly lines from 1847 to 1860. The Walker model (1847) found its way to the side of many Texas Rangers.

Some of Colt's pistols had an attachable shoulder stock intended to transform them into pistol-carbines. Colt also produced smaller caliber guns such as the .36 Colt Navy pistol, named for the naval scene engraved on the cylinder.

The advent of metallic cartridges represented a great improvement over cap-and-ball firearms technology. (Thereafter cowboys would refer to a backward ranching outfit as a "cap-and-ball layout.") Fortunately, most of Colt's older guns could be modified from percussion ignition to use the new cartridges. One of his conversion models was the .44 Rimfire Colt, a precursor to the famous Peacemaker that would appear in 1873.

The Single Action Army revolver (also known as the Frontier or the Peacemaker), proved enormously popular. More than 300,000 of these Model P six-shooters came from Colt's factory. The Peacemaker, more than any other firearm, became *the* cowboy's companion.

Colt's revolvers had a light trigger pull that permitted accurate shooting. A gunman could fire rapidly by "fanning" (holding the trigger back while slapping the hammer with the free hand). One interesting variation was the Buntline Special, a revolver with an exceedingly long barrel of 12 inches or more.

The first Colt double-action weapons emerged in 1876. They took such forms as the .38 Lightning and .41 Thunderer, as well as the .45 Army-Frontier. In 1889, swing-out cylinders came to Colt handguns. One of the most famous of these was the Officers Model Colt Double Action .38, which saw action in the Spanish-American War.

The old Colts retain their attraction to gun buffs, and models in good condition command high prices. According to Bill Mackin, "of all cowboy collectibles, simply nothing transcends the Colt revolver." (Mackin 1989; Serven 1979)

—*Mark Mayer*

COMANCHE

See Indians as Cowboys.

COMB

See Rodeo.

COMPADRE

Term the cowboy picked up from the **vaquero,** meaning friend, companion, pardner.

COMPAÑERO

Same as *compadre.*

CONCHAS

Small, round, etched silver decorations stitched onto clothing, saddles, and other tack. The cowboy borrowed conchas and many other things from the Mexican **vaquero.** The term *conchas* (meaning shell) was anglicized to conchos.

CONTRACT BUSTER

Bronc buster who contracts to break a given number of **horses** for a given fee.

CONVERTER

Colloquial term for a preacher.

COOK, JAMES HENRY
(1857–1942)

Cowboy, writer. See Autobiographies by Cowboys.

COOK, WILL
(1922–1964)

Novelist who wrote formula westerns under various names.

"COOL WATER"

Song written by Roy Rogers in 1936. See Rogers, Roy.

COOLIDGE, DANE
(1873–1940)

Writer. See Historiography of the Cowboy.

COOPER, GARY
(1901–1961)

Actor. See Films, Cowboy.

COOSIE

Also cusie; colloquial terms for cook from the Spanish *cocinero.*

CORONA

Saddle pad. See Saddle.

CORPORAL

See Caporal.

CORRAL DUST

Colloquial term for tall tales or lies. See Humor.

CORRER EL GALLO

Chicken pull. See Equestrian Games.

COSÍO GONZÁLEZ, RAMÓN

See *Charro.*

COW GREASE

Also cow salve; colloquial terms for butter.

COW TOWNS

Abilene, Baxter Springs, Caldwell, Dodge City, Ellsworth, Hays City, Newton, Wichita—these Kansas cow towns became famous and infamous during the 1870s. So did other little towns at the ends of cattle trails, including Sidney and Ogallala, Nebraska, Pine Bluffs and Cheyenne, Wyoming, and Glendive and Miles City, Montana. Most of the boomtowns served as railheads, points where trail drivers from Texas deposited their herds and railroads carried the bounty of beef back east for processing.

Also called trail towns or cattle towns, these lively spots drew every type of westerner, from the dregs to the elite of society. Wild Texas hands painted the town red at the end of months on the trail. Stock buyers from the East exchanged gold, cash, and checks for beef on the hoof. Fancy-dressed gamblers and prostitutes, saloon keepers, land speculators, rank-smelling freighters and buffalo hunters, and naive, young soldiers from frontier army posts jostled one another in the streets.

First among the great cattle towns, Abilene is located on the Smoky Hill River in east-central Kansas. It is the county seat for Dickinson County. As a drop-off point for the famous Chisholm Trail, the town boomed from 1867 through 1871. Cattleman Joseph G. **McCoy** played a leading role in turning Abilene, and later Newton and Wichita, into cow towns.

Frontier boomtowns attracted gamblers, thieves, prostitutes, and others looking to separate cowboys and others from their money. McCoy hired James Butler ("Wild Bill") Hickok to serve as town marshal during the 1870s. William Matthew Tilghman, Jr., served ably as a Kansas lawman until 1889. Fellow lawman William Barclay ("Bat") Masterson described Tilghman as "the greatest of us all."

The local business community had something of a love-hate relationship with the Texas cowhands who brought them prosperity but also trouble. A reporter for Colorado's *Gunnison Review* (14 August 1880) described the business community's attempts to attract Texans on "Saturday Night in a Kansas Cattle Town":

> Everywhere the cowboys made themselves manifest, clad now in the soiled and dingy jeans of the trail, then in a suit of many buttoned corduroy, and again in the affluence of broadcloth, silk hat, gloves, cane and sometimes a clerical white necktie. And everywhere, also, starred and shone the Lone Star of Texas—for the cowboy, wherever he may wander, and however he may change, never spends his money or lends his presence to a concern that does not in some way recognize the emblem of his native State; so you will see in towns like New Sharon a general pandering to this sentiment, and lone stars abound of all sizes and hues, from the big disfiguring white one painted on the hotel front down to the little pink one stitched in silk on the cowboy's shilling handkerchief.

The *Dodge City Times* (28 April 1877) described the preparations made to impress the town's fun-seeking guests:

> Dodge City is bracing herself up for the cattle trade. Places of refreshment are being gorgeously arrayed in new coats of paint and other ornaments that beguile the festive cowboy. Materson & Springer's place can scarcely be recognized since the bar has been moved and operated upon by Mr. Weaver's brush. The graining is finely executed. Charley Lawson's orchestra are mounted on a platform enclosed by and tastefully ornamented with bunting.

In contrast, the *Caldwell Post* (2 September 1880) issued a stern warning to merrymaking cowboys who blew into town:

> We are very sorry that some of the cowboys who come in here allow whisky to get the better of them; because when sober, they are as are the majority of them, as nice fellows as ever lived. We expect them to have all the fun they can get, but they must acknowledge that the citizens of our town have a right to insist upon a strict compliance with the city's laws. Visitors had better bear that in mind, and also the fact that we have a police force determined to do their duty.

Cowboys earned their reputation for drunken, violent, and disorderly conduct during their blowouts at cow towns. Like sailors home from sea, hands fresh off the trail had lots of pent-up energy and desires. The effects of cowboy fun could be very destructive. One of the most graphic depictions of such "fun" is the scene from the **film** *Monte Walsh* in which Walsh rides a wild bronc to submission, destroying most of Main Street in the process.

Cowboys indulged themselves in whatever vices a cow town could provide. Local businesses willingly and profitably fulfilled the cowboy's desires for everything from a bath and shave to cheap whiskey, gambling, and prostitutes. One old hand explained cowboy behavior this way (*Overland Monthly*, November 1902):

> We're not near so bad as we're painted. We like to get up a little racket now and then, but it's all in play. Of course, sometimes we fall out amongst ourselves and then there is a corpse.

Many cow towns, such as Ellsworth, enjoyed only a few years of prosperity. Pulling strings in the Kansas state legislature and working in cooperation with the Kansas Pacific Railroad, Ellsworth city fathers engineered a successful trail season in 1872. A harsh winter and outrage among farmers, whose crops and fences suffered mightily from the Texas herds, quickly reversed cattle industry fortunes. The ever-fickle railroads also pushed westward, leaving Ellsworth, deserted and dusty, in favor of Wichita.

In 1877 Wichita suffered the same fate as the cattle trade pushed on to Dodge City. Cattle shipping replaced the traffic in buffalo hides that had sustained Dodge during the 1870s. Nearly 200,000 buffalo hides had been shipped east from Dodge during its first winter in existence, 1872–73. By 1884 sagging livestock prices and **fencing** and political opposition from farmers brought an end to Dodge City's boom. It was then Caldwell's turn for a short time in the sun.

The cow towns flourished briefly, but changing markets and the building of more railroads stemmed the great Texas **trail drives** by the mid-1880s. Most of the towns slipped back into obscurity. Once the beef bonanza burst, Abilene went back to being a subdued spot. Today, the town's 7,000 inhabitants lead much quieter lives than their predecessors did in its heyday.

Beginning in the 1950s, however, city fathers in many old cow towns struck upon the idea of using history to attract tourists. With westerns dominating **television** programming, boosters created "Old Abilene," "Cowtown Wichita," Dodge City's "Front Street Replica," and other recreations of wild, bygone days. Like many elements of cowboy culture, the cow towns passed quickly from the realm of history to legend. (Dykstra 1976; Forbis 1978)

See also Prostitution; Saloons.

COWBOY ARTISTS OF AMERICA MUSEUM

In April 1983 the Cowboy Artists of America Museum opened its doors in Kerrville, Texas. The museum exhibits western **art** by contemporary painters, who, according to executive director Gene Ball, "build on the legacy of Frederic **Remington** and Charles **Russell**."

The museum came about through the efforts of several Texas businessmen who collect contemporary western art. L. D. Brinkman, Robert Shelton, and others wanted a place where the public could enjoy the works they cherished.

A sculpture by Fritz White greets visitors at the entrance. The museum features works by a select group of two dozen to three dozen artists, members of the Cowboys Artists of America (CA). The group had made its home in Arizona, but the attractive offer of a museum site in Texas moved them east. Texas CA members include Tom Ryan (Midland), Melvin Warren (Clifton), Robert Pummill (Kerrville), and James Boren (Clifton, deceased 1990).

Gordon Snidow, another early CA member, was born in 1936 in Paris, Missouri. He grew up in Tulsa admiring the western art at the Gilcrease Museum. After studying art in Hollywood in the late 1950s, Snidow found little market for his photorealistic paintings of contemporary cowboys. Things have changed, however, and Snidow's paintings now command top dollar. Like C. M. Russell, Snidow thinks of himself as a storyteller. He seeks to go further, however, "to find some insight into the characters I paint. I guess I'm seeking the soul."

In addition to contemporary works, the museum houses fine historical paintings, the legacy that inspires CA members. The collection includes works by the founder of the Taos Society of Artists (1912), Joseph Henry Sharp. Sharp is among America's premier painters of the American Indian. There are three works by Oscar Edmund Berninghaus, another original member

of the Taos Society of Artists. Berninghaus left a good selection of representational paintings.

In addition to art works, the museum serves as an educational resource. CA members give several workshops each year. The small research library includes a good range of books about the **beef cattle industry.** Rotating exhibits depict the studios of prominent western artists, including that of Bavarian-born Nick Eggenhofer, who has been a CA member since 1970. "The West got hold of me at a very early age," he noted, "and it hasn't turned loose yet."

Address: P.O. Box 1716 (1550 Bandera Highway), Kerrville, TX 78029-1716; tel. 210-896-2553. Museum supporters receive a newsletter, *Visions West*.

COWBOY COCKTAIL

Straight whiskey.

COWBOY HALL OF FAME

See National Cowboy Hall of Fame.

COWBOY TURTLE ASSOCIATION

See Rodeo.

THE COWBOYS

Film (1972). See Wayne, John.

COWBOYS FOR CHRIST

See Religion.

COWBOYS OF CANADA

Canada's ranching frontier boomed from the 1880s through the early twentieth century. Southwestern Saskatchewan, along with southern and central Alberta and British Columbia, flourished as cattle country. Cowboy culture remains a vibrant, living part of these areas of western Canada.

Canadian cowboys are the only cowboys of the Americas to have little negative imagery associated with them. Canadians go to considerable pains to distinguish their civilized and cultured West from the violent, rough-and-tumble frontiers to the south. John R. Craig *(Ranching with Lords and Commons)* insisted that "there was very little of what is termed the 'wild and woolly' West in evidence; the people were law-abiding, and there was absolute freedom from such objectionable incidents as were encountered south of the boundary line."

Nineteenth-century sources contrasted cowboys north and south of the 49th parallel. The Calgary *Herald* (12 November 1884) contrasted the cowboys of Canada and the United States: "The rough and festive cowboy of Texas and Oregon has no counterpart here. Two or three beardless lads wear jingling spurs and ridiculous revolvers and walk with a slouch." The paper added with a touch of prideful chauvinism that "the genuine Alberta cowboy is a gentleman."

Similarities between Canadian and U.S. Cowboys

Canadian cowboys shared many similarities with their cousins south of the border. They dressed in the standard cowboy outfit: broad-brimmed **hat,** durable jeans, and high-heeled **boots.** An anonymous, itinerant cowhand of the early twentieth century provided a down-to-earth description of his fellows *(Canadian Cattlemen,* March 1943):

Attire was not nearly as picturesque as we are led to believe; 10 gallon hats of today would have been more ornamental than useful. The narrow-brimmed gray Stetson, a shirt open at the neck, sometimes a scarf about the neck, pant overalls with a leather belt, and hand-made riding boots with **spurs** completed the outfit. In winter weather hair **chaps** were worn over the pants, giving added protection to the legs.

Many hands from the United States rode north to work the Canadian ranges during the late 1880s. Overstocking the range and the sting of the raging blizzards of the mid-1880s put many U.S. outfits out of operation; the demand for ranch hands in many areas of the West dropped sharply. At about the same time, however, the Alberta ranch industry began expanding.

In contrast to Latin American riders, cowboys in Canada generally treated their horses well. John David Higenbotham *(When the West Was Young)* complained that "cowboys who own their mounts almost 'baby' them with kindness." Some ranch foremen preferred not to hire hands who brought their own mounts. The foremen believed that the men did not ride their own animals hard enough to do the strenuous work required on the range. Of course, this practice also tied the worker to the ranch by making him dependent on the outfit for his mounts.

Canadian hands, like all cowboys, hated footwork. At Macleod, an early Alberta **cow town,** a policeman complained that he could not hire someone to dig a well: "A man cannot dig a well from a horse's back." In 1888 a Mounted Police commissioner repeated complaints from ranchers that "cow-boys will not work on foot." Despite their dislike of such things, haying, **fencing,** and even milking became increasingly commonplace as a part of the cowboy's work.

Attitudes haven't changed much. Cowboys interviewed during the 1980s for *The Working Cowboy,* a delightful documentary narrated by singer Ian **Tyson,** express a century-old opposition to footwork. A cowboy is happy if he spends most of his time in the saddle. The day is not nearly as cheery if he finds himself atop a tractor, swinging a pitchfork, or stringing fence.

In *Wolf Willow,* Wallace **Stegner** argued convincingly that cowboy culture and character transcended the boundary between the United States and western Canada. He pointed out that the American cowboy's Stetson, bandanna, **chaps, saddle, rope, roundup,** and much more readily crossed the border into Canada:

The outfit, the costume, the practices, the terminology, the state of mind, came into Canada ready-made, and nothing they encountered on the northern Plains enforced any real modifications. The Texas men made it certain that nobody would ever be thrown from a horse in Saskatchewan; he would be piled. They made it sure that no Canadian steer would ever be angry or stubborn; he would be o'nery or ringy or on the prod. Bull Durham was as native to the Whitemud range as to the Pecos, and it was used for the same purposes: smoking, eating, and spitting in the eye of a ringy steer.

They honored courage, competence, self-reliance, and they honored them tacitly. They took them for granted. It was their absence, not their presence, that was cause for remark. Practicing comradeship in a rough and dangerous job, they lived a life calculated to make a man careless of everything except the few things he really valued.

Canadian cowboy life rarely reached the hell-raising pitch made famous by Texas punchers who lit up a cow town after a **trail drive.** In 1905 Sir John Fraser (*Canada As It Is*) offered a view of the Canadian cowboy far different from the wild images of popular fiction:

The "broncho-buster," the "cow-puncher," and the men who ranch among the foothills of the Canadian Rockies are neither so picturesque in garb, so lurid in language, nor so daring in performance as the stay-at-home imagines. The days of "raising hell and playing Cain" are nigh over. Cowboys no longer—if they ever did— spend their time riding unrideable horses, which rear and plunge and roll, or whoop across the boundless prairie swinging lassoes over their heads to catch stampeding cattle by the hind hoof and down them. Nor are they any longer in the habit of dashing from camp into the nearest town to make the townfolk dance on the sidewalk by playing bullets round them. Nor do they ride their horses into the drinking saloon, knock off the neck of a bottle of rye whiskey with a revolver, or guess they'd have a drink of that.

Wages

The earnings of Canadian cowboys generally paralleled those of cowboys in the United States. The heady agricultural demands of World War I pushed cowboy wages upward, and as elsewhere, except for a privileged few permanent hands, most cowboys worked as migrant laborers.

The account books of Canadian cowboy Harry Denning, housed at the Glenbow Archives in Calgary, illustrate his wanderings as a hand. Among other odd jobs, he earned $2 castrating colts in June 1908. In March and May 1909, he did the same thing at different ranches. He made $12.30 breaking horses in July. From January through April 1910, he worked on a ranch and made $40 per month. In May 1910 he earned $4 castrating colts. In July he worked fighting a fire and made $29. At various times, he also worked at a mill, on farms haying and threshing, and on a road crew. Clearly, a cowboy had to be willing to take whatever work was available.

For cowboys everywhere, no work generally meant no pay. Cowboy Ralph Clifton Coppock worked for $25 per month in Alberta from July through September 1905, but he got hurt on 29 August and missed more than a week's work. Those days were deducted from his pay. A stove-up cowboy—one who had been hurt too seriously to continue working on horseback— faced bleak prospects. He might land a job as a cook, but otherwise, he had to make do with charity and odd jobs.

Chivalry

Like their American counterparts, Canadian hands held **women** in almost reverential awe. Mary Ella Inderwick, an English bride, arrived on her husband's ranch in the mid-1888s. She described the extremes to which the hands would go to show her courtesy. She wrote in a letter to a friend dated 13 May 1884:

They are a nice lot of men. I love their attempts to help me to appear civilized. Though they ride in flannel shirts they never come to the table in shirt sleeves.

They have a black alpaca coat hanging in the shack and each one struggles into it to live up to the new regime which began with a bride at the ranche—and this is done so enthusiastically and with such good will that I have no qualms of conscience that I am a nuisance.

Sometimes, however, the burdens of chivalry taxed the good will of the most gentlemanly Canadian cowboys. Monica Hopkins (*Letters from a Lady Rancher*, 1981), another frontier bride, recalled a cowboy rebellion on her ranch near Priddis in 1909. In the name of good breeding and civilization, she decreed that everyone would dine using napkins and napkin rings at every meal. Although they complied with this extreme request, the hands made their true feelings known:

Deadly silence followed this announcement, but at least they did put the napkins into their laps. After they left I retrieved [the napkins] from the floor. They looked as if the men had wiped their feet on them. I put out clean napkins for the next meal and the same thing happened so I picked them up, and put them in the rings, and there they have stayed ever since.

About the only type of Canadian rider to be criticized was the **remittance man**, a young English gentleman seeking his fortune on the frontier. Few of these men succeeded; many ended up squandering the remittances sent by their families. Frank Gilbert Roe (*Alberta Historical Review*, January 1954) painted an unflattering portrait of these equestrian dandies. He concluded that many were little more than ignorant, drunken wastrels. He found their wasteful ostentation especially galling: "Although in many cases anything but the most docile old sheep of a horse was beyond their skill, nothing less in saddlery than a sixty-pound Cheyenne steel tree was worthy of their patronage. They were seldom seen, and never in the public eye, without the full regalia of the range."

Canadian Cowboys in Film

Hollywood also took a hand in misshaping images of the Canadian West. Eager to expand the popular cowboy **film** market, filmmakers extended their imagination to western Canada as early as 1910. The Edison company produced two one-reel westerns supposedly set in Canada: *The Cowpuncher's Glove* and *Riders of the Plains*. Silent cowboy film stars such as Hoot Gibson, Ken Maynard, William S. Hart, and Tom Mix made a dozen Canadian westerns. Later Gene **Autry** and Roy **Rogers** added their versions of Canada's cowboy past.

Pierre Berton (*Hollywood's Canada,* 1975) sharply criticized Hollywood's deformation of the Canadian past. To Berton, Hollywood's mythic Canadian frontier, "complete with **saloons, gambling,** and six-gun violence," bore no resemblance to actual history. In reality, gambling and saloons were outlawed and gunplay was rare. Calls for historical reality seldom fazed filmmakers, however. Hollywood churned out some 575 films depicting Canadian life and history with varying degrees of error. Even the Mountie, the quintessential western Canadian figure, had his uniform and **hat** altered to suit Hollywood cowboy film fashion.

The cultural elite of Montreal or Quebec looked down on the Alberta or British Columbia ranch hand, just as the New Yorker disdained the American cowboy. Most eastern Canadians knew nothing firsthand of the western ranges. Their conception was built upon a crazy quilt of images from scattered news reports, bad movies, and simple prejudice.

A ride through the ranch country of Alberta, British Columbia, or Saskatchewan today, however, reveals a vibrant, positive, active cowboy culture. Many forces keep Canada's range culture alive and well. Ian Tyson and other cowboy singers and a host of cowboy poets commemorate the traditions. *The Puffin' Blow Boys,* a play by Alberta writer Val Jenkins, likewise memorializes cowboy culture.

Since 1912 the Great **Calgary Stampede** has helped preserve ranch and cowboy traditions in Canada. The **Stockmen's Memorial Foundation** likewise works on behalf of the past and future of the **beef cattle industry.** Cowboy work persists side by side with cowboy culture. Hands still work, much as they have for a century, at the Gang Ranch, the Spruce Ranching Co-op, the Y Cross, and the Douglas Lake Calico. (Brado 1984; Breen 1983; Kelly 1965; MacEwan 1975)

COWBOYS OF NORTH AND SOUTH AMERICA

The table below lists the major types of cowboys in the Western Hemisphere, the countries in which they roam, and the term for the plains region where ranching takes place.

Group	Location	Region
Charro	Mexico	
Cowboy	Western Canada	Prairie
Cowboy	Western United States	Plains
Gaucho	Argentina, Uruguay	Pampas
Gaúcho	Rio Grande do Sul, Brazil	Pampas
Huaso (guaso)	Chile	
Llanero	Venezuela, Colombia	Llanos
Paniolo	Hawaii	
Vaqueiro	Northern Brazil	Sertão
Vaquero	Mexico, Southwestern United States, and California	

COWBOYS OF THE UNITED STATES

Etymologists trace the use of the term *cowboy* back to 1000 A.D. in Ireland. Swift used it in 1705, logically enough, to describe a boy who tends cows. Modern usage, first in hyphenated form, dates from the 1830s in Texas. Colonel John S. ("Rip") Ford used the word *cow-boy* to describe the Texan border raider who drove off Mexican cattle during the 1830s. The term carried a tinge of wildness, of life at the fringes of law and civilization.

After the American Civil War, westerners applied the term *cowboy* to ranch hands rather than cattle thieves. The Denver *Republican* (1 October 1883) observed that "it matters not what age, if a man works on a salary and rides after the herd, he is called a 'cowboy.'" A cowboy, then as now, is a man who works at least part of the year as a salaried ranch hand. Ranchers or "cowmen" owned land and cattle; cowboys did not own land and seldom owned cattle.

The cowboy of the American West, a dashing figure in popular novels and films, was in reality a poorly paid laborer engaged in difficult, dirty, often monotonous work. During the years after the Civil War, the **beef cattle industry** spread northward from Texas. During the 1870s cowboying spread to the Southwest and the northern plains. Although some of the young men who worked on these ranches were from the northeastern states, a majority were probably southerners. Many had fought for the Confederacy.

Unlike most movie depictions, not all cowboys were white. Racial distribution varied from place to place. Mostly Anglo cowboys worked the Montana ranges. Farther south, however, such as in Texas, perhaps one-third of the hands may have been African Americans or Mexican Americans.

The cowboy's work year centered on two big events, the **roundup** and the **trail drive.** Roundups were held in the spring and often also in the fall. After cowboys had herded cattle to a central location, they branded newborn calves, castrated and dehorned older animals, and, in spring, chose the cattle to be taken to market.

From 1865 to 1880 at least 3.5 million cattle were driven in herds of between 1,500 and 3,000 from southern Texas to **cow towns** on rail lines in Kansas, Nebraska, and Wyoming. The route most frequently used was the Chisholm Trail, which went to Abilene, Kansas. Working up to 20 hours a day, cowboys drove the animals from one watering place to the next. They had to guard against predators (two-and four-footed), straying cattle, and stampedes at night. For his hard and dirty work the typical cowboy earned the low wage of $25 to $40 a month.

By about 1890 much of the range had been fenced. The westward extension of the railroads eliminated the need for long cattle drives. The good old days of epic drives and open-range riding came to an end. At this point, however, **pulp novels,** Wild West shows, and books such as Owen Wister's *The Virginian* (1902) offered the nostalgic public a stalwart, romantic cowboy hero. Although far removed from the drab truth, the image of excitement, freedom, and drama continues to dominate popular accounts of the cattle frontier.

Cowboys generated conflicting appraisals. When observed at the end of a long trail drive "hellin' 'round town," they attracted little praise. The *Topeka Commonwealth* (15 August 1871) painted an unflattering portrait of the cowboy on a tear:

> The Texas cattle herder is a character, the like of which can be found nowhere else on earth. Of course he is unlearned and illiterate, with but few wants and meager ambition. His diet is principally navy plug and whiskey and the occupation dearest to his heart is **gambling.** His dress consists of a flannel shirt with a handkerchief encircling his neck, butternut pants and a pair of long **boots,** in which are always the legs of his pants. His head is covered by a sombrero, which is a Mexican **hat** with a high crown and a brim of enormous dimensions. He generally wears a revolver on each side of his person, which he will use with as little hesitation on a man as on a wild animal. Such a character is dangerous and desperate and each one has generally killed his man.

The unsympathetic writer went on to catalog the cowboy's additional sins of swearing, fighting, and aversion to authority.

As the ranching industry matured during the 1880s, many observers saw little improvement in cowboy character. The *Las Vegas Optic* (New Mexico, 28 June 1881) reported an unfavorable opinion:

> It is possible that there is not a wilder or more lawless set of men in any country

that pretends to be civilized than the gangs of semi-nomads that live in some of our frontier States and Territories and are referred to in our dispatches as "the cow boys." Many of them have emigrated from our States in order to escape the penalty of their crimes, and it is extremely doubtful whether there is one in their number who is not guilty of a penitentiary offense, while most of them merit the gallows. They are supposed to be herdsmen employed to watch vast herds of cattle, but they might more properly be known under any name that means desperate criminal. They roam about in sparsely settled villages with revolvers, pistols and knives in their belts, attacking every peaceable citizen met with. Now and then they take part in a dance, the sound of the music frequently being deadened by the crack of their pistols, and the hoe-down only being interrupted long enough to drag out the dead and wounded.

A similar assessment of cowboys appeared in the *Rio Grande Republican* (Las Cruces, New Mexico, 13 December 1884):

> Out in the Territories there are only two classes—the "cowboys" and the "tenderfeet." Such of the "cowboys" as are not professional thieves, murderers and miscellaneous blacklegs who fled to the frontier for reasons that require no explanation, are men who totally disregard all of the amenities of Eastern civilization, brook no restraint, and—fearing neither God, nor man or the devil—yielding allegiance to no law save their own untamed passions. He is the best man who can draw the quickest and kill the surest. A "cowboy" who has not killed his man—or to put it more correctly his score of "tenderfeet"— is without character, standing, or respect. The "tenderfoot" who goes among them should first double his life insurance and then be sure he is "well-heeled."

These negative portrayals are not unlike those depicting Latin American horsemen as violent frontier criminals and ruffians living beyond the pale of civilization. While some cowboys in both hemispheres fit this mean stereotype, the majority did not. In fact, some writers recorded in glowing images the character of the American cowboy. William G. (Billy) Johnson worked the range during the 1880s and recalled that "cowpunchers were square shooters, upright, and honest men. I never heard of a cowpuncher insulting a woman. If they were not up to par they were soon run out of the country" (Rollinson 1948).

Other sources from the 1880s likewise reveal positive appraisals of cowboy character. The *Texas Live Stock Journal* (21 October 1882) wrote glowingly of the cowboy's courage, chivalry, and loyalty:

We deem it hardly necessary to say in the next place that the cowboy is a fearless animal. A man wanting in courage would be as much out of place in a cow-camp, as a fish would be on dry land. Indeed the life he is daily compelled to lead calls for the existence of the highest degree of cool calculating courage. As a natural consequence of this courage, he is not quarrelsome or a bully.

As another necessary consequence to possessing true manly courage, the cowboy is as chivalrous as the famed knights of old. Rough he may be, and it may be that he is not a master in ball room etiquette, but no set of men have loftier reverence for **women** and no set of men would risk more in the defense of their person or their honor.

Another and most notable of his characteristics is his entire devotion to the interests of his employer. We are certain no more faithful employee ever breathed than he; and when we assert that he is, *par excellence,* a model in this respect, we know that we will be sustained by every man who has had experience in this matter.

John Baumann *(Fortnightly Review,* 1 April 1887) decried the myth of the cowboy as a "long-haired ruffian. He is in the main a loyal, long-enduring, hard-working fellow, grit to the backbone, and tough as whipcord; performing his arduous and often dangerous duties, and living his comfortless life, without a word of complaint about the many privations he has to undergo."

How can we account for such sharply conflicting visions of cowboy character? First, where the writer observed cowboys is important. Writers who saw cowboys in town, letting off steam after months on the trail or range, saw only lawlessness and debauchery in the cowboy's life. The few journalists who actually spent time on the range and saw hands riding, roping, and branding formed a positive view, remarking of the cowboys' strength, skill, courage, and hard work.

The time period of the observation can also be significant. The heyday of cowboy life lasted only a few brief decades. In the early 1870s, when Texas cowboys drove hundreds of thousands of cattle north to various railheads, unbridled frontier exuberance dominated their lives and actions. As a British traveler noted, "The Texans are, as far as true cowboyship goes, unrivaled: the best riders, hardy, and born to the business, the only drawback being their wild reputation. The others [from Missouri and Oregon] are less able but more orderly men."

Joseph G. **McCoy** offered the wealthy cattleman's vision of the cowboy. He recorded a reasonably balanced, if slightly condescending, view in his 1874 treatise on the cattle trade:

He lives hard, works hard, has but few comforts and fewer necessities. He has but little, if any, taste for reading. He enjoys a coarse practical joke or a smutty story; loves danger but abhors labor of the common kind; never tires riding, never wants to walk, no matter how short the distance he desires to go. He would rather fight with pistols than pray; loves tobacco, liquor and women better than any other trinity. His life borders nearly upon that of an Indian. If he reads anything, it is in most cases a blood and thunder story of a sensational style. He enjoys his pipe, and relishes a practical joke on his comrades, or a corrupt tale, wherein abounds much vulgarity and animal propensity.

Anglo cowboy dress varied with climate and terrain. Cowboys in Canada and the United States had access to mass-manufactured equipment and clothing. As a result, Anglos made far fewer items by hand. **Vaqueros** would weave intricate leather lariats; cowboys bought hemp rope. Argentine **gauchos** fashioned their boots from the leg skins of a colt; cowboys in the West purchased high-heeled boots at the store.

William Timmons (*Twilight on the Range,* 1962) recalled from his days on the range that cowboys had a particular ritual for dressing and undressing:

A cowboy undresses upward: boots off, then socks, pants, and shirt. He never goes deeper than that. After he has removed the top layer he takes his hat off and lays his boots on the brim, so the hat won't blow away during the night. Spurs are never taken off boots. In the morning a cowboy begins dressing downward. First he puts on his hat, then his shirt, and takes out of his shirt pocket his Bull Durham and cigarette papers and rolls one to start the day. He finishes dressing by putting on his pants, socks, and boots. This is a habit that usually stays with a cowboy long after his days in the saddle are over.

While the cattle frontier in the United States featured more **firearms** than any other, cowboy gunplay has been exaggerated to titillate movie and pulp novel fans. Most hands were not particularly good shots nor were sidearms very accurate. Self-conscious of their image, most cowboys strapped on a six-shooter for photographs, but a sidearm was heavy and uncomfortable. On trail drives or roundups,

most cowboys left their pistols in the chuck wagon.

During the 1880s, particularly on the northern ranges, cattle raising took on the trappings of big business. Cowhands were employees in large corporate enterprises. These big businesses had obligations to eastern and foreign stockholders who expected handsome returns on their investments. Ranchers under these circumstances ran businesses that showed little evidence of the wildness of the Old West.

Few ranchers in the American West faced labor shortages. Green kids, college graduates, immigrants, and sundry other men seemed willing to try their hand at cowboying. Ranchers could impose restrictions on their hands, such as forbidding gambling and drinking, and make them stick. Any grumblers or violators could be replaced quickly and easily with other men. Joseph Nimmo recorded that "organization, discipline, and order characterize the new undertakings on the northern ranges" (*Harper's New Monthly Magazine,* November 1886). The northern cattle industry made cowboys less independent and more akin to other regimented workers of their time. The supposedly wild, hard-riding Texas cowboy gave way to responsible, loyal ranch hands.

Cowboys were no paragons of virtue, as many romantics and popularizers would have it, nor were they the uncouth barbarians of the plains described by self-anointed spokesmen of civilization and culture. While externalities—principally the law and employers—imposed restrictions that shaped their lives, cowboys lived as much as possible by their own internal codes of conduct. The cardinal virtues for the American cowboy were to do his best and to be cheerful, courageous, uncomplaining, helpful, and chivalrous. Of course, few cowboys maintained these ideals at all times in their lives.

Honesty, a man's word as his bond, is also associated with the cowboy in the popular mind, but examples exist of cowboy indifference to the truth and to the rights of others. A diary kept by cowboy Perry Davis describes a trail drive from

South Dakota to Texas in 1894. Davis notes that in Wyoming they passed "a nice stream through a pasture where they charge twenty dollars for watering a herd. Watered before anyone sees us; no pay." A little farther along, their horses ran through a fence. "Didn't pay for fences" records Davis. In fact, this trail crew committed so many misdemeanors that they became notorious. In northern Colorado the boss of the "7D" outfit passed the crew Davis worked with, and, as Davis recorded, "Says he is glad to get ahead because we left a hard name and everyone was watching him whenever he stopped fearing he would steal fence posts or water as we did."

It may be that Davis simply fell in with a trail boss who was a cut below the standards of the range, but his comments reveal a sense of use rights—open access to resources on the plains—typical of an earlier era in cowboy life. They believed in open access to animals, water, and grass on the plains. Latin American cowboys held the same opinion. As laws imposed a private property ethic in place of communal use rights, conflict between politically dominant ranchers and range cowboys increased.

The cowboy's low socioeconomic status didn't give him many life options. Generally not considered a good catch, a cowboy often could not marry. Women, a scarce commodity on the cattle frontier, married ranchers and merchants, not poor, itinerant cowhands. Few hands could save enough of their meager wages to become ranchers themselves.

Despite the lack of social and economic benefits, lots of men, mostly young, reveled in the cowboy life. The occupation continues to appeal to the individualist. Cowboy wages remain low. A 1989 summary of salaries by occupation placed the cowboy 247 out of 250 on the list. Men (and on occasion women) don't cowboy to get rich. Many want to avoid the shackles of modernity that fetter urbanites.

Good hands require little, but they do demand respect. If they don't get it, they are willing to say, along with singer Johnny Paycheck, "take this job and shove it." Good hands working for good ranchers will "ride for

the brand," however. As a century ago, they'll ride the extra mile to find one lost calf. While cowboys are fewer these days, the cowboy spirit remains alive and well. (Dary 1981; Forbis 1978; Frantz and Choate 1955; Savage 1975, 1979; Slatta 1990)

See also African-American Cowboys.

COWCHIPS
Dried cattle dung used for fuel.

COWGIRLS
See Women.

COWHAND
Also cowpoke, cowprod, cowpuncher; synonyms for cowboy.

COWHUNT
See *Vaquería*.

COWJUICE
Milk.

COWPENS THEORY
See Historiography of the Cowboy.

CRABBE, LARRY
(1908–1983)
B-western film actor known as Buster.

CRACKERBOX
Rodeo rider's term for bronc **saddle.**

CRITTER
Any cow.

CROSS HOBBLE
To hobble or tie a horse's front foot to the opposite hind foot.

CROW HOP
A horse's short, stiff-legged jump.

CRUPPER TRICKS
Fancy riding tricks performed back on the hips of a horse.

CRYING ROOM

Colloquial term for **rodeo** headquarters office.

CUSTOM-MADES

See Boots.

CUTTING HORSE

Also cut horse, cutter, chopping horse, carver, chopper; terms for a horse trained to move an individual animal out of a cattle herd. Cutting **horses** are important as ranch work animals and for reining competitions.

See also Quarter Horse.   (Campion 1990)

CYRUS, BILLY RAY
(1961–)

Singer. See Hat Acts.

D RING

Flat-sided or round metal ring on each end of a **cinch.** Straps pass through these rings to secure a **saddle** to a horse.

DAKOTA HAT

See Hat.

DALE, EDWARD EVERETT
(1879–1972)

Historian. See Historiography of the Cowboy.

DALLY

Term describing a **rope** technique; derived from the Spanish *dar la vuelta.*

DALLY TEAM ROPING

Tied team roping. See Rodeo.

DALLY YOUR TONGUE

Colloquial for shut up, quit talking.

DANA, RICHARD HENRY, JR.
(1815–1882)

Sailor and writer Richard Henry Dana was born in Cambridge, Massachusetts, and attended a variety of schools during his youth. At one time Ralph Waldo Emerson taught his class. Dana went to Harvard in 1831 and left in 1833 because of failing eyesight after an attack of measles.

Frustrated by inactivity at home, Dana joined the crew of the *Pilgrim* in 1834 and sailed from Boston to California. He arrived in California in January 1835 and spent the next few months loading hides and tallow and trading items of cargo up and down the coast. (The local economy depended heavily on the cattle industry, especially the hides trade. Hides were used as a form of cash.)

Dana did not see much of California besides the coastal area. He explored some rocky cliffs not far from San Juan Capistrano, recalling that "I separated myself from the rest, and sat down on a rock, just where the sea ran in and formed a fine spouting horn." This majestic ocean overlook is now called Dana Point, in Orange County, California.

His account of this naval adventure is told in *Two Years before the Mast* (1840), the first book to expose the often grueling existence of a sailor and the injustices a captain could inflict on his men. Dana is credited with making the public aware of how the common sailor lived aboard ship.

Two Years Before the Mast offers vivid, opinionated descriptions of California during the 1830s under Mexican rule. Dana described the important cattle hides trade, Mexican horsemen, the **vaquero,** and other elements of early California society. He also outlined the history of California, critiqued the form of government the Mexicans had imposed, summarized the state of the economy, and recorded his impressions of the people who lived there.

Dana did not have a very high opinion of California's Mexican population, known as *Californios.* He mirrored the racial prejudices of his time, writing that "the men are thriftless, proud, extravagant, and very much given to gaming; and the women have but little education, and a good deal of beauty, and their morality, of course, is none of the best." He also noted with proper Yankee disapproval the Californio affection for sport and **gambling,** including horse races, "bull-baitings," "cockfighting, gambling of all sorts, fandangos, and various kinds of amusement and knavery."

Dana did not find the Californios lacking in horsemanship. "There are probably no better riders in the world," he concluded, adding:

> The men in Monterey appeared to me to be always on horseback. Horses are as abundant here as dogs and chickens were in Juan Fernández [Chile]. There are no stables to keep them in, but they are allowed to run wild and graze wherever they pleased, being branded, and having long leather ropes, called lassos, attached to their necks and dragging along behind them, by which they can be easily taken.

Dana also described Californio riding gear of the era:

> The stirrups are covered or boxed up in front, to prevent their catching when riding through the woods; and the **saddles** are large and heavy, strapped very tight upon the horse, and have large pommels, or loggerheads, in front, round which the lasso is coiled when not in use. They can hardly go from one house to another without mounting a horse, there being generally several standing tied to the doorposts of the little cottages. When they wish to show their activity, they make no use of their stirrups in mounting, but striking the horse, spring into the saddle as he starts, and, sticking their long **spurs** into him, go off on the full run. Their spurs are cruel things, having four or five rowels, each an inch in length, dull and rusty. The flanks of the horses are often sore from them, and I have seen men come in from chasing bullocks, and their horses' hind legs and quarters covered with blood.

After his return to the East, Dana reentered Harvard in 1837 and attended law school. In 1839 he received an appointment as instructor in elocution at Harvard but resigned the next year. He opened his law practice in Boston in 1840 and that September published *Two Years before the Mast*. In 1841 he published *The Seaman's Friend*. That December he began a journal that he kept until September 1860. In 1859 he traveled to Cuba and published his observations in *Cuba and Back*.

It is in his *Journal* that Dana recounts his return to California in 1859 and his trip to Hawaii and Asia. He enjoyed a more leisurely pace during his second trip to California than his first. He also explored more of inland areas. He spent some time with John Frémont, the Republican candidate in the 1856 presidential election. He rode horseback through the Sierra Nevada and visited Yosemite, later to become a national park.

Dana visited a camp of Digger Indians, a group of several hundred people who had been captured and taken to a camp. He found them living in "very ugly and squalid" conditions. By this time mining, agriculture, and commerce had become well developed in California. Agriculture, to him, was "the richest and most numerous, but divided into various interests, grain growing, vine growing, cattle raising, and large rancheros and small yeoman."

Despite his condescending, racist views toward Californios and Indians, Dana fervently opposed slavery. He took part in the Rescue Trials in Boston in 1851. This case involved defending several persons who were accused of rescuing Shadrach, an apprehended fugitive slave. In 1854 Dana unsuccessfully defended fugitive slave Anthony Burns and suffered an assault for doing so.

In April 1861 President Lincoln appointed Dana U.S. district attorney for the District of Massachusetts, a post he held until 1866. In 1863 he successfully argued before the Supreme Court in the Prize Cases. In 1868 Dana lost an election for the House of Representatives. In 1876 President Grant nominated him to be ambassador to England, but the Senate blocked his appointment.

After retiring from law practice in 1878, Dana spent the remainder of his years studying and traveling. He died in Rome in 1882 while writing a book on international law. He is buried in Rome in a Protestant cemetery. (Dana 1964; Gale 1969)

—*Janine M. Cairo*

DANGERS OF COWBOY LIFE

Cowboys faced a wide range of dangers on the job. Nature might confront them with lightning, fires, floods, hail, snow, or tornadoes. Disease, injury, suicide, hunger, and thirst took many lives. Cowboying was hard work for young men. Long hours in the **saddle,** falls and other injuries, and inclement weather took a toll on the health of ranch hands. In *Ranching with Lords and Commons* (1903), John R. Craig of the Oxley

Ranche in Alberta described the Canadian cowboy's average day. "The cowboy is in the saddle twelve to fourteen hours on the stretch, with a bite from hand to mouth, caught at odd intervals, as his only sustenance." This description could fit a hand working virtually any range from Alberta to Argentina.

An old song, "The Texas Cowboy" (credited to Al Pease) warned against the hardships of the cold, northern ranges:

> But stay home here in Texas
> Where they work the year around
> And where you'll not get consumption
> From sleeping on the ground.
> Montana is too cold for me,
> And the winters are too long,
> Before the round-ups have begun,
> Your money is all gone.

Cowboys in Canada and the northern ranges of the United States got their fill of winter riding. Livestock faced the threats of freezing and starvation, and men faced the additional hazard of snow blindness. In *Impressions of Pioneers of Alberta* (ca. 1916), Canadian Duncan McEachran emphasized the importance of getting men on the range after a winter storm:

> Much therefore, depends on the activity and interest of the cowboys, not during, but immediately after a storm. Sometimes a bunch of cattle are hemmed in by deep snow in the coulees, which require a path to be tramped down by the man for himself and horse. Many a cow and calf if driven in, sheltered and fed for a few days would live and do well, but unassisted they die.

Another Alberta rancher, John Macoun, in *Manitoba and the Great North West* (1882), explained why cattle and snow did not mix. "As cattle use the nose instead of the hoof to clear away snow, they cannot support themselves when the snow gets too deep." Thus, in Canada, cowboys had to perform one of the most hated of chores—putting up hay. If snow became too deep, hands had to put hay out for the stock—bone-chilling work. Men made repeated, tedious trips hauling hay. If struck by painful snow blindness, a cowboy had to spend several days in a darkened room, eyes bandaged.

Once **fencing** became common, hands had to ride fence year-round. On large spreads like the Spur Ranch in Texas, **line riders** covered up to 30 or more miles a day from their lonely line camps. Range riding, more interesting work, occupied hands in any season. Cowboys checked for predators, strangers, and sick or injured animals. Injured or thrown from a horse, a cowboy faced a bleak future alone on the range.

Blizzards could sweep in and kill men and animals on the northern Great Plains. On the southern ranges, "blue northers" (aptly named for the color of the threatening northern sky) brought freezing temperatures and high winds. Cowboys had to find drifting cattle and try to turn them from fences, ravines, and other obstacles; otherwise, herds would stack up and perish in the cold. Charlie **Russell**'s famous watercolor *Waiting for a Chinook* (1886) provides a vivid picture of the results of a prolonged winter storm. (A chinook is a warm, dry wind that blows down the east slope of the Rockies and quickly melts away the snow covering the ground.)

Wallace **Stegner** (*Wolf Willow*, 1955) described a Canadian cowboy's day on the trail when overtaken by cold weather:

> By day the labor and the cold and the stiffness of many hours in the saddle, the bawling of calves, the crackle and crunch of hoofs and wheels, the reluctant herded movement of two or three hundred cows and calves and six dozen horses, all of whom stopped at every patch of grass blown bare and had to be whacked into moving again. By night the patient circling ride around the herd, the exposure to stars and space and the eloquent speech of the wolves, and finally the crowded sleep.

Horses could step into gopher holes and throw their riders. A foot tangled in a stirrup meant death or injury as the cowboy was dragged across the ground; Eli Lucero, an excellent **vaquero** in Arizona, met his death this way. Richard Deane, a Mounted Police officer, offered an understated opinion on the rigors of trail driving. "For the benefit of those who have not tried it may I say that driving refractory cattle on a tired horse is very poor fun."

Working cattle in the brush country of south Texas held its own hazards. Concealed in a thicket, a ringy (angry) **longhorn** bull could blindside a rider. Throwing **ropes** in thick brush required special techniques and care. A hand and his mount could be dragged into cactus or brush by a roped animal, and thorns and branches could quickly poke out an eye. Vaqueros of Baja California and **gauchos** of Salta in northern Argentina both used stiff leather "fenders" *(armas)* to protect their legs from cacti.

Cowboys feared river crossings, because they generally could not swim. If cattle began milling in the water or were swept downstream, men and animals could be lost. Larry McMurtry captured the terror of a young hand's first river crossing in *Lonesome Dove* (1985), in which one hapless youth dies after falling into a nest of water moccasins. Swollen rivers might delay a herd for days and result in injured and lost animals. Also at river crossings, cowboys had to ride into the center of a milling herd to straighten out the leaders. In the opinion of cattleman Joseph G. **McCoy,** the lack of sizable river crossings on the Chisholm Trail gave the route a distinct advantage.

The *paniolo* faced special conditions in the Hawaiian Islands. Because he worked on islands, this Hawaiian cowboy had to develop special skills to work cattle around water. In the nineteenth and early twentieth century, paniolo transported cattle by small boat from land to awaiting steamers. Cowboys lashed the animals by the horns to the gunwales, and upon reaching a steamer, hoisted the animals aboard with a sling.

Llaneros of Colombia and Venezuela also learned to work cattle around water in their tropical plains environment. During the six-month rainy season, llaneros faced a variety of dangerous water hazards. Crisscrossed by rivers, much of the llanos lay inundated each year between April and September. Llaneros had to be expert swimmers and boatmen as well as horsemen.

Breaking horses, a very important ranch chore, held plenty of dangers. Rancher Bert Sheppard, writing in *Canadian Cattlemen* (March 1949) described many hazards suffered by a **bronc buster** riding six or eight horses in a day:

> He was in constant danger of being kicked when pulling up the **cinch.** Sore horses would bite and chase a man out of the corral. If a horse started in to buck before the rider was on, it was sometimes necessary to hang and rattle with only one stirrup till he quit. There was no whistle in ten seconds, no pick-up men and no Boy Scouts to run out and help him if he got his wind knocked out. The horse might start the ball rolling either by bucking, falling over backwards or stampeding. These riders had to be masters of every situation that arose and they came out on top most of the time.

As a seventeen-year-old, William Easley Jackson helped trail cattle from eastern Oregon to Cheyenne, Wyoming, in the summer of 1876 *(Agricultural History,* October 1949). He complained of choking alkali dust and giant mosquitoes near the Snake River. Greenhead flies, he said, "nearly set the horses crazy." In 1882 Jack Porter drove cattle from Wyoming to Oregon and recorded another disastrous plague of the plains (quoted in Jack K. Rollinson, *Wyoming Cattle Trails,* 1948):

> About noon that day we encountered what in that country were called "Mormon crickets" [likely locusts or grasshoppers]. They migrate in untold millions. Every blade of grass was gone, having been devoured by this army of big, dark-brown

crickets, each as large as a small mouse. We could see that every bit of brush was thick with these destroying pests. The farther we went, the more dense were their numbers, and our horses and cattle tramped on and killed millions of them.

Stampedes posed a grave threat to the herd and its keepers. Nightriders especially feared stampedes. A coyote's call, a lurking mountain lion, or a flash of lightning could startle a herd. Cowboys had to dash to the head of the herd and turn or stop the leaders.

An anonymous witness to an Idaho stampede in 1889 reported the grisly details. The stampede killed 341 cattle, two horses, and one cowboy. Several men suffered broken legs. The dead cowboy "was literally mangled to sausage meat. His horse was little better, and mine was crushed into a bloody mass. I found that I could not get up, for my leg was broken just below the thigh" (quoted in Clifford Westermeier, *Trailing the Cowboy*, 1955).

On balance, then, cowboys faced a multitude of dangers—and they faced them for very meager wages. Good hands, however, "**ride for the brand**"—loyally work hard for their employer's ranch. They took the hazards of their work in stride and took pride in overcoming them without complaints. (Francis 1989; Slatta 1990, 1992)

DANGLERS
See Spurs.

DART, ISOM
(ca. 1849–1900)
See African-American Cowboys.

DARY, DAVID
(1934–)
Journalist, historian, author of *Cowboy Culture* (1981). See Historiography of the Cowboy.

DEADSHOT
Colloquial term for strong liquor. See Saloons.

DEADWOOD DICK
See African-American Cowboys.

"DEATH VALLEY DAYS"
Popular **television** program.

DEHORNING
See Roundup.

DENHARDT, ROBERT
(1912–)
Historian. See Historiography of the Cowboy.

DESERT SOLITAIRE
Book. See Abbey, Edward.

DESJARRETADERA
Hocking blade used during the colonial era. See *Vaquería*.

DIABLO
The horse ridden by the Cisco Kid in western **film**.

DICE HOUSE
Colloquial term for bunkhouse.

DIE-UP
A large number of dead cattle, often killed by snow, ice, or other inclement weather.

DIGGERS
One of many colloquial terms for **spurs**.

DILLON, MATT
(1964–)
Star character of "Gunsmoke." See Television.

DIME NOVELS
See Pulp Novels.

DINNER
The hearty noon meal. Cowboys don't eat "lunch." See Food.

DISCRIMINATION
Canada
Racist attitudes toward nonwhites in Canada closely resembled those in the United States. The big difference, however, was that vaqueros and black cowboys only rarely made their way so far

This weathered cowboy enjoys the afternoon dinner in typical fashion, sitting legs folded under him, on the ground.

north. The Cochrane Ranch, one of the first in the Calgary area, hired a vaquero as foreman. He worked hard and ably, and even headed a ranch roundup. The Anglo cowboys resented him, perhaps envious of his extensive knowledge of livestock.

The most famous African-American cowboy of Alberta, ex-slave John Ware, had earlier cowboyed in Texas and Idaho. After cowboying at the Quorn and Bar U ranches, Ware saved enough money to stock his own ranch, and he worked it until his death in 1905. In 1933, in what was considered a compliment in that time, rancher Fred Ings recalled Ware as having "black skin, but he was all white in spirit, courage and nerve" *(Canadian Cattlemen,* June 1941). Albertans named some landmarks after him.

Anglos on both sides of the 49th parallel generally found Indian culture and customs distasteful. Cattleman Duncan McEachran complained in 1881 that "the practice of selling their daughters is very common among the Indians," often for one to six ponies. He added that in southern Alberta, white men cohabited with Native American women "at almost every ranch which we passed." With buffalo herds decimated by 1879, some tribes migrated to Montana, while others sometimes killed cattle for food since they considered free-roaming animals fair game. McEachran listed the ranchers' major complaints as "stealing by Indians, prairie fires, and mosquitoes."

Rancher William F. Cochrane recorded a problem with Indians from a reserve near the Cochrane spread in 1885. "The boys surprised the Indians after they killed a cow Thursday, but the Indians got away. They had a pack horse with them."

Occasional hunting of cattle by Native Americans continued into the early 1890s. *The Macleod Gazette* (2 October 1890) editorialized against lax policies toward Indians who left the reservations. The paper recommended a pass system to control tribal movements.

Compared with the American West, where white migration preceded Anglo-Indian conciliation, serious conflict between the two peoples in Canada was relatively rare. Mounted Police had imposed European law and implemented an Indian governing policy, including reservations and government food subsidies, before the cattle industry was introduced. Canadian Indian policy may not have always been farsighted and just, but compared with the violence and ruthlessness of American western policy, Canada's actions appeared much more restrained.

Latin America
Colonial Anti-Indian Discrimination
Lines of color and class divided societies in South America just as they did in North America. Whites and mestizos drew sharp distinctions between themselves and full-blooded Indians. Despite racial mixing and cultural borrowing, mestizo plainsmen took pains to differentiate themselves from Indians. **Gauchos** referred to themselves as Christians and to Indians as savages or infidels. The distinction was more cultural and racial than religious. On occasion, however, repression by central governments could push gauchos to cross the frontier line and live with Indians.

Eighteenth-century Capuchin priests in the **llanos** described their Indian charges in unflattering terms. A report of 1745 complained that the Indians were "indolent, much given to idleness, and great lovers of liberty, like the wild beasts of the forest." Similar descriptions of mestizo plainsmen abounded.

Indigenous peoples throughout the region suffered at the hands of Europeans. Spaniards in the Río de la Plata and Chile, and Portuguese in São Paulo, Brazil, carried out slaving expeditions against Indians. The Spanish in Chile launched raids (called *malocas* or *campeadas)* against the Indians from the late sixteenth through the seventeenth century. Bandeirantes of São Paulo made Indian slaving the mainstay of their existence. This set the tone for racial antagonism that kept Europeans and Indians warring for several centuries.

Chilean colonial officials faced difficulties in their efforts to subdue the fierce Araucanians.

These people were much more skillful horsemen than the Spanish soldiers and repeatedly defeated the cavalrymen in battle. In 1566 they forced the Spanish to abandon two forts at Arauco and Cañete and gained 360 horses in the bargain. By the early seventeenth century, the Spanish adopted the tactic of the maloca, scorched earth raids that destroyed Indian crops and villages. The Spanish also enslaved Araucanians for labor. As in Argentina, frontier troops were often criminals or the rural poor pressed into service. Ill-fed and poorly supported, they offered little impediment to speedy, mounted Indian warriors.

The failure of Chilean and Argentine frontier defense points out the inherent problem of rural conflict between the elite and the masses. Forced recruits saw little incentive to serve. Soldiers faced harsh treatment, abysmal conditions, and late or nonexistent pay. Why should they trade a largely self-sufficient existence as wild-cattle hunters for the privations and dangers of military life? Gauchos and *huasos* saw little reason for defending the economic interests of the same landed elite that outlawed their access to wild livestock. Frontiersmen were economic competitors and political enemies of the landed elite.

Post-Independence Indian Wars

Racial strife became even more polarized during the independence and civil wars of the early nineteenth century. White elites, whether Spanish colonizers or creole patriots, feared the nonwhite masses. Neither the Spaniards nor the creoles wanted a social revolution. Both depended on nonwhites as a source of cheap labor, and both strenuously avoided granting nonwhites any real measure of political power or economic progress.

Efforts to enlist gauchos against Indians fared no better during and after the independence wars with Spain beginning in 1810. The new Argentine government reestablished *blandengue* units (irregular gaucho troops) in December 1816. Military patrols were ordered into the countryside to recruit vagrants and deserters —that is, gauchos—for frontier military service.

The new leadership faced the same dilemma as had colonial officials. Gauchos were not inclined to fight Indians to defend the interests of the landed elite. As a result, Argentine officials faced Indian incursions with a shortage of troops until the latter decades of the nineteenth century.

Even orders about caring for their **horses** might be met with gaucho hostility or indifference. Articles 9 through 14 of the orders issued by Colonel Conrado Villegas in 1876 required that troops care for and groom their mounts. Soldiers were forbidden to ride horses with sore backs. "Without horses there is no cavalry," affirmed Villegas. Commanders had to insist on these matters, because gauchos customarily gave their mounts little care, knowing that they could be replaced easily and cheaply. Gauchos could ride anything and so wasted little effort in breaking or training their mounts. Short of manpower, frontier commanders had to make do with immigrant volunteers who could not ride and indigenous troops who abused and injured mounts.

The racial element of the independence wars emerges clearly on the **llanos**. Mestizo and black cavalrymen from the plains, led by regional caudillos, battled the forces of the creole elite in Caracas. José Tomás Boves, the wily and terrible Spanish army officer, ably manipulated racial hatreds to rally **llaneros** behind his standard. It took the prowess of a llanero caudillo, José Antonio Páez, to swing the fierce cavalrymen of the llanos to the patriot cause.

General Julio A. Roca launched Argentina's "final offensive" against its Plains Indians at the same time the United States Cavalry was busy opening up the American West. Roca brought together for the first time sufficient commitment, materiel, technology, and planning to accomplish what had been talked about for centuries— security against Indian attack.

In 1878 Roca vowed "to break the spirit of the Indian and keep him full of fear and terror of us. That way, instead of thinking to invade us, he will only think of fleeing, seeking his salvation in the depths of the forest." He ordered villages leveled and *caciques* (chiefs) exiled to Chile along with the *chusma* (a disparaging term for Indian women and children). This repressive policy was meant to destroy Indian morale, like earlier scorched earth raids practiced by the military in Chile.

In 1883 Roca stated somewhat prematurely that "the wild Indians, then, have disappeared, with no danger that they can return." In April of that year a band of 50 braves attacked German immigrant ranchers on the frontier in Buenos Aires province. They killed and mutilated at least eight ranchers, injured others, and stole an estimated 3,000 cattle. One Buenos Aires newspaper, *La Campaña* (25, 29 April 1883), reported that "with the band of Indians went some gauchos." Argentine officials had yet to subdue entirely the Indian or gaucho population.

Chronic labor shortages plagued military commanders and rendered inoperative strategies that required large numbers of troops. Officials from the colonial period on faced the problem of how to mobilize unwilling gauchos to fight Indians. In terms of class, culture, and economic interests, gauchos had more in common with the Indians than with the elite leaders giving the orders. Vagrancy laws, passports, and arbitrary conscription antagonized gauchos and hindered frontier settlement. The government held no legitimacy in the eyes of the best cavalrymen—the gauchos of the **pampa.**

The Argentine military faced a cultural gap between its leadership and its enlisted men. Gaucho troops, accustomed to traditional ways of surviving on the pampa, did not always readily accept army mandates. Any orders involving footwork, such as digging defensive ditches, aroused gaucho ire. They considered such work servile and unmanly, and preferred to leave it to immigrant laborers. (In fact, a life in the **saddle,** grasping a small stirrup with the big toe, rendered some gauchos virtually unable to walk.) Neither would gauchos take to **firearms;** many preferred the traditional **bolas** and **facón.**

In the final analysis, the major shortcoming of Argentine frontier strategy lay in conceptualization, not in technology, tactics, or military intelligence. The racial and cultural

prejudices of Spanish and then creole elites precluded a comprehensive, positive frontier policy.

From the days of sixteenth-century slaving expeditions, policy served negative goals: to exterminate and subjugate—but never to integrate—the indigenous peoples of the pampa. Indians had formulated a sophisticated cattle trade that might well have evolved into economic partnership, not conflict, had the Argentine leadership been so inclined. In Argentina, the American West, and Chile, white expansionists created frontiers of exclusion to push aside existing Amerindian cultures.

The intermittent success of treaties showed that adaptation was possible, but national elites, from the sixteenth through the nineteenth centuries, conceived the frontier as an uncrossable line dividing the forces of civilization and barbarism.

The gaucho, the elite's most potent force against the Indian, also came to be considered a barbarian, outside the pale of acceptable society. Had accommodation and integration played larger roles in formulating strategy than marginalization and extermination, perhaps the prolonged frontier conflict in Argentina would have taken a different direction.

The dynamics of Indian-white relations in Argentina and Chile bear a strong resemblance to events in the United States. An examination of the final Indian wars of Argentina offers a case study of an expanding livestock economy in conflict with a contracting Amerindian world.

Argentina's elite leadership in Buenos Aires despised and feared the provincial masses, calling them *cabecitas negras* (little black heads). To the centralizing elite, the masses in the interior provinces, mounted and armed *montoneros,* provided the basis of popular and military support for disruptive caudillos. Racism pervaded and shaped elite policies toward labor, immigration, and other matters throughout the nineteenth century. Even today the topic of race relations, particularly concerning the Indian population, remains taboo in Argentina.

In both North and South America (Canada excepted), cattle frontiers represented theaters of racial and cultural mixing and conflict. In Latin America, indigenous, black, and mixed-blood cowboys first worked as wild-cattle hunters. Gradually, whites established control over the resources of land, livestock, and water. With the rise of systematic ranching and domesticated stock, nonwhites continued to labor as ranch hands. Amerindians found themselves pushed back and then aside by the expanding livestock industry.

In the Southern Cone countries of Argentina and Chile, the violent conquest of resistant indigenous cultures did not succeed until the latter decades of the nineteenth century—about the time of the last Indian wars in the United States. In both North and South America, the expansion of the ranching frontier contributed to the decline of Amerindian cultures. In turn, the livestock industry suffered encroachment and then decline in the face of agriculture.

Conscripted cowboys in several Latin American nations were instrumental as the cavalrymen who defeated and pushed aside the Plains Indians. The cowboy, however, was himself going into eclipse. Rapid changes during the late nineteenth century brought traditional cowboy life and open-range ranching in most of the Americas to an end.

Discrimination against Blacks

Blacks, first as slaves and runaways and later as freed people, added to the cultural mix of frontier regions. Convicts exiled from Portugal, runaway slaves, and other uprooted wanderers populated the Brazilian backlands. One-sixth of the inhabitants of sixteenth-century New Spain may have been vagrants. White urban elites came to view plains regions as bastions of dangerous nonwhite criminals who threatened their power and competed for frontier wealth.

Frontier regions gave rise to populations consisting of Spanish, Indians, and blacks. **Gauchos** and **llaneros** had a similar ethnic makeup, but local differences altered the proportions. In Venezuela, the greater number of runaway slaves who escaped from coastal plantations probably increased the black influence. Estimates for Venezuela in the early nineteenth century place the white population (Spaniards and creoles, or American-born Spaniards) at about 20 to 25 percent of the total, with *castas* (nonwhite lower classes), slaves, and Indians comprising the balance.

Often faced with labor shortages, Latin American ranchers availed themselves of another labor pool—slaves. Debt peonage and various types of working papers were common means of compulsion. Slaves remained in bondage through legal subterfuge for decades after abolition in Argentina. The dictator Juan Manuel de Rosas employed slaves on his **estancias** through the 1840s, and on at least one of his ranches, slaves comprised a majority of the workers.

Slaves worked throughout the **llanos** of Venezuela as well. In 1791 some 180 slaves lived on or near 16 ranches in Tucupido. The same records list only ten resident free peons, so most ranchers relied on slave labor. On his visit to the llanos in 1799, scientist Alexander von Humboldt described the ranch workers of the llanos: "These Mulattoes, who are known by the name of Peones Llaneros, are partly freed men and partly slaves." Despite abolition, slaves remained in the llanos after independence came to Venezuela. In 1831 the province of Apure included 193 slaves, but eight years later Apure had only 158, Barcelona 941, and Barinas, 1,458. The llanos moved steadily away from slave labor, although more than 11,000 slaves still lived in Venezuela in 1858.

Despite discrimination and oppression, black gauchos and llaneros played important cultural and historical roles. A large Venezuelan black known as El Negro Primero served as bodyguard for the liberator Simón Bolívar. Many of Argentina's best gaucho folksingers *(payadores)* were black.

In both North and South America, Indians and blacks suffered greatly from racial discrimination, but in most cases their cultures and languages survived.

The American Frontier

Historian Frederick Jackson Turner and other frontier boosters depicted the frontier as a place of social leveling. Unfettered by the social conventions of settled society, the frontier supposedly offered great opportunity and equality to all, regardless of race or gender. The reality of the Old West is that ethnic minorities and **women** faced discrimination, just as they did elsewhere in American society.

Cattle frontiers were regions of racial mixing and tension. In general, as explorers, ranchers, miners, trappers, and others sought to extract wealth from the frontier, white Europeans came into violent conflict with Native Americans. Blacks, through the institution of slavery, also became part of the cattle culture. Frontier democracy is a myth—the livestock industry developed clear, discriminatory color lines. As in society at large, whites imposed their will and rule on nonwhites.

Hispanics

Anglos in California also applied negative racial stereotypes to the Hispanic population, and racial mythology in California takes yet another twist. Self-proclaimed **Californios** celebrate their pure Spanish heritage, ignoring that the vast majority of the population of Spanish California originated from mestizo and Native American cultures. Indians at California's missions were the region's first **vaqueros.**

Vaqueros of northern Mexico faced double discrimination. First they suffered social and legal disadvantages because of their status as *castas* (nonwhites) in highly stratified Spanish colonial society. After the United States warred successfully to annex northern Mexico in 1845, vaqueros suffered new forms of racism, discrimination, and derision from Anglos. These negative forces persisted well into the twentieth century.

Texas history reflects a bias based on the victory of European immigrants over Mexicans. Anglo-Texan mythology has built up Anglo contributions and often ignored or denigrated preexisting Hispanic foundations.

In the borderlands of Mexico and the United States, Europeans stereotyped Hispanics. During the 1840s the notion of Anglo-Saxons as a race became popular in the United States. Armed with a sense of racial superiority, European Americans found all sorts of negative characteristics in people of color. Nineteenth-century writings by Richard Henry **Dana,** Francis Parkman, Clarence King, and others depicted Hispanics as lazy, thieving, untrustworthy, and incompetent. These negative images attached themselves to vaqueros in California, the Southwest, and Texas.

In the nineteenth century, the western white population exhibited blatant racism against Mexican Americans, **African Americans,** and Native Americans. Racially mixed persons, referred to as half-breeds in the United States and Canada, also suffered social stigma. Vaqueros earned only one-third to one-half the wage of white cowboys, and some Anglo ranchers preferred to hire vaqueros to save money. Despite their reputation as superior ropers and horsebreakers, vaqueros seldom rose above the common cowboy ranks to become foremen or trail bosses. Even the **King Ranch** of Texas, home to the famous Kineños (vaquero ranch hands), hired only Anglos as foremen.

The law also weighed more heavily on the vaquero than on his European-American counterparts. The predations of the Texas Rangers against Mexicans during the Mexican War and against Mexican Americans north of the border are well documented. Happy in their work as agents of Manifest Destiny, Texas Rangers crossed the Mexican border with impunity. They worked assiduously on behalf of powerful Texas ranching interests to the detriment of Hispanics on both sides of the border.

Despite racial prejudice, vaqueros worked on ranches throughout the West and Northwest. In 1837 Philip Edwards drove cattle from California north to Oregon with the help of California vaqueros. Eastern Oregon ranchers employed Mexican-American cowboys during the late nineteenth and early twentieth centuries. In 1869, for instance, Juan Redón and six vaqueros drove 3,000 head of cattle belonging to John Devine into Oregon. They established the first ranch in eastern Oregon's Harney County. Redón continued to work as Devine's foreman on what was at the time Oregon's largest ranch. Devine himself wore hacendado garb. The terrible winter of 1888 put Devine out of business, so Redón hired on as cattle superintendent for the Miller and Lux outfit (Pacific Livestock Company). Other Oregon ranchers, including Peter French and Dick Anderson, also hired Mexican cowboys. Vaqueros comprised up to half of the cowhands on many large ranches in the area until the big operations disappeared in the 1920s and 1930s.

African Americans

Black cowboys faced racial violence on the frontier as they did elsewhere in the United States. On an 1878 trail drive from Texas to Kansas, an Anglo cowboy named Poll Allen harassed an African-American hand. Allen refused to let the black cowboy eat or sleep with the other hands. Allen fired shots at the man and finally drove him off.

African-American cowboys seem to have suffered the same social discrimination but slightly less economic discrimination than vaqueros. Like an aging white hand, a good black cowboy might be rewarded with the job of cook after his riding days were done. Wages for African-American cowboys generally matched those of white cowboys. Both received raises with experience. On the other hand, blacks frequently occupied the lowly job of horse **wrangler** and seldom rose to the level of foreman.

African Americans found no more upward social mobility on the frontier than elsewhere in society. Jim Perry worked at the giant XIT ranch for 20 years. That outfit included seven divisions or ranges by 1900, each requiring a foreman. "If it weren't for my damned old black face," lamented Perry, "I'd have been boss of one of these divisions long ago." Instead he ended his days at the ranch as a cook.

Women

Many politicians have pointed proudly to the West as the region that first gave women the vote. In 1869 Wyoming Territory became the first area in the nation to grant women's suffrage. Women, however, faced de facto discrimination, especially during the nineteenth century. In cattle country, even jobs routinely assigned to women went to men. Men did the cooking at **roundup** and on **trail drives**—there is no record of a female trail drive cook. Likewise cowboying was man's work. Female family members might help out, but until the discrimination lessened in the twentieth century, women did not work as hired hands.

Lingering Discrimination

The famed Texas Rangers remained among the last western institutions to drop discriminatory practices. Proud of their tradition and steeped in Old West machismo, the Rangers kept out ethnic minorities and women long after most of society had abandoned such discrimination.

The Rangers did not hire a black officer until 1988, under threat of a federal job discrimination complaint filed by the National Association for the Advancement of Colored People (NAACP). In 1993 the Rangers finally admitted two women to their ranks. Two veteran law enforcement officers, Cheryl Steadman, age 32, and Marie Garcia, age 38, joined the force. In mid-1993 the 96 members of the Texas Rangers included two women, two African Americans, and five Hispanics. (Andrews 1980; DeLeon 1983; Durham and Jones 1965; Katz 1977; MacEwan 1974; Savage 1976; Slatta 1989, 1990, 1992; Somora 1979)

DIXON, MAYNARD
(1875–1946)
Artist. See Art of the Cowboy.

DOAN'S CROSSING
A location on the Western Cattle Trail. See Trail Drive.

DOBIE, JAMES FRANK
(1888–1964)

Texas folklorist. See Historiography of the Cowboy.

DODGE CITY, KANSAS

See Cow Towns.

DOFUNNIES

Miscellaneous personal belongings.

DOG FIGHT

Colloquial term for fist fight. See Violence.

DOGGER

A bulldogger. See Rodeo.

DOG-HOUSE STIRRUP

An old-fashioned wooden stirrup wider at the base than the top. See Saddle.

DOGIE

Also dogey; an orphaned or abandoned calf.

DOINGS

Cooked **food**, also called fixins.

DOMADOR

Term used in Argentina for a gaucho horse tamer or **bronc buster.**

DON SEGUNDO SOMBRA

Novel. See Güiraldes, Ricardo.

DOÑA BÁRBARA

Novel. See Gallegos, Rómulo.

"DON'T FENCE ME IN"

Popular western song from 1935.

DOUBLE RIGGED

Also double fire, double-barreled. See Saddle.

DOUGH WRANGLER

Also dough puncher—colloquialisms for the camp cook.

DRAG

See Trail Drive.

DRAGO, HARRY SINCLAIR
(1888–1980)

Author of formula westerns published under various names.

DRIVE

See Trail Drive.

DROVER

Cowboy who herded (drove) cattle north from Texas to Kansas and other points. See Trail Drive.

DRURY, JAMES

Actor in "The Virginian." See Television.

DUDE RANCHES

Tanque Verde, Flathead Lake, Lazy K Bar, Lazy L and B, Skyline, Hot Springs, Vista Verde—these are some of the dude ranches that dot the West from Arizona through Colorado and Wyoming to Montana and western Canada. Dude ranches have been attracting tenderfoot dudes to come and live the western life for more than a century.

Lawrence R. Borne is one of a very few historians who has studied the dude ranch. In his fine book, *Dude Ranching: A Complete History* (1983), he lays out the "most important features of a dude ranch":

(1) It was generally a year-round home of the owner where the visitor was considered a guest; (2) it was located in western North America, usually in the United States but occasionally in Canada; (3) it offered food, lodging, and horseback riding, most often at one price (i.e., the American Plan); (4) in location or in its outdoor activities it was remote from crowded areas; (5) its main activities have been horseback riding, fishing, hiking, hunting, sightseeing, and ranch work, although few of these activities were regimented and none mandatory; simply relaxation was always an

option for the dude; (6) reservations were required, and transient trade was refused or formed little of the ranch's business; (7) atmosphere was the key ingredient; it was informal in manners and dress, people were on a first-name basis, hospitality was genuine, and guests did things together as part of a ranch family.

The nineteenth-century roots of dude ranching lie in the tourist appeal of magnificent western landscapes, in wilderness hunting parties, and in the extension of railroads westward, which made the region accessible to easterners. The term *dude ranch* appeared in the early 1870s, well before the large-scale tourist industry developed in the West. Griff Evans and Abner Sprague ran dude ranches in the Estes Park area of the Colorado Rockies in the 1870s. Howard Eaton and Dick Randall also number among the pioneering dude ranch operators in Colorado. In neighboring Wyoming the Davis Ranch and the Gros Ventre Lodge, run by William Wells, entertained guests in the 1890s.

From these scattered ranches, the business grew gradually and then quickly in the 1920s. Irwin H. (Larry) Larom and his wife Irma developed the Valley Ranch near Cody, Wyoming. Larom, Ernest Miller of Bozeman, Montana, and others founded the Dude Ranchers Association in 1926. Larom served as president and principal spokesman for the industry until 1944. Dude ranches appealed to middle- and upper-class easterners who wanted to taste western life without suffering its rigors.

Thriving on repeat customers, ranchers offered a comfortable, casual atmosphere, but they controlled conditions carefully. Many dude ranches kept their guest lists exclusive to whites, keeping out Jews, blacks, and Hispanics. Some ranches refused to hire Hispanic cowboys. Native Americans, however, often found a place in the dude ranch environment because they represented an exotic part of the Old West with strong tourist appeal.

Acutely aware that their business lives depended upon the pristine natural beauty of the West, many dude ranchers worked ardently on behalf of conservation. Larom, Howard Eaton, Dick Randall, Struthers Burt, Charles Moore, and others lobbied strenuously to preserve the fish, wildlife, and beauty of the West from excessive, destructive development and exploitation. Larom also played a leading role in preserving Old West culture and artifacts. He worked hard on behalf of what became the **Buffalo Bill Historical Center** in Cody, Wyoming. The center now houses Larom's papers.

Dude ranching remains a multimillion-dollar industry. Boulder-based Old West Dude Ranch Vacations (tel. 800-444-DUDE), a division of American Wilderness Experience, Inc., helps families book their ranch stays all over the West. Their 1993 catalog listed 54 ranches in Arizona, Colorado, Idaho, Montana, Oregon, Texas, Wyoming, and British Columbia. Colorado and Wyoming lead the listing with 27 and 10 ranches respectively. Western state tourist offices also publish guides to dude ranches and outfitters.

Business is still thriving, as the film *City Slickers* (1991) reminds us. Dude wranglers charm and entertain large herds of dudes, dudettes, and dudines every year. (The latter two terms refer to female dudes.) Strap on your fancy dude **chaps,** mount your very tame dude **horse,** and have a fine old western time. (Borne 1982, 1983)

DUDE WRANGLER
Cowboy who works at a dude ranch tending tourists (dudes) rather than horses and cattle.

DUNTON, W. HERBERT
(1874–1939)
Artist. See Art of the Cowboy.

DUTCH OVEN
See Food.

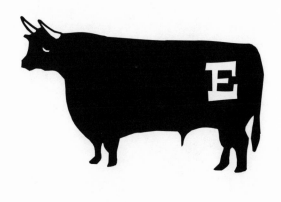

EAGLE BILL

A type of *tapadero*. See Saddle.

EARMARK

See Roundup.

EASTWOOD, CLINT

(1930–)

It usually takes American cultural leaders a few extra decades to accept and recognize the worth of something western. John **Wayne** had to wait until the very end of his life to gain recognition of his stature as an actor. Likewise, actor and film director Clint Eastwood worked in the film business with little critical acclaim for 35 years. In 1992, however, Motion Picture Academy members recognized Eastwood's talents by Oscars for best film and best director for *Unforgiven*. Film critic Roger Ebert described it as "an uncommonly intelligent and beautiful film about the death of a way of life." Only two previous westerners have won the Oscar for best picture: *Cimarron* (1931) and *Dances with Wolves* (1990).

In his 36-film career (to date), Eastwood has displayed his talents in a wide range of memorable characters and styles. He has played the violent cop and soldier, a comic truck driver, a disk jockey, and a convict. "I'm very close to the Western," says Eastwood. "That's where my roots are."

After military service during World War II, Eastwood followed the stars to Hollywood. Handsome, athletic, and tall (6′4″), he began his career in 1955 in Universal's B movies. The role of Rowdy Yates in the CBS **television** series "Rawhide" (1959–1966) allowed Eastwood to leave behind *Revenge of the Creature, Tarantula,* and *Francis in the Navy.* He still looks back at those days of shooting the series in Arizona and riding with real cowboys as the happiest of his life.

Spaghetti Westerns

Warm public response to Eastwood in "Rawhide" opened new opportunities. Italian director Sergio Leone (1921–1989), impressed with Eastwood's catlike indolence and nonchalance,

offered the young actor a role in his first spaghetti western—*A Fistful of Dollars* (1964). These Italian films featured lots of violence and gore, with a solitary hero or antihero emerging victorious. Was Eastwood interested? "Not particularly," he said. His wife Maggie's urging and his own growing fascination with the script (a remake of the Japanese film *Yojimbo* (1961), originally directed by Akira Kurosawa) changed Eastwood's mind. He agreed to go to southern Spain to begin what became a series of three low-budget westerns. The rest, as we say, is history.

Leone and Eastwood together crafted the enigmatic ponchoed, cigar-smoking, laconic character that appeared in a number of films, including *A Fistful of Dollars* (released in the United States in 1966), which enthralled moviegoers in Italy and around the globe. "Get three coffins ready," Eastwood tells the undertaker. He then dispatches four gunman because "my mule don't like people laughin'." Catching his math error, Eastwood provides a measure of extra-dry, black humor. "My mistake. Four coffins."

For a Few Dollars More (1965) followed. Then came *The Good, the Bad, and the Ugly* (1966); Eastwood hardly qualified as "good," but Eli Wallach played a sinister "bad" and Lee Van Cleef a convincing "ugly." Van Cleef went on to make a long string of mostly dreadful pasta oaters (spaghetti westerns).

From Spaghetti Westerns to Directing

Film violence remained a staple for Eastwood. "I'm appalled by violence in films," he says, "but you have to tell the drama and if the basis of the drama is conflict then sometimes a certain amount of violence is justified."

With his newfound international stature, Eastwood could shape his own career. After acting in a variety of films in the late 1960s, he moved behind the camera to add directing to his credits. In 1971 he directed and starred in *Play "Misty" for Me.* Some of his most powerful performances have come in films that he directed: *High Plains Drifter* (1972), *The Outlaw Josey Wales* (1976), and *Unforgiven* (1992).

The enigmatic loner—Shane with an attitude—remained a common character for Eastwood. His antiheroes or unusual heroes stood in sharp contrast to the kind of characters John Wayne played. "People don't believe in heroes," says Eastwood. "I disagree with the Wayne concept. I do the stuff Wayne would never do. I play bigger than life characters but I'd shoot the guy in the back."

Eastwood also showed a flair for humor. In *Bronco Billy* (1980) the leading character presides over a tattered Wild West show. The wacky film, replete with oddball characters, gives Eastwood a chance to present yet another side of cowboy mythology. Bronco Billy McCoy is also a wonderful, hilarious self-parody of Eastwood.

Hollywood's belated recognition of Eastwood's directing ability should further fuel his creativity. The Cannes Film Festival has also honored Eastwood. He served as head of the 1994 jury, the first American to do so since 1986. (Johnstone 1988)

See also Films, Cowboy.

EATIN' IRONS

Colloquial term for silverware.

EDSON, JOHN THOMAS
(1928–)

British author of formula westerns.

"EL PASO"

Popular Marty Robbins song from 1957. See Music.

THE ELECTRIC HORSEMAN

A 1979 film starring Robert Redford. See Films, Cowboy.

ELKO, NEVADA

See Poetry.

ELLIOTT, WILLIAM
(1903–1965)

B-western film actor known as Wild Bill.

ELLSWORTH, KANSAS

See Cow Towns.

EQUALIZER

Colloquial term for pistol. See Firearms.

EQUESTRIAN GAMES

Cowboys everywhere enjoyed pitting their strength against **horses,** bulls, steers, and each other. Highly competitive, prone to **gambling,** and enjoying danger, cowboys played a wide range of inventive, often risky horseback games.

Man and Horse

Horse races, often accompanied by heavy betting, provided entertainment throughout the Americas. Argentine **gauchos** and Chilean *huasos* enjoyed a dangerous contest called "crowding horses," in which two riders sharply spurred their horses in an attempt to crowd or push the other in a specified direction or toward a marked point. In a variation, two riders galloped down a narrow track and tried to push each other's mounts off the track as they raced.

George A. Peabody, a Massachusetts sportsman on a hunt in South America, watched a gaucho horse race in Argentina in 1859. He described the race in his *South American Journals:*

> The track is of a certain width, & if one of the horses is able to crowd the other off the acknowledged track, he wins the race: they accordingly run down the course, each horse pushing with all his might, & it is frequently not the fastest, but the best trained and strongest horse that wins.

Vaqueros and **charros** enjoyed a very old horseback game of tag called *juego de la vara* (rod game). This contest dates back centuries to the Moorish occupation of Spain. Riders arranged themselves in a circle with their mounts facing the center. A vaquero outside the circle would thrust a wooden rod into the outstretched hand of another man and quickly ride around the circle. The player in possession of the rod galloped in pursuit. The pursued rider dashed for an opening in the circle. If he was caught, the man with the rod beat him over the head and shoulders, a painful penalty for the slow rider. Riders continued the games of pursuit, beating, and riding for hours.

Many contests required great stamina of the gaucho's *pingo* (horse). Contestants in the *cinchada* fastened their horses together tail to tail with stout rawhide lassos tied to the **saddles.** The rider who could pull the other backward past a mark won this equestrian tug-of-war. This contest grew out of the need for mounts strong enough to pull against a wild, lassoed bull.

Chilean horsemen practiced a hazardous form of equestrian combat not unlike the gaucho's cinchada, but in the Chilean version, rawhide thongs bound together riders instead of horses. Despite its name, *tirar al gallo* or *tiro al gallo* (rooster shoot), this game did not actually involve a bird. A rawhide thong was lashed to the

right wrists of two mounted contestants. At a signal the bound men began to race. The race continued until one man pulled the other from the saddle, to the applause of spectators. Strength and agility were necessary to keep one's seat and win the contest.

Gauchos also competed at *pechando* (breasting), an even more dangerous and macho game than the cinchada. Two mounted gauchos faced each other over a distance of up to 220 yards. At a signal, they galloped at top speed directly toward one another. The concussion of the head-on crash usually tumbled one or both riders (and often their mounts) to the ground. Recovering and remounting, the combatants quickly charged again until stopped by exhaustion or serious injury. Chilean huasos also battled with their mounts until one dropped from exhaustion.

Mexican vaqueros performed dangerous combat similar to breasting. Samuel C. Reid, Jr., in *The Scouting Expeditions of McCulloch's Texas*

La sortija, *painted by F. Molina Campos, portrays a gaucho crossing the finish line on horseback during an Argentine ring race in which the winner received the gold ring as a gift for his girlfriend.*

Rangers (1847), described this event during the fiesta of San Juan in Mexico:

> Single horsemen sometimes meet in full career, and as it is disgraceful to give the road on such occasions, they ride directly upon one another, and the consequence is, that the weakest horse or the most unskillful rider is dashed to the ground, while the victor rides on in triumph, rewarded for his gallantry and skill by bright smiles from the balconies above. Occasionally large rival parties meet in the narrow streets, and then a scene of wild confusion ensues. Like madmen, they yell and rush together; and when the horses are not overthrown by the shock, they grasp each other by the neck or waist, and attempt to drag their antagonist from the saddle to the ground.

Huasos also developed contests to test the strength of their mounts. In the *topeadura* or *topeo,* riders positioned their horses side by side, with the animals' heads over a railing. The object was to push the opponent's horse beyond the end of the railing or to unseat the opponent.

By the eighteenth century, **violence** had spread from the contests to spectators. The disorder, fighting, and drunkenness that accompanied horse races and other equestrian contests became a serious problem to colonial authorities. Officials eventually introduced regulations to maintain order.

Mexican vaqueros passed some of their horseback games on to the American cowboy. In the ring race, galloping riders tried to skewer tiny dangling rings with a short lance. The game can be traced to medieval Spain and is likely of Moorish origin.

Of course, Spain held no monopoly on horseback fun. Similar practices appeared in the antebellum American South. The southern fixation on medieval chivalry extended to replicating a tamer version of a jousting tournament, which rose to great popularity in the 1840s in Virginia. Riders used 11-foot-long lances to spear a series of rings ranging in diameter from one-half inch to two inches. The rings dangled from supports spaced 25 to 30 yards apart. A rider would cover the 100-yard course in about ten seconds, skewering as many of the elusive rings as possible. Such contests are still held in some parts of the South.

Another contest passed from the Mexican vaquero to the Anglo cowboy was called "picking up." The object was to pluck from the ground a small coin, handkerchief, arrow, or even a potato, at a full gallop. Texas Rangers, Indians, and Hispanics competed at picking u p in San Antonio in 1844. Picking up contests were also part of the first Texas State Fair in 1852. California vaqueros competed often, even at the 1891 Tournament of Roses in Pasadena—well before football became the main event. Wild West shows also featured vaquero riders performing this impressive feat.

Man versus Bull

Gauchos jumped onto the backs of wild bulls. After riding the bull around for a while, the gaucho would kill the animal with a knife thrust into the throat. Much like modern **rodeo** bull riders, the **llanero** tied a stout rope around the bull's girth just behind the front legs. Using the rope as a handhold, the llanero would ride the wild bull to exhaustion or until he was thrown. The Mexican version of bull riding resembled that of the llanero. After mounting a lassoed bull, the vaquero would hang on for dear life and ride the animal to submission—or until he was thrown or injured.

Contests between man and bull had many variants. *Colear* (tailing the bull) dates from early colonial times. Llaneros first performed the feat in pairs. One rider would gallop up behind the bull, grasp the tail, and twist the animal off balance. Before the bull could recover, the other rider jumped down and deftly castrated the hapless animal. Here again, work skills had become stylized into a recreational pastime. In later versions, riders simply tumbled the bulls without castration.

In *Rambles and Scrambles in North and South America* (1852), Sir Edward Sullivan described the popular practice of bull tailing in Venezuela:

The colleador, mounted on a good horse that knows his business, gallops close up to the bull, when catching hold of the tail he clenches it under his knee, and the horse darting off at right angles pulls the bull's legs from under him, and he comes to the ground with crashing force. This art of throwing bulls by the tail is all knack, and the slightest men generally make the best colleadors. They say that, as in bull fighting, there is a certain fascination in the danger, and though many lose their lives every year, it is a favourite sport amongst the wild riders of the plains; and the reputation of being the best colleador of a district, ensures the happy possessor the admiration of his comrades and the prettiest partners at the fandangos. An expert colleador will by himself throw and brand fifty wild cattle on a day.

Venezuelan writer Ramón Paez *(Wild Scenes in South America,* 1863) left a similar description:

The rider first gallops close to the rear of the bull, and seizing his tail with one hand, gives it a turn or two around his wrist to prevent its slipping. When thus prepared, he urges his horse forward, until the heads of the two animals are on a "dead-heat;" then quickly turning in an oblique direction, and exerting all his strength, he pulls the bull toward him, and does not relinquish his hold until he perceives that the enemy is tottering, when he is easily overthrown from the great impetus imparted by their rapid pace. Some men are so dexterous that they can colear with both hands at the same time.

If too powerful resistance is offered at the outset by the bull, as is sometimes the case, the rider still clings to the tail of his adversary, and throwing himself off his horse while at full speed, the impetus combined with his weight and strength never fail in bringing the bull like a fallen giant to the ground; then the man quickly drawing the tail between the hind legs, awaits the arrival of his companions to assist in securing the prize.

By excelling at dangerous equestrian feats, caudillos (military strongmen) could gain recruits among plainsmen. José Antonio Páez, the Venezuelan caudillo, tailed bulls. Argentine dictator Juan Manuel de Rosas likewise competed in dangerous gaucho horseback games. They won adherents among the llaneros and gauchos with daring, skilled horsemanship.

In late 1827 a British diplomat watched Páez tail a bull and daringly jump on its back. Unfortunately for the caudillo, the bull "took revenge with his horns in the fleshy part of the Chief's person," and Páez was unable to ride for some time. As the Briton noted, on the llanos "the play is dangerous and often both horse and man get gored to death."

British traveler James W. Wells watched *vaqueiros* tail bulls in northern Brazil in 1886. The rider, "dashing alongside a galloping bull, seizes its outstretched tail with his hand, and lo! the astonished animal is capsized on the ground."

Vaqueros in Mexico and old California also enjoyed tailing bulls and became very adept at it. Horsemen would pursue a herd of wild bulls. The toss was made by passing the bull's tail under one's right leg, turning it around the pommel of the **saddle,** then wheeling one's mount sharply away. With this type of leverage, even youngsters could fell large bulls. As with the chicken pull, cowboys of the American West learned tailing from the vaquero. The sport never reached the popularity that it achieved in Mexico or Venezuela, however.

Man versus Bear

Grizzly bears offered an attractive adversary to the California vaquero looking for thrills. Spotting a grizzly, several riders would lasso him by neck and feet. Choking off his air to subdue him, the vaqueros then trailed him back to a village to be pitted in battle against a wild bull. Along the way, they would take turns riding in front of the bear and provoking a charge. Anglo cowboys in the mountain states of Colorado, Wyoming, and Montana also roped grizzlies for fun. California fiestas often featured bull and bear fights, in which the grizzly usually killed several bulls before being gored mortally.

Man versus Fowl

A number of cowboy games involved fowl. The ostrich hunt or *boleada* provided gauchos with fun and profit. Whirling their *bolas* overhead, gauchos chased herds of rheas across the **pampa**. After catching and killing the large birds, gauchos gathered the ostrich feathers to sell to local merchants.

El pato (duck) was probably the most famous of all gaucho equestrian games. Riders fought for control of a duck sewn into a rawhide bag with several handles. The struggle might take them over miles of plains. Exhausted, sore, and bruised, the gauchos gathered at a rural tavern or *pulpería* after the contest to toast the winner.

Vaqueros in Mexico and the American Southwest developed their game involving a fowl. The chicken race *(correr el gallo)* used an unfortunate rooster, duck, or chicken. The fowl was tied to a tree or more commonly buried up to its neck in the ground. Horsemen galloped after the bird. Whoever succeeded in grabbing it then became the object of pursuit. Sometimes riders followed a set course. If the vaquero with the chicken crossed the finish line without being caught, he kept the fowl as a prize. As in pato, the racers rode miles cross-country and pulled one another off their mounts. As with pato in Chile, the Mexican chicken race was often held on San Juan's feast day. The victor presented the prize to a woman he wished to impress, and fandango street dancing often followed.

So much of the American cowboy's equipment, language, and work habits comes from the Mexican vaquero that it is not surprising to see games carry over north of the border. By 1888 the chicken race had made its way north to Gunnison, Colorado. At a fair held in that town, five cowboys competed in a "chicken pulling" after other horse races had been concluded. (Slatta 1990, 1992)

ESPUELAS

Spanish term for **spurs**.

ESTANCIA

A Latin American cattle or sheep ranch. During the early colonial period the Spanish crown gave grants of land to conquistadors and others to reward their service. A grant of an *estancia de ganado mayor* (large livestock ranch) encompassed 6.7 square miles. Over time, the term *estancia* became more generalized in many countries to mean a ranch of any size. Many other regional terms for ranch developed, including *hacienda, fundo* (Chile), and *hato* (Venezuela).

Traditionally, **gauchos** had considered the resources of the plains to be in the public domain. Wild cattle and grasslands were available to all. On the **pampas** of Argentina and Uruguay, the livestock ranch became the most important rural socioeconomic institution. Estancias developed greater importance during the eighteenth century, when large ranchers *(estancieros)* established private control over land, water, and cattle.

The headquarters at some poor estancias consisted of little more than a humble adobe shack. A few cattle skulls served as chairs. On more substantial estates, a watchtower or *mirador* topped the central ranch house. From this perch, ranchers could spot the dust of approaching raiders. A modest bunkhouse and kitchen served the needs of the gauchos.

Ranchers on larger estancias divided their ranges into many units, each under the charge of a manager. Many ranches included a *pulpería,* a combination general store and tavern, where gauchos gathered to drink, gamble, and sell produce. Although subdivision reduced many of the larger estates in the twentieth century, the estancia remains a place of power and prestige in cattle regions throughout Latin America. (Sáenz Quesada 1980; Slatta 1992)

ESTRIBO

Spanish term for stirrup.

EVANS, DALE

(1912–)

Singer, actress. See Rogers, Roy.

EVANS, EVAN

Pseudonym used by pulp writer Frederick **Faust.**

EVENT

See Rodeo Events.

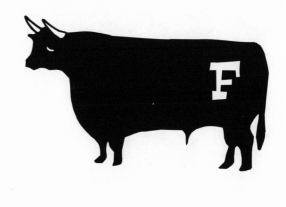

FACÓN
Long swordlike **gaucho** knife.

FACUNDO
Influential Argentine book. See Sarmiento, Domingo Faustino.

FANDANGO
Lively dance or party.

FARO
Card game. See Gambling.

FARR, KARL
Member, along with Hugh Farr, of singing group Sons of the Pioneers. See Rogers, Roy.

FARR, HUGH
See Farr, Carl.

FASHIONS
While cowboy garb is always in style in most parts of the West, cowboy fashion elsewhere waxes and wanes. For working cowboys, **rodeo** riders, and ranch folk, **boots,** jeans, and **hat** are regular work clothes. According to a 1991 Professional Rodeo Cowboys Association (PRCA) survey, 61 percent of rodeo fans regularly wear western clothing.

Thanks to the line-dancing craze and **hat acts,** demand for cowboy and cowgirl fashions has increased dramatically. Quick to recognize market openings, western clothiers set their sights on new customers. Weekend cowboys and cowgirls now deck themselves out as folks did following the *Urban Cowboy* fad. As one clothing executive put it, "Country dancing and country music has never been more popular than it is now, and they are driving the market. Western wear is being perceived less as costume dressing and more as weekend casual wear."

Some years crossover cowboy fashion takes new and often unusual turns. Kim Long, author of *The American Forecaster Almanac,* predicted that used cowboy boots would be a fashion hit for 1993. Long predicted that purchasers would want to say, "I've been doing this for awhile."

Sure enough, cult markets developed for used jeans and used boots. The broken-in, authentic look appealed to many folks whose only riding comes in Ford Mustangs or on swivel office chairs.

Wah-Maker takes authenticity more seriously than any other clothing manufacturer. Slim Jim Rodgers and Wahoo Allen Wah recreate historical clothing from the last century. No slick polyester and pearl snaps here. Instead, they recreate the canvas pants, wool vests, and bib-front shirts of the past century. Clint **Eastwood**'s film, *Unforgiven,* sports some Wah-Maker fashions.

In addition to cowboy fashion, cowboy memorabilia and ranch house furnishings made a 1990s comeback. Michael Friedman, author of *Cowboy Culture: The Last Frontier of American Antiques* (1992), sells cowboy memorabilia. His interest stems from childhood experiences, which parallels the interest of many forty-something or older males in **B westerns.** In childhood, "the games we played were about cowboys, and our heroes were cowboys like the Lone Ranger and Hopalong Cassidy."

In the late 1980s Southwest (Santa Fe) style marked the first phase of the cowboy fashion revival. Lodge or log cabin furnishings popped up in the early 1990s. Then in 1992 "pure straight cowboy" made an appearance.

These trends gave welcome market opportunities for western craftsmen. Makers of boots, **saddles, tack,** and furniture enjoyed growing sales. New magazines, such as *Western Styles* and *That's Country,* cater to the new country and western tastes. *Western English World* is a trade magazine that tracks the cowgirl/boy fashion world. According to Christine Mather *(True West,* 1992), "All of a sudden, they are being inundated with people who now see these crafts as something unique."

As in authentic cowboy garb, cowboy furnishings vary widely and exhibit many different influences. The sturdy, simple pine furniture, Mexican-inspired wrought iron, Native American textiles designs, and other influences may again be found. In short, the early 1990s provided some exciting fun and fashions for wanna-be and real-life cowboys alike. (Beard 1993; *Cowboys & Indians* magazine; Friedman 1992; *Western Styles* magazine)

FAST DRAW

The gunman's life often depended upon his ability to draw and fire his gun with incredible speed. The type of **firearm** and draw he chose hinged on personal preference. Though no two styles matched exactly, several broad categories of fast draws (quick draws) exist.

Many real gunfighters used the traditional Hollywood depiction of the hip **holster** with the gun butt facing back. The gunman then performed the draw with the hand on the same side as the holster. (Watch the opening scene on the old television program "Gunsmoke" for a good look at this technique.)

The cross-draw, with either one or two guns, required the butts of the weapons to point forward. The hand then crossed the body to reach the butt of the gun and draw it up to horizontal firing position.

The importance of wearing the holster at the proper height cannot be overemphasized. If the gun did not clear the holster easily, the draw would be too slow. If a weapon actually got caught on the holster, the undertaker made his rounds. To prevent this problem, some gunfighters greased their holsters or filed down the sight at the end of the gun's barrel.

Fast-draw duels on Main Street quickly became a staple of **B westerns**. "Fanning" is a shooting technique that has added excitement and action to many movie shootouts. The term means to hold down or tie back the trigger while repeatedly pulling back the hammer with the palm of the other hand, allowing a shooter to fire several shots in rapid succession. Also known as "flip-cocking," fanning is very inaccurate—a gunman could only hit a target at extremely close range. This shortcoming prevented any real gunman with an interest in living from adopting the technique.

Cowboys packed iron on their hips. Others interested in shooting used other equipment.

Fast draws done with a shoulder holster required a special spring shoulder holster. This arrangement invariably meant a cross draw, with the butt of the gun pointed forward in the holster. A shoulder holster could be concealed under a coat, thereby giving the shooter an added element of surprise. Likewise a small derringer could be concealed in the sleeve with a wrist holster, ready for action with a flip of the wrist.

All fast draws, of whatever kind, required practice on an everyday basis. Any gunfighter who broke this cardinal rule lived only until he came up against one who followed it. Quick-draw artists needed plenty of practice to put the hand on the gun, pull it from the holster while cocking the hammer, bring it to a level horizontal position, and fire. Only by repeating the maneuver again and again could a gunfighter attain the skill and speed necessary to survive.

Modern fast-draw competitions perpetuate the old-time gunfighter skills with a notable difference. Today's quick-draw artists compete against targets and the clock. Unlike the duels of yesteryear, all contestants can walk away alive. In an interesting variation, artists and illustrators engage in quick-draw competitions to see who can draw a western scene the fastest. (Cunningham 1934, 1962; Rosa 1969)

—Mark Mayer

FAUST, FREDERICK SCHILLER
(1892–1944)

Pulp novelist Frederick Faust wrote under some 20 pseudonyms. His best and most widely read westerns appeared under the pseudonym Max Brand. The prolific Faust worked in many genres, including westerns, and richly deserves his title, King of the Pulps. He wrote more than 500 books. At least seven of his works made it to film, including *Destry Rides Again* (1932, 1939).

Born in Seattle, Faust grew up in California's San Joaquin Valley. He attended college at the University of California, Berkeley, worked as a reporter, and served in the military during World War I. He sold his first western in 1917, and the rush of words continued for nearly three decades.

During World War II, Faust took his writing talents to the front. He died in action in 1944 while working in Italy as a correspondent for *Harper's Magazine.*

No one would accuse Brand pulps of an excess of authenticity or literary style. Dashed off quickly, the works perfectly suited their medium and audience. In Berkeley, Faust had hoped to become a classical poet. He laced his works with classical allusions, reflecting that early interest. Along with Louis **L'Amour** and Ned **Buntline,** Brand is one of the foremost creators of the mythical pulp West. (Nolan 1985; Thrapp 1988; Tuska and Piekarski 1983, 1984)

FEED LOT

Enclosed area for fattening cattle on special feed. See Beef Cattle Industry.

FEEDER

Person who fattens cattle; also cattle being fattened. See Beef Cattle Industry.

FELLOWSHIP OF CHRISTIAN COWBOYS

See Religion.

FENCE RIDER

See Line Rider.

FENCING

Farmers and ranchers have used fencing to separate livestock and crops for thousands of years. In the eastern and southern United States, herders held livestock in fenced cow pens. The **beef cattle industry** that developed in Texas and the Great Plains operated very differently. Ranchers in the arid western country followed the Mexican practice of open-range grazing.

Nevertheless, within a decade after the start of the great **trail drives** north from Texas, the Great Plains began to feel the transformation brought on by the fence and the **windmill,** and these changes began to alter the Great Plains by the mid-1870s. The disastrous droughts from 1886 to 1888 further speeded the trend. The huge wave of western bankruptcies convinced most ranchers to forsake the open range for fenced operations. On fenced range, cattle couldn't always get to water, so they needed windmills to bring water to the herd. The old and somewhat wild and hazardous livestock industry gave way to haying, irrigation, controlled grazing and breeding, and supplemental feeds.

In 1874 an Illinois farmer named Joseph F. **Glidden** received a patent on a type of barbed wire still used today. He began marketing his wire the following year. Glidden manufactured his fencing from strands of steel wire. The long strands had sharp wire barbs twisted or welded to them. After a little learning, cattle prudently avoided contact with the wire. Barbed (also bob or barb) wire proved perfect for the wood-short western **plains,** where all-wood fences could not be constructed.

Within a decade after Glidden began his business, annual U.S. output of barbed wire jumped from 300 to 100,000 tons. In one year alone (1885) the U.S. Patent Office issued some 400 patents on barbed wire and machines to produce it.

Many cattlemen and cowboys initially opposed barbed wire because its strands literally cut them off from the open range. Fencing and the encroachment of farmers pushed back the open-range cattle frontier and hastened its demise. Fencing, along with the westward and southward extension of railroads, also doomed the great cattle drives that once employed tens of thousands of hands.

Once they had accepted the notion of fencing, however, ranchers quickly saw its benefits. Wire let ranchers reduce the number of hands and cut labor costs. They could also manage the range more efficiently. Breeding control could be maintained. Losses due to theft and straying were reduced. With water pumped by windmills, ranchers could stock the range with more animals than when only surface water was available. In some states, large outfits fenced public lands, thereby cutting off access to smaller ranchers.

Along with fencing came another innovation, the cattle guard, a series of round metal poles that stretched across a roadway between two sections of fence. Space between the bars and a moat underneath prevented livestock from crossing the cattle guard. Meanwhile, vehicles could pass through unimpeded. Gates could provide access, but stopping to open gates was time-consuming, and not everyone remembered to close them again. Cattle became so wary of cattle guards that some ranchers merely painted black stripes across the road. The stripes looked like a cattle guard and worked just as well as the real thing.

In the twentieth century, building and tending fence became a part of cowboy work, although many old hands avoid it if possible. On some ranches, different hands worked in the saddle and on foot. Cowboy Oscar Wright described the division of labor at the Chapman-Barnard Ranch in Oklahoma's Osage country.

We had the cowpunchers and the shoe-and-sock outfit. The shoe-and-sock outfit was the working guys, the ones who built fence, fed cattle in the winter, all that. Ben Johnson and Mr. Chapman would take that crew to work cattle, and Mr. Barnard would take the regular cowboys.

The Chapman-Barnard cowpunchers could not always avoid working with wire. Building new fence got top priority from all hands. Fencing crew veteran Marvin Griffin recalled what a huge task it was: "We followed every fenceline on this whole ranch. At that time it was 115,000 acres. That's a lots of land. Then when we got that out-side fenced, why, then we'd take in all the cross fences. Mister, we put *lots* of fence posts in."

Oklahoma Cowboy Adary Hull remembered that the regular cowboys rode fence as often as

With the invention of barbed wire, many cattle ranch owners fenced off their property, and some angry cattlemen took it upon themselves to engage in fence-cutting to demonstrate their disapproval as shown in this staged photograph, which was taken in 1885.

the fencing crew did. "We used to ride the fence onc't every week. We were looking for holes, steeples [staples] out, this 'n' that. I carried a pair of pincers and a hammer on my saddle all the time. And every spring before we got the cattle in receivin', we walked 'em [the fences]. And steepled 'em. Every steeple."

Fencing brought similar changes in Canada. Unlike the American Great Plains, Alberta enjoyed an abundance of trees in the western hills, and wooden fences appeared well in advance of barbed wire. Rancher Fred Ings described fence building in the mid-1880s. Hands constructed calf pens and fences from "poles, cut in the hills and sawed into post lengths. The ends of these poles we rested on the ground on a slant; in a hole drilled through them with a two inch auger. We inserted a brace, then nailed on thin poles. This made a strong efficient fence."

Barbed wire and farmers followed soon thereafter. In 1906 the superintendent of mines in Calgary reported that "the farmer and his fences are gradually driving the big rancher further and further back, and it is only a question of years when the real ranche will have ceased to exist." Within a year, an extremely harsh winter further reduced the attractiveness of ranching in Alberta.

Many western museums feature barbed wire collections. The Barbed Wire Museum in La Crosse, Kansas, is devoted entirely to this important piece of western history. (See Appendix B.) (McCallum 1985; Slatta 1990)

FENDERS
See Saddle.

FERBER, EDNA
(1885–1968)
Author of *Cimarron* (1930) and *Giant* (1952).

FIADOR
Spanish term anglicized to theodore. See Tack.

FILMS, BEST COWBOY
Westerns are as old as the film industry itself. Films with western settings or documenting western life appeared in the 1890s. Edwin S. Porter made film history in 1903 with eight minutes of film called *The Great Train Robbery.* Thousands of westerns have followed: a few very good, many very bad.

What exactly is a cowboy film? This is akin to asking where the West is. The following criteria identify outstanding cowboy films. The film must have (1) horses and preferably cattle, (2) cowboys or outlaws, and (3) a western location. Note that the relative dearth of horses and cattle eliminates *The Virginian* (1929) from contention. Using these criteria, the following are the ten best classic cowboy films, arranged chronologically.

1939 *Stagecoach*
This is a winner from the opening strains of the theme song, "O, Bury Me Not on the Lone Prairie," to the final, exciting Indian attack in Monument Valley. Director John Ford keeps the several "lifeboat-style" plot lines running strong. He fosters empathy for the social outcasts, Dallas, Ringo, and the drunken Dr. Josiah Boone. The potpourri of engaging and interesting characters draws the viewer into their lives. We quickly get to know them. Gatewood, the nasty, blowhard banker, is obviously a crook.

Ford draws on some cliches that ring true in this fanciful tale. Luke Plummer draws a dead man's hand, aces and eights, before facing Ringo in a gunfight. **Horses** ride over the camera so the thundering hooves are right in our faces. The sweeping grandeur of Monument Valley looms, huge and foreboding, in the background. Most importantly, John **Wayne** shows that he can act and establishes a credible basis for his long, distinguished career.

1946 *My Darling Clementine*
John Ford, like many other filmmakers, took up the challenging mythology of the Earps, Clantons, and the shootout at the O.K. Corral in Tombstone. Henry Fonda stars as Wyatt Earp in this beautifully filmed picture (again in Monument Valley). Ford, who helped create much of the drama of the mythical West, makes

the audience care about Earp as a person while building him into an even greater legend.

Ford also contrasts the closeness and loyalty of the Earps with the bickering and nastiness of the Clantons, a truly dysfunctional family. Fonda is joined with a strong performance by Victor Mature as Doc Holliday, the antihero who comes through in the end. The film also features veterans Walter Brennan, Tim Holt, Ward Bond, and John Ireland.

1948 *Red River*

This list limits itself to just two John **Wayne** top-ten picks—that's real restraint. *The Searchers* (1956) is one the very best Ford/Wayne efforts. Wayne's latter-day characters, Rooster Cogburn in *True Grit* (1969) and J. B. Books in *The Shootist* (1976), are wonderfully and engagingly wrought.

Nevertheless, *Red River* is at the top of the John Wayne list. This classic **trail drive** film includes a host of wonderful actors and dramatic, poignant generational conflict. Howard Hawks provided superb direction in this, his first western. Montgomery Clift shines as Matthew Garth, his first role. Harry Carey acted in his final role in the film, dying before the film's release. Shots of the trail drive have a docudrama quality enhanced by great black-and-white photography by Russell Harlan.

Red River has it all—the dust, danger, and death. The story also takes up another epic western theme, the use of **violence** and force to maintain order and protect property on the frontier. Wayne is powerful and threatening as the maniacal Tom Dunson. He represents the Old West where might made right. The young Clift, portraying Wayne's stepson, represents the future of rule by law and reason. Their conflict comes to a dramatic end in the film's final riveting fight scene. Like the **B westerns** of yesteryear, the film has a happy ending.

1952 *High Noon*

Picking Gary Cooper's best film is a challenge. *The Westerner* (1940), with Cooper bantering with Walter Brennan as Judge Roy Bean, is a charmer. For powerful acting and drama, however, Cooper's portrayal of the besieged Will Cane, in *High Noon,* is his best. Under Fred Zinnemann's skillful direction, Cooper won the second of his three Oscars.

High Noon skillfully combines traditional and modern elements. We see good fighting evil against great odds. Grace Kelly's character, a devout, pacific Quaker, must choose between religion and love. The bad woman with a good heart (Katy Jurado as Helen Ramirez) interjects a note of complexity.

The community in *High Noon* leaves the hero alone to face overwhelming odds. Both women leave in the face of the conflict, but the good woman returns and saves the hero. She resorts to violence, which goes against her faith, to save the man she loves. Right wins over wrong; love conquers. The cowardice of the good Christians in the community stands in sharp contrast to traditional views of the city and city folk as civilizers. The white hats and black hats are blurred a bit.

1952 *The Lusty Men*

A top-ten list must have a stand-out **rodeo** film. The Steve McQueen/Sam Peckinpah collaboration in *Junior Bonner* is a contender—the rodeo scenes are first rate. The year 1972 brought forth three good rodeo films: Cliff Robertson as an ex-convict rodeo rider in *J. W. Coop, The Honkers* with James Coburn and Slim Pickens, and *When the Legends Die,* with Richard Widmark as a drunken rodeo promoter.

The Lusty Men, however, offers stellar performances by Robert Mitchum and Arthur Hunnicutt, who carry the day. Aging rodeo star Mitchum becomes Arthur Kennedy's mentor. Sexual tension unfolds as Mitchum gravitates toward the younger man's wife, played by Susan Hayward. All in all, we get a real sense of life "goin' down the road."

1953 *Shane*

Homesteaders besieged by ruthless gunmen, working for big ranchers, is a common western plot line. *Shane,* with Alan Ladd as the one-name hero, is the best execution of this kind of tale.

Director George Stevens does justice to the Jack **Schaefer** novel. An ex-gunfighter, Ladd's Shane takes up his six-shooter again in defense of good, decent people.

The strong cast (Jean Arthur, Jack Palance, Van Heflin) draws the audience into their characters. The powerful, unrequited attraction between the characters played by Arthur and Ladd adds to the film's tension. Stevens keeps the story moving. Cinematographer Loyal Griggs won an Oscar for his fine effort.

Acclaim for *Shane* is not universal. Feminist critic Joan Mellen *(Big Bad Wolves: Masculinity in the American Film)* finds little merit in the film:

> *Shane* has been an overrated film, embodying as it does virtually every stock attitude and cliché of the "B" Western: wicked large ranchers hiring guns to terrorize small homesteaders, who are often defended by a cool superman with the fastest gun around. It offers an unabashed celebration of the most destructive emblems of maleness in the fifties.

1962 *Lonely Are the Brave*

This black-and-white film brilliantly captures the venerable theme of a cowboy in conflict with modernity. Kirk Douglas stars as the rebellious anti-modern hero, Jack Burns. The film, adapted from Edward **Abbey**'s *The Brave Cowboy,* does justice to Abbey's wonderfully wrought characters.

Douglas remains mostly at center stage. Supporting performers include Walter Matheau, George Kennedy, Carroll O'Connor as the truck driver, and Bill Bixby. Director David Miller successfully conveys the dignity and strength of the stubborn cowboy's rock-steady traditional values. *Lonely are the Brave,* like *Ride the High Country* and *Monte Walsh,* provides a touching treatment of the clash between old cowboy values and the changing West.

1962 *Ride the High Country*

Sam Peckinpah certainly deserves to appear in the top-ten list. This film is his best. His sensitive treatment of two aging cowboy/gunslingers is masterful. The main plot line anticipates by three decades Clint Eastwood's *Unforgiven.* The oldtimers have outlived their time. In the opening sequence, Joel McCrae rides into town. He is almost run down by a bizarre race pitting a camel against a horse. On the heels of that encounter, he survives a near miss with an automobile. Modernity is not kind to old cowpokes.

Randolph Scott, in his last role, and McCrae make us care about their crusty characters. The film also introduces young Mariette Hartley as Elsa. The innocent woman joins the two old hands to escape her tyrannical father, a religious fanatic.

Like any good western, indeed any good film, this one poses a moral dilemma. The two oldtimers are guarding a gold shipment. Scott is tempted to steal the gold. He reminds McCrae that when a poor man dies, all he has are "the clothes of pride." McCrae, poor but proud, refuses to stoop to theft. His honor tattered but still in tact, he says "I just want to enter my house justified."

Peckinpah had worked mostly as a television writer. He showed his capabilities in several ways. He spent four weeks rewriting and enlivening the script. "We didn't know he was such a good writer," recalled McCrae. Taking the advice of expert technicians, he used creative flash cutting and montages to heighten the film's tension, using impressive rising shots from a crane. The beauty and ruggedness of the high Sierra Nevada (Inyo National Forest) provide an impressive backdrop for the action.

1969 *Butch Cassidy and the Sundance Kid*

Paul Newman and Robert Redford provided two great sidekick films, *The Sting* and *Butch Cassidy and the Sundance Kid.* In *Butch Cassidy,* chosen here as one of the top ten westerns, Katherine Ross as a runaway schoolteacher adds grand entertainment. The film deftly blends witty comedy, tragedy, and Old West fact and legend. The outlaw trio trail from the Hole in the Wall in Wyoming to the outback of South America.

Joan Mellen again provides a critical counterpoint:

Poorly directed and tiredly resurrecting old stereotypes buried with the Western of the forties, *Butch Cassidy and the Sundance Kid* would have us look once again with nostalgia upon a male image in danger of extinction. Yet despite its amateurishness and banality, it set the tone for buddy films to come in the seventies.

Mellen roundly condemns westerns for the secondary roles they assign to women. While she may not like it, many good western films reflect a historical demographic reality. Men formed close bonds with other men because women were few, far between, and usually out of reach for a working cowhand. Much as during wartime, men develop close, but not necessarily sexual, relationships with other men. Their lives often depend on their pards.

The film won four Oscars, and the awards point to its many strengths. Oscars went to William Goldman for the fine script, to Conrad Hall for cinematography, and to Burt Bacharach and Hal David for the wonderful score. George Roy Hill was nominated as best director. "Raindrops Keep Fallin' on My Head" will ever conjure memories of old-fashioned bicycles.

1970 *Monte Wash*
Based on a Jack Schaefer novel, *Monte Walsh* portrays an aging cowboy in conflict with a changing West of the late 1880s. In the title role, Lee Marvin arouses our sympathy and our support. Perennial bad guy Jack Palance adds interest by playing a good guy, Walsh's sidekick Chet Rollins.

The movie is a happy blend of gritty realism and touching sentimentality. Arriving at a ranch, the cowboy's first question as he gets off his horse is "How's the grub?" The ranch scenes, from the bunkhouse to mustang and cattle **roundups,** ring true. The cattle boom has gone bust, so everything is fraying around the edges. As

Palance observes philosophically, "Nobody gets to be a cowboy forever."

Walsh faces many losses in his life. He loses the two people he most loves, Martine Bernard, played by Jeanne Moreau, and Rollins. He also loses his job and his way of life. Cowboy proud to the end, Walsh turns down the chance to earn big money as a performer in Colonel Wilson's Wild West Show. "I ain't spittin' on my whole life." Walsh shares much in common with the lone wolves that open and close the film.

The production has many fine touches. Mama Cass sings John Barry's sad, ironical theme song, "The Good Times Are Comin'." Veteran actor Richard Farnsworth appears in a cowboy role. David Walsh's cinematography looks like Charlie **Russell** paintings come to life. Indeed, the credits appear over Russell drawings. The film well conveys the starkness of life in a dying little **cow town** and the unhappy prospects for cowboys whose golden days have past.

1985 *Silverado*
Produced and directed by Lawrence Kasdan, *Silverado* opens with a blazing gunfight and never slows its breakneck pace. Kevin Kline and Scott Glenn star, but the supporting cast deserves equal billing. Kevin Costner makes a delightful young lady's man/gunfighter. Danny Glover plays a strong role in his righteous, no-nonsense quest to revenge his father's murder. Linda Hunt plays a **saloon** girl with her heart in the right place. Brian Dennehy is downright chilling as the homicidal sheriff.

The heroes, badly outnumbered but inventive, use a massive stampede to flush out the bad guys. Their smarts and superior gunplay allow them to cut down the crooks, over a period of several minutes, one by one. The action sometimes takes on a *Batman* socko flavor, but it remains absorbing. In one of the closing scenes, a hero loses his weapon. He rides up a ramp, hides, then jumps his horse down onto the bad guy, killing him.

There is lots of **violence,** but also lots of laughs. The film does a great job of using western cliches in a refreshing and entertaining fashion.

The plot is outlandishly **B western,** but the actors make it A quality.

1992 *Unforgiven*

William Munny is another in a long line of Clint **Eastwood**'s cold, quiet avenging killers. He raises his two kids on a forsaken Wyoming pig farm after his wife dies of smallpox. The big-talking Schofield Kid (Jaimz Woolvett) comes along with news of a $1,000 reward for killing two cowboys who cut up a prostitute. Munny sets aside his vows to his dead wife and rides off to Big Whiskey, Wyoming, to collect the reward.

The movie has comic moments like another western spoof, *The Over-the-Hill Gang* (1969). The aging Munny has great difficulty mounting his skittish horse. The big-mouthed Schofield Kid, a would-be gunslinger, is woefully nearsighted. Only Munny's black sidekick, Ned Logan (Morgan Freeman), seems to have weathered the years gracefully.

Between these three and the reward, however, stands sadistic Sheriff Little Bill Daggett (Gene Hackman). The sheriff first kicks gunfighter English Bob (a flamboyant Richard Harris) nearly to death and runs him out of town. He gives Eastwood the same treatment. As in many previous films, Eastwood's righteous wrath brings him back from near death. He avenges wrongs and rides out of town, alone, as always.

Unforgiven earns its R rating for language and violence. Eastwood's character is familiar. The plot and some of the scenes are absurd and a bit tasteless. (The Schofield Kid kills his first and only man as the victim sits relieving himself in an outhouse.) Despite its cliches and preposterous elements, the film is powerful and compelling. Eastwood masterfully conjures many images of western mythology—violence, justice, and loyalty.

Many of the best cowboy films pit individualism and respect for tradition against the growing constraints of modernity. Anyone who likes *Monte Walsh* will also enjoy Charlton Heston's leading role in *Will Penny* (1968). Heston acted badly in his share of turkeys, but here he is first rate.

Two other lighter treatments of the same theme are enjoyable. Clint Eastwood does a wonderful job as *Bronco Billy* (1980). *The Electric Horseman* (1979), with Robert Redford and Jane Fonda, also highlights cowboy independence.

A limited number of gunfighter films, like *The Gunfighter* (1950) and *The Magnificent Seven* (1960), would make the top twenty list.

Audiences get a concentrated dose of old-time B-western stars in three films. Several greats perform in *The Over-the-Hill Gang* (1969). *The Wild West* (1975) and *Meanwhile Back at the Ranch* (1976) splice together footage from oaters of the 1930s and 1940s into hilarious new plots.

Well there you have it, pardner. Keep an eye on late-night TV listings, and you'll still see these and other classics. Ride on over to the local video outlet and rent a few for a gala evening of cowboy fun. You'll enjoy them, maybe even more than you did a few decades ago. Better yet, add a few to your own video archive. For a few dollars, you can own a piece of western movie history. (Everson 1992; Garfield 1982; Mellen 1977)

FILMS, COWBOY
Film History

Early filmmakers quickly learned that crowds flocked to see action-packed cowboy movies. From the silent era on, westerns have been a mainstay of the industry. Films with identifiably western themes or settings appeared as early as 1894. Thomas Edison's film company produced short vignettes during the 1890s about Buffalo Bill **Cody,** Annie **Oakley,** and other western topics. Other filmmakers quickly followed.

The year 1903 looms large in western film history. The first plotted, copyrighted westerns appeared that year, *Kit Carson* and *The Pioneers.* The production of the year, however, came from director Edwin S. Porter, whose *Great Train Robbery* was produced in New Jersey for less than $150. The short film (about eight minutes) became a prototype for the western genre. It followed what became a timeworn narrative: a holdup by bad guys, a frantic horseback chase, a final blazing shootout, and the good guys defeating the crooks. Porter's formula of crime, chase, and retribution served as a model for countless **B westerns** and serials.

Films in general and westerns in particular quickly became big business. In the first decade of the twentieth century, nickelodeons sprang up everywhere. By 1908 an estimated 10 million Americans each year fed change into machines to watch nickelodeon films. In 1921 filmmakers released a record 854 westerns. In 1926 westerns comprised 28 percent of feature films. That proportion fell for the next decade, but jumped back to 28 percent in 1935, and percentages remained in the high twenties and low thirties through 1956. The genre has lost its mass-market clout since then, but western film is still very much alive and well.

Silent Era

Actor Max Aronson (1882–1971) played four small parts in *The Great Train Robbery.* Born in 1882 in Little Rock, Arkansas, the Jewish actor began his career in vaudeville. In 1907 he starred in *The Girl from Montana,* the first western actually shot in the West. In 1908 he became one of the first filmmakers to shoot his one-reelers at western locations instead of in a studio. Aronson (who changed his name to Gilbert M. Anderson) got his first starring role in *The Bandit Makes Good* (Essanay, 1908). Al Jennings shot *The Bank Robbery* on location at Cash, Oklahoma, the same year.

One of Aronson's greatest contributions to western film was his creation of a star performer. According to William K. Everson *(The Hollywood Western),* he first used the new name Broncho Billy in a 1908 film. Everson explains what happened:

Without any inkling of the impact it would have, he made a short Western entitled "Broncho Billy and the Baby," playing the lead himself. The title and the story itself came from a published Peter B. Kyne story. Anderson neglected the niceties of acquiring legal rights to the story before he filmed it, and he was soon visited by Peter B. Kyne himself. The author for-

tunately liked the film well enough to take no legal action, while making it plain that Anderson couldn't expect such generosity to apply in the future.

Aronson purchased for $50 the rights to the literary character Broncho Billy. He then changed his name to Gilbert M. ("Broncho Billy") Anderson. He first appeared using his new name in the 1910 film *Broncho Billy's Redemption.* He went on to become the first bona fide celluloid cowboy hero. From 1908 to 1915, he made a prodigious number of one-and two-reel westerns—at least 376 and possibly as many as 500. His last and only feature-length film was *The Son-of-a-Gun.* Like William S. Hart, Anderson captured a realistic-looking West of dust and run-down buildings. (Such realism, however, did not extend to his contrived, romanticized plots.) Anderson also helped found the Essanay Film Company, which produced many westerns and other silent films. His contributions to the film industry earned him a place in the Jewish-American Hall of Fame (see Appendix B).

In 1914, a year that looms large in film history, Cecil B. DeMille directed the first feature-length western, *The Squaw Man.* Dustin Farnum starred, as he did in DeMille's first screen portrayal of *The Virginian.* In that year D. W. Griffith also produced some westerns, including *The Battle at Elderbush Gulch,* and William S. Hart appeared in his first feature-length western, *The Bargain.*

The year 1915 saw the creation of Universal City by Carl Laemmle, whom critic Jon Tuska called "the single most important figure in the history of the silent Western." Laemmle, who began life as a poor immigrant, eventually made assembly line production and stock companies essential parts of the Hollywood film industry. Under his guidance, John Ford and Thomas Ince got their starts; many silent stars acted in his pictures. He gave directors and actors the freedom they needed to prosper.

From 1915 to 1925, William Surrey Hart (1870–1946) became the silver screen's biggest cowboy star; indeed he would become the biggest film star of his time. A stern, steely-eyed presence who could freeze a bad guy with his chilling stare, Hart served as role model for a horde of successors. He established his star status in 1916 with three long features. Fanatical about authenticity, Hart came into conflict with his film industry bosses. Unwilling to bow to demands for phony but popular productions, he disappeared from the western film scene. *Tumbleweeds* (1925), which Hart codirected, was his last and finest effort. In 1939 United Artists rereleased this great saga of the Oklahoma land rush. At age 69, Hart added a touching eight-minute prologue to the film in which he fondly remembered "the thrill of it all."

During film's second decade, longer features replaced short films. The 1920s brought the first big epic westerns, *The Covered Wagon* (1923) and *The Iron Horse* (1924). A young John Ford directed the latter film, already his 40th western. Ken Maynard (1895–1973), Harry Carey (1878–1947), Hoot Gibson (1892–1962), Buck Jones (1889–1942), and Tim McCoy (1891–1978) rose to stardom. McCoy, an expert in Indian languages and history, brought 500 Indians to Hollywood to act in *The Covered Wagon.* He stayed on to enjoy a fine career in B westerns. Maynard, the screen's first singing cowboy, also excelled at trick riding and stunts.

Hard-riding Tom Mix (1880–1940), however, succeeded Hart as the nation's leading cowboy hero. Mix injected myth and flashy dress in place of the dusty, dour, authentic look favored by Hart. He would order a lemonade at the saloon and dare anyone to snicker. He donned satin shirts with piping. He wore fancy, fringed gloves, reportedly because he had very sensitive hands. Mix sometimes gave equal billing to his horse Tony (he rode Old Blue until late 1914). Born in Mix Run, Pennsylvania, he made more than 170 westerns. No overnight success, Mix had appeared in movies since 1910, when he played in a Wild West documentary called *Ranch Life in the Great Southwest.*

Like many previous and subsequent cowboy stars, Mix manufactured a colorful history for himself. He reputedly was a **rodeo** rider, served in the Spanish-American War and the Philippine insurrection, broke horses for the British in the Boer War, was a deputy U.S. marshal, and had his own Wild West show. He often portrayed a lawman in roles capitalizing on his horsemanship. He and Tony left films for circus life in 1935.

Some stars of the B westerns came from cowboying or ranch backgrounds. Nebraska-born Hoot Gibson worked as a **bronc buster** and rodeo performer. Gibson mixed plenty of comedy and action in his features. He began in pictures as a stuntman for Tom Mix. Oklahoman Jack Hoxie (1890–1965) rode with Wild West shows and worked as a stuntman before gaining the lead in **B westerns.**

Great stuntman Yakima Canutt (1896–1986) was born in Colfax, Washington. Born Enos Edward Canutt, he came by his horseback skills honestly. He won honors as world champion All-Around Cowboy at Pendleton for five years beginning in 1917. He began making films in 1924 and did his own trick riding and other stunts.

With the transition to talkies, Yak concentrated on stunt work and directing action sequences more than acting. Together with director Robert North Bradbury, Canutt developed the "pass system," in which actors threw near-miss punches that, owing to the camera angle, looked very realistic. He continued to perform stunts until 1947. Filmmakers recycled some of his great scenes into many different movies. He often doubled for John **Wayne** and many other actors. Wayne imitated Yak's posture in the saddle. Canutt received a special Academy Award in 1966 for his stunt work. *Stunt Man* (1979), his autobiography, offers a good glimpse inside the world of B westerns.

"Talkies"

The Rivoli Theater in New York City presented the first sound on picture in April 1923, and the first all-talking picture appeared in July 1928. The year 1929 marked the advent of western "talkies." Historian Ray White names *Overland*

Bound as the first B western with sound. Soon came *In Old Arizona,* with the Cisco Kid; *The Virginian,* with Gary Cooper; *The Big Trail,* with John Wayne; and an Academy Award winner, *Cimarron,* with Richard Dix and Irene Dunne.

The transition from silent to sound pictures created great new opportunities. It also spelled doom for actors who could not make the change. Of the old silent film stars, Hoot Gibson, Buck Jones, Ken Maynard, Tim McCoy, Bob Steele (1907–1988), and Tom Tyler (1903–1954) made the transition most successfully. Other silent-era stars—Jack Perrin, Wally Wales, Buddy Roosevelt, Lane Chandler, and Jack Hoxie—saw their careers decline with sound.

The talkies added the exciting sounds of galloping hooves, gunshots, and furniture-smashing fistfights to westerns. The essential plot line, however, remained much the same: A strong, lone hero defeats the forces of evil (after a lengthy chase and fight) and wins the girl. Although it might be touch and go, right prevails over wrong.

Hollywood cranked out more than 100 westerns every year during the 1930s. Kids and many grownups thrilled to fast action and bigger-than-life heroics. The 1930s also brought a new twist to the western—singing cowboys. Republic Pictures, formed in 1935 through the efforts of Herbert J. Yates, quickly became the premier producer of B westerns and serials. Republic played a key role in the careers of many cowboy stars, including John Wayne, Gene **Autry,** and Roy **Rogers.**

Cowboy heroes came to the cinema from many walks of life. Sports stars sometimes attracted the eye of directors or talent scouts. Pasadena-born Fred Thomson (1890–1928) was one of the first college sports stars to reach the silver screen. A great amateur athlete before World War I, he began his movie career in 1921. By the late 1920s, Thomson, mounted on Silver King, rivaled Tom Mix as the country's leading cowboy star at the end of the silent era. Pneumonia cut short his life and career.

Several stars moved from the gridiron to film. Johnny Mack Brown's (1904–1974) great Rose Bowl performance gave the Alabama Crimson Tide a victory in 1927. His key interception also paved the way to a Hollywood career. John Wayne's football career at the University of Southern California gave him a boost in Hollywood. Charles Starrett (1903–1986) played football at Dartmouth, and Larry ("Buster") Crabbe (1909–1983) had a standout football and swimming career at the University of Southern California.

The 1930s saw the emergence of a new generation of stars: John Wayne, Gene Autry, Roy Rogers, Gary Cooper, and others. Born Frank James Cooper in Helena, Montana, in 1901, Gary Cooper brought back the quiet strength made famous by William S. Hart. His career began in 1925 with a bit part in *The Thundering Herd,* and he appeared as an extra in other silent films. We first see his skill and charisma in *The Virginian* (1929). In *The Westerner* (1940), Cooper is a heroic cowhand who takes on the legendary Judge Roy Bean (Walter Brennan). He won Academy Awards for his strong, silent heroes in *Sergeant York* (1941) and *High Noon* (1952). He also played some light comic and romantic roles.

Singing cowboys created a world in which cowhands alternate between strumming the ever-present guitar and chasing after bad men. Ken Maynard made the first singing cowboy film in 1929. Little Bob Steele sang in *Oklahoma Cyclone* (1930). A chorus of singing cowboys followed: Gene Autry, Tex Ritter, Dick Foran, Roy Rogers, and more. Autry and Rogers each made more than 90 films. Tex Ritter made some 60 films, cowboy crooner Jimmy Wakely starred in about 30 films, and Eddie Dean and Rex Allen made about 20 each. For Maynard and Steele, music provided but a brief interlude, but song became the mainstay of Gene Autry westerns. Roy Rogers and Dale Evans made some films that are not musical westerns, they are western musicals.

The John Ford Era

In the 1940s and 1950s great westerns came from many excellent directors: Howard Hawks

(Red River, 1948), John Sturges *(Gunfight at the O.K. Corral,* 1957), Henry Hathaway *(True Grit,* 1969), Anthony Mann *(Man of the West,* 1958), and Budd Boetticher *(Ride Lonesome,* 1959).

Born Sean Aloysius O'Feeny, John Ford (1895–1973) worked in the newly empowered sound medium and took the western to new heights. He directed his first western in 1917 and two more in the 1920s. Not until 1939, however, did he return to the western genre. The classic *Stagecoach* established Ford as the premier director of westerns. It also launched John Wayne from B-movie obscurity to stardom.

Following World War II, John Ford concentrated on the western genre. He made the landscape a vivid part of his films, thanks to his skill at painting with the camera. Henry Fonda starred in the beautifully filmed *My Darling Clementine* (1946). Ford next directed John Wayne in his cavalry trilogy, *Fort Apache* (1948), *She Wore a Yellow Ribbon* (1949), and *Rio Grande* (1950). Ford worked with the leading western stars of the day: John Wayne, Henry Fonda, James Stewart, and Ward Bond. He won four Oscars, but none for his westerns.

Ford's early westerns exalted the victories of eastern civilization over a barbaric West. A regrettable racism against Native Americans pervades many of his works, especially the cavalry movies and *The Searchers.* He depicts Comanches as subhumanly evil. According to critic Jon Tuska, Ford even had racially segregated outhouses on location. During the 1950s, however, his vision of the West seems to have changed. He raised dark, troubling questions and presented a more complex vision of the Old West. *The Man Who Shot Liberty Valance* (1962) reminds viewers that western heroic myth can have an unsavory reality behind it.

During the 1950s, **television** offered stiff competition to neighborhood movie theaters. Some western heroes, like Roy and Dale, Gene, and Rex Allen, adapted well to the change. The Lone Ranger, Cisco Kid, Sky King, and Annie **Oakley** entertained in living rooms, not darkened theaters. William Boyd as Hopalong Cassidy made the transition successfully. He provided a stern, moral father figure for kids similar to the image cultivated later by Lorne Greene as Pa Cartright on "Bonanza."

Television and fast-rising production costs spelled the end of B westerns. What is generally acknowledged as the last B western, *Two Guns and a Badge,* with Wayne Morris, appeared in 1954.

Modern Westerns

Perhaps a mark of distinction and affection is the appearance of oddball westerns. By the 1950s, westerns had established enough of a presence to be parodied. For example, in 1956 came a sci-fi western, *The Beast of Hollow Mountain,* in which cowboy Guy Madison takes on a prehistoric monster attacking a Mexican village. Horror flick fans got several westerns tailored to their interests. *Curse of the Undead* (1959) pitted cowboys against vampire zombies. *Billy the Kid vs. Dracula* (1966), in which Dracula was played by John Carradine, also combined the two venerable genre. The same producer followed up the same year with *Jesse James Meets Frankenstein's Daughter.*

If imitation is the sincerest form of flattery, then the western is a much-flattered genre. Nearly everyone in show business tried a hand at making a western. In *Ride 'em Cowboy* (1941), Abbott and Costello ride the range with Dick Foran and Johnny Mack Brown. In 1958 a young Dan Rowan and Dick Martin "acted" in *Once Upon a Horse.* Fortunately, they deserted westerns for "Laugh In." Even Andy Warhol left soup cans long enough to direct *Lonesome Cowboys* (1968).

The western also went international. In 1952 Peter Lawford, Maureen O'Hara, and Richard Boone took the western to Australia in *Kangaroo.* In *The Americano* (1954), Texas cowboy Glenn Ford takes on the bad guys in Brazil. In 1961 Stewart Whitman starred in a South African western in which Boer settlers replaced the Conastoga wagon train, and Zulus stood in for murderous Apaches.

Since the 1950s, western films have become less predictable and stereotypical. Directors have stretched the genre well beyond the narrow confines of traditional formulas. Every few years, a special gem appears. In 1962, *Lonely Are the Brave* brilliantly captured the old theme of the cowboy in conflict with modernity. Kirk Douglas starred in this adaption of Edward **Abbey**'s novel *The Brave Cowboy.* Other movies echoed the theme. Robert Redford played an aging rodeo star in *The Electric Horseman* (1979). Clint Eastwood provided another example of trying to recapture the cowboy past in *Bronco Billy* (1980).

Traditional westerns relied on limited **violence,** with lots of shooting and fighting but few deaths and no blood. In the 1960s we got the ultraviolent spaghetti westerns with Clint Eastwood. Sam Peckinpah's *The Wild Bunch* (1969) topped all westerns for stylized gore. Some black westerns of the "blaxploitation" genre also reveled in violence (see African-American Cowboys). Another new ingredient, raw sex, accompanied the violence. This combination of sex and violence gave these so-called adult westerns R ratings.

Midnight Cowboy (1969) brought together the cowboy innocence of Texas Joe Buck (Jon Voight) and the urban angst of Ratso Rizzo (Dustin Hoffman). The only X-rated film to win an Academy Award for Best Picture, the screenplay was based on a novel by James Leo Herlihy. The film poignantly, powerfully, and tragically juxtaposed stereotypically eastern and western figures.

Black-hat/white-hat melodrama took flight into space with the "Star Wars" series. In 1981 Sean Connery starred in *Outland,* a space version of *High Noon.* Like Will Kane, Connery got little help fighting the bad guys on one of the moons of Jupiter.

The western has proved a very flexible genre. Revisionist visions of history were depicted in *Little Big Man* (1970). Urban, yuppie malaise fell to the magic of life in the saddle *(City Slickers,* 1991). Sci-fi, vampire, and cartoon westerns, such as *Fievel Goes West* (1991), have been produced.

The recent boom in westerns kicked off by *Lonesome Dove, Dances with Wolves,* and

Unforgiven continued into 1994. As Associated Press writer Bob Thomas put it, "Westerns are in." Western films for the year included *City Slickers II, Wyatt Earp, Maverick, Bad Girls, Savage Land, Tall Tale, The Quick and the Dead, Legends of the Fall, Cowboy Way,* and *Silent Tongue.* In February 1994 the evocative *Midnight Cowboy* enjoyed a rerelease on its 25th anniversary.

After nearly a century of western films, it is clear that there will always be westerns. Some years will yield more, some less. The film industry finally recognized and applauded the art of John Wayne and Clint Eastwood. Perhaps their belated acceptance by the American Academy of Motion Pictures will inspire a new generation of actors and directors. As new technologies create a truly global audience, westerns continue to attract the fascination of armchair cowboys of all ages around the world.

Continuing Appeal

Many western movies have received belated critical acclaim. Once dismissed as kid stuff, westerns are now studied and appreciated. The quantity, not the quality, of western films makes them important in American culture. Their imagery is pervasive and long-lived. Western myth resonates with Americans. Images from film and television have shaped the way Americans (and people in countless other countries) like to think about themselves, their characters, and their histories.

The iconography of western films has taken on a life and reality of its own. For many Americans, the cowboy is John Wayne or some other silver-screen favorite. Westerns offer escapism, action, and uncomplicated entertainment. Perhaps one reason that westerns translate so well into other cultures is their simplicity and predictability; most are mounted morality plays. The success of westerns does not depend upon innuendo, subtle plots, dense dialogue, or complex character development.

Members of the Western Film Preservation Society of North Carolina, mostly men aged 40 to 65, cite escapism, nostalgia, and the desire to recapture the joys of lost youth as "front-row kids" as the reasons for their ongoing appreciation of westerns. Many fans appreciate the traditional values and role models projected by the B westerns: individualism, fair play, honesty, integrity, and clean living. They also applaud the inevitable triumph of right over wrong.

The late Tom Walters, a talented North Carolina writer and "ex-front-row kid," penned a volume of poems about film. *Seeing in the Dark* (1972) captures many memories and sentiments common to B-western fans. In a poem titled "Grade B Westerns," Walters wrote:

> How the grainy gray was colored
> By eager eyes.
> Saturday mornings we lived in the dark:
> The garish posters,
> Hoky poses announced a world of thrills
> At thirty cents.
> Ah, the purity of punishment
> Meted by cartridged centaurs
> (Lord, there were guns
> And stallions everywhere)
> Right prevailed among
> Hard-ridden horsehair seats.
> In colors all our own, in
> The flickering opalescent light,
> We believed, we believed, we believed. . . .

Jon Tuska (*A Variable Harvest*) reminds us that the goal of formula western filmmakers "had never been to depict the West as it once was, but rather to interpret its spirit and give it a new meaning. For them, the Western represented an enduring myth and they were part of a living tradition bound up in the articulation of that myth." (Everson 1992; Garfield 1982; Miller 1979; Thomas 1989; Tuska 1984, 1985, 1990)

See also African-American Cowboys in Film; B Westerns; Films, Best Cowboy; Films, Documentary; Women in Western Film.

FILMS, DOCUMENTARY

Filmmakers have produced a legion of A and B westerns. Paradoxically, the cowboy has attracted the attention of relatively few documentary filmmakers. To be sure, some films have a docudrama quality or are based on historical events. *Heartland* (1979), for example, gives a very realistic sense of the loneliness and hardship of plains ranch life during the past century.

A documentary, however, seeks to document—portray without embellishment—cowboy history and culture. Some of the very earliest film shot by Thomas Edison and other crews documented Buffalo Bill **Cody**'s Wild West Show. Others focused on Annie **Oakley** and other western celebrities of the time.

The earliest cowboy documentary, as we know the genre today, appeared in 1954. William Conrad, John Dehner, Larry Dobkin, and Tex Ritter narrated a loving look at *The Cowboy,* produced and directed by Elmo Williams. The highly romanticized script sometimes detracts from good visuals of cowboy history and life. The film emphasizes the real dangers of cowboy life and the courage required to face them.

In 1961 Gary Cooper narrated an hour-long, black-and-white look at *The Real West.* The program sweeps over the entire westward movement. Cooper, looking haggard, already knew he was dying of cancer as he made this final appearance before the camera. His memorable voice and his death the same year give the documentary a special poignancy. In 1969 the University of Arizona produced a 30-minute film called *Bellota: The Story of Roundup.* Directed by Harry Atwood, the film accurately details the work life of Anglo cowboys and **vaqueros.** *Vaquero: The Forgotten Cowboy* (1987) looks at contemporary ranch life in Hebronville, south Texas. Henry Darrow narrates.

A more recent, but unfortunately disjointed production is *The Real American Cowboy* (1992). Aired on the Discovery Channel and unevenly narrated by Roger Kennedy, the film is a pastiche of images, music, and sundry information. Despite appearances by cowboy poets Baxter **Black** and Wally **McRae,** the production never quite gels. The script jumps around too much to provide much of a sense of the cowboy's historical development. The history of the cowboy often seems little more than an excuse for jokes and musical interludes.

Kennedy narrated another documentary in 1993 entitled *The Frontier.* The program provides a passable survey of the fur, mining, and farming frontiers. Incredibly, however, it jumps right over the ranching frontier. The livestock industry is not mentioned. There is no discussion of the cowboy or ranching.

The most sweeping and ambitious documentary of cowboy life to appear so far is *Cowboys of the Americas* (Warner Western, 1993). Canadian filmmaker Doug Hutton took crews from the Alberta prairies to the American West, northern Mexico, and Argentina. The beautifully filmed documentary captures the work and play of cowboys (including Indian cowboys), vaqueros, **charros,** and **gauchos.** The script by Val Jenkins is based on *Cowboys of the Americas* (1990), by Richard W. Slatta, who also served as historical consultant to the project. Singer Michael Martin **Murphey** narrates.

Rodeo has attracted a few skilled filmmakers. Jeff Kanew directed a 1972 film, *Black Rodeo.* Filmed at a black rodeo in New York, the documentary includes appearances by Muhammad Ali and Woody Strode. Canadian rodeo gets its due in *Here's to the Cowboy* (1982). Director Paul Jay takes the viewer "down the road" to small-town rodeos in Alberta. The 30-minute documentary is informative and realistic in its portrayal of the appeal and difficulties of rodeo life. Viewers get a good look at some "mutton bustin'" kids riding sheep. Ivan Daines provides the songs.

Joel McCrea narrated an exciting look at *The Great American Cowboy* (1973). Winner of an Academy Award for best documentary, the film focuses on the contest between Larry Mahan and Phil Lyne to become the World Champion Cowboy.

Cowboy Up (198?) offers a fast-paced 30 minutes of rodeo. Produced and directed by Rodney Jacobs, the film includes many comments from rodeo performers, including Leo Camarrillo (team roping), J. C. Trujillo and Bruce Ford

(bareback bronc riding), Dan Gay (bull riding), and Rick Chatham (rodeo clown). Cliff Robertson, who appeared as a rodeo rider in the movie *J. W. Coop* (1972), narrates from Old Tucson.

Cattle drives, the stuff of legend and many a **B western,** also provide great visuals for documentaries. *Born to Buck* (1975) provides a variation on the theme. Henry Fonda and Rex Allen narrate. The film traces a 400-mile **trail drive** of wild horses through Montana.

Biographical documentaries are also in short supply. One of the best is the Galen Films production, *Roy Rogers: King of the Cowboys.* Directed by Len Morris, the film premiered in 1992 on American Movie Classics. Roy narrates the one-hour production, which features plenty of music, film clips, and never-before-seen home movies.

Not surprisingly, the Duke has been the subject of several documentaries. *John Wayne: Standing Tall* appeared on PBS in 1989. James Arness narrates this retrospective of the Duke's career. The documentary covers Wayne's major film roles, his marriages and romantic involvements, and his very conservative politics. In 1990 Burbank Video distributed *John Wayne: Bigger than Life.* This posthumous production lacks the intimacy of the Roy **Rogers** biography, but it competently traces the Duke's film career.

A better effort is *Young Duke,* which traces Wayne's early B-western career through 1939, when he achieved stardom in *Stagecoach.* We see lots of clips from the Duke's years with Republic Pictures, including his work with *The Three Mesquiteers.* The biography aired in June 1993 on the Arts and Entertainment Network series "Biography" (A&E Biography, 235 East 45 Street, New York 10017). Film critic and author Leonard Maltin produced and narrated the show.

Sam Peckinpah: Man of Iron (A&E, 1993) takes a hard look at the controversial director. The two-hour documentary captures the complex psyche of the man who gave us *Ride the High Country, The Wild Bunch,* and many other memorable westerns.

Ranch life received documentary attention during the 1980s. *On the Cowboy Trail* (1981) shows both traditional and modern ranching techniques in the Tongue River valley of southeastern Montana. The traditional ranching techniques of Ellen Cotton are contrasted with the new technologies of Bill and Ann McKinney. Waylon Jennings provides the **music.** Cowboy Ray Holmes and his wife Pauline (see Autobiographies by Cowboys) are among the ranch people interviewed. Margot Liberty and Barry Head collaborated on this unsentimental look at ranch life. They later assisted Holmes in publishing his memoirs in *Working Cowboy* (1994).

Tom Brokaw surveys *The Changing West* (1988) for NBC, exploring the problems facing ranchers in Stillwater County, Montana. Actress Glenn Close narrates the PBS documentary, *Do You Mean There Are Still Cowboys?* (1988). In that film, director Jon Blair lets residents of Big Piney, in western Wyoming, tell their stories in their own words. Close, whose family lived there in the 1970s, explains the changes coming to the tiny ranching community.

Cowboy folklore has also attracted some attention. In *The Last Wagon* (1971), director Harry Atwood looks at the Old West through the eyes of folksinger Katie Lee. Like *Belotta,* the film is beautifully photographed. In 1991 the PBS-TV program "Austin City Limits" broadcast *A Salute to the Cowboy,* a fine musical review including performances by Michael Martin **Murphey, Riders in the Sky,** cowboy poet Waddie **Mitchell,** and many others. Kim Shelton's PBS film *Cowboy Poets* (1988) focuses on Wally **McRae,** Slim Kite, and Waddie Mitchell.

Ben **Johnson, Jr.** narrates *The Legendary West,* which aired on the Discovery Channel in 1992. It examines how filmmakers and other mythmakers have portrayed western history. The clear, analytical script deftly contrasts history and cinema myth. The script and excellent film clips combine to make this a superior documentary. We see young John **Wayne**'s exhortations to pioneers struggling along in *The Big Trail* (1936), and we get a good look at Buffalo Bill **Cody**'s transformation into frontier hero.

While cowboys receive the lion's share of the attention, PBS produced a 30-minute documentary entitled *Cowgirls* (1991). Directed by Nancy Kelly and written by Teresa Jordan, the program provides glimpses into the lives of several ranch women, young and old. *Cattle Drive* (1980) features two women among a crew of seven moving cattle to winter range in the Montana-Idaho border area. Ann Reynolds is one of the buckaroos and Judy Neuhauser is one of two cooks on the drive.

During the 1980s and early 1990s, several documentary series appeared on television. Five 30-minute programs appeared in 1992 in the series "Legends of the American West." A bearded Harry Carey, Jr. hosted the series produced by Cabin Fever Entertainment. The series mixes recreations, feature film footage, vintage photographs, paintings, and brief comments by experts. Three programs focus on gunfighters, lawmen, and outlaws.

Cowboys & Indians (1992) makes a notable, if brief, effort at presenting a historically accurate view of cowboy and Indian life on the frontier. It quickly traces the westward movement in order to set the cowboy in proper historical context. Singer Charlie Daniels and actor Ben Johnson, Jr., add a few comments about the hardships of cowboy life. Only about six minutes of the half-hour program focuses on the cowboy.

The West Remembered (1992) focuses on western memorabilia. Buffs will enjoy seeing some of John Wayne's film gear, artwork by Russell, **Remington,** and others, and weapons belonging to some of the Old West's bad men. It opens with a rapid-fire two-minute vignette of the cowboy as portrayed in western film. The film also takes viewers on a good tour of the **National Cowboy Hall of Fame** and the Gene Autry Museum.

The best documentary series on the cowboy is the five-part "Great West Collection," which maintains a tight focus on cowboy and ranch life. Telecast in the 1980s, the series appeared for sale in video stores in 1992. Singer Ian **Tyson** narrates *The Working Cowboy,* and takes the viewer to several ranches in Alberta and British Columbia.

Singer Michael Martin Murphey leads a tour of four *Great Ranches of the West.* One of the ranches visited is the famous Parker Ranch in Hawaii. A third cowboy singer, Waylon Jennings, takes viewers to a West Texas roundup in *My Heroes Have Always Been Cowboys.* The final two programs hold the focus on working ranches. In *The Last Cowboys* and *Ranch Album,* we get to ride with working cowboys on ranches in Arizona, Nevada, and Utah.

Another singer, Kenny Rogers, narrates a multi-part series titled "The Real West" (1992–1993). Production is similar to the "Legends of the American West" series. Topics range widely, but one program, *Wild, Wild Women,* provides a revisionist view of the role of women. Historian Dee Brown and others provide commentary.

In the fall of 1993 Ted Turner's TBS station offered a three-part debunking series, "The Untold West." The first program, narrated by Lou Diamond Phillips, is the best. Titled *Outlaws, Rebels and Rogues,* the documentary examines the lives and myths of Billy the Kid, Jessie James, Belle Star, and other infamous outlaws. The production mixes historical photographs with Wild West recreations. It also features interpretations by many prominent historians of the American West.

The second program focuses on *The Black West.* Danny Glover narrates and singing cowboy Herb Jeffries, an African American, provides wonderful commentary. (See African-American Cowboys in Film.) The presentation documents the fact that American racism did not stop at the frontier. Regrettably, the director of this segment included no views from western scholars, so the opinions expressed create a very impressionistic tone.

Keith Carradine and Dee Hoty narrate the final episode titled *Hot on the Trail.* The program examines western "love, sex, and romance," both historical and contemporary. The rather ragged production jumps around from Calamity Jane to modern rodeo **buckle bunnies** to nineteenth-century whorehouses to a modern cowboy/cowgirl wedding. As in episode two, we get no interpretations from scholars of the West, but the film makes a serious attempt to treat sometimes taboo subjects, including Indian-white marriages, **prostitution,** mail-order brides, and the general problem of sexual imbalance on the frontier. (Garfield 1982)

FIRE ON THE MOUNTAIN

Novel. See Abbey, Edward.

FIREARMS

When people think of cowboys they often think of guns. Much of the mystique of the Old West comes from the imagined or real activities of the gunslinger. Hollywood depicts the man who always carried a gun, on the range, in the **saloon,** or even in bed. In fact, this characterization carries a grain of truth. Seldom did anyone heading west of the Mississippi venture forth without a good rifle or two and a handgun. Hunting for meat, killing rattlesnakes and other varmits, and defending oneself and one's property gave most westerners ample reason to travel armed.

Many of the weapons used in the West achieved legendary status. Weapons also reflected many important inventions in American industrial technology. The names Colt, Winchester, and Sharps will long be remembered as fine, innovative firearms important in the settlement of the West.

One common misconception about western firearms pertains to the use of metallic cartridges. Percussion weapons remained prevalent well after the end of the Civil War. Whether muzzle or breech loaded, these weapons required several steps in preparation for firing. The exact method varied with the type of firearm. All percussion weapons needed three components to load: a slug (ball or conical), powder, and a percussion cap. A pull of the trigger resulted in billowing clouds of choking black smoke. (The invention of smokeless powder came late in the nineteenth century.) Paper and linen cartridges facilitated reloading by placing the slug and powder together, but the weapon still required a separate cap to fire.

Tyler Henry's invention of the rimfire cartridge made reloading much simpler. This type of ammunition put the slug, powder, and primer into one casing. The later centerfire cartridge grew out of Henry's original invention. Initially, the expense of metallic cartridges deterred many from giving up percussion guns. Many westerners converted percussion weapons to use the new ammunition rather than purchasing new guns. Ultimately, metallic cartridges ensured the predominance of breech-loading weapons and facilitated the manufacture of magazined guns. The Henry rifle led the way with its under-the-barrel 15-shot magazine and lever-loading action.

Cowboys could choose from a wide variety of weapons. Manufacturers produced muskets, shotguns, rifles, carbines, and many types of pistols— even the tiny derringer. Old-time cowboys used the word *gun* to refer only to pistols. Muskets and shotguns share a common attribute: they both have smooth-bored barrels. Rifles, carbines, and many pistols have rifled barrels. Rifling is grooving inside of the barrel that imparts a spin to the slug. The rotational inertia imparted by the grooves gives the slug a straighter, truer course.

Rifles and carbines achieved much greater popularity in the West than did smoothbores. Some famous figures, such as Doc Holliday, used

shotguns. The primary distinction between rifles and carbines is the length of the barrel. Generally, carbines had barrel lengths of 24 inches or less; rifles had longer barrels. The demand for carbines came from cowboys, cavalrymen, and others who spent time on horseback. The lighter weight and shorter length of the carbine allowed the cowboy to handle it more easily. Some carbines came fitted with saddle rings to allow simple storage. Almost every manufacturer that produced rifles offered them as carbines as well.

Many companies competed in producing rifles and carbines sold in the West. Some of the biggest names were Sharps, Remington, and Winchester. Popular among big-game hunters, Sharps rifles played a major part in the quick decimation of the buffalo herds. These single-shot rifles had a huge bore and a heavy slug capable of stopping a charging beast.

Remington also produced a single-shot rifle that attained fame. The company's Rolling Block rifle was constructed so the breech actually tightened during firing. This innovation enhanced safety and allowed the use of larger powder charges. Many shooters considered the Remington breechloader to be one of the most accurate rifles of the time.

Nevertheless, Remingtons could not compare with the sales volume of Winchester Model 1873

The Colt Peacemaker was one of the most popular guns carried by cowboys. The Frontier model .44 caliber, pictured here, was introduced in 1873. It used the same ammunition as another popular weapon, the Winchester '73 rifle.

rifles. These lever-action weapons loaded rounds from a tubular chamber under the barrel. Their reliability, power, and accuracy over moderate distances made the Model '73 *the* rifle of the West.

Handguns or pistols (guns in cowboy parlance), not carbines, became dominant in the cowboy mystique. Typically we think of revolvers, guns that incorporated a cylinder that revolved so that another cartridge could be fired. Another type of gun, the pepperbox, had multiple barrels that revolved. Pepperboxes never attained great popularity because they suffered from the dual problems of high weight and poor balance. Pepperboxes are not considered to be true revolvers.

Gunfighters depended upon their revolvers and their own skill to survive. Hours spent practicing the fast draw raised one's odds of living through a fight. Reputedly, gunslingers put a notch in their gun for each man they killed, though in fact, they rarely did so. Among other things, excessive notching could unbalance a weapon. Nevertheless, the **notcher** became part of western folklore.

Pistols could be of either single action or double action. Single-action guns required the operator to pull back the hammer into a cocked position before the trigger could be pulled to fire the round. The design of double-action guns allowed a pull of the trigger to rotate the cylinder, then cock and drop the hammer all in one motion. Despite the introduction of double-action guns in the 1850s, single-action guns remained dominant for decades.

Many companies manufactured pistols. Many westerners used Remington handguns, and some people considered the Smith and Wesson the finest revolver of the time. No other manufacturer gained the name recognition of Colt, however. The most famous model is the Colt Single Action Army, called the Peacemaker in its .45 caliber variety and the Frontier in its .44–40 form. The latter model could share ammunition with the popular Winchester Model 1873. With the introduction of the Frontier model in 1873, Colt achieved lasting fame.

Many pistols carried the Army and Navy designation. Army models had a .44 caliber bore, while Navy models used a smaller .36 caliber slug. The Army model was so named because it was made to U.S. Army specifications and often sold to the military. Navy models got their name in two ways. First the U.S. Navy contracted for the weapons; second, the first Colt Navy model had a cylinder engraved with a naval scene. Various other sizes of pistols also flowed from the factories, including pocket and holster pistols of many different calibers, beginning as small as the .22.

Guns took on many variations. One of the more interesting and storied was the Buntline Special. These revolvers have exceptionally long barrels, often more than a foot long. This variation takes its name from the pulp writer and promoter **Ned Buntline.**

The tiny derringer spread throughout the West as well. This large-bored, short-barreled weapon could be easily concealed almost anyplace on the body, ready for action in an instant. Because of its inaccuracy, the derringer could only be used reliably in close fighting. In popular western culture, the derringer is portrayed as a puny, cowardly weapon suitable only for **women,** cheating gamblers, and low-lifes. Real cowboys packed a Colt, not a derringer. (Cunningham 1962; Rosa 1969; Tractman 1974)

See also Colt; Fast Draw; Holster; Remington; Winchester.

—*Mark Mayer*

FIREWATER

Colloquial term for liquor. See Saloons.

FISH

Colloquial term for a yellow, oilskin slicker often used by cowboys.

A FISTFUL OF DOLLARS

Film (1966). See Eastwood, Clint.

FIVE BEANS IN THE WHEEL

Colloquial term meaning five cartridges in the six chambers of a revolver. Westerners often left the chamber under the hammer empty for safety reasons.

FIVE-EIGHTHS RIG

See Saddle.

FIXINS

This term usually meant tobacco and paper to roll cigarettes. It could also refer to **food**.

FLANK MAN

Also flank rider. See Trail Drive.

FLEA-TRAP

Accurate colloquialism for a cowboy's bedroll.

FOOD

Cowboys everywhere had only a few basic necessities. One was beef, preferably fresh. Another was cigarettes or cigars. Finally, cowboys liked **coffee** or another hot drink with plenty of caffeine.

Given his free choice, a cowboy anywhere in the Americas would eat beef several times a day. Cowboys spent their days herding and caring for cattle. It shouldn't surprise us that beef would suit the cowboy palette. The type of beef consumed by cowboys varied from country to country, however.

Cowboy Cuisine: United States and Canada
Breakfast Call

In the December 1938 issue of *Canadian Cattlemen,* rancher Fred Ings recalled a typical breakfast during a roundup in Canada in the 1880s:

Breakfast at daybreak was eaten in the mess tent, a hot substantial meal of meat, potatoes, bread, jam, with strong black coffee. Our dishes were tin and we ate sitting around on bed rolls or a box if one was handy, or on the ground.

Cowboys in the United States had similar **chuck** (also called grub or chow): canned and dried fruit, "overland trout" (bacon), beans, fresh meat, soda biscuits, tea, and coffee. Breakfast might include eggs or salt pork. Eggs, sometimes shipped west for considerable distances, tended to go bad. According to Winfred Blevins, westerners called an old, spoiled egg a "souvenir." Hands relished sourdough biscuits, which they favored over those made with buttermilk or baking powder. Ranch cooks baked biscuits in the versatile Dutch oven.

Dinner (the noon-time meal) and supper (evening) often looked very similar to breakfast, with the addition of beef and beans. As Puny Martin, an Oklahoma cowboy, put it, "Beef, beans, taters. That's what you had to have." One source attributed the often bowed legs and lean physique of the cowboy to his calcium-and calorie-deficient diet, although long hours on horseback likely played a bigger role.

Chuck-Wagon Cooking

Cowboys owe a hearty thanks to Charlie **Goodnight,** credited with inventing the chuck wagon. Needing to transport and cook food for a trail crew, Goodnight bought an Army surplus supply wagon and reinforced it. He replaced wooden axles with iron. He built a pantry-like chuck box on the back and strapped a water barrel on one side and a toolbox on the other. Six oxen pulled his chuck wagon.

The chuck box held cast-iron kettles, Dutch ovens, a three- to five-gallon coffee pot, and even such luxuries as sugar. The cook also carried medical supplies, including at least one bottle of whiskey "for medicinal purposes." Goodnight's creative invention plus the availability of "airtights" (canned goods) gave cowboys in the United States a diet much more varied than that of Latin American ranch hands.

Over the years, wagon manufacturers refined the original design. C. J. Christianson, who

Chuck Box and Boot Storage

1. Dried fruit
2. Flour
3. Sugar
4. Pinto beans
5. Roasted coffee beans
6. Plates, cups
7. Cutlery, flatware
8. Possible drawers:
   bandages, calomel, castor oil, needle, thread
9. Razor, strop, salt, lard, baking soda
10. Sourdough keg, matches, molasses
11. Coffee pot, whiskey
12. Skillets, Dutch ovens, iron pots, pot hooks
13. Wagon repair equipment:
    canvas bolts, hammer, nails, fitted lumber, wool
    batting, tar or fat for weatherproofing, saw blades,
    iron stakes

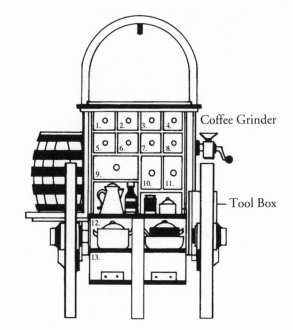

Coffee Grinder

Tool Box

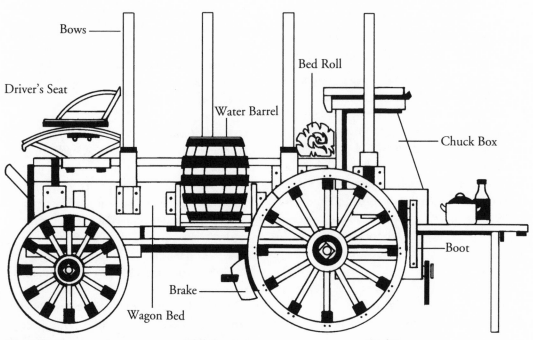

Bows

Driver's Seat

Bed Roll

Water Barrel

Chuck Box

Boot

Brake

Wagon Bed

Wagon Bed	Bulk Storage	Tool Box
Axle grease	Dried beef	Ax, shovel
Bedrolls	Dried fruit, apples	Branding irons
Extra wagon wheel	Flour	Extra pots, skillets
Guns, ammunition	Green coffee beans	Hobbles
Lantern, kerosene	Onions	Horseshoeing equipment
Raw beef, salt pork	Pinto beans	Rods for pot rack
Slickers	Potatoes	
Wagon sheet	Salt, sugar	
1/2 in. corral rope		

cowboyed in Canada from 1904 to 1909, described an early twentieth-century chuck wagon *(My Life on the Range,* 1968):

I want to say a word about the wagons used on a **roundup** in those days. Don't get them confused with the skeletons used in the chuckwagon races at the Calgary Stampede, pulled around the track by four trained race horses.

The wagon used on the range was a heavy ironed-up affair, but light running, high narrow wheels, narrow tires and wide gauge. There seemed to be two favorite makes used in those days, the "Studebaker" made in South Bend, Indiana and the "Peter Schuttler" made in Chicago, Illinois, both made to stand the roughest of use. Those wagons had to withstand a lot. They were loaded to the extent of about two ton at all times. The mess wagon was loaded with the cook stove, cook tent, a mess box, provisions of all kinds, enough to feed from 16 to 20 men for five or six weeks at a time without restocking. The bed wagon had all the bed rolls, rope or rawhide corrals, horseshoes, rope and tackling of all kinds and often wood.

Sometimes things could go wrong around the chuck wagon. Coosie would get ringy (the cook would get mad), and the hands would suffer. Dallas Poteet, who cowboyed in the Osage country of Oklahoma, recalled one chuck-wagon disaster:

There come a storm that first night we was out. Dang, it blowed everything away. Blowed the chuck box away on that covered wagon. Next morning that old cook, he just went out there and gathered that stuff up, just scooped it up off the ground, because [it] spilt the coffee, the sugar and everything else. So the rest of the way, the next two or three days, we had coffee [that was] half dirt and half coffee, and that old sourdough bread, it was part flour and part dirt.

Despite such adversity, inventive and adaptive ranch cooks created their own special cuisine from the basics of beef, beans, and bread. Cowboys branded cooks with a wide range of inventive names, some of which are fit to reprint: bean master, pot rustler, biscuit shooter, dough puncher, grub slinger, and coosie (from the Spanish term for cook, *cocinero).*

Range Fare

While riding the range, a cowboy's noon dinner might include some dried beef, dried fruit, sourdough biscuits, and perhaps a cup of coffee if he carried a pot in his saddlebags. According to cowhand Philip Ashton Rollins *(The Cowboy,* 1922), the bare necessities rolled into a slicker might include a "frying-pan, some flour, bacon, coffee, salt, and, as a substitute for yeast, either a bottle of sour dough or a can of baking-powder."

Meals at camp or at the bunkhouse offered greater variety and abundance. Pauline Barham cooked for Chapman-Barnard hands in Oklahoma during the 1940s. She recalled the following:

They were hungry. They would eat everything, and they enjoyed it. Beef roast and beans is the main thing for cowboys, I think. Hot biscuits. We made our own biscuits. And potatoes fixed some way. Always coffee. The coffee pot was on all the time.

Hot coals were placed on the lid of a biscuit kettle to create a more even distribution of heat.

Food was cooked in large cast iron pots hung over or placed on top of shallow fire pits dug in the dry soil.

Syrups and stewed prunes usually served as dessert. Coosie might also make a fruit pie, perhaps a "boggy-top" (open-faced with no top crust.). A real range cooking artist might even dress up a pie with "calf slobbers" (meringue.) Another challenge was "son-of-a-bitch-in-a-sack" (not to be confused with the stew described below), in which Coosie would sew dried fruit and dough into a sack and steam the concoction.

On the trail, canned tomatoes helped to quench thirst. Rollins notes that acidic tomato juice counteracted the ill effects of alkali dust inhaled by men on the trail. Even the greenest cook could whip up a batch of "pooch"—stewed tomatoes mixed with bread and sugar.

Make Mine Beef

Cowboys everywhere liked fresh beef and lots of it. Steaks, fried well-done in a cast-iron skillet, ranked high. A good cook would toss flour into the beef grease, let it brown up good, and serve up tasty gravy (called "Texas butter" or "sop") for the biscuits.

Almost any beef cut imaginable went into the legendary "son-of-a-bitch stew." (In polite company, cowboys would call the dish "son-of-a-gun" stew.) As Ramon F. Adams notes, "You throw everything in the pot but the hair, horns, and holler." Cooks preferred to have meat and parts from an unweaned calf. To the choicest meat, they added sweetbreads, marrow gut from between the two stomachs, kidneys, heart, liver, and tongue. Brains and flour thickened the mix, and onions and chilis sometimes added flavor. This was cowboy cuisine at its finest.

Profit-minded ranchers and trail bosses did not always provide a bounty of fresh beef. Granville Stuart, the well-known Montana rancher and politician, recorded that cowboys on the trail ate corn meal, sorghum molasses, beans, salt, and bacon. Game—including deer or, while they lasted, buffalo—might add meat to the regimen. As one cowboy—John K. Rollinson— remarked in *Wyoming Cattle Trails* (1948), "We could not keep ourselves in fresh meat like a cow outfit does on a roundup for the reason that we had a smaller crew than the average roundup uses, and we had no visitors to drop in for a meal. Another reason was that our animals were of large size, and with the weather so very hot, meat would not have kept fresh." Some ranchers practiced what the old range adage preached: "Only a fool eats his own beef!"

Calf Fries

At roundup, cowboys enjoyed another delicacy, variously called calf fries, mountain oysters, or prairie oysters. Whatever the term, these fried or roasted calves' testicles made gourmet eating for cowmen. Obviously, a large number of these prize delicacies could be gathered when hands castrated calves during roundup. Cowboys attributed to calf fries an amazing number of benefits. Some considered it a wonderful elixir or aphrodisiac.

Preparation might consist of nothing more than tossing the testicles into a branding fire and waiting for them to pop open, ready to eat. Stella Hughes, in *Chuck Wagon Cookin'*, offers a tastier recipe. She suggests soaking the mess in saltwater for an hour and then drying them. The oysters are then seasoned, rolled in flour or cornmeal, and fried in hot grease until crisp—a great end to a long day of branding. Another variant suggests soaking the harvest in buttermilk instead of salty water.

Mexican Vaquero Food

Mexican **vaqueros** also liked beef. F. Warner Robinson (*Scribner's Magazine* correspondent in Mexico in 1912) found vaqueros carrying fresh beef on their saddles (as did **gauchos**). "They sat gracefully astride mules, with their *serapes* [blankets] wound closely about them, each with a chunk of raw beef, bleeding and uncovered, dangling from his saddle. Starting for the mountains just at nightfall, with the raw freshly killed beef dripping blood from the saddle, the *maleta* [saddle bags] filled with cold *tortillas* and *frijoles* and tobacco, and the little tin cup covered with dirt and dust dangling from the saddle strings."

Mexican vaqueros cooked a special dish using only the head of a freshly killed yearling.

Wrapped in hide and a wet gunnysack, the head was buried in a shallow hole. It cooked slowly all night under a roaring fire. The meat, brains, and tongue provided a delectable repast the next day.

Vaqueros and Anglos in south Texas made and ate beef jerky as well. (Today German immigrants to such towns as Fredericksburg and New Braunfels continue to produce jerky in large, savory, sweet chunks.) The export of dried beef along with hides and tallow represented a major part of the pre-Anglo economy of California well into the nineteenth century. An average carcass might yield about 200 pounds of meat suitable for *carne seca* (jerky).

Llanero and *Huaso* Food

Instead of the biscuits favored by Canadian and American cowboys, **llaneros** ate *arepas* (thick corncakes). Thicker and harder than the Mexican corn tortilla, white- and yellow-corn arepas remain a popular food in Venezuela today. Beans were as much a mainstay on the llanos as on the North American ranges. In the United States, cowboys preferred red beans, but in Latin America, the choice might well be black beans. Llanos cuisine also developed dishes in addition to the staples of meat, beans, coffee, and corncakes. *Sancocho,* for example, is a tasty stew of meat or chicken and vegetables. The numerous rivers of the tropical plain also yielded a variety of fish. In fact, llaneros had to be expert swimmers and boatmen because of the annual floods that swept the lowland plains. These skills were not generally shared by other cowboy types.

Exploring the **llanos** in the late eighteenth century, German scientist Alexander von Humboldt noted of the inhabitants that "their food is meat dried in the air, and a little salted; and of this even their horses sometimes eat." If freshly killed beef was available, it was spitted and roasted by an open fire. Llaneros prized the kidney, liver, and ribs. George D. Flinter visited the llanos during the stormy independence wars and described, in his 1819 *History of the Revolution of Caracas,* the llanero method of cooking beef: "The general way of preparing the meat, is by cutting it up in large pieces of ten or twelve pounds each, and putting it on a huge wooden spit, and placing between every two pieces of meat, pieces of the heart, the liver, and large lumps of suet, this they call entreverado; they roast it before an immense wood fire." Lacking wood, llaneros used cow dung for the fire. They sometimes hunted jaguars, using dogs to track the quarry. The jaguar meat was either sold or eaten.

Huasos and llaneros often had to eat dried beef *(tasajo* or *charqui,* hence jerky). For them, fresh meat of any kind was a rare luxury. The tropical climate of the llanos made it impossible to preserve fresh meat, so the llanero often consumed dried beef. The tough, rangy creole cattle that dominated the Chilean range until the 1870s were better suited for dried than fresh meat. John Miers visited Chile in 1819, and in *Travels in Chile and La Plata* (1826), reported favorably on the jerky that "requires no salt, and will keep sweet many years if preserved in dry places." We should remember, however, that most of the dried beef went to slaves in Brazil and Cuba. That should leave little question about its palatability compared with other foods.

Gaucho Food

The gaucho had the most limited of all cowboy diets. Beef, *mate,* tobacco, and nothing more nourished gauchos for months at a time. Gauchos shared the disdain for milk found in **plains** regions elsewhere, but, unlike his counterparts, the gaucho also refused vegetables. Bread remained scarce on the **pampas** until the arrival of European farmers late in the nineteenth century. One British visitor, Alexander Caldcleugh, in the early 1820s remarked that gauchos viewed vegetables "with eyes of ridicule" and considered a man who would eat them "as little superior to the beasts of the field."

Many South American cowboys, including gauchos, llaneros, and huasos, spitted beef on a metal rod or *asador* and cooked it beside open coals. An entire calf, sheep, or goat might be spitted and roasted in this same fashion. Gauchos cut and consumed their *asado,* or beef roast, using a long swordlike *facón.* Like gauchos,

huasos used only long knives to eat their meat. The Argentine gaucho probably ate more beef than anyone else in the world.

Beef, washed down with highly caffeinic *mate* tea, constituted the gaucho's favorite meal. The temperate climate of the pampa permitted gauchos to carry fresh meat with them for a few days. They simply tied a few pieces to the saddle and cooked it briefly whenever and wherever hunger overtook them. Denied wood as fuel on the largely treeless pampa, the gaucho sometimes used dung or dried bones to build a fire. Wild cattle abounded on parts of the pampa through the mid-nineteenth century. Unmindful of waste, gauchos would rope and kill a cow only to consume some choice morsel and leave the remainder to rot. Gauchos favored the tongue and what they called *matambre,* the meat between the ribs and hide.

For special occasions, gauchos and huasos prepared a delicacy called *carne con cuero* (literally, meat with a hide). Chilean cooks stuffed a calf with a variety of foods, wrapped it in a cowhide, and slow-cooked it by a fire. The Argentine version of this dish often omitted the stuffing, but the hide still held in the juices and flavor. (Adams 1952; Anon. 1978; Blevins 1993; Brown 1971; Hughes 1974; Slatta 1992)

FOOT-AND-MOUTH DISEASE

See *Aftosa.*

FOR A FEW DOLLARS MORE

Film (1967). See Eastwood, Clint.

FORD, JOHN
(1895–1973)

Film director. See Films, Best Cowboy; Films, Cowboy.

FOREFOOTING

Roping an animal by the front legs.

FOREMAN, LEONARD LONDON

(1901–)

British-born author of formula westerns.

FOREMAN

Person in charge of assigning and directing daily work at a ranch.

FORK A HOSS

Colloquialism meaning to ride a horse.

FORMULA WESTERNS

See Pulp Novels.

FORTY ROD

Also forty rod lightning. Colloquial terms for liquor. See Saloons.

FOUND

Colloquial term for food.

FOX, NORMAN ARNOLD

(1911–1960)

Novelist who wrote formula westerns.

FOX FIRE

See Saint Elmo's Fire.

FRANTZ, JOE BERTRAM

(1917–1993)

Historian. See Historiography of the Cowboy.

FRENO

Also *brida*. Spanish term for bridle. See Tack.

FRIGORÍFICO

Chilled meat-packing plant. See Beef Cattle Industry.

FRITZ

William S. Hart's pinto pony that he rode in his movies.

FULL-RIGGED

A **saddle** that is completely leather-covered.

FUN

See Humor.

FUNDO

A *fundo* is a Chilean rural estate that often includes both ranching and farming. Chile's long, narrow central valley enjoys a temperate climate and good soils. These virtues make it excellent for agriculture and grazing. Since colonial times, a small number of landowners has controlled most of Chile's thin band of arable lands. In the seventeenth century, *fundos* raised mostly food for local markets and cattle for tallow exports to Peru. Wheat production picked up at the end of the century, but the small internal market limited production.

Scholars differ on the precise definition and size of a fundo. Historian Arnold J. Bauer says the term did not come into general use until the nineteenth century. It referred to a smaller farm, often devoted to irrigated agriculture. Estates of more than 5,000 hectares qualified as haciendas. In contrast, historian Brian Loveman says the terms *fundo* and *hacienda* are synonymous, both referring to large landed estates.

Regardless of the term used, it is clear that large estates dominated the Chilean countryside. In 1866 a visitor from the United States noted that "the farms are usually very large, frequently comprising several thousand acres, and herds of cattle five, ten, or twenty thousand in number are pastured on the elevated plains and tended by the rough huasos, till the period of their slaughter arrives."

Some fundos were subdivided during the latter half of the nineteenth century. The divided lands often took the form of tiny plots called *chacras* or *minifundia*. These holdings lacked the size necessary for profitable farming or grazing.

Land concentration increased in the early twentieth century. The gulf between Chile's small landed elite and the **huasos** and rural poor widened. Socialist Salvador Allende attempted to enforce land reform legislation passed under his predecessor Eduardo Frei, but the brutal military overthrow of his government in 1973 eliminated, for the time being, threats to the fundos of the rural elite. (Bauer 1975; Loveman 1976)

See also Huaso; Latifundia.

FUSTE

Anglicized to fusty; a Mexican **saddle** or wooden saddletree.

GAD

Colloquial term for **spur.**

GAFF

To **spur** a **horse.**

GALLEGOS, RÓMULO
(1884–1969)

Although he served briefly as president of
Venezuela in 1948, Rómulo Gallegos is best
remembered as the author of the widely praised
novel, *Doña Bárbara* (1929). This novel captures
the wildness and mystery of Venezuela's cowboy
country, the **llanos.** Interestingly, Gallegos spent
only eight days in the llanos prior to writing the
novel. He made up for this lack of firsthand
experience by studying **llanero** folklore and
legends extensively.

The novel gives a good sense of old-time
ranch life on the llanos. The hero (Santos
Luzardo), a city dweller, understands he has
to prove himself worthy if he is to command
the llaneros. The task is, of course, the
"Horsebreaking! the great test of the cowboy,
proof of the courage and skill these men were
waiting to attribute to him."

Gallegos also conveys much of the stark
beauty as well as the dangers of life on the llanos.
As a llanero sings while herding cattle through
the wet, tropical plain, "his song could be heard
from the middle of the wide river, in whose
muddy waters were lurking the treacherous
alligator, the electric eel, the ray, and voracious
schools of caribs, with the vultures hovering
overhead."

Gallegos was one of many writers in both
North and South America to explore conflict
between the frontier and the city. Like Domingo
Faustino **Sarmiento**'s *Facundo,* the Gallegos
novel pits civilization against barbarism. The
terrifying, powerful, and autocratic ranch
woman, Doña Bárbara, represents the power
of llanos barbarism. Civilization triumphs in
the person of Santos Luzardo. "Progress will
come to the Plain," says the civilizing hero, "and
barbarism will be conquered and retreat. Perhaps
we shall not see it, but our blood will sing with

the emotion of the ones who do." Resolution of
the struggle comes when Luzardo falls in love
with Marisela, Doña Bárbara's beautiful daughter.
(Liscano 1970)

GAMBLING

Balzac believed "the gambling passion lurks at
the bottom of every heart." While that is a bit of
an overstatement, it is certain that many cowboys
enjoyed betting. Whenever cowboys gathered,
odds were that money would change hands.
Cowboys bet on horse races and other **equestrian
games,** on cards, cock fights, and just about
anything you can imagine.

The Spanish contributed much to New
World culture, including a love of card games.
Tavern keepers were more than happy to host
games of chance. Many card games enjoyed on
cattle frontiers came from European origins.
Spain may have ranked as the card-playing
capital of medieval Europe—soldiers, sailors,
clerics, the rich, and the poor played cards often
and enthusiastically. Many Spaniards favored
canasta, a variant of rummy. That popular game,
along with many others, traveled from Spain to
the New World with the conquistadors. Despite
repeated prohibitions, games of chance remained
very popular throughout the Americas during
the colonial and modern periods.

Gambling in Latin America

Cowboys in different countries had their favorite
forms of gambling. In Mexico both men and
women of all classes patronized gambling halls
(salas). Women often worked as dealers. Spanish
monte, played like short faro, was the most
popular card game of Mexico. Far to the south,
Chileans enjoyed cards and a variety of dice games.

William MacCann, a nineteenth-century
visitor to Argentina, noted that the gaucho's
"chief amusement is card-playing, and they are
confirmed gamblers." A British consul, Thomas
J. Hutchinson, agreed: "Gambling is their life,
soul, and very existence." Gauchos favored a card
game called *truco.* Played with a 40-card deck,
the game included clever signaling and witty
table talk, with verbal sparring adding spice to

the game. In some cases, players even sang verses back and forth.

Gauchos created a wide range of gambling games. They enjoyed playing *taba* by the hour. The game was played with an abundant resource of the South American plains, the anklebone (talus or astragalus) of cattle or horses. Players tossed a bone. As with dice games, the outcome of the throw, heads or tails, determined the winner. Chilean *huasos* also played taba.

Cowboys everywhere participated in and bet on equestrian contests. Tavern owners often sponsored a horse race, ostrich hunt, or similar horseback event. Gauchos would converge from miles around to compete, gamble, and drink.

Gambling in the American West and Canada

Americans acquired a passion for gambling from both Spanish and English sources. Except for the Puritans, Englishmen of all social classes held gambling to be among the "lawful recreations."

The Puritans carried their reservations about gambling to the New World. In neither England nor the colonies, however, did they succeed in their efforts to banish gambling.

When we think of gambling in the United States, we often think of a dandified Mississippi riverboat gambler. Games of chance, however, traveled far west of the Mississippi. Every western **saloon** included a number of busy card tables. According to a Denver pioneer, writing in an 1859 letter, "There is more drinking and gambling here in one day than in Kansas City in six—in fact about one-half of the population do nothing else but drink whiskey and play cards."

During the 1870s, Kansas City, the "Cowboy Capital," offered a great choice of lavish saloons famed for gambling—the Crystal Palace, Alhambra, Lady Gay, Alamo, and Lone Star. In Cheyenne, gamblers enjoyed the hospitality of the Gold Room. The Bull's Head in Abilene drew crowds of professional gamblers, eager to separate a cowboy from his meager wages.

North and south of the border, cowboys spent much of their free time engaged in some form of gambling. Gauchos play truco *in this F. Molina Campos painting.*

Most cowboys who played cards preferred the simplicity and clarity of poker, especially draw and stud. Faro and monte also found favor. Cowboys distrusted complicated gambling machinery or fancy card games, just as they disliked most gadgets from the East. Many cowboys lost their hard-earned wages to more skillful gamblers at saloon tables.

Cheating was a commonplace business practice. A "card mechanic" might "jump the cut" and deal himself an especially good hand. "Buying chips" came to mean jumping into a fight—evidence of the close relationship between gambling and fighting. Ralph Compton's novel, *The Goodnight Trail* (1992), includes a delightful episode in which cowboys and an Apache take revenge on cheating gamblers in Santa Fe. A sharp-eyed Apache named Goose exposes a cheating dealer in front of a judge. With a Bowie knife, he punctuates the lesson by chopping off the dealer's little finger, and then removes a ring containing a tiny, embedded mirror. Goose has learned to count cards. He wins back several thousand dollars in gold that the saloon owner had previously stolen from the cowboys.

Cowboys would play poker each evening by the **roundup** camp fire, if the roundup boss permitted it. The *Kansas Cowboy* (28 March 1885) warned sternly that "gambling in cow camps is an evil which is commencing to attract the attention of thinking stockmen."

Many ranchers prohibited gambling at the home place and at roundups. Ranchers feared divisive fights among the men, and some opposed gambling as morally debasing. Furthermore, hands who played cards all night could not be expected to work well all day. Texas stockmen prohibited card playing during roundup. R. G. Head, manager of the Prairie Cattle Company, minced no words in his 1885 warning to his hands: "If you feel like you cannot live without gambling, be man enough to say so, get what is due you and go to town, or some place, where you can gamble unmolested. You cannot play cards in camp during the working season and do your work properly at the same time. It will not be tolerated, and any employee knowingly violating this rule will be subject to discharge" (*Trinidad Daily Advertiser,* 27 May 1885).

Gambling and drinking did not seem to be as widespread among Canadian cowboys as among their American counterparts, but Canadian cattleman Duncan McEachran, a generally reliable source, compared Alberta cowboys of the 1880s with sailors. Both worked very hard, but would then "blow it in," drinking and gambling in town. On the other hand, "George," a Montana cowboy who went to Alberta, described considerable differences between the two regions. In Montana, he said, "when I would get into a town I wanted to have a good time. I usually took a few drinks, and sometimes got into a game of poker, and generally left town 'broke.'" In sharp contrast, he found neither gambling nor whiskey readily available in Alberta. George actually saved some of his wages while working there.

Gambling, particularly mixed with drink, raised the specter of violence. A verse from the traditional song, "The Cowboy's Lament," warned of the perils of gambling and drink:

> It was once in the saddle I used to go
>   dashing,
> Once in the saddle I used to go gay;
> First to the dram house, then to the card
>   house,
> Got shot in the breast, I am dying today.

One has only to eye the giant neon signs of Las Vegas and Reno to see that the cowboy remains closely tied to western gambling. In Las Vegas, huge neon cowboys beckon the public into the Pioneer Club and other casinos along Glitter Gulch.

Cockfights

A cockfight *(riña de gallos)* would draw a large, boisterous crowd in either North or South America. Officials alternated between banning and trying to regulate fights. Whether legal or illegal, raising and fighting cocks absorbed the energy and attention of multitudes. Some municipal governments licensed and taxed the fights. Some towns even constructed special cockfight arenas. This was the case in Santiago, Chile. British Captain Allen F. Gardiner visited the Chilean capital in 1838. He recalled that on Sunday "from first dawn of daylight we were disturbed by the shrill crowing of the numerous cocks." By late Sunday morning, the first fights had begun. On the Venezuelan llanos, a good fight might draw a crowd of 200 to 300 fans, most eager to place bets. Matched for combat by weight, the ferocious birds usually gave spectators their money's worth.

Vaqueros in Mexico also enjoyed cockfights. On his *Old Corrals and Sagebrush* album, Ian **Tyson** sings a wonderful Mexican *corrido* (folk song) about a cock named Gallo de Cielo. The tale is something of a cockfighting parallel to Sylvester Stallone's *Rocky.* A young Mexican named Carlos Zaragoza steals the bedraggled rooster, who rises to become a champion fighting cock. Zaragoza hopes to win a fortune and "get back the land that [Pancho] Villa stole from father long ago." The corrido ends tragically with the death of the brave, fighting bird. Zaragoza loses his $50,000 bet and sadly buries his rooster.

John M. Findlay *(People of Chance)* points out that the English enjoyed many blood sports, including cockfights. The southern colonies of the eighteenth century provided most of the cockfighting fans in the colonial United States. Cockfighting marked a departure from the usually sharp lines of race and class that divided the South. Rich and poor cheered and bet on the fighting cocks. One observer noted with obvious distaste that in colonial Virginia, "genteel people" mingled at cockpits with "vulgar and debased whites" and slaves. Indeed, the University of South Carolina's mascot is the fighting gamecock.

As southerners migrated westward, they toted along cultural baggage, including a taste for cockfighting. In the West, some southerners set aside their racism and found a common bond with Mexicans in the cockpits. Despite bans, the contests remained popular into the twentieth

century. Indeed, their increasingly clandestine character added another element of excitement to the fights. (DeArment 1982; Findlay 1986; Jones 1973; Slatta 1992)

See also Saloons.

GARFIELD, BRIAN
(1939–)

Novelist who wrote formula westerns under various names. He also wrote some film scripts and an excellent summary of *Western Films* (1982).

GAUCHESCO

Fictional literature about the **gaucho,** sometimes written in his dialect, is known as *gauchesco.* The genre achieved national recognition and appreciation in Argentina, with poems, plays, and novels making the gaucho a hero. By comparison, most American cowboy literature was traditionally held in critical contempt.

We can trace published gaucho literature back to the late eighteenth century. Wherever gauchos gathered, someone would strum a *charango* (ukelele-style guitar) and sing traditional and improvised verses. Poetry and song formed an important element of traditional gaucho culture. In 1777 an anonymous artist published a poem written in gaucho dialect. It celebrated a Spanish victory over the Brazilian Portuguese.

Poet Bartolomé Hidalgo (1788–1823) succeeded in moving gaucho poetry from a lower-class pursuit into more respectable literary circles. Born in Montevideo, Uruguay, he forsook his occupation as a barber to fight for Argentina during the independence wars. During the early 1820s he wrote patriot verses in which two ex-soldiers (Ramón Contreras and Chano) recalled great battles. These *Diálogos patrióticos* became an important part of Argentina's early national literature. Hidalgo's ear for dialect and his firsthand war experiences gave his works a compelling, authentic ring.

Hidalgo's works inspired a rash of successors in both Uruguay and Argentina. In the mid-nineteenth century Hilario Ascasubi (1807–1875), a political activist as well as a writer, opposed the dictatorship of Juan Manuel de Rosas. The dictator responded to Ascasubi's criticism by jailing him and condemning him to death. The plucky poet made a daring escape and continued writing anti-Rosas verse in Montevideo, home to many liberals exiled by the dictator.

Ascasubi injected sharp political commentary into traditional gaucho verse. Some of his works, such as "Media Caña del Campo," became widely popular. Illiterate gauchos heard such verses recited, then memorized and repeated them. Ascasubi's publications include *Paulino Lucero* (1852, the year of Rosas' fall from power), *Aniceto el Gallo* (1864), and *Santos Vega* (1872).

Some writers, steeped in European cultural models, rejected gaucho dialect as lowbrow and unliterary. Esteban Echeverría (1805–1851) wrote romantic gaucho verse but eschewed dialect for a standard Spanish vocabulary. His poem "La cautiva" (1837) gained wide critical acclaim from the Francophile literati of Buenos Aires as well as the unlettered gauchos of the pampas. Like Ascasubi, Echeverría had to flee the wrath of Rosas. From exile in Montevideo, he wrote an important short political novel, *El matadero,* a powerful attack on the bloodthirsty Rosas dictatorship.

The greatest gauchesco poet, politician José Hernández (1834–1886), published *Martín Fierro,* a two-part epic poem, in 1872 and 1879. Using authentic dialect, Hernández recorded the injustices and persecution visited upon the gaucho by unscrupulous, oppressive civil and military officials. Elite critics again blasted the use of dialect. People and events in the poem ring true when compared with historical sources of the time. The masses recognized the truths expressed by Hernández; the poems became wildly popular and quickly went through dozens of authorized and unauthorized printings.

Argentine nationalism in the first decades of the twentieth century brought belated critical acclaim to *Martín Fierro.* Leading writers, such as Leopoldo Lugones, heaped praise on the work. Jorge Luis Borges, the quintessential cosmopolitan, used to enthrall audiences by quoting stanzas of the poem from memory. *Martín Fierro* became the national poem of Argentina. Walter Owens published a wonderfully wrought English translation in 1936.

No poet has equaled the achievements of Hernández. Estanislao del Campo (1835–1880), however, left a single contribution also worth mentioning. After a military career, del Campo became a politician and journalist. Most of his works are not memorable, but *Fausto* (1866), a hilarious spoof of the famous opera, is the great exception. The plot is simple. A gaucho wanders into a performance of *Faust* at the famous Colon Theater in Buenos Aires. Later he retells the story to a friend, giving the opera a unique, outrageous gaucho interpretation. Although lacking the depth and authenticity of Hernández, del Campo made a delightful contribution to Argentine popular letters. Again, Walter Owen provided an excellent translation into English (1943).

The outpouring of gaucho prose has been as extensive as that of verse. Uruguay produced a number of outstanding novelists writing in the gauchesco genre. A strong, brave, and free gaucho hero appears in novels by Eduardo Acevedo Díaz (1851–1921). His trilogy—*Nativa* (1880), *Grito de Gloria* (1884), *Ismael* (1888)—makes the gaucho a hero in Uruguay's struggle for independence. His fourth major work, *Soledad* (1894), reflects a warm understanding and sympathy for the gaucho and his culture.

Acevedo inspired an entire generation of writers working in the *nativista* tradition, one which explored sympathetically the lives and problems of Uruguay's traditional rural society and its typical figure, the gaucho. In the naturalistic works of Javier de Viana (1869–1926), the gaucho has lost his freedom and is reduced to peonage. The works of Acevedo and Viana accurately mirror the historical reality of changing conditions during the nineteenth century. Among Viana's strongest novels are *Campo* (1896), *Guri* (1898), and *Gaucha* (1899). Carlos Reyles (1868–1938), Justino Zavala

Muñiz (1898–1968), and others also contributed to Uruguay's vast fictional literature of gaucho life.

Neighboring Argentina produced its own stable of talented gaucho novelists. *Juan Moreira,* by Eduardo Gutiérrez (1851–1889), appeared in 1879. Based on the life of a famous gaucho outlaw, it is Argentina's first significant gaucho novel. (Domingo Faustino **Sarmiento** had treated the gaucho at length in 1845 in *Facundo.* This fascinating, rambling book, however, is a polemic against the Rosas dictatorship rather than a novel.)

Many quaint, romanticized tales of gaucho life, similar to **pulp novels** of the American cowboy, also appeared in Argentina. Several important writers, however, took gaucho prose several levels above the pulps. Benito Lynch (1885–1951) sensitively probed the motivations and mentality of his gaucho characters. His first novel, *Los Caranchos del "La Florida,"* appeared in 1916. Two years later he followed up with *Raquela.*

Lynch returned to the successful ploy used by Campo, the gulf of cultural misunderstanding between the gaucho and European culture. Lynch, however, wrote a realistic novel, not a humorous satire. *El inglés de los güesos* (1924) examines mutual misunderstandings between people of the **pampas** and a visiting English archaeologist, Mr. James Gray. The title comes from Gray's halting Spanish explanation of his work, "I look for old bones" *(güesos).* In 1930 he published the skillful *El romance de un gaucho,* written entirely in dialect.

Leopoldo Lugones, Ricardo Rojas, Manuel Gálvez, Ezequiel Martínez Estrada, and other leading Argentine writers also treated and lauded gaucho themes. The high-water mark of the gaucho novel, however, came in 1926, when Ricardo Güiraldes published his classic *Don Segundo Sombra.* This touching tale of a boy learning the ways of gaucho life is still appreciated by readers in Argentina and abroad. Güiraldes sketched a memorable portrait of Segundo Sombra, the gaucho *domador* (**bronc buster**):

He was not really so big. What made him seem so, as he appears to me even today, was the sense of power flowing from his body. His chest was enormous and his joints big-boned like those of a horse. His feet were short and high-arched; his hands thick and leathery like the scales of an armadillo. His skin was copper-hued and his eyes slanted slightly toward his temples.

A plain pigskin belt girded his waist. The short blouse was caught up by the bone-handled knife from which swung a rough, plaited quirt, dark with use. His *chiripá* [baggy pants] was long and coarse, and a plain black kerchief was knotted around his neck with the ends across his shoulders. He had split his *alpargatas* at the instep to make room for the fleshy foot.

Regrettably, Güiraldes died within a year of the publication of his wonderful novel. According to self-trained historian Edward Laroque Tinker, "250 sad and silent gauchos, mounted on horses of every color, their silver bridles scintillating through the thin dust raised by thousands of hoofs, followed his coffin to the grave."

Gaucho literature remains a beloved, vibrant part of the national cultures of Argentina and Uruguay. Argentines celebrate November 10, the birthday of José Hernández, as the "Day of Tradition." Even urban sophisticates who get no closer to gaucho life than a giant steak at a Buenos Aires restaurant identify with the literature and mythology of the gaucho. (Borges and Bioy Casares 1955; Nichols 1968; Slatta 1992; Tinker 1967)

GAUCHO

From the 1600s on, gauchos—South American cowboys—roamed the broad plains or pampas of the Río de la Plata through what is today Argentina, Uruguay, Paraguay, and Rio Grande do Sul, Brazil. Early gauchos hunted the prolific herds of wild cattle and horses of the plains. They believed in use rights—free access to the pampa's resources of land, water, and livestock.

Feral livestock was common in the gaucho's realm. Eighteenth-century observers recorded that some herds took hours to pass, much like the early bison herds of the Great Plains. Indians of the **pampas,** who traditionally had hunted the *guanaco,* expanded their hunting activities, capturing and taming wild horses to use as mounts for hunting cattle. They developed equestrian skills that made them dangerous adversaries to the encroaching Spanish.

Markets for hides and by-products offered a ready source of income to anyone with the skill and energy to chase, kill, and skin cattle. By the mid-eighteenth century, these wild-cattle hunters had developed a subculture well suited to the plains they inhabited.

Some riders worked for merchants who held official hunting licenses *(acciónes).* Others free-lanced illegally. During the colonial era the vast herds of wild cattle and horses on the plains seemed inexhaustible. Gauchos scorned or ignored the restrictions of remote government officials who tried to monopolize the killing of cattle.

Riders would use long lances tipped with hocking blades to hamstring fleeing cattle. After felling many, they returned to slit each animal's throat and stripped off the hide. A gaucho might slice out the tongue, considered a delicacy, for a meal. Staked out on the plains to dry, the hides would later be collected for export to Spain. Organized ranches, domesticated cattle, slaughterhouses, and the production of beef jerky would come later.

Gradually, the depletion of livestock and the desire to extract greater profits brought changes to the livestock economy. Spanish colonial officials sought to limit access to the wild-cattle herds. Wealthier ranchers and merchants began to extend their domination over the resources of the **plains,** including labor. The rise of ranches and an organized livestock industry profoundly changed the gaucho's life and work.

The gaucho borrowed freely from Indians of the pampa. He usually wore a poncho over a *chiripá* (baggy, diaper-like pants). Both garments came from South American Indians. A stout leather belt *(tirador)* held up his pants. Soft **boots** made from the leg skins of a colt **(botas de potro)** and dangling iron **spurs** covered his feet. He armed himself with the *bolas* (or *boleadoras),* a dangerous weapon developed by Indians. A long, swordlike knife *(facón)* was secured through the back of a rider's leather belt so it would not kill a gaucho who accidentally pitched forward off his horse.

Colonial officials branded most wild-cattle hunters as outlaws. The terms *gaucho* and *gauderio* appear in print during the 1740s. As used by Spanish colonial officials, both terms meant vagrant or rustler. To officials, the unlettered, uncultured, uncivilized gaucho was not significantly better than the Indians of the **pampas,** who were considered savages.

Gauchos became the targets of vagrancy and military conscription laws designed to end their free-riding life-style. During the eighteenth century, Argentine gaucho conscripts fought as **blandengues,** irregular frontier militiamen. Military service against Indians on the frontier, during the British invasions of 1806 and 1807, and against the Spanish during the independence wars improved the gaucho's image somewhat. In Uruguay, José Gervasio Artigas ably led his gaucho army. The word *gaucho* came to mean a plainsman who hunted or tended cattle on horseback and who wore traditional dress.

William Henry Webster, a British naval surgeon, described the traditional dress and demeanor of an Uruguayan gaucho of the late 1820s in his 1834 *Narrative of a Voyage to the Southern Altantic Ocean:*

> His complexion is a swarthy brown, his hair is generally black and long, sometimes platted and surmounted by a small-brimmed neat-looking hat. His shoulders and body are concealed by his poncho, and by the variety and mixture of its colours, in which bright scarlet and yellow are sometimes particularly conspicuous, adds much to the general effect. It descends only low enough to leave the fringe of his white trousers conspicuous, over the feet, which frequently are uncovered.

Charles Darwin visited the pampa in the early 1830s, a critical period in Argentine political life. Rancher Juan Manuel de Rosas had become governor of the province of Buenos Aires and de facto dictator of the young Argentine nation. Darwin recorded his impressions of gaucho character and appearance in his *Journal of Researches* (1839):

> At night we stopped at a *pulpería,* or drinking-shop. During the evening a great number of Gauchos came in to drink spirits and smoke cigars: their appearance is very striking; they are generally tall and handsome, but with a proud and dissolute expression of countenance. They frequently wear their mustaches and long black hair curling down their backs. With their brightly-coloured garments, great spurs clanking about their heels, and knives stuck as daggers (and often so used) at their waists, they look a very different race of men from what might be expected from their name of Gauchos, or simple countrymen. Their politeness is excessive: they never drink their spirits without expecting you to taste it; but whilst making their exceedingly graceful bow, they seem quite as ready, if occasion offered, to cut your throat.

Somewhat later Scottish writer Robert B. Cunninghame Graham recorded a memorable if slightly romanticized vision of the gaucho in his essay "La Pampa."

> Nothing could be more typical of the wild life of forty years ago [about 1862] upon the plains than was the figure of a Gaucho dressed in his poncho and his *chiripá* [baggy, diaper-like pants], his naked toes clutching the stirrups, his long iron spurs kept in position by a thong of hide dangling below his heels, his hair bound back by a red silk handkerchief, his eyes ablaze, his silver knife passed through his sash and *tirador* [belt], and sticking out just under his right elbow, his *pingo* [horse] with its mane cut into castles and its long tail floating out in the breeze, as, twisting *las tres Marías* [bolas] round his head, he flew like lightning down a slope, which a mere European horseman would have looked on as certain death, intent to 'ball' one of a band of fleet *ñandús* [rheas, ostriches] all sailing down the wind.

As established ranches replaced the wild herds, gauchos began working as ranch hands. At most times of the year, ranch day labor was not needed. A small staff of permanent peons could tend the animals adequately. Most gauchos found ranch employment for only a few months a year. That was all that ranchers required. Gauchos hired themselves out by the day during the **roundup** and branding season.

All gauchos could ride reasonably well. A highly skilled horseman would work as a *domador* or **bronc buster.** A domador could tame any wild horse to the **saddle.** As long as wild horses remained plentiful, the domador worked with brutal efficiency. Horses often suffered injury or death. The demand for his special skills earned the bronco buster premium rural wages. By the late nineteenth century wild horses became scarce and mounts became more costly. Harsh, traditional *criollo* taming methods gave way to gentler ones.

A small minority of gauchos held permanent positions as year-round ranch peons, but even permanent workers were prone to quit their jobs and ride off. In some cases, such departures were prompted by the chance to earn higher wages by the day during roundups. Many ranchers felt that both day laborers and permanent peons drank and gambled too much. The landed elite worked assiduously to tame the free-riding gaucho. They wanted docile peons who were willing to work hard for low wages.

Unemployed gauchos hunted rheas for the prized feathers that were exported to satisfy the vanities of European fashion. Gangs of ostrich hunters drew the wrath of ranchers because they scattered livestock and sometimes set range fires

This no-nonsense South American cowboy wears traditional gaucho attire, including a brimmed hat, a vest, bombachas—*baggy trousers from the nineteenth century—and a belt decorated with silver with a* facón *hanging from the belt at his side.*

to drive ostriches (technically rheas) into the open plains where the bolas could do their work.

Wild cattle remained on much of the pampas through the mid-nineteenth century. Gauchos would kill these animals and sell their hides and tallow at the local pulpería. These migratory types, whom Charles Darwin found lounging about the tavern, smoking, drinking, and **gambling,** were widely held to be responsible for most rural crimes, especially **rustling.**

To be sure, some gauchos became bandits and rustlers. A gaucho named Juan Moreira, for example, worked as a bandit and "enforcer" for a political party. After his death at the hands of the police, he came to be celebrated in Argentine poetry and prose. In the early 1880s, a bandit gang led by the Barrientos brothers terrorized the Tres Arroyos area of Buenos Aires province. Such gaucho criminals were in the minority, however. More often, gauchos' lawbreaking reflected their traditional belief in common-use rights. They became bandits because legitimate alternatives proved very few.

Throughout their history, gauchos have held to simple, clear values and a simple set of goals. They wished to ride freely about the plains wherever and whenever they chose. They rejected and resisted as best they could attempts to alter or regulate their lives. The abundance of the plains permitted gauchos to live doing little or no wage labor, as long as wild livestock and game animals roamed the plains. Gauchos could exchange hides or ostrich feathers for *mate* (a bitter, caffeine-rich tea), tobacco, and liquor. The toss of a lasso brought a tasty beef dinner, washed down with large amounts of *mate*.

During the colonial era of wild-cattle hunts, hostile Indians, and weak governmental authority, gauchos stood a chance of maintaining their free-riding lives. A horse, a knife, beef, *mate,* and tobacco accounted for most of the gaucho's worldly needs, and these the pampa provided.

While independence wars raged elsewhere in Latin America, Argentina escaped any direct attack and devastation. Except for short-lived, localized invasions by the British in 1806 and 1807, Argentina suffered only the self-induced

pillage of civil war during the nineteenth century. During the fight against the Spanish, the able gaucho cavalry of Martín **Güemes** held off royalists in the north. The towering Andes protected the west, and unsettled Patagonia buffered the south.

The Argentine pampa emerged from the independence period with its livestock richness intact. Wild herds, if somewhat less plentiful than during the eighteenth century, still represented a considerable source of wealth. Many *estancieros,* or ranchers, began to tame the wild cattle and claim exclusive grazing rights to choice areas of the pampa and ownership of all cattle thereon.

Buffered from the ravages of the independence wars, the livestock industry of the Río de la Plata expanded. British and Argentine investors established a new *saladero,* or meat-drying plant, around Buenos Aires. Dried beef exports joined the traditional trade in hides and tallow.

Merchants and prestigious ranchers on the Argentine pampa engaged in widespread "contraband capitalism," wherein they bought stolen wool, hides, and other goods from gauchos and Indians. These profit-minded middlemen then brokered the fruits of the countryside to export merchants in Buenos Aires. Outlaws, whether deserters, bandits, or worse, could sometimes count on protection from chronically labor-short Argentine ranchers. An estanciero in need of temporary hired hands during the busy roundup and branding season would ask few questions about a gaucho's background.

The nation's growing prosperity carried with it changes that threatened the gaucho's traditional way. The landed elite, masters of a burgeoning livestock industry, instituted repressive measures to control rural labor, always in short supply in the region. They began husbanding livestock wealth more carefully and asserting control over the land itself. Both of these concepts were alien to the gaucho.

From the 1820s on, elites ruling from the port city of Buenos Aires waged military and political war against the gaucho population. They passed a plethora of restrictive laws. Internal passports, working papers, military conscription, and vagrancy laws curtailed the movements of gauchos. Elite policy had two main goals: to make the gaucho fight in the frontier militia against another threat—the Indians of the plains—and to transform him into a docile, obedient ranch peon.

Military patrols scoured the countryside to recruit vagrants and deserters—that is, gauchos—for military service. Leaders in newly independent Argentina faced the same dilemma that had bedeviled colonial officials. Gauchos had no interest in fighting Indians to protect the interests of the landed elite. As a result, Argentine officers faced repeated Indian incursions shorthanded until the latter decades of the nineteenth century.

Nineteenth-century administrations, including the long dictatorship of Juan Manual de Rosas during the 1830s and 1840s, extended the efforts to subdue the gaucho. Beginning with Buenos Aires province in 1865, officials formulated comprehensive rural codes that sounded the death knell for the gaucho way of life. These broad-ranging codes, backed with better-armed and more diligent police and military forces, virtually outlawed the gaucho life.

No area of gaucho life went untouched. The ranching elite meant to expunge all relics of the gaucho's alleged barbarism. Some ranchers forced diet changes to save money and improve worker efficiency. The traditional fare of self-service beef and *mate* around an open fire gave way to measured cafeteria-style rations. Cecilio López, a landowner in Buenos Aires province, estimated that the changes cut his expenses by 40 percent. López also banned the drinking of *mate*—a move akin to denying **coffee** to Texas cowboys—on the grounds that it wasted too much time.

New laws forbade the gaucho's traditional homemade boots, crafted from the leg skins of a colt. As early as 1856, ranchers demanded laws against homemade boots and leather saddle linings. Ranchers charged that gauchos stole and killed horses simply to make boots.

Imported textiles and manufactured boots appeared throughout the pampa. The traditional chiripá yielded to bloused trousers imported from Europe *(bombachas)*. (These pants are the model for the high-fashion women's gaucho pants that make an appearance every decade or so.)

In stripping the gaucho of his traditional dress, diet, and pursuits, the landed elite made his self-sufficient survival impossible. By the 1880s gauchos faced few viable legal options. They also faced military conscription under penurious conditions. Soldiers encountered harsh corporal punishments, meager and late pay, and few incentives to do anything other than desert. Forced recruits saw little incentive to serve.

Many gauchos deserted and fled to the remote frontier, beyond the pale of the law. These frontiersmen usually led an outlaw existence to survive. Some of the last groups of gauchos were illegal bands of rhea hunters and rustlers who killed cattle illegally in remote frontier areas.

The landed elite working with Europeanized politicians gradually subdued the gaucho and radically altered his life. The gaucho retained his long hair, beard, and poncho. To be sure, gauchos remained, just as cowboys persisted after the closing of the open range in the American West. Their ability to maintain the traditional way of life on the open range, however, largely disappeared during the last third of the nineteenth century.

Writer John H. White painted an unhappy portrait of the transition from gaucho to docile ranch peon in *Argentina* (1942): "The last gaucho has galloped across the far-away horizon of the pampas and into the twilight of history, and Argentina has lost its most characteristic and attractive citizen. His successor is a poor, miserable, underpaid peon who is called a *paisano* [countryman] but never a gaucho." By the late nineteenth century, the gaucho had passed from the realm of history into folklore. (Nichols 1968; Slatta 1992; Tinker 1967)

See also Vaquería; Gauchesco.

GAÚCHO

The *gaúcho,* the cowboy of Rio Grande do Sul, Brazil's southernmost state, developed along lines very similar to his Spanish cousin, the **gaucho.** Similarities in dress, language, and custom tie the two groups together. Both groups began as seventeenth-century wild-cattle hunters exploiting vast herds of feral livestock. The *campanha,* the lush, rolling grasslands of southern Brazil, held a bounty of wild livestock. This frontier abundance shaped the gaúcho's life and values, just as the abundance of animals on the **pampas** to the south shaped the gaucho of Argentina and Uruguay. Fiercely independent, the gaúcho resisted the constraints of law, but owing to his superb horsemanship and cavalry skills, he often faced military conscription.

Origins of Ranching in Southern Brazil

In Brazil, as in Mexico, missions played an important role in the growth of the livestock industry. Priests trained Indian novices to work cattle. On Argentina's pampas, in contrast, religious missions played virtually no frontier economic or social role.

Beginning in 1535, Jesuits began raising livestock on their missions in the interior of South America (southern Brazil, Paraguay, northern Argentina, and Uruguay). The Jesuit missions soon faced a dangerous threat from *bandeirantes* (slave raiders) based in São Paulo, Brazil. Every few years these slave hunters launched massive expeditions into the interior. Thousands of Portuguese men and captive Indian bearers comprised an expedition. They scoured the South American interior for anything of value, including Indian slaves. These slaving expeditions might last for several years before the hunters returned to São Paulo with their booty.

Bandeirantes found it difficult to chase down and capture scattered nomadic tribes. They learned that it was much easier to capture and enslave sedentary mission Indians. Bandeirantes destroyed many Jesuit missions, carried off the

neophytes, and left thousands of **cattle** abandoned.

Jesuit missionaries moved some livestock into southern Brazil in the 1620s. Ranchers and priests brought many more animals during the following decade. The Brazilian southern plains, called Campo Gerais during the colonial era, had an abundance of well-watered pastureland. From about 1637 to 1687, frontiersmen considered feral cattle in Rio Grande do Sul part of the public domain. Anyone could avail themselves of these wild animals. As in Argentina, only the hides of wild cattle held any market value.

Wild-cattle hunting began to give way to more settled ranch life during the eighteenth century. Juan de Magalhaes established his *estancia* (cattle ranch) in Rio Grande do Sul in 1715. The rise of such ranches set up conflict with wild-cattle hunters. Ranchers challenged free access to wild animals and claimed title to land and cattle.

Despite setbacks suffered at the hands of raiders, the Jesuits continued their missionizing efforts. In about 1720, Jesuits drove an estimated 80,000 to 100,000 head of cattle from Vaquería del Mar in Uruguay north to Campos da Vacaria. The impressive drive covered more than 300 miles, and the hardy drovers had to cut a 17-mile stretch of trail through dense forest. The mission the Jesuits established became the town of Vacaria dos Pinhais in Rio Grande do Sul.

Static Frontier

The cattle frontier of southern Brazil and northern Uruguay remained relatively static from the late eighteenth century through much of the nineteenth century. Beef jerky *(charque)* joined hides as a marketable product. Brazilian ranchers enjoyed an internal market for jerky. Slave owners fed the tough, stringy meat to their slaves (slavery lasted in Brazil until 1888).

In 1793 the captaincy of Rio Grande exported 13,000 arrobas of dried meat. (An arroba is a unit of weight equalling 11.5 kilograms or about 25 pounds.) About a decade later the figure had jumped to 600,000 arrobas as *charqueadas* (beef-drying plants) multiplied. Slaves in Cuba provided a ready market throughout the nineteenth century.

French traveler Auguste Saint-Hilaire visited Rio Grande do Sul, Brazil, in the early 1820s. He commented that "the cattle are left completely to the laws of nature. They are not cared for in any way. They are not even given salt as the cattle in Minas [Gerais] are. They are almost wild." A German visitor to the region commented in 1829 that "the cattle are not well cared for" and "horses are badly treated too."

Not until the mid-nineteenth century did ranchers in southern Brazil begin to furnish cattle with salt. Some ranchers added wire **fencing** after the 1880s, but borderlands cattle production, work techniques, and social relations changed very little. Ranchers in Rio Grande and northern Uruguay continued to raise cattle for the traditional hide and jerky markets for decades after ranchers elsewhere diversified into the more lucrative chilled beef trade.

During the nineteenth century, a robust if primitive dried-beef industry developed in Rio Grande do Sul and northern Uruguay. Open-range ranching and mostly unimproved livestock characterized this border region into the twentieth century.

Gaúcho in Literature and Mythology
Both the Brazilian gaúcho and the *vaqueiro* to the north remained regional types. Neither gained the national stature enjoyed by gauchos of Uruguay and Argentina or the cowboy in the United States. The mythology surrounding the bandeirante slave hunters of colonial São Paulo looms much larger in the nation's culture. The mythical bandeirante became the moral equivalent of historian Frederick Jackson Turner's hardy frontiersman, an archetype of Brazilian national identity, and a force in cementing Brazilian national unity.

João Capistrano de Abreu, Cassiano Ricardo, Gilberto Freyre, and Euclides da Cunha and other Brazilian intellectuals came to believe that the miscegenation in Brazil gave rise to more democratic race relations. The mestizo bandeirantes became heroes of this myth.

Ricardo depicted the slavers as explorers who successfully bridged the cultural and racial gap between the Portuguese and indigenous cultures.

Some Brazilians sought to transform the slave hunter into a national paradigm of democratic frontier spirit and enterprise. Bandeirantes explored and expanded the national territory (at the expense of Spanish America) and stimulated the economic development and settlement of the frontier. As noted above, the historical reality of these rapacious, brutal, plundering raiders was quite different from Brazilian mythology.

Although the gaúcho did not become a national hero in Brazil, he did attain important regional status. A vibrant literature developed on the southern plains of Brazil. The *campanha* of Rio Grande do Sul and its gaúchos became storied figures in regional literature and folklore. (Chasteen 1988; Prado, Jr. 1967; Slatta 1990)

GAUDERIO
Early pejorative term for the rural poor of the **pampas,** later replaced by the term *gaucho.*

GENTLE A HORSE
To break a horse to the **saddle,** using one of a variety of techniques. See Bronc Buster.

GIBSON, HOOT
(1892–1962)
B-Western movie actor (also known as Edmund Richard).

GIG
To **spur** a horse.

GILLEY, MICKEY
Country singer, club owner. See Music.

GIRLS OF THE LINE
Prostitutes.

GIRLS RODEO ASSOCIATION
See Rodeo.

GIRTH

Pronounced as girt, a Texas term for the cinch on a **saddle.**

GLIDDEN, FREDERICK DILLEY
(1908–1975)

Novelist who wrote formula westerns under various names.

GLIDDEN, JOSEPH
(1813–1906)

See Fencing.

GOAT MEAT

Colloquial term for venison killed out of season.

GOOD NEWS

Novel. See Abbey, Edward.

THE GOOD, THE BAD, AND THE UGLY

Film (1966). See Eastwood, Clint.

GOODNIGHT, CHARLES
(1836–1929)

Cattleman and trailblazer Charles Goodnight was born in Macoupin County, Illinois, but his family headed west to Milam County, Texas, in 1846. In 1857 he moved to Palo Pinto County, Texas, where he later worked as an Indian scout and Texas Ranger. During the Civil War he continued his work as a scout for a Confederate frontier regiment, and he saw considerable action against Indians.

After the war Goodnight planned to raise and sell **cattle.** In 1866 he formed an informal partnership with Oliver Loving. The Kentucky-born Loving moved to Lamar County, Texas, in 1845, then resettled in Collin County a year later. In 1855 he moved west again and built a home and general store in Palo Pinto County on the Red Fork of the Brazos River near Fort Belknap, Texas. He made his mark as a trail driver by moving a herd of **longhorns** all the way from west Texas to Chicago. He supplied beef to the Confederacy during the Civil War.

Goodnight and Loving teamed up to drive cattle from Fort Belknap to Fort Sumner, New Mexico. This route became known as the Goodnight-Loving Trail and became a heavily traveled cattle route. The inventive Goodnight is credited with creating the first chuck wagon by modifying a covered wagon for cooking on the trail (see Food).

Goodnight showed his intelligence and ingenuity in another way. On an 1867 **trail drive,** he observed that a bull's testicles became battered and bruised as the animals lumbered down the trail day after day. Two of his bulls died and a third had become quite ill from enlarged testicles. Goodnight decided that lancing the wound might ease the animal's suffering. Then he struck upon a way to solve the problem itself.

Goodnight pushed the bull's testicles up against its belly and cut off the scrotum. He then sewed the wound closed, leaving the testicles riding close to the abdomen instead of swinging low between the bull's legs. The bull recovered, and Goodnight repeated the operation on his other bulls. Other ranchers also began performing the operation, which came to be known as "Goodnighting," in honor of the inventor.

Loving died in 1867 of complications from wounds inflicted by a Comanche raiding party. Goodnight then joined up with cattleman John **Chisum** and continued to drive cattle to New Mexico. In the mid-1870s, Goodnight extended his cattle trailblazing from Alamagordo Creek, New Mexico, to Granada, Colorado, a route later extended north to Cheyenne, Wyoming. His ranching efforts in Colorado, however, did not meet with the great success of his Texas operations.

In 1876 Goodnight moved his operations to Palo Duro Canyon, about 12 miles east of Canyon, Texas. Kent Ruth (*Landmarks of the West,* 1963) described his arrival:

Palo Duro, nearly a thousand feet in depth and varying in width from a few hundred yards to several miles, had the water, wood, and grass to provide an unexcelled winter range for cattle, and here, in late 1876, Goodnight ran his herd down a 700-foot rockslide to the grassy bottom of the canyon. The dismantled chuck wagon and a supply of provisions were packed down and the "Old Home Ranch"—first in the Texas Panhandle—was established: a few corrals and picket houses built with nearby timber.

In 1877 Goodnight formed a partnership with Scotch-Irish financier, John George Adair. Adair had left his New York brokerage in 1874 to participate in a buffalo hunt. He shot his own horse and nearly killed himself, however, and the buffalo remained unscathed. Nevertheless, Adair liked the West and moved his business to Denver, where he met Goodnight. Their JA Ranch grew to include over 1,000,000 acres and 100,000 head of cattle.

Beginning in 1880, Goodnight pushed hard to create the Panhandle Stock Association of Texas. Through this organization, ranchers sought to improve cattle breeds and end **rustling**. Goodnight served as the first president of the association and always maintained that it benefited all ranchers, large and small.

Throughout his life Goodnight had turned his creative mind toward nature. At the JA he raised many different **cattle breeds** and undertook some breeding experiments. He managed to save and maintain a small herd of southern buffalo stock on his ranch. In his most ambitious project, he tried to crossbreed Angus cattle and buffalo to create "cattalo." The offspring proved mostly sterile, so this expensive experiment earned Goodnight no money. His buffalo herd, however, played a key role in the preservation of plains buffalo in the face of almost complete extinction. Another invention proved more successful. Goodnight created a side saddle for horsewomen that enjoyed great popularity in the West.

Two years after Adair's death in 1885, Goodnight divided the JA with his partner's widow, Cornelia. Five years later he sold his

With the invention of the chuck wagon by Charles Goodnight, meals became slightly more elaborate. More food and utensils were available to cook for the hungry cowhands. This photograph shows a group of cowhands relaxing with a little grub.

share. In his remaining years Goodnight invested in a Mexican mine and worked the Goodnight Ranch in Goodnight, Texas. He continued to spend most of his time, however, at the Old Home Ranch in Palo Duro Canyon, near present-day Canyon, Texas. In 1929 he died of a heart attack in Tucson, Arizona, three years after the death of his wife. Goodnight's legacy is that of one of the most successful and innovative cattlemen ever. In 1985 Larry **McMurtry**'s novel *Lonesome Dove* used incidents from the lives of Loving and Goodnight to construct his memorable heroes, Augustus McCrae and Woodrow F. Call. (Haley 1949; Thrapp 1988; Webb 1965)

—*Nils E. Mikkelsen*

GOODNIGHTING
See Goodnight, Charles.

GOODNIGHT-LOVING TRAIL
See Goodnight, Charles.

GOUGE
To **spur** a horse.

GRAB THE APPLE
Also grab the nubbin—taking hold of the **saddle** horn to avoid falling off. This is something no self-respecting cowboy wants to be caught doing.

GRAHAM, ROBERT BONTINE CUNNINGHAME
(1852–1936)
Writer and horseman Robert Bontine Cunninghame Graham came by the love of international travel honestly. He was born in London to a half-Spanish mother and a Scottish father. After enjoying an elite education, he headed off at the age of 17 to ranch in Argentina. This early experience on the **pampas** marked him for life. "Don Roberto" continued to wear elements of **gaucho** dress throughout his life.

Graham spent his life in quest of adventure. He also engaged in a number of international business endeavors, none very successful. An acute observer, he recorded vivid sketches of many of the people and places he visited. He served in the British Parliament from 1886 to 1892 championing progressive causes.

In 1878 he married Gabrielle, who, like Graham, came from an international background (born in Chile of a Spanish mother and a French father). She could also capture vivid landscapes in words. Here she describes their trip down a dusty Mexican trail in "Waggon-Train" (1880):

We can scarcely breathe for the fine dust, which penetrates to the lungs. It is so penetrating that the train men on the San Luis Potosí road to Mexico rarely if ever live long, and nearly all die of consumption. On either side of us we see nothing but scorched plains, covered with many different kinds of cactus and thorny brushwood. Dim blue mountains rise in the distance, but the cactus is certainly the chief feature of the landscape. Hedges of palm and cactus enclose huge flat fields of tall magueyes (the species of aloe from which the Mexican drink, mescal, is made, and the finer quality, tequila), and this is the only vegetation that there is between San Luis and the capital.

During his long life Graham wrote some 30 books of descriptive sketches and works of history, most dealing with the New World. He died at age 84 in Buenos Aires, Argentina, and is buried in Scotland.

His historical studies remain well worth reading for their engaging styles and original thought. He wrote *Hernando De Soto* (1903), *Bernal Díaz del Castillo* (1915), a study of Antonio Conselheiro, leader of the Canudos revolt, entitled *A Brazilian Mystic* (1920), *The Conquest of New Granada* (1922), *The Conquest of the River Plate* (1924), *Pedro de Valdivia* (the conqueror of Chile, 1926), *José Antonio Páez* (Venezuelan caudillo, 1929), and *The Horses of the Conquest* (1930).

Of even greater interest are Graham's many vignettes of **plains** life and cowboys in both North and South America. John Walker, literary scholar at Queens University in Kingston, Ontario, has written widely about Graham and his works. He has edited two superb samplers of Graham's writings, *The South American Sketches of R. B. Cunninghame Graham* (1978) and *The North American Sketches of R. B. Cunninghame Graham* (1986).

Graham generally wrote in long, rambling sentences, spiced with lots of adjectives and detail. In *A Hegira,* he offers a quick glimpse of Mexican **vaqueros:** "Horsemen rode out, sitting erect in their peaked saddles, toes stuck out and thrust into their curiously stamped toe-leathers; their chaparreras giving to their legs a look of being cased in armour, their poblano hats, with bands of silver or of tinsel, balanced like halos on their heads." Graham's ardent spirit, quick eye, and fascile pen combined to leave us delightful descriptions of ranch life in both Americas. (Graham 1936, 1978; Watts and Davies 1979)

GRAMA GRASS

Also gramma grass; a tall, nutritious **plains** grass (species *Bouteloua),* good for grazing livestock. The grass even retained its nutritional value after it turned brown and dry in the winter. Thanks to this grass, ranchers could graze their animals through winter as far north as Alberta. Grama grass grows to a height of two feet or, with excellent conditions, even three feet. The term was originally Spanish.

GRANGER

Derogatory term for farmer.

GRAPPLING IRONS

Colloquial for **spurs.**

GRASS ROPE

See Rope.

GREASER

Derogatory Anglo term for Mexican or Mexican American. See Discrimination on the American Frontier.

THE GREAT AMERICAN COWBOY

Film. See Rodeo.

THE GREAT TRAIN ROBBERY

Historic 1903 film. See Films, Cowboy.

GREEN, BEN K.
(1912–1974)

Author of fine nonfiction and fictionalized works about **horses** and cowboy life.

GREEN, DOUGLAS BRUCE

Singer known as Ranger Doug. See Riders in the Sky.

GREENE, LORNE
(1915–1987)

Actor who starred as Ben Cartwright in "Bonanza." See Television.

GREENHORN

Also greener, green pea, tenderfoot—an easterner innocent of cowboy ways.

GREY, ZANE
(1872–1939)

Born Pearl Zane Gray in Zanesville, Ohio, novelist Zane Grey would later drop his first name and change the spelling of his last name. Never a very good student, young Zane excelled as a fisherman and athlete. He loved to play baseball, and once pitched the new curve ball throughout a game. The skill so infuriated the opposing team's fans that they started a riot and tried to run him out of town on a rail.

As a youth, Grey read the dime novels of the 1890s, exciting tales of the mythical adventures of Buffalo Bill, Deadwood Dick, and Jesse James. **Pulp novels** gave him his first glimpse of the

West. At age 15, the youngster decided to try his hand at writing. His first manuscript, "Jim of the Cave," ended in disaster. His strict father tore it up after he read it. He beat the boy with a strip of carpet and demanded that he forget such nonsense. Zane was to become a dentist, like his father.

Grey attended the University of Pennsylvania on a baseball scholarship. The obedient son graduated in 1896 with a degree in dentistry. After graduation he went to New York City to open a dental practice. He was not one to give up; he still harbored dreams of becoming a writer. Grey spent considerable time fishing with his brother along the Delaware River, and in 1902 he published his first article, "A Day on the Delaware," in *Recreation Magazine.*

This success encouraged Grey to take up writing as a second career. He next attempted a novel, *Betty Zane,* inspired by one of his ancestors. The book became the first part of his Ohio River trilogy. After many rejections by publishers, Grey finally paid to have the manuscript published in 1903. Two years later a publisher accepted his second book, *Spirit of the Border.* Grey quit dentistry for good and devoted himself to writing.

During the early years of his writing career, he had the predictable difficulties getting his novels published. As has often occurred, a trip to the West changed his fortunes for the better. He visited California for the first time in 1906 with his new bride, Dolly. On a 1907 trip to Arizona, the beauty of the desert captivated Grey. He learned old western tales about Indians, outlaws, and rangers, and now knew he wanted to write about the West.

He wrote his first western novel, *The Last Plainsmen,* on his return to New York. Publishers rejected it, but he succeeded in 1909 with *The Heritage of the Desert.* This book set the tone for many of Grey's romanticized western novels. He stressed the themes of rugged individualism and the healing powers of the desert. His stories showed how the West built character and turned weaklings into strong men. He followed with other desert novels, including *Desert Gold* (1913) and *The Call of the Canyon* (1924).

Grey spent a decade (1907–1917) traveling throughout the Southwest, Mexico, and Cuba gathering material for his novels. In 1912 he published *Riders of the Purple Sage,* considered among the best western novels ever written. This novel centered on the Mormons. Grey illustrated another important theme, that people often must pay a high price for their beliefs.

Grey appreciated the value of **horses** and used them in many of his novels. In *Last of the Plainsmen,* he described futile efforts to capture a wild horse named Silvermane. Grey owned several horses himself and featured his favorites in some of his books. He again made a horse the central character in *Wildfire* (1917). The horse hero elicits varied feelings and reactions in the human characters.

Grey greatly romanticized the West and its central icon, the cowboy. In his novels, he presented cowboys as part of the ranch family. He imbued them with predictable characteristics: loyalty, intemperateness, and deadliness. Grey used the cattle industry as a setting for *Knights of the Range* (1939) and *The Trail Driver* (1936).

Unlike many pulp and even more polished western writers, Grey did not create an artificially lily-white West. **African-American cowboys,** ignored and omitted by most other western authors, appear in *West of the Pecos* (1937). Neither did Grey ignore the importance of Native Americans. He depicted conflict between whites and Indians in *Fighting Caravans* (1928) and *The Lost Wagon Train* (1936). Grey seemed to sympathize with the plight of Native Americans, and criticized white treatment of them. (Grey himself was $\frac{1}{32}$ Indian.) He examined Native American customs and culture in several short stories, including "The Great Slave" and "Blue Feather."

Grey wrote 89 books in all, including 56 books on the West. The rest were short stories and hunting, juvenile, and fishing books. Forty-six of Grey's works have been made into motion pictures. From 1956 to 1961 the popular "Zane Grey Western Theater" brought his works to **television.** In the last decade or so, several of his previously published works, such as *Maverick Queen* and *30,000 on the Hoof*, were reprinted. The modern editions restore some rather tame material that had been edited out of earlier versions as being too risque.

Grey reached the height of his popularity between 1914 and 1928. He offered readers a thrilling escape from urban life and a nostalgic look at a mythical western past. Grey excelled at vividly describing colorful landscapes and rousing action. His romantic depiction of the West and of the cowboy has shaped the vision of several generations of readers. He died in 1939 at his home in Altadena, California, after suffering a heart attack. (Gruber 1970; Jackson 1989)

—*Janine M. Cairo*

GRINGO

Colloquial Spanish term for any foreigner, including North Americans. In Argentina, for example, the term was applied to Italians in the nineteenth century. There is absolutely no truth to the oft-given story that the term originated during the Mexican-American War. The word *gringo* was in use in Mexico and elsewhere well before U.S. troops showed up singing "Green Grow the Lilacs."

GRUB

Also grub pile; colloquialism for **food** or a meal.

GRUB SLINGER

Also grub spoiler or grubworm; colloquialisms for cook.

GRUB-LINE RIDER

See Chuck-Line Rider.

GUASO

Archaic variant of *huaso*, the Chilean cowboy.

GÜEMES, MARTÍN
(1785–1821)

Martín Güemes was a caudillo (military-political leader) who led the **gauchos** of Argentina's northwestern Salta province during the independence wars against Spain. Güemes joined the patriot (independence) forces in 1810.

The camp cook, often referred to as a grub slinger, used the equipment carried on the chuck wagon to create hearty meals of beef, biscuits, chili, coffee, and more. This 1907 Erwin E. Smith photograph pictures a JA Ranch wagon cook inspecting his stew.

In March 1814 Argentine General José de San Martín appointed Güemes general commander of patriot forces in Salta. Güemes and his gaucho cavalry fought well and hard and expelled royalist troops from Salta. His military prowess kept the Spanish forces from entering Argentina from the north and made Argentina a secure pocket of independence. (Haigh 1968)

GÜIRALDES, RICARDO
(1886–1927)
Argentine novelist, author of *Don Segundo Sombra*. See *Gauchesco*.

GUMBO GRASS
Blue stem grass. See Plains.

GUN
A pistol (not a rifle). See Firearms.

GUNFIGHT
Another term for gunplay. See Fast Draw; Firearms.

GUNFIGHT AT THE OK CORRAL
Film (1957). See Films, Cowboy.

"GUNSMOKE"
See Television.

GUT HOOKS
Also gut lancers; colloquialism for **spurs**.

GUT LINE
Colloquial term for rawhide **rope**.

GUT WARMER
Colloquial term for whiskey.

HAAS, BENJAMIN LEOPOLD
(1926–1977)

Novelist who wrote formula westerns under various names.

HACENDADO

Owner of a large ranch or estate. See Estancia; Latifundia.

HACIENDA

A large ranch or estate. See Estancia; Latifundia.

HACKAMORE

Also hackamer. See Tack.

HAIR CASE

Colloquial term for **hat.**

HAIR PANTS

Chaps made from a hair-covered hide.

HAIR ROPE

Also lariat or reata; a **rope** made from horsehair.

HANDLE

Colloquial term for **saddle** horn.

"HAPPY TRAILS"

Song (1950). See Rogers, Roy.

HARD TWIST

See Rope.

HARD-AND-FAST

See Rope.

HART, WILLIAM S.
(1870–1946)

Actor. See Films, Cowboy.

HASHER

Colloquial term for cook or waitress.

HAT

Along with his **boots,** a cowboy's hat is one of his most distinguishing features. The utility of a broad-brimmed hat is immediately obvious to anyone who has spent a day outdoors in one of the semi-arid regions of the ranching frontier. The hat protects the wearer's head, face, and neck from the sun's heat and glare. It keeps the rain out of his eyes. Held down around his ears with a rawhide thong, it protects against freezing weather. In short, the hat helped keep the cowboy from frying or freezing, depending on the whims of the weather.

Many early Texas cowboys adopted the venerable Spanish sombrero (literally a "shader"—*sombra* is Spanish for shade). The hat has a flat crown and a wide, flat brim. Also called *poblanos,* these hats came from Spain and continue to be used there. They worked well in the hot ranges of north Mexico. Wealthier Spaniards had their hats embellished with silver **conchas** and silver or gold braid.

The Mexican variation of the sombrero added an even wider brim and a high, conical crown. These are the hats worn by *mariachi* musicians and *charros.* They are too large, heavy, and unwieldy for ranch work. Both types of sombreros usually include a *barboquejo* or chin strap. Cowboys would adopt and generalize the word *sombrero* to mean just about any broad-brimmed hat.

Hat making is one part art, one part science. The brims on early, cheap American-made hats often lacked rigidity. Some were made from wool, which could not be stiffened. Such low-quality headgear marked the wearer as part of the "wool-hat bunch"—not a compliment. Thus we associate slouch hats with floppy brims with the early Texas cowhands who could not afford the more elegant-shaped sombreros. Some cowboys pinned the front brim back to keep it out of their eyes. Hands with a little more money would purchase better quality headgear.

With the advent of the great Texas **trail drives,** drovers began demanding better quality, more serviceable equipment, including a better pair of boots and a better "hair case" (hat). John Batterson Stetson, a New Jersey–born hat manufacturer, came to the rescue. He had learned his trade from his family. Like many other easterners, he traveled West for his health. This combination of western experience and family skills came together in the most famous cowboy hat of all, the Stetson. Stetson designed a large, broad-brimmed "ten-gallon hat" and began manufacturing it in Philadelphia in 1865. His attention to quality and durability quickly established his company as the leading hat manufacturer in the country. A good John B. might cost a month's wages, but it would last a lifetime.

Stetson made hats, usually from felt, of varying price and quality. Felt from rabbit or beaver fur provided the raw material. The 5X and 7X beaver were the finest quality hats available to the old-time cowboy. Later inflation would strike the beaver X scale. At one time a 20X meant 100 percent beaver felt. Today, however, you can purchase a 30X or even jump to a 100X beaver at a cost of $1,000 or more.

Cowboys added their own individual and regional variations by creasing the crown or adding distinctive hat bands. Some of the creases gained names, so that today you might favor the cattleman, centerfire, two dot, peak, Montana, or foreman crease. Likewise, brims can take on a rodeo, ranch, snap, or Aussie look.

Stetson also paid attention to style, creating a wide range of looks. He followed up his early Boss of the Plains with many popular styles, including the Carlsbad (extremely popular among cowboys) and the Buckeye, which stood

The hat was an indispensable element in the costume of the cowboy. Work on the hot, open prairies and ranches demanded their use, and, as this motley crew demonstrates, cowboys did not leave them behind on their jaunts into cow towns.

even higher and wider than the original Boss. By the time of his death in 1906, Stetson was selling two million hats per year worldwide. His name had become synonymous with cowboy hats. Hat evolution continued in the twentieth century, with Stetson's Tom Mix and Columbia styles and many more.

As in the boot industry that followed Justin's lead, competitors entered the hat business. American Hat, Resistol, Bailey, and others joined in. Today far more "pilgrims" wear cowboy hats than do cowboys. Some hands, ever individualists, have even switched over to baseball caps. Winfred Blevins tells the story of a tourist who asked a cowboy in Jackson Hole why he was wearing a baseball cap instead of a cowboy hat. The hand replied, "Don' wanna look like a goddam truck driver." (Blevins 1993; Van Deventer 1994)

HAT ACTS

The connection between country **music** and western music goes back to at least the 1930s. Sensing the popularity of cowboy western dress, country singers began donning fancy **boots** and broad-brimmed **hats.** Some performers, such as Michael Martin **Murphey,** are bona fide western singers. In most cases, however, neither the singer nor the songs had anything western about them. We give the name "hat acts" to country singers who dress cowboy but sing country. This entry profiles a few of the most popular hat acts of the past decade.

The most wildly popular hat act of the late 1980s and early 1990s was (Troyal) Garth Brooks. Born in Tulsa, Oklahoma, in 1962, Brooks grew up in the town of Yukon. A legitimate westerner, he can sing a cowboy song, but his stock-in-trade is a dazzling mix of rock 'n' roll guitar-smashing and strobe lights with good old-fashioned country themes and tunes. It took two abortive moves to Nashville and lots of support from wife Sandy before Brooks pushed his way into the country music scene.

A talented songwriter and spirited performer, Brooks prospered in Nashville. He became the 65th member of the Grand Old Opry in 1989.

His songs enjoyed wide appeal, so many of his hits crossed over to the pop charts. Brooks has won a roomful of music awards and become far and away the leading money-maker for Capitol Records.

Born in New Jersey in 1962, Clint (Patrick) Black grew up in Houston. At age 15 he graduated from the harmonica to the guitar and began writing songs. In 1987 he teamed up with songwriter Hayden Nicholas, and together they've prospered. Black's debut album, *Killin' Time,* included five number-one hits, many of them cowritten with Nicholas.

In 1991 Black followed Brooks into the select membership of the Grand Old Opry. That same year American Society of Composers, Authors and Publishers (ASCAP) honored him as Songwriter of the Year, one of his many writing and performing awards. He sang at halftime during the 1994 Super Bowl in Atlanta. He also made his acting debut as a gambler in the movie *Maverick* (1994). The film, starring Mel Gibson and Jodie Foster, is based on the **television** character made famous by James Garner.

Brooks and Dunn are another popular hat act. Louisiana-born Leon Eric ("Kix") Brooks (1955–) teamed up with Texas-born Ronnie Gene Dunn (1953–) in 1990. They began by writing songs together, but their demos attracted the right attention from Arista Records. Four of the singles from their first album, *Brand New Man,* went to number one. As a vocal duo, they have won several Academy of Country Music (ACM) awards.

Like Dunn, Mark Chestnutt was born in Texas (1963). Growing up in Beaumont, he carries on the musical tradition of his father Bob, a country-and-western singer. As a teenager, Chestnutt cut several albums on independent Texas labels. With his father's constant encouragement, he hit the big time in 1990 with his debut album, *Too Cold at Home,* on MCA. He followed up with *Longnecks and Short Stories* and shows no signs of letting up.

"The Mysterious Rhinestone Cowboy," David Allan Coe, was born in Akron, Ohio, in 1939. His troubled early life, a broken home and a stint in prison, gave him plenty of firsthand experiences for country songwriting. He wrote some winners, such as Johnny Paycheck's smash hit, "Take This Job and Shove It." In 1974 he made the country charts as a singer. He has continued to write and sing ever since. He wrote all 20 songs on his 1991 album, *1990 Songs for Sale.*

Billy Ray Cyrus led a rambling life for his first 20 years. Born in Kentucky in 1961, he says an "inner voice" prompted him to try his hand at entertaining. He played clubs around the country until about 1991 when Mercury Records offered him a contract. His debut album, *Some Gave All,* quickly topped the country charts. The single "Achy Breaky Heart" crossed over to the pop charts and touched off the line-dancing craze of the early 1990s. The song became the Country Music Association's (CMA) Single of the Year for 1992.

Alan Jackson (born in Georgia in 1958) grew up loving cars, but he also loved country music. He played clubs for three years before joining Glen Campbell Music as a songwriter. Jackson became the first artist signed by Arista's country music division. Each of his several albums has done well. The ACM named him Top Male Vocalist for 1990. The following year he became the 68th member of the Grand Old Opry.

Born in Grit, Virginia, in 1952, Ricky Van Shelton always loved music. His father gave him a guitar when he was 12 and taught him to play. Along with wife Bettye, Van Shelton moved to Nashville in 1986. Beginning with *Wild Eye Dream,* he quickly turned out four platinum albums. The multi-talented Shelton also writes, illustrates, and publishes children's books. Country music organizations have showered awards on his songs and videos.

Born in Poteet, Texas, in 1952, George Strait today makes his home in San Antonio. He worked on the family ranch near Big Wells, Texas, during his youth. Unlike many country stars, he did not grow up with a musical dream. With time on his hands in the army, however, he taught himself to play the guitar. In the mid-1970s, he formed the Ace in the Hole Band

that performed at clubs in the San Marcos, Texas, area. He patterned his group after The Texas Playboys, of Bob Wills fame.

After a couple of unsuccessful forays into Nashville, Strait was ready to quit music and stick with the cattle business. With help from fellow Texan Erv Woolsey (nightclub owner, record promoter, and later Strait's manager) Strait landed an MCA contract. ACM executive director Bill Boyd credits Strait with kicking off the wave of hat acts that swept the country in the 1980s. Strait performed "in the starched shirt, the starched pants and the hat," says Boyd. "He opened the door for the hat acts like Garth Brooks, Clint Black, Brooks and Dunn, and Mark Chestnutt." Several songs from *Strait Country,* his 1981 debut album, hit number one. Even with his busy life in music, he continues to enjoy team roping and ranching.

A North Carolinian, Randy Travis was born Randy Bruce Traywick in 1959. As a youngster he loved **horses** and music. He had a pony by age three and a guitar at age eight. With the help of Mary ("Lib") Hatcher, Travis left behind a wild teenage life of scrapes with the law and began performing. She became his manager and the two married in 1991.

Travis turned out a steady stream of winners through the 1980s. His stock-in-trade is the standard country tearjerker. His albums *Storms of Life* and *Always and Forever* enjoyed great success. On the 1990 *Heroes and Friends* album, he sings with George Jones, Willie Nelson, Roy **Rogers,** Tammy Wynette, and others. He also collaborated at songwriting with Alan Jackson. His many recording honors included induction into the Grand Old Opry in 1987.

In 1993, Travis delivered his first non-country album, *Wind on the Wire,* for the **television** movie of the same name. This soundtrack included a variety of moods, including the popular old swing tune, "Cowboy Boogie." Roger Brown wrote many of the songs.

A Georgian, George Travis Tritt was born in 1963. He sang as a youngster, taught himself to play the guitar, and wrote his first song at age 14. He enjoyed all kinds of music, from rock to country. The "Outlaw" movement from Austin in the early 1970s captivated and influenced him. He worked hard at his craft through the 1980s and garnered a top-ten single, "Country Club," in 1989. Successful albums followed, and in 1992 he became the 71st member of the Grand Old Opry.

Like Billy Ray Cyrus, Dwight Yoakam is Kentucky-born (1956). Like Alan Jackson, he has a passion for collecting cars. As a teenager, he played with rockabilly bands. It took two shots to make it in Nashville, but he broke in with his 1986 debut album, *Guitars, Cadillacs, Etc. Etc.* In 1988 he teamed up with one of his heroes, Buck Owens, with the successful duet, "Streets of Bakersfield." His popularity and awards have continued to grow.

It was obvious that hat acts had really arrived when in 1992 Alvin and the Chipmunks came out of retirement. Alvin, Simon, and Theodore paid the genre a high compliment with *Chipmunks in Low Places,* a spoof of the Garth Brooks smash hit, "Friends in Low Places." The album cover featured Alvin dressed in a huge red cowboy hat and boots, along with a world champion–sized belt buckle adorned with a giant A. Writer Joe Edward well summarized the album in an Associated Press news story (9 October 1992):

On this album, Alvin leaves behind his classic "The Chipmunk Song" (1958). He takes up new western tunes, like "Achy Breaky Heart" (Billy Ray Cyrus) and "Stand by Your Man" (Tammy Wynette). The album breaks achy breaky new ground for cowboy-dressing songsters. The Chipmunks surround themselves with hot talent, including Cyrus, Wynette, Waylon Jennings, Charlie Daniels, and other stars.

Alvin and the gang had cashed in earlier on the *Urban Cowboy* mania kicked off by the John Travolta movie of 1980. The enterprising trio sold a million copies of *Urban Chipmunk.*

In 1994, hat acts continued to be hot. Country music and line dancing drew fans to clubs across the country. It seemed that lots of folks agreed with Toby Keith's song, "Should Have Been a Cowboy."

Female Hat Acts

By definition "hat acts" are male; they are also referred to as "country hunks" in the popular press. A new generation of country female singers, however, appeared along with the male hat acts on the music scene in the 1980s. These **women,** mostly born in the 1950s, joined the grand dames of country music, June Carter Cash (1929–), Emmylou Harris (1947–), Brenda Lee (1944–), Loretta Lynn (1935–), K. T. Oslin (1941–), Dolly Parton (1946–), and comedian Minnie Pearl (1912–).

Country music has broadened its decidedly male bias throughout the 1980s and 1990s. The new breed of female country vocalist includes: Mary-Chapin Carpenter (1958–), Carlene Carter (1955–), Rosanne Cash (1955–), Patty Loveless (1957–), Kathy Mattea (1954–), Reba McEntire (1954–), Lori Morgan (1959–), Pam Tillis (1957–), Tanya Tucker (1958–), and Trisha Yearwood (1964–).

As during the early 1970s, outlaw music rebellion (see Music) in Austin continues to lend its distinctive western voice to the music scene. Austin-born Nancy Griffith (birth date unknown) moved out of nightclub singing and recorded five albums by the mid-1980s. She signed with MCA in 1986 and has recorded in Nashville and Los Angeles. *Other Voices, Other Rooms,* according to entertainment writer Michael McCall, is "an album exploring her folk roots."

Born to Mexican immigrants, Tish Hinajosa (1956–) brings a Hispanic beat to her eclectic style. Although she has lived in New Mexico since 1979, she recorded her first album, *Aquella Noche,* live in Austin. The songs are all in Spanish. "Though I deal with some Hispanic themes," she says, "I also include elements of folk, pop, western swing, and everything in between." She often performs to enthusiastic crowds at Michael Martin Murphey's WestFest concerts.

The most unusual of the new female western stars is Canadian singer k. d. Lang. She was born Kathy Dawn in Alberta's cowboy country in 1962. Lang honored her childhood singing idol Patsy Cline (1932–1963) by naming her backup group the "Reclines." Her early albums, *A Truly Western Experience* (1984) and *Angel with a Lariat* (1987), had a western flair. Her very strong, soaring voice and rollicking stage presence make her a favorite among country-and-western music fans.

As in **rodeo, poetry**, and other aspects of cowboy culture, women are playing increasingly visible and creative roles. (Flint and Nelson 1993; McCall 1993; WestFest 1993 program)

HATO
Llanero term for ranch.

HAWKS, HOWARD
(1896–1977)
Film director. See Films, Best Cowboy.

HAY BALER
Also hay burner; colloquial terms for **horse.**

HAYCOX, ERNEST
(1899–1950)
Oregon-born novelist who wrote formula westerns.

HAYS CITY, KANSAS
See Cow Towns.

HAYSEED
Also hay shaker; derogatory terms for farmer.

HAZER
The hand who assists a **bronc buster;** also a **rodeo** rider who keeps a bulldogging steer running straight so the steer wrestler can grab it.

HEADER
See Rodeo Events.

HEADSTALL
See Tack.

HEEL
To **rope** a cow by the hind feet.

HEELER
See Rodeo Events.

HELL ROUSERS
Colloquial term for **spurs.**

HEMP
Colloquial term for **rope,** coined because cowboys used ropes made of Manila hemp.

HERD
A group of animals, **cattle, horses,** sheep, etc.; also the act of bunching animals or guiding them from one point to another.

HEREFORD CATTLE
See Cattle Breeds.

HERNÁNDEZ, JOSÉ
(1834–1886)
Argentine writer, politician. See *Gauchesco.*

HIDE AND TALLOW FACTORY
See *Vaquería.*

HIERRA
Also *yerra,* a **gaucho** term for **roundup** and branding season.

HIGH NOON
Film (1952). See Films, Best Cowboy.

HIGH TAIL
To leave or ride off in haste.

HIGHBINDER
A dangerous, vicious horse or man.

HILL, THOMAS
(1829–1913)
Artist. See Art of the Cowboy.

HISPANIC

See Vaquero.

HISTORIOGRAPHY OF THE COWBOY

The history of the cowboys of the Americas covers many centuries, cultures, and countries. As with many storied figures, myth and legend threaten to overwhelm serious historical studies of the cowboy. Historiography is the examination of the written histories about a topic. It examines how interpretations and approaches by historians change over time. Following is a summary of highlights in the evolution of historical writings about cowboys in the United States, Canada, and South America.

United States

Several classic primary sources about the **beef cattle industry** remain basic references. (Primary sources are eyewitness accounts that come from the place and time under study.) In *Historic Sketches of the Cattle Trade of the West and Southwest* (1874), Joseph G. **McCoy** reveals a decidedly condescending attitude toward the cowboy. His views, however, along with those of James Cox *(Historical and Biographical Record of the Cattle Industry and the Cattlemen of Texas and Adjacent Territory,* 1895) are important contemporary accounts.

For information on the great cattle drives, look at *The Trail Drivers of Texas* (1920, 1925). This two-volume compilation by J. Marvin Hunter includes hundreds of autobiographical sketches of old-time drovers and cattlemen.

Not long after Hunter's second volume appeared, E. Douglas Branch provided the first major summary and review of writings about the cowboy. *The Cowboy and His Interpreters* (1926) is an uneven guide to the early literature, fiction and nonfiction. Branch showed himself a bit gullible in taking some wild cowboy yarns as fact, but he did approach the literature about the cowboy with seriousness and appreciation.

Firsthand descriptions of nineteenth-century cowboy life vary in their accuracy, but they are a joy to read (see Autobiographies by Cowboys).

Likewise, accounts by outsiders, often foreign or eastern tourists, provide good descriptions of dress, equipment, roundups, and the like.

Many factors introduce bias into the writing of history. One reason for bias is that winners (in this case the Anglo-Americans of the United States) record the official history. Views of Mexicans, Native Americans, and African Americans generally come down to us with an Anglo bias.

The makers of myth and legend kept their heroes white and male. Traditional western American history, using the model of Frederick Jackson Turner, has been depicted as the inevitable victory of white civilization over nonwhite savagery. Modern historians are trying to restore the real-world complexities of ethnic and other relations to western historiography.

Despite the general shortcomings in the early historiography, some good studies appeared. *The Cowboy: An Unconventional History of Civilization on the Old-Time Cattle Range* (1922), by Philip Ashton Rollins, is the first major attempt to treat the cowboy as a historical rather than a romanticized figure. Rollins drew upon firsthand experiences in the West during the 1890s. On page one, he forthrightly summed up the cowboy's debt to the Mexican **vaquero:**

> He obtained from Mexican sources all the tools of his trade, all the technic of his craft, the very words by which he desig-nated his utensils, the very animals with which he dealt; but as one of the dominant figures in the development of the United States, he was self-made.

Charles Willington Furlong focused in the ranch country around Pendleton in eastern Oregon in his book, *Let 'er Buck: A Story of the Passing of the Old West* (3d ed., 1923). Furlong broadens the scope of cowboy literature by taking a Pacific Northwest focus. Most of the early literature focused on Texas and the Great Plains.

Two pioneering studies of western ranching appeared within a year of one another. Ernest Staples Osgood published *The Day of the*

Cattleman in 1929. He focused on the rise of open-range ranching in the mid-nineteenth century and took the story into the early twentieth century. Osgood noted the impact on cowboy life of the end of the open range and the rise of farming and sheep ranching. "Mowing machines, hay rakes, and ditching tools became as important a part of ranch equipment as the chuck wagon, the lariat, and the branding iron."

In 1930 Texas-born Edward Everett Dale provided another major cattle industry study, *The Range Cattle Industry: Ranching on the Great Plains from 1865 to 1925*. Dale studied with Frederick Jackson Turner at Harvard and spent most of his career at the University of Oklahoma. His fine description of ranching is based on extensive archival sources. Unfortunately, he ignored those who actually worked the range, the cowboys. Dale later wrote another ranching study titled *Cow Country* (1965). Both Osgood and Dale overlooked important Hispanic contributions to the open-range ranching complex.

Dale's contemporary and fellow Texan J. Frank **Dobie** made up for these and other shortcomings in historical scholarship. His pioneering work in folklore and oral history placed great importance on the Hispanic culture in Texas. In 1930 he published an important essay, "Ranch Mexicans." With this essay and other works, Dobie showed an understanding of and appreciation for the Hispanic component of Southwest culture.

In *Guide to Life and Literature of the Southwest* (1952) Dobie describes and critiques a wide range of western literature of all types. A good Texan, Dobie spoke his mind and bluntly criticized books he found lacking. Largely an annotated bibliography, the book devotes chapters to a wide range of topics from Mountain Men and the Texas Rangers to Spanish-Mexican Strains and Negro Folk Songs and Tales. Chapters 21 and 22 focus on the cowboy.

Dobie pulled no punches. Here is his comment on Frederick R. Bechdolt's *Tales of the Old Timers* (1924): "Research clogs the style of many historians; perhaps it is just as well that Bechdolt did not search more extensively into the arcana of footnotes." Dobie also left other classic studies, including *The Longhorn* and *A Vaquero in the Brush Country*.

Mari Sandoz was one of relatively few women to write histories of cowboy and ranch life. In 1935 she published her first book, *Old Jules*, a biography of her father. The book is rich in details of rural life in western Nebraska. A prolific writer, Sandoz went on to write many more fascinating regional studies. In 1958 she published a sweeping study, *The Cattlemen from the Rio Grande across the Far Marias*. Both books contain a wealth of detail and make delightful reading.

Jo Mora's *Trail Dust and Saddle Leather* (1946) is an enjoyable fount of information written in a folksy style. Mora also wrote several books about the California vaquero. Born in Uruguay in 1876, Mora worked the range from Mexico to Canada. He also illustrated his books with his own drawings.

Very similar in knowledge, detail, and style to Mora is Ramon F. **Adams**. *The Old-Time Cowhand* (1948) is written in Adams's attempt at heavy cowboy dialect, which gets in the way of the information. Reacting to overblown fiction and movie depictions, Adams wanted to point out some of the cowboy's good points. He stated his goal on the book's concluding page. "I'm not tryin' to make a hero of the old-time cowhand, but I want to show you that he had some virtues too."

In two books, he pilloried many a writer for straying from the truth as Adams saw it. He published two volumes of criticisms, *Burs under the Saddle* (1964) and *More Burs under the Saddle* (1979). Unfortunately, Adams wrote these works more as a buff than a serious analyst. He focused on rather trivial errors of fact related to the lives and actions of gunmen and outlaws. Larger, more significant interpretative points did not seem to interest him. Even a first-rate scholar might slip up on a small point or two, but it need not invalidate his or her larger interpretation of past events.

The American Cowboy (1955) by Julian Choate and Joe B. Frantz was the first serious modern historical study of cowboy myth and reality. The last four chapters also critique literature about ranching and cowboys, updating Branch and Dobie. Choate and Frantz recognized the need to undertake a multifaceted examination of the cowboy:

> The American cowboy exists on three distinct levels—the historical level, about which the average American cares and knows no more than he does about any other phase of nonmilitary or nonpolitical history; the fictional level, in which the cowboy occupies a not quite respectable but highly popular position; and the folklore level, on which the cowboy sits as an idealized creation of the American folk mind.

With such a daunting interpretive task, it's not surprising that the historiography has found a place for more attempts to analyze the cowboy.

Fay E. Ward's *The Cowboy at Work* (1958) is an excellent, knowledgeable, accurate, down-to-earth work. The book tells "all about his job and how he does it, with 600 detail drawings by the author." Ward "worked as a horse wrangler, cowhand, bronc breaker and roughstring rider for cow outfits in Canada, and for outfits extending from there to the border of Mexico, for a period of over forty years." He worried not at all about the legendary or symbolic elements of cowboy life. He kept his seat firmly planted in the saddle and provided an excellent how-to manual for working or prospective hands.

Newspapers offer additional glimpses into western social, economic, and political life. Clifford P. Westermeier gathered original nineteenth- and early twentieth-century newspaper reports into topical chapters and reprinted them as *Trailing the Cowboy: His Life and Lore as Told by Frontier Journalists* (1955). The sampler offers firsthand descriptions of the cowboy at work and play. Then, as now,

journalists varied widely in their accuracy and perspicacity. Westermeier's collection, however, remains a convenient window on cowboy life a century ago.

Cowboy Life: Reconstructing an American Myth (1975), edited by William W. Savage, Jr., offers a more recent, stimulating collection of firsthand descriptions and opinions. Savage has excerpted selections from many important sources, including Joseph G. McCoy, Richard Irving Dodge, W. S. James, Baylis John Fletcher, and Andy Adams. The editor's brief introduction offers an excellent summary of how the attitudes toward and mythology surrounding the cowboy have changed over time.

The Cowboy Hero: His Image in American History and Culture (1979), also by Savage, probes the cowboy's cultural significance. He provides an excellent critique of cowboy historiography, frankly and correctly laying out the dilemma for scholars trying to give the cowboy serious historical treatment:

> The romanticized view of the cowboy is less prevalent than it once was, since truth is the historian's stock in trade and myths are his principal enemies. But the historian's influence seldom extends into society beyond the texts that he writes for the hasty perusal of freshmen, and the public will preserve its myths elsewhere. Thus the historian's statements that cowboy life was "dirty and hard" or that cowboys came in colors other than white may be revelation to the undergraduate, but they cannot negate the lessons learned from a lifetime of exposure to comic-book, **radio,** motion-picture, and **television** cowboys.

Ethnicity and Gender

Like legends of popular culture criticized by Savage, older, traditional historiography focused rather narrowly on white males. The first two generations of professional western historians seldom mentioned blacks, Hispanics, or women.

More recently, scholars have sought to restore social complexity and reality to western history.

Several books have documented the importance of Hispanic influences on the cowboy and the open-range cattle industry. Junior Jean Wagoner's *History of the Cattle Industry in Southern Arizona, 1540–1940* (1952) is an important regional study. In *Cowboy Culture: A Saga of Five Centuries* (1981), David Dary does a masterful job of placing the American cowboy in the proper Hispanic context. Kathleen Mullen Sands examines the history and folklore of Mexican **rodeo** in *Charrería Mexicana* (1993). She draws evidence from both the southwestern United States and Mexico.

For a more general history of early Texas ranching, readers should consult Jack Jackson's well-documented study, *Los Mesteños* (1986). Thanks to his intensive use of an impressive array of Spanish-language archival sources, Jackson's extensive research effectively refutes Terry Jordan's erroneous depiction of the evolution of Texas ranching in *Trails to Texas* (1981). Jordan tries to trace the roots of western ranching to "cowpens" of the colonial Carolinas. The meager cultural trickle from the Carolina Piedmont through the Old South to the coast of east Texas was a minor sideshow.

Cattle herding in the United States did begin at several different poles. The Spanish brought livestock to Florida in the sixteenth century. These early efforts had little long-term impact. Aside from a few "Spanish ponies" that reached Indian hands, Spanish Florida little influenced the course of ranching in British North America. The British colonies also developed their own version of the cattle culture.

In 1611 cattle were first imported to Jamestown colony. Herders on foot tended cattle in enclosed "cowpens" of seventeenth-century South Carolina. The practice spread north to North Carolina and Virginia and southwest to Georgia during the eighteenth century. These "cattle hunters" (more rarely called cowboys) worked on foot for the most part. Black slaves often performed the hard labor of hunting wild cattle. They also used stock dogs and whips.

Herders in the southeastern piedmont branded their animals to show ownership, a common practice dating back thousands of years. Herds of 100 to 300 head of cattle appeared in the Ohio Valley by the 1820s. By the 1830s herding techniques had diffused through the Deep South into the humid coastal plains of east Texas. Moving farther west to the semi-arid plains, the habits and techniques of southeastern Anglo cowboys changed substantially under the influence of Mexico's vaqueros.

As Jackson and others illustrate, Spanish influence dominated and shaped the western open-range cattle frontier. The Anglo-American cowboy learned his trade from the vaquero. Spanish terminology, **tack,** and technique spread from Texas and California throughout the western United States.

In the 1880s a ranch foreman was called "major domo" (from the Spanish term *mayordomo)* whether he was in eastern Oregon, southern Idaho, or Nevada. Cowboys in that region were called vaqueros. Hispanic influences also crossed the border into Canada, carried by cowboys from the United States. David Weber's *The Spanish Frontier* (1992) adds rich historical detail and a sweeping interpretive vision to the study of the borderlands.

We now have a growing body of scholarly literature on Hispanic influences in western ranch culture. More work remains to be done about other issues of frontier ethnicity. African-American cowboys need more probing treatment. The literature has gone little beyond the pioneering but limited *Negro Cowboys* (1965) by Philip Durham and Everett L. Jones. The two English teachers did a good job insofar as their secondary sources permitted. Additional research into primary sources should reveal more about realities of frontier **discrimination** against black cowboys. Bulldogger Bill **Pickett** has a biographer, but many other African-American frontier figures remain more legendary than historical.

Scholars are employing diverse perspectives to the cowboy with varying results. Mary Lou LeCompte brings a background in the history of sport to her study of *Cowgirls of the Rodeo* (1993). This is the first serious look at pioneering rodeo

women of the early twentieth century. As LeCompte clearly shows, women's opportunities in rodeo fell sharply beginning in the mid-1930s.

Literature scholar Jack Weston presents a revisionist, multicultural perspective in *The Real American Cowboy* (1985). He depicts cowboys as oppressed workers and, drawing mostly on secondary sources, describes their grim lot. He includes a chapter entitled "Minority Cowboys and Women Cowhands." Like most previous analysts, he takes a shot at explaining the enduring myth of the cowboy.

Weston provided an honest, accurate self-evaluation of his book in the preface. "I am proud of my contributions to Afro-American and Chicano history in this book, but I feel my neglect of two other aspects of the history of the dispossessed." Weston considered his omission of Native American cowboys and his segregation of women from the book's main narrative to be failings.

Surely the strangest cowboy study yet penned comes from another literature scholar, Blake Allmendinger. His book, *The Cowboy* (1992), is noteworthy only because it takes the reader into the arcane and bizarre world of postmodernist literary analysis.

Canada

The American cowboy becomes a national cultural icon and as a result generates a huge historiography. Cowboys in Canada remain regional figures, associated only with the western provinces of Alberta, British Columbia, and Saskatchewan. As a regional rather than a national phenomenon, Canada's cowboy history and culture has stimulated far fewer studies than in the United States. Frontier imagery and the Turner thesis did not capture the Canadian mind the way it did the American. As a result, Canada's frontier literature is much less extensive than that of the United States.

The Range Men, by L. V. Kelly, appeared in 1913, not long after the decline of open-range ranching in Alberta. Paul D. Sharp's wonderful *Whoop-up Country* (1955) covers range life on both sides of the U.S.-Canadian border.

Wallace **Stegner**'s stimulating *Wolf Willow* (1955) gives insights into the same region covered by Sharp.

Canada's livestock industry is the subject of several excellent books and articles. Most important is David Breen's outstanding study, *Canada's Prairie West* (1984). Geographer Simon Evans has written many useful articles on Alberta ranching. Less scholarly but useful is Edward Brado's *Cattle Kingdom* (1984). Grant MacEwan's many books, such as *Blazing the Old Cattle Trail* (1975), give enjoyable, often humorous sketches of cowboy and ranch culture in Alberta.

Latin American Cowboys

Frontier history poses peculiar problems and difficulties because of the lack of traditional archival sources. The lack of sources and other research difficulties means that many cowboy types still need substantial scholarly investigation. Chile's *huaso,* Brazil's *vaqueiro* and *gaúcho,* Mexico's vaquero, and the llaneros of Colombia and Venezuela lack intensive historical studies supported by research into primary sources.

Many existing studies in Spanish and Portuguese are highly impressionistic, romantic, or polemical. (This discussion is limited mostly to English-language studies. Readers of Spanish or Portuguese may consult the bibliographies in the books discussed below.)

As with Canada, we find studies of ranching in Latin America, but far fewer works specifically about the cowboy. The Mexican *charro* (gentleman rider) has attracted more attention than the Mexican vaquero (working cowboy). We do not have a study of the Mexican vaquero to equal *Charro: Mexican Horseman* (1969) by James Norman.

We do have several studies of vaqueros in California written by Jo Mora and Arnold R. Rojas. The Spanish borderlands have gotten much more attention than comparable frontier regions in South America.

The history of Hawaii's cowboy, the *paniolo* (or *paniola)* remained largely unknown outside the islands until recently. *Nā Paniolo o Hawai'i*

(1987), edited by Lynn J. Martin, covers much of the folklore of the Hawaiian cowboy and something of his history. *Aloha Cowboy* (1988), by Virginia Cowan-Smith and Bonnie Domrose Stone, is a popular history of horsemanship in Hawaii.

Like the American cowboy, the **gaucho** of Argentina and Uruguay (and the gaúcho of Rio Grande do Sul, Brazil) have generated enormous fictional and folklore literatures. We find novels, poems, plays, memoirs, and more. The broad basis of literary representations attest to the gaucho's cultural significance.

A horse lover, Robert Bontine Cunninghame **Graham** left us some very enjoyable and evocative vignettes of cowboy life in both North and South America. The delightful *Don Segundo Sombra* (1926), by Ricardo Güiraldes, offers a wonderful introduction to the gaucho in literature. This touching story describes a boy's journey to manhood on the pampas of Argentina. It captures the flavor of gaucho character and values.

Gauchos and the Vanishing Frontier (Slatta 1983, 1992) describes the changes in nineteenth-century gaucho life and explains the forces leading to his decline. Madaline Wallis Nichols provides an extensive bibliography of hundreds of items in her brief study, *The Gaucho* (1942, 1968). *Historia social del gaucho* (1968), by Ricardo Rodríguez Molas, is far and away the best Spanish-language study. The literature in Spanish on the Uruguayan gaucho is extensive, but little is available in English.

The Chilean huaso still awaits substantial treatment in either English or Spanish. Aside from brief glimpses by European travelers and impressionistic works of folklore, little has been written. Thus far, huaso myth holds sway over huaso history.

As with many cowboy figures, we know more about llanero folklore and mythology than about history. As with Argentina, the study of the llanero might begin with a novel, *Doña Bárbara* (1935, 1966). This rich, powerful novel by Rómulo **Gallegos** conveys the power, mystery, and superstitions of the llanos. Jane M. Rausch has written two fine studies of llanos history, but she includes relatively little about the llanero or ranch life.

Broader, Comparative Studies

Several researchers have provided important overviews of horsemen and ranching in North and South America. Edward Larocque Tinker genuinely loved horses and equestrian cultures. The well-traveled New Yorker accumulated an impressive library and artifact collection representing horsemen around the world. His artifacts and books are housed on the fourth floor of the undergraduate library building at the University of Texas in Austin. Appropriately enough, the J. Frank Dobie Collection adjoins the Tinker Collection.

Tinker did more than travel and collect. He wrote an important, pioneering work entitled *Horsemen of the Americas* (1967), in which he compares the lives, literature, and legends of cowboys in North and South America. The book concludes with a very useful bibliography. Robert Denhardt, who helped found the American **Quarter Horse** Association, also wrote a very fine historical study, *The Horse of the Americas* (1975).

Man on Horseback (1964) by Glenn R. Vernam traces equestrian history to the earliest origins with Chinese, Sythian, and other horsemen. On livestock, the basic reference is John E. Rouse's *The Criollo: Spanish Cattle in the Americas* (1977).

Herbert Eugene Bolton, the great historian of the Spanish borderlands, urged the comparative study of frontiers in the Americas. He posed a question and a challenge to scholars in his 1932 address as president of the American Historical Association. "Who," Bolton asked, "has written the history … of the spread of cattle and horse raising from Patagonia to Labrador?" *Cowboys of the Americas* (Slatta 1990, 1994) attempts to cover that vast topic. (Limerick 1991; Nash 1991; Walker 1981)

See also Autobiographies by Cowboys; Pictorial Books.

HITCH

To knot, tie, or fasten something, such as a horse to a wagon.

HOBBLE

See Tack.

HOE-DOWN

Also hoe-dig; colloquial terms for a dance.

HOG RANCH

Colloquial term for crude **saloon,** often located near a military fort. Such establishments often housed prostitutes.

HOGAN, (ROBERT) RAY
(b. 1908)

Novelist who wrote formula westerns.

HOLMES, LLEWELLYN PERRY
(b.1895)

Colorado-born novelist who wrote formula westerns under various names.

HOLMES, RAY
(1911–)

Cowboy, author. See Autobiographies by Cowboys.

HOLSTER

Also known as a scabbard, the holster serves as the primary method of carrying guns. Made of leather, the basic holster often had a strap going over the gun that secured it and kept dust from the gun. If worn on the hip the holster could also be tied to the leg with a skirt (leather thong). The specifics of the holster depended upon the needs of the owner, especially the style of his draw.

The two major types of holsters are hip and shoulder holsters. The latter concealed the weapon and were not used by cowboys. They became popular after cities began passing laws against carrying guns. Westerners sometimes called a shoulder holster (or other concealed weapon) an "ace in the hole."

Each type of holster had variations making it more suitable for **fast-draw** action. The swivel hip holster was a variation of the hip model. Being attached at only one point, the entire holster could be swiveled to a horizontal position. A gunman could fire through a hole at the bottom of the holster without drawing the weapon. With the advent of the dual action revolver, holsters again needed modification. This time, the leather around the trigger disappeared.

To facilitate faster action from the shoulder holster, manufacturers developed the spring shoulder holster. Essentially the entire front of the holster was missing, except for the bottom tip, which served to hold the muzzle in place. A spring held the cylinder to the holster. With such a setup, the gun could be drawn without having to clear as much leather.

No hard-and-fast rules exist about holsters. The gunman used whatever suited him, arranged in the manner he desired. Some cowboys used no holster at all, preferring to carry a revolver tucked into their belts. The discomfort and possibility of accident, however, convinced most cowboys who carried a six-gun to tote it in a holster. (Cunningham 1934, 1962; Foster-Harris 1955; Rattenbury 1993)

—*Mark Mayer*

HOMBRE

Spanish for man, this term is sometimes modified by derogatory adjectives such as *malo* (bad).

HOMBRE DEL CAMPO

Literally a "man of the countryside;" someone knowledgeable about nature and animals.

HOME END

The end of the **rope** held by the thrower.

HOME RANGE

Also accustomed range; the usual grazing area for a herd of cattle.

HONDA

Also hondo. See Rope.

THE HONKERS

Film. See Rodeo.

HOOEY

See Rodeo Events.

HOOF-AND-MOUTH

A cattle disease. See *Aftosa*.

HOOKER, HENRY CLAY
(1828–1907)

Henry Clay Hooker, a pioneering Arizona rancher, moved to Arizona from San Francisco and established the well-known Sierra Bonita Ranch. His Crooked H brand eventually covered some 20,000 head grazing over a quarter of a million acres. His ranch house is among Arizona's oldest. In 1907 he died and was buried in Los Angeles. (Thrapp 1988)

HOOKS

Colloquial term for spurs.

HOOKSHOP

Colloquial term for brothel. See Prostitution.

HOOLIHAN

Also hooley-ann. See Rope.

HOOSEGOW

Jail; a corruption of *juzgado*, the Spanish term for courthouse.

HOPPLE

Variant of hobble. See Tack.

HORN, TOM
(1860–1903)

Tom Horn—cattle detective, cowboy, scout, and convicted killer—was born to a poor family and grew up in Missouri in the post–Civil War era. During this violent and lawless time, gangs led by Jesse James roamed the state. At the age of 14 Horn headed west on foot after getting in a fight with his father. He worked a variety of jobs—on the Santa Fe railroad, as an overland mail and stage driver, night-herding cattle, and herding cavalry horses. He learned both Spanish and Apache, and in 1876 Al Sieber, chief of government scouts at San Carlos Apache Indian reservation, gave him a job as a government interpreter. On one of his first assignments, he lived with the Apache on their reservation for about a year. According to his autobiography (not always a reliable guide), they nicknamed him the "Talking Boy."

Horn gained a reputation as an excellent steer roper and won numerous contests. He quit the scouting business and sold his mine in 1890 and went to work for the Pinkerton National Detective Agency in Denver. On his first case he tracked train robbers. The work lacked the excitement he relished, so he quit after four years.

The Wyoming Cattle Grower's Association hired Horn as a cattle detective to gather evidence of **rustling** and to track and kill the culprits. Such a job had many names, including "regulator" or range, stock, or livestock detective. In many cases, unwanted settlers and small ranchers also became targets of a regulator. Horn earned $500 for every cattle thief he killed.

Horn returned to military service in 1898 during the Spanish-American War, serving as master of transportation for Shafter's Army. After the war, he returned to Wyoming and worked for the Swan Land and Cattle Company in Wyoming as a cattle detective. He ruthlessly and successfully tracked rustlers and gained a reputation as a killer. As a trademark, he set two stones under the head of each victim.

In 1901 Horn investigated a rustling problem near Iron Mountain, Wyoming. A feud between two cattle ranchers, Miller and Nickell, complicated the situation. Someone murdered a 14-year-old boy, Willie Nickell, on 18 July, probably mistaking the lad for his father. Horn stood accused. A jury tried and convicted him, but considerable doubt still exists about his guilt. The deputy marshal obtained a confession while Horn was drunk. The prosecution never established a reasonable motive for Horn to

These weapons were used by the famed Tom Horn, a stock detective and convicted killer.

kill the boy. Horn was hanged in Cheyenne, Wyoming, on 20 November 1903. His last words are reputed to be "That's the sickest-looking lot of damned sheriffs I ever saw."

Horn's death did not end the controversy that surrounded his life. Filmmakers have found his violent, somewhat tragic life an appealing topic. McDonald Carey played him as a hired killer named Bus Crow in the 1953 film *Hannah Lee.* David Carradine starred in *Mr. Horn,* a 1979 **television** movie based on the stock detective's life. A year later Steve McQueen played the role in *Tom Horn,* an exquisitely photographed but rambling and boring film. As with many other figures of western history, myth and mythmakers continue to shape our vision of the past. (Burroughs 1962; Coolidge 1968; Horn 1964; Nunis 1992; Raine 1929)

—*Janine M. Cairo*

HORSE THIEF SPECIAL

Colloquial term for a raisin and boiled rice dish.

HORSE WRANGLER

See Wrangler.

HORSES

One simply cannot imagine a cowboy without a horse. (By the way, when a cowboy says "horse," he generally means a male animal, not a mare.) Cowboys, however, were not the first to discover and enjoy riding horses for work and pleasure. Riding and pack animals have played a long role in human history. The two main domesticated species of the genus *Equus* are horses and ponies *(E. caballus)* and asses *(E. asinus).* Records of horses, ponies, asses, and the mule (a cross between a horse and an ass) date back thousands of years. Riders of Central Asia and North Africa probably first domesticated the horse. Many breeds can be traced to Arabian origins, dating back to at least 500 B.C.

About 55 million years ago, after roughly 120 million years of mammal existence, *Hyracotherium,* or *Eohippus,* the earliest ancestor of the modern horse, appeared. Eohippus stood only 15 inches high. The animal had 4 toes on each front foot and 3 on each hind foot. From its tooth type, it appears to have been a leaf eater. Remains have been located in Wyoming and Utah.

Over a long period of time, horses evolved into the larger animals that we would recognize today. The grass-eating *Equus caballus* appeared in Central Asia, probably as "Przhevalski's horse." Other species such as the ass or donkey, the onager, and zebras also evolved. Four to five millennia ago, Sumerians used onagers to pull vehicles. Glaciation rendered the genus *Equus* extinct in North America about 1.7 million years ago during the Pleistocene Epoch.

Horses in the wild depended on keen senses and speed for survival. Horses have keener senses of smell and hearing than humans. A long neck with large eyes placed high provides a superior view of the horizon. Wide-set eyes give a broad field of vision to the side and rear. The horse's long, slender, lower legs and heavily muscled upper legs are built for speed. Large lung capacity increases endurance.

The swift and powerful horse has long been domesticated by human beings for use as a draft animal, for transportation, and in warfare. It also has figured notably in art and mythology. The riding of horses was not practical until suitable bits and other controlling devices were invented. The horse did not supplant humans and oxen at heavy farm labor until the appearance of an efficient harness about 2000 B.C.

The Spanish reintroduced domesticated horses as they explored and conquered New Spain (Mexico) and Florida in the sixteenth century. This reintroduction profoundly changed many American Indian cultures. Some animals escaped to form the **mustang** or wild horse herds. Domesticated horses descended from those of the conquistadors are termed Spanish horses. They are often bays or sorrels.

Today horses are used primarily for sports such as racing, show competition, **rodeos,** and simple riding for pleasure. Horseflesh has occasionally been consumed by humans since prehistoric times. Some Indian cultures in the Americas preferred horseflesh to beef. It is still used as pet food.

Breeds

Horses are commonly measured in terms of hands. One hand equals about 4 inches. If a horse is said to stand 10-2 hands, that means it is 42 inches tall (40 plus 2) at the withers. (The withers is the highest point on the horse over the shoulders when the animal's head is bent down as when grazing.)

There are three major groups of horses and about 100 different breeds. Small ponies, like the Shetland or Welsh, stand only 10 to 14-2 hands and weigh less than 850 pounds. A light horse, the type a cowboy would generally ride, stands 14-2 to 17 hands and weighs 800 to 1,300 pounds. Large draft horses, such as the Belgian or Percheron, tower 15-2 to 19 hands and weigh 1,500 to 2,600 pounds.

In the United States light horse breeds, especially the thoroughbred and **quarter horse,** are widely used for pleasure riding. Saddle horses vary widely in type, ability, and temperament. The standardbred is used mainly for harness racing and trotting.

Historian J. W. Grant MacEwan provided excellent thumbnail sketches of various North American breeds in the *Canadian Cattlemen* (March 1949), and these are quoted below.

Nez Perce Indians, excellent horse breeders, apparently developed the versatile Appaloosa, a distinctively spotted horse. According to MacEwan, "they possess vigor, hardiness, light tails and manes, and spotted coats, especially over the rumps." Fans can visit the Appaloosa Museum, 5070 Highway 8 West, P.O. Box 8403, Moscow, ID 83843; tel. 208-882-5578.

Morgans can trace their lineage to a single stallion, Justin Morgan, foaled in Massachusetts in 1793. "The horses are usually smaller than Standard Breds, but possess symmetry and great courage."

The Tennessee walking horse combines a comfortable gait with a gentle disposition. Their running walk "is a characteristic gait with long stride and one which possesses an unusual degree of utility, being easy on both horse and rider." The adaptable quarter horse likewise originated in the American South.

The American saddle horse is light, strong, fast, and generally taller than the quarter horse. It is comfortable to ride over long distances. "They are primarily show horses, with long necks, high carriage of head, exaggerated flexion when in action and superb grace."

Imported breeds have also played important roles in the Americas. Spaniards treasured the golden-colored palomino, and the breed has remained very popular. Hernán Cortés brought at least one with him on his invasion of the Mexican mainland in 1519. The animals have a refined and lively manner.

Among imported breeds, the Arabian is one of the oldest. It is ancestor in part to every modern riding, harness, or coach horse. Fast, compact, and beautiful, Arabians make excellent mounts. A hot blood, it tends to be nervous, but it has great endurance. By crossing the Arabian and the thoroughbred, breeders produce the strong, intelligent Anglo-Arabian.

Some breeds, like the palomino, have a standard color. Many breeds, however, include animals of varying colors from jet black to gray or white. Bays are brownish with some auburn or red shades. The mane, tail, and stockings are black. Chestnuts are similar to bays, but mane, tail, and stockings are the same color as the coat or lighter. Duns are grayish-yellow to grayish-gold, with black mane and tail.

Rider and Mount

In cowboy mythology, a horseman usually shows special affection for his mount. Famous horse and rider duos of the western movies, like Roy **Rogers** and Trigger, perpetuate this notion. Cowboys, however, needed fresh, strong mounts for strenuous ranch work, so they rode a number of different animals. In fact, most cowboys didn't even own their own mounts. Ranchers generally supplied working horses for their hands. American cowboys were unlikely to mistreat their mounts; ranchers would not countenance destruction of valuable property.

Argentine **gauchos,** on the other hand, routinely maltreated their horses. If a mount was injured or even killed in a drunken contest, the rider simply abandoned him and got a fresh mount. Vast herds of wild horses roamed the **pampas** during the eighteenth century, and a rider could quickly and easily enlarge his herd *(tropilla)* with the toss of a lasso. Owing to their great abundance, horses cost next to nothing until the mid-nineteenth century. Even the humblest gaucho maintained a string of perhaps a dozen animals, matched by color if possible.

Cowboys everywhere shared many superstitions concerning their horses. The color of a horse was important to a cowboy. The **vaquero,** for instance, retained a Spanish prejudice, perhaps traceable to Arab roots, against spotted or yellow mounts, preferring chestnuts, blacks, and grays.

Vaqueros in turn passed their superstitions along to Anglo cowboys. Many cowboys in the United States believed that paints (also called pintos by oldtimers) did not make good cutting horses. They considered solid-colored mounts to be better work animals. Cowboys preferred darker horses and avoided pintos, palominos, and Appaloosas. Interestingly, the Nez Perce Indians of the Pacific Northwest bred Appaloosas and believed them superior as war-horses.

Cowhand Jack Porter reported that these color preferences extended to the northern ranges of the United States. He helped trail a herd from Oregon to Wyoming in 1883. "A rangeman," recalled Porter, "would rarely ever buy a horse for his cavvy [band of saddle horses, from the Spanish *caballada*] unless it was a 'straight-colored' one, so that was the reason our cavvy, like most all others, was composed of bays, browns, grays, sorrels, blacks, whites, and roans."

South American cowboys also developed superstitions and preferences about the color of horses. **Llaneros** believed that white or silver-gray *(rucio)* horses were better swimmers. In the tropical **plains,** subject to seasonal flooding and crisscrossed with rivers, swimming was a necessary and important skill for man and horse. Mounts with four white hooves, however, were to be avoided because they were weak. Argentine gauchos liked roans and tried to gather a matched herd.

North America's horse population peaked about 1910, when there were about 20 million domestic horses. Although the horse's use as a draft animal is now negligible, the animal remains very popular for ranch work and recreational riding. China, however, remains the leading horse-producing country in the world, followed by the United States, Mexico, Brazil, and the former Soviet Union. (Denhardt 1975; Edwards 1987; Hayes 1969; Taylor 1961; Vernam 1964)

HORSES OF THE MOVIES

Horses are a requirement of cowboy life on the range or in the movies. Some **B-western** film cowboys even gave their mounts equal star billing. Trigger, for example, often enjoyed costar status with Roy **Rogers.** Roy and Trigger began working together in 1938 *(Under Western Skies).* The palomino, according to Rogers, was "the greatest horse that ever came along." Trigger went on to make 87 films and 101 **television** programs before retiring in 1957. He died on 3 July 1965 at the ripe old age of 33. Thanks to taxidermy, he can still be seen at the Roy Rogers and Dale Evans Museum in Victorville, California.

By granting starring roles to their horses, cowboy actors recognized the importance of their audience. B westerns appealed to youngsters, especially boys, and children enjoyed the heroic feats of movie horse stars. A brave, intelligent horse might save his master and the day. Horses could untie knots, gallop for help,

neigh a warning, and perform other wonderful feats.

The list below pairs B-western and other film stars with the names of their trusty steeds.

Horse Name	Rider Name
Buttermilk	Dale Evans
Cactus	Sunset Carson
Champion	Gene **Autry**
Copper	Eddie Dean
Diablo	Cisco Kid
Fritz	William S. Hart
Ko-Ko	Rex Allen
Lightnin'	Monte Hale
Midnight	Tim McCoy
Mutt	Hoot Gibson
Raider	Charles Starrett
Rebel	Johnny Mack Brown
Ring Eye	Smiley Burnette
Rush	Lash LaRue
Scout	Tonto (Jay Silverheels)
Silver	Buck Jones
Silver	The Lone Ranger
Silver Bullet	Whip Wilson
Silver King	Fred Thomson
Tarzan	Ken Maynard
Trigger	Roy **Rogers**
Tony	Tom Mix
Topper	William Boyd (Hopalong Cassidy)
White Dust	Fred Scott
White Flash	Tex Ritter

(Cary 1975; Everson 1992; Miller 1979; Starlog Press 1981)

See also Films, Cowboy.

HOSS

Colloquial term for **horse.**

HOT ROCK

Colloquial term for biscuit.

HOT ROLL

Colloquial term for bedroll.

HOUGH, EMERSON
(1857–1923)

Writer Emerson Hough was born in Newton, Iowa. His family left Virginia prior to the Civil War because of their antislavery beliefs. His father never held a steady job so poverty marred his childhood. He did, however, manage to attend Iowa State University where he played football.

Hough graduated with a degree in philosophy but decided to pursue a career in law. He passed the bar in 1882. That same year he published his first article, "Far from the Madding Crowd." In 1883 he went to New Mexico and opened a law practice in a mining town in Lincoln County, just two years before Billy the Kid was killed there.

Practicing law, Hough became very critical of the legal profession. In his autobiography he wrote about a time he and another lawyer encouraged a client to jump bail and flee to Mexico. Later in life he would attack the law profession in his novels *John Rawn, The Law of the Land,* and *The Broken Gate.*

After returning east Hough began a career in journalism. He worked for both the *Des Moines Times* and the *Sandusky Register.* A Chicago publisher hired him and an artist friend to write and illustrate the histories of western counties and cities. This job allowed Hough to travel extensively. His business failed, however, when his partner embezzled funds and fled. Hough then found work in Chicago as the western editor of *Forest and Stream* magazine.

Hough disliked the influx of immigrants that arrived in eastern cities in the early twentieth century, bringing new cultures and traditions. He joined anti-immigrant organizations, such as the Author's League of America and the American Protective League. As his aversion for changing eastern urban life grew, so did his appreciation of the West.

According to Hough, a book by Henry Howe, *Historical Collections of the Great West* (1851), exerted an early, powerful influence on him. He used it as a reference for many of his novels and essays. Hough felt nostalgic about the West and contrasted it favorably with urban life.

Hough's western novels emphasized a strong sense of community. He admired the people who lived on the frontier and their ability to endure hardship. He published his first book, *The Story of the Cowboy,* in 1897. It details the cowboy's life on the ranch and on the cattle drive, as well as his social activities. Hough described to his readers how the cowboy dressed, how he rode his horse, and how he performed his job.

While Hough depicted the cowboy as an honorable and even romantic figure, he made it clear that the life of the cowboy was not an easy one. Dangers and hardships abounded. Theodore **Roosevelt** reportedly lauded the book: "Now, thank God, it has been done better than I could have done it myself." This book opened Hough's career as a serious author.

Eight of Hough's 18 novels directly involved the West. They include *Heart's Desire, The Way of a Man, The Sagebrusher,* and *North of 36.* Several of his novels were turned into motion pictures, including *The Covered Wagon,* which reaped immediate financial success. Hough died in 1923, the same year *The Covered Wagon* was released. (Hough 1897, 1915, 1923; Wylder 1981)

—*Janine M. Cairo*

HUARACHES

Crude leather sandals worn by Mexican **vaqueros** and other poor Latin Americans.

HUASO

Chile's cowboy, the *huaso,* engendered a variety of identities and characteristics—outlaw, vagrant, or ranch hand. The term carried the same negative connotations as did the term *gaucho.* Indeed, horsemen in Chile were sometimes referred to as gauchos.

Uneducated and landless (as were the vast majority of Chileans), the huaso strongly preferred to work on horseback. If necessary, he would stoop to mundane agricultural labors as well. Like the gaucho, he faced limited avenues of legal work. Like many cowboy types, he served as a soldier, and the long wars against the Araucanian

Indians in the south of Chile put the huaso in great demand as a frontier cavalryman.

The working ranch hand in Chile wore simple, functional riding clothes. The huaso went barefoot or wore sandals *(ojotas).* He wore a simple apron or flour sack tied about his waist to protect him during his arduous labors. The high-crowned **hat** worn during the colonial era gave way to one with a lower crown during the nineteenth century. His knee britches became full-length trousers. High-heeled **boots** became more common, in place of the colonial sandals and low-heeled shoes. His large Chilean ceremonial **spurs** *(marinos* or *moriscos)* dragged the ground. Regular working spurs *(medio celemin)* were not so large. Brightly colored **ponchos** served many purposes—from protection from rain and wind to being a blanket at night. Leather **chaps** protected the legs from raking thorns and brush, particularly during busy **roundups.** At ranches near the coast, huasos also used chaps fashioned out of sealskin.

Thomas Sutcliffe, who lived in Chile and Peru from 1822 until 1839, described the huaso's skill with the *bolas,* a weapon generally associated with the gaucho:

In the southern provinces [of Chile] a missile is used, called "bolas," that are made from three stones, or round pieces of iron or lead, enclosed in a piece of leather; these weigh from six to eight ounces each, and are attached to thongs of about three feet in length, which, when knotted together, complete the bolas. The person who uses this missile takes the bolas by the knot, and gallops after the animal, or ostrich, he may be in pursuit of, and when he arrives at a convenient dis-tance he lets two of the balls slip through, and retains the other in his hand, and begins twirling them round his head, and casts them from him, as a stone would be propelled from a sling. An expert hunts-man, or what is called a good "boleador," can almost ensure his aim at the distance of one hundred paces. The bolas generally entangle the legs of the animal, and causes it to fall, or otherwise impede its flight; then the huaso is enabled to secure it with his lasso; the bolas is also used in warfare both by the Chilian [*sic*] cavalry and the Indians, and is a fearful missile.

The many similarities between huasos and gauchos show that the Andes did not form an impenetrable barrier. By 1603, Spaniards in Chile had established horse breeding ranches. A shortage of mounts in the sixteenth century forced Chilean riders to the unthinkable and unmanly expedient of riding mares. Herds of horses multiplied, and by the nineteenth century huasos reasserted the cultural prejudice against mares. Cowboys throughout Latin America refused to ride mares. The Mexican **vaquero** passed this aversion along to Anglo cowboys in Texas.

In northern Mexico, on the Argentine **pampa,** and in southern Chile, hostilities with Indians made cattle and horses important allies in the conquest of frontier regions. By 1568 the fierce Araucanians had become dangerous cavalrymen, often armed with weapons captured from the Spanish. By 1600 the Indians had more horses than the Spanish. Repeated and prolonged conflict with the Araucanians created a sizable internal market for livestock to mount and feed the Spanish armies in Chile.

The independence wars that swept Chile in 1817 and 1818 hurt the livestock industry, particularly in the southern part of the nation. Production fell during the 1820s to less than half of what it had been during the first decade of the century. Taking advantage of the turmoil, Indians in the south pushed the frontier of European settlement back farther to the north. Like the **llaneros,** huasos found themselves fighting as cavalrymen rather than working on ranches.

What never failed to impress observers, regardless of their estimates of the huaso's social status and character, was his ability to ride and rope. Thomas Sutcliffe visited the ranch of Juan de Dios Correa de Saa and watched the huasos at work during a *rodeo* (cattle **roundup**).

It is during a rodeo that the Chilian Huassos [*sic*] are seen to advantage, whilst they are scouring the woods, and riding at full gallop up and down the steep hills, and almost impervious thickets of thorns, "algaroba" [*algarroba,* a variety of vetch], and patches of cardoon [perennial thistle related to the artichoke], where a stranger could scarcely find a passage, or be able to ride without incurring the danger of breaking his neck, or being sorely lacerated. I have often seen them throw their lasso at full speed, and entangle and secure the wildest animal in situations that have surprised me; and still more so, to see them bring a strayed one back to the herd in perfect safety.

Chilean romanticizers tend to have their cowboy dressed in fine silks trimmed in silver or gold braid, along with huge silver spurs. The "postcard huaso" could well afford such expensive ceremonial trappings and blooded horses, but

This Chilean huaso, pictured on horseback enjoying a smoke, wears the traditional brimmed straw hat, poncho, tight trousers cinched with a sash at the waist, and knee-high boots gaitered just below the knee and adorned with large spurs.

the huaso of reality was an ill-dressed, lower-class mestizo cowhand.

As in Argentina, the elite in Chile viewed their land as perhaps overly abundant. Landowners complained that the benign climate and fertile land permitted the shiftless rural population to subsist with little or no labor. To the jaundiced elite eye, the rural poor enjoyed a secure life of fiestas and merriment. They worked only long enough to earn a few coins to be squandered at the next celebration.

The rich valleys of central Chile occupied a middle ground between the pampas and the llanos in terms of nineteenth-century change. Ricardo Price imported purebred Durham bulls during the 1840s. Tomás Gallo and Anacleto Mott followed suit in 1850. The Agricultural Society, the political organization of the Chilean landed elite, established a Durham registry in 1883. Nevertheless, many *fundos* (ranches) continued to produce traditional mestizo cattle for the internal market.

Ranching became increasingly marginalized in the Chilean economy during the late nineteenth century. The Chilean landed elite failed to modernize either ranching or agriculture. As a result, they could not compete against more efficient producers in the United States, Argentina, and Australia. They fought protectionist rear guard actions to keep out superior, cheaper Argentine beef.

Controlling national politics, the landed elite kept internal beef prices artificially high to guarantee themselves a good return. The huaso faced shrinking economic prospects and higher food prices as the protected livestock industry failed to compete internationally. Late in the century, the rise of the nitrate industry and copper mining pushed northern Chile to economic prominence and further marginalized the ranching sector.

The failure of the livestock industry to compete brought even harder times to the huaso. Some left the countryside for work as day laborers in Santiago and other cities. Others migrated north to work in the mines. Economically reduced, the huaso did not rise to the cultural prominence achieved by some other cowboys. Nevertheless, calling someone a huaso remains a compliment to the person's strength and determination. (Lago 1953; Moody 1986, 1987; Slatta 1990)

HUDDLESTON, NED

Birth name of Isom **Dart.** See African-American Cowboys.

HULL

Colloquial term for **saddle.**

HUMOR

Contrary to their laconic image, cowboys love to talk. They're just choosy about who they talk to. Conversations and story-telling offered a welcome relief from often solitary ranch labors. A cowboy who spends weeks alone out at a line shack might welcome the chance to exercise the jaw a bit around the campfire or back at the bunkhouse. "Sometimes," says John O. West *(Cowboy Folk Humor,* 1990), "in the daily round of herding cattle, looking for screwworms in cows' hides, riding fence, greasing windmills, and cleaning out stock tanks, the cowboy's spirit simply has to break out." That's when the cowboy's sense of humor shines—in tall tales, practical jokes, and witty conversation.

Cowboys and ranchers often use humor to cope with the troubles and tragedy all too common on the range. Folklorist and storyteller Jim Garry relates the tale of one old rancher who got yet one more loan from the bank. Asked why he was so happy to be even further in debt, he said, "Don't you see? I've won." When asked what he meant, he replied with glee, "There's just no way I can live long enough to have to pay this note off at the bank."

Among themselves, cowboys passed long hours exchanging jokes and tall tales, but outsiders often missed out on cowboy humor. To the stranger, cowboys often appeared taciturn in the extreme. For example, outsider William T. Hornaday misread cowboy character during his visit to cow camps *(Cosmopolitan,* December 1886):

I never saw elsewhere in this country a set of men that were so careful in the avoidance of sarcasm and smart sayings likely to give offense. They are severely matter-of-fact in everything, and very little given to joking. Indeed, where every man carries a six-shooter, jokes are not safe things to handle, unless they are of mighty small calibre. Any joke, no matter how old and rusty, if pointed at a cowboy, is liable to go off, and kill the very man that "didn't know it was loaded."

Gauchos in Argentina and **vaqueros** in Mexico likewise exhibited a reserve toward strangers. Their common response to the questions of a prying outsider was "¿Quién sabe?" ("Who knows?"). Cowboys shared their humor and private thoughts with their pards. Most outsiders had difficulty seeing and understanding the real cowboy and his culture.

A few cowboy humorists attained fame. Edgar Wilson ("Bill") Nye (1850–1896) became the best paid humorist of the late nineteenth century. He began writing humorous stories in 1876 in Laramie, Wyoming. As he honed his skills, more than 60 newspapers carried his columns. By the early 1890s, he earned $30,000 a year from his writing and lecturing. Declining health and a stroke ended his life at age 45.

Oklahoman William Penn Adair (Will) **Rogers** (1879–1935) became America's most beloved cowboy humorist, philosopher, and roper. Rogers came from a ranching background and earned his **spurs** as a performer with Wild West shows and **rodeos.** Beginning in 1915, he turned banter with the audience into the mainstay of his stage presence. Like Bill Nye, he used his down-home wit and tales to comment on contemporary politics. In the early 1920s, he wrote a syndicated column. He starred in several films from 1929 until his tragic death in an airplane crash. Images of Rogers grinning shyly and scratching his head remain part of the wonderful world of cowboy culture.

Vaqueros and Anglo cowboys would swap tall tales and ghost stories around the campfire. Superstitious vaqueros enjoyed frightening tales of spirits and buried treasure. *Doña Bárbara,* the famous novel of Venezuela's llanos, is filled with superstition and the supernatural. The leading female character in this fine Rómulo **Gallegos** novel is a powerful witch.

Tall Tales

"Windies," tall tales filled with exaggeration, held a special attraction for cowboys. Tales about the exploits of Pecos Bill are probably the most famous of the genre. Jim Garry provides some fine examples of windies in his collection of stories of the American West. His title is a great statement of ranch humor: *This Ol' Drought Ain't Broke Us Yet (But We're All Bent Pretty Bad)* (1992).

Cowboys found simple ways to spend their free time. "Oh, we just set around and lied to each other, that's all," says Raisins Rhoads, who worked at the Chapman-Barnard Ranch in Oklahoma. "We raised hell with each other. We kidded each other a lot. That's the only thing we had to do."

Horse trading gave rise to its own entire genre of humor and folklore. Roger L. Welsch has collected old-time horse trading tales in his book, *Mister, You Got Yourself a Horse* (1981). "Skinnin', skunkin' or trimmin'" someone in a swap, he points out, brought profound joy to the heart of a real horse trader. A wily horse trader might say with straight-faced honesty, "You'll be surprised to see the way he works." The way the horse works, of course, is not at all. Earl Conrad *(Horse Trader,* 1953) offers a few jewels of horse humor. "A hoss don't have to talk for hisself very often but when he does he's got two advisers in back and two spokesmen in front." Horses and **women** often appear together in cowboy jokes, songs, and conversation. Conrad commented on

Story-telling and humor kept cowboy spirits up. Many tales were told around evening campfires on the range. In this 1908 Erwin E. Smith photograph, a group of L. S. Ranch cowboys gather 'round for a tall tale or two.

the difference between his argumentative wife and a horse. "One thing about a hoss—you can always swap her!"

Practical Jokers

When a cowboy had a few dollars in his pocket, he would avail himself of the popular vices of his day, but cowboys also invented their own low-cost fun. From Argentina to Alberta, cowboys enjoyed practical jokes. Writing of life on the Midway Ranch in Alberta, rancher Fred Ings recalled that "the cowboys used to have great fun—always up to some prank. A tethered horse at night might have his saddle reversed, particularly if its rider was paying court to some girl. A horse and buggy left standing would be found seemingly intact, but with the horse on one side of the fence and the buggy on the other." "Snipe hunts," popular in Canada and the United States, left the victim afoot far from help with nothing but a candle and a bag for comfort.

Baby swapping is one of the most storied cowboy pranks. Every part of the range has a tale about a cowboy switching the blankets of babies sleeping at a dance. In his famed novel, Owen **Wister** has the Virginian play this trick when the schoolmarm refuses to dance with him.

Cowboys might haze a tenderfoot or a new hand to test his mettle. One anonymous cowboy writer recalled a cow outfit's reaction to a newcomer's fear of panthers. They convincingly faked a panther attack on one of their comrades, complete with terrifying howls. They carried the "victim" of the attack into camp, having smeared him with beef blood to heighten the effect. The new hand became one of many, many victims of ingenious cowboy pranks.

Sticking unlikely or uncomfortable objects in a cowboy's bedroll or **boots** was popular. Cowboys and vaqueros loved roping one another from ambush. At spring **roundup,** kangaroo courts might be held. Goading a coworker's horse, just as the man was lighting a cigarette or otherwise occupied, provided great fun. The cook became a favorite target of pranksters, but given the cook's importance to the outfit, hands took care not to go too far.

Profanity

Real cowboy speech (as opposed to that manufactured by Hollywood or New York), humor, and song often reveal a flair for the obscene. Only a cowboy could come up with the name "son-of-a-bitch stew" (see Food). Owing to Victorian morality and a century of sanitizing the cowboy's image, profanity became a forgotten part of his public persona.

With characteristic wit and bluntness, singer Katie Lee explained the eastern impulse to bowdlerize in her book, *Ten Thousand Goddam Cattle* (1976). The book title is a line from an old range song.

> We'll let the title of this book serve as an example—it comes from the cowboy's camp. The other title, *Ten Thousand Cattle Straying,* comes from the literary camp, and seventy-five years ago the Eastern dudes who were writing about the cowboy wouldn't have said shit if they'd had a mouthful of it. Also, at the time our cowboy was saying the most with his flamboyant tongue, decency was heading West with Victorian codes, breathing fire and damnation on the songs and verses of the nation's last great individual.

Ramon Frederick **Adams** enriched the literature of the cowboy in many ways. Readers interested in authentic cow country profanity may consult his book titled *The Cowman Says it Salty* (1971). Like Katie Lee, folklorist Guy Logsdon examined the cowboy's bawdy humor in *The Whorehouse Bells Were Ringing* (1989). Logsdon spent years collecting and recording more than 60 bawdy ballads sung for him by old-time cowboys. As Logsdon explains, "While some readers will see only offensive words, others will surely discern the genius of humor."

Cowboy Humor Today

Cowboy humorists, storytellers, and poets perpetuate the comedy of the range. Poet and "one-time large animal veterinarian" Baxter

Black is currently the nation's best-known cowboy humorist.

Black's success prompted many other cowboy humorists to try their hand. Wallace D. ("Wally") McRae and Waddie Mitchell have gained national reputations as cowboy poets. McRae's hilarious "Reincarnation" is probably the most recited cowboy poem.

Humor can take many forms. Artists and cartoonists visually tickle the western funnybone. Ace Reid, Lloyd Mitchell, Mad Jack Hanks, Herb Mignery, Chris Hammack, Bonnie Shields, Paul Crites, Doc R. M. Miller, and others paint or draw comical depictions of the West. Walt LaRue, Mike Craig, Dwayne Brech, Justin Wells, and Dick Spencer also sketch funny cowboy cartoons. Argentine artist Florencio Molina Campos created entertaining gaucho caricatures for several decades. Mike Scovel sculpts distinctive western caricatures. Curt Brummett and Viv Spencer write humorous short stories. In sum, humor in its many forms has long been and remains a great survival mechanism on western ranges.   (Allen 1933; Hoig 1958; Larson 1968; Rogers 1919, 1924, 1949; Rollins 1984)

HUNG UP

When a rider falls from the saddle and catches a foot in the stirrup. The rider is in grave danger of being dragged if the horse bolts.

HURRICANE DECK

An apt term for the saddle on the back of a wildly bucking horse.

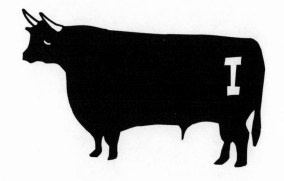

"I WANT TO BE A COWBOY'S SWEETHEART"

Hit song by Patsy Montana. See Music.

IKARD, BOSE

(1847–1929)

See African-American Cowboys.

INDIAN BROKE

A horse trained to be mounted from the right side. Cowboys mounted from the left side.

INDIAN LIQUOR

Also Indian whiskey—cheap, adulterated liquor. See Saloons.

INDIAN SIDE

Also off-side—the right side of a horse.

INDIANS AND THE HORSE

As historian Peter Iverson well illustrates in *When Indians Were Cowboys* (1994), many Plains Indian cultures developed sophisticated equestrian cultures long before the heyday of ranching in the American West. The horse revolutionized many native economies and cultures. It became central to Plains Indian buffalo hunting, raiding, and religion. Some Indians also took up cattle ranching, and, in the case of the Navajo, sheep herding.

Prehistoric Period

The Bering Land Strait served as the link between the fauna of the Siberian savanna and the inviting tundra of the North American continent during the Pleistocene era. Across this frozen land bridge traveled herds of giant elk, super bison, woolly mammoths, and small horses. In pursuit of these animals came people of Mongolian ancestry, the nomads believed to be the ancestors of Indians who populated the North and South American continent in the centuries to come. Scholars generally believe that most of the Indian population arrived on the North American continent between 25,000 B.C. and 10,000 B.C.

Small prehistoric horses served only as a source of food and resources for the first Indians of the Pleistocene. Prehistoric Indians used most of the ancient mammals for food. Archeological evidence and Indian oral tradition indicate that they did domesticate dogs as hunting aids and beasts of burden, practices inherited from their Mongolian ancestors. Scientists theorize that warming trends in the climate and the pressure of human exploitation were primary factors in wiping out the North American horse and other mammals.

Indian Acquisition of the Horse

The horses Plains Indians employed in hunting and warfare in the eighteenth and nineteenth centuries did not evolve on the North American continent. These creatures arrived with the Spaniards and other Europeans. Scholars once believed that Plains Indians acquired horses from the strays whose original herds had been imported from Spain for the disastrous exploration led by Hernando de Soto from 1539 to 1543.

The "stray theory" has since fallen to the wayside. Out of de Soto's 223 horses, 150 perished, 15 were slaughtered as the expedition's food supply dwindled, 22 returned to Spain, and a few wandered off. Reports suggest that nearby Indians ate these strays.

According to scholar John C. Ewers, tribes in the Plains acquired their horses through trade, theft, or as rewards. While the Spanish set very strict rules concerning horse trade, they often gave horses to Christianized Indians. At stock ranches near the Rio Grande, the Spanish trained Native-American captives as stable hands. Some of these young men may have escaped, bringing both horses and valuable knowledge back to their tribes. **Mustangs,** thought to be running wild, may have actually been horses left to roam tribal territory until the time came for their training or horses left to spend the season when buffalo migrated out of the tribal hunting grounds.

Many Plains Indians proved themselves astonishing masters of equestrian skills. As keen observers they copied Spanish training techniques, improvising where they saw fit. Oral traditions recall that the people of the Flathead, Nez Perce, and Coeur d'Alene tribes spent much time observing the horse, its movements, and how it might react around people before attempting to master it. Often substituting buffalo hide and wool for the leather used in Spanish equestrian equipment, the Plains Indians modeled their own gear after the **saddles** and **tack** of the Spanish.

In the varied cultures and languages of the native population, no tribe possessed a word to describe the strange animals they saw Spaniards riding. Since the dog was the only animal they associated with domestication, Native Americans often used the root word *dog* to describe horses. A Cree Indian related his first encounter with a horse to a white trader in 1730. He and his war band happened upon a horse killed in battle with a mounted tribe. "Numbers of us went to see him," he recounted, "and we all admired him. He put us in mind of a stag that had lost his horns; and we did not know what name to give him. But as he was a slave to Man, like the dog, which carried our things, he was named the Big Dog."

Hidatsa, Atsina, and Sioux Indians described the bizarre animals owned by white men as "great-dog," "elk-dog," or "mysterious dog." One of the chief advantages Europeans had over Indians was their use of the horse in warfare. Even so, Indians knew well their homeland and its many secret avenues for escape or ambush. To the dismay of many Spaniards, **Plains** Indians constructed thin, especially powerful arrows that could penetrate Spanish armor. Furthermore, Indians fired their bows faster than the Spanish could reload a crossbow or harquebus.

The Comanche obtained horses by about 1700. Once mounted, they left their homeland in the semidesert west of the Rockies and moved south onto the plains. Their sweep to the south and east drove out many Apache groups, such as the Jicarilla and Lipan. Thanks to their superb horsemanship, they made themselves masters of a huge territory. Comanche control ran from the Arkansas River in southeastern Colorado south to the Pecos River in Texas and east into western Oklahoma and southwest Kansas.

Adapting the Horse to Indian Culture

The horse made possible the trade and commercial boom in the Spanish borderlands. Thanks to the horse, Native Americans faced fewer periods of famine. Mounted hunters could efficiently bring down buffalo, deer, and other large animals. Such mobility, of course, also encouraged more warriors to raid distant enemies. Able to create a surplus of goods, Plains Indians traveled long distances to participate in trade fairs. They exchanged their hides and dried meat for the agricultural produce of more sedentary Indian peoples. Spaniards brought a wealth of trade goods, from baubles and beads to very useful metal tools. Alas, Spanish slaving and other abuses often undercut such budding trade relations.

Eventually Native Americans conquered their fear of the horse, accepting it into their cultures as they had accepted no other animal. The impact of the horse in Plains Indian culture permeated all aspects of warfare, social life, transportation, religion, and food-gathering. No other animal had so profound an effect on Plains Indian life-style. Before the horse era, most Plains Indians followed on foot the migratory patterns of big game herds like the long-horned bison or survived as semisedentary agriculturists. In the pre-horse era, the buffalo hunt was an exhausting procedure requiring the exertion of every able-bodied member of the tribe, male and female.

Once a tribe acquired horses, the hunt became infinitely easier and far more efficient. On horseback, the buffalo hunt required fewer hunters, ensured that more meat could be taken from a herd, and made transportation of the meat much simpler.

Some scholars suggest that the horse merely fulfilled the same jobs fulfilled by dogs. Yet, as anthropologist Elizabeth Atwood Lawrence ascertains, dogs required very different care than their horse replacements. Dogs ate meat like their masters. They were inherently more submissive and could be trained in shorter periods of time than the horse. Horses, on the other hand, were not naturally submissive. They required rigorous training sessions and enormous pasture to sustain them. The arrival of the horse disrupted the Plains Indian way of life as tribes abandoned older migratory routes in order to incorporate the horse into their new life-styles.

The horse also changed the life of tribes who practiced forms of agriculture. When the Blackfeet acquired the horse, the tribe's traditional way of life vanished and an entirely new method of survival emerged. The Blackfeet abandoned their crops, supporting themselves predominantly with the spoils of the buffalo hunt. The horse replaced both the canoe and the dog as their primary method of transportation. A man's wealth and honor became measured by the number and health of his horses. Horses became an essential element of trade.

Lawrence writes, "The horse has been credited with bringing about for the Crows the vast cultural changes from semi-sedentary horticultural life to nomadic hunting and gathering." As Plains Indians tossed aside old ways for new, the horse became the symbol of wealth. Plains Indians paid for brides, shaman services, and valuable objects with the Big Dog.

The Comanche also altered their economy radically. Buffalo hunting remained their mainstay. They also traded horses, mules, and captives obtained in raids against white settlements in Texas and New Mexico. Through trade, the Comanche turned the Kiowa from an enemy to an ally. The Kiowa originally lived near the headwaters of the Arkansas, Cimarron, Canadian, and Red rivers. In the eighteenth century, they met and fought the Comanche. Beginning about 1790, however, the two tribe agreed to share territory and cooperate on raids against settlements in Texas and New Mexico. They then traded the horses, mules, captives, and other booty to other plains tribes, including the Wichita.

In the horse cultures, Plains Indian tribes ventured into new territory in search of better pasture. Wealthier nomads may have herded their horses to pastures much like sheep or cattle. Each family took care of its own animals. When traveling, Indians moved their horses in small groups, allowing horses to follow their instincts. Small families of horses trailed an older mare with a stallion guarding the rear.

Observers could determine the wealth of a tribe by the number of women riding horses. If women walked or led packhorses and dogs, the tribe suffered in poverty or was just returning from a successful buffalo hunt. Women and men were both mounted in a prosperous, horse-rich tribe.

Nomadic tribes required up to ten horses per male. Aside from the buffalo horse and the war-horse, a male family leader needed at least five packhorses to carry 250 pounds of camping equipment. Each member of the family, children included, often possessed their own steeds. Wealthier tribes exchanged extra horses for items brought by white traders.

Military Impact of the Horse

The need for more grasslands both intensified rivalries between tribes and helped Indians from one tribe to establish new trade contacts with friendly tribes. Raiding other tribes for horses became an accepted means of replenishing the herd. Aside from successful battle, horse raiding was one of the chief pursuits for young Indian warriors. With each raid came prestige and honor—keys to proving manhood and gaining acceptance into one's tribe. Intertribal warfare became more frequent and eventually replaced even the buffalo hunt as the highest test of Plains Indian manhood.

Acquisition of the horse altered the basic elements of Indian warfare. Bows, arrows, and shields had to be constructed out of lighter material as the horse became central to Plains Indian warfare. Shamans conducted sacred war ceremonies, blessing battle steeds with strength, endurance, speed, and a safe return.

Men openly grieved for days if their horses died in battle, just as they might mourn a lost relative or best friend. An entire war complex emerged, placing extraordinary importance on the horse. A warrior's identity became closely linked to his horse. Before battle, Indians bedecked both warrior and steed in the same paint designs, feathers, and beads, and blessed each pair with the same prayers. If a man wanted to insult a warrior, he would slap the warrior's horse in the face.

In the horse era, Native-American warfare was not the total warfare known to white men of the day. Often a successful battle occurred if warriors from one tribe managed to merely strike or touch their opponents. Some "wars" involving counting coup seem more like glorified games of tag. Warriors often valued the acquisition of horses in warfare over how many enemies they slaughtered. The recapture of horses previously stolen by an enemy became more important than acquiring new steeds. Horses helped to transform intertribal warfare into something

of a sport—just as the buffalo hunt had become more sport than necessity.

During the early eighteenth century, French firearms reached plains nomads. These firearms greatly enhanced Native-American hunting and military capability. With the gun and horse, the Comanche became known as the "Lords of the South Plains."

Indians used ambush, sneak attack, and their extraordinary horsemanship to wage war effectively. Apaches often ambushed Spanish forces. In 1780 Apaches disguised themselves as Spanish soldiers by donning the appropriate leather jackets, hats, and muskets, then completely surprised Pima Indians at Gila River, Arizona, killing or capturing 120 people.

During the eighteenth century, the mounted Comanche closed off both French and Spanish expansion into their bastion, the southern plains.

Native Americans also tended cattle on the western plains. This photograph of Indians, possibly Caddo or Kickapoo, and their horses was taken circa 1890 in Oklahoma.

Not until the Medicine Lodge Treaty of 1867 did whites force the Comanche (along with their allies the Kiowa and Kiowa Apache) to restrict themselves to reservation land in southwestern Oklahoma. Warfare with whites continued, however, and decimated the Comanche—an estimated 20,000 Comanche roamed the plains in the eighteenth century, but in 1910 only 1,500 remained. By 1987 about 4,650 Comanche lived on or near their Oklahoma reservation.

Like other Plains Indians, Plenty Coups, chief of the Crow in 1930, believed horses to be spiritual intelligent beings. Before battle, Crow warriors spent time alone with their horses. In Plenty Coups' words, "such a time teaches them (the battle steeds) to understand us, and us to understand them." The Crow warriors fasted with their horses before battle to ensure that both achieved a mutual bond of understanding. As the Crow chief observed, the horse "must know my heart and I must know his or we shall never become brothers.... I have many times seen my horse's soul in his eyes."

Religious Impact of the Horse

The horse became an important element of Native-American belief systems. In many Plains Indian cultures, like the Crow and the Apache, people worshipped horses, particularly war-horses. They believed that horses possessed intelligence, souls, and the ability to speak to sensitive members of the tribe. Horse spirits appeared in dreams or visions. The horse came to represent the link between the spiritual and temporal world. Among the Crow, it was considered blasphemy to eat horseflesh. Only in times of severe famine did the Crow break this taboo. The Comanche ate horse meat only if the hunt had been unsuccessful and dog meat was unavailable.

Most Plains Indian beliefs stressed that horses should be treated with respect and even reverence. Some contemporary Crow still believe that if a horse is not treated properly it will seek vengeance on its owner. In the Crow culture, a man could be killed for abusing a horse.

Just as a horse could punish its owner, it could also provide awards. Many tribal legends describe a Spirit-Horse, a being that watches over all horses and rewards men and women who have given special care to their steeds. To reward a man, the Spirit-Horse might appear to him in a dream and give him the secrets of multiplying his herd.

Plains Indians believed horses possessed the ability to cure people injured in raids and battle. In the Apache culture, rituals known as horse ceremonies attempted to ensure success, safety, and well-being in the buffalo hunt, the battle, and the capture and training of horses, and to cure those who had been injured after falling from their mounts.

Demise of the Plains Indian Horse Cultures

Three main factors contributed to the demise of the Plains Indian horse era: (1) The late-nineteenth-century Indian reservation policy of the United States; (2) increased Anglo-American expansion into the West; and (3) depletion of the once-plentiful buffalo herds.

Inheriting the British Indian policy, American officials continued the practice of isolating Native American tribes in areas where they could conduct their own affairs away from white contact. In the removal period of American Indian policy, many Native Americans moved to reservations far from their ancestral lands, usually without their consent. As the "Indian frontier" continued to grow smaller, outbreaks of hostilities between free-roaming tribes, reservation tribes, and white settlers forced American officials to reevaluate their Indian policy.

Tribes with horses and **firearms** put up the best resistance against the reservation policy and the United States Army. Most people recall this era with fanciful visions nourished by Hollywood and pulp westerns. In truth, bloody Indian war raids against whites were few and far between. Most resistance took the form of guerrilla-style fighting. Plains Indians mastered camouflage and escape methods rather than developing disciplined maneuvers like those of the U.S. Army.

The Sioux and Apache proved themselves the most difficult tribes to subdue. At a time when many Native Americans in the West complied with the American reservation policy, leaders of Indian resistance, the brilliant Sioux Sitting Bull for example, refused to abandon older ways of life for the stark existence they witnessed on reservations. To those who sought temporary shelter, food, and clothing from federal Indian agencies, Sitting Bull taunted, "You are fools to make yourselves slaves to a piece of fat bacon, some hard tack, and a little sugar and **coffee**."

Despite General Custer's famous defeat in the Battle of Little Bighorn in 1876, the United States conquered the Sioux nation. After the Ghost Dance Massacre of 1890, the government confined rebellious Indians to reservations. The lures of game and land that might have once tempted them off the reservation were quickly disappearing.

Throughout 1867 and 1868, the Union Pacific Railroad divided the massive western bison herd into two separate entities. In 1871 an eastern tannery company discovered the vast market for buffalo hides. Hide hunters and "sportsmen" descended on the plains in droves, killing buffalo at a rate of three million a year. By 1883 a western scientific expedition could account for only 200 surviving buffalo.

Joseph Medicine Crow, commenting on the slaughter of his people's precious horses, writes, "The whole affair was a great shock to the tribesmen, just as much as the previous clearing of the Crow range of buffalo was a sad blow.... The destruction of the horse was one of the basic factors detrimental to the Crow's problem of adjustment for the Crow culture was based primarily on the horse." (Collier 1947; Dobie 1950; Ewers 1955; Getty 1963; Haines 1938, 1971; Iverson 1994; Lawrence 1985; Medicine Crow 1992; Roe 1955)

See also Arapaho; Cheyenne.

—*Corinne Frist Glover*

INDIANS AS COWBOYS

The horse remains important to many Indian cultures. In the mid-1980s, anthropologist Elizabeth Atwood Lawrence conducted fieldwork among the Crow to find what place the horse held in their contemporary culture. She demonstrated that horses still play important roles in Crow society.

Many of the tribe's men favored working as cowboys or ranchers over working in factories. Factory work to them seemed a degrading job, void of the challenge and contact with **horses** inherit to ranching. Ranching requires much physical activity and working with the elements of nature. It emphasizes tasks to be mastered by individuals. Unlike other American cattlemen, Crow ranchers do not raise their cattle entirely for profit, but work instead towards acquiring more horses. Wealth is still measured by the number of horses an individual owns, not by the size of his income. One Crow remarks, "I love horses, and I have a bunch of them at my place. They mean a lot to me. I would have them even if I were broke, as long as there is grass. Horses have status here."

Crow children learn to ride at a very young age. Non-Indian neighbors remark that Crow children are riding before they learn to walk. Indian parents encourage both girls and boys to ride and compete in equestrian contests. Missionary work and the establishment of 4-H clubs helped to bring young girls out of the traditional domestic roles Crow culture previously imposed upon them. The horse provides activities for children who do not have swimming pools, basketball courts, or Little League to occupy them.

Indian **rodeo** mixes Native American and white equestrian cultures. Edison Bisuie, president of the American Indian Rodeo Cowboy Association, went so far as to say, "In today's modern setting there's no such thing as Indians and Cowboys." In his view, the two have fused into a single rodeo culture. Both Native Americans and whites wear the same rodeo cowboy dress. Both take on the same challenges against horses, livestock, and the clock. The appearance in 1993 of a glossy, new magazine, *Cowboys & Indians,* reflects a similar belief in the convergence of cultures in the West. A mix of

Anglo-American cowboy and Native-American artwork and artifacts decorate many homes.

Horses still serve as extensions of an Indian's personality. A good racehorse reflects the value and importance of its owner. The Crow are renowned for nursing lame or sick horses back to health; some of these horses become champions. As in the old days, mastering the skills required to ride still provides many Crow with a sense of self-confidence and achievement. A Crow teacher remarked, "Bicycles and Hondas just don't give them (kids) a sense of who they are. The kids are looking for something to make them Indian. Long hair, beads, and floppy hats don't do it. Those things make you a hippie, not an Indian. An Indian is an individual. With the horse, he gets a sense of his own identity and individuality." (Iverson 1994; Lawrence 1985; Medicine Crow 1992)

INGRAHAM, PRENTISS
(1843–1904)

Author and publisher of **pulp** fiction. See Autobiographies by Cowboys.

IRON

Short for branding iron or six-gun.

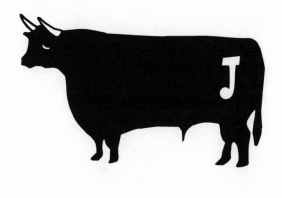

J. W. COOP

Rodeo film directed by and starring Cliff Robertson.

JA RANCH

See Goodnight, Charles.

JACKEROO

Also buckaroo; colloquial terms for cowboy.

JACKSON, ALAN
(1958–)

Singer. See Hat Acts.

JACKSON, HARRY
(1924–)

Artist. See Art of the Cowboy.

JACKSON, JACK

Texas historian. See Historiography of the Cowboy.

JAMES, WILLIAM RODERICK
(1892–1942)

Writer, illustrator. See Autobiographies by Cowboys.

JÁQUIMA

Spanish term anglicized to hackamore, jacamore, headstall, halter. See Tack.

JAVA

Colloquial term for **coffee.**

JEANS

See Levi's.

JEFFRIES, HERB
(1916–)

Actor, singer. See African-American Cowboys in Film.

JENNINGS, WAYLON
(1937–)

Singer. See Music.

JERKY

Dried meat, usually beef. The name comes from the Spanish word *charqui.* See *Vaquería.*

JINETE

Spanish word meaning horseman.

JINETEA

A short-stirruped riding style passed from Moors to Spaniards. See *Charro.*

JINGLEBOB

This melodic term has two meanings. First, it refers to a deeply cut earmark used by John **Chisum,** who ranched in Lincoln County, New Mexico. Because of the deep cut into the cow's ear, the lower portion of the ear flops downward. Consisting of a single, long slit along the full length of the ear, the mark was quick to make and identifiable at a considerable distance. Many ranchers used earmarks, but most favored smaller notches and designs.

The term's second meaning refers to danglers, little pear-shaped pendants that dangle from a cowboy's **spurs.** Most of the cowboy's equipment is strictly functional. Jinglebobs, however, serve only to add a little jingling **music** to his walk and ride. (Branch 1961; Watts 1977)

JOHN B.

Colloquial term for cowboy **hat,** after hatmaker John B. Stetson.

JOHNSON, BEN, JR.
(1922–)

Born in Pawhuska, Oklahoma, Ben Johnson, Jr., was called "Son" in his youth as he grew up on the Osage. Cowboying in Oklahoma honed the riding and roping skills that later served him well in Hollywood westerns. He enjoyed fame and fortune as a daring stuntman, memorable character actor, and **rodeo** performer.

Johnson came by his horseback skills honestly. His father, Ben Johnson, Sr., served as ranch foreman at the Chapman-Barnard Ranch in northeastern Oklahoma from the 1930s through the 1950s. Ranch cowboys recalled the champion steer roper and master cowboy with great affection. The father passed his savvy and skills along to his son, who also worked on the ranch.

The hands at the Chapman-Barnard liked working for Ben, Sr. One hand, Oscar Wright, summed it up this way: "He knew the business better than anybody that ever rode a horse, I guess. He knew the livestock business, and he could ride a horse. He could ride a buckin' horse just as easily as he could one that you was working cattle on."

In 1939 Howard Hughes talked Ben, Jr., into leaving Oklahoma ranch life for Hollywood. Hughes purchased a string of mounts from Ben Johnson, Sr., and suggested that his teenage son go along as top wrangler. Ben's first weekly paycheck of $175 convinced him to stay in Hollywood. "With pay like that, they couldn't have run me off with a stick. You can make more falling off *one* horse out there [in Hollywood] than you can make in two months back here."

Hands who knew young Ben at the Chapman-Barnard were not the least bit surprised at his Hollywood success. They saw his talents early on. "Son was interested in ropin' hisself," recalled Oscar Wright. "He started out when he was just real young, and he wanted to rope everything he come to, you know. Whether they needed ropin' or not! And Son was a good rider. He still is."

Oklahoma cowboy Marvin Griffin put it this way: "He was a damn good cowboy, mister. He was, well, I guess one of the best as far as I was concerned. He wasn't afraid of no horse, and he'd a-roped a freight train if somebody said catch it."

Stories about Ben point to a young stuntman in the making. Cowhand Dink Talley recalled a time when Ben, Sr., told his son to bulldog a steer from a car fender. Ben, Sr., drove right up next to a steer and yelled, "Git 'im, Son." Young Ben jumped off the fender and dogged the steer. When someone suggested that such activity might be dangerous, his father replied that his son "just as well die young, as wait till he gets old."

Ben Johnson, Jr., appeared in dozens of feature **films,** mostly westerns. His film credits range from *The Outlaw* (1943) to *The Shootist* (1976). His memorable performance as Sam the Lion in *The Last Picture Show* won him a well-deserved Oscar in 1972. In 1991 he appeared in the popular rodeo film, *My Heroes Have Always Been Cowboys.* (Miller 1979; Ronda and Slatta 1993)

JOHNSON, FRANK TENNEY

(1874–1939)

Artist. See Art of the Cowboy.

JONES, BUCK

(1889–1942)

B-western film actor.

JORDAN, TERRY G.

(1938–)

Geographer. See Historiography of the Cowboy.

JOSLYN ART MUSEUM

Omaha, Nebraska, museum opened in 1931. See Appendix B.

JUAN MOREIRA

Novel by Eduardo Gutiérrez. See *Gauchesco; Gaucho.*

JUDAS STEER

A steer that led other animals to the slaughterhouse.

JUDSON, EDWARD Z. C.

See Buntline, Ned.

JUNIOR BONNER

Film. See Rodeo.

JUNIPER

Derogatory term for an easterner or novice cowhand.

JUSTINS

Synonym for cowboy **boots.**

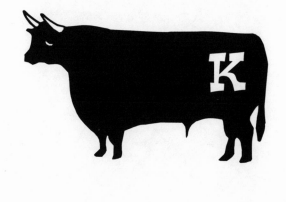

KANSAS CITY FISH
Colloquial term for fried side pork.

KELLY'S
See Spurs.

KELTON, ELMER
(1926–)
Texas novelist Elmer Kelton was born to and grew up in a ranch family in Andrews County, Texas. "With all that heritage," he says, "I should have become a good cowboy myself, but somehow I never did, so I decided if I could not do it I would write about it." After studying at the University of Texas at Austin he pursued a career in journalism and wrote fiction on the side.

By the 1970s Kelton's fiction began to receive praise. He writes historical fiction often based on events in Texas. His books are far more believable than the work of pulp novelists. "I have always believed we can learn much about ourselves by studying our history, for we are the products of all that has gone before us."

Kelton has authored nearly 20 novels. Folklorist Guy Logsdon (see Humor) is one of his many fans. "Three novels by Elmer Kelton that are excellent in catching the real cowboy spirit and reflecting their culture and thought process are *The Time It Never Rained* [1973], *The Good Old Boys* [1978], and *The Man Who Rode Midnight* [1987]." The **National Cowboy Hall of Fame** awarded Kelton its Western Heritage Wrangler Award to the latter novel. Another excellent work of historical fiction by Kelton is *The Day the Cowboys Quit* (1971), based on a failed Canadian River cowboy strike in 1883. (Kelton 1992; Tuska and Piekarski 1983)

KETCH ROPE
A lariat used to catch animals.

KETCHUM, PHILIP
(1902–1969)
Colorado-born author of formula westerns.

KETTLE
To buck.

KING, PEE WEE
(1914–)
Singer. See Music.

KING, RICHARD
See King Ranch.

KING RANCH
The current owners of the King Ranch, the Klebergs, are among the world's largest landowners. Their total holdings include over 11 million acres. About one million of those are part of the King Ranch in Texas.

The founder of the King Ranch, Captain Richard King, was born on 10 July 1824. The title of captain came from his command of riverboats, not from any military experience. His aptitude for riverboating allowed him to form a successful business, along with Charles Stillman and Mifflin Kenedy, after the Mexican-American War.

In 1852 King took advantage of extremely low land prices in Texas. For two cents an acre he purchased 15,500 acres in an area called Rincón de Santa Gertrudis (aka Wild Horse Desert) between the Nueces River and the Rio Grande. This purchase formed the basis of what would become one of the largest holdings in the country.

King's cattle business started in 1854 when he purchased his first herd of somewhat dilapidated **longhorns.** He hired local **vaqueros** (Mexican cowboys) to maintain both the herd and ranch. **Fencing** the property became a priority for King. In this sense he would not seem to be a proponent of open-range ranching as practiced at the time, but in reality his huge acreage gave the cattle virtually free range. Fences merely kept others out, a point King wanted to make. By the end of the Civil War, the R. King & Co. ranch consisted of more than 8,000 acres. On that land, vaqueros tended huge herds of cattle, over 50,000 strong.

At the time of King's death in 1885 the R. King & Co. ranch consisted of half a million acres stretching almost from Corpus Christi to Brownsville. King left it all to his wife, Henrietta Chamberlain King. Two years later she appointed her favorite daughter's husband, Robert Kleberg, general manager of the ranch. Kleberg added to the holdings. He called for the drilling of wells and the construction of **windmills,** thereby assuring water for the herds. He also designed the town of Kingsville (seat for Kleberg County) and instituted all operations the town needed.

When Henrietta died in 1925, the will she left behind probably came from Kleberg, a lawyer by training. It called for a ten-year waiting period before partition of the million-acre estate. During that time, Kleberg's wife, Alice, bought 200,000 acres from her siblings, making the already considerable holdings even larger.

With the death of his father, Robert Kleberg, Jr., known as Bob, took over the affairs of the ranch. Bob assured the success of the cattle operation by developing a new **cattle breed,** the Santa Gertrudis. This breed fared better on the poor land of the King Ranch. Bob also helped ensure the financial success of the ranch by signing a drilling rights agreement with Humble Oil (later Exxon). The discovery of oil in 1939 added immensely to the value of the land.

The King Ranch has become one of the most storied and sometimes reviled in Texas history. Its vaqueros are famous for their skill and loyalty. Today the family empire stretches from Texas around the globe.   (Frost 1985; Lea 1957)

—Mark Mayer

KNIBBS, HENRY HERBERT
(1874–1945)
Author of ranch romances and other western novels.

KNOB
See Spurs.

KOERNER, W. H. D.
(1879–1938)
Artist. See Art of the Cowboy.

KOKO
Horse ridden by **B-western** film star Rex Allen.

KUCZYNSKI, FRANK ANTHONY
Singer Pee Wee **King**'s given name. See Music.

LABOUR, FRED

Singer known as Too Slim. See Riders in the Sky.

LADIES OF THE LINE

See Prostitution.

LAMA, TONY

Manufacturer of cowboy **boots**.

LAMB LICKER

Colloquial, uncomplimentary term for a sheepherder.

L'AMOUR, LOUIS
(1908–1988)

Born in Jamestown, North Dakota, novelist Louis L'Amour (Louis Dearborn LaMoore) became the most prolific pulp western author of all time, selling more than 200 million books by the time of his death. His westerns reach fans worldwide, translated into Swedish, Japanese, Italian, Portuguese, and several other languages.

As Jon Tuska (*A Variable Harvest*, 1990) points out, the early L'Amour wrote mostly ranch romances and related formula westerns. Using the pseudonym Tex Burns, he penned four brief Hopalong Cassidy books. He wrote other stories under the name Jim Mayo. His characters and plots had the predictability of the **B westerns;** you know the hero will prevail and be rewarded with the heroine. Action-packed range wars and other conflicts came to life on his pages. His fast pacing, with new action or a twist every 800 words or so, kept millions of readers turning pages. His characters often delivered homespun homilies reflecting the author's conservative political and social values.

In an 1980 interview, Jon Tuska asked L'Amour to comment on the near-extermination of the buffalo. The writer replied with Darwinian clarity and simplicity:

They had outlived their usefulness. It was necessary that they be killed. Now there are farms throughout that whole area, farms that grow food to feed one third of the world. It's a matter of progress. The Indians didn't own the lands they occupied. Many of the tribes, in fact, had only recently occupied certain regions before the white man arrived. The Indians took the land from others, the cliff dwellers, for example. And the white man took the land from the Indians. It wasn't the Indians' to claim or to sell. It went to the strongest. The white men were stronger.

This strident social Darwinism did not appear in his first original paperback novel, *Westward the Tide* (1950). In this early novel, the author shows great sympathy for the Indians and criticizes the destruction and rapine attendant to the westward movement. Within a few years, however, the sentiments in his novels reflected the opposite view. Having achieved a measure of success, L'Amour preached the social Darwinist gospel. His views are a belated echo of an earlier age found in Zane **Grey** novels.

No overnight success, L'Amour had begun writing book reviews and poetry in the 1930s. His big break came because of the popular John **Wayne** film *Hondo* (1953). James Edward Grant wrote the screenplay based on a L'Amour short story. L'Amour in turn used the movie screenplay to write his first big-selling novel by the same name. L'Amour did not acknowledge his reliance on the screenplay. All told, more than 30 of his stories made it into the movies.

A genial self-promoter and prolific writer, L'Amour toured the country selling his books in his big bus, the "Overland Express." The heart of his appeal comes from his great ability as a storyteller. As one of his editors noted, "You may find writers who produce a better book in terms of pure literary quality, but I don't think you'll ever find a better storyteller." Because of the uneven literary quality of his works, the immensely popular artist never received critical acclaim. He also faced the unhappy cultural bias of the United States: "Things Western are relegated to the ash heap."

L'Amour trumpeted the historical grounding of his fiction. "Every incident in any story I write is authentic and usually based either on something I personally experienced or something that happened in history." The truth is quite different. Like all pulp novelists, L'Amour created a fictive West. Unlike most novelists, however, L'Amour seemingly came to believe his own fiction.

When Tuska pointed out to L'Amour a discrepancy in one of his books, L'Amour took it in stride. "You know, I don't think the people who read my books would really care." L'Amour wrote and dictated his novels at tremendous speed. Given his haste and aversion to revising, it is entirely understandable that inconsistencies arose.

Indifference to accurate detail and internal contradictions extended to L'Amour's autobiographical statements. Depending on the version, he won between 51 and 58 of his 59 boxing matches. Like other western mythmakers, he created his own mythical, variable past. He apparently spent time as a drifter, boxer, miner, lumberjack, laborer, World War II tank officer, and adventurer. According to L'Amour, a Sioux war party scalped his great-grandfather, and his grandfather fought in the Civil War. He also recalls that as a boy he met frontier marshal Bill Tilghman in Oklahoma City.

Fans overlook mistakes and "misstatements" because L'Amour offered them an exciting, moral West they wanted to believe in. He admired western writer Jack **Schaefer** but claimed he avoided reading westerns. "I'm worried about subconsciously picking up someone else's plot accidentally, and using it as my own a few years later." As the line from "Who Shot Liberty Valance" reminds us, when the legend becomes fact, print the legend. Workaholic to the end, L'Amour was working on his autobiography when he died in 1988 of lung cancer. (Cozzens 1988; L'Amour 1981; Tuska 1990; Tuska and Piekarski 1983; Weinberg 1992)

LANE, ALLAN
(1904–1973)
B-western film actor known as Rocky.

LARIAT
A **rope,** anglicized form of the Spanish words, *la reata.*

LASSO
See Rope.

LATIFUNDIA
A system of land tenure dominated by large rural estates (latifundios). Concentration of land ownership in Latin America began with large royal grants given to conquistadors during the Spanish Conquest.

Chile is among the extreme cases of a nation where the latifundia system prevailed. From colonial times onward, a rural elite owned **fundos** of the best lands in the central valley around Santiago. In 1924 fewer than 3 percent of farms in the fertile central valley controlled 80 percent of the arable lands. The rural poor, including the *huaso,* remained subservient to a powerful patrón. The regime of Salvador Allende (1970–1973) attempted unsuccessfully to reform the latifundia system.

Mexico's landowners established the first association in the western hemisphere to promote the interests of the landed elite. In 1529 town councilmen in Mexico City organized the Mesta, patterned on a powerful organization of sheep ranchers in Spain. While not as powerful as its Spanish predecessor, the Mexican Mesta appointed many important rural officials and shaped rural legislations. As a public official recorded in 1594, ranching and agriculture were "in the hands of the rich and of those possessing Indians under the *encomienda* system" (royal grants of Indian labor made to Spaniards in the New World).

Latifundia was not universal in Mexico, but in the north large haciendas dominated into the twentieth century. Even the great upheaval of the Mexican Revolution only replaced one set of *latifundistas* with another. The outbreak of revolutionary violence in the southern state of Chiapas in 1994 attests to the continuing problem of landlessness.

Similar circumstances occurred in Uruguay and Argentina. Spanish colonial policy promoted land concentration and the marginalization of **gauchos** and others of the rural lower classes. Rich, landed Uruguayan families—the Viana, de la Quadra, and others—dominated the countryside and, after independence, the country.

Argentina, with vast lands and a small population, also experienced latifundia, especially on the **pampas.** Colonial and national policies granted control of the vast **plains** to the few.

Great estates *(hatos)* also developed on the Venezuelan and Colombian **llanos** during the early eighteenth century. Around 1750 in Venezuela, 30 families owned 40 ranches covering 219 square leagues. About 300,000 cattle grazed on these estates.

Independence speeded land concentration in much of Latin America. Land granted to war veterans quickly passed to the hands of caudillos and wily speculators. Venezuelan caudillo José Gregorio Monagas distributed land to followers in 1848, but more than half the total went to ten concessions.

Owing to the income and prestige of land ownership, latifundistas have retained strong political clout. Through rural societies and associations, they continue to promote their interests at the regional and national level.

Land concentration persists in Latin America today. In 1978 about 60 percent of rural Mexican households were landless or near landless as were 66 percent of Colombian households and 70 percent of Brazilian households. Latifundia has been especially persistent in cattle ranching regions. Brutal military governments frequently have repressed the landless poor and supported the latifundistas.

Land laws in the United States did not encourage latifundia. On the contrary, law and political sentiment favored smaller family farms. Jefferson/Jacksonian agrarian idealism assumed family farms essential to the national well-being. Many ranchers scratched out a meager living with small herds and crude accommodations.

Huge ranches did develop in Texas and elsewhere. By the end of the nineteenth century, the **King Ranch** had accumulated 1.27 million acres in south Texas. It employed 300 **vaqueros**

who worked 65,000 cattle and 10,000 horses. John Simpson **Chisum**'s well-named Rancho Grande stood on the west Texas-New Mexico border. In a single season before Chisum died in 1884, his cowboys branded 18,000 calves. Charles **Goodnight**'s XIT outfit in the Texas Panhandle covered approximately 700,000 acres in 1883.

Large outfits also developed on the northern plains. In 1884 ten Montana companies owned 90 percent of the livestock in the area of Fort Benton. The Swan Land and Cattle Company herded 65,000 cattle and 10,000 horses. In some cases wealthy ranchers illegally fenced public lands, thereby extending their holdings. Land fraud was common in all frontier regions. Up to 95 percent of the final titles under the Desert Land Act of 1877 probably were fraudulent. (Dale 1960; Esman 1978; Frost 1985; Haley 1967; Holden 1970; Slatta 1990)

See also Beef Cattle Industry; *Estancia.*

LÁTIGO

Also anglicized to latigo and larigo. See Saddle.

LAW AND ORDER

See Violence.

LAZO

Spanish term for a **rope,** anglicized to lasso.

LEA, TOM
(1907–)
Illustrator, writer, artist. See Art of the Cowboy.

LEDOUX, CHRIS
(1948–)
Singer. See Music.

LEE, JOHNNY
(1946–)
Singer. See Music.

LEGGINS

South Texas term for **chaps,** usually close-fitting shotgun chaps that covered the entire leg.

LEI

Garland of colorful flowers or shells that Hawaiian cowboys *(paniolo)* use to decorate their **hats**.

LEONE, SERGIO
(1921–1989)

Italian film director. See Eastwood, Clint.

LEVI'S

Sturdy denim pants made by Levi Strauss (1829–1902) became closely associated with the cowboy. Strauss, a German-Jewish immigrant, made the long voyage around Tierra del Fuego to San Francisco in 1849. The following year he began making pants for miners, reinforcing stress points with copper rivets. By the time cowboys began heading up the trail from Texas after the Civil War, Strauss's sturdy pants already had a following in the West.

Cowboys gave up their war-surplus wool pants to adopt Levi's. The popularity of hard-wearing canvas and later denim clothing spread. Denim, first made in Nimes, Frances, had been widely used in Europe since the seventeenth century. In the United States, denim originally came in light blue, gray, and brown colors. Indigo blue eventually became the great favorite.

Farmers would wear bib overalls made of denim. Cowboys, of course, would never be caught dead in bib overalls, but they favored the same fabric in their jeans. Competitors such as Wrangler, Lee, and others, cropped up. Wranglers, in particular, have won over the **rodeo** crowd. Levi's, however, remains a synonym for blue jeans around the world. Today Levi Strauss and Company has more than 150 facilities operating in 19 countries. The company annually sells some 250 million items totaling $2.7 billion worldwide. The founder is honored in the Jewish-American Hall of Fame in Berkeley. (Cray 1978; Foster-Harris 1955)

LIBERTY, MARGOT

Writer. See Autobiographies by Cowboys.

LICK

Colloquial term for molasses.

LILLIE, GORDON WILLIAM
(1860–1942)

Born in Bloomington, Indiana, Wild West showman Gordon Lillie spent much of his childhood attending local schools. He also worked in his father's mill in the evenings and on Saturdays. A visit from cousins living in Kansas sparked his interest in the West. He began reading pulp fiction extolling the exploits of William Frederic "Buffalo Bill" **Cody** and James Butler "Wild Bill" Hickok. When his father's mill burned in 1874, the family moved to Wellington, Kansas. Lillie spent much of his time visiting the nearby Pawnee Indian camps.

At the age of 15, Lillie left home intending to be a cowboy. He returned home soon after killing an opponent in a gunfight. Acquitted by a coroner's jury, he spent a year working in a Pawnee rock quarry in Indian Territory and in a government sawmill. After brief stints as a hunter and rancher, he worked for the government as a schoolteacher and interpreter at the Pawnee Agency.

His fortunes changed for the better in 1883. The federal government appointed him as interpreter and escort to a group of Pawnee performing with Buffalo Bill Cody's Wild West show. Thanks to his good working relationship with Indians, he acquired the nickname Pawnee Bill.

While on tour that first summer, he met Mary Emma Manning in Philadelphia. They married three years later. As his knowledge of the Wild West business grew, Lillie began to think bigger. In 1888 he and his wife broke with Cody and started their own show, Pawnee Bill's Historic Wild West. The company lasted only a few months. In 1889 he formed the Pawnee Bill Oklahoma Colonization Company. He hoped to capitalize on the "Boomer" movement to open unassigned lands in Indian Territory to whites.

He revived his Wild West show in 1890 with much better success. He spent the next 20 summers touring the United States and Canada. In 1894 he performed at the International

Exposition in Antwerp, Belgium, and later toured Holland and France. When not on the road, he spent winters on his 2,000-acre ranch near Pawnee, Oklahoma.

Wild West shows ran up huge bills, because they included hundreds of performers and much livestock. Both Lillie and Cody ran into financial problems. After many years of competition, the two merged their shows in 1909. The partnership dissolved four years later, ending the great heyday of the Wild West shows. The fame of Cody and Lillie led people to call all types of wild west extravaganzas "Bill shows."

Lillie retired to his ranch and joined the national effort to preserve the buffalo. He kept a large herd of bison on his land. He also helped establish a national game reserve in the Wichita Mountains and became Director of the Historical Society of Oklahoma. He converted part of his ranch into Pawnee Bill's Buffalo Ranch, Oldtown, and Indian Trading Post to attract tourists in Oklahoma.

An automobile accident in 1936 injured Lillie and killed his wife. He spent the remainder of his life in poor health and died in 1942. Like Cody, Lillie played a key role in moving the cowboy and American western life from the realm of history to mythology and popular culture. (Russell 1970; Shirley 1958; Thrapp 1988)
—*Stephen C. Keadey*

LINE CAMP

Line riders, or outriders, had some of the loneliest work on the ranch. They stayed, usually by themselves, at crude line shacks or camps that dotted the farthest ranch boundaries. Some camps were nothing more than dugouts, holes dug into a hillside. Each day the line rider ate a solitary breakfast that he had to cook himself. Then he patrolled the ranch's boundaries. He herded outfit cattle back onto the ranch and chased strays away. (Grass was too valuable to let neighboring cattle feed.) Line riders also tried to discourage **rustling.** Cattle seem bred to get into trouble. An outrider would have to pull animals from bogs, treat sick animals, and shoot an occasional wolf.

The advent of barbed wire added repair of **fencing** to the chores. As a result the line rider also became known as a fence rider. The wire barrier ended the cowboy's freedom to chose his route, so the job became more monotonous. On larger outfits a line camp might hold two cowboys who rode fence each day in opposite directions. At least that meant someone to talk to, which could be a mixed blessing. (Blevins 1993; Forbis 1978)

LINE RIDER
See Line Camp.

LINING HIS FLUE
Colloquial term for eating.

LIQUOR
See Saloons.

LITERATURE
See Autobiographies by Cowboys; *Gauchesco;* Historiography of the Cowboy; Pulp Novels.

LITTLE BRITCHES RODEO
See Rodeo.

LIVESTOCK
See Cattle Breeds.

LIVESTOCK DETECTIVE
Also stock detective. See Horn, Tom.

LIZZY
Colloquial term for **saddle** horn.

LLANERO
The llanero is the cowboy of the tropical plains (llanos) of Colombia and Venezuela. Descriptions of the llanero show that his dress and habits changed relatively little from the early nineteenth to the early twentieth centuries. The llanero adapted his dress to the necessities of his tropical plains environment—searing heat during the dry season alternated with massive floods during the rainy season.

Colonial Origins of the Llanero

Historians generally credit Spanish explorer Cristóbal Rodríguez with first importing livestock into Venezuela during his expedition in 1548. In neighboring Colombia, cattle were driven over the Andes from Santa Marta to Santa Fe in the llanos in 1541. In 1569 Diego Fernández de Serpa brought in 800 head via the island of Margarita. The important livestock center of San Sebastian de los Reyes was founded in 1584 or 1585, and *hatos* (ranches) proliferated thereafter.

By the early seventeenth century, ranches had extended to the areas of Tocuyo, Barquisimeto, Valencia, and the valley of Caracas. By 1665 hides ranked first among Venezuela's exports. On the Colombia llanos, herds of Casanareño (a small jersey-tan breed) and San Martinero (a larger, dark red breed) became common. Over time, coastal cacao (chocolate) plantations overtook livestock in importance. Hide prices tended to fluctuate much less than those for cacao, however, so the livestock industry enjoyed gradual, relatively stable growth during most of the colonial period.

Franciscans and Capuchins established mission villages in the llanos by the mid-seventeenth century. Cattle herding became an important economic activity for profit and for indoctrinating the Indians. During the eighteenth century, the original mission villages gradually became secularized. After independence came to Venezuela in 1821, the authority of the religious orders in the llanos gave way to that of caudillos, local political bosses backed by private armies.

The independence wars devastated the plains livestock industry, and the economic fortunes of the llanero went into decline. Many turned to banditry or joined the marauding army of some local strongman.

Nineteenth-Century Descriptions

Soldier Richard L. Vowell, who observed the llanero at work in 1818, wrote in *Campaigns and Cruises in Venezuela and New Granada* (1831): "Although usually styled and considered herdsmen, their habits and mode of life were in reality those of hunters; for the cattle, which constituted their sole wealth, being perfectly wild, the exertions requisite to collect a herd, and to keep it together in the neighbourhood of a farm-house, were necessarily violent and incessant."

In *A History of the Revolution of Caracas* (1819), George D. Flinter detailed the llanero technique of wild-cattle hunting. The llanero "at full speed, hamstrings the animal in both legs, which brings it immediately to the ground; he then alights, and, with the point of his spear, strikes the bull in the nape of the neck.... He next skins it, takes out the fat, and, after having cut up the flesh in long pieces, brings it to the hato, where it is sprinkled with salt, and hung up to dry in the sun."

Venezuelan Ramón Páez *(Wild Scenes in South America,* 1863) described llanero appearance during the early 1860s:

... breeches tightly buttoned at the knee, and a loose shirt, usually of a bright checkered pattern. Shoes are altogether dispensed with in a country like the Llanos, subject to drenching rains, and covered with mud during a great portion of the year, besides the inconvenience they offer to the rider in holding the stirrup securely when in chase of wild animals. The leg, however, is well protected from the thorns and cutting grass of the savannas by a neat legging or *botín,* made of buffskin, tightly buttoned down the calf by knobs or studs of highly polished silver. Another characteristic article of dress, and one in which the wearers take great pride, is the linen checkered handkerchief, loosely worn around the head. Its object is ostensibly to protect it from the intensity of the sun's rays; but the constant habit of wearing it has rendered the handkerchief as indispensable a headdress to the Llaneros as is the cravat to the neck of the city gentleman.

With his keen eye to equestrian life, the Scottish writer Robert Bontine Cunninghame **Graham** left memorable portraits of many cowboy types.

In *South American Sketches* (1978), he described the llanero manner of roping in the late nineteenth century:

> He, of all wielders of the rawhide noose, alone secures it, not to the saddle, but to his horse's tail, fishing for, rather than lassoing, a steer, playing it like a salmon with a rope a hundred feet in length, instead of bringing it up with a smart jerk, after the fashion of the Argentines or Mexicans.

Llaneros often rode half-naked and barefoot in the tropical heat. All carried the indispensable **poncho** or *cobija,* well adapted to the vicissitudes of the tropical plains. Ramón Páez described the garment and its utility:

> It is fully six feet square, with a hole in the centre to admit the head, and its office is twofold, viz., to protect the rider and his cumbrous equipment from the heavy showers and dews of the tropics, and to spread under him when there is no convenience for slinging the hammock. It also serves as a protection from the scorching rays of the sun, experience having taught its wearer that a thick woolen covering keeps the body moist and cool by day, and warm by night. The poncho in Venezuela is made double, by sewing together two different blankets, the outside one being dark blue and the inner one bright red, which colors, as is well known, are differently acted upon by light and heat.

Like cowboys everywhere, the llanero subsisted on a rather meager diet. Graham listed the essentials of food and equipment:

> Beef is the staple, almost the only food of the Llanero; his ordinary drink is the muddy water of the neighboring stream or the lagoon. His luxuries, coffee, and the rough brown sugar full of lye, known as Panela; his bed a hammock, that he carried rolled up, behind his saddle; his pride, his horse, the companion of his dangers and his toil, sober and hardy as himself.

Like the gaucho, the llanero always carried a knife or machete. British diplomat Robert Ker Porter, writing in his diary, termed the knife "an appendage no llanero ever is without, and which amongst the poorest classes, answers likewise for a spear head." Laws in some parts of Venezuela long prohibited llaneros from wearing the shirt outside the pants. Officials imposed this odd dress code to prevent llaneros from concealing machetes under their shirts.

Europeans and Venezuela's own elite looked disdainfully upon the backward llanos and its crude inhabitants. Ramón Páez, European-educated, found many shortcomings in the "barbarous" life of the "mongrel breed" inhabiting the **plains,** but like other educated observers, notably the Argentine **Domingo Faustino Sarmiento,** he found strengths and virtues in the primitive cowboy.

> The Modern Centaur of the desolate regions of the New World, the Llanero spends his life on horseback; all his actions and exertions must be assisted by his horse; for him the noblest effort of man is, when gliding swiftly over the boundless plain and bending over his spirited charger, he overturns an enemy or masters a wild bull.... Like the Arab, he considers his horse his best and most reliable friend on earth, often depriving himself of rest and comfort after a hard day's journey to afford his faithful companion abundance of food and water.

Like the Mexican **vaquero,** the llanero was very superstitious. Both feared ghosts and evil spirits. The powerful novel of the llanos, *Doña Bárbara,* by Rómulo **Gallegos,** highlights the prevalence of superstition on the plains. The novel is filled with supernatural happenings. The leading lady, Doña Bárbara, is a witch in league with a wizard (Melquíades) and the Devil (her "Partner"). In the novel, mysterious dancing lights, generated by decomposing matter in swamps, are only one of the apparitions imbued with supernatural meaning.

Despite his penchant for romanticism, typical of his epoch and class, Ramón Páez identified the raison d'être of the llanero—remaining on horseback. Indifferent to **religion**, political philosophy, education, and "high culture," the llanero lived to ride. Strong of body and spirit, he clung to his life in the **saddle** despite sharp outside pressures. He also pursued another passion—**gambling**—with a zeal common to cowboys in both North and South America. A card game or a cockfight was sure to attract his interest and absorb his meager earnings.

Life changed far less on the llanos than on the Argentine plains over the course of the nineteenth century. Following a visit to the llanos in 1925, Graham (1978) described the llanero in terms that might well have been used a century earlier:

His well-greased *lazo* ready coiled in front of his right knee, his brown, bare toes sticking out through his alpargatas [sandals], clutching the light llanero stirrup with its crown-like prolongation underneath the foot, the llanero scans the horizon as his horse paces rapidly along, leaving a well-marked trail upon the dewy grass. He sits so loosely in the saddle that one would think if his horse shied it must unseat him, but that he also shies. High on his vaquero saddle, so straight and upright that a plummet dropped from his shoulder would touch his heel, he reads the llano like a book.

Llanero's Cultural Significance

In Venezuela and Colombia, the llanero is associated with the interior tropical plains. Some writers, however, have tried to propel the llanero to national significance as a symbol of independence and valor. As early as the 1860s José María Samper looked to the llanero as a national archetype for Colombia. Manuel Tejera presented similar images of the Venezuelan

llanero during the 1870s. The llanero came to epitomize fervent patriotism as a result of his role in the victories over the Spanish, such as the battles at Boyacá in 1819 and at Carabobo in 1821.

Mythmaking accompanied these efforts to make the llanero a national symbol. In an essay published in 1861, the Colombian José María Samper lauded the llanero for his fight against Spanish oppression: "The llanero is the union between civilization and barbarism, between society with all its more or less artificial conventions and the imposing solitude of the deserts, where only nature rules with her immortal grandeur and solemn majesty."

As in the United States and Argentina, political conservatives in Venezuela have most often used the cowboy figure for partisan purposes. Intellectual Laureano Vallenilla Lanz, an apologist for the dictatorship of Juan Vicente Gómez (1908–1935), described the llanero as an important ingredient in Venezuelan national identity. He wrote that "in Venezuela even those of us born in the mountains and the coasts have something of the llanero."

For the most part, however, such nationalistic rhetoric convinced relatively few. Some elements of llanero folklore, especially dances and music, do appeal to Venezuelans outside the plains, but few Venezuelans view the llanero as the symbol of national virtue. He remains a regional figure, and that region, the llanos, plays a less important national role than it did in the nineteenth century. (Izard 1981, 1982, 1983, 1985; Rausch 1984, 1993; Slatta 1990)

See also Llanos.

LLANOS

The tropical plain of interior Colombia and Venezuela, the llanos, is topographically very different from the vast **pampas** of the Río de la Plata and the Great Plains of the United States. The latter two regions lie within the temperate zone. The llanos is tropical, crisscrossed by many rivers and shrouded by forests of dense trees and shrubs *(matas)*. The high peaks of the Andes surround the llanos to the north and west. Tropical rain forests along the Guaviare and Amazon rivers bound it to the south. The lower Orinoco River and the Guiana Highlands form the eastern boundary of the llanos.

The llanos itself is drained by the Orinoco River and its western tributaries. The llanos covers about a quarter of a million square miles divided about equally between Venezuela (56%) and Colombia. The prevalence of trees or shrubs, almost always in sight, contrasts markedly with the pampas and the Great Plains.

Two seasons, a dry summer *(verano,* October–March) and a rainy winter *(invierno,* April–September), divide the year. These seasons are extreme and inhospitable. Drought conditions and high temperatures alternate with torrential downpours and mass flooding. The llanos averages about 47 inches of rainfall per year. All the rain falls within a six-month period, during which vast low-lying areas are inundated. Some areas, such as Guanare and occasionally Barinas, receive up to 79 inches of annual rainfall. Within the llanos, subregional variations exist, but the livestock industry developed throughout the tropical plains.

The Scottish aficionado of equestrian life, Robert B. Cunninghame Graham, rode most of the plains regions of North and South America in the late nineteenth and early twentieth centuries. In *Rodeo* (1936), he left a vivid description of the foreboding yet fascinating llanos:

> ... A very sea of grass and sky, sun-scourged and hostile to mankind. The rivers, full of electric eels, and of caribes, those most ravenous of fish, more terrible than even the great alligators that lie like logs upon the sandbanks or the inert and pulpy rays, with their mortiferous barbed spike, are still more hostile than the land.

Many Venezuelans and Colombians hold an entirely negative view of the llanos. They emphasize the vile, extreme climate, unhealthy for man and beast. The region has suffered from repeated, devastating epidemics. Novelist and one-time Venezuelan president, Rómulo **Gallegos,** strongly molded his countrymen's perceptions of the llanos. His wonderful novel *Doña Bárbara* (1929) depicts many powerful negative elements in the plains. In his romantic optimism, however, he hoped the obstacles would be overcome. In his novel *Cantaclaro* (1934), Gallegos has a dying man utter this lament: "But we're in a completely savage desert! The desert! The enemy against which we should first fight! The cause of all our problems."

The tropical climate of the llanos made infection and disease constant threats to riders and their animals. Travelers found themselves under constant attack by what Karl Sachs, a German physician, termed "monstrous armies of insects." He found that "the feeling of solitude and forlornness that in these desert plains overwhelms the traveler who moves completely alone, is difficult to paint."

The llanos served as the site of an expanding colonial livestock industry. During the independence wars, it became a major battleground. Its livestock provided food and mounts for both royalist and independence forces. Fierce llanero cavalrymen finally turned the tide of battle in favor of independence. No sooner had independence been won than a new cycle of **violence** began between competing caudillos, regional strongmen who filled the power vacuum in the new republic. Civil war became a way of life on the llanos.

Much fighting occurred in the llanos, sparked by the need to have access to livestock, and the region suffered grave devastation. The number of cattle in the Venezuelan llanos fell from about 4.5 million in 1812 to 2.5 million a decade later. Between 1814 and 1820 on the Colombian llanos of Casanare, the estimated number of cattle dropped from 273,000 to 50,000; the number of horses fell from 30,000 to 4,000.

The llanos was home to many prominent caudillos (military chieftains), such as José Antonio Páez. The llanos shaped Venezuela's political destiny. Despite its historical significance, however, the tropical plain and its inhabitants remain enigmas in Venezuelan historiography. Few substantial studies exist of the horsemen, cattle ranches *(hatos)*, or geopolitical and economic development of the llanos.

The Colombian llanos also faced disruptions from nineteenth-century civil wars. Competition for labor from the burgeoning coffee sector drew workers away from the llanos. Ranches in the Casanare region of Colombia operated from the colonial period through the twentieth century. By 1907 the region held only about 150 ranches with 250,000 cattle and 50,000 horses. Some Colombian ranchers modernized their operations to produce higher-grade beef for local markets. The number of cattle in Colombia grew slowly from about 4.4 million in 1898 to some 6.7 million in 1925. In Colombia coffee was king, however. As in Venezuela, ranching had become a small, backwater segment of the national economy.

Despite the harsh extremes of its climate, some observers viewed the tropical plain as an untapped fount of abundance. Writing in 1875, Manuel Tejera painted a glowing portrait of the llanos, "the immense plains where, without any work by man, livestock multiply, grazing on the abundant grass."

Some optimists held a vision of the underpopulated llanos as the key to Venezuela's future greatness. Augustín Codazzi, a French geographer, estimated in 1841 that the llanos, with only 390,000 people, could support a population of six million. In 1872, Luis J. Alfonso stressed that in view of "the fertility of the land, its vast extension, varied climates" and other advantages, Venezuela needed only capital, roads, and labor to prosper.

The great potential, however, remained untapped. In Colombia, the towering Andes cut off the llanos of Casanare from the rest of the country. The region remained, in Jane Loy Rausch's term, a backward, "static frontier" well into the twentieth century. Ranching techniques on the llanos remained backward. Many llanos ranches suffered from overgrazing and lack of fences and roads.

Ranchers *(hateros)*, indifferent to the niceties of selective breeding or careful husbandry, made very few changes to their approach to ranch management from the eighteenth through the twentieth centuries. As one nineteenth-century rancher, Zoilo Navarro, observed, "God nourishes the cattle and I sell them. It's a profitable deal." (Izard 1985; Rausch 1993, 1984; Slatta and Alvarez d'Armas 1985)

LLORONAS

Large **spurs** worn by **gauchos** of the Río de la Plata. The word literally means "mourners," which may reflect their effect on a horse.

LOCKED SPURS

See Spurs.

LOG OF A COWBOY

See Autobiographies by Cowboys.

LOGSDON, GUY

Folklorist, writer. See Humor.

LOMAX, JOHN AVERY
(1867–1948)

Folklorist, music collector. See Musicology.

LOMILLO

See Saddle.

"THE LONE RANGER"

See Television.

LONELY ARE THE BRAVE

Film (1962) starring Kirk Douglas; based on Edward **Abbey**'s novel, *The Brave Cowboy.*

LONG RIDER

Colloquial term for an outlaw.

LONGHORN CATTLE

The longhorn is, without question, the most storied **cattle breed** in history. Several generations of painters, sculptors, writers, and more recently photographers, have created countless images of them. These big, wiry, muscular, hardy animals dominated the golden age of open-range ranching from 1865 through 1885.

Longhorn history, however, goes back several centuries. They are descended from the creole cattle brought to Mexico and South America during the sixteenth century. During the eighteenth century, Spanish priests brought the breed to missions they established in Texas, New Mexico, and California. Unlike many breeds, longhorns come in an amazing variety of colors and patterns.

Although cattle with long horns appeared elsewhere in the country, the breed became closely identified with Texas. Longhorns likewise provided the basis for the **beef cattle industries** of Brazil and Argentina. Their hardiness made the longhorn well-suited to less hospitable ranges, such as the semidesert regions and the south Texas brush country.

Major William H. Emory submitted a report on the Texas-Mexican border region in 1857. He noted the great abundance of livestock in the Longhorn State.

The numbers of horses and cattle that ranged here under Spanish rule are incredible. To this day remnants of this immense stock are running wild on the prairies between the two rivers. Hunting the wild horses and cattle is the regular business of the inhabitants of Laredo and other towns along the Rio Grande.

Growing up wild on open range or in the dense thickets of the Texas brush country, longhorns did not take kindly to being herded. With horn spreads sometimes exceeding ten feet, they posed dangers to horses and riders. Fiercely protective, they used their horns against wolves and other enemies. In 1876 Col. R. I. Dodge judged "wild cattle of Texas" to be "fifty times more dangerous to footmen than the fiercest buffalo."

In at least one case, however, the very size of the horns saved a cowboy's life. The *Cheyenne*

Daily Leader (2 August 1882) reported the incident:

Not long since a herder was knocked down by a wild steer and his faced disfigured for life. His nose was torn completely from his face. That he was not killed was owing to the fact that the long horns, wide apart, touched the ground on either side of the poor fellow's head as he lay prostrate.

Besides their long horns and generally nasty, independent disposition, Texas longhorns posed another problem to the beef cattle industry. The animals carried but were themselves immune to Texas fever, a disease caused by a microscopic tick-born parasite related to those that cause malaria. Longhorns carried the fever north with them on the great **trail drives.**

Ranchers and farmers demanded quarantines on the Texas cattle. The ticks die within three or four months if they cannot attach themselves to an animal, so quarantines provided the time needed for the ticks to die. Needless to say, this proved very unpopular with Texas cattlemen. To escape the quarantines in Kansas and points east, Texans began blazing new cattle trails farther to the west.

Despite their virtues, longhorns had deficiencies that ultimately doomed them as the mainstay of the beef cattle industry. First, they take longer to mature; ten years versus six years for so-called American breeds such as the Hereford, Angus, Devon, and shorthorn. Second, they are a lean breed, and the American palate demanded fatty, marbled beef. Heavier animals meant more profits to producers. Third, the unwieldy horns created havoc in close quarters, such as the confines of feedlots. During the late nineteenth century, American breeds pushed aside the venerable longhorn.

In 1927 the U.S. Forest Service acted on a congressional mandate to establish a national herd of longhorns. Rangers could locate only three bulls, 20 cows, and four calves. They removed those animals to the Wichita Mountains Wildlife Refuge at Cache, Oklahoma. During the following decades, government and private efforts established the "Seven Families" of different gene pools to rebuild the breed.

The picturesque longhorn has been a favorite subject of many western artists. In the late nineteenth century, Frank Reaugh and Harvey Wallace Caylor painted the great beasts. Both Charles Marion **Russell** and Frederic **Remington** captured elements of the longhorn's power and majesty. Since those days, the longhorn has remained a mainstay of trail drive, ranch, and stampede scenes.

What goes around comes around, goes the old saying. During the 1980s, concerns about heart disease and cholesterol turned the public against fatty beef. Some beef producers turned to the rangy old longhorn as a source of lean beef. Other breeders kept the animals for their intrinsic and historical interest. The Texas Longhorn Breeders Association maintains a registry. By the early 1990s, the association identified about 150,000 longhorns grazing in many different parts of the nation. The animal is, appropriately enough, the mascot of the University of Texas at Austin. (Dobie 1941; Rouse 1970)

LOOMIS, NOEL MILLER
(1905–1979)
Oklahoma-born author of formula westerns.

LOVE, NAT
(b. 1854)
See African-American Cowboys.

LOVE APPLES
Colloquial term for canned tomatoes.

LOVING, OLIVER
(1812–1867)
See Goodnight, Charles.

THE LUSTY MEN
Classic **rodeo** film (1952) starring Robert Mitchum.

LUTZ, GILES ALFRED
(1910–1982)
Missouri-born novelist who wrote formula westerns under various names.

LYNCHING
See Violence.

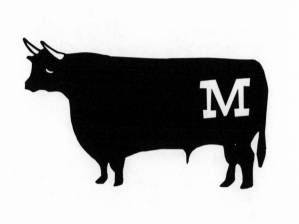

MCCARTY

Fine horsehair **rope,** from the Spanish word *mecate.*

MCCLURE, JAKE
(1903–1940)

See Rodeo Events.

MCCOY, JOSEPH G.
(1837–1915)

One of 11 children, Joseph Geiting McCoy was born in Sangamon County, Illinois, and spent his childhood on his family's farm. He attended local schools, except for one year at the Knox College Academy in Galesburg. He married Sarah Epler in 1861 and entered the mule- and cattle-raising business around the same time.

During the Civil War, McCoy became interested in the feeding and transporting of livestock. He conceived the idea of a main western loading station to ship cattle via railroad to packing centers in the East. This idea became reality in 1867 when he selected Abilene, Kansas, as the endpoint of the "Long Drive" from Texas. He established good relations with the Kansas-Pacific and Hannibal-St. Joseph railroads, which let him ship large numbers of cattle at low rates. He transformed relatively unsettled Abilene into a booming **cow town.** He constructed stockyards, loading chutes, pens, barns, a livery stable, and even a hotel for the drovers arriving from Texas. McCoy's railhead became very popular, because it was farther west than other towns on the line.

Only 35,000 head of cattle arrived the first year. Between 1868 and 1871, however, over 1,500,000 head of cattle moved through Abilene. Drovers liked the flat, unsettled, open land that was the standard terrain along the route, known as the Chisholm Trail. As the town grew, so did the problem of law and order. After he became mayor in 1871, McCoy appointed James Butler ("Wild Bill") Hickok as City Marshal.

Unfortunately for McCoy, the same factors that fueled Abilene's success also caused its decline. The **trail drives** shifted farther west as settlement became thicker in east Kansas. Railroads also pushed farther west. Having sold much of his land in Abilene, McCoy adjusted to this transition by supervising the construction of stockyards in Newton, Kansas, and promoting the town of Wichita to cattle buyers in 1872.

McCoy wrote *Historical Sketches of the Cattle Trade of the West and Southwest* (1874), which chronicled his success in Kansas and described the rise of the **beef cattle industry** and many of its pioneers. He well describes the rigors of the great drives up the Chisholm Trail and other routes. As his book shows, however, McCoy suffered from the lamentable racial and environmental determinism that typified his era:

> The average New Mexican is a bad mixture of Spanish, Indian, and sometimes negro blood, producing in that warm sunny clime, a degenerate, unenterprising, go-easy specimen of the *genus homo,* who is in his seventh heaven when he can get enough to eat and an opportunity to "trip the fantastic toe" nightly at the fandango, to lascivious music, in company of maidens to whom virtue is an unknown and unrespected grace, and to whom modesty is a lost sensibility.

He remained active in the livestock industry and reported on it for the 1880 United States census. He worked briefly for the Cherokee Nation and ran an unsuccessful campaign for Congress in 1890. He spent most of the rest of his life at various occupations in Wichita and Kansas City, where he died on 19 October 1915. (Dykstra 1976; McCoy 1966; Thrapp 1988)
> —*Stephen C. Keadey*

MCCOY, TIMOTHY J.
(1891–1978)

Actor. See Films, Cowboy.

MACDONALD, WILLIAM COLT
(1891–1968)

Prolific Michigan-born novelist and screenwriter.

MACEWAN, GRANT
(1902–)
Canadian writer and historian. See
Historiography of the Cowboy.

MCMURTRY, LARRY JEFF
(1936–)
Born in Wichita Falls, Texas, writer Larry
McMurtry grew up in and around the small
town of Archer City. His family included its fair
share of cowboys and ranchers. Memories of
small-town life fueled many of his early novels
and shaped a theme common to many of his
works. He often examines a fundamental
conflict, depicting the tensions between a
waning, traditional frontier spirit and rising
modern, urban values. He often presents this
conflict set amidst the loneliness and boredom of
small-town life. A fascination with sexuality also
pervades McMurtry's works.

He set his earlier works, such as *Horseman,
Pass By* (1961), *The Last Picture Show* (1966),
and *Terms of Endearment* (1975), in the
twentieth century. In 1985, however, he returned
to the nineteenth century with *Lonesome Dove.*
This epic, which won a Pulitzer Prize, chronicles
a long **trail drive** from Texas to Montana. By
mid-1993 it had sold 300,000 copies in hardcover
and 1.2 million paperbacks. *Lonesome Dove*
creates a vivid, realistic portrait of frontier life. It
also evokes nostalgia for the vanishing frontier
spirit. The novel made a very successful transition
to film as a popular **television** miniseries starring
Tommy Lee Jones and Robert Duvall.

In *Lonesome Dove,* Augustus McCrae reveals
an acute sense of the passing of his time and the
cattle frontier. "Why women and children and
settlers are just cannon fodder for lawyers and
bankers ... Every bank in Texas ought to pay
us a commission for the work we done. If we
hadn't done it, all the bankers would be back in
Georgia, living on poke salad and turnip greens."

McMurtry returned to the Old West with
Anything for Billy (1988), in which he reinvents
the legend of Billy the Kid through the eyes of a
first-person narrator, a dime novelist. The book
reads like a **pulp novel** and makes no attempt to
portray accurately people or events. Instead
McMurtry adds another layer of myth to the
Lincoln County War and Pat Garrett's hunt for
Billy the Kid.

In *Buffalo Girls* (1990) McMurtry probes the
last years of Calamity Jane and returns to the
theme of the passing of the frontier. His vehicle
this time is Buffalo Bill's Wild West Show and its
role in preserving the western mystique.

In *Lonesome Dove* and *Buffalo Girls,*
McMurtry accurately depicts frontier life. His
characters ring true but often also seem bigger
than life. When he sets his mind to it, McMurtry
skillfully molds elements of real historical figures
into believable characters. This is particularly
true in *Lonesome Dove.* The characters of
Augustus McCrae and Woodrow Call seem
loosely based on Charles **Goodnight** and Oliver
Loving. In *Anything for Billy,* however, his
portrayal of John S. **Chisum** through the
character of Will Isinglass does not ring true.

In mid-1993 McMurtry followed up
Lonesome Dove with *Streets of Laredo.* The latter
is a sequel only in the sense that characters from
the former book reappear. The story lines are
very different. Like several of his earlier works,
Streets reflects McMurtry's interest in the
collision of the Old West with the New.
Woodrow Call, nearing age 70, is still chasing
bad guys. This time he hunts Joey Garza, a train
robber and murderer, and his sadistic
pyromaniac sidekick, Mox Mox.

McMurtry wrote the book after recovering from
quadruple bypass surgery. He admits that the heart
surgery was difficult to cope with psychologically.
He offers a rather mystical explanation of how he
wrote the book. "It was coming to me from afar,
sort of, from a writing persona that was mine, or
that had been mine, and was still coming across
the wire somehow, but without my having much
control over it. I really feel like this novel was
faxed to me by my former self."

Like the original, the sequel includes very bad
bad guys and human but admirable heroes. Pea
Eye Parker, one of the *Lonesome Dove* cattle
drovers, has settled down and married Lorena,

the ex-prostitute who is now a schoolmarm. The book maintains the author's claim (closely followed by Cormac McCarthy) as today's foremost novelist of the Old West. (Peavy 1977; Tuska and Piekarski 1983)

—*Nils E. Mikkelsen*

MCRAE, WALLACE D.
(1936–)

Montana rancher Wallace (Wally) McRae is a humorous and entertaining cowboy poet who is also a philosopher and environmentalist. He has written a wide range of fun and profound poems. He comes from a family of ranchers: his Scottish grandfather, John B. McRae, bought 160 acres in Montana in the early 1880s to start the McRae Ranch.

McRae runs the Rocker Six Cattle Company, a 30,000-acre ranch in Rosebud County, Montana. When McRae rhymes cowboy thoughts, he writes from experience. Thus far he has published four volumes of poetry, with one of the better collections, *Cowboy Curmudgeon and Other Poems* (1992), published by **Peregrine Smith Books.**

Much cowboy **poetry** is lyrically descriptive. It evokes places, people, or events that have slipped into the past. McRae skillfully and powerfully records pieces of Montana ranch life, but his poems go far beyond the nostalgic. McRae is a poetic conscience for the West, the land, and the people. His "Things of Intrinsic Worth" captures the bitter sense of losing the beauty and majesty of western lands.

> Great God, how we're doin'! We're
>   rollin' in dough,
> As they tear and they ravage The Earth.
> And nobody knows ... or nobody
>   cares ...
> About things of intrinsic worth.

In "Our Communion," he mixes environmental and religious sentiments:

> The water is our life-blood.
> Our bodies are the land.

> Why can't they comprehend this?
> Why don't they understand?

McRae is equally eloquent about the human cost of economic progress in the West:

> "Sold to the highest bidder!"
> The gavel crashes down.
> Another rural family
> Goes shamblin' into town.

Lots of cowboy poetry contains **humor.** The funniest cowboy poem is, hands down, McRae's "Reincarnation." McRae goes far beyond cheap laughs, however, by mixing everyday cowboy common sense and dialect with abstract philosophical issues. "Reincarnation" humorously reduces the issue of immortality and the afterlife to a pile of horse manure. In another work, McRae humorously and logically explains why there "Ain't No Cowboy Heaven."

In spite of his philosophical bent, McRae has never gotten too big for his John B. (Stetson hat). His humor often is self-deprecating. In "Clint" he chronicles the misadventures of his son Clint, but concludes by admitting: "I wasn't like him, growing up. I was a whole lot worse."

New York photojournalist Bernard Wolf spent some time with McRae at the Rocker Six Cattle Company in the mid-1980s. In 1985, he published *Cowboy,* a beautiful photojournalistic piece based on his conversations and black-and-white photographs. Wolf concludes his book with these lines:

> Some evenings, when the weather is fine, Wally likes to go out walking on the land, just for the pure pleasure of it. There's always so much to see: sometimes a fresh wildflower; or maybe an old Indian bead from someone long ago. Words are not enough to say what he feels. "God," Wally murmurs. "God, how I love it!"

I met Wally McRae at the 1991 Elko Cowboy Poetry Gathering. I had the great pleasure and honor of hearing him recite "Reincarnation."

With typical modesty, he insists, "It's a superficial poem; I don't know what the attraction is." His conversations with singer Ian **Tyson** inspired McRae to write a wistful poem dedicated to Tyson entitled "We Never Rode the Judiths." The poem reflects one of life's fundamental realities: We never experience or accomplish everything we would like. One line expresses the stark reality for most people as they move beyond middle age: "Seems we're not as scared of 'dyin' as we are of growing old." Another line reflects the wistfulness: "And we'll never ride the Judiths before they carry us away."

"I think the cowboy tradition has things of value inherent in it," says McRae, "and poetry lets me share that. I also think there's a search for roots, a more simple life and maybe personal freedom and my poems speak to that."

No cowboy poet has stirred, instructed, and entertained us more than Wally McRae. If you haven't had the pleasure of hearing or reading his poems, you've missed a wonderful, vibrant part of today's cowboy culture. *(American Cowboy Poet* magazine; *Cowboy Magazine;* Logsdon 1988; Martin 1992)

MAGGOT

Derogatory term for sheep.

MAGUEY

Century plant. See Rope.

MAHAN, LARRY

See Rodeo.

MAJOR DOMOR

Also mayor domo, meaning ranch foreman (from the Spanish term *mayordomo).*

"MAKE ME A COWBOY AGAIN FOR A DAY"

Anonymous song. See Music.

MAKINS

Tobacco and papers used to roll cigarettes.

"MAMAS, DON'T LET YOUR BABIES GROW UP TO BE COWBOYS"

Song. See Music.

MANGANA

Forefooting, a **rope** throw that catches a horse by the front feet.

MANILA

A **rope** made of Philippine hemp.

MANNING, DAVID

One of the many pseudonyms used by Frederick **Faust.**

MANTA

Finely woven **poncho** worn in Colombia and Venezuela.

MANZANA

Spanish word for apple, also applied to the **saddle** horn.

MARINOS

See Spurs.

MARLBORO MAN

See Pitchmen.

MAROMA

See Equestrian Games.

"MARTÍN FIERRO"

Epic poem written by José Hernández. See *Gauchesco.*

MASSACRE

Early (1934) social protest film about a Native American **rodeo** star.

MATADERO

Slaughterhouse. See Beef Catttle Industry.

MATANZA

See *Vaquería.*

MATE

Strong, highly caffeinic tea enjoyed by **gauchos**. See Coffee.

MATRERO

Gaucho outlaw, fugitive, or murderer.

MAVERICK, SAMUEL A.
(1803–1870)

See Maverick.

MAVERICK

An unbranded or "slick" calf is known as a maverick. In spring on the open range, cowboys sometimes found calves that did not follow a mother. Ranchers followed the usual practice of marking the calf with the brand of its mother, so this left the ownership of an orphaned calf an open question. Cattlemen provided the answer: finders keepers. An unowned calf or maverick (pronounced "mav rick") could be claimed and branded by whoever found it.

Some cowboys scoured the range for mavericks and built modest herds. Some unscrupulous riders preferred to give mother nature a hand by creating mavericks. One particularly disgusting tactic was to slit a calf's tongue. Because it could not nurse, the calf might separate from its mother. It could then be claimed as a maverick. Rustlers might also kill cows to make their calves orphans. This practice was known as "running a maverick factory," an unhealthy business if caught.

J. Frank **Dobie** traces the origin of the term to a Texas lawyer named Samuel A. Maverick and relates much of the folklore associated with him in *The Longhorns* (1941). According to the tale, in 1845 Maverick received a herd of cattle in payment for a debt. As a lawyer, he had no interest in tending the herd. He let them wander free on Matagorda Island off the Texas coast. In 1853 he had his 300 head brought to the mainland.

An **African-American** family tended the herd and branded some of the animals. When neighboring ranchers spotted unbranded calves, they began referring to them as "Maverick's." Because the animals lacked brands, other cowmen put their own brands on them. As Dobie reminds us, "This was not thought of as stealing—it was not stealing; it was the custom of the range at the time."

Gradually the term came to mean any unbranded cattle of unknown ownership. Such animals were fair game for the first branding iron. As applied to people, the term took on the connotation of extreme individualism, applied to those who strayed from the herd. (Dobie 1941; Marks 1989)

MAVERICK BRAND

An unrecorded brand. See Maverick; Roundup.

MILLER BROTHERS' 101 RANCH WILD WEST SHOW

George W. Miller founded the famous 101 Ranch near Ponca City, Oklahoma, in 1892. He and his sons built it into a 110,000-acre operation, part of a vast commercial network. In 1908 his sons George Lee, Joseph, and Zack kicked off the famous Miller Brothers' 101 Ranch Wild West Show. William M. (Bill) **Pickett,** "The Dusky Demon" and inventor of bulldogging, performed as a star attraction. Like many of the performers, Pickett actually worked on the Miller ranch. Future silent **B-western** film stars Buck Jones, Tom Mix, and Mabel Normand also performed with the show.

The 101 also got into the movie business. Pioneer filmmaker Thomas Ince found the troop during a winter layoff near Los Angeles. He hired the full cast at $2,500 per week and had all the cowboys, Indians, and livestock he needed for his pictures. After a wartime break to raise livestock for the government, the 101 reopened in 1925, embellished with ballet, Ziegfeld dancers, and elephants. Like earlier shows headed by Buffalo Bill **Cody** and Pawnee Bill **Lillie,** the 101 fell to bankruptcy, a victim of the Depression in 1931. (Gipson 1946; O'Neil 1979; Russell 1970)

MILONGA

Typical **gaucho** song.

MIRADOR

Watchtower on a ranch house in Argentina. See Beef Cattle Industry.

THE MISFITS

Film (1961) directed by John Huston and starring Marilyn Monroe and Clark Gable.

MISSIONS

See Vaquero.

MITCHELL, WADDIE
(n.d.)

Along with Wallace D. (Wally) **McRae** and Baxter **Black,** Waddie Mitchell has become one of America's best-known cowboy poets. Son of a Nevada cowboy, Mitchell quit high school at age 16 to follow in his father's footsteps. Along with cowboying, young Mitchell enjoyed collecting and reciting old cowboy poems. "I can't ever remember 'find' cowboy poetry," he says. "It was always there." He also began writing original poems.

Mitchell helped organize the first cowboy **poetry** gathering at Elko in 1985. Inspired with the warm reception, he gradually shifted his attention away from ranching and more toward performing. His trademark handlebar mustache and ready grin became familiar to millions from appearances on the Johnny Carson Show and elsewhere.

Mitchell's poetry is available to a broader audience through books, videotapes, and audiotapes. His first two albums on the Warner Western label, *Lone Driftin' Cowboy* and *Buckaroo Poet,* blend cowboy **humor,** witty commentary, and wisdom. He also recites on the Michael Martin **Murphey** *Cowboy Christmas* album.

Mitchell lives in Jiggs, Nevada, and retains his love of ranching as well as cowboy poetry. He wants to buy his own ranch: "I'm hoping for the opportunity to go broke on a ranch by myself instead of helping somebody else do it." (*American Cowboy Poet* magazine; *Cowboy Magazine;* Flint and Nelson 1993)

MIX, TOM
(1880–1940)

Actor. See Films, Cowboy.

MOCHILA

See Saddle.

MONKEY NOSE

Type of *tapadero.* See Saddle.

MONTANA, PATSY
(1912–)

Singer also known as Rubye Blevins. See Music.

MONTANA, THE MAGAZINE OF WESTERN HISTORY

See Western History Association; Appendix C.

MONTANA RIG

See Saddle.

MONTE

Card game. See Gambling.

MONTE WALSH

Film (1970). See Films, Best Cowboy.

MONUMENT VALLEY, ARIZONA

Scenic mountain and desert location used by John Ford and many other directors to shoot western films.

MOORE, CLAYTON
(1914–)

Actor who played the Lone Ranger. See Television.

MORA, JOSEPH J.
(b. 1876)

Historian also known as Jo Mora. See Historiography of the Cowboy.

MORAN, THOMAS
(1837–1926)

An artist with a keen eye and uncanny ability to recreate the sublime in his depictions of western countryside, Thomas Moran took long sojourns throughout the West and painted such sites as the Grand Canyon and Yellowstone.

See also Art of the Cowboy.

Thomas Moran not only painted awe-inspiring western nature scenes but he also took advantage of them. Here he is seen resting by a stream after fishing, one of his favorite pastimes.

MORGAN, MARK

Pseudonym for author Wayne D. Overholser.

MORGAN

See Horses.

MORISCOS

See Spurs.

MORLAND, PETER HENRY

Pseudonym for Frederick Schiller **Faust**.

MORMON TEA

Colloquial term for liquor. *See also* Saloons.

MORRAL

A horse's feed bag or nose bag, a Spanish term adopted by Texans. If a cowboy rode a grain-fed (as opposed to grass-fed) horse, he carried a fiber bag of grain strapped to the **saddle** horn. To feed the animal, he strapped the bag onto the head over the nose. This may be the origin of the expression "tie on the feed bag," meaning to eat. "Put on the morral" or "put on the nose bag" likewise meant to eat. (Blevins 1993)

MORRISON, MARION MICHAEL

John **Wayne**'s given name.

MOSES, ANNE

See Oakley, Annie.

MOSS HEAD

Colloquial term for a very old steer.

MOTHER HUBBARD

See Saddle.

MOTHER HUBBARD LOOP

A very large loop in a lasso.

MOTION PICTURE INDUSTRY

See Films, Cowboy.

MOUNTAIN OYSTERS

Fried or roasted calves' testicles. See Food.

MOUNTAIN PRESS PUBLISHING COMPANY

Over nearly half a century, Mountain Press has evolved into one of the more interesting active western publishers. The press publishes books on geology, natural and earth science, horsemanship, and western Americana, including the fur trade and cowboy culture.

The press's origins lie with Pennsylvania-born David P. Flaccus, who began an offset printing company in Missoula, Montana, in 1948. In the mid-1960s, Flaccus began printing a few books, the first titled *The Psychology of Coronet and Trumpet Playing*. The current president of Mountain Press, John Rimel, explains what happened next. "Soon the publishing business had outgrown the printing business. Books interested David more than letterheads and thus the printing part of the business was sold. It was, as David said, 'a case of the tail wagging the dog.'"

One of the press's major franchises began in 1972 with the publication of *Roadside Geology of the Northern Rockies*. Since that year Mountain Press has added many volumes to its Roadside Geology series, numbering 17 by fall 1993. The press added a companion Roadside History series, which includes Arizona, New Mexico, Oklahoma, Oregon, South Dakota, Texas, Vermont, and Yellowstone Park.

Flaccus retired to Bend, Oregon, in the spring of 1992 because of failing health. The press expanded to new facilities in July 1993. At the time, it was publishing a dozen new volumes each year and had nine full-time employees and a backlist of about 100 books.

Cowboy Culture

Mountain Press publishes or distributes a wide range of books treating horsemanship and cow culture. The fall 1993 catalog included 28 books on western Americana and classics of the fur trade. Several titles should interest readers of this encyclopedia. *Behind the Chutes: The Mystique of the Rodeo Cowboy* (1993), by Rosamond

Norbury, is a handsomely produced exercise in photojournalism. The book, published by arrangement with Whitecap Books in Vancouver, British Columbia, consists mainly of the author's evocative Canadian **rodeo** photographs, reproduced in attractive deep sepia tones. Brief text and captions tie the photographs together into a very enjoyable whole. Norbury, a freelance photographer, well captures the thrills and spills of rodeo. Ian **Tyson**'s cover blurb says it well: "If you ever fantasized about goin' down the road with the wild young riders but you know you'll never do it—Rosamond Norbury's book is the next best thing."

Beginning in the 1980s, western collectibles became very hot. Among the Mountain Press titles is *Cowboy and Gunfighter Collectibles: A Photographic Encyclopedia with Price Guide and Makers Index* (1989), by Bill Mackin, a useful, attractive book for the collector or would-be collector. The author is a collector of western Americana who lives in Meeker, Colorado. He describes himself as "a devotee of Will James, but a student of Jo Mora." If cowboys or gunfighters used it, you'll find it pictured, described, and priced in this guide. Mackin offers an alphabetical sampling of cowboy artifacts, from advertising, badges, and belts to tapaderos, watch fobs, and Winchesters. Prices, of course, change over time, but the new collector, in particular, should benefit from Mackin's guidance.

Mountain Press also published Jim Bramlett's *Ride for the High Points: The Real Story of Will James* (1987), a loving literary biography. The author's own artistic and cowboying background serve him well in treating a cowboy/writer/illustrator like James. The author did not attempt to write a complete biography. He "wanted to capture him [James] at his prime, when his genius was surfacing and he was contributing color and a historical record to the cowboy's West through his writings and art." The book is not a whitewash to James's checkered life; Bramlett covers fully the cowboy's arrest and conviction for cattle rustling in 1915. Sources for the book include interviews with James's ex-wife, Alice James Ross, and with Abe Hays, "a living

authority on Will James," as well as the files of James specialist Anthony Amaral. Black-and-white photographs enliven almost every page. The book lacks notes or bibliography but does conclude with a useful glossary and index.

The tragic death of Wallace **Stegner** in 1993 gives special significance to another Mountain Press book, *The Range* (1990) by Sherm Ewing. Stegner grew up along the Saskatchewan-Montana border and evoked life in that region in his delightful memoir, *Wolf Willow* (1955). Ewing has gathered firsthand observations about life in northern Montana, southern Saskatchewan and Alberta—Wallace Stegner country. After retiring from ranching, Ewing spent two years interviewing ranchers and another two years organizing their stories into topical chapters. The result is an interesting combination of history, memoir, and range management handbook that illuminates a century of ranch life (about 1880 to 1980) on both sides of the U.S.-Canadian border. Why don't we hear the voices of many **women?** "In the period I selected," says Ewing, "few women were prominent in range management. A history of the years after 1980 can draw on the experiences of many women who have made the range their business and career."

Students of cowboy history and culture will enjoy these and other Mountain Press books.

Address: 2016 Strand Avenue, P.O. Box 2399, Missoula MT 59806; tel. 800-234-5308; fax 406-728-1635.

MOVIES
See Films, Best Cowboy; Films, Cowboy; Films, Documentary.

MOZEE, PHOEBE ANNE
See Oakley, Annie.

MUD FENCE, UGLY AS A
A "cowboyism" that is not a compliment.

MULE-EARS
See Boots.

MULEY
A one-horned or hornless cow.

MULEY SADDLE
A hornless **saddle**.

MULFORD, CLARENCE EDWARD
(1883–1956)
Novelist and creator of Hopalong Cassidy.

MURPHEY, MICHAEL MARTIN
(1945–)
With his highly successful 1990 album, *Cowboy Songs,* singer-songwriter Michael Martin Murphey became the country's leading evangelist for western **music**. It is, he says, the "music of my people, of my land." Murphey has won millions of converts who agree with his choice. "This is not the hot new country. This is the great old western."

Murphey grew up hearing and singing cowboy songs around campfires at Sky Ranch, near Lewisville, Texas. He left Texas to attend the University of California, Los Angeles (UCLA) in the late 1960s. "I went out there to study Greek and Latin and Roman history and medieval history. I was interested in the classical world, the ancient world, and the medieval world. And I'll tell you my reasoning for that. I feel like I was the wandering minstrel of today, and I really wanted to study the wandering minstrel of the ancient times, and so, I got into all that because I was interested in actually digging up more stuff on the early, early singer-songwriters and minstrels. And I had a great time doing that." At UCLA Murphey set his studies to song with a folk-rock group called the Lewis and Clark Expedition.

Murphey's love for and knowledge of history continues. He often gives audiences intriguing glimpses into the history behind his songs. In 1971 Murphey returned to Texas, just in time for the great outlaw music rebellion.

Like Willie Nelson, Jerry Jeff Walker, and Waylon Jennings, Murphey shunned Nashville's constraints and conservatism in favor of the West's wide-open spaces. His 1973 tune, "Cosmic Cowboy," became a counterculture cowboy anthem:

I just wanna be a Cosmic Cowboy.
I just wanna ride and rope and hoot.
I just wanna be a Cosmic Cowboy.
A supernatural country rockin' galoot.
Lone Star sippin' and skinny dippin'
and steel guitars and stars
Are just as good as Hollywood
and them bullshit disco bars.

During the 1970s Murphey enjoyed great commercial success with beautiful ballads. Audiences continue to thrill to his great melodies like "Wildfire," "Carolina in the Pines," and "What's Forever For." Of the latter song, Murphey jokes, "It was hard for me to write about romantic love since I was raised a southern Baptist."

Murphey's music blends western images, old and new. Like many old-time cowboy songs, his lyrics often belie a nostalgia for times past. "Texas Morning," "Another Cheap Western," and "Geronimo's Cadillac" all evoke powerful images from western myth and history. In 1978 Murphey left Texas for Taos, New Mexico. He still writes his music and ranches there.

Cowboy Songs
In the mid-1980s, the rise of cowboy **poetry** festivals signaled a major western cultural revival. The joyful enthusiasm of the crowds "got me so fired up you can't believe it," said Murphey. He decided to join in the fun. "I wanted to revive this cowboy spirit, and I found myself almost operating like an evangelist." He began performing old cowboy standards like "Red River Valley." Audiences, young and old, loved the traditional songs.

Does Murphey have an old-time favorite?

Absolute number one favorite is "When the Works All Done This Fall." I'm fascinated with the man who wrote it, D. J. O'Malley. Not very much is known about him.... It deals with the true danger of being a cowboy. The real risk involved is with the animals themselves and the possibility of getting hurt just in an accident. So much focus was put for so many years on getting shot in a duel or a stagecoach robbery or a train robbery or something like that. People missed out on the real message of the cowboy.... It's a tragedy of a death in a stampede and symbolically, I think, represents all that danger that a cowboy takes on. And plus it's a wonderful melody.

Murphey "discovered that there was a thread that tied the whole thing together that I'd been missing." That thread, he says, "was that I am absolutely rooted in the American West." At that point, he conceived his *Cowboy Songs* album.

Besides his strong voice and captivating songs, Murphey's warm stage presence delights fans. Ever gracious, he has a wonderful self-deprecating sense of humor. Murphey switches guitars between virtually ever number so the instruments can be kept closely tuned. He explains the practice this way: "I saw Eric Clapton do it," he says wryly, "so I thought it might work for me."

Like many westerners, Murphey traces his roots to the South. His great-great-great grandfather, Archibald Murphey (1777–1832), was a prominent North Carolinian. "He was a statesmen, lawyer and sort of a public transportation engineer. He also founded the public school system of North Carolina," says Murphey, with understandable pride. Murphey Hall at the University of North Carolina campus in Chapel Hill stands as a tribute to Archibald.

Family ties are very important to the Murpheys. The *Tonight We Ride* album includes several dedications—"Innocent Hearts" for daughter Laura Lynn's christening, "Close to my Heart" for wife Mary. Murphey dedicated his entire *Americana* album to Mary.

At WestFest 1993 Murphey dedicated several songs to his parents, P. L. and Lois. They have been married for more than 50 years. He dedicated another song to his step-grandfather,

Ed Gross. With his love for family, friends, and the land, Murphey embodies the basic values of the Old West.

Family ties now reach into music. Murphey and his oldest son Ryan have become musical collaborators. In 1993 Ryan took over full time as lead guitar in Murphey's Rio Grande Band (along with David Cole, fiddle; Gary Roller, bass; Joey Miskulin, keyboards; LeRoy Featherston, drums).

Spokesman for Western Culture

Murphey has taken a leading role in many aspects of western culture. He often appears at the **National Cowboy Hall of Fame** in Oklahoma City, which honored *Cowboy Songs* with its prestigious Western Heritage Wrangler Award in 1991. He serves on the board for the Elko Cowboy Poetry Gathering.

WestFest, which Murphey began at Copper Mountain, Colorado, in 1987, is the ultimate western celebration—a cowboy Woodstock with music, poetry, literature, and horses. Red Steagall, Don Edwards, Bill Miller, Sons of the San Joaquin, Baxter **Black,** and many, many other western stars have performed. Many of the artists perform for the Warner Western label, which Warner Brothers formed after the success of Murphey's *Cowboys Songs.*

As a composer, singer, musicologist, and rancher, Murphey wears lots of **hats.** At WestFest, his big black Stetson seems the perfect fit. He loves "standing on a stage singing a Western-style song. That's what makes me happy," he says. "It's what I do best." Audiences at WestFest couldn't agree more. They stamp, clap, howl, and whistle their delight after every song.

Murphey uses WestFest to show people that western "tradition and heritage is fun and it's alive. I think much like many people who have put living history into museums. We try to do that at WestFest. We also really try to showcase the contemporary, which is going to be tradition."

Murphey has narrated several documentaries about ranch life. In 1989 he hosted visits to four ranches in *Great Ranches of the West,* a PBS **film documentary.** In 1993 he narrated *Cowboys of the Americas,* a sweeping look at ranch life from Tierra del Fuego to Alberta.

Murphey's "Cowboy Songs" series skillfully blends history, myth, and melody. His music reflects many influences in his life. He's a fan of Buffalo Bill **Cody** and wears a long buff-colored buckskin jacket reminiscent of the great Wild West showman. *Rhymes of the Renegades* (1993) includes two Marty Robbins hits, "Big Iron" and "El Paso." Robbins, says Murphey, "is one of my heroes" and "El Paso" is "the greatest song of my life." Through multi-track technology, Murphey sings "Big Iron" as a duet with Robbins, "probably the greatest honor I've been afforded in my life."

Murphey's 1994 album, *A Night in the American West,* combines two of his favorite types of music—symphonic and cowboy. "We are going to go back and reprise a lot of the western albums. Boil it down. It's going to be like a best of the cowboy songs album done with the symphony."

Who enjoys western music today? According to Murphey, "Probably ten percent have a real tie to ranching and cowboying and the actual life-style day to day. Ninety percent of the rest are people who are interested in it to participate in some way, or they are just vicarious."

Fans old and new will keep Murphey center stage for a long time to come. True to his roots, Murphey's music of choice remains cowboy. He's been a cosmic, urban, and outlaw cowboy. "From now on," he says, "it's just COWBOY!"

For the future? "Give me a good steel-string guitar, a good pony, nights under western stars, and a 'home on the range' when I'm too old to ride," Murphey says.

Discography
1973 *Cosmic Cowboy Souvenir*
1974 *Michael Murphey*
1975 *Blue Sky, Night Thunder* ["Carolina in the Pines," "Wildfire"]
1975 *Swans against the Sky*
1976 *Flowing Free Forever*

1978 *Lone Wolf*
1979 *Peaks, Valleys, Honky-Tonks & Alleys* [includes five live performances]
1982 *Michael Martin Murphey* ["What's Forever For?," "Still Taking Chances," "Ring of Truth"]
1984 *Best of Michael Martin Murphey*
1986 *Tonight We Ride* ["Innocent Hearts," "Fiddlin' Man"]
1987 *Americana* ["A Face in the Crowd," sung with Holly Dunn; "Almost Free"]
1988 *River of Time*
1989 *Land of Enchantment* ["The Heart Knows the Truth," "Desperation Road"]
1990 *Cowboy Songs*
1990 *The Best of Country* [greatest hits collection]
1991 *Cowboy Songs II: Cowboy Christmas*
1993 *Cowboy Songs III: Rhymes of the Renegades*
1994 *America's Horse*
As narrator of videotape documentaries:
Great Ranches of the West, Atlas Video, Inc., 1992.
Cowboys of the Americas, Warner-Western, 1993.

(Murphey 1991, 1994; *Songs of the West* magazine)

MUSEUMS
There is a multitude of institutions with collections that allow the general public to enjoy cowboy history and culture. See Appendix B for a listing of cowboy museums.

MUSIC
Cowboy music is laboring man's music. Like slaves, miners, seamen, and other laborers, cowboys created songs that reflected the realities of their working lives. Lyrics recorded the difficulties, tragedies, and **humor** of daily life on the range. Music served as both memory and therapy. Cowboys memorialized special events, friends, **horses,** and other things dear to them. They used music to ward off the loneliness and sadness they often faced in their difficult occupation. **Trail drives,** stampedes, bronco busting, gunfighters, outlaws—all elements of cowboy life—may be found in the lyrics of old cowboy songs.

Folklorist Charlie Seemann estimates that three-fourths of original cowboy songs began as verses composed by working cowboys:

> In the relative isolation of the long trail drives, cowboys found they had to provide their own entertainment, and in this setting a rich folklore grew up, including tales and stories, jokes, recitations, and songs. Most cowboys probably knew at least snatches of songs, but not many could carry a tune.

Poetry sometimes found its way into print, often in western newspapers or stockmen's publications. When set to traditional folk tunes, often of Irish, Scottish or English origin, the poems evolved into cowboy songs. Some cowboy songsters adapted earlier compositions. "The Dying Cowboy" ("Bury Me Not on the Lone Prairie") is a rewrite of "The Ocean Burial," a poem written by Reverend E. H. Chapin in 1839. "The Streets of Laredo" comes from a British ballad of a soldier's death and burial. "The Dying Ranger" is an adaptation of a Yankee Civil War song, "The Dying Soldier."

Spanish words worked their way into many songs, especially on the southern ranges. Like the Anglo cowboy's general working vocabulary, his songs also showed Hispanic influences. Famous cowboy poet Badger **Clark** wrote a poem called "Spanish is the Lovin' Tongue." Singer Bill Simon gave the poem a haunting melody in the 1920s and produced a beautiful love song, with a strong Spanish flavor. Michael Martin **Murphey** gives a splendid interpretation of the song on his *Cowboy Songs* album (1990). Canadian cowboy singer Ian **Tyson** has recorded a wonderful Mexican *corrido* (folk song) about a fighting cock, "Gallo de Cielo."

Popular cowboy songs generated innumerable variations and verses as different singers forgot, altered, or added to the lyrics. Cowboys added their own verses to popular tunes, so that some songs, such as "The Old Chisholm Trail," have literally hundreds of known verses.

Instrumentation was simple. Traditional cowboy music revolved around a few key instruments. Three of them were stringed—the guitar, banjo, and fiddle. Two were played with the mouth—the harmonica and Jews' harp. The latter two had the special virtue of small size, portability, and durability. Few cowboys could manage to pack bulky instruments around the range.

The guitar remains the instrument most associated with cowboy music. The guitar or some close musical relative graced bunkhouses throughout the Americas. It became even more strongly associated with the cowboy during the rise of the singing cowboys of the movies during the 1930s and 1940s.

Journalist John Baumann (*Fortnightly Review,* 1 April 1887) listened to cowboys singing on the Texas range. "The younger hands are whiling away the time 'whittling' and 'plug chawing,' drawling out yarns of love and sport and singing ribald songs, until someone strikes up the favorite wail, 'Oh, bury me not on the lone prairie, Where the coyotes howl and the winds blow free.'"

Did cowboys really sing at night to soothe their restless bovine charges? Some writers find the notion of singing to cattle preposterous. Jack Thorp, one of the nation's first authorities on cowboy songs, had this to say (*Pardner in the Wind,* 1945):

> It is generally thought that cowboys did a lot of singing around the herd at night to quiet them on the bed ground. I have been asked about this, and I'll say that I have stood my share of night watches in fifty years, and I seldom heard any singing of that kind.

Most authorities, including Jules Verne Allen, "the Singing Cowboy," insist that cowboys used steady, low, melodious tunes to keep cattle from starting at unexpected sounds. This serenading helped keep the herd under the compelling spell of the human voice. It also kept the puncher's silhouette against the skyline or the noise of his moving pony from startling the animals.

In his *Dictionary of the American West,* Winfred Blevins includes several entries that mention singing to cattle. He defines "hymn" as "cowboy talk for a song he sings to the cows." Under "night herd," he opines that "in the night herder's singing was the cradle of the one art of the West, the cowboy song." "Singing to them" meant riding night guard.

Many sources mention that night riders sang, usually unaccompanied, to the herd. When a night herder ran out of songs he knew, he patched together a miscellany of words and music, mixing the sacred and the profane. One might hear gospel strains mixed with bawdy poems. As Jack Thorp put it delicately, many songs "were full of the vernacular of the range, and it wasn't always parlor talk." Hands might incorporate accounts of horse races, unflattering opinions about cattle, strings of profanity, the text from canned goods, or simply humming.

Cowhand Harry Stephens claimed authorship of "The Night-Herding Song." He explained the song's origin to John Lomax this way.

> Well, we always got night-herd years ago when they didn't have so many fences and corrals, and that was the biggest job for the cowboy. We generally have a two-hour shift, and two to four men on a shift according to the size of the herd. And when I made up this song, why, we always had so many different squawks and yells and hollers a-trying to keep the cattle quiet, I thought I might as well have a kind of song to it.

Contrary to the plots of Gene **Autry** or Roy **Rogers** movies, cowboys did not burst into song every ten minutes. Quiet conversation, not songs around the campfire, commonly marked the end of the day. William G. Johnson, who worked as a cowboy during the 1880s, recalled "there was no singing or playing the fiddle around the campfire as the story writers and the movies would have

you believe." After a hard day in the saddle, men played poker. "There is little else but hard work in the life of a cowpuncher," Johnson concluded (Rollinson 1948).

The heyday of cowboy life in the United States passed quickly within a single generation. Not surprisingly, a longing for bygone days became the refrain of many old cowboy tunes. One American song of unknown authorship wistfully asks, "Make me a cowboy again for a day:"

> Thunder of hoofs on the range as you ride,
> Hissing of iron and sizzling of hide,
> Bellows of cattle and snort of cayuse,
> Longhorns from Texas as wild as the deuce.
> Mid-nite stampedes and milling of herds,
> Yells of the Cow-men too angry for words,
> Right in the thick of it all would I stay,
> Make me a Cowboy again for a day
> Under the star-studded Canopy vast,
> Camp-fire and coffee and comfort at last,
> Bacon that sizzles and crisps in the pan,
> After the round-up smells good to a man.
> Stories of ranchers and rustlers retold,
> Over the Pipe as the embers grow cold,
> Those are the times that old memories play,
> Make me a Cowboy again for a day.

Beginning in the late nineteenth century, song collectors, writers, and singers kept cowboy music alive. John A. Lomax, N. Howard ("Jack") Thorp, Charles Nabell, Carl T. Sprague, Jules Verne Allen, and Mac McClintock collected, recorded, or performed traditional tunes and in some cases penned new ones.

Some profanity laced the lyrics of many cowboy songs. (See Guy Logsdon's *The Whorehouse Bells Were Ringing,* 1989, for example.) Some puritanical spirits "sanitized" latter-day versions of many cowboy songs. John A. Lomax removed much profanity when he compiled his famous anthology, *Cowboy Songs* (1910). Many mythmakers have expended considerable energy cleaning up the cowboy's image.

During the late 1920s, the Carter family, James Charles (Jimmy) Rodgers (1897–1933), and other country singers gained large audiences. Rodgers, "the Father of Country Music," grew up working on the railroad with his father. His "blue yodel" could be heard above the noise of the train until tuberculosis struck him in 1924. He gave up the railroad but kept on yodeling and singing. His illness killed him at the tender age of 35.

During the early 1930s, western swing blew in from the Texas plains. James Robert (Bob) Wills (1905–1975), who played mandolin and fiddle, formed the Texas Playboys in 1933. Known as the King of Texas Swing, Wills blended driving fiddle music with strains of jazz and popular music of the day. He sometimes brought in brass and saxophones, common in jazz, but unusual in country music. Wills exerted a powerful, pioneering influence on country-and-western music, recording some 550 recordings and starring in 25 films.

At the same time, the singing movie cowboys burst on the scene. The first singing cowboy of the movies, Ken Maynard, warbled his way through two songs in *The Wagon Master* (1929), singing "The Lone Star Trail" and "The Cowboy's Lament." Maynard helped introduce Gene Autry to audiences in the 1934 film, *In Old Santa Fe*. Soon, Tex Ritter, Roy Rogers, the Sons of the Pioneers, Dick Foran, Bill Boyd, and a host of other cowboy crooners could be heard on **radio,** records, and movies. Rex Allen, Jimmy Wakeley, Monte Hale, and Ken Curtis joined the chorus in the 1940s.

Maurice Woodward ("Tex") Ritter (1905–1974) was a major musical force, helping establish the Country Music Foundation and the Country Music Hall of Fame. He is most notable for his rendition of the theme song to the film *High Noon* (1952).

During the 1930s, the cowboy replaced the hillbilly as the dominant country music persona. Country singers who had never been near a ranch recognized the popular appeal of cowboy **boots, hats,** and western-cut clothing. Their music became country and western.

Many memorable stars arose during the golden age of country-and-western music from the 1930s through the 1950s. Frank Anthony Kuczynski (1914–), better known as Pee Wee King, played with Autry's band, the Range Riders, during the early 1930s. When Autry headed out to Hollywood, King took over the band and rechristened it the Golden West Cowboys. Many country-and-western stars, including Ernest Tubb, Eddie Arnold, and Cowboy Copas, played with the band over the years. Among Pee Wee King's many musical achievements is the "Tennessee Waltz," cowritten with Redd Stewart.

"The Texas Troubadour," Ernest Tubb (1914–1984), idolized Jimmy Rodgers as a child. He began recording in 1936 and went on to become the first country performer to grace the stage at Carnegie Hall. "I'm Walking the Floor Over You" sold more than three million copies. His long career earned him deep respect and many awards from the country-and-western music community.

Eddie Arnold (1918–1990), "the Tennessee Plowboy," played nightclubs and radio. In 1945 he cut his first album and went on to sell more than 85 million records. (Only the Beatles and Elvis Presley surpass that number.)

Hank Williams (1923–1953) dominated the charts in the late 1940s until his premature death from alcohol. As a teenager, he formed a band called the Drifting Cowboys. He began recording songs in 1946 and turned out a string of country hits. Along with Fred Rose and Jimmy Rodgers, he became one of the first members of the Country Music Hall of Fame in 1961. He wrote more than a dozen million-selling songs. His son, Hank Williams, Jr., (1949–) carries on the family musical tradition, giving it his own unique spin.

Martin David (Marty) Robbins (1925–1982) added his unforgettable gunfighter ballads, notably "El Paso" and "Big Iron." The Arizona-born singer wrote more than 500 songs and reaped many awards, including two Grammys. Michael Martin Murphey brought back the two gunfighter ballads on his 1993 album, *Rhymes of the Renegades.*

Cowboys dominated country and western, but Rubye Blevins, better known as Patsy Montana (1912–), has certainly left her mark. She sang with the Prairie Ramblers on Chicago's WLS during the 1930s. In 1935 they recorded "I Want to be a Cowboy's Sweetheart," believed to be the first million-seller by a female country singer. The Academy of Country Music (ACM) honored this yodeling cowgirl with a Pioneer Award in 1970.

Over the years, many distinctly noncowboy songwriters tried their hand at western tunes. As Jim Bob Tinsley has pointed out, many memorable cowboy ballads "came from the imagination of Tin Pan Alley writers in New York City." This is the case with the 1912 hit song, "Ragtime Cowboy Joe." Dance band leader Jack Breckenridge Tenney wrote "Mexicali Rose" (1923).

A few "cowboy" tunes originated even farther away from the West than Tin Pan Alley. "Ole Faithful" (1934), an ode to the loyal cowboy pony, came from England. Michael Maurice Cohen, a Jew born in Leeds but raised in Dublin, changed his last name to Carr in 1933. He composed the song along with Hamilton Kennedy, born in Northern Ireland.

Many composers, however, had firsthand experience in the West. Bob Nolan of the Sons of the Pioneers grew up in Tucson. Young Jimmy Rodgers spent the winter of 1923–24 looking for railroad jobs in Arizona and the West. Stan Jones, who wrote "Riders in the Sky" (1947), was born in Douglas, Arizona, and learned guitar-playing from Arizona cowboys. Marty Robbins was born in Glendale, Arizona.

Traditional western music continues to be performed. Glenn Ohrlin, Slim Critchlow, Van Holyoak, Red Steagall, Don Edwards, Dallas ("Nevada Slim") Turner, and a handful of other singers kept performing the old tunes through

the 1960s, '70s, and '80s. Ramblin' Jack Elliott has been entertaining audiences with his tall tales and guitar playing for four decades.

New Jersey–born Don Edwards (1939–) grew up admiring writer Will James and silver screen cowboys Tom Mix, Tex Ritter, and Gene Autry. He came from a show business family. His father performed as a vaudeville magician, so he heard a wide, wonderful variety of music as a child. At the tender age of ten he began teaching himself to play the guitar. His family moved to Texas when Don was 16. He worked on Texas and New Mexico ranches as a teenager and participated in some **rodeos.** In 1961 he began singing (and performing stunts) as part of his job at Six Flags over Texas. Three years later he recorded his first album. Two Edwards albums are among the Folklore Archives of the Library of Congress. His 1993 album, *Goin' Back to Texas,* combines traditional with contemporary cowboy songs. His earlier albums include *Happy Cowboy, Desert Nights and Cowtown Blues, Chant of the Wanderer,* and *Songs of the Trail.*

Edwards has won widespread praise for his strong, melodious voice and his sensitive handling of cowboy songs. Michael Martin Murphey said it well when he described Edwards as "one of the finest pure cowboy singers I've ever heard." "In listening to Don's fine voice," said Roy Rogers, "I hear a little bit of some of my favorites, like Marty Robbins and my good friend Bob Nolan." The **National Cowboy Hall of Fame** honored Edwards with a Western Heritage Wrangler Award for Outstanding Traditional Western Music.

Red Steagall has worked many different jobs, including rancher, agrochemical salesman, poet, and singer. Born in Gainesville, Texas, he grew up in the Panhandle town of Sanford. As a teenager, he rodeoed (bull riding) until a bout of polio hit him. He took up guitar playing as part of his therapy, and cowboy music has been much the better ever since. Steagall has recorded some 200 songs of all types. It is cowboy music, however, that holds a special place in his heart. "The cowboy image has always exemplified independence and individualism, and that's the thing that's made it endure," he says, "because everybody wants to feel independent." His 1992 album, *Born to This Land,* exemplifies that feeling.

In contrast, humor is the stock-in-trade for the **Riders in the Sky.** They also feature the close harmonies of the Sons of the Pioneers. Formed in 1977, the group has become widely popular with radio, television, and live audiences of all ages.

The cowboy music genre has continued to evolve. Chris LeDoux *(Rusty Spurs,* 1977) used his rodeo experiences and put his own special brand on cowboy music. Born in 1948, LeDoux grew up loving horses and wanting to be a cowboy. By age 14 he was competing ably in the national finals of the Little Britches Rodeo. He continued to rodeo through high school and college in Wyoming. Along the way, he found time to take up guitar playing and songwriting. LeDoux kept winning at rodeo (1976 National Finals Rodeo [NFR] World Championship Bareback Rider). His family also began producing his albums on their independent American Cowboy Songs label. By 1984 two decades of rodeo injuries convinced him to turn his attention from professional riding to singing. His star rose quickly, hastened by the mention of his name in a Garth Brooks song. The two then recorded a smash duet, "Whatcha Gonna Do with a Cowboy?"

Johnny Lee (1946–) broke into performing in the early 1970s in a club owned by singer Mickey Gilley (1936–). He hit the big time in 1980 by singing "Looking for Love" in the film *Urban Cowboy.* The same movie put Louisiana-born Gilley and his Pasadena, Texas, club on the nation's cultural map. Debts, lawsuits, and fire closed the club, but the enterprising singer and promoter joined the exodus to Branson, Missouri, where he opened the Gilley Family Theater in 1989.

Nashville, the country music center, exercised a conservative musical influence that many artists found too constraining. Some singers and songwriters wanted to stretch and grow beyond the Grand Old Opry model. In the early 1970s,

Austin, Texas, became the center of progressive "outlaw" music, a reaction against Nashville.

Willie Nelson led the charge with his album *Red Headed Stranger.* Nelson and Waylon Jennings, singing Ed Bruce's lyrics, warned "Mamas, Don't Let Your Babies Grow Up To Be Cowboys" (1978). Born in Abbott, Texas, in 1933, Nelson was already performing with a Bohemian polka band at age ten. He became know as a songwriter during the 1950s and early '60s ("Crazy," "Funny How Time Slips Away," "Night Life," "Hello Walls.") He left Nashville and returned to Texas in 1970. Five years later *Red Headed Stranger* finally earned him respect as a performer as well as a songwriter. Neither marital ups-and-downs (he married for the fourth time in 1991) nor IRS troubles (an $18 million tax debt) have kept Nelson down. He performs widely and remains a vibrant part of the musical scene.

Texan Waylon Jennings (1937–) rose as another leader of the outlaw gang. He struck a resonant chord with "My Heroes Have Always Been Cowboys." Jennings began singing as a youngster and in the mid-1950s played bass as one of Buddy Holly's Cricketts. He narrowly escaped disaster when, in February 1959, he gave up his seat on the ill-fated flight that killed Holly and J. P. ("Big Bopper") Richardson. In 1969 Jennings married country singer Jessi Colter. Their 1976 album, *Wanted—The Outlaws,* eventually went beyond double platinum—more than two million copies sold.

Sons of the San Joaquin is a family affair, consisting of brothers Jack and Joe Hannah and Joe's son Lon. All three have well-trained voices, and their fine, close harmonies are reminiscent of the Sons of the Pioneers. They do a great job of classics, such as "Cool Water." Michael Martin Murphey produced their first album, *A Cowboy Has To Sing,* for Warner Western. Jack Hannah is also a talented songwriter. The group's second album, *Songs of the Silver Screen,* says Lon, is "something collectible for Sons of the Pioneers fans, or for fans of the songwriting of Tim Spencer and Bob Nolan."

Some country singers have discovered the attraction of western songs. In 1993 Randy Travis took a stab at western with his soundtrack to the television film *Wind in the Wire*. During the 1930s, Rex Allen was one of the original singing cowboys of the silver screen. His son, Rex Allen, Jr. (1947–) began his career in country music during the 1970s. More recently, he has taken up traditional cowboy songs.

Music and cowboy life have been an important part of Texas-born Buck Ramsey's entire life. As a youngster he learned songs, lore, and tack braiding from his uncle Ed. Ramsey only began performing in public during the 1980s. His low-key renditions of cowboy standards, accompanied by banjo or guitar, are very popular with music traditionalists. Ramsey is also a talented poet, so he mixes poetry with song in his performances. Owing to a bronco-riding accident in the early 1960s, Ramsey is confined to a wheelchair. With typical cowboy spirit, however, he did not let physical adversity stymie him. He overcame anger and depression at his condition and remained an active part of the "cowboy tribe." His album, *Rolling Uphill from Texas* garnered the 1993 Western Heritage Wrangler Award for Outstanding Traditional Western Music.

Many cowboy singers who performed throughout the West began releasing albums in the early 1990s. In 1993 Bob Campbell released *Roll On, Cowboy*. Best known as a songwriter, Campbell had written songs previously recorded by Chris LeDoux, Fletcher Jowers, Ed Stabler, Chuck Milner, and other western singers. He wrote all of the songs on his debut album, with the exception of the "Streets of Laredo." Randy Elmore and Rich O'Brien joined gravelly voiced Campbell on some of the tunes.

Coloradan Ed Stabler brought his excellent guitar work and polished performances to *Partner of the Wind* (1993). Instead of old-time standards, Stabler sings many original compositions, mostly the works of other contemporary songwriters. He often sets the lyrics of others to his own fine tunes. On this album he provided the tunes for two poems by Darrell Arnold ("Colorado Skies" and "Windmill"). (Arnold publishes and edits *Cowboy Magazine*.) Stabler's previous albums include *Ponies* and *His Knibbs and the Badger* (with Arizona singer Katie Lee). The latter album is comprised entirely of adaptations of poems by Henry Herbert Knibbs and Charles Badger Clark.

In contrast, Robert Wagoner's *Heart of the Golden West* (1993) includes many old songs that will sound "new" and unfamiliar to most listeners. Some of the 16 titles on the album include "Blow Wind Blow," "Open Range Ahead," "Prairie Echo," and "I Belong to the Range."

Fletcher Jowers *(Songs of a Texas Cowboy, Sing Me a Cowboy Song)* has earned the praise of none other than Buck Ramsey. "Fletcher, with just his guitar," says Ramsey, "is as pure and authentic as anyone. His voice is appropriate, and his guitar playing is clean. He is right at the top of the heap as far as I'm concerned." Jowers cites Gene Autry and Jimmy Rodgers as the big influences on his musical life.

Many other cowboy singers appear regularly at songfests and poetry gatherings. Tom Hiatt *(Rugs, Wranglers and Rodeos)*, Joel Reese *(Cowboy Up!)*, Chuck Milner *(Live from the Buffalo Pavillion)*, Jesse Ballantyne, R. W. Hampton, yodeler Gary McMahan, and many more singers are reaching larger audiences each year.

Female vocalists are also becoming more numerous—Katie Lee, Trudy Fair, Canadian Cindy Church, and Suzy Bogguss, to name just a few. As in poetry, **women** add their special views and voices to the music scene. Of course, k. d. lang and the reclines put their own special twist on western music. Family acts also take the stage. Tom and Becki Chambers *(West by Southwest)* perform as a duo. So do tenor Max and alto Cindy LaBry *(For the Cowboy's Sake)*. As noted above, the Hannahs *(Sons of the San Joaquin)* are all related. Likewise, Muzzie Braun and the Boys all come from a single family. Muzzie and his four sons form the core act. Muzzie's two brothers joined in on the *West Tunes* album.

In 1993 a four CD or cassette collection called *Songs of the West* appeared. The set covers mostly silver screen and television cowboy music. The four volumes include *Cowboy Classics* (Gene Autry, "Back in the Saddle;" Roy Rogers and Dale Evans, "Happy Trails," etc.), *Silver Screen Cowboys* (Rogers, Tex Ritter, and many more), a special selection of tunes by *Gene Autry and Roy Rogers,* and *Movie and Television Themes,* such as "Bonanza" and "Rawhide."

Strong attendance at musical gatherings of western song, like WestFest, attests to the growing popularity of western music. Cowboy music even has its own publication, *Songs of the West* (see Appendix C). Like other elements of cowboy culture, the musical roots run deep and the future holds continued promise. (Bane 1978; Dellar and Cackett 1986; Flint and Nelson 1993; McCall 1993; Malone 1985; Rollinson 1948; Seemann 1983; Tinsley 1981, 1991; Tosches 1985)

See also Hat Acts; Musicology.

MUSIC ROOT
Colloquial term for sweet potato.

MUSICOLOGY
Much cowboy music flowed naturally from the lives and poems of working cowboys. We do not know the composer of some songs, such as "Make Me a Cowboy Again for a Day." In other cases, we can trace the composers of both lyrics and tune. Some songs got written down in newspapers or stockmen's publications, but many remained in the oral culture.

For more than a century, a dedicated band of folklorists and musicologists have done field research to uncover the roots of cowboy music. Some of the song collectors came from backgrounds in ranching, cowboying, or **rodeo.** Others were performers who sang cowboy songs for a living. Still others had academic training and brought an outsider's perspective to the music.

In 1897 Clark Stanley published a pamphlet that mixed song texts with ads for his business. Annie Laurie Ellis of Uvalde, Texas, submitted the words and music to "Oh, Bury Me Not on the Lone Prairie" to the *Journal of American Folklore.* The journal published the song in 1901. Eight years later the journal published "Songs of the Western Cowboy," collected by G. F. Will in North Dakota.

N. Howard (Jack) Thorp (1867–1940) compiled and published the first significant collection of cowboy lyrics. His 50-page booklet, *Songs of the Cowboys,* appeared in 1908. Born in New York City, Thorp spent summers as a teenager working on his brother's Nebraska ranch. At age 19 he took up cowboying and horse trading in New Mexico. He became fascinated with the songs that cowboys sang around the campfire. After a couple of years riding the range, he decided to hunt songs instead of cattle and horses. He became the first person to travel the West seeking out and collecting cowboy songs. Thorp also added to cowboy culture by writing the famous poem "Little Joe, the Wrangler."

In 1910 John Avery Lomax (1867–1948) published a second major collection, *Cowboy Songs and Other Frontier Ballads.* Unlike Thorp, Lomax was college-educated. He had studied folklore at the University of Texas, Harvard, and the University of Chicago. Products of the Victorian era, both Thorp and Lomax decided they could not print authentic, often profane, cowboy lyrics. Both men cleaned up (bowdlerized) the lyrics of some of the songs they reprinted.

Despite his scholarly training, Lomax failed to credit sources for the songs he reprinted. As folklorist Guy Logsdon has pointed out, at least 19 of his songs first appeared in very similar form in Thorp's earlier book. (An angry Thorp later repaid the favor by failing to credit Lomax's book.) Despite his early, sloppy scholarship, Lomax went on to become president of the American Folklore Society. His son Alan (1915–) worked with him on many later projects and publications.

Margaret Larkin provided the first major anthology to include tunes for every song. Her *Singing Cowboy* appeared in 1931.

Jules Verne Allen (1883–1944) published *Cowboy Lore* in 1933. Born in Waxahachie, Texas, Allen was working cattle at age ten and bustin' broncs at 14. He wrangled horses on five different **trail drives** from Texas to Montana. He also sang and grew up to record cowboy songs for RCA-Victor.

Allen's book includes a smattering of history and folklore, including brands and cowboy lingo. He even has a list of 21 Spanish words commonly used on the range. Part four of the book provides words and music for 38 traditional cowboy songs, of which Allen writes:

Most of these songs of the range so far as I know have come down from generation to generation—here and there a verse or two added or changed to suit the fancy of whoever may be singing it, however in the main most of them are presented here just as I learned them on the range; in the ranchhouse or near the corral years ago. The authors are unknown to me except those where I have given credit. One of my contemporary cowboy singers says that in most instances many of the old cowboy songs "just grew." I think so, too.

The folk music revival of the 1960s stimulated greater study of and interest in cowboy music. Richard E. Lingenfelter, Richard A. Dwyer, and David Cohen published *Songs of the American West* in 1968. Folklorists Austin E. and Alta S. Fife provided two useful compilations: *Cowboy and Western Songs* (1969) and *Heaven on Horseback* (1970).

Glenn Ohrlin (1926–) grew up performing cowboy songs and continues to do so. Like Thorp, Ohrlin knew ranch life from the inside out. He compiled the many songs he had collected and sung into *The Hell-Bound Train: A Cowboy Songbook* (1973). The book is part of a fine series, "Music in American Life," published by the University of Illinois Press. It includes transcriptions of nearly 100 songs that Ohrlin had recorded. The book also includes an extensive discography and bibliography.

Born to a Swedish-Norwegian family in Minnesota, Ohrlin grew up in the West. His family moved to California while he was a teenager. He cowboyed in Nevada and rodeoed during the 1940s. Since the mid-1950s he has lived on a ranch near Mountain View, Arkansas. Since the 1960s he has performed widely at folk festivals and more recently at cowboy songfests and poetry gatherings. He closed *The Hell-Bound Train* with this brief poem titled "Cheers!"

We sang of Windy Billy, High Chin
    Bob, and all the rest,
And some of their adventures were just
    a shade out west.
They might awake a memory and
    maybe a laugh or two,
So try to sing 'em all again, and boys,
    "Here's luck to you!"

In 1975 John Irwin White (1902–) added his contribution to the Illinois "Music in America Life" series: *Git Along, Little Dogies: Songs and Songmakers of the American West*. Like Allen, White was a cowboy singer. Born and raised in the Washington, D.C., area, White received a trip to Arizona in 1924 as a college graduation present. An Arizona cowboy named Romaine H. Lowdermilk introduced him to cowboy life, humor, and music. They used Lomax's volume of songs for reference. White traded in his ukulele for a guitar and began singing cowboy songs. Within a couple of years, he had jobs singing cowboy songs on radio. He had also acquired a new handle, "the Lonesome Cowboy."

White performed on radio until 1936. Family and business occupied the next three decades. After his retirement in 1965, he returned to cowboy music, this time researching and writing about it. *Git Along, Little Dogies* includes fascinating information on singers, songs, collectors, and more. It also includes good chapters on the pioneering cowboy poets Gail Gardner (b. 1892), Badger **Clark**, and D. J. O'Malley (1867–1943).

Arizona singer and song collector Katie Lee delivered on her title in *Ten Thousand Goddam*

Cattle: A History of the American Cowboy in Song, Story and Verse (1976). Unlike Lomax, Lee did not "prettify" the language of cowboy songs. "We're going to let the cowboy talk the way he talks, really, without laundering his lingo." Lee, a veteran performer of western music since the 1940s, included scores to more than 50 songs in her book. Like Guy Logsdon, Lee wanted to present the cowboy's culture authentically, not colored by proper eastern prejudice, and she succeeded.

Lee's book illustrates many diverse elements of real cowboy life and music. She reprints "Lavina's Parlour," by Travis Edmonson, which takes us to a brothel. She clearly shows the importance of Spanish language and culture in western music. Her compendium of songs includes "Adios," "El Corrido de Bartolo Negro," "La Firolera," "José Cuervo," "Lolita," "A Peon Named Pancho," "The South Coast," and "Spanish is the Lovin' Tongue."

Like Lee, Guy Logsdon provides unsanitized versions of 61 songs, many of them bawdy (*"The Whorehouse Bells Were Ringing" and Others Songs Cowboys Sing*, 1989). The book culminates 40 years of song collecting and is comprised of two main sections, "Songs about Cowboys" and "Other Songs Cowboys Sing." Logsdon scoured the western countryside collecting these authentic gems. He explains an important truth that guided his efforts.

A friend and noted western historian asked me why I have included bawdy songs, which challenge the cowboy's romantic image. The question shocked me, for I thought all scholars sought the truth. I did not write the songs; I make no apology for the content. The desire for recreation is the motive behind all bawdy songs; while some readers will see only offensive words, others will surely discern the genius of humor. Traditional songs, bawdy and otherwise, persist because people value them.

Jim Bob Tinsley (1921–) has made many contributions to the study and performance of cowboy songs. His 1981 book, *He Was Singin'*

This Song, includes 48 traditional songs sung by cowboys. In 1991 he published a beautifully produced volume, *For a Cowboy Has To Sing: A Collection of Sixty Romantic Cowboy and Western Songs, Covering the Fifty-year Golden Era of Popular Standards between 1905 and 1957.*

If you rode horse-hair-stuffed seats enthralled in **B-western** shoot-'em-ups, if you hum along with singing cowboys from Sons of the Pioneers to Marty Robbins, if you enjoy the trivial and the touching about songs, songwriters, and singers, then you will enjoy Tinsley's fine book. As Roy **Rogers** and Dale Evans note in their two-page foreword, reading the book is "like saddling up a good cow horse and riding back along the western music trail."

Tinsley has been preserving and performing cowboy music since the 1930s. *For a Cowboy Has To Sing* contains reprints of complete sheet music for 60 songs. The delightful melodies are arranged chronologically, beginning with "Cheyenne" (1905) and "San Antonio" (1907) and running through "High Noon" (1952) and "El Paso" (1957). Most of the tunes are immediately recognizable, including "Rag Time Cowboy Joe" (1912), "Tumbling Tumbleweeds" (1932), "Wagon Wheels" (1934), "Cool Water" (1936), "San Antonio Rose" (1938), "Happy Trails" (1950), and many more. According to Roy and Dale's forward, their friends, the Sons of the Pioneers, "recorded more than half the songs in this collection and sang nearly all the rest at rodeos and shows."

In the all-too-brief four-page introduction, Tinsley places cowboy music into the context of movies and popular culture. In spite of the brevity of the text, the book does a good job of reminding readers that professional songwriters, not working cowboys, created many popular western songs.

The ethnic richness of western culture remains a fertile area of research. Américo Paredes analyzed southwestern Hispanic music in *A Texas-Mexican Cancionero: Folksongs of the Lower Border* (1976). A full-scale examination of Spanish influence on western and cowboy music remains to be written.

Thanks to the efforts of these and other musicologists and song collectors, we retain a wide range of traditional cowboy music that might have otherwise disappeared. Many of the old-time songs retain their popularity and provide inspiration for new generations of singers and songwriters. (Manson 1985; Seemann 1983; Stambler and Landon 1983; Tinsley 1981, 1991)

See also Music.

MUSTANG

Horses and cattle managed to escape from Spaniards in what is now the United States as early as the mid-sixteenth century. Indians killed and ate some of those escaped animals, but eventually some survived. Spaniards called wild horses and cattle *mesteños,* which became anglicized to mustang or mestang. The small, fast horses descended from the hardy Spanish mounts brought by the conquistadors. The cattle likewise descended from hardy *criollo* stock and became the storied **longhorn cattle** of Texas. The terms *longhorn* or *Spanish cattle* referred to cattle after the Civil War, and the term *mustang* became associated solely with horses. (Dobie 1952; Worcester 1986)

MUTTON-PUNCHER

Derogatory term for sheepherder.

MYERS, HARRY

Founder and publisher of *Western Styles* magazine. See Appendix C.

MYRAH, NEWMAN
(1921–)

Artist. See Art of the Cowboy.

MYTHOLOGY OF THE COWBOY

Few figures in American mythology loom as large as the cowboy. He is part of our collective, mythical past. He is part of the way we define ourselves. Everyone has some acquaintance with cowboy culture, whether through novels, **film, television,** or history. Speaking of the cowboy, Alvin Davis, of the **American Cowboy Culture Association,** said "We recognize that much is myth, but we love it. And we'll defend it till we die."

The Mythmakers

Cowboy mythology developed in stages from the 1880s on. Much credit for popularizing the cowboy must go to Buffalo Bill Cody's Wild West Show. **Cody** and his star Buck **Taylor,** "King of the Cowboys," brought the romanticized, shoot-'em-up horseman to America and Europe. The cowboy shed the image of an uncouth rowdy and became a national hero. **Pulp novels** (penny press and dime novels), such as Prentiss Ingraham's 1887 potboiler about Buck Taylor, brought exciting mythical cowboy action to a mass audience.

Theodore **Roosevelt** greatly enjoyed his years among cowboys in the Dakota Badlands. He helped make cowboy mythology more palatable to proper eastern society. "I do not believe there ever was any life more attractive to a vigorous young fellow than life on a cattle ranch in those days," he wrote. "It was a fine, healthy life, too; it taught a man self-reliance, hardihood, and the value of instant decision" *(The Outlook,* 24 May 1913).

Cowboy literature extolled the virtues of courage, honor, chivalry, individualism, and the triumph of right over wrong. Wild West shows, circuses, films, pulp novels, **radio,** and finally television perpetuated cowboy mythology.

Cowboys are viewed as representing rugged individualism, unbending principle, frontier spirit, and manly courage. In the United States, politicians from Chester Arthur and Theodore Roosevelt to Henry Kissinger and Ronald Reagan have manipulated cowboy imagery for political purposes.

Many Americans still believe in the efficacy of what they define as the frontier experience. They yearn for the simpler days when the good guys always defeated the bad. Cowboy films and cowboy politics appeal to this desire for a clear, uncomplicated, black-and-white world. The cowboy has supplanted the sturdy yeoman farmer as the foremost symbol of the nation's mythical past.

Cowboys and Animals

One of the best summaries of mythical cowboy virtues is Gene **Autry**'s Ten Commandments of the Cowboy. One commandment states that "a cowboy is kind to small children, to old folks, and to animals." Historically speaking, cowboys have never been very staunch animal rights advocates. Bear-baiting, cockfighting, and abuse of stubborn livestock all have a part of cowboy history. The cowboy-horse bond, so prevalent in **B-western** movies, is largely imaginary. Working cowboys used ranch mounts, and several per day were required. They rode them hard. Horses were a tool of the cattle trade, not pampered pets and companions.

Cleanliness

"A cowboy is clean about his person and in thought, word, and deed." Unlike Autry's cowboy, most working cowboys probably scored low on cleanliness of body and language. Cowboys did not worry themselves unduly about daily or even weekly bathing. Cowboy culture was a masculine culture. **Women** in ranch country were few and far between. Like locker room and barracks humor, cowboy **humor** and language was often obscene. When in town, most cowboys enjoyed plenty of whiskey, **gambling,** and a visit to the local brothel.

Discrimination

"A cowboy is free from racial and religious prejudices." Once again, Autry's idealized cowboy did not reflect the reality. Racial **discrimination** blemished frontier society, just as it did elsewhere. Anglo cowboys discriminated against **vaqueros,** blacks, Asians, and anyone else who wasn't white. Some cowboys, especially those from the Old South and Texas, retained the pre–Civil War racial attitudes of their region. Cowboys applied names like "Nigger John" to **African Americans.** Well into the twentieth century, "greaser" remained a common label for Hispanics. Nonwhites earned less and generally got less desirable jobs. Despite their skills, they seldom rose to become ranch managers or **trail drive** bosses.

White Cowboy Heroes

If we believe many B westerns and pulp novels, cowboys were always white. Novels by Louis **L'Amour** and other pulp writers, as well as most western films, generally depict white heroes, Indian savages, and sometimes a few bad Mexican bandidos. More recent films and literature have departed from this racial formula. In reality, many cowboys were nonwhite, especially on the southern ranges. Hispanic, black, and Native American cowboys worked the range in Texas, Oklahoma, and the southwestern borderlands. According to rancher John M. Hendrix of Abilene, Texas, writing in 1936,

Henry McCarty, better known as Billy the Kid, has been built up by western mythology as a dangerous outlaw and killer, although he had far fewer victims than thought by most.

"nearly every old cow outfit had one or more" black cowboys.

Periodization

We customarily link the cowboy to a few hectic decades following the Civil War, when open-range ranching and trail drives employed tens of thousands of cow hands. Part of our mythology is that this eventful period is the "birth" of the American cowboy. A more appropriate historical beginning point is 2 January 1494. On that day Christopher Columbus unloaded 24 stallions, ten mares, and an unknown number of cattle on the Caribbean island of Hispaniola. Within a few decades, horses, cattle, and ranching spread throughout South America and into Mexico.

In 1519 Hernan Cortés brought horses into New Spain (Mexico). Spanish explorers took horses and cattle northward to Florida, beginning with Ponce de León's second trip in 1521, and some stock raising was established around 1565 near St. Augustine and Tallahassee. Hernando de Soto followed, with more than 300 horses and some cattle, in 1539. This marked the first stock raising and hence the first cowboys in what is now the United States. Mexican vaqueros were the first cowboys in Texas, California, the southwestern borderlands, and Hawaii. They worked cattle in these areas long before the arrival of Anglo Americans.

Frontier Opportunity

The cattle frontier was not a land of opportunity and upward mobility. Few cowboys earned enough money to establish their own ranches. Low wages of $30 per month (1880–1900), long, seasonal layoffs, and the cowboy penchant to blow it all on a lively weekend in town inhibited savings. Most cowboys faced a life of hard work, primitive conditions, the risk of injury or death, and little chance for improving one's lot.

Rugged Individualism

Part of western mythology is a self-reliance and rugged individualism that takes a sharply antigovernment stance. In reality the federal government was and is a major actor in western economic development. Western entrepreneurs enjoyed federal subsidies and assistance at all turns. The U.S. Cavalry cleared out Native American populations and provided ranchers with a local market for beef to feed soldiers and reservation Indians. Railroads, with the exception of the Great Northern, received heavy subsidies, to the tune of 200 million acres of land. Federal lands were open to free or cheap grazing, mining, and lumbering. The government expanded the water supply through dams and irrigation projects.

Cowboys are Dead and Gone

As with Mark Twain, rumors of the cowboy's demise have been greatly exaggerated. Today westerners of all types perpetuate cowboy culture and live the cowboy life. Cowboy culture exists in poets, like Wally **McRae** and Baxter **Black,** singers like Ian **Tyson** and Michael Martin **Murphey,** and **saddle** makers, like Wyoming's Don King. **Spur, hat, boot,** saddle, and **tack** makers perpetuate old skills. If you are willing to look hard, you'll still find plenty of ranch people riding horses and herding, branding, and nursing cattle as cowboys have for a very long time.

Truth in Myth

Some parts of cowboy mythology did rest on a bedrock of historical fact. As in pulp novels, cowboys everywhere hated fences, farmers, and sheepherders. For example, in 1896 ranchers in Paulina, Oregon, organized the Crook County Sheep Shooters Association. The conflict between rancher and farmer or rancher and sheepman depicted in many a movie was very real.

Cowboys really dressed that way. Cowboy film and country **music** stars certainly have embellished cowboy dress, but cowboys of a century ago really did wear high-heeled boots, broad-brimmed hats, and jangling spurs.

Conclusions

Historians are working hard to correct myths about the cowboy. We must remember, however, to guard against the dangers of "over-revisionism." We face the danger of trivializing larger events and issues by trying to cram everything and everybody into cowboy history. Some level of generalization is needed. Politically correct concerns of today can serve as a distorting filter on the past.

Without question, traditional western mythology excluded or ignored **women** and ethnic minorities. We should not overcompensate by interjecting social groups where they did not actually exist. Some women, in modern times, work as cowhands. Georgie Sicking, a poet from Fallon, Nevada, worked most of her adult life as a hand. Ranching records of the nineteenth century (in both North and South America) rarely list women as ranch hands.

Revisionist historian Patricia Nelson Limerick offered a good commentary on fiction and history: "If you were to read a science-fiction novel, you wouldn't say, 'Well, that's Mars. Now I know all about life on Mars.' But people often read Western novels and say, 'Well, that was the West, the real West.'" Fiction may convey some elements of historical truth, but fiction is not history. Mythology, like history, can be beguiling and entertaining, but we should distinguish between them. (Forbis 1978; Limerick et al. 1987; O'Neil 1979; Slatta 1990; Taylor and Maar 1983)

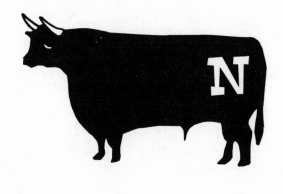

ÑANDÚ

Gaucho term for rhea, a large ostrich-like bird hunted by gauchos for its feathers. See Pampas.

NATIONAL BLACK COWBOYS ASSOCIATION

See African-American Cowboys.

NATIONAL COWBOY HALL OF FAME AND WESTERN HERITAGE CENTER

This fine institution plays a major role in preserving and promoting cowboy culture. Seventeen western states and countless private benefactors provide support and sponsorship. Chester A. Reynolds of Kansas City provided the inspiration for the center, formally dedicated on 26 June 1965. Located on Persimmon Hill in northeast Oklahoma City, the 37-acre site affords a good view of the surrounding countryside and city.

This impressive collection of galleries and exhibits includes something for everyone. Western **art** fans can view exhibits of historic and contemporary works. You'll marvel at sculptures and paintings by Frederic **Remington** and Charles Marion **Russell.** You can also enjoy the impressive collection of paintings by Albert Bierstadt, Carl Wimar, Thomas **Moran,** and many other artists. The hall created the National Academy of Western Art to promote continuing excellence. Outstanding contemporary artists are invited to exhibit their works each June.

Those more interested in authentic **saddles** and **tack** will enjoy the great saddle collection and the Luis Ortega Collection of rawhide tack. Visitors can also view the bane of the cowboy, the Robert O. Campbell barbed wire collection. This exhibit of some 16,000 items is probably the largest such collection in the world.

Children and most adults will enjoy stepping back in time in the "West of Yesterday" exhibit. Visitors can walk through recreated buildings from an Old West town—a sod hut, jail, telegraph office, and gold mine. The exhibit also features an authentic stagecoach, chuck wagon, and sheepherder's wagon.

Among the galleries and exhibits is the Rodeo Hall of Fame, which commemorates the champions of the all-American sport. Displays highlight outstanding performers in the five major **rodeo events:** bull-riding, saddle bronc riding, bareback bronc riding, calf-roping, and steer-wrestling. The Hall of Great Western Performers honors Tom Mix, Gary Cooper, Gene **Autry,** and other stars of western **film** and **television.** John **Wayne** fans will be particularly pleased to view an extensive array of the Duke's memorabilia, including his fine collection of kachina dolls.

The exhibits focus appropriately enough on the American West. The vast collection, however, includes saddles and tack of Argentina's **gaucho.** Two Mexican **vaqueros** are honored at the Hall of Fame. Born in Sonora in 1868, Ramón Ahumada worked as a ranch foreman for some 40 years in Arizona. An expert rider and roper, who was knowledgeable about brands and was a good tracker, Ahumada impressed his fellow cowmen greatly. Vicente Oropeza is honored for his superb roping. African-American cowboy Willie M. (Bill) **Pickett** is recognized for the invention of bulldogging.

Each spring the Hall of Fame honors a wide range of contributors to cowboy culture. Artists, actors, writers, and others receive Western Heritage "Wrangler" awards honoring their contributions to cowboy history or culture. Winners receive handsome, personalized bronze Wrangler sculptures, modeled on a work by C. M. Russell.

Writers who have been honored include James Michener, Louis **L'Amour,** Elmer **Kelton,** Harry Sinclair Drago, Angie Debo, and Robert Utley. Richard Slatta had the honor of receiving the 1991 Wrangler Award for nonfiction literature for *Cowboys of the Americas* (1990). Screen personalities, including Ben **Johnson, Jr.,** Roy **Rogers** and Dale Evans, Gene Autry, Henry Fonda, and Tex Ritter have been honored by the Hall of Fame awards. The Hall of Fame is a fitting memorial to the cowboy in all his historical and mythical incarnations.

The Western Heritage Research Library includes thousands of important historical books. The Hall of Fame's quarterly publication, *Persimmon Hill,* is a good way to monitor events there. Editorial quality and content has been uneven over the years, however. Financial problems forced suspension of the magazine in 1985, but it rebounded thereafter. Executive Director B. Byron Price has rejuvenated operations at the Hall of Fame.

Address: 1700 NE 63d St., Oklahoma City, OK 73111; tel. 405-478-2250.

NATIONAL COWGIRL HALL OF FAME

See Rodeo.

NATIONAL FINALS RODEO

See Rodeo.

NATIONAL LITTLE BRITCHES RODEO ASSOCIATION

See Rodeo.

NAVY MODEL

See Colt Firearms.

NEAR-SIDE

Left side of a horse from which the rider mounts.

NECK OIL

Colloquial term for whiskey.

NECKTIE PARTY

A hanging, more often a vigilante hanging without sanction of the law. See Violence.

NEGRO

See African-American Cowboys.

NELSON, WILLIE

(1933–)
Singer. See Music.

NESTER

Derogatory term for squatter, farmer.

NEWTON, DWIGHT BENNETT

(1916–)
Missouri-born author of formula westerns.

NEWTON, KANSAS

See Cow Towns.

NICHOLS, MADALINE WALLIS

Historian and bibliographer of the **gaucho.** See Historiography of the Cowboy.

NIGHT HAWK

Also night **wrangler**—a rider who watches the horse herd *(remuda)* at night.

NIGHT-GUARD

Cowboy who watches the trail herd at night.

NO TIME

When a rider receives no score for an attempt in a timed **rodeo event.** Aside from injury, this is the last thing a contestant wants.

NOLAN, BOB

Singer and songwriter in the original Sons of the Pioneers. See Rogers, Roy.

NORTHERN TRAIL

See Trail Drive.

NOSE PAINT

Colloquial term for whiskey.

NOTCHER

Drawing upon Ramon Adams *(Western Words,* 1968) as he often does, Winfred Blevins *(Dictionary of the American West,*1993) offers a good, concise definition of notcher: "A killer, a gunman (from their reported practice of notching their guns to keep count of their murders). A killer horse was said to have a notch in his tail."

See also Fast Draw; Violence.

NUBBIN'

Colloquial term for **saddle** horn.

NYE, EDGAR WILSON (BILL)
(1850–1896)

Wyoming journalist. See Humor.

NYE, NELSON CORAL
(1907–)

Illinois-born novelist who has written formula westerns under various names.

OAKLEY, ANNIE
(1860–1926)

Shootist and Wild West performer Annie Oakley was born Anne Moses in Darke County, Ohio. Little Annie grew up shooting wild game for Cincinnati markets. Her youth, sex, and skill made her an oddity. In 1876 she beat a marksman named Frank E. Butler in a competition. They married the following year and performed together for a time.

Annie Oakley, a gun-toting cowgirl, became famous for her shooting ability, and she performed with Buffalo Bill Cody's Wild West Show.

In 1885 they joined Buffalo Bill **Cody's** Wild West. Oakley spent the next 17 years as a shooting superstar of Cody's show. Immensely popular with fans, she executed incredible shooting feats. Biographer Walter Havinghurst describes her act:

While the band increased tempo she jumped off her pony and ran to the gun-covered table. Guns smoked in her hands and targets shattered in air. She shot on foot, on horseback, from a bicycle; she shot from both shoulders and behind her back. While six glass balls went up she turned a handspring and seized a repeating rifle; the six ball vanished. She caught her pony, leaped to the saddle, and raced away.

Another famous Wild West cast member, Chief Sitting Bull, adopted her and dubbed her "Little Sureshot." Not even a serious injury during a 1901 train wreck deterred her. She endured several operations and for a time walked with a leg brace and cane. She recovered to perform her miraculous shooting feats even after leaving the Wild West. She continued to perform until the early 1920s, when ill health overtook her. Butler died only three weeks after Oakley, and both were buried in the Brock Cemetery in Darke County.

Like many legendary westerners, Oakley took a hand in creating her own **mythology.** In her autobiography, she shaves six years from her age by giving her birth date as 1866. As her given name she lists Phoebe Anne Oakley Mozee. Cody helped the process of mythmaking by creating a fictive western past for the midwestern girl. (Havinghurst 1954, 1992; Russell 1960, 1970; Vonada 1990)

OATERS
Colloquial term for **B-western** films.

O'BRIAN, FRANK
Pseudonym for western novelist Brian **Garfield.**

OCEAN WAVE
See Rope.

OFF-SIDE
The right side of a horse from which one does not mount. Native Americans, however, did mount from the off-side, so it is also called the Indian side.

OHRLIN, GLENN
(1926–)

See Musicology.

OJOTAS

Chilean term for crude sandals worn by *huasos*. Mexican **vaqueros** wore similar sandals called **huaraches.**

OLD BLUE

The roan horse used by silent movie star Tom Mix from 1909 until 1919.

OLD WOMAN

Humorous term for the cook. The phrase offers clear insight into the cowboy's gendered division of labor. Often forced to cook for themselves, cowboys still considered the act to be woman's work.

OLIVE, PRINT
(1840–1886)

Rancher and gunman Print Olive was born Isom Prentice in Louisiana and grew up cowboying on the family ranch in Williamson County, Texas. His father Jim opposed secession, but young Print fought for the Confederacy. Union forces captured him at Vicksburg and paroled him back to Galveston. He returned to ranch work after the war and spent the next several years trailing cattle and shooting people. In some cases, he exchanged fire with suspected rustlers. In others cases, he got into gunfights in **saloons.** Tried for murder on several occasions, he never served time in prison for his **violence.**

In March 1876 officials in Lee County found two dead men wrapped in green hides carrying the Olive brand. Everyone took it as a clear message to would-be rustlers. In the early 1880s Olive moved his herd to Kansas and settled in Dodge City. He diversified his operations and built stables, a wagon yard, and a saloon in the new **cow town** of Trail City. Joseph J. Sparrow, Olive's one-time trail boss, operated a competing saloon. Following a dispute over a small sum of money, Sparrow shot and killed Olive. He is buried in Dodge City. (Chrisman 1962; Thrapp 1988)

OMOHUNDRO, JOHN BURWELL, JR.
(1846–1880)

Wild West showman "Texas Jack" Omohundro rose from obscurity, born near Palmyra, Virginia, to become a legendary figure in the Old West. He served on the side of the Confederacy during the Civil War. Writer Joel Chandler Harris embellished on his military service, making Omohundro a master spy in a series of short stories. After a stint teaching school in Florida, he headed west to Texas.

From Texas, Omohundro trailed cattle north to Nebraska. He joined William F. **Cody** and others as a scout at Fort McPherson from about 1870 to 1872. He and Cody met Ned **Buntline** while working for the army. Buntline used the greatly exaggerated exploits of both men in some of his **pulp novels.**

Buntline's farcical play, *The Scouts of the Prairie* (1872), catapulted both Cody and Omohundro into careers as western showmen. The play, awful as it was, brought "Texas Jack and His Lasso" to national attention. Omohundro became the first nationally known Wild West cowboy performer. Within a few months of the play's opening, he also married the Italian leading lady, Giuseppina Morlacchi. She played an Indian maiden, Dove Eye, in the Buntline production.

Texas Jack and Cody continued to appear together on stage until 1875. The following year Omohundro and his wife launched their own stage company. They performed from New York to Denver and Leadville. Their plays included *Texas Jack in the Black Hills* and *The Trapper's Daughter.* Texas Jack died a living legend a month before reaching his 34th birthday.

Texas Jack's death did not deter Buntline and others from their pulp labors. In 1883 Buntline published *Texas Jack's Chums; or The Whirlwind of the West.* In 1891 Prentiss Ingraham joined in with *Texas Jack, the Mustang King.* Beginning in 1900, Joel Chandler Harris made Texas Jack the hero of several short stories set during the Civil War.

Texas Jack Omohundro, a noted scout and friend of Buffalo Bill Cody, not only trailed cattle but also became a legendary showman. He is photographed here backstage on the set of Scouts of the Prarie *with Ned Buntline, Buffalo Bill, and Giuseppina Morlacchi, an Italian dancer (ca. 1870).*

During his short life, Texas Jack, like Cody, lived the life of a frontier cowboy and scout. Both also played important roles in moving the cowboy from plains history to the realm of American **mythology.** (Russell 1960; Thrapp 1988)

ONCE UPON A TIME IN THE WEST

Film (1969).

OPEN-FACED CATTLE

Another term for white-faced Hereford cattle. See Cattle Breeds.

OREJANO

Spanish term meaning an unbranded calf (*orejana* if female). Since *oreja* means ear, the origin of the term would seem to lie in the calf's lack of earmarks. Peter Watts (*A Dictionary of the Old West,* 1977) gives an excellent summary and list of synonyms:

The old Tejano word for the **mustang** cattle, meaning "the eared ones": those that had not been marked or cut on the ears. They were also called black cattle, cimarrones, mesteñas (mustangs) cattle, Spanish cattle, wild cattle.... In later years, orejanos became the Southwestern equivalent of the Northwestern slick-ear, meaning an unbranded and un-earmarked cow-crittur.

OSGOOD, ERNEST S.
(1888–1983)

Historian. See Historiography of the Cowboy.

OSTRICH

See Pampas.

OTERO

Colloquial term for a very large steer. The term is a Spanish word meaning hill, height, or knoll. This probably explains why it came to be applied to an animal as "big as a mountain."

OUTLAW

A horse that cannot be tamed to ride.

OUTLAW MUSIC

See Music.

OUTRIDER

See Line Camp.

OUTSIDE MAN

See Roundup.

OVERHOLSER, WAYNE DANIEL
(b. 1906)

Washington-born novelist who wrote formula westerns under various names.

OVERLAND TROUT

Colloquial term for bacon. See Food.

OVERO

A Spanish term that refers to a dappled or speckled pinto horse with white spots and smaller, more numerous black spots. A female is an *overa*.

THE OXBOW INCIDENT

A powerful 1943 film based on a lynching. See Violence.

OXBOWS

Large, old-time wooden stirrups also known as oxyokes. See Saddles.

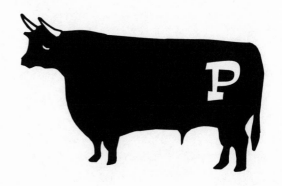

PACK IRON

Colloquial term meaning to carry a revolver or "shooting iron." See Fast Draw.

PAINT

See Horses.

PAINTING

See Art of the Cowboy.

PAINTING HIS TONSILS

Also painting his nose; colloquialisms for drinking whiskey.

PAIR OF OVERALLS

Colloquial for two drinks.

PALOMINO

See Horses.

PAMPAS

The term *pampas* refers to a large, flat plain that covers nearly 300,000 square miles in Argentina and Uruguay. The pampas are home to the **gaucho,** the cowboy of the Río de la Plata. The word probably comes from a Quechua term meaning "plain." The land slopes upward, rising from near sea level in the east to about 2,000 feet in the west. The vast plain stretches through the Río de la Plata from Patagonia in the south to the Andean foothills in the west to the Chaco in the north. The pampas reach through Uruguay to the rolling hilly grasslands of the *campanha* in Rio Grande do Sul, Brazil.

Scottish writer Robert B. Cunninghame Graham rightly described the pampa as "all grass and sky, and sky and grass, and still more sky and grass." Ranging from flat to gently rolling terrain, the pampas stretch nearly unbroken by hills for several hundred miles from the Atlantic Ocean inland. Only two ranges of hills, one in southern Buenos Aires province and another in Córdoba province, interrupt the vast grasslands. Fanning out from the Atlantic coast, the fertile, humid plain is well watered and subject to seasonal flooding, offering immensely rich agricultural and grazing lands. Farther west,

beginning in Argentina's Córdoba province, the pampa becomes drier, the grasslands thinner, and the water sources fewer.

Divided into the eastern humid pampas and western dry pampas, the region has an average annual temperature of 60°F. Annual rainfall totals 38 inches in the east but drops to 15 inches in the arid west. The Paraná, Uruguay, and Río Salado are some of the main rivers that drain the pampas.

One of the richest agricultural areas in the world, the eastern pampas support most of Argentina's population. The fertile plain supplies 80 percent of Argentina's farm products, especially beef and wheat. Farmers also produce linseed oil, corn, and dairy products. The richness of the area made Buenos Aires and La Plata major meat-packing and food-processing centers.

Much of the region remained sparsely populated until the late nineteenth century. Then railroads opened up the interior, and millions of European immigrants arrived to work in agriculture. The pampas are probably the world's richest natural grazing lands. A temperate climate and adequate, but not excessive, rainfall combine to provide a near ideal environment for livestock. Control of this rich grassland gave the landed elite economic and political power in the Río de la Plata.

An oddity of the pampas, compared with other **plains** regions, is its nearly total lack of trees. This condition may be natural or induced by man. An occasional, twisted ombú tree *(Phytolacca dioica)* rises from the flat plain. This giant, highly adaptable shrub may have been transplanted from the Andean foothills. Its soft spongy wood is worthless for building or firewood. The leaves, fruit, and flowers have little use except as purgatives. The overhanging branches do provide shade to people and livestock. Skilled **gaucho** guides *(baquianos)* used the distinctive trees as landmarks to help them navigate across the trackless plains. According to Indian folklore, the plant could cause a person harm or make someone fall in love.

This mid-nineteenth-century painting by Jean León Pallière shows two gauchos wearing the traditional garb of the pampas. The one in the foreground wears a narrowly brimmed hat, a poncho over a short jacket and vest, and a wide leather belt decorated with silver coins holding up baggy chiripás. *A sword or* facón *hangs at his side.*

Tall, coarse grasses, thistles, wildflowers, and low shrubs in swampy areas *(pajonales),* cover the plains. Rich, natural grasses covered vast stretches until the advent of alfalfa, wheat, and corn farming in the latter half of the nineteenth century.

Cattle, introduced in the mid-1500s, have traditionally been tended by gauchos, the cowboy of the pampas. One reason that wild cattle and horses flourished was a lack of major predators. During the colonial periods, however, packs of wild dogs attacked livestock.

The pampa held its share of unusual animals, however. Rheas (pampas ostriches) are large, flightless birds native to the region. Indians and gauchos hunted the big birds for food and fun, using the *bolas* (leather thongs tipped with stones). During the nineteenth century, European fashion demands gave rhea feathers some market value.

The *guanaco (Lama guanacoe)* is another animal native to the pampas and other areas of South America. This small mammal is probably related to the llama and vicuña. It grows to 4 to 6 feet in length and about 3.5 feet tall at the shoulder. The animals provided soft pelts, meat, and bones. People have hunted the animals to near extinction in the wild.

The pampas were also home to the *vizcacha,* a South American version of a prairie dog. Numerous vizcacha burrows caused many falls and injuries to man and mount. Charles Darwin visited the pampas in the early 1830s and observed that "the holes caused by this animal yearly cause the death of many of the gauchos."

American painter George Catlin visited the pampas in the 1860s. He compared the region with the Great Plains, which he had also traversed.

The pampas in various parts of South America are vast level plains, not unlike the great prairies of the Platte and the Arkansas, excepting that they are covered with high weeds instead of short grass; and amongst these weeds, of which there are many kinds, there are wild flowers of all colors. And on the eastern borders of the great pampas, stretching off from Buenos Ayres to Patagonia on the South and to the base of the Andes on the west, there are vast forests of thistles, which, sometimes for a great many miles together, though they grow in patches and as high as a horse's back, are almost impassable, even for a man on horseback.

These thistles are the covers and asylums for the ostrich, which feeds mostly out in the open plains and in the ravines; and when pursued runs for the thistles for cover, where it is excessively difficult to follow it.

Conflicting Images of the Pampas

Argentine intellectual Ezequiel Martínez Estrada believed that the vast pampas possessed telluric powers—almost magical energy arising from the earth. He expressed the mystical forces of the plains in his brooding, masterful, existential *X-Ray of the Pampa* (1971).

The vastness of the horizon, which always looks the same as we advance, as if the whole plain moved along with us, gives one the impression of something illusory in this rude reality of open country. Here prairie is expanse, and expanse seems to be nothing more than the unfolding of the infinite within, a colloquy of the traveler with God. Only the knowledge that one is traveling, fatigue, and the longing to arrive give scale to this expanse seemingly without measure. It is the pampa, the land where man is alone, like an abstract being that will begin anew the story of the species—or conclude it.

The pampas and its native inhabitants long stood as hostile, forbidding barriers to European settlement. Spaniards had to make two determined attempts before the backwater settlement of Buenos Aires could be established in Argentina. Compared with the human and mineral riches of Upper Peru (present-day

Bolivia) and Mexico, the pampas seemed singularly unappealing for conquistadors bent on New World glory and wealth. Once they acquired **horses,** the many Indian tribes of the plains became even more formidable opponents to Spanish expansion.

The image of the pampas as a desert persisted long after the vast plains had been explored. In reality, the humid pampa, radiating out in a semicircle from the Atlantic coast, had nothing in common with a true desert except for its flatness and sparse population. To Europeans and city dwellers, however, it constituted a geographical and cultural desert. Argentines refer to the military incorporation of the dry pampa into the national patrimony as the "conquest of the desert."

Argentine intellectuals and politicians developed views of the pampas similar to those expressed in Venezuela toward the **llanos.** Domingo Faustino **Sarmiento** best expressed Argentina's perceived struggle between civilization and barbarism. He viewed the plains as the bastion of barbarism. The pampas sheltered disruptive caudillos who stifled progress. He found the strength and skill of the gaucho strangely compelling, however. Argentine political development was the struggle between caudillos and gauchos of the backward pampa and civilizing, Europeanizing leaders of Buenos Aires. Only by pacifying and repopulating the plains with "civilized" European immigrants would Argentina enjoy progress and prosperity.

Positive images of the pampa also developed alongside such disparaging views. Observers expressed amazement at the prodigious livestock wealth. Ironically, some considered the Argentine plains to be too rich: the natural bounty of the region was seen as the root cause of the gaucho's perceived indolence. Henry Marie Brackenridge (*Voyage to South America*, 1817) noted that in Uruguay "horses [were] so cheap and abundant that the best [could] be had for only a few dollars." Cattle remained so plentiful in Buenos Aires province through the mid-1800s that meat was not even sold in some areas. Anyone with a lasso could find his own dinner.

After downing an animal and consuming a few delicacies, the gaucho left the remainder of the carcass to scavengers.

The modernizing liberal elites of the nineteenth century viewed the pampa as an area of great abundance. According to them, the rich land needed better people—white people. The primitive mestizo population of the plains held back progress. Several administrations hatched a variety of colonization schemes to populate and cultivate the frontier. Argentine leaders, including Juan Bautista Alberdi, Sarmiento, and Julio A. Roca, all believed that large numbers of European immigrants could almost magically turn the desert into a garden. According to liberal dogma, sturdy European yeomen would push aside the racially and culturally inferior Argentine rural natives and regenerate the nation economically and socially. Unfortunately for the immigrants and for the nation, very few success stories emerged from these quixotic racist dreams of agricultural paradise.

The dream of pioneering on the plains has not died. Like many other South American nations, Argentina continues to view its vast, sparsely populated hinterland as the key to future national greatness. Brazilian politicians in 1964 made faith in the frontier a matter of public policy. They moved the national capital from coastal Rio de Janeiro to the new city of Brasilia in the interior backlands. Likewise in 1987 Argentina contemplated moving its national capital from the megalopolis of Buenos Aires south across the pampas to the Patagonian "desert." The move is unlikely to occur, but the plan shows that plains regions, like the pampas, remain a symbol of progress for the future. (Catlin 1959; Graham 1936, 1978; Martínez Estrada 1971; Slatta 1992; Williams Alzaga 1955)

See also Beef Cattle Industry.

PANCAKE
Colloquial, derogatory term for small English **saddle.**

PANELA
Llanero term for unrefined sugar used in **coffee.**

PANIOLO

The least known cowboy of the United States is also among the most colorful, the *paniolo* of Hawaii. British navigator George Vancouver first brought cattle to Hawaii in 1793 as a gift to King Kamehameha I. Under royal protection, the animals multiplied quickly. Within a couple of decades, vast herds of wild cattle grazed contentedly in their new fertile island environment. In 1803 Richard J. Cleveland brought a gift of horses (**mustangs** from Spanish California) to the Hawaiian king. The islands now had the raw materials for a ranching industry—land, water, and livestock. All that was lacking was the cowboy.

(A lexicographical note: In official Hawaiian lexicography, the terms *paniola* and *paniolo* are synonyms. The latter is the preferred official spelling. The term is both singular and plural; no "s" is added. The origin of the term is from the word *español,* meaning Spanish.)

By the late 1820s, European pioneers and native Hawaiians began hunting the island's wild cattle for their hides, tallow, and meat. As in South America, the island livestock industry progressed from wild-cattle hunts toward domesticating animals and organizing ranches. King Kamehameha III recognized that he needed a more skillful labor force to handle his burgeoning herds. He arranged for **vaqueros** to come from Spanish California to Hawaii in 1832 to teach ranch skills to Hawaiians. The Hawaiians learned quickly and well. In 1908 paniolo Ikua Purdy competed in Cheyenne, Wyoming, and won the World's Steer Roping Championship. **Rodeo** and ranching remain important in the islands.

Pioneers of the Hawaiian livestock industry, such as John Palmer Parker, also benefited from vaquero expertise. A Massachusetts seaman, Parker bought land on the island of Hawaii in 1815. He married a princess and acquired more land. The Parker Ranch came to encompass 225,000 acres, the largest ranch under single ownership in the United States. Today 50,000 head of cattle still graze on Parker lands.

By the mid-nineteenth century, an estimated 35,000 to 40,000 cattle, about one-third of them tame, roamed the volcanic slopes of Hawaii. The vaquero passed along his cattle-handling and leather-working techniques and much more. The paniolo adapted the vaquero **saddle,** sombrero and **spurs** to the Hawaiian environment. By the twentieth century, ranches existed on six of Hawaii's eight islands (all but tiny Lana'i and Kaho'olawe).

The California vaqueros carried to the islands more than cowboying skills. Their cultural baggage included attitudes about animals as well as their distinctive dress. The paniolo adopted Mexican techniques and dress to suit local conditions. For example, the Hawaiian cowboy retained the general shape of the vaquero's sombrero, but he constructed his **hat** *(papale)* from locally available materials. The woven leaves of the *hala* (pandanus tree or screw pine) proved well suited to hatmaking.

The paniolo also added his own touches to the quintessential cowboy headgear. Hawaiian cowboys decorated their hats with beautiful, richly hued local shells and feathers. They bedecked their hats and necks with lei of vivid flowers, vines, or feathers. The paniolo is a colorful figure, but very different in dress from other cowboys. One old cowhand, sensitive to his image, defended the practice of using the lei: "Even the roughest, toughest, rowdiest, most rugged and most manly of us wear *lei.* We do it for the pure joy and pleasure of it and you cannot tell me that we don't look handsome as men should!"

At least two practical reasons have been suggested for wrapping a cowboy hat with a lei. The first and more convincing is that the costume is useful for impressing women. "The flower lei makes you feel good, special, and *paniolo* like to make fancy sometimes. We like to show off. The girls all look at you when you wear lei!" said one paniolo (Martin 1987).

Another explanation is that the flower wreath helps secure the paniolo's hat in the gusty island winds. Since a simple chin strap would do that job better, this argument seems a bit weak.

Making a lei on the job gives the paniolo another way to help pass the time; the lei also provides a memento of a place and perhaps a special event. There is no denying the alluring beauty and fragrance that a well-constructed lei adds to a hat. Regrettably, the custom is not as popular with youngsters today as it was earlier in the century.

The vaquero also brought his knowledge of leather work to the islands. Like his Mexican mentor, the paniolo learned to work rawhide into functional but intricately decorated tools. The making of **saddles, ropes,** bullwhips, bridles, and other riding gear became a specialized craft in Hawaii. Nineteenth-century paniolo made and used braided rawhide ropes *(kaula 'ili)* or ropes made of horse or cow hair *(kaula hulu).* The islands' saltwater, rain, and tropical heat took a toll on rawhide, however; today's Hawaiian cowboys have switched to nylon ropes.

Vaqueros also brought guitars with them, and Hawaiians quickly put their distinctive stamp on guitar playing. They developed a unique style of slack-key guitar **music** called *kiho'alu.* The guitar is tuned so the open strings produce a chord. What we now call the Hawaiian guitar style developed during the 1890s as the forerunner of the country music sound produced with slide- and steel-guitar styles.

The craft of guitar making developed on the islands. Craftsmen use both native and imported woods and local shells in their beautifully styled instruments. The ukulele typifies Hawaiian music even more than the guitar, but even this quintessential island instrument has Iberian roots. It evolved from the Portuguese *braguiha* introduced to Hawaii in the 1870s.

Many Hawaiian songs celebrate persons, places, or events associated with ranching in the islands. Unlike cowboys in most other cultures, however, the paniolo usually did not compose songs. Hawaiian singers developed a vocal style, yodeling, that is often associated with cowboy music. Hawaiian music included yodeling in the 1890s, but the technique did not appear in cowboy music on the mainland until Jimmy Rodgers popularized it in the 1920s. "Cattle Call" (first recorded in 1935 by Tex Owens and popularized by Eddie Arnold in 1955) is one of the best-known cowboy yodeling tunes.

The folklore and history of the paniolo is attracting increased interest. Much remains to be learned about his daily life. Little of the negativity associated with most other cowboy types appears to be connected to the paniolo. He is a positive figure of Hawaiian folklore. The existence of a number of large, working ranches in the islands should ensure the perpetuation of paniolo culture and skills. (Berney 1993; Brennan 1978; Cowan-Smith and Stone 1988; Martin 1987)

See also Vaquero.

PARD

Also pardner (variants of partner); colloquial terms for friend, companion.

PARKER RANCH, HAWAII

See *Paniolo.*

PASO DE MUERTE

See *Charro.*

PATERSON REVOLVER

See Colt Firearms.

PATO

A horseback **gaucho** and **huaso** game in which riders fought for possession of a duck *(pato)* stuffed in a hide. Gauchos enjoyed challenging others and showing their courage and skill in a variety of **equestrian games.** Pato, the most popular and storied of the gaucho games, has been played since at least the early seventeenth century in both Argentina and Chile. The contest usually ended in a cross-country equestrian free-for-all.

William Henry Hudson *(Tales of the Pampa,* 1916) described the game as played in the 1840s:

Pato means duck; and to play the game a duck or fowl, or, as was usually the case, some larger domestic bird—turkey, gos-ling, or moscovy duck—was killed and sewn up in a piece of stout raw hide, forming a somewhat shapeless ball, twice as big as a football, and provided with four loops or handles of strong twisted raw hide made of a convenient size to be grasped by a man's hand. A great point was to have the ball and handles so strongly made that three or four powerful men could take hold and tug until they dragged each other to the ground without anything giving way.

On the appearance of the man on the ground carrying the duck the others would give chase; and by-and-by he would be overtaken, and the ball wrested from his hand; the victor in his turn would be pursued, and when overtaken there would perhaps be a scuffle or scrimmage, as in football, only the strugglers would be first on horseback before dragging each other to the earth. Occasionally when this happened a couple of hot-headed players, angry at being hurt or worsted, would draw their weapons against each other in order to find who was in the right, or to prove which was the better man. But fight or no fight, some one would get the duck and carry it away to be chased again. Leagues of ground would be gone over by the players in this way, and at last some one, luckier or better mounted than his fellows, would get the duck and successfully run the gauntlet of the people scattered about the plain, and make good his escape.

Riders fighting over the duck would range for miles, scattering livestock, destroying fences, and wreaking havoc. Like ostrich hunts, pato attracted the ire of ranchers and government officials because of livestock loss and property damage. Authorities of first Spain and then Argentina banned the contests at least six times between 1799 and 1899. Pato's popularity persisted as long as the gaucho roamed.

In Chile the game became a traditional event on June 24, the Feast of San Juan. Huasos played the game as rambunctiously as did gauchos. The games became so scandalous that in 1748 church officials asked that it be regulated. "Horse races held in all the streets more resembled bacchanal feasts." By the late eighteenth century, rules governed most horseback contests. Officials banned pato in 1768, following the death of a participant. The law threatened pato riders with a 500 peso fine.

By the late nineteenth century, government officials succeeded in banning or altering many elements of traditional gaucho life, including pato. The contest acquired regulation playing fields, league competition, and written rules. The modern domesticated game, somewhat akin to polo, retains some of the form but lacks the danger and vitality of the **gaucho** original.

The Argentine Pato Federation wrote rules and set up leagues. In civilized pato, two four-man teams compete on a field 90 yards wide and 230 yards long. Players carry a six-handled leather ball with arm outstretched, and opponents try to snatch it. By tossing the ball into a net suspended on a 9-foot pole, a contestant earns a point. The federation even developed a handicapping system, similar to polo. Like the gaucho himself, the gaucho's favorite game lost its wildness and vigor. (Slatta 1986, 1992)

See also Equestrian Games.

PATRÓN

Literally patron, used to refer to the owner of a large estate or ranch.

PATTEN, LEWIS BYFORD
(1915–1981)

Colorado-born author of formula westerns.

PAYADOR

Like cowboys everywhere, **gauchos** of the Río de la Plata enjoyed **music.** Gauchos held the *payador,* an itinerant troubadour skilled at musical improvisation, in highest esteem. He excelled at singing duels *(payadas),* in which two contestants exchanged witticisms and insults. Singers accompanied themselves on the *charango,* a small guitar-like instrument fashioned from the shell of an armadillo.

Writing in the mid-1840s, Domingo Faustino **Sarmiento** described the poems and songs created by the *payador* as "replete with imagery relating to the open country, to the horse, and to the scenes of wilderness, which makes it metaphorical and grandiose." In addition, "He can tell of a couple of stabs he has dealt, of one or two *misfortunes* (homicides!) of his, and of some horse or girl he has carried off."

Many of the most famous *payadores* were black. Two singing duels became especially celebrated in **gauchesco** literature. Santos Vega lost a singing duel to the devil in the poem "Santos Vega" by Rafael Obligado. In the famous epic "Martín Fierro" by José Hernández, Fierro challenges a black payador. He then kills the black singer in a knife fight. Leopoldo Lugones titled his influential interpretation of the Hernández poem *El payador* (1916). (Paullada 1963; Sarmiento 1971; Slatta 1992; Tinker 1967)

PEACEMAKER REVOLVER

See Colt Firearms.

PECHADA

Also *pechando.* See Equestrian Games.

PECKINPAH, SAM
(1925–1984)

Film director. See Films, Best Cowboy.

PEE WEE KING AND HIS GOLDEN WEST COWBOYS

See Music.

PEEL

To break (tame) a horse. See Bronc Buster.

PEON

The landless rural worker of Latin America is known as the peon (*peón* in Spanish). The person might work in agriculture or ranching. A *peón de campo* is a ranch worker, not a peasant farmer.

PERIODICALS

Many western culture magazines continue to be published today. See Appendix C for a listing of popular cowboy periodicals.

PERRYMAN, LLOYD

Member of the singing group Sons of the Pioneers. See Rogers, Roy.

PERSIMMON HILL

See National Cowboy Hall of Fame.

PIAL

Also *peal, piale.* See Rope.

PIALAR

See Equestrian Games.

PICKENS, SLIM

B-western film actor.

PICKETT, WILLIE M.
(circa 1870–1932)

Willie M. (Bill) Pickett, a Wild West show and **rodeo** performer credited with inventing bulldogging, was born in Travis County, Texas, 30 miles northwest of Austin. One of 13 children, his mostly black ancestry also included white and Cherokee forebears. As a youngster in rural Texas, he learned to read brands and toss a **rope.** One day, he said, he watched a small dog bite a cow's lip and thus control the large animal. According to Pickett, he decided that a person could do likewise. He first demonstrated his technique—bulldogging—to a group of cowboys in 1881.

Pickett worked on central Texas ranches during the late 1880s and 1890s. He married Maggie Turner in 1890, and they had nine children. With his brothers, he started the Pickett Brothers Broncho Busters and Rough Riders Association in Taylor, Texas. "We ride and break all wild horses with much care," read their ad. "Catching and taming wild cattle a specialty."

By the early twentieth century, Pickett bulldogged steers with his teeth at county fairs and other gatherings in many western states. He

Bill Pickett, an African-American cowboy, is credited with the invention of bulldogging. This 1923 poster announces a movie in which he performed many of his dangerous and entertaining rodeo feats.

performed at the 1904 Cheyenne Frontier Days celebration. *The Wyoming Tribune,* reporting on the celebration, claimed that Pickett would

> ... attack a fiery, wild-eyed and powerful steer, dash under the broad breast of the great brute, turn and sink his strong ivory teeth into the upper lip of the animal, and throwing his shoulder against the neck of the steer, strain and twist until the animal, with its head drawn one way under the controlling influence of those merciless teeth and its body forced another, until the brute, under the strain of slowly bending neck, quivered, trembled and then sank to the ground.

Rodeo announcer Frederick Melton ("Foghorn") Clancey reported seeing Pickett bulldog a steer in Dublin, Texas, in 1905. Some cowboys, including Lon Seeley and Milt Hinkle, began using Pickett's technique as well. The same year Pickett tied in with the **Miller Brother's** 101 Ranch Wild West Show. He performed with Tom Mix, Guy Weadick, Milt Hinkle, and other cowboy stars.

Pickett dressed like a Spanish bullfighter. He performed his brand of bulldogging in Calgary, Sonora, Mexico, and throughout the United States. The 101 program listed him as "the Dusky Demon who throws steers with his teeth." In late 1908, he accepted a challenge to take on a Mexican fighting bull. The bull gored both Pickett and his prized mount Spradley. (This was one of several incidents in which the athlete suffered injury.) From late 1913 to 1914 the 101 troop toured South America and Europe.

In the 1920s Pickett retired from competitive bulldogging but continued to give exhibitions. He also starred in a few black western movies that highlighted his rodeo skills. Pickett returned to work for Zack Miller and continued to break horses. His wife Maggie died in 1929, a devastating loss to Pickett.

Pickett died on the 101 Ranch on 2 April 1932 after being kicked by a horse several days before. Miller eulogized Pickett as the "greatest sweat and dirt cowhand that ever lived—bar none." In 1971 Bill Pickett became the first **African-American** cowboy admitted to the select company of the **National Cowboy Hall of Fame.**

In 1994 another attempt at honoring Pickett went awry. The U.S. Postal Service planned to commemorate Pickett, along with 19 other famous western figures, with a stamp series called "Legends of the West." Unfortunately, stamp designers picked an erroneously labeled picture as the basis for the stamp. The picture, which appears in a number of western history books, actually depicts Ben, one of Pickett's three brothers.

Authorities learned of the error too late to rectify the mistake. For the first time in history, the Postal Service recalled an entire stamp series. Azeezaly Jaffer, manager of stamp services, explained the action this way:

> Why would we want to do that if our whole premise for recalling the stamps is to set history straight? The whole concept of the "Legends of the West" stamps was to recognize the contributions of people. Unfortunately, history did not serve the African-American very well.

Stamp flap or not, Pickett remains a rodeo legend. (Hanes 1977; Russell 1970)

PICTORIAL BOOKS

Picture books have their place in historiography. Images from painting and photography capture and preserve elements of cowboy culture that are difficult to convey with words. We can also examine similarities and differences in artistic depictions over time.

Once in the Saddle: the Cowboy's Frontier, 1866–1896 (1973), edited by Laurence Ivan Seidman, features nineteenth-century prints and photographs of the period. The photographs of Ray Rector, featured in *Cowboy Life on the Texas Plains: the Photographs of Ray Rector* (1982), edited by Margaret Rector, take up about where the Seidman volume leaves off.

Other pictorial books focus more on ranch houses than cowboys per se. An oversized and beautifully produced book, *Ranch: Portrait of a Surviving Dream* (1983), features photographs by Dudley Witney and text by Moira Johnston. It covers ranch houses and scenes in the American and Canadian West. *Arizona Ranch Houses: Southern Territorial Styles, 1867–1900* (1974, 1987) has historical photographs taken by Louis Bencze. Janet Ann Stewart wrote the text, and John Bret edited the work.

John R. Erickson has contributed two major pictorial works. He wrote the first, *Panhandle Cowboy,* in 1980. Larry McMurtry provided a foreword, and Bill Ellzey took the photographs. Erickson followed up the next year with *The Modern Cowboy* (1981), which provides good photographs of today's working cowhand.

American Cowboy in Life and Legend (1972), by Bart McDowell, blends paintings, photographs, and a lively text. William Albert Allard took the photographs and historian Joe B. Frantz wrote the foreword. The handsomely produced book was prepared by the Special Publications Division of the National Geographic Society.

Michael Rutherford's contemporary photographs are shown to good advantage in *The American Cowboy: Tribute to a Vanishing Breed* (n.d.).

William D. Wittliff published one of the few pictorial books to turn a lens toward the Hispanic West. *Vaquero: Genesis of the Texas Cowboy* (1972) provides a good photographic record of modern-day Texas vaqueros.

New York photojournalist Bernard Wolf carried his camera west and produced a modest volume called *Cowboy* (1985). The 76-page book is of interest because it focuses on Montana rancher and cowboy poet Wallace D. (Wally) McRae.

The American Cowboy (1983), by Lonn Taylor and Ingrid Maar, includes a wonderful variety of images, historical and modern. It is based on an exhibit of the same name held at the Library of Congress. The book mixes historical and modern images of the cowboy.

The Spirit of the West (1987), with photographs by Dudley Witney and text by Ted Barris, is a loving look at the region in the twentieth century. A brief section titled "The Beginnings" features historical black-and-white photographs of Native Americans and pioneers. The remaining sections use Witney's color photographs to highlight "The Land" and "The Life" (people) of the West. The book is really a pastiche of often unrelated imagery, but it creates a nostalgic feeling for the many faces of the western United States.

Many museums have created exhibitions about the cowboy, and the catalogs to those shows provide useful images. One example is *The Cowboy,* a catalog and exhibition of nineteenth- and twentieth-century artwork sponsored by the San Diego Museum of Art in 1981.

A "weightier" book is Russell Martin's *Cowboy: The Enduring Myth of the Wild West* (1983). This massive coffee table tome includes about 400 illustrations, half of which are in full color. Virtually all of the photographs are modern, diminishing the book's use for historical analysis.

Both the Taylor/Maar and Martin books offer some assistance in understanding the cowboy's historical and cultural significance. A recent contribution to the cowboy coffee table genre is *Way Out West* (1993), by Jane and Michael Stern. Although the text is largely dependent on a handful of secondary sources, it offers a pictorial history of the cowboy and helpful lists of publications, organizations, and stores. Such books perpetuate the view of the cowboy and the West as weird and quaint rather than real, tangible, and worthy of serious consideration.

The renaissance of interest in cowboy culture during the 1980s spurred a welcome publishing boom. James H. Beckstead's *Cowboying: A Tough Job in a Hard Land* (1991) is an excellent history of ranch life in Utah. It includes 250 illustrations, most of historical interest. Beckstead covers all areas of cowboy culture and life—work on the range and fun in cow towns. He covers ranchers, outlaws, lawmen, and the cowboy's transition from history to popular culture. The lively text includes enough anecdotes to satisfy any history buff. Beckstead bases his narrative mostly on printed sources, but he also uses recollections of frontier life drawn from interviews and archives.

We have many publications that focus on the works of a single author. For example, *Trails Plowed Under* (1927), by Charles Marion **Russell**, offers a good sampling of imagery by Montana's foremost cowboy artist. A more unusual view of his work comes in *Good Medicine: The Illustrated Letters of Charles M. Russell* (1929). Humorist Will **Rogers** penned the introduction and wife Nancy C. Russell added a biographical note.

Many volumes of Frederic **Remington** works are available. Two good collections are Matthew Baigell's *The Western Art of Frederic Remington* (1976) and Henry C. Pitz's *Frederic Remington: 173 Drawings and Illustrations* (1972).

Other books, such as *The Cowboy in Art* (1968) by Edward Maddin Ainsworth, offer a broader sampling of art and artists. *The Cowboy in American Prints* (1972, 1985), edited by John Meigs, reproduces a wide range of black-and-white etchings and drawings dating back to the 1860s.

Another well-illustrated volume with good accompanying text is *The Cowboys* (1973), by journalist William H. Forbis. Forbis did a commendable job of drawing together a good body of secondary sources and summarizing what was known about the cowboy in very readable prose. The book is especially strong in its use of nineteenth- and early twentieth-century photographs from a very wide range of collections. The volume is part of the Time-Life series, "The Old West." Companion volumes by other authors include *The Ranchers, The Gunfighters, The Spanish West,* and *The End and the Myth.* All remain enjoyable, useful reference works.

In sum, the cowboy's picturesque life has generated far more pictorial works than serious scholarly study. Historians can analyze paintings and photographs as historical evidence, however, so picture books can enlighten scholarship and entertain.

PIG

One of many colloquial terms for **saddle horn.**

PIGGING STRING

Also piggen string, hogging string, hogging **rope.** See Rodeo Events.

PILGRIM

Cowboy term for an easterner or novice cowhand.

PIMPLE

Derogatory term for the small eastern **saddle.**

PINGO

Gaucho term for his small, strong horse. These hardy *criollo* mounts were like the Spanish ponies of Mexico.

PINTO

See Horses.

PISTOL

Colloquial term meaning a young, inexperienced hand. Cowboys never used the word to mean a handgun.

PITCHMEN

Merchandisers in many countries have used the cowboy's appeal to pitch products. People around the world immediately recognize the American cowboy and the Argentine **gaucho** as national symbols. Advertisers, politicians, and others quickly learned to cash in on the cowboy's image. Advertisers throughout the western hemisphere have used heroic cowboy imagery to promote a bewildering variety of products. By linking a product to the cowboy's image, advertisers created an association between a product and the strength, manliness, courage, patriotism, and other virtues attributed to the cowboy.

Purveyors of whiskey, tobacco, and **food** products used the cowboy to peddle their products as early as the 1870s. Like dime novelists, advertisers recognized the cowboy's immense marketing appeal. Ads often featured a hard-riding, lasso-twirling cowboy chasing a herd of cattle.

Many cowboy ads showed only a tenuous link to cowboy reality. A color ad for Clark's O. N. T. Spool Cotton thread (circa 1880) depicted a Mexican **vaquero** roping a long-horned bull. A closer look shows that the horseman has tossed a rope of Clark's thread instead of the customary rawhide reata. Another lithograph from 1880 had plainsmen lassoing buffalo. A **longhorn** lurks dangerously in an insert. The ad is for Seth Norwood & Co., Manufacturers of Fine Shoes. Obviously both Clark's and Norwood believed the ads would project an image of strength for their product.

Even when a cowboy figure had a logical product tie-in, advertising creativity found a way to give it a bizarre twist. Cowboys surely fit in logically and closely with the meat-packing industry. An 1886 lithograph for Halstead & Co., a meat-packing company, had five Mexican vaqueros herding a gaggle of cattle and pigs. The riders are depicted in action on the New York pier that housed the Halstead main office.

Advertisers continued to use the cowboy to promote a wide range of products in the twentieth century. No less an artist than N. C. Wyeth painted an ad for the National Biscuit Company. The oil painting shows a cowboy on horseback delivering the mail. The title of the painting is "Where the Mail Goes, Cream of Wheat Goes." The ranch mailbox is made from a wooden Cream of Wheat box.

From colorful lithographs, cowboy figures hawked Buckaroo Apples, Lasso Brand Sweet Corn, Westernaire Brand Yellow Free Peaches, Cowboy Brand Prunes, and Libby's Ox Tongues. Liquor companies also recognized the appeal of linking their beverages to the cowboy. A bewhiskered old cowboy wearing a contented smile and holding a glass of Wiedeman's Fine Beer appeared in an 1897 lithograph. A cowboy mounted on a buffalo promoted Bob Yokum's Blended Buffalo Whiskey.

During the 1930s and 1940s, cowboy movie stars—including Tom Mix, Roy **Rogers,** Hopalong Cassidy, and the Lone Ranger—huckstered a variety of products. Tom Mix munched Cheerios. Gene **Autry,** with his winning smile, munched Wrigley's gum. Roy Rogers backed many products over the years, including Quaker Oats (later pushed by Wilford Brimley), Dodge cars, Goodyear tires, and roast-beef sandwiches.

Film cowboys proved especially attractive in promoting breakfast cereals. Children, particularly boys, consumed lots of cereal and cheered their silver-screen heroes each Saturday. Cereal boxes often included coupons good for premiums. Young would-be cowboys and cowgirls could exchange coupons for a Roy Rogers badge and whistle, a Lone Ranger pedometer, a Tom Mix decoder badge, and many more exciting premiums. Cereal manufacturers regarded clean-cut cowboys as positive role models who would appeal to adolescent boys and perhaps even a few girls. The use of professional athletes to promote cereals today reflects a similar mentality.

Retailers went well beyond simple appeals to adolescent boys. Cowgirls, for instance, have also been visible marketing icons. A 1937 ad for Coca Cola pictured a horsewoman (in eastern rather than western dress) standing in front of her horse sipping her favorite soft drink. Much of today's high-fashion western clothing is pitched to women by cowgirl models.

Perhaps the most famous cowboy advertising icon in the world is the Marlboro Man. Leo Burnett USA, a Chicago-based ad agency, developed the original concept in 1954 for Philip Morris. They created ads depicting rugged, smoking outdoorsmen, including the cowboy. The ads tied smoking to a macho, outdoor image. The company needed a gimmick to give their new filter-tipped cigarette a more masculine appeal. (As Camel smokers of the day knew, filtered cigarettes were for women and sissies.) By the early 1960s, the agency dropped the other outdoor characters, making the cowboy the lone master of Marlboro Country. Photographer

Norm Clasen shot many of the memorable scenes used in billboard and magazine ads.

Beginning in 1992 the Marlboro ads dropped the traditional living cowboy icon and instead used closeups of **boots, spurs,** and other cowboy paraphernalia to promote the now many varieties of Marlboro cigarettes. In a sense the ads went full circle back to their 1950s origins. They returned to the broader outdoor adventure theme (including the sale of related outdoor gear).

Even the high-tech microcomputer industry found the cowboy to be a helpful pitchman. An ad for Northern Telecom, a communications firm, displayed a computer keyboard sticking out of a Pony Express rider's **saddle;** the caption reads "The data must go through." Kodak likewise stretched the cowboy connection to the breaking point in order to cash in on western imagery. They depicted the Lone Ranger and Tonto holding a portable computer and Kodak's portable printer. The caption read "Corral a Trusty Sidekick for Your Laptop."

Ads during the 1980s for computers from Compaq and Dell, both Texas companies, featured illustrations of cowboy dress and equipment. Dell used old western prints, one of a train robbery and another of cowboys sitting by a chuck wagon, to emphasize the Americanness of its products. The ad caption read, "You can't get good chili in Taiwan."

Other companies played up the cowboy's association with Americanness. A 1980 ad showed a Volkswagen Dasher Diesel with five ranchers and cowboys in the background. The copy read "It has a way of going much like that of a fine horse, precise and proud."

In many cases, we find no logical connection between true, traditional cowboy culture and the items being packaged or promoted. A 1979 ad showed three cowboys by a horse corral at sunset—all dressed in fashionable bathrobes designed by Oleg Cassini. A 1981 Kohler ad displayed a blood-red hot tub in the middle of a desert—two cigar-smoking ranchers, complete with Stetsons, play poker while sitting in the tub. "At the edge of your

imagination lies a new frontier of comfort," reads the ad copy.

The Duke University basketball team's annual team poster for the 1990–91 season depicted Christian Laettner and his teammates in western wear, with horses grazing in the background. The poster carried the caption "Duke's Young Guns." It's a long way from the western Pony Express routes of the 1860s to Durham, North Carolina, but the distance was not too great for some enterprising ad writer to connect the two. In a slightly less preposterous stretch, the Portland Trailblazers, a National Basketball Association (NBA) team, also used a cowboy motif for publicity photos.

Miller Lite beer put an unusual twist to cowboy advertising with their summer 1993 television ads for "the Big Lawyer Round-Up." This take-off on a **rodeo** theme featured a roping competition. In this case, however, a cowboy rode down and roped a fat, briefcase-toting lawyer. Attorneys protested the insulting ads, but the public, never in love with lawyers, loved them. Virginia attorney Neil Kuchinsky decided to turn the tables. He targeted Miller's parent company, Philip Morris, with a TV spoof. A rodeo cowgirl easily roped a businessman named Phillip Millerd, who, of course, smokes. A "cancer widow" cheered on the cowgirl with a "Git 'em." A voice-over reminded viewers that the tobacco industry had contributed "to the untold misery, suffering, and deaths of smokers worldwide."

Cowboy imagery remains strongly masculine. **Television** ads during professional football games used cowboy imagery to push items such as pickup trucks, beer, and chewing tobacco (smoking tobacco ads now being banned on television). Clothing companies such as Wranglers and **Levi's** have spent countless millions to associate their jeans with the rodeo and ranch cowboy. The cowboy is likewise a mainstay of ads for **boot** manufacturers.

Cowboy marketing, however, aims at both blue-collar and upscale urban (yuppie) audiences. Male-oriented advertisements tie cowboy manliness to a plethora of products.

Some manufacturers have created special upscale products to appeal to the city slicker crowd. Ralph Lauren has produced cowboy fashions suitable for the yuppie market, complete with Chaps cologne. According to advertisements, "Chaps is a cologne a man can put on as naturally as a worn leather jacket or a pair of jeans. Chaps. It's the West." Appropriately enough, Stetson is a competing brand of cologne.

The late 1980s and early 1990s witnessed a strong revival of cowboy culture. A Yakelovich Partners survey, commissioned by Cowles Magazines, found 31 percent of Americans (57.4 million people) to be "Western enthusiasts." Even used jeans and cowboy boots found a special market niche. Cowboy collectibles, fashion, and furniture enjoyed a strong resurgence. New magazines, films, and television shows brought back the country's leading cultural icon.

Today Wah-Maker produces authentic-looking, historically accurate clothing for men or women. Old West Outfitters, Cheyenne Outfitters, Buck-N-Bum, and a host of other companies distribute a wide variety of western wear. Advertisers, ever attentive to what sells, will keep finding new ways to use (and often abuse) the cowboy and his image. (Martin 1983; Taylor and Maar 1983; *Western Styles* magazine)

See also Fashion; Tobacco; Appendix C.

PLAINS

The Great Plains region of the United States is a broad strip of semiarid land 500 miles wide that extends from the Central Lowlands to the foothills of the Rockies. The eastern boundary lies around the 98th or 100th meridian. The plains range in elevation from 2,000 feet in the east to more than 5,000 feet around Denver.

The term *prairie* became a synonym for plains in both the United States and the Canadian West. The term is of French origin, meaning meadow. Many names including the term became very common. Cowboys called buffalo grass prairie wool and sometimes picked low-growing prairie tomatoes. Prairie chickens

(grouse), prairie dogs, and prairie rattlers (sidewinders) lived on the plains. The cowboy diet included prairie oysters (calf fries), prairie strawberries (beans), and prairie dew (liquor).

Isolated mountain ranges break up the generally flat topography of the plains. The Black Hills, Sweetgrass Hills, Judith Mountains, and other ranges rise up sharply. Much of the plains, however, consists of grasslands. A wide variety of plains grasses have nourished large numbers of deer, antelope, buffalo, cattle, and sheep. Some western prairie grasses cure rather than decay in winter, preserving their nutritional value so animals can forage most of the year. Abundant needle grass cures well after being cut as hay.

Short buffalo grass fed the vast herds of bison and later **longhorns.** Many ranchers considered bluegrass (especially *Poa secunda)* excellent for grazing **horses.** Bluegrass comes in more than 60 varieties. Gumbo grass or bluestem, so named for its color, proved nourishing for cattle. Little bluestem, less than two feet high, grows on the "short-grass prairie." Big bluestem, which can tower up to 6 feet high, grows in the "tall-grass prairie," such as the Osage hills of Oklahoma. In the Osage, the Nature Conservancy has created the Tall Grass Prairie Preserve, complete with bison and native grasses.

Of course, not all plains plant life is benign and nourishing. Sharp little bristles that can injure grazing cattle top some types of needle grass. Poisonous plants, including loco weed, horsetail, plains larkspur, poison vetch, bitterweed, death camass, and Johnson grass, can harm and even kill horses and cattle. No one who's ever been there would claim that life on the plains is easy.

Rainfall on the plains is light, less than 20 inches per year, and not very dependable. Thanks to the Rocky Mountain watershed, however, major rivers flow through the Great Plains from west to east. In the north flow the Missouri, Platte, and North Platte; in the south, the Red and Canadian. Access to water shaped the direction of many cattle trails and the locations of many ranches.

Cowboys are strongly and correctly associated with vast plains regions in both North and South America. Horsemen lived their lives on plains frontiers from the prairies of Alberta to the Great Plains to the **pampas** of Argentina. In the United States, the Texas **trail drives** after the Civil War quickly spread open-range ranching across the Great Plains.

A vast web of famous cattle trails (Goodnight-Loving, Western, Chisholm, Shawnee) criss-crossed the plains. Much of the imagery associated with cowboys, especially his shortcomings, originated in Abilene, Dodge City, and other **cow towns** on the Kansas plains.

Plains regions tend to be areas of conflict and **violence.** Different social groups contest control of plains resources. Indians fought against white encroachment and the decimation of buffalo herds. Cowhands fought against rustlers. Cowmen quarreled with farmers, sheepherders, and each other over water and grass. The many western "wars," such as the Fence Cutter's War of 1883 or the Johnson County War a decade later, attest to the often conflictive nature of plains life.

During his explorations in 1541, Francisco Vásquez de Coronado described what is now the American Southwest as "these deserts." Desert imagery would remain associated with the Great Plains, arising due to sparse population, lack of eastern-style civilization, and little rainfall. Texas historian Walter Prescott Webb aroused a storm of controversy in 1957 by asserting that "the heart of the West is a desert, unqualified and absolute.... Once we recognize the desert as the major force in the American West, we are able to understand its history" *(Harper's Magazine,* 1957).

For many people, however, the plains represented freedom and opportunity, not a bleak desert. Generations of optimists traveled to the plains to ranch, farm, or otherwise make a living. The Great Plains has been a boom-bust region, but it remains a vital part of American society and life. By serving as a major theater of the cowboy's brief heyday, the plains also passed into **mythology** and folklore. (Blouet and Lawson 1975; Hollon 1966; Webb 1957)

THE PLAINSMAN

Film (1936) starring Gary Cooper.

PLOW CHASER

Derogatory term for farmer.

PLUNDER

A cowboy's miscellaneous personal belongings generally kept in a bag, which he called his war bag.

POETRY

Cowboys have been entertaining one another with stories, songs, and poems for as long as they've built campfires. Miles from any other sources of entertainment, cowboys had to come up with ways to pass the time. Evenings, particularly in winter, could get very long. Poet Waddie **Mitchell** explained the origins this way:

When you live in close proximity like that with the same folks month after month, one of your duties is to entertain each other, and I suppose that's where the whole tradition of cowboy poetry started. You find out that if you have a rhyme and a meter to start that story, people will listen to it over and over again.

Some cowboy poetry got set to music, and Jack Thorp and other experts in **musicology** collected and published it. Much of the genre, however, remained unknown outside of intimate circles of friends and family. Some poets contributed original verse to stockmen's publications, such as the *Stock Grower's Journal.* This weekly, published in Miles City, Montana, reprinted poems in the 1890s. D. J. O'Malley (1867–1943) contributed many works, including "When the Work is Done Next Fall" (first called "After the Roundup").

During the twentieth century, poems by Curly Fletcher (1892–1953) and Bruce Kiskaddon (1878–1949) found their way into print. Paul Patterson (1909–), a Texas high school teacher, wrote poetry during the 1930s. In addition to writing poetry, he taught Spanish and journalism to young Elmer **Kelton.** "Everything I write," said Kelton, "has a little bit of Paul Patterson in it, because without his early encouragement and pointing of the way, none of it might ever have found its way to paper." Most cowboy poems, however, remained part of regional oral or family tradition.

In the early 1980s, folklorist "Big Jim" Griffith of the University of Arizona suggested moving cowboy poetry out of the bunkhouse and onto the stage. Hal Cannon, of the Western Folklife Center in Salt Lake City, picked up on Griffith's idea and ran with it. The result was the first Cowboy Poetry Gathering in Elko, Nevada, in late January 1985. Skeptics termed the idea in Cannon's words, "the most hare-brained scheme in the world."

The folklorists interested in collecting and disseminating cowboy poetry first had to define it. They came up with this official definition:

Cowboy Poetry is rhymed, metered verse written by someone who has lived a significant portion of his or her life in the Western North American cattle culture. The verse reflects an intimate knowledge of that way of life, and the community from which it maintains itself in tradition.

The official demand for rhymed, metered verse caught some **maverick** poets wrong. Since that first gathering, free verse and other varieties have made inroads. So have dozens of cowgirl poets. The Elko gatherings have grown greatly in the past decade. The Western Folklife Center has branched out into hosting a summer songfest as well as the annual poetry gathering. The January 1988 meeting included the premiere of Kim Shelton's film, *Cowboy Poets.* Other gatherings have taken up broader themes, such as the Hispanic culture and Australian drovers.

Most poets have experience as cowboys or ranchers. **Rodeo** performers constitute a sub-genre writing about their all-American sport. Poems often mix nostalgia and humor. Baxter **Black** is one of the masters of humorous cowboy poetry. Some poets tackle serious concerns about

contemporary western problems, such as environmental pollution. As Wallace D. (Wally) **McRae** says, "There isn't anybody else out there who can represent us and speak to who we are, so we do it ourselves."

The tenth gathering in 1994 included some 150 poets and drew thousands of people. These popular Elko gatherings have spawned similar events throughout the West. *American Cowboy Poet* magazine and other publications now disseminate the works by the West's "poet lariats."

A few poets, Wally McRae, Baxter Black, and Waddie Mitchell, have achieved national renown. Folklorist Guy Logsdon, however, reminds us of what's really important.

Cowboy poetry has traditionally been tagged as doggerel, verse, or mere rhymes. However, as with all poetry through the ages, there are excellent as well as far-from-excellent poems. But the cowboy writes and recites for cowboys, not literary acclaim, and the measure of success is when cowboys absorb a poem into their traditional culture.

Hal Cannon has edited several cowboy poetry books, which have been published by Peregrine Smith. Two convenient pocketbooks include *Cowboy Poetry: A Gathering* (1985) and *New Cowboy Poetry* (1990). In addition Smith published *Songs of the Sage: The Poetry of Curly Fletcher* (1986) and *Rhymes of the Range: A New Collection of Poems by Bruce Kiskaddon* (1987). In 1992 Phil Martin compiled an anthology entitled *Coolin' Down.* Cowboy poetry remains alive and well and more popular than ever. *(American Cowboy Poet* magazine; Logsdon 1988; White 1967)

POETRY AND MUSIC GATHERINGS

The first Cowboy Poetry Gathering at Elko, Nevada, in 1985 launched a huge western cultural revival. Old-time and neophyte poets began gathering throughout the West to share their work. By the 1990s the revival had moved from a regional to a national phenomenon. The popularity of Michael Martin **Murphey**'s 1990 album, *Cowboy Songs,* and the birth of the Warner Western label are two of the most visible pieces of evidence of the movement's success. Today hundreds of locales throughout the West host cowboy **poetry** gatherings and songfests. (See Appendix D.)

POINT MAN

Also pointer. See Trail Drives.

PONCHO

Traditional garment worn by many Latin Americans, including cowboys. A poncho is a large square of either cotton or woolen cloth. A hole in the middle permits the garment to be slipped over the head. It protects the wearer from rain and cold and serves as a blanket.

PONDEROSA RANCH

See Television.

PONY

See Horses.

POP SKULL

Colloquial term for whiskey.

PORTER, WILLIAM SYDNEY
(1862–1910)

William Sydney Porter was an author of short stories and creator of the Cisco Kid. He wrote under the pen name O. Henry. Born in Greensboro, North Carolina, Porter quit school at age 15. He traveled west to Texas in 1882 where he worked as a bank teller in Austin (1891–1894) and journalist in Houston (1895–1896). Unfortunately, he embezzled money while working as a teller and served three years in prison following his conviction in 1898.

Following his release from prison, he returned east to New York City. He spent the rest of his life writing stories for a variety of popular magazines. He wrote delightfully detailed and witty stories of working people. His intelligent plots often

included a bit of irony or a surprise ending. To western literature fans, he is best remembered for creating the character of the Cisco Kid. Cisco, with his sidekick Pancho, migrated from O. Henry's short stories to silent film, talkies, and television. The durable character's latest incarnation came in an early 1994 television movie—*The Cisco Kid. (Microsoft Encarta* 1993)

See also Television.

PORTIS, CHARLES MCCOLL
(1933–)

Reporter and novelist who wrote *True Grit* (1968). John **Wayne** starred in the movie based on the book.

POT RUSTLER

One of many colloquial terms for cook.

POTRO

A colt.

POWDERSMOKE RANGE

Film (1936).

PRAIRIE

See Plains.

PRAIRIE DEW

Colloquial term for whiskey.

PRAIRIE OYSTERS

Fried calves' testicles. See food.

PRAIRIE WOOL

Cowboy term for buffalo grass. See Plains.

PRANKS

See Humor.

PRAYER BOOK

Also dream book—colloquial terms meaning a packet of papers used to roll cigarettes.

PRODDY

Also on the prod; colloquialisms meaning spoiling for a fight.

PROFANITY

See Humor.

PROFESSIONAL RODEO COWBOYS ASSOCIATION

See Rodeo.

PRORODEO HALL OF CHAMPIONS AND MUSEUM OF THE AMERICAN COWBOY

Since opening in August 1979, the Prorodeo Hall of Champions has attracted crowds of **rodeo** fans, some 50,000 per year. It sits on a 5-acre site in Colorado Springs, with the Front Range of the Rockies as an impressive backdrop.

Each year a selection committee nominates additional rodeo stars for the Hall of Fame. Performers who qualify for at least ten National Finals Rodeos gain automatic nomination. The hall honors rodeo greats well known to the public. Exhibits at the site honor All-Around Cowboys Larry Mahan and Leo Camarillo.

The hall also salutes the legendary Casey Tibbs, who won world saddle bronc honors in 1949 and several times in the following decade. Tibbs ranked as All-Around Cowboy in 1951 and again in 1955. A rider must win the most money in two or more events during the season to become an All-Around Champion.

Actor Ben **Johnson, Jr.,** is honored at the Hall of Fame, and legitimately so. In 1953 Johnson's performance in the rodeo arena earned him the title of world champion team roper.

Exhibits feature photographs, but also rodeo **tack** and other equipment. Giant 10- by 30-foot multimedia projection screens evoke rodeo excitement. Animals are not forgotten: Tornado, a bull, bucked off more than 200 riders in his 14-year career; Oscar, another famous bull, remained undefeated, that is, unridden. Famous bucking horses Midnight and Five Minutes to Midnight also get their due. Visitors can also see live rodeo stock in paddocks on the grounds. Descent, a six-time Bucking Horse of the Year, lived out his retirement here. A large bronze sculpture memorializes the palomino gelding.

The museum shows rodeo's historical ties, and the Wild West exhibit links many rodeo performers to the Wild West shows of the past. The hall also includes a research library.

See also Rodeo Events; Appendix A.

PROSTITUTION

Richard Erdoes notes that "Westerners divided women into two categories—good ones and bad ones." The preponderance of males in cattle frontier regions dictated that poor, working cowboys socialized mostly with "bad ones." One commentator estimated that there were six to ten men per woman on the American ranching frontier.

The ratio was probably even more skewed toward males in many Latin American frontiers. Some ranchers in Argentina, for example, banned women entirely (except for the rancher's own family). Ranchers feared that **gauchos** would get into fights with one another over **women.** In both North and South America, machismo and sexism kept women from employment as working cowhands.

Because of the lack of women, prostitutes found many doors open to them. Alfred Doten, a newspaperman from Virginia City, Nevada, left a revealing journal entry in 1870. At a benefit ball held to aid Benito Juárez and the Mexican liberals, "the women were principally whores, although there were some decent women among them." "Fallen angels," "soiled doves," or "calico queens" of the West graced most **cow towns.**

The term "red light district" supposedly originated in one of the foremost cow towns, Dodge City. The *Rocky Mountain News* (23 July 1889) lamented that **saloons** "were the most fruitful source for breeding and feeding prostitution." Many sanitized cowboy memoirs discreetly omit this element of cowboy life.

Teddy Blue Abbott devoted several pages of *We Pointed Them North* (1939) to the cowboy's

Cowboys blew into cow towns expecting to indulge in a little hedonism—liquor, baths, and women. Charles Russell's Just a Little Pleasure *(ca. 1898) depicts a drunken cowboy with a "lady of the line."*

relationship with prostitutes. Why did cowboys seek out prostitutes? "Well, they were women. And we didn't know any others," says Abbott. "We'd go to town and marry a girl for a week, take her to breakfast and dinner and supper, be with her all the time." Cowboys socialized openly with prostitutes in Miles City, Montana. In Lincoln, Nebraska, however, "you couldn't walk around with those girls in the daytime like you could in Miles City."

Frontier saloons offered many activities to attract customers and generate additional profits. Prostitution provided a natural adjunct to liquor and **gambling.** Besides prostitutes, saloons employed "hurdy-gurdy" girls who danced with patrons and brought them drinks—for a price.

Town leaders often licensed and regulated prostitution. Increasingly, however, western towns outlawed prostitution, spurred by determined protests from civic and religious reformers. Reformers in Abilene, Kansas, launched a largely successful effort to exclude prostitutes very early—in 1870. The practice remained legal (or accepted) well into the twentieth century, however, especially in parts of Nevada and Texas.

Hollywood **films** have not been reluctant to include saloon girls and prostitutes. Directors have presented western prostitutes in a variety of lights. *The Cheyenne Social Club* (1970) takes a decidedly humorous approach. In the film, James Stewart, a down-on-his-luck cowhand, inherits a house of prostitution. Gene Kelly directed the film, which starred Henry Fonda and Shirley Jones.

Director Robert Altman took up the topic the following year. *McCabe and Mrs. Miller* cast Julie Christie as a madam and Warren Beatty as her partner. This serious film, often dark and brooding, drew kudos and brickbats. Christie succeeded in breathing humanity into her character.

Canada and Latin America

An imbalance between the sexes also characterized western Canadian ranching country. Only the most puritanical Albertans at the turn of the century attached any stigma to a cowboy's visit to a "sporting house." Alberta at the time held few unmarried women other than prostitutes. The town of Lethbridge had a special section of brothels. The sporting houses stood on "The Point," a spit of land, jutting out into Oldman Coulee to the west of town. The section drew cowboys, miners, and settlers like a magnet. Madams reportedly liked cowboys. Men of the range tended to spend money a bit more freely than many other workers.

As on other cattle frontiers, women were in short supply on the Argentine **pampas.** The demands of ranch work as well as powerful negative pressures from the landed elite condemned most gauchos to enforced bachelorhood or occasional liaisons. Gauchos lived mobile lives. They rode from ranch to ranch in search of work at **roundup** time. Many also stayed mobile in order to escape military conscription. With little hope of owning land, gauchos had few opportunities for a stable home life. Prostitutes often provided their only female companionship.

Itinerant madams loaded up their girls and traveled the plains. The arrival of an entourage in a high-wheeled oxcart at a saloon *(pulpería)* kicked off an impromptu fiesta. Word spread and gauchos rode in from far and wide. The women worked in small tents. The madam sold candles of varying lengths that measured the time purchased by each patron.

The lack of employment opportunities for women in the countryside forced many rural women to move to towns. Some took work as prostitutes. Most nineteenth-century towns regulated the business and required the women to undergo periodic health inspections. With a nod to social propriety, some municipalities prohibited solicitation on the street. (Butler 1985; Erdoes 1969; Goldman 1981; Guy 1991; Lamar 1977)

PULL LEATHER

To grab onto the **saddle** when a **horse** bucks. Pulling leather shows a lack of skill or courage or both.

PULP NOVELS

Pulp novels, especially those with cowboy heroes, are a highly conventional romantic literary form. Larger-than-life cowboy heroes protect heroines and other weaker figures from despicable villains. Readers get stylized **violence** and lots of action. Important imagery and settings, six-guns, **horses,** saloon brawls, stampedes, and lots of open prairie surround the characters.

Pulp fans wanted pure escapism, a chance to ride the range with the cowboy hero. The David Crosby and Phil Collins song "Hero" (1991) well captured the essence of this kind of appeal. "The hero knew what he had to do and wasn't afraid to fight.... I wish it were that simple for me.... And the reason that she loved him was the reason I loved him too. He never wondered what was right or wrong; he just knew."

Critics have rightly attributed a decidedly second-class status to cowboy literature. Publishers reinforced the low-brow image by printing their products on second-class pulp paper. The penny press and dime novels of the late nineteenth century had no literary pretensions. Like other products of the country's expanding mass market economy, they were aimed at volume sales to an undiscriminating consumer. Purveyors of pulp worried more about increasing circulation and sales than about raising the nation's literary standards.

Pulp magazines, forerunners to comic books, appeared along with novels. Men and boys (and a few girls and women) read *Dime Western, Western Story Magazine,* and *Wild West Weekly.* Some 200 different magazine titles appeared, delivering cowboy action and adventure for a few cents. The likes of Deadwood Dick, who first rode in 1884 in Beadle's Pocket Library, captivated boys and men who wanted to be boys again. The pulp magazines disappeared, along with **B-western** movies, in the 1950s, victims of **television**'s growing appeal.

Ned **Buntline** pioneered the genre and eventually authored 400 dime novels. Like Buffalo Bill **Cody,** Buntline led a colorful life that he embellished in pulp fiction. In the hands of Buntline and his heirs, the pulp cowboy lost his earlier negative trappings of outlaw and renegade and became a strong, courageous, virtuous hero.

Unlike Buntline, Zane **Grey** had led a very conventional eastern life. His formula novels posed stereotypical cowboy heroes against stereotypically dastardly villains. He often paired his strong, capable quick-draw heroes with civilizing heroines. Fans loved his vivid sense of local color and forgave him for his cardboard characters. His first big success, *The Heritage of the Desert,* appeared in 1910.

Frederick Dilley Glidden (1908–1975) used the pen name, Luke Short, to write very popular formula westerns. He sold more than 30 million copies, and many of his tales reached the cinema. Raw violence made his stories attractive to filmmakers. He married Florence Elder in 1934 and began writing pulp stories sometime thereafter. He explained his move to literature this way:

> Newly married and lacking any kind of job, let alone the newspaper job I wanted, I decided I'd write for the Western pulp magazines. Their contents seemed simple-minded to the point of idiocy; their stories appeared easy to write if you could complete a sentence. I studied them with a secret contempt since I'd graduated from Zane Grey at the age of twelve. Then I hacked out Western pulp stories that sold.

Although characters, dialogue, and setting remained predictable, Short did work at revising and polishing his prose. Unlike Louis **L'Amour,** he made no pretense of historical accuracy. He told stories well. His first novel, *The Feud at Single Shot,* appeared in 1935; his final one, *Trouble Country,* in 1976. The **National Cowboy Hall of Fame** recognized his literary contribution to cowboy mythology and literature in 1975, the year of his death.

Writer (Daniel) Dane Coolidge (1873–1940) worked as a naturalist after studying at Stanford. He made field trips to Baja California and Mexico in the late 1890s. Coolidge married

Frank Leslie's Illustrated Newspaper *"reported" the escapades of larger than life cowboy heroes, North America and South America alike.*

Mary Elizabeth Burroughs Roberts in 1906 and settled down in Berkeley. He wrote more than 40 books, mostly formula westerns. Coolidge based *Arizona Cowboys* (1938) on notes he took in 1903 at his first **roundup** at Pinal, Arizona. Jon Tuska *(A Variable Harvest,* 1990) well captured the writer's approach: "Coolidge was not an historian; he was a romantic." He had little understanding of or appreciation for working cowhands. He also wrote other pseudohistorical works: *Texas Cowboys* (1937) and *Old California Cowboys* (1939).

Male authors dominated the pulps, but Bertha Muzzy (B. M.) Bower (1871–1940) left her mark. She created the durable character *Chip of the Flying U.* Her ranch romances broadened the market for pulps beyond the traditional shoot-'em-ups to "ranch romances." This genre aimed at drawing **women** readers into the pulp marketplace with books that spiced up western action with traditional love stories. These fanciful tales often plunged to new lows in both artistry and authenticity. Writers simply moved their love stories from drafty old Gothic houses to the range.

Frederick Schiller **Faust** wrote under as many as 20 pseudonyms, the most famous being Max Brand. His prodigious output of more than 500 books exceeded even Buntline's. He earned his title as "King of the Pulps."

Louis **L'Amour** succeeded Brand as the modern king. Beginning with *Hondo* in 1953, he published a long string of formula westerns. Like previous pulp novelists, he peopled his books with figures bordering on caricatures, but his action plots, homilies of folk wisdom, and pretensions of historical accuracy captivated his fans.

Although the heyday of the pulps has passed, it is far too soon to pronounce a final eulogy. Paperback editions of books by Brand, Grey, L'Amour, and others continue to sell well. Virtually every bookstore sets aside space for western pulps.

Pulps have even ridden off into some strange, new directions. Bernard A. Drew *(Western Series and Sequels,* 1986) summarized some of the recent odd hybrids: "Since the 1970s, there have appeared Spectros, the magician cowboy; Six-Gun Samurai, the martial arts gunslinger; Claw and Leatherhand, the disabled cowboys; Gold, the Jewish cowboy; and Breck, the born-again Christian gunfighter." Every social group, it would seem, needs its own cowboy hero.

Graphic sex appeared in cowboy pulps during the 1980s, giving rise to "adult" westerns. Cowgirl heroines are finally getting their day in the sun. Fancy Hatch, Lone Star, and Molly Owen now ride and shoot on the range once dominated solely by males.

To be sure, skilled latter-day writers have raised the esteem accorded to western literature. Larry Jeff **McMurtry,** Edward **Abbey,** Jack Warner **Schaefer,** Cormac McCarthy, and others have achieved national critical acclaim. Writer, editor, and critic Don D. Walker is correct to lament, however, "the persistence of a sad statistical fact about cowboy novels: out of every hundred written perhaps only one has literary sophistication." Neither fans of Buntline nor L'Amour, however, open a book looking for great, timeless art. They want action and a cowboy hero they can admire, and they get it. (Bold 1987; Dinan 1987; Milton 1980; Tuska and Piekarski 1983, 1984)

PULPERÍA
Rustic tavern and general store. See Saloons.

PULPERO
Saloon keeper. See Saloons.

PUNCHER
Short for cowpuncher—a cowboy.

PUNCHY
Colloquial term meaning good, just fine, as a punchy day or a punchy time.

PYLE, HOWARD
(1853–1911)
Artist. See Art of the Cowboy.

QUARTER HORSE

Visit a working western cattle ranch and you will most likely see hands riding quarter **horses.** Attend a reining competition, and you will again see quarter horses. Like many other elements of western history, however, the roots of the quarter horse go far back and far away.

The American quarter horse originated during the latter half of the seventeenth century in colonial Virginia and Carolina. Southern breeders developed the animals to race on straight quarter-mile tracks, hence the name. Unlike the taller thoroughbred, the quarter horse could start very fast and quickly reach top speed. Quarter horses have a relatively short body. They usually stand from 14-2 to 15-2 hands high (58 to 62 inches at the withers). A large animal might reach 16-1 hands (65 inches). The horse has broad, well-muscled hindquarters and strong shoulders and feet. They come in virtually any solid color from buckskin and smoky to palomino. Paints or pintos, however, are not permitted to be registered as quarter horses.

According to Nelson C. Nye, "The real Quarter Horse must be a hot blood."

Quickness is his stock in trade.... He has three gaits, each of them natural; the walk, trot, and gallop. The short gallop, or lope, is unequaled for pleasure riding. He is ridden with a loose rein and responds to signals given with the rider's knees or posture. If he's been raised by a rancher he'll be neck reined.

The breed we now call the quarter horse carried various names before getting its official designation in 1940. In the 1700s, the horse carried the rather ungainly name of "quarter of a mile running horse." In his 1833 *American Race-Turf Register,* Sir Patrick Nisbett Edgar wrote about the "famous and celebrated American Quarter Running Horses." The initials CAQRH or CAQRM (mare) became commonplace in the 1700s. All these tags referred to the same breed.

Whatever they have been called, quarter horses have always been fine all-around animals. They are well suited for riding, pulling, and all ranch work, especially roping and cutting. Their strength and burst speed make them excellent for many types of competition: reining, short-track racing, barrel or cutter racing, pole bending, and as show horses. A good rustler (capable of finding grass to eat), the quarter horse is easy to keep. The animal also has great cow sense.

English Sires

According to Robert Denhardt, a fine historian and first secretary of the American Quarter Horse Association, breeders in colonial Virginia and the Carolinas produced the first quarter horses by mixing imported English sires and native mares. Horse importation did not begin auspiciously in Virginia. Settlers at Jamestown imported six mares and a stallion from England in 1610. Unfortunately, the starving settlers had to eat all seven animals that winter. In following years, however, additional imports survived.

English blood-horse stallions, such as Bulle Rock, began appearing in the 1730s. Breeders in colonial Virginia imported many great sires. Mordacai Booth imported Janus, the great thoroughbred, sometime between 1752 and 1755. Edgar's 1833 registry identified more than 100 of Janus's progeny, many extremely fast at the quarter mile. Janus was bred in Chowan, Halifax, and Bertie counties of North Carolina.

Jolly Roger, a chestnut sire, was imported in 1746 at the age of five. According to John Goodrum, "He produced most excellent bottomed stock in Virginia." Denhardt ranks Sir Archy as the most important thoroughbred sire after Janus. Sir Archy stood 16 hands high, weighed 1,400 pounds, and ran four-mile races.

The disruptions of the revolutionary war pushed Virginia horse breeding farther south from its traditional center along the Rappahannock River to the lush pastures along the banks of the Roanoke River on the Virginia-North Carolina border. This valley—including the North Carolina counties of Northampton, Granville, Warren, and

Halifax—became prime racehorse breeding territory in the late eighteenth century.

Leading planter and horse breeder Wyllie Jones of Halifax County, North Carolina, purchased Spadille, bred from Janus and Selima. Joseph John Alson, also among the premier breeders in Halifax County, raised horses descended from Janus's Nancy Willis and Morton's Traveler.

Spanish/Indian Dams

Much less is known about the dams that give birth to quarter horses. The names of the native dams generally went unrecorded. Breeders imported some English mares, such as Mary Gray, brought to Middlesex County, Virginia, in 1748. Most dams, however, were so-called Chickasaw Indian ponies, probably of Spanish ancestry.

Spanish horses came to the colonies as early as did English stock. Yankee traders imported Spanish horses from the West Indies during the 1600s. New England "Jockey Ships" carried horses back and forth. In 1665 the governor of New York laid out a two-mile track at Hempstead Heath on Long Island.

In 1565 Pedro Menendez de Aviles had established the colony of Guale in Florida. By 1650 the Spanish had built 79 missions, eight towns, and two royal ranches in the southeastern regions. English and Indian attacks resulted in escaped horses that went wild. These Spanish ponies probably descended from barbs, fast desert horses from Africa that reached Spain with the Muslim invasion of 711.

The Chickasaw and some Cherokees traded Spanish horses to colonists in the Carolinas. The colonists called such horses Chickasaw mares. These short, heavily muscled animals were quick, but short on long-distance endurance. The *South Carolina Gazette* (3 December 1763) reported the racing victory of Bonnie Jane, a five-year-old "Chicasah mare" owned by Edmund Bellinger, Jr.

Dr. John B. Irving (*The Turf in South Carolina*, 1857) described the Chickasaw breed. This was a stock of horses originally introduced into Florida by the early Spanish. They were in general well formed, active and easily kept, but small. The mares seldom exceeded thirteen and a half hands, but being remarkable for their muscular development and great endurance."

Horse expert Paul Laune offers an alternative explanation of the origins of these Spanish ponies. They did not come from Florida, he says. Instead the Chickasaw or Choctaw ponies came from west of the Mississippi in the late 1600s and early 1700s. They passed from Spanish colonists in Texas and the borderlands into the hands of Plains Indians and then to French traders at Natchez and Mobile Bay.

Sol Torrey (*The Western Horseman,* July 1942) wrote that "before the 'gentlemen breeders' became more enamored with racing for its own sake than as a proving ground for breeding horses, a large number of Chickasaw mares, and other fast mares which could not be called Chickasaws, were crossed with the line-bred Orientals such as Janus."

Dr. George H. Conn (*The Arabian Horse in Fact, Fantasy, and Fiction,* 1959) also argues for extensive Indian pony influence. "The native American horses in Virginia and surrounding states at the time of the importation of English blood horses were chiefly of Chickasaw breeding. There was a marked improvement both in size and speed of these horses after the Chickasaw mares were cross-bred with English stallions."

Denhardt surveyed all colonial horse breeding, not just animals bred for racing. Using this broader base of evidence, he attributes a large role to Chickasaw mares. Alexander Mackay-Smith disagrees with Denhardt, Conn, and others who give great importance to native mares. Mackay-Smith looked at only racehorses and argues that the Indian-Spanish infusion did not reach the eastern seaboard. According to Mackay-Smith, breeders from Tennessee westward used the Chickasaw or Spanish mares as well as mares from Mexico during the nineteenth century but not earlier.

Unfortunately, racism and xenophobia have shaped the folklore of the quarter horse (and much else). Nineteenth-century conflict with Mexico as well as Anglo racism led many

Americans to minimize Spanish contributions. They did not want to see Spanish links to the quarter horse or anything else of value. Paul Laune reports a typical attitude from one old-time breeder who said "he never saw a **mustang** or Indian pony that was worth a bowl of jailhouse chili."

Colonial Era Racing and Betting

With the felicitous mating of thoroughbred studs and Spanish/Indian dams, the horse population of Virginia grew quickly in the seventeenth century. The number of horses rose from 200 in 1649 to around 10,000 in 1671.

Horse racing remained a sport for gentlemen during the seventeenth and early eighteenth centuries. The sport was considered the exclusive privilege of the upper class. In 1674, for instance, a York County, Virginia, court fined a laborer for engaging in a horse race. In the South, white masters owned the horses and placed the bets. Black slaves, however, served as jockeys, trainers, and grooms.

Northerners preferred more traditional long races of up to four miles, but short races were more popular in the South for a number of reasons. The heat and humidity took a dreadful toll on horses in a long race. Virginia's dispersed, rural population offered no central site to build a long, large track. Short races could be held on any little stretch of road, offering great impromptu entertainment. These match races often took place near taverns and always included heavy betting.

Englishman J. F. D. Smyth (*A Tour of the United States of America*, 1784), writing in 1769, described southern horse racing:

> In the southern part of the colony [Virginia], and in North Carolina, they are much attached to quarter-racing, which is always a match between two horses, to run one quarter of a mile straight out.... They have a breed that perform it with astonishing velocity, beating every other for that distance, with great ease; but they have no bottom. However, I am confident

that there is not a horse in England, nor perhaps the whole world, that can excel them in rapid speed, and these likewise make excellent saddle horses for the road.

So-called short horses sped over many short tracks, winning and losing considerable sums for their owners. William Ransom Johnson of Warrenton, North Carolina, earned the title "Napoleon of the Turf." During the 1807–08 racing season, his horses won 61 of 63 races. Hogsheads of tobacco served as currency for the gambling planters.

Willie (Wyllie) Jones was a Halifax, North Carolina, politician and planter and probably the most successful of all colonial quarter horse racers. Jones owed much of his success with horses to his skillful black trainer/jockey/groom, Austin Curtis. A very wily and resourceful rider, Curtis mixed trickery with good riding. In an ask and answer start, one rider would ask if the other was ready. If the answer came yes, the race began. Catching the other off guard was part of good strategy, since a quick start counted heavily in the outcome of a quarter-mile race. Curtis mastered this quick-start strategy.

The Modern Quarter Horse

The quarter horse breed and breeders, like many Americans, moved progressively westward during the nineteenth century. Horse raising expanded into Tennessee, Kentucky, and on into Texas and the West. The quarter horse's virtues—intelligence, strength, agility, and cow sense—made it the horse of cowboys working cattle in the American West.

Robert Denhardt pushed successfully in the 1930s and 1940s for the term *quarter horse* to become the breed's official name. Other breeders of the time used other terms. Jack Casement called his father Dan's horses "Steeldusts." George Clegg and Ott Adams called their horses "Billys."

In 1940 Denhardt, Robert J. Kleberg, Jr., of the **King Ranch,** W. B. Warren, and other aficionados formed the American Quarter Horse Association (AQHA) and made the name official. They shared a common bond in their admiration for the horses they bred. Dan Casement, writing in the first edition of the *American Quarter Horse Association Stud Book* (1940), described the ideal quarter horse:

> There is a small, sensitive, alert ear, his wise bright eye, the amazing bulk and bulge of his jaw which seems to betoken his bulldog tenacity and resolution. There is his short back, deep middle, and long belly, his low-slung center of gravity, and the astonishing expanse of his britches, seen from the rear, surpassing the width at the croup.

The American Quarter Horse Association remains a vibrant, active force in promoting the breed, sponsoring some 2,000 events each year. Their Heritage Center and Museum houses a Hall of Fame that honors people and horses important in the history of the breed. The association sponsors "America's Horse," an ESPN television program devoted to quarter horse competitions. For membership information contact AQHA, P.O. Box 200, Amarillo, Texas 79168; tel. 806-376-4811. Museum tel. 806-376-5181. The National Cutting Horse Association encourages riders and cutting competitions. Many good cutting horses, as noted, are quarter horses.

Address: 4704 Highway 377S, Ft. Worth, TX 76116; tel. 817-244-6188. (Denhardt 1970; Laune, 1973; Mackay-Smith 1983; Nye, 1978; Osborne 1977)

See also Horses.

QUERENCIA

In Latin America, especially in Argentina, this word means a cattle herd's accustomed range. In Mexico it also applied to a person's home territory *(pago* in Argentina), often one's birthplace. When the term *querencia* crossed the border into the American Southwest, it became generalized even further to mean one's favorite haunt.

QUIRT

A riding whip generally made of plaited leather. Some quirts had handles weighted with lead, serving as effective close-range weapons or a means to get the attention of a difficult horse. The word comes from *quarta,* the Spanish term used in Mexico for quirt.

The **gaucho** of the Río de la Plata also used a rawhide riding whip called a *rebenque.* Often two feet long, this whip also had stout handles and consisted of a single rawhide strip about two inches wide. (Slatta 1992; Ward 1958)

RACISM

See Discrimination.

RADIO WESTERNS

On Christmas Eve in 1906 Reginald A. Fessenden made the nation's first experimental radio broadcast from Brant Rock, Massachusetts. The medium did not take off until after World War I, but 30 stations were in operation in 1921 and 500 stations had been licensed by 1922. A little more than a decade later, President Franklin D. Roosevelt would address an estimated 60 million Americans over the radio through his "fireside chats."

Radio stations quickly discovered the appeal of singing cowboys. John White (see Musicology) began singing his cowboy tunes on New York's WEAF in 1926. A few years later Gene **Autry** got his start singing on KVOO (Tulsa). He then moved to Chicago's WLS.

Cowboy melodrama followed the cowboy crooners. "Death Valley Days," sponsored by Pacific Coast Borax, began airing in the fall of 1930.

WXYZ (Detroit) listeners first heard "The Long Ranger" in late 1932. George W. Trendle created the character, Fran Striker joined the show as a main scriptwriter a few weeks later, and James Jewell directed the series until 1938. Faithful companion Tonto made his debut in the tenth script. The masked figure, inspired by Zorro and Robin Hood, caught on immediately. In July 1933, some 70,000 fans showed up for the Lone Ranger's first public appearance at Belle Islands in Detroit. The last episode aired on 4 September 1954.

The 1930s and '40s represented the golden age of the radio cowboy. In 1933 "The Tom Mix Ralston Straightshooters" premiered. Along with the Lone Ranger and Tom Mix, Red Ryder, Buck Jones, and eventually Sky King sang, rode, shot, and even flew airplanes on radio. Cowboy crooners and action heroes thrilled millions and pitched products each week. (Ralston Purina sponsored Mix on the radio from 1933 to 1938 and again from 1940 until 1950. Thanks to Mix's effectiveness as a **pitchman**, the program

continued for a decade after his death in 1940.) Gene Autry's "Melody Ranch" appeared on radio in 1940, Roy Rogers took to the airwaves four years later, and William Boyd as Hopalong Cassidy followed in 1950.

During the early 1950s both cowboy radio programs and **B westerns** fell victim to **television**'s growing appeal. Rogers, Autry, King, and other radio cowboys migrated to the new medium and prolonged their careers for a few more years, but the age of radio drama had ended. Music, news, sports, and talk shows remained, but radio cowboys had ridden off into the sunset. (Aylesworth 1986; Dunning 1976; Savage 1979; Weissman 1981)

RAIDER

Movie horse of **B-western** film star Charles ("the Durango Kid") Starrett.

RAILHEADS

Towns with facilities for loading cattle onto trains. See Cow Towns.

RAINE, WILLIAM MACLEOD
(1871–1954)

Prolific author of western fiction.

RAKING

Also scratching—spurring a horse to encourage it to buck.

RAMADA

A thatched roof set on poles. **Llaneros** and **vaqueros** sometimes slept under an arborlike *ramada*, which kept off the rain but let fresh breezes in.

RANCH WORK

Cowboys throughout the Americas cared for large herds of cattle from horseback. They faced the caprice of wild beasts and encountered choking alkali dust, swollen rivers, blinding rainstorms, or howling blizzards. Regardless of weather or obstacles, cattle had to be tended. Few

Among a cowhand's tasks was the slaughtering of cattle for food, hide, and tallow. This 1910 photograph, taken by Erwin E. Smith, depicts two Arizona cowhands butchering cattle.

men have labored so faithfully under such harsh conditions for such meager pay.

The cowboy's morning began with a predawn breakfast (see Food). Hands then selected their first mount of the day from the *remuda,* the herd of horses tended by a **wrangler.** They then dispersed over the range to perform a variety of tasks. On open ranges, cattle had to be gathered. After the advent of barbed wire, fences had to be checked and mended. During rainy weather, animals might bog down in marshes, bogs, and swamps. (No hand relished the muddy task of the bog rider.) To the outsider, cowboying might appear monotonous, but hands knew better. They faced new problems and incessant challenges each day.

The essential cowboy chores of **roundup** and branding persist through today. Ranching economics and markets, however, have changed over time. Early wild-cattle hunters in Texas and

California killed animals for their hides and tallow. A gaucho might slice out a tongue for dinner, but he left most of the meat to rot because no market existed. During the late nineteenth century, new refrigeration technology opened markets for chilled meat. By this time, most of the cow was utilized. The rising value of cattle meant that ranchers became more concerned about their care. Infections and disease no longer went untreated. Most cattlemen began dipping their animals to kill ticks. Inoculations became a standard part of the branding routine.

The diaries of rancher H. M. Hatfield (Glenbow Archives, Calgary) offer insight into ranch work in Alberta during the mid-1890s. Like many cowboys and ranchers, Hatfield had to perform a wide range of chores to survive. Spring plowing began in March and continued through May. Once the fields were ready,

Hatfield planted rye and wheat. Animals also needed attention, with branding in April and May. Hatfield spayed the heifers in May. By late May and early June, it was spring roundup time. July found Hatfield back in the fields, cutting hay and rye. He mixed pleasure with pragmatism, shooting ducks and geese for the larder during the hunting season in August and September. Late September and early October found Hatfield joined with his neighbors for the fall roundup. They gathered again for one final, smaller roundup in November. During the winter months, Hatfield earned extra cash hunting wolves and coyotes for bounty.

Most cowboys lost their paychecks during the winter months. Ranchers kept only a skeleton crew to handle repairs, routine chores, and the exigencies of bad weather. The lucky few who escaped winter layoffs faced cold, difficult chores. John Baumann *(Fortnightly Review,* 1 April 1887) recorded the winter discontent on a Texas ranch: "We have nothing before us but the long dreary winter months, which will be spent in cheerless dug-outs, line-riding, repairing fences and corrals, killing wolves, and turning the heavy drift of starving cattle, which must inevitably take place, as much as possible off our range."

The early twentieth century brought little change. Regardless of the weather, animals needed tending. The worse the weather, the greater the need. For year-round hands, the chores didn't end. Texan James C. Dahlman worked on the western Nebraska range. He recalled *(Nebraska History Magazine,* October 1927) that "those kept during the winter months chopped and hauled logs, corral poles, posts; they built barns, houses, ice-houses, corrals, or anything the foreman ordered done. The Texas Puncher was always sighing for spring."

Cowboys, then, worked within nature's cycles. The reproductive cycles of livestock and the changing seasons shaped the rise and fall in their activities. Modern technology has not altered ranch work nearly as much as it has urban or factory labors. Four-wheel drive or all-terrain vehicles, helicopters, and cellular phones have appeared on some ranches, but the essence of ranch work remains cowboys on horseback caring for cattle that many times don't wish to cooperate fully. (Adams 1989; Dary 1981; Mora 1973)

See also Bronc Buster; Roundup; Trail Drives.

RANCHERO
Rancher.

RANCHO
Ranch.

RANGE BOSS
Cowboy in charge of work on a given section of range.

RANNY
Also ranahan—colloquialisms for a top hand, a skilled cowboy.

"RAWHIDE"
See Eastwood, Clint; Television.

REAGAN, RONALD WILSON
(1911–)
Born in Tampico, Illinois, Ronald Reagan grew up with and never abandoned small-town, middle-American values. After college (B.A., 1932, Eureka College), he worked as a sportscaster. In 1937 he began his acting career with Warner Brothers, going on to make more than 50 films.

Reagan's first major role came in 1940. He played George Armstrong Custer in a western *(Santa Fe Trail),* which also starred Errol Flynn as Jeb Stuart. As a child he "had only a yen to be like Tom Mix."

Reagan wanted to star in big-budget westerns, but studios kept him in Bs. All told, however, only about six of his 54 films were westerns. In the 1953 film *Law and Order,* he played a thinly disguised Wyatt Earp. Posters announced that "his guns were the only law." He also played opposite Barbara Stanwyck in *Cattle Queen of Montana* (1954). Other westerns included *The Bad Man* (1940), *The Last Outpost* (1951), and

Tennessee's Partner (1954). Reagan failed in his childhood dream to be Tom Mix. With characteristic humor, he noted that "if someone was casting a Western, I'd be the lawyer from the East."

During the 1950s Reagan politically moved to the right, leaving behind his father's New Deal liberalism and taking up an increasingly strident conservatism. He served as president of the Screen Actors Guild in 1952 and again in 1959–1960. In 1955 he moved into **television,** hosting "General Electric Theater" and serving as company **pitchman.** He then hosted another popular weekly show, "Death Valley Days," from 1962 to 1965. That program made Reagan familiar to millions of Americans and closely identified him with western images.

The Goldwater fiasco of 1964 brought down many political conservatives, but not Ronald Reagan. Two years later he defeated Pat Brown to become governor of California, serving from 1966 to 1974. That experience combined with tirelessly delivering "the speech" (his litany of liberal ills) gave him increasing political credibility and support. He gained visibility by voicing vocal opposition to the new Panama Canal treaty in 1976. ("We stole it fair and square!")

An increasingly conservative nation brought Reagan to the presidency in 1980; at age 69 he became 40th president and the oldest man to ever take the oath. During his frequent breaks from Washington, Reagan was often photographed chopping wood at his California ranch. He donned jeans and cowboy **boots** for leisure-time activities, becoming the first president since Lyndon Johnson to cultivate a cowboy image.

Reagan's rhetorical imagery resounded with cowboy cliches. He proclaimed Louis **L'Amour** his favorite author. He skillfully painted political issues in simple black-and-white terms, not unlike the old **B-western** plot lines. He played on the public's desire for simple, easy answers to frustratingly complex problems. Reagan looked and acted like a cowboy hero, with plenty of seemingly straight talk and decisive action. He appealed to conservatives in all sections of the nation, but the West in particular gave him strong support.

Reagan helped fuel the "Sagebrush Rebellion," a western backlash against federal legislation. He named James G. Watt secretary of the interior. The abrasive Watt resigned in disgrace after just two years. Both Watt and Reagan supported opening western lands and resources to corporate exploitation. In B-western terms, Reagan worked on behalf of the cattle and mining barons, not the working cowboy or the family ranch. Author Wallace **Stegner** termed Reagan an "ersatz Westerner" who affected the style but had little regard for protecting the region's special qualities and treasures.

In "Western Film, Ronald Reagan, and the Western Metaphor," a chapter in *Shooting Stars* (McDonald 1987), historian Michael E. Welsh noted that "not since Theodore **Roosevelt** had a chief executive of the United States attached himself so closely to the myths of the American West." Reagan did conjure a mythical West, indeed a mythical past, that appealed strongly to many people. Unfortunately, mushrooming budget deficits, financial scandals, growing mass poverty, and the sordid Iran-contra affair marred Reagan's presidency. Unlike B-western plots and cowboy **mythology,** national problems did not lend themselves to neat, simple solutions. (Rogin 1987; McDonald 1987)

REATA

Also *riata*—a braided rawhide **rope.** Texans anglicized *la reata* to *lariat,* one of countless ranching terms originating from the Spanish language.

REBEL

Johnny Mack Brown's famous movie horse.

REBENQUE

See Quirt.

RECADO

Soft multilayered **gaucho saddle.**

RED EYE

Also red disturbance and red ink—colloquial terms for whiskey.

RED RIVER

Film (1948). See Films, Best Cowboy; Wayne, John.

RELIGION

It appears that most cowboys of both North or South America spent little time worrying about or practicing organized religion. Much of their fun, especially at **saloons** and brothels, fell far short of the standards of religious morality. The lack of missions and churches on most ranching frontiers makes this indifference to religion more understandable.

Even where mission activity flourished, however, cowboys seldom exhibited interest in religion. Eighteenth-century reports from clerics on the Venezuelan **llanos** are uniformly uncomplimentary concerning **llanero** morals and behavior.

Most cowboys held views that could be described as superstitious rather than religious. Llaneros, **gauchos,** and **vaqueros** believed in a wide range of supernatural forces. The Devil and other vestiges of Christianity might figure into some superstitions, but the mysteries of nature often had superstitious explanations based on Indian cosmology or on fetishistic beliefs developed by cowboys themselves. We therefore find an ironic juxtaposition of strong mission activity (directed toward Indian populations) and unchurched cowboys sharing the same frontier.

Missions made few inroads onto the **pampas** of Argentina, so it is not surprising that gauchos remained mostly ignorant of religious matters. True, gauchos used the term *Christian* to distinguish themselves from the Indians, whom they called savages. These terms denoted cultural rather than religious categories, however. Latin American cowboys, indeed males in general, seldom entered a church. Machismo left religious matters to women and old men.

Cowboys in the United States likewise worried little about theology. The vast distances and sparse populations of the West gave rise to circuit riders and itinerant evangelists who visited various locales, but few hands of the range had regular contact with preachers or churches. An anonymous cattle dealer in Texas put it this way (*Texas Live Stock Journal,* 21 January 1888):

> The average cowboy does not bother himself about religion. The creeds and isms that worry civilization are a sealed book to the ranger, who is distinctively a fatalist. He believes that when the time comes for him to go over the range nothing can stand death off, and no matter what danger he faces previous to that time no deadly harm can come.

T. L. Shepherd of West Plains, Saskatchewan, published "The Cowboy's Religion" in *Canadian Cattlemen* (December 1939). He repeated a skepticism about religion often heard on the range:

> My brother was talking to a real old time cowpuncher, who was a stranger to him. Soon the rider produced a sack of Bull Durham and a packet of papers. These he offered to my brother so that he too could roll his own, but my brother didn't happen to smoke. The cow-hand was a little surprised at this, so offered a plug of chewing. "No thanks," to this too. Not to be outdone, our Western friend offered a drink, but that too was declined. Eying him with suspicion the cowhand said, "Say, you ain't Religious, are you?"

Cowboy singer Don Edwards made a similar distinction. In describing himself, he said "I'm spiritual, but I'm not religious." A closeness to nature and participation in its natural cycles gave the cowboy a feeling about nature and the forces driving it, but cow work couldn't be put on hold to trek into town and hear someone preach a sermon.

Cowboys may not have been religious, but they certainly had a clear sense of morality. Shepherd well captured the essence of a cowboy's moral code:

Those who live in the West don't call for help until they really need it, but when they call we sure expect to answer it. For we are bound to help those who need help, governed only by their need and our opportunity. That, to my way of thinking, is the Cowboy's Religion.

Given the cowboy's general lack of interest in institutional religion, some organizations have seen cowboys and **rodeo** riders as a fertile field for proselytizing. One group that has taken the cowboy's spiritual needs to heart is the Fellowship of Christian Cowboys. Based in Colorado Springs, the group is a branch of the larger nondenominational Fellowship of Christian Athletes. As Dan Semrad, the group's publicity manager, put it, "The lifestyle that cowboys are famous for definitely demonstrates the need" for religion.

Cowboys for Christ (CFC), based in Fort Worth, Texas, is the best-known group of this kind. Christian evangelist Ted K. Pressley founded the group in 1972. He still serves as CFC president and editor/publisher of the group's monthly tabloid, *The Christian Ranchman.*

CFC hosts nondenominational religious services at rodeos, cutting horse and quarter horse competitions, and other places where ranch people gather. It is organized into local chapters in 18 states.

Cowboy Jim Eicke explained why he participates in CFC:

I'm not a religious person. I'm not a nonbeliever either. I believe there's somebody looking after us somewhere. But I don't go to church every Sunday and every Wednesday. We've got a thing called Cowboys for Christ. It's nondenominational. People give testimonies about what they've done and how it's changed their

life. I've never given one yet. [smiles] I don't think they're ready for mine.

(Adams 1989; Allmendinger 1992; Slatta 1990)

RELOADING OUTFIT
Colloquial term for eating utensils, cup, and plate.

REMINGTON, FREDERIC S.
(1861–1909)
New York–born Frederic S. Remington became the leading artistic recorder of the vanishing American Wild West. After studying at Yale School of the Fine Arts, Remington made an abrupt career change. In 1880 he went to Kansas to begin sheep ranching, but he sold the ranch after four years and traveled around the West. In the fall of 1884 he returned to the East and married Eva Caten, but in 1885 he traveled west and sketched Apaches on the San Carlos Reservation in Arizona. His authentic-looking illustrations of Native Americans and cavalrymen impressed eastern magazine editors. He was on his way.

Theodore **Roosevelt** was among those impressed with young Remington's work. The future president commissioned the artist to draw sketches for his book, *Ranch Life and the Hunting Trail* (1888). Roosevelt's endorsement assured Remington's reputation. He took up writing himself, publishing *Pony Tracks* (1895) and *Crooked Trails* (1898). He also illustrated books for his friend Owen **Wister.**

By 1891, Remington settled in New Rochelle, New York, where he filled his studio with western materials that provided the detail for his paintings. His skill and concern for authenticity raised his work well above that of romantic pulp illustrators of the day.

In 1895 Remington observed sculptor Frederic Ruckstull at work. This inspired him to expand into a new medium. Remington's bronzes, such as *Bronco Buster* (1895), retain and even expand the realism of his paintings. He

Western artist Frederic Remington photographed in his New Rochelle studio with a work in progress,
The Buffalo Horse.

often told stories with his works. *Comin' through the Rye* (1902) depicts a quartet of hell-raising cowboys flying along on mounts whose hooves barely touch the ground.

Remington's only novel *(John Ermine of the Yellowstone,* 1902) shows considerable compassion and sympathy for the Native American way of life. It is his powerful images, however, not his prose, that most clearly remain with us. His works form a major part of cowboy **mythology.** As death neared he reportedly cried, "Cowboys! There are no cowboys any more!" His style and subjects remain an inspiration to many, including the **Cowboy Artists of America.** (Baigell 1976, 1988; McCracken 1947; Samuels 1982; White 1968)

REMINGTON FIREARMS

Eliphalet Remington began his arms-making career early in the nineteenth century by making rifle barrels. In the 1850s he expanded to form the E. Remington and Sons Company. They produced many types of **firearms,** of which rifles and revolvers received the most use in the West.

In 1857 Fordyce Beals patented a percussion revolver for the company. Produced first as a .31-caliber pocket revolver, it later came out in standard army (.44) and navy (.36) calibers. Remington also produced the first double-action revolvers. In these weapons the trigger both cocked the hammer and rotated the cylinder. Remington handguns gained a loyal band of aficionados, but they never attained the vast popularity of **Colt** revolvers.

While losing out to Colt in handguns, Remington excelled in the production of rifles. The introduction of the Rolling Block Sporting Rifle represented a major advance in breech-loading technology. This 1866 design actually caused the breech parts to tighten during firing, thus reducing safety problems and allowing for larger powder charges.

Remington's association with the Union Metallic Cartridge Company aided in the design of their weapons. Accurate and possessing a great range, the Rolling Block nevertheless lost out to the **Winchester** Model '73, except among sharpshooters and some big-game hunters.

The Remington-Lee bolt action rifle in 1880 provided another innovation, the box magazine. Thanks to this improvement, the time-consuming reloading of cylinder magazines became unnecessary. Fully loaded magazines could be carried for quick replacement when needed. Such ingenuity made Remington one of the three big names in firearms used in the West. (Hatch 1956; Karr and Karr 1960)

—*Mark Mayer*

REMITTANCE MEN

Remittance men were young European gentlemen, usually English, who came to make their fortunes in the American or Canadian West. The term carries a negative connotation owing in part to the men's dependence on family money (the remittance).

Some remittance men showed up in ranch country, generally overdressed and underskilled. Most preferred investing in cattle ranching to the sweat and dust of cowboying. Winfred Blevins quotes Steward Edward White, an Arizona rancher, on remittance men: "I had a son of a duke drivin' wagon for me; and he couldn't drive nails in a snow-bank." (Blevins 1993; Dunae 1981; Roe 1954)

REMUDA

String of replacement mounts tended by a horse **wrangler.** Cowboys used this Spanish term or the word *cavvy* (from *caballada)* as synonyms.

REP

Also stray man or outside man—a cowboy who represents his ranch at a general **roundup.**

RESERO

Gaucho term for trail driver.

REVOLVER

See Colt Firearms; Firearms.

RHEA

Large ostrich hunted by **gauchos** for its feathers. See Pampas.

RHODES, EUGENE MANLOVE
(1869–1934)

Writer Gene Rhodes was born in Tecumseh, Nebraska, but his family soon moved to Cherokee, Kansas. Rhodes's father served briefly in 1890 as agent to New Mexico's Mescalero Apaches, and the Rhodes family moved to Fort Stanton, New Mexico. The time he spent in New Mexico would mark Gene Rhodes for life.

From age 13 to 28, Rhodes worked as a cowboy, eventually hiring on as a **wrangler** at the famous Bar Cross ranch. During this time he encountered the many unforgettable men who entered his writings, including such notorious outlaws as Bill Doolin and Sam Ketchum.

Chronically short of money, Rhodes had to educate himself. He attended the University of the Pacific at Stockton, California, in 1889–1890, but lacked the funds to complete his degree. After leaving college he garnered a reputation as a voracious reader of the classics. He acquired some books by exchanging Bull Durham coupons for literary classics. His companions at the Bar Cross claimed that Rhodes could read while riding 50 miles through a snowstorm.

In 1896 Rhodes published his first work, a poem. Six years later he published his first short story, "Once in the Saddle." He met his future wife, May Davison Purple, thanks to his poetry. After reading one of his works, the widow with two children wrote him a complimentary note. Rhodes hopped a freight train east to meet his pen pal. They married in 1899. May and Gene lived in New Mexico for three years. May, however, felt lonely for her parents and life in the East, and the couple moved to Apalachin, New York. Rhodes's nostalgia for life in New Mexico strongly shaped his later writings.

A cowboy of the Argentine pampas takes part in a popular high-speed equestrian game, balling ostriches (rheas) in this early nineteenth-century painting by Emeric Essex Vidal.

Like many western writers, Rhodes often depicted actual events, with little or no changes in the characters involved. At that point, however, he parts company with genre writers. Rhodes disdained simple plots. His stories have a complexity that breathed greater life into his characters. Rich authentic language, dialogue, and character development distinguish his works.

Rhodes also differed in his choice of villains. Unlike many contemporaries, he avoided stereotyping Mexicans as stupid or villainous. He engendered some outlaws with the heroic status of social bandits. His experiences with ranch life and the people he encountered led Rhodes to conclude that eastern bankers, speculators, and monopolists, rather than outlaws, were the true villains of the West.

Rhodes made no apologies for the sometimes harsh nature of frontier life. He celebrated the virtues of the frontier as superior to all others. His ability to blend complex plots, realistic

characterization, and frontier realities make Rhodes one of the best western writers. Many of his stories originally appeared in *The Saturday Evening Post*. His works of fiction include *Good Men and True* (1910), *Stepsons and Light* (1921), *Beyond the Desert* (1934), and *The Proud Sheriff* (1935).

In 1926, after May's parents had died, Gene's poor health prompted the couple to move to Santa Fe and then Alamogordo, New Mexico. His degenerating health forced a final move to Pacific Beach, California, in 1931.

The richness of Rhodes's writing never translated into riches. He died, nearly destitute, in 1934, after a series of heart attacks. He is buried in the San Andres mountains of New Mexico. His epitaph reads Pasó Por Aquí (He passed this way), taken from his greatest short story, published in 1926.

Rhodes has gotten the literary attention he deserves, thanks in part to another writer and literature scholar, William Henry Hutchinson. Both Hutchinson and his father greatly admired Rhodes's work. After Rhodes's death, Hutchinson gathered a book's worth of his favorite writer's stories and published them as *The Little World Waddies* (1946). During the next decade he published a biography of Rhodes, *A Bar Cross Man* (1956), and compiled *The Rhodes Reader* (1957) and *A Bar Cross Liar* (1957), a bibliography of Rhodes's writings. (Hutchinson 1956; Rhodes 1975; Tuska and Piekarski 1983)

—*Nils E. Mikkelsen*

RIB WRENCHES
Colloquial term for **spurs**.

RICHTER, CONRAD
(1890–1968)
Pulitzer Prize–winning author of *The Sea of Grass* (1937).

RIDE FOR THE BRAND
A cowboy saying, "ride for the brand" means to be loyal to the ranch and rancher that pays you. Cowboys took a great deal of pride in giving their all for the brand. They would ride the extra mile and fight, if necessary, for their outfit. Singer and poet Red Steagall wrote a poem titled "Ride for the Brand," and recorded it on his 1993 album, *Born to This Land.* The poem well expresses the heartfelt sentiment of loyalty evident in a century of top hands:

Son, a man's brand is his own special mark,
It says this is mine; leave it alone.
If you hire out to a man, ride for his brand,
And protect it like it was your own.

RIDE THE HIGH COUNTRY
Film (1962). See Films, Best Cowboy.

RIDERS IN THE SKY
Cowboy singer Douglas Bruce ("Ranger Doug") Green brought together the original Riders in the Sky in 1977 in Nashville. A talented vocalist, yodeler, and guitarist, Green left a position at the Country **Music** Foundation to take up full-time performing. Joining him at that time were bassist Fred ("Too Slim") LaBour and Bill Collins. After various personnel changes in the 1980s, Green and LaBour added fiddler Woody Paul (Paul Woodrow Chrisman).

Their first album, *Three on the Trail* (1980), appeared on the independent Rounder label. They recorded a total of eight Rounder albums. Success did not come overnight. Green recalls the difficulty of winter layoffs, much like those suffered by old-time cowboys. "Several winters Woody fixed Volkswagens, Slim did puppets at the public library and galvanized metal, I did freelance writing and cut and sold firewood, not to mention those Sunday nights playing banjo at Shakey's."

The trio signed with MCA and in 1987 issued *The Cowboy Way.* Their performances mix comical high jinks, lowbrow puns and props, and great musical talent. Their popular **radio** program, "Riders Radio Theater," attracts a mostly adult audience that enjoys their great singing and zany humor. Their crazy characters are now familiar to millions—Too Jaws, Joey the Cowpolka King, High Sheriff Drywall, Sgt. Dudley, Sidemeat, and more. Texas Bix Bender, "the Voice that Sold a Million Baby Chicks," serves as announcer.

In 1991 the group began a children's Saturday morning television program, with music, zany props, and improbable skits. Ranger Doug, "the Idol of American Youth," usually saves the day.

Their wide audience appeal reflects the broad influences that have shaped the group—everything from kid's cartoons to cowboy folklore and old **B westerns.** It also reflects their intelligence. All three are college-educated: LaBour has a bachelor's degree in wildlife management, Green hold's a master's degree in literature, and Chrisman has a doctorate in nuclear engineering.

The group performs its own songs in addition to the western classics. Woody Paul wrote the beautiful ballad, "Cowboy Song," in 1980. Folklorist Charlie Seemann rightly calls it "a model for western songs; not only does Paul evoke the coyotes, prairies, Texas, the moon, western skies, horses, buffalo and women, but he offers his six-gun, his saddle, spurs, roping and steer-wrestling as well." That same year Paul and LaBour teamed up to write the rousing "Cowboy Jubilee." Who except Too Slim could write the 1986 song titled "The Salting of the Slug"? In 1991 the **National Cowboy Hall of Fame** honored their song, "The Line Rider," with a Western Heritage Wrangler Award. Doug Green wrote the words and music.

Green sums up the trio's attitude today:

We still love bringing the West to the people of this country, and others, making audiences misty-eyed one moment, roll with laughter the next, smile in appreciation the next. You couldn't plan a career like this, but we're sure glad it happened. All along, it's been The Cowboy Way.

(Flint and Nelson 1993; Too Slim, Ranger Doug, and Woody Paul 1992)

RIDING LINE

Also riding fence. See Line Camp.

RIG

Colloquial term for **saddle.**

RIMFIRE SADDLE

Also rimmy. See Saddle.

RING BIT

See Bit.

RING EYE

Horse ridden by comic sidekick Smiley Burnette in **B-western** movies.

RING RACE

See Equestrian Games.

RINGOLD, CLAY

Pseudonym for writer Ray **Hogan.**

RINGY

Also ringey—colloquial term applied to angry or ornery man or animal.

RITTER, MAURICE WOODWARD ("TEX")
(1905–1974)

Singer, actor. See Music.

ROBBINS, MARTY
(1925–1982)

Singer, composer. See Music.

ROBERTS, WAYNE

Pseudonym for writer Wayne D. **Overholser.**

ROCK HOPPER

A term applied to hands who hunted wild cattle in the rock country of Arizona. Like the Texas **brush popper,** a rock hopper operated in very difficult terrain under difficult conditions.

ROCKWELL MUSEUM

See Appendix B.

ROCKY MOUNTAIN SCHOOL

See Art of the Cowboy.

RODEO

Let's rodeo! Rodeo is a set of competitive events pitting people against livestock. Modern rodeo flourishes in all 50 states of the U.S., most of Canada, and parts of Europe and Australia. Each year an estimated 16 million fans cheer at more than 800 sanctioned rodeos around the world. About 2,000 rodeos of all types are held annually in the United States and Canada.

Origins

Many rodeo events originated from traditional cowboy skills—riding horses and roping cattle. The word's Spanish origin points to another important influence from south of the border. In Spanish the term *rodeo* means a gathering place of cattle (a **roundup**). Cowboys used the term in that sense in the nineteenth century. Gradually in the United States the term came to mean the dazzling cowboy and cowgirl contests now enjoyed by millions.

Mary Lou LeCompte (*Journal of Sport History,* Spring 1985) has shown that the "all-American sport" of rodeo owes a strong debt to Mexican equestrian displays and competitions. Riders in Mexico competed in *charreadas* long before rodeo appeared in the United States. Early cowboy tournaments or contests in the Southwest often included **vaqueros** and Anglo cowboys. These contests included ranch work skills, but some events came directly from earlier vaquero and *charro* practices in Mexico.

Another point of origin probably stems from the great Texas **trail drives** after the Civil War. Drovers would gather at corrals in **cow towns** to see who was top hand. In Abilene, Dodge, and elsewhere, cowboys climbed aboard **mustangs** and roped wild cattle.

Hands also competed against one another at ranch rodeos. On 4 July 1869 Mill Iron, Camp Stool, and Hash Knife cowboys got together at Deer Trail, Colorado. Clifford Westermeier reprinted a contemporary journalist's account of the exciting saddle bronc ride in *Trailing the Cowboy* (1955):

The prize was a suit of clothes, and the conditions were that the horses should be ridden with a slick saddle, which means that the saddle must be free from the roll usually tied across the horses, and that the rider must not wear spurs.

Those in charge made no secret of the fact that all the horses they had were outlawed horses, which it had been impossible to break, and the conditions made it dangerous riding. Many of the boys shook their heads, but Will Goff, a slim, young cow puncher from the Bijou jumped out and said he'd ride anything with hair on it.

Swish! and his felt hat whistled through the air and caught the broncho across the side of the head. The pony hitched violently for fifty yards, making about 300 revolutions to the minute.

Emilnie Gardenshire let it be known that he wanted the worst animal in the pen, and he got it in the shape of a bay, from the

Hashknife ranch, known throughout the section as the Montana Blizzard. Gardenshire, rawhide whip in hand, crawled aboard cautiously and, once firm in his seat, began to larrup the bay unmercifully.

For fifteen minutes the bay bucked, pawed, and jumped from side to side, then, amid cheers, the mighty Blizzard succumbed, and Gardenshire rode him around the circle at a gentle gallop. It was a magnificent piece of horsemanship, and the suit of clothes, together with the title "Champion Bronco Buster of the Plains," went to the lad from the Milliron ranch.

Buffalo Bill **Cody**'s Old Glory Blowout of 4 July 1882 in North Platte, Nebraska, provides another important rodeo landmark. He convinced local merchants to donate prizes for a variety of riding and roping contests. Pecos, Texas, held another early competition—the West of the Pecos—on 4 July 1883. Held every Fourth of July since, Pecos Rodeo was the first to award a cash prize. According to Charlie **Siringo**, a "grand cowboy tournament" was held in Caldwell, Kansas, in May 1885.

The *Denver Republican* (30 September 1887) reported a near-tragedy in Montrose, Colorado:

The cowboys' tournament in which roping from the ground, from the saddle, heading and heeling, riding bucking bronchos, etc., afforded much sport, but well nigh terminated fatally. One of the cowboys was riding a bucking broncho when the animal made a dash towards where the ladies were seated and could not be checked before he struck Mrs. James A. Ladd, who was thrown violently to the ground beneath the animal's hoofs. The horse struck the lady with its front feet on her chest and pinioned her to the earth for a second or two, but he was quickly grasped by one or two gentlemen who stood near the lady and prevented from trampling her to death. Every lady on the grounds screamed and one or two fainted.

The Prescott (Arizona) Frontier Days Celebration on 4 July 1888 holds claim as the first rodeo to charge admission and present a trophy—a silver-mounted medal won by contestant Juan Leivas. The town of Payson, Arizona, also began celebrations that included rodeo competition during the early 1880s.

Rodeo appropriated entertainment styles from Wild West shows, drawing upon Buffalo Bill Cody's flair for showmanship in promoting their attractions. The last of the great old troops, the **Miller Brothers'** 101 Ranch Wild West Show, closed in 1931, and some contract performers (as opposed to contestants) moved their acts from Wild West shows to rodeos. Trick riding at rodeos showed the common heritage and crowd-pleasing showmanship of rodeos and Wild West shows. Trick riders, such as Dick Griffin, Don Wilcox, and Bernice Taylor delighted audiences in the early twentieth century with their skill and courage on horseback. Trick ropers, such as Chester Byars and Jim Eskew, Jr., likewise amazed crowds with their talents.

Early rodeo and Wild West show performers shared some characteristics with the working cowboy: they gained unsavory reputations for wildness, fighting, and drunkenness, and most of them remained poor. Like the people who stick with cowboying because they love the life, many rodeo riders today participate for the sheer thrill of it. Of course, everybody hopes to make it big one day.

Cheyenne, Pendleton, and More

In the United States, rodeo has become the "all-American sport." Rodeos in Pendleton (Oregon), Cheyenne (Wyoming), and elsewhere have gained international fame. First held in 1897, Cheyenne's Frontier Days has become one of the biggest western spectacles. Early boosters tried a variety of crowd-pleasing acts, including Buffalo Bill's Wild West in 1898. At various times, promoters also added balloon flights, parachute drops, masquerade balls, and wolf roping. Some couples even decided to take their wedding vows in front of enthusiastic crowds in the grandstand.

Rodeos were quickly recognized as a means of promoting tourism and business. Businessmen in Pendleton planned their cowboy extravaganza, which they called a "roundup," in 1910. According to original publicity, early events included "roping, racing, and relays, by cowboys, Indians and cowgirls; steer roping, maverick races, steer bulldogging, riding bucking horses, steers, bulls, buffaloes, and cows; stagecoach racing, Indian ceremonial and war dances, trick riding, mounted tug of war, the grand parade, and that wonderful finale, the wild horse race." What more could an audience want? Let 'er buck!

By 1915 major rodeo events had become annual occurrences in Cheyenne, Pendleton, Salinas (California), and Calgary (Alberta). The following year, Guy Weadick, a Wyoming rider and promoter, took rodeo performers to Brooklyn for the New York Stampede. **Rodeo events** became more standardized over the decades.

Along with big, famous shows like the Stampede, Roundup, and Frontier Days, many smaller events came into being. Amateur rodeos, often during summer holidays, became commonplace throughout the western United States and Canada. Today every rodeo season finds a crowd of ever-hopeful would-be champions "goin' down the road."

It took a while for rodeo stars to emerge. Rough stock, however, quickly became legends in their own time. Bucking horses—like Steamboat, Midnight, Tipperary, and Five Minutes to Midnight—became more famous than the men who challenged them. According to rodeo legend, Tipperary first met his match in Yakima Canutt, who went on to become a legendary stuntman and film actor.

Getting Organized

As rodeo's popularity grew, so did the opportunity for fraud. Corrupt promoters sometimes ran off with the gate and left competitors unpaid and stranded. Fake rodeos raised questions in the public mind about the legitimacy and honesty of rodeo contestants. To counter these problems, honest rodeo boosters formed the Rodeo Association of America (RAA) in 1929. The RAA gave its stamp of approval to legitimate rodeos and blacklisted dishonest promoters.

Meanwhile, rodeo riders also saw the need to organize on their own behalf. In 1936 they organized the Cowboy's Turtle Association, often referred to as "the Union." The turtle moniker reflected the fact that it took performers a long time to get organized. The group formed when sixty competitors demanded a bigger slice of the gate and walked out on Col. W. T. Johnson's rodeo at the Boston Garden. At the time the total purse was less than the sum of their entry fees. The union prompted Johnson to agree to their demands and grant them a $14,000 purse.

The RAA's name changed to the Rodeo Cowboys Association (RCA) in 1945. Members won an important victory over rodeo management in 1955. The RCA point system and standings became the single measure for naming rodeo world champions. In 1974 the RCA adopted its present name, the Professional Rodeo Cowboys Association (PRCA).

Hawaiian riders formed the Hawaii Rodeo Association in 1966; the group presently numbers about 250 members and sanctions eight or nine rodeos per year.

Rodeo performers can start young. In 1968 Anne Lewis became the youngest national rodeo champion ever. She won the barrel racing crown that year at the ripe old age of ten. The National Little Britches Rodeo Association sponsors events for boys and girls aged 8 to 18. The first such competition took place in Littleton, Colorado, on 29 August 1952. The National Finals, held at Colorado Springs, attract hundreds of young competitors.

Little Britches Rodeo can include up to 22 events, so there's plenty of action. Many of the events are modeled on adult rodeo, but goat tying and goat tail tying add new twists. "Mutton bustin'" (sheep riding) gives youngsters plenty of spills and thrills. Girls hone their skills at barrel racing in hopes of graduating to adult competition later. Girls in Little Britches Rodeo also compete in riding events, including pole bending and trail course, an obstacle race.

Today's rodeo riders, like other professional athletes, follow preprofessional training in schools, since direct opportunities to work on the range are relatively few. Many people work their way up through high school and intercollegiate rodeo competition. The best youngsters compete annually at the Collegiate National Rodeo Finals.

Rodeo has generated its own mystique, with a bit of glamour, life on the open road, and the potential for hefty winnings. The rodeo rider's once unsavory reputation has been replaced by an all-American image.

Women

Women quickly found a place in rodeo, just as they had on the frontier and in Wild West shows. Mary Lou LeCompte (Cowgirls of the Rodeo, 1993) found records of at least 16 women who competed in rodeos or Wild West shows during the 1880s. In early rodeos, women competed head to head with men in what later became men's events, such as saddle bronc riding.

May Lillie, married to Wild West show entrepreneur Pawnee Bill **Lillie,** captured the allure of horseback life: "Let any normally healthy woman who is ordinarily strong screw up her courage and tackle a bucking bronco, and she will find the most fascinating pastime in the field of feminine athletic endeavor."

Prairie Lillie Allen, Fox Wilson, and other daring cowgirls competed in early rodeos. Missouri-born Lucille Mulhall became the best-known rodeo cowgirl of the early twentieth century. She also became friend and mentor to Ruth Roach and other young female competitors of her day.

Bertha Kapernick gave the first bronc riding exhibition by a woman at Cheyenne Frontier Days in 1904. She later married bulldogger Dell Blancett and rode as his hazer. (Some sources state that in 1901 Prairie Rose Henderson became the first woman bronc rider at Cheyenne. Mary Lou LeCompte found no evidence of her participation there before 1910.)

Guy Weadick included a full range of women's events for the September 1912 **Calgary Stampede.** The program listed the following: "Fancy and trick riding by cowgirls, Cowgirls relay race, Fancy roping by cowgirls, Bucking horse riding by cowgirls."

Beginning in the 1930s, rodeo promoters reduced women's participation. When men riders organized their union in 1936, they excluded women. Women no longer competed against men. Rodeo promoter and singing star Gene **Autry** played a leading role in marginalizing rodeo cowgirls. Autry took control of major rodeos in the early 1940s and reshaped them to reflect his conservative, strongly gendered values. In 1942 he eliminated women's bronc riding from competitions in New York and Boston. Rodeo cowgirls found themselves relegated to the sidelines as rodeo queens or to special events, such as barrel racing.

Faced with the setbacks of the 1940s, a group of Texas women organized the Girls Rodeo

Association in 1948. This organization later became the Women's Professional Rodeo Association (WPRA). Since that time women have worked to close the gender gap in rodeo. They have competed in all-girl rodeos and sought to reestablish their lost status in men's rodeo, and in this they are succeeding.

Women's rodeo is slowly making its way into popular culture. The 1980 television movie, *Rodeo Girl,* starring Katharine Ross and Jackie Cooper, was based on the career of world champion Sue Pirtle. The National Cowgirl Hall of Fame and Western Heritage Center, at Ft. Worth, Texas, is dedicated to perpetuating the history and legacy of rodeo cowgirls.

Charmayne James Rodman and other modern cowgirls have pushed far beyond the rodeo queen role. In 1992 Rodman rode Scamper to her ninth straight barrel racing title at Las Vegas—not bad for a 22-year-old! Her string of wins is a rodeo record for men and women. (Bull rider Donnie Gay and calf roper Dean Oliver each

Bronc riding is a dangerous sport not exclusive to men. This cowgirl was thrown from Silver in a Cheyenne, Wyoming, rodeo.

managed eight straight.) The first and so far only "million-dollar cowgirl," Rodman drives her own rig some 90,000 miles each rodeo season.

Rodeo culture is very traditional, as reflected in the rodeo queen competitions, which are still held. A Miss College Rodeo is chosen each year. Contestants must excel in appearance, sportsmanship, personality, congeniality, and horsemanship.

Not all women are content to limit their rodeo participation to a horseback beauty pageant. Increasing numbers of women have made their way back into the rough stock events. In the early 1990s, Tonya Butts (age 21), for example, ranked among the leading bull riders of the Women's Professional Rodeo Association. Tammy George won the 1992 women's bull riding championship. Veteran Jan Youren was twice WPRA world champion bareback bronc rider and has been inducted into the Cowgirl Hall of Fame.

As sexist barriers fall throughout society, rodeo fans will see a blurring of the sex-segregated lines in rodeo events. Women in rodeo likely will narrow the gap between their earnings and visibility, just as women have in other professional sports.

To contact the Women's Professional Rodeo Association, write Rt. 5, Box 698, Blanchard, OK 73010; tel. 405-485-2277.

Rodeo and Popular Culture

Hollywood also recognized the fan appeal and entertainment value of rodeo. Bing Crosby (that's right) played a rodeo star/crooner in the 1936 film *Rhythm of the Range*. Dean Martin and Jerry Lewis starred in a 1956 remake titled *Pardners*, in which Martha Raye made her debut and Roy **Rogers** and the Sons of the Pioneers added their voices. *The Cowboy and the Lady*, a 1939 comedy, had rich Merle Oberon falling in love with rodeo rider Gary Cooper. Walter Brennan and Fuzzy Knight added to the humor.

Two good, similar rodeo films appeared in 1952. Budd Boetticher's *Bronco Buster* included good rodeo action and starred Casey Tibbs, John Lund, and Chill Wills. In the film, rodeo veteran Wills taught newcomer Lund the ropes. *The Lusty Men*, a rough-and-tumble classic, conveyed much of the dust, hurt, and hubris of rodeo life. Robert Mitchum starred as a beat-up, broken-down rodeo veteran. Arthur Kennedy played the up-and-comer, with Susan Hayward as his wife. Another film simply titled *Rodeo*, with Jane Nigh and John Archer, appeared the same year.

Arena appeared as a 3-D movie in 1953. Lee Van Cleef gave a good performance as a rodeo rider. Gig Young and Polly Bergen starred in a script that included too much soap opera romance. The plot reappeared in 1972 as *The Honkers*. *Born Reckless*, another rodeo soap opera appeared in 1958. Arthur Hunnicutt reprised his role from *The Lusty Men*. Mamie Van Doren and Jeff Richards also starred.

For some reason the years 1972 and 1973 produced a bonanza of rodeo films. Steve McQueen starred in Sam Peckinpah's *Junior Bonner* (1972), with first-rate rodeo scenes. Cliff Robertson starred as an ex-convict rodeo rider in *J. W. Coop* (1972). The heroes in both of these movies faced the harsh reality of fast-changing times.

The Honkers (1972), starred James Coburn and Slim Pickens. Not very memorable, the film was based on a tried-and-true rodeo plot: the rodeo rider's conflict between spending time with his wife and spending time on the road. *When the Legends Die*, with Richard Widmark as a drunken rodeo promoter, also appeared in 1972. *The Great American Cowboy*, a very fine documentary film about rodeo, appeared a year later.

My Heroes Have Always Been Cowboys (1991) returned to a theme much like that of *Junior Bonner*. The film, hokey at times, was something of a *Rocky* with spurs. It opened and closed with wild, dangerous bull-riding action. In between, we had the slowly unfolding story of conflict and love between H. D. Dalton (Scott Glen) and his father Jesse (Ben **Johnson**). The cast also included Mickey Rooney, Gary Busey, and Kate Capshaw.

Depending on national cultural attitudes, rodeo stars sometimes reached celebrity status; Casey Tibbs, for example, struck a macho pose for the cover of *Life* magazine (22 October 1951). Some rodeo announcers also became celebrities in their own right. Frederick ("Foghorn") Clancy built his reputation before the advent of loudspeaker systems. His memoir, *Fifty Years in Rodeo* (1952), provides lively insights into the sport. Clem McSpadden followed Clancy as a popular, sought-after announcer.

Rodeo Today

It has been a long road from "the Union" of 1936 to today's Professional Rodeo Cowboys Association, which is headquartered next door to the Prorodeo Hall of Champions. About 10,000 riders hold PRCA memberships. In 1992 total PRCA prize money approached $20 million, double the 1980 figure. Only about 300 members, however, compete full time. The rest support their rodeo habit with other jobs.

The PRCA sanctions most rodeos held in the United States (770 in 1992). (The smaller International Professional Rodeo Association also sanctions events.) The PRCA sponsors the National Finals Rodeo (NFR) each year. Dallas hosted the first NFR in 1959. The contest later moved to Oklahoma City. After a 20-year tenure there, the NFR moved to Las Vegas in 1985. The year's top 15 money-winners compete in nine days of events. Leading WPRCA barrel racers also ride for the national crown. By the early 1990s, NFR prize money neared $3 million.

Like any sport, rodeo has its groupies. "Buckle bunnies" flock to rodeo stars just as groupies do to other professional athletes.

Rodeo is popular and big business from Pendleton, Oregon, to Paris and Tokyo. In 1990 world champion Ty Murray won more than $213,000. Murray became the PRCA's youngest all-around champion in 1989 at age 20. In 1992 Murray became one of only three cowboys to qualify for all three NFR rough-stock events: bull riding, bareback riding, and saddle bronc riding. Winning his fourth straight title in 1992, the 22-year-old won $225,000.

Few riders hit the big time, but the average rodeo winner makes about $29,000 annually. Not every rider has a winning season. Six-time all-around world champion Larry Mahan explained the basics of rodeo "survival skills." You have to learn to travel without a car, borrow clothes, and put up with ten men in a motel room. Competitors also subsist on a diet heavy in "rodeo steak" (hot dogs.) Contestants pay a fee to compete and earn no salary. On a bad day, riders end up several hundred dollars poorer.

Rodeo has millions of fans, but the sport also has its detractors. Elizabeth Atwood Lawrence *(Rodeo,* 1984) argues that rodeo has institutionalized macho values and attitudes of the Old West. Man reenacts the taming of the West through his mastery over wild animals. As Lawrence points out, however, rodeo people strongly identify with the livestock. Famous rodeo animals share the spotlight with humans at the Prorodeo Hall of Champions.

Mastery over animals can involve what appears to be cruel, violent treatment. The Fund for Animals, People for the Ethical Treatment of Animals, and other groups strongly criticize rodeo. They argue that the flank strap inflicts pain to the genitals of a bucking bronc or bull. (A flank strap or scratcher cinch extends around the animal's body at the flanks.) Critics take strong exception to calf roping, since calves can be injured when the taut rope pulls them sharply to the ground. Animals rights advocates also object to using electric cattle prods or twisting an animal's tail in the chutes to get it to buck more wildly.

Rodeo fans will reject such criticism, but rodeo is definitely hard on man and beast alike. In a 1937 California rodeo, a horse named Duster bucked off four-time world champion saddle bronc rider Pete Knight, planting a hoof in his ribs. Knight walked away from the ride but died that night of internal injuries at age 33. Roper Bob ("Wild Horse") Crosby became a legend for competing while seriously injured. A charging bull gored and killed 1987 world champion bull rider Lane Frost. The 25-year-old Texan died before a horrified crowd at Cheyenne Frontier Days in 1989.

Arena dangers created another job, the rodeo clown. These funny, entertaining figures have a serious task. They distract animals from fallen performers in the arena. Clowning and humorous bullfighting date back to at least the 1920s, when a Wild West performer and bronc rider named Red Sublett turned his talents in that direction. John Lindsey and Hoyt Hefner became well-known rodeo clowns of the 1930s and '40s. Today rodeo clowns have their own bullfighting championships and remain crowd favorites.

Rodeo performers project a toughness, endurance, and stoicism. Some working cowboys still become rodeo performers, but many rodeo stars never work cattle on a ranch. Both working cowboys and rodeo riders, however, share a common culture and exhibit similar values. Rodeo people would agree with writer Gene Lamb: "Rodeo is the last Frontier for the individual." (Fredriksson 1984; Hoy 1990; Lamb 1956; Lawrence 1984; LeCompte 1985, 1993; Pointer 1985; St. John 1977; Savitt 1963; Tinkelman 1985)

See also Charro; Rodeo Events.

RODEO COWBOYS ASSOCIATION

The name of the professional **rodeo** riders association from 1945 to 1974. The organization is now called the Professional Rodeo Cowboys Association.

RODEO EVENTS
Traditional Standard Events

By the 1920s, sanctioned rodeo's five standard events had taken shape: bareback bronc riding, saddle bronc riding, bull riding, calf roping, and steer wrestling (bulldogging). Team roping and, less often, steer roping competitions are also part of some **rodeos.** Rodeo performers specialize, but they must have skills is several events to become all-around champions. Oklahoma-born Jim Shoulders, for example, excelled at both bull and bronc riding. He earned five All-Around Championships from 1949 through 1959.

Participation by **women** in American rodeo has grown steadily in recent decades. Federally mandated equal opportunity programs for intercollegiate sports and the erosion of sexism have forced changes in rodeo. Currently in collegiate rodeo men have the five standard rodeo events. Women compete in barrel racing, goat tying, and breakaway tying. Both men and women participate in team roping.

The bareback bronc rider takes on an untamed bucking horse. He holds onto a special leather bareback rigging with one hand. With no reins, **saddle,** stirrups, or bridle, the rider must stick with the bronc for eight seconds, which seems like eternity on the back of a bad one.

Saddle bronc riders use a special lightweight rodeo saddle and, in lieu of a bridle, hold a single piece of **rope.** The rider clutches this rope or bucking rein and cannot change hands. If a rider "blows a stirrup" (lets his foot slip out), he is disqualified. Touching anything with the free hand also earns disqualification. Great work by both man and animal is required to score well. A perfect score is 100 points, and contestants have only eight seconds to show their stuff. The ranker the horse (harder to ride), the better. It should kick and buck high and hard. The rider must comb the horse, that is, rake it with his **spurs** from the shoulder back to the flanks. He also must time his spurring to the horse's bucks.

In 1920 rodeo associations set the standard for saddles used by saddle bronc riders. The so-called Association saddle (also called Committee or contest saddle) favors the horse. The rider has little to give him leverage. According to Ramon F. Adams *(Western Words,* 1968), the original saddle had a 14-inch swell and a 5-inch cantle. Saddle makers built it around a modified Ellenburg tree—a wooden frame that lies under the saddle leather. Riders gave the minute seat an appropriate name, a crackerbox.

Because rodeo features people and animals, some horses became as famous as the stars riding them. According to rodeo records, only five cowboys ever stuck with Midnight during the black gelding's long career (1920s and 1930s).

Another powerful black horse, Five Minutes to Midnight, became popular at the time and also challenged the best riders. Both animals are buried on the grounds of the **National Cowboy Hall of Fame** in Oklahoma City.

Bull riders face ferocious Brahman bulls and other breeds. The event is acknowledged as the most dangerous in rodeo. According to a Justin Sportmedicine Program study, bull riders suffered 43 percent of all rodeo injuries. In the event, the rider holds onto a bull rope with one hand. The rope encircles the bull's body behind the hump. A bell hangs from the rope underneath the bull and excites him to greater efforts.

Rodeo clowns haze the bull in an attempt to get the animal to spin. A spinning bull gets the rider more points. A particularly "rank" bull provides a greater challenge but higher marks to the cowboy who stays on. Like bronc riders, bull riders must stay on deck for eight seconds. Riders score extra points for sticking with an animal that puts up a good fight. Only eight of 300 riders stuck with fast-spinning Oscar during his fine career in the 1970s. He lived out his days until

1982 as a show guest at the Professional Rodeo Cowboy Association in Colorado Springs.

Calf roping is one rodeo event with very clear roots in actual **ranch work**. The event mimics the work done during **roundup** to brand calves. At roundup, a hand would carry a pocketful of short rawhide strings for tying the calves' feet. These strings are known on the ranch or in the rodeo arena as hog ties, hogging **ropes**, hogging strings, or pigging strings.

In the rodeo event, ropers chase a calf into the arena. The rider ropes the calf by the neck, then jumps to the ground and runs to the calf. He throws the calf to the ground and ties three of its feet together in the shortest possible time. Scores under six seconds are excellent. Competitors usually take two wraps around three legs. A half hitch, called the hooey, around two legs secures the job. All the while, his mount keeps the calf under control by keeping the rope taut. A "buford" (weak, easily thrown steer or calf) does not score a cowboy championship points. The luck of the draw plays a role in who wins and who loses. Of course, the rodeo stock come out the winners on many occasions.

This cowboy is in the midst of championship bronc riding—one of the five traditional rodeo events.

Especially talented performers help develop any sport. Jake McClure, born in Amarillo in 1903, made important contributions to calf roping by developing his trademark tight "McClure loop." He worked very well with talented mount Silver, earning several different championships. Thrown from a horse, McClure died in 1940 of a concussion.

(Lewis) Edward Bowman, born in 1886, also played an important role in the development of calf roping. A Texas cattleman, Bowman excelled as a relay rider and roper. He is credited with developing the first rope-working horse in calf roping. In addition, he and his mount Sonny teamed up to win the National Cutting Horse Championship. His impressive rodeo and cutting horse careers earned him a place in the National Cowboy Hall of Fame in 1962.

Steer wrestling (bulldogging), like calf roping, is a timed event; the quicker the better. The bulldogger rides after a steer while a hazer on the other side keeps the steer running in a straight line. The steer wrestler jumps from his horse to the steer's neck and grabs its horns. He digs his heels into the dirt to slow down 750 pounds of hard-charging animal. The next move is to twist the horns so the steer falls to the ground. Bill **Pickett,** an **African-American** cowboy who rode with the **Miller 101 Wild West Show** in the early twentieth century, is generally credited with inventing bulldogging. He could grab a steer by the horns, bite the animal on its lip, and force it to the ground.

Other Events

In addition to the five standard events, many other competitions enliven rodeo. Some events have survived from the early days of rodeo. Three-man teams still compete in the wild horse race, although no championship is awarded. The cowboys, perish the thought, are unmounted. They must catch, saddle, and ride a wild horse across a finish line. Another recognized event with no champion is wild cow milking. A two-man team rides after and ropes a wild cow. They must squeeze a little milk into a bottle and carry it across the finish line. Best times

determine the winners in both wild horse races and wild cow milking.

Team roping is a recognized, timed event for which a world champion team is named. In the event, the "header" first ropes a steer's head and the "heeler" ropes one or both hind legs. Both competitors get to throw two loops, if necessary. In dally team roping, the riders take their dallies, that is, they wrap the rope around the saddle horn rather than tying it fast. In tied team roping, the competitors tie their ropes to the saddle. These variations reflect the two roping traditions that developed in western ranch work, dally and hard-and-fast.

Steer roping or single steer tying is a less common event. It resembles calf roping, with a big exception. The roper's horse, not the man, drops the steer. After roping the steer, the rider runs his horse off at a sharp angle. The taut rope jerks the steer to the ground. The roper then dismounts and ties the steer's feet with a pigging string. Many states banned this event because the hard jerk from the horse sometimes broke the necks of steers. At some rodeos, hands carried all steers out of the arena on a sled, a ploy that kept the crowd from knowing whether or not an animal's neck had been broken. (Lamb 1956; Lawrence 1984; Savitt 1963)

RODEO STEAK
A hot dog, the staple food of **rodeo** contestants.

RODGERS, JAMES CHARLES (JIMMY)
(1897–1933)
Singer. See Music.

RODRÍGUEZ MOLAS, RICARDO
Historian of the **gaucho.** See Historiography of the Cowboy.

ROGERS, ROY
(1912–)
Born Leonard Slye in Cincinnati, Ohio, Roy Rogers became the singing "King of the Cowboys." Wielding a guitar as often as a

six-shooter, Roy and second wife Dale Evans have sung and ridden their way into the hearts of several generations of armchair cowpokes.

Len Slye grew up with his family in Duck Run, Ohio. At age 17, he went to work with his father in a shoe factory. In 1929 Len purchased his first guitar, secondhand, for $20. A letter from an older sister in California beckoned the family west, where they headed in the spring of 1930.

In California, Len drove a gravel truck and rolled greens on a golf course—anything to bring in money during the Depression. He also kept strumming the guitar and singing. He began his entertainment career at age 18, performing on an amateur **radio** program. Thanks to a good performance, he was asked to join a group called the Rocky Mountaineers. He performed with many western bands during the early 1930s, playing for dances and on the radio.

Walter E. Whitmore at KGFL radio in Roswell, New Mexico, gave young Len Slye a regular singing slot three times per week. He also gave Slye a new name, Dick Weston, the "Texas Troubadour."

Rogers joined with other talented western musicians in the early 1930s. They sang in various combinations and under several different names. He sang with Bob Nolan (born Robert Clarence Nobles in New Brunswick, Canada) and Vernon Harold (Tim) Spencer as the Pioneer Trio on KFWB in Los Angeles in 1934. Nolan's tunes "Tumblin' Tumbleweeds" and "Cool Water" remain western classics. Tim's brother, Glenn Joseph Spencer, wrote many songs and served as musical director for the group. The trio added talented fiddler and bass player Hugh Farr and his younger brother, guitar-playing Karl Farr. Lloyd Perryman, vocalist, rounded out the famous group—the original Sons of the Pioneers. Combining strong voices and good songwriting, the group became a major influence in western music. Pat Brady replaced Rogers in 1937 when he left the group to pursue his **film** career. Both Rogers and the Sons of the Pioneers went on to highly successful film and music careers. They often appeared together.

Rogers appeared in motion pictures under at least three different names. As Len Slye, he appeared in three Columbia pictures, *The Gallant Defender* (1935), *The Mysterious Avenger* (1936), and *The Old Wyoming Trail* (1937). As Dick Wooten, he appeared in two Republic pictures, *Wild Horse Rodeo* (1937) and *The Old Barn Dance* (1938). All told, Rogers starred in more than 100 films. He legally changed his name to Roy Rogers in 1938 while working for Republic Pictures. He got his first lead role in Republic's *Under Western Skies* (1938).

Rogers had learned a bit about riding horses and cowboying while living in Roswell. After signing with Republic, he spent some time at a Montana ranch to hone his on-screen skills, riding, roping, shooting, and boxing. With the famous moniker Roy Rogers, he went on to enjoy a half century in film, radio, **music,** and **television.**

Rogers married his first wife, Arlene Wilkens, in 1936. Arlene died in 1946, however, and Rogers married Dale Evans the following year. They had three children from previous marriages. Their only child together, Robin, died at age two of Down's Syndrome. They raised five more children, however—four adopted and one foster child. As of 1993, Roy and Dale's family numbered six children (Tom, Dusty, Linda Lou, Cheryl, Dodie, Marion), 16 grandchildren, and 26 great-grandchildren.

Rogers and Evans, "Queen of the West," became well known role models of strong, loving family life. They first appeared together in the 1944 film, *Cowboy and the Senorita.* As his popularity grew in the late 1930s, fans invariably compared Rogers to the other leading singing cowboy, Gene **Autry.** World War II proved important to the careers of both. With Autry in uniform for several years, Rogers gained the number one position as "King of the Cowboys."

The advent of television in the 1950s opened yet another door. Rogers and Evans enjoyed several successful specials and a six-year run of their half-hour series. Roy, Dale, Trigger, Buttermilk, and Pat Brady driving a Jeep named Nellie Belle (with Bullet in the passenger seat) became known to millions of fans. Their popularity never waned. Syndication now brings their television shows to succeeding generations.

Like his fellow singing cowboy, Gene Autry, Rogers took his job as a role model for youngsters seriously. Rogers avoided excessive gunplay on his show. He often handled the bad guy neatly with his fists rather than **firearms.** "We'd shoot the gun out of their hands and stuff," says Rogers, but they kept **violence** minimal. Rogers understood the essence of being a role model: "Kids would listen probably to me better than they would their Pa."

During the 1950s members of the Roy Rogers Riders Club agreed to obey the following rules. The rules are very similar to Autry's earlier "Ten Commandments of the Cowboy."

1. Be neat and clean.
2. Be courteous and polite.
3. Always obey your parents.
4. Protect the weak and help them.
5. Be brave but never take chances.
6. Study hard and learn all you can.
7. Be kind to animals and care for them.
8. Eat all your food and never waste any.
9. Love God and go to Sunday School regularly.
10. Always respect our flag and our country.

Rogers keeps a hand in the entertainment business at an age when most people are content with retirement. In 1990 Rogers survived heart surgery and a bout of pneumonia. Then in 1991 he completed yet another album, *Tribute.* Son Dusty wrote a tune on the album entitled "King of the Cowboys." K. T. Oslin, Randy Travis, Kathy Mattea, and other country-and-western stars also performed.

Appearances at fairs and **rodeos** draw fans, young and old. Like Autry, Rogers has an excellent business acumen. He merchandises more than 400 products, from clothing to restaurants.

The Roy Rogers and Dale Evans Museum includes much of their professional memorabilia. They sometimes personally greet some of the 200,000 guests who visit annually. Visitors can also see faithful companions Trigger, Buttermilk, and Bullet the Wonder Dog, thanks to the skills of taxidermists. The still-active couple has plans to expand the museum grounds into a 35-acre theme park. It would include elements important to their film lives—a Spanish village, a frontier fort and **cow town,** and a 1950s walk down memory lane.

The museum houses a collection of some 300 firearms. The Rogers/Evans gift shop, however, does not sell toy guns for children. Rogers supports the rights of gun owners, but he wants children to understand that firearms are serious, dangerous business. "The shows you see now," says Rogers, "with all that killing and everything, I just don't know. Now you hear about all these guns at school, and it makes you sick."

Rogers has received many professional awards for his long career. In 1975 he received the Pioneer Award from the Academy of Country Music. He is a two-time member of the Country Music Association's Hall of Fame. He was honored in 1980 as a member of the Sons of the Pioneers and eight years later as a solo performer. In 1992 TNN/MCN gave Rogers their Living Legend Award. Roy and Dale have enjoyed many, long, happy trails. (Flint and Nelson 1993; Miller 1979; Rothel 1987)

ROGERS, WILL
(1879–1935)

America's beloved cowboy humorist of the 1930s, Oklahoman Will Rogers (Penn Adair), began his entertainment career as a Wild West show trick roper. He had cowboyed and managed the family ranch in his youth, so he came by his roping skills honestly. In 1902 he joined Texas Jack's Wild West Show and toured as "the Cherokee Kid." He later worked for the Mulhall Wild West Show and then took his talents to the vaudeville stage.

Rogers rode well, but his roping skills became legend. He could throw three ropes at one time, dropping loops over a galloping horse's neck, front legs, and the rider. Fans can still enjoy his amazing rope feats in the silent film, *The Roping Fool.*

In 1905 Rogers appeared in New York City in Hammerstein's Roof Garden. He quickly became a Broadway star and appeared in musical revues. In 1915 he appeared in *Midnight Frolic* and subsequently became a regular in Florenz Ziegfeld's follies. During this time he began injecting political **humor** into his act and strengthened his audience appeal even more.

Through his stage performances, newspaper columns, 15 movies, and many books, Will Rogers raised lively, funny political commentary to an art form. He helped Americans retain their sense of humor during the depths of the Great Depression. Rogers could deliver great one-liners and was a master of extemporaneous humor. His head-scratching modesty ("All I know is what I read in the newspapers") charmed millions.

Rogers freely engaged in political commentary and good-natured, but sharp, political satire. "I do not belong to an organized political party; I'm a Democrat." He kept the crowd in stitches when he introduced Governor Franklin Delano Roosevelt to the 1932 Democratic convention.

Rogers published many books of his wit and wisdom, including *Rogers-isms: the Cowboy Philosopher on Prohibition* (1919), *The Illiterate Digest* (1924), *There's Not a Bathing Suit in Russia* (1927), and *Ether and Me* (1929). He appeared in motion pictures as early as 1918, but given his charm and wit, the "talkies" proved a far better medium. His movies included *A Connecticut Yankee* (1931), *State Fair* (1933), and *David Harum* (1934).

Tragedy cut short his brilliant career. Rogers died on 15 August 1935 in a plane crash near Point Barrow, Alaska, with his friend, aviator Wiley Post. Memorials remain to Rogers at his ranches (Oologah, Oklahoma and Santa Monica, California) and at Claremore, Oklahoma. (Rollins 1984; Rogers 1949)

ROJAS, ARNOLD
(1899–)
Historian of the California **vaquero**. See Historiography of the Cowboy.

ROLLINS, PHILIP ASHTON
(1869–1950)
Historian. See Historiography of the Cowboy.

ROMAL
From Spanish *ramal*. See Tack.

ROOKUS JUICE
Colloquial term for liquor.

ROOSEVELT, THEODORE
(1858–1919)
New York–born Theodore Roosevelt (TR) is best remembered in history as the 26th president of the United States, serving from 1901 to 1909. It is not, however, his colorful political career that interests us here. Our concern is his western experiences and the impact of his writings on America's vision of the cowboy.

When Roosevelt graduated from Harvard University in 1880, he had no clear vocation in mind. He did, however, have clear personal plans. He married Alice Hathaway Lee, but after only four years together, tragedy struck when Alice died within hours of TR's mother. The double disaster crushed young Roosevelt, who threw his energies into politics and writing.

Ranching in the Badlands
After a stint as a New York assemblyman, Roosevelt purchased two ranches in the Dakota Badlands near Medora. The Elkhorn Ranch overlooked a bend of the Little Missouri River. He lived there from 1884 until 1886, then returned east and ran for mayor of New York City in 1886. The Cowboy Candidate suffered a stinging political defeat and turned his attention full-time to writing.

He remarried in 1886 to Edith Kermit Carow. TR fathered one daughter, Alice Lee Roosevelt (1884–1980), with his first wife. Edith and TR had several more children: Theodore, (1887–1944), Kermit (1889–1943), Ethel Carow (1891–1977), Archibald Bulloch (1894–1979), and Quentin (1897–1918).

Roosevelt's first trip west for a buffalo hunt had whetted his appetite for more. "There are few sensations that I prefer," he wrote in a letter to politician Henry Cabot Lodge, "to that of galloping over these rolling, limitless prairies, rifle in hand, or winding my way among the barren, fantastic, and grimly picturesque deserts of the so-called Bad Lands."

Colonel Theodore Roosevelt leads his famous Rough Riders on horseback.

TR had many adventures and showed considerable courage during his western stay. He knocked out a drunken bully who hazed him in a **saloon.** That feat moved him quickly out of the tenderfoot ranks. As a deputy sheriff, he captured three thieves at gunpoint. His order to a cowboy to "hasten forward quickly there" became a call echoed fondly by Dakota ranch people thereafter. Dakotans remained loyal friends and supporters throughout TR's life.

In the late 1880s Roosevelt visited his Elkhorn Ranch only for brief hunting trips. He liquidated his operation in 1889, with estimated losses of $50,000. Like many ranchers before and since, TR learned that teasing profit out of a hard land can be mighty difficult.

Despite the briefness of his ranch experience, the West left an indelible mark on Roosevelt. His perception that the western landscape was being destroyed by overgrazing and unwise development spurred his conservationist politics. He perceived the West as having a tremendous impact on his character and on how people perceived him. He believed he would never have become president if not for his western experience. The ranch years transformed his image from an effete, sickly eastern dude to a rough-riding cowboy.

Roosevelt conveyed the full weight of his considerable enthusiasm for western life in print. Thanks to his stature, the cowboy and the West became topics acceptable to the eastern cultural elite. Before the 1880s ended, TR had published *Hunting Trips of a Ranchman* (1885), *Ranch Life and the Hunting Trail* (1888), and *The Wilderness Hunter* (1893). He recorded his western adventures with a reasonable level of veracity.

Roosevelt also wrote the four-volume *Winning of the West* (1889, 1894, 1896). He put much more work and research into his history than he did into his light, episodic writings. He wanted to be taken seriously as a writer and historian, and he achieved his goal. Young historian Frederick Jackson Turner approved of TR's effort. All told, TR wrote or edited more than three dozen books.

Thanks to attention from Roosevelt, the western cowboy became an acceptable literary topic to the eastern cultural establishment. Having been properly introduced by Roosevelt, the eastern elite was ready to accept and laud **Remington**'s images and **Wister**'s novel. Indeed, Remington's big artist break came when Roosevelt commissioned him to illustrate *Ranch Life and the Hunting Trail.*

Roosevelt shared the regrettable racism of his day. His condescension toward Hispanics, obvious in his Big Stick foreign policy, surfaced earlier in his writings. "Some of the cowboys are Mexicans," he wrote in 1888, "who generally do the actual work well enough, but are not trustworthy." Roosevelt worried about the welfare of Anglo-Saxons in the era of massive foreign immigration. He chided Steven Crane for writing a story in which a gang of Mexicans kills an Anglo-American. He urged Crane to write "another story of the frontiersman and the Mexican Greaser in which the frontiersman shall come out on top; it is more normal that way!"

TR romanticized and internalized his western experience:

We led a free and hardy life with horse and rifle. We worked under the scorching midsummer sun, when the wide plains shimmered and wavered in the heat, and we knew the freezing misery of riding night guard around the cattle in the late fall roundup. In the soft springtime the stars were glorious in our eyes, each night before we fell asleep; and in the winter we rode through blinding blizzards, when the driven snowdust burned our faces. There were monotonous days, as we guided the trail cattle, or the beef herds, hour after hour at the slowest of walks; and minutes or hours teeming with excitement as we stopped stampedes or swam the herds across rivers treacherous with quicksand, or brimmed with running ice. We knew toil and hardship and hunger and thirst; and we saw men die, violent deaths as they worked among the horses and cattle, or fought in evil feuds with one another, but we felt the beat of hardy life in our veins, and ours was the glory of work and the joy of living *(The Outlook,* 24 May 1913).

Rough Riders

Roosevelt strongly supported intervention against Spain in Cuba in 1898. He formed the Rough Riders (First U.S. Volunteer Cavalry Regiment) for the Spanish American War. The regiment showed the impact of his western experience. The Rough Riders, one part cowboys, one part Harvard gentlemen, gathered in San Antonio, Texas, on 1 July 1898. After a month of horseback drill, they traveled by rail to Tampa, Florida. Transport problems there forced them to leave most of their mounts. Such logistical problems abounded during the war. Observing the military chaos, one reporter observed, "God takes care of drunkards, sailors and the United States."

Roosevelt led the Rough Riders as a lieutenant colonel under the command of Leonard Wood. Fighting mostly on foot, the Rough Riders battled alongside a contingent of **African-American** troops commanded by Lt. John J. Pershing. Together they took Kettle Hill and a spur of San Juan Hill. Roosevelt led the charge mounted on Little Texas. Looking back at the battle, he commented, "We have had a bully fight!" He later referred to the battle as "the great day of my life." The decommissioned Rough Riders presented TR with a two-foot-high casting of Frederic Remington's statue, *Bronco Buster.*

As a doting father, Roosevelt passed along to his children his enthusiasm for cowboy life. Even during the presidency, he was the center of his children's world. He would mark their toy horses and cattle with the brand of his western ranch. He delighted in telling them stories about his childhood heroes. On rainy days they played hide-and-seek in his Gun Room. TR had filled that special room with his gun collection and other western memorabilia.

Politician Mark Hanna once labeled Roosevelt "that damn cowboy." Like many easterners, TR took to western life. Although brief, his Badlands days marked his life indelibly. Covering 110 square miles of North Dakota Badlands, Theodore Roosevelt National Memorial Park commemorates his stay at his ranches. (Collins 1989; Miller 1992; Roosevelt 1966; White 1968)

ROOSTER COGBURN

Film (1975). See Wayne, John.

ROPE

One cannot imagine the cowboy without a horse and a rope. The type of rope and the manner of using it varied widely, however.

South America

In South America, cowboys braided ropes from rawhide or horsehair. The **llanero** had a distinctive roping style. He braided the end of the lariat into the tail of his horse—a tactic that took its toll in horsehair. Llaneros, however, used dexterity and balance, not brute force, against a lassoed animal because their lightweight, tropical **saddles** did not offer sufficient bulk or strength to secure the rope.

British visitor Sir Edward Sullivan *(Rambles and Scrambles,* 1852) marveled at the success of this roping style:

> I could never believe this till I saw it. It always struck me that it would either pull the horse's tail out by the root, or else throw him down; and so it would, but the horses become so cunning and so fond of the sport, that the moment the lasso leaves the hand of the rider, instead of stopping short, as I always imagined was the method, they gallop off at a slight tangent as fast as they can, when if the lasso is round the leg, the slightest jerk brings the bull to the ground. So little actual force and so much knack is there in it, that many men will throw bull after bull with a mere jerk from the shoulder, without laying any strain whatever on the horse. Great misapprehension exists as to the

distance the South Americans throw the lasso; seven or eight paces is a good long cast, and four or five not a bad average.

Argentine **gauchos,** like some Anglo cowboys, tied the lasso to their saddles. Gauchos used a comparatively short rope, about 12 yards in length, for working cattle in corrals. On the open **pampas,** they wielded ropes 20 yards long. Gauchos carefully cut a single piece of cowhide into strips and braided it into a strong lasso, with a small iron ring often attached to form the noose. Gauchos began practicing with the rope as youngsters. As William MacCann recalled in *Two Thousand Miles' Ride* (1853), "The natives are extremely expert in using the lazo; it is their earliest toy in childhood; and to lazo cats, dogs, and sheep, is the delight of children."

Mexico

Concerned that wild-cattle herds would be decimated, the ranchers' organization (Mesta) in New Spain banned the hamstringing of cattle in 1574. It outlawed the use of lances and hocking knives on pain of a 20-peso fine or 100 lashes. These restrictions promoted greater use of the lasso by **vaqueros** hunting wild cattle. Until the late eighteenth century, the vaquero, like the llanero, tied the lariat to the horse's tail. The development of heavier, more substantial saddles changed this technique, however, and vaqueros began wrapping the end of the rope around the horn of their considerable saddles. This wrapping technique, called *dar la vuelta* (take a turn), passed over to Anglo cowboys, who corrupted the Spanish term into "dally" or "dally welter." Vaqueros and the cowboys who copied the practice could slip the rope against the saddle horn and gain leverage against a roped animal. Faulty technique could be hazardous. A thumb caught between the lariat and saddle horn might be amputated by the whizzing rope. Even today many an old-time dally man has a missing thumb to mark his profession.

Vaqueros skillfully braided long reatas from four rawhide strips. They could make much of their equipment from leather. They also wove

horsehair into a fine rope called a *mecate.* (Anglos corrupted that Spanish term into McCarty.) Not strong enough for catch ropes, hair ropes found their use in hackamores and halters. A *cabestro* (anglicized to caberos) is a soft horsehair halter.

Lariats in Spanish California ran from 65 to 110 feet in length and about five-eights of an inch in diameter. In the Texas brush country, vaqueros used shorter ropes that were less apt to become entangled in the underbrush. Vaqueros threw a variety of loops, according to the task at hand. A figure eight would bring down a running animal. The *piale* (also peal or pial), an underhand toss, caught the animal's hind legs as it stepped into the noose. The *mangana,* an overhand throw, opened to catch the animal's forefeet.

In addition to rawhide and horsehair ropes, vaqueros used the tough, stringy fiber of the maguey or century plant to make ropes. (The same versatile plant is used to make a popular alcoholic beverage called mescal.) Because maguey fiber stiffens in damp weather, vaqueros used it only on dry ranges. Sisal, from the leaves of the agave plant, ran a distant third to rawhide and maguey as material for ropes.

Fay E. Ward, in *The Cowboy at Work* (1958), well summarized the pride taken by vaqueros in their roping ability:

> The experienced Mexican vaquero can make more different catches than the American cowhand because the vaquero practices more and takes great pride in making difficult and artistic catches. The difficult catches perfected by the Mexican ropers have been used as the basis for the trick and fancy rope stunts which have been developed to a very high degree of perfection.

The vaqueros who sailed to Hawaii in the 1830s to train ranch hands also transmitted their skills in rope making and throwing. Thus the Hawaiian cowboy *(paniolo)* became a "dally man." Clyde ("Kindy") Sproat, a cowboy from North Kohala, explained the rationale for dally roping *(hawili).* Because it was dangerous to tie the rope fast to the saddle when facing a heavy animal like a wild bull, the paniolo wrapped the rope *(kaula 'ili)* a few turns around the saddle horn "and let it slide along and smoke da' pommel!"

American West and Canada

Like the paniolo, Texans and other Anglo cowboys benefited from the vaquero's expertise with the rope. Some Anglo cowboys, particularly in the West and Northwest, used reatas and worked as dally men. A new hand might be guilty of "coffee grinding," that is, wrapping the rope the wrong way (clockwise) around the saddle horn.

The advent of grass ropes (made from sisal or hemp) altered roping technique. Cowboys could tie the "home end" of these stronger grass ropes hard-and-fast to their saddle horns. This practice became known as a "Texas tie," and a practitioner was a "tie-hard" or "tie-hard-and-fast" man. These hard twist ropes, unlike braided rawhide, would not break when tied hard-and-fast. Hands also used a loosely twisted grass rope called a seago (from the Spanish *soga).*

We know less than we would like about early roping techniques. The Anglo cowboy's debt to the vaquero remains clear. The backhand forefooting catch, for example, is the vaquero's mangana. Texas cowboys after the Civil War used a variety of catches, including the pitch, slip, heeling, backhand slip, and forefooting.

Each catch begins with "building a loop." The cowboy shakes out a coil of rope in preparation for roping. The loop is formed by passing one end of the rope through the honda (or hondo), a knotted or spliced eyelet in the other end. Then the hand makes the rope sing with one of a number of different throws.

Cowboys have long used the hoolihan, in which the roper swings the loop only once above his head before letting fly. This fast throw is used by hands on foot to catch horses by the head in a corral. The same throw can be used from horseback to catch a calf.

Some throws developed in the American plains. John Blocker, a Texas roper, created the extra-large blocker loop. The rope travels over a steer's shoulders and snares both front feet. Cowboys also developed some rope tricks. One might make an "ocean wave" by flipping a noose with an undulating motion back and forth. The "wedding ring" is another favorite rope trick—a roper (either mounted or on foot) encircles himself with a large, horizontal loop.

Some Anglo cowboys learned to make rawhide lariats and horsehair McCartys. They also used maguey ropes from Mexico. The importation of so-called Manila hemp, however, made ropes of that fiber the most common in the American West. Three-strand Manila hemp ropes, produced by the Plymouth Cordage Company in Massachusetts, became the cowboy's favorite by the late nineteenth century. Purchased in large rolls, the rope was simply cut to the needed length to replace limp, worn-out lariats. Once stretched and conditioned with tallow and paraffin, the rope was ready for action.

The terms used by cowboys for various types of ropes varied by region and time. The term *lasso* (from the Spanish *lazo)* might be heard. Cowboys might term a rawhide reata a "skin string," "catgut," "gut line," or "whale line." He might call his grass rope a "clothesline" or "coil."

Cowboys continued to use strong, hard twist hemp ropes into the twentieth century. Synthetics, primarily nylon and propylene, then began replacing hemp. Synthetics became especially useful in wet climates and when working animals around water.

Canadian cowboys had access to the same range of ropes and roping techniques as did their American counterparts. Cowboys had strong opinions about what equipment worked best. Cowman Fred Ings favored rawhide over hemp ropes. In the 1880s, he recalled, cowboys "used strong light rawhide ropes more exact on the throw than the coarser hemp ones commonly used today" *(Canadian Cattlemen,* December 1938). The cheapness and ready availability of manufactured hemp ropes, however, made them the standard on both Canadian and U.S. ranges. (Adams 1989; Byers 1966; Mora 1973; Slatta 1990; Ward 1958)

ROSADEROS

Also *sudaderos*. See Saddle.

ROUGH NECK

Another term for a dude wrangler, a cowboy who works at a **dude ranch.**

ROUGH RIDERS

See Roosevelt, Theodore.

ROUGH STOCK EVENTS

In **rodeo,** bareback bronc, saddle bronc, and bull riding. See Rodeo Events.

ROUGH STRING

See Ranch Work.

ROUNDUP

Working cattle was the cowboy's main job. As ranching evolved, specialized tasks developed on ranches in North and South America. Cattle had to be herded from one place to another. Wild horses had to be broken to **saddle.** The roundup (from the Spanish *rodeo)* became the central event in the ranch work cycle.

Seasonal roundup and branding required extra manpower and long days in the saddle. Sorting and branding cattle on the open range required cooperation and trust between different ranches. Roundups also provided an opportunity for the unscrupulous to enlarge their herds at their neighbors' expense, if they could get away with it.

Roundup customs and techniques passed from Mexico to the United States. We find remarkably similar descriptions of the busy branding season throughout the Americas. Cowboys everywhere used the same essential equipment: **ropes,** branding irons, hot fire, and sharp knives for earmarks and castration.

The practice of branding extends far back into history. Since at least 2000 B.C. in Egypt, herdsmen have used hot irons to sear through the hides of animals, thereby marking them for identification. The Spanish conquistadors first brought the practice of branding to the Americas in the early sixteenth century. Some societies also used brands to mark humans. Greeks, Romans, and Anglo-Saxons branded criminals, military deserters, and slaves. Fortunately, this practice declined around the mid-nineteenth century.

Latin American Roundups

At first glance, roundups looked and sounded much the same everywhere: cattle, **horses,** riders, dust, smoke, and noise. British diplomat Robert Ker Porter described a Venezuelan roundup in 1832 in his diary. He was awed by the "almost incredible looking mass of animation and dust, where I beheld thus co-mingled 12,000 head of noble cattle." He recalled the extraordinary sight of a "multitudinous gathering of heads, and horns; bellowing, lowing, and a mingled melancholy crying, set forth by bulls, cows, calves, and oxen."

Roundups consisted of several stages of action. First, riders gathered at a central point. Each large ranch sent a team of riders, often from considerable distances. Ranchers hired extra riders, paid by the day, to work alongside their year-round hands.

Once the cattle had been rounded up, cowboys sorted them by owner (called the *aparte* in Spanish) for branding and earmarks. The hands castrated and dehorned most bulls. In the nineteenth century, castrated bulls received no medical treatment. Infection and maggot infestations were commonplace among animals on the tropical **plains** of Venezuela and Colombia.

American visitor Isaac F. Holton *(New Granada,* 1857) described a *rodeo* on the Colombian llanos:

> Now begins the business of the day. What calf has not his ear-mark? What youngster of two months has not his little brand on his cheek? What yearling not branded for life in his side? A lazo on his head, another on his heels. A fire burning by the division fence, and the irons are hot. Here is a calf with a sack of morbid growth. A spatula

of wood is whittled out with a machete; fifty maggots of all sizes are dislodged from the cavity, and it is filled with the first dry, soft absorbent substance at hand.

Rules of etiquette guided roundups everywhere. A rider from one ranch never cut in front of a hand from another ranch when cutting an animal out of the herd. Teamwork was important. Hands covered for one another when an animal broke and ran from the herd. Cowboys rode special cutting horses, held in reserve, during roundup. In such close quarters, the end of the roundup offered workers an excellent opportunity to show their stuff. Horseback competition between rival ranches and a grand fiesta usually marked the end of roundup.

Argentine roundups differed little from those in Colombia and Venezuela. **Gaucho** techniques of roundup and branding (the combined process known as *hierra* or *yerra)* changed little during the nineteenth century. In his fine novel, *Don Segundo Sombra* (1926),

A handwritten list of brands (1886) demonstrates the sense of ownership ranchers felt when it came to their cattle. Cows were branded with the owner's personal brand in an attempt to curtail rustlers.

Argentine writer Ricardo **Güiraldes** provided a memorable description of a roundup:

> With their old wild instinct flaring they began to mass and to feel out the weakest spot in the circle around them. First they milled from the middle toward the sides; then they seemed to come to an understanding and stampeded with irresistible speed and determination toward a single point. The scrimmage was terrific. The bulls, blind with rage, charged straight ahead, horns lowered. The calves leaped into the chaos, stiff-legged and with tails up. The others rushed about bewildered, charging wherever they could. The men shouted; ponchos whirled in the air; whips cracked on leather. Collisions and falls reached their height; at times horse, rider and bull rolled to the ground together in one mad maze.

Wild-cattle hunts *(vaquerías)* represented the first type of roundup held in Chile, as in other livestock regions of South America. These hunts took *huasos* (Chilean gauchos) into wooded areas where horses found it difficult to work. As a result, ranchers also hired foot peons and dogs to work cattle in the woods. Roundups replaced wild-cattle hunts as ranchers established legal claims to land and began to tame their livestock. Huasos on Chilean ranches *(fundos)* worked tame cattle much as their counterparts did elsewhere.

The biggest Chilean roundups came during springtime (September) when huasos located and marked newborn calves. Englishman Thomas Sutcliffe lived in Chile from 1822 to 1839. He watched huasos round up cattle at a number of Chilean ranches. As elsewhere, hands dehorned and castrated bulls, marked calves, and branded animals. "The animals when set at liberty, are so enraged, that they run about bellowing with pain, and attack such as are near them, to the no small diversion of the bystanders" *(Sixteen Years in Chile and Peru,* 1841).

In late December ranchers again rounded up mature animals for slaughter. Chileans used most parts of the animal. Hides and horns went to foreign merchants for export. Dried meat, fat, and suet went to local markets. Like llaneros and vaqueros, huasos ate dried beef. According to Sutcliffe, Chileans ate dried beef roasted, boiled, or combined with vegetables into stews.

Like cowboys everywhere, huasos were skillful ropers. Sutcliffe also described the Chilean lasso and its use:

> The lasso is a strip of green hide of considerable length, and made pliable, some are plaited, at one end there is a running noose, the other is fastened to the girth of the saddle; few Chilians [*sic*] travel without their lasso, in the use of which they are uncommonly expert; in fact they ought to be so, for when children their amusement is the ensnaring of cats, dogs, and even poultry, with the lassito. The lasso has often been used in warfare, and many a Spaniard has been dragged from the ranks, or gun, dismounted by the intrepid huassos [*sic*].

In Mexico, as with other parts of Latin America, land and cattle accrued to the rich through careful control of the legal machinery. Early regulations controlled who could harvest wild livestock. Subsequent rules dictated who could hold roundups, as well as where and when. During Mexican roundups, vaqueros from a number of different outfits worked under the direction of a rodeo judge. Vaqueros would sweep the brush in a crescent-shaped line, herding cattle toward a central location. The rodeo judge protected the interests of the large hacendados. In colonial Mexico the *alcalde de Mesta* directed the rodeo; after independence, the official became known as the *juez de campo.*

In terms of technique, Mexican roundups changed little from colonial days to the early twentieth century. Equipment did change, however. Most vaqueros in Mexico dropped the use of lances or spears *(picas* and *garrochas),*

which dated from early colonial wild-cattle hunts. In California, however, lances remained in use as late as the 1880s. The lasso, however, increasingly became the tool of choice in handling cattle. Vaqueros still applied large brands, cut earmarks, and castrated bulls. The old practice of tailing remained common as a work technique. It also became a popular and dangerous equestrian game. In *Pony Tracks* (1895) Frederic S. **Remington** vividly described a Mexican roundup:

> In the morning we could see from the ranch-house a great semicircle of gray on the yellow plains. It was the thousands of cattle coming to the *rodeo.* In an hour more we could plainly see the cattle, and behind them the *vaqueros* dashing about, waving their *serapes.* Gradually, they converged on the *rodeo* ground, and, enveloped in a great cloud of dust and with hollow bellowings, like the low pedals of a great organ, they began to mill, or turn about a common centre, until gradually quieted by the enveloping cloud of horsemen.
>
> You see a figure dash about at full speed through an apparently impenetrable mass of cattle; the stock becomes uneasy and moves about, gradually beginning the milling process, but the men select the cattle bearing their brand, and course them through the herd; all becomes confusion, and the cattle simply seek to escape from the ever-recurring horsemen. Here one sees the matchless horsemanship of the punchers. Their little ponies, trained to the business, respond to the slightest pressure.
>
> The process of "tailing" is indulged in, although it is a dangerous practice for the man, and reprehensible from its brutality to the cattle. A man will pursue a bull at top speed, will reach over and grasp the tail of the animal, bring it to his saddle, throw his right leg over the tail, and swing his horse suddenly to the left, which throws the bull rolling over and over.

Llaneros of Colombia and Venezuela would also "tail" *(colear)* animals. The practice eventually worked its way into *charreada* or Mexican rodeo.

Roundup in the United States

Anglo ranchers and cowboys adopted the organization of the Hispanic rodeo as well as Spanish conventions for hip brands and earmarks. Cowboys generally branded animals on the left hip where the mark would be visible to an approaching right-handed roper. By 1848 Texas law required that ranchers register their brands with the county clerk. Brand design varied with the creativity and needs of the rancher. Pictographs, letter and number combinations, and plays on words were common. Letters might be tilted off center, denoting brands that were read as tumbling, rocking, flying, running, or lazy.

Anglo ranchers also saw the wisdom of a **stockmen's association.** Regional or statewide stockmen's or livestock associations adjudicated the proceedings, with roundups conducted by superintendents. The bylaws and activities of many stockmen's organizations strongly resembled those of the Mexican *Mesta* (a powerful colonial rancher's group). Livestock associations furthered the interests of big outfits, just as the Mexican Mesta had represented the most powerful *hacendados.*

The Anglo cowboy adopted the vaquero's lasso, but some modified his way of tossing it. The lasso was the cowboy's main tool for working cattle, but Anglos also wielded **quirts** (a corruption of *cuarta de cordón,* meaning horsewhip) to control their horses. Anglos did not use lances, spears, or hocking blades on cattle (although they might use sticks to prod the animals), nor did they tail bulls, except for fun.

Spring roundups came in April or May, depending on how far north the range was located. Given the vastness of the West, roundups could become big affairs. A Wyoming roundup, for instance, held in May 1880 included 150 riders and 1,200 work horses from 18 outfits. On the first day, the hands gathered between 5,000 and 6,000 head. The logistics of such vast operations posed serious problems and stimulated innovation.

Stockmen's associations divided the range into roundup districts, using rivers and creeks as dividing lines. Given the considerable logistics, preparations began weeks in advance. Men from the various outfits gathered at a predetermined point and prepared for the intense 16- to 20-hour workdays. At daybreak circle riders fanned out across miles and miles of often rugged terrain. Cowboys had to be more stubborn and persistent than the cattle they hunted. They combed ravines, bogs, thickets, prairie dog towns, and alkali flats. Hands had to scour all hiding places and drive every animal to the rendezvous.

Cowboys at the rendezvous point had to control thousands of head. Night guards, working two- to four-hour shifts, slowly circled and sang to their bovine charges. A nighthawk watched over the remuda (the herd of spare mounts). Stampedes could happen by day, or worse, by night. Semiwild **longhorns,** trailed north from Texas, were particularly prone to stampeding.

Having assembled the herd, cowboys began cutting out the stock by outfit to be branded and otherwise treated. Cattle on western ranges usually got modest medical attention, a practice uncommon in Latin America.

Records from the Spur Ranch in northwest Texas indicate that roundups absorbed one-fifth of the ranch labor required for the entire year. Extra hands came on board April 1. Equipment repair and other preparation occupied the men until the action began. Roundup superintendents checked to see that hands observed the regulations of the Northwest Texas Stock Raisers Association.

Depending on terrain and visibility, riders rode anywhere from a hundred yards to half a mile apart. Reps (representatives) of other ranches observed the cutting out of strays. Because they represented other outfits, reps were also known as outside men.

Once the cattle were gathered, branding chores began. A skilled roper first "heeled" a calf, catching the animal's hind legs with a loop and dragging it to the "wrestlers." An open fire (or more recently a propane-fueled flame) heated the branding irons. Two wrestlers threw the calf on its side and removed the heeler's rope. The roper reported the brand he spotted on the calf's mother. Another hand burned the appropriate brand into the calf's flank. Some ranchers cut earmarks to help identify an animal when the brand could not be seen in a crowded herd. In the case of most young bulls, castration added the final indignity before the bawling calf was loosed to return to its mother.

On big outfits like the Spur, roundup might take months. After three months, the hands and their horses took a six- to eight-week break. Ranchers tried to avoid working cattle during the very hot summer months when they would lose valuable weight. Range work on the southern plains resumed in September and continued through mid-December.

Roundup in Canada

The vaquero passed his expertise and equipment to the American cowboy, who in turn carried them north to the western Canadian ranges. A good bit of "homegrown" technique also developed in Alberta. Ranchers held Alberta's first roundup in the summer of 1879, and 16 riders gathered some 500 to 600 head near Fort Macleod. This did not represent a very auspicious beginning for Alberta's livestock industry, but the herds and roundups grew larger. Some ranchers gave up and moved their herds back south to Montana, but others held on.

The Canadian ranch calendar resembled that of the northern American ranges. Rancher Fred Ings worked his first roundup at the Bar U Ranche in the spring of 1884. The first general roundup on the Alberta range came the same year. "We adopted pretty much the same system as was carried on across the border," recalled Ings. "Our roundups were community affairs."

Ranchers called a general roundup to brand and castrate calves each spring. Smaller fall sweeps in September collected late calves and removed spring calves from their mothers for weaning. Mature animals were taken from the range for slaughter in the fall. For district and general roundups, a range boss presided, as in the United States.

By 1885 roundups on the Macleod range had increased greatly over the meager return in 1879—100 cowboys, 500 mounts, and 15 chuck wagons gathered in May. Jim Dunlop, from the Cochrane Ranche at Kootenay Lakes, served as roundup captain. The riders gathered about 60,000 head. The operation proved so big as to be unwieldy, and Alberta ranchers turned to smaller district roundups to keep it more manageable. The districts included Fort Macleod, Pincher Creek, Willow Creek, High River, Medicine Hat, Red Deer River, Cypress Hills, and Whitemud River.

Mrs. Lynch-Stauton of Pincher Creek described the frantic roundup routine: "The cowboy's life was a strenuous one while on the round-up; nothing but eat, sleep and ride, ride, ride from start to finish; but through it all he was the most happy-go-lucky individual living, always joking or 'swapping yarns' or 'kidding' someone who had a 'bad actor' to 'wrangle' with in the chilly morning."

Ranchers south of the border formed groups to organize roundups and to promote their interests. In its issue of 1 July 1882, the *Fort Macleod Gazette* expressed hope for "a strong and compact Cattle Association such as is in existence in Montana." Such a group quickly arose, the Western Stock Association. Canadian lease laws favored very large operations. As in the rest of the Americas, extensive outfits dominated the Alberta range.

George Lane, for example, bought the Bar U in southern Alberta in 1904 for $220,000 (Canadian). The ranch included some 1,800 acres of deeded and leased land. About 5,000 cattle and 1,000 horses grazed its ranges. With a spirited program of shorthorn breeding, Lane increased the herd to 25,000 cattle. His cowboys branded up to 8,000 animals during spring roundup.

Roundup Today

Today's roundup reflects some changes. Cowboys now regularly medicate animals. Purebred show or breeding stock might have ear tattoos, chemical marks, or metal tags instead of burned brands. Cattle raised for beef, however, continue to receive brands. Pickups pulling trailers haul cowboys and their mounts to the roundup site. Propane gas might heat the branding irons instead of cow chips or wood, but the sights, smells, and noises of roundup today are strongly reminiscent of the past century.

"The Great West Collection," five videotapes from Atlas Video, provides strong evidence of the continuities of roundups past and present. In *The Working Cowboy* (1989) Ian **Tyson** narrates a look at work life on four ranches in Alberta and British Columbia. Waylon Jennings takes part in a West Texas roundup in the video *My Heroes Have Always Been Cowboys* (1981). Michael Martin **Murphey** leads a tour of four *Great Ranches of the West* (1989). *Ranch Album* (1987) and *The Last Cowboys* (1991) complete the series, offering further looks at roundup and ranch work throughout the West. (See Films, Documentary). (Brado 1984; Breen 1983; Dary 1981; Remington 1961; Slatta 1990; Ward 1958)

ROWEL

Round wheel attached to the back of a **spur**.

RUANA

Heavy woolen **poncho** used in Colombia.

RUNNING IRON

See Rustling.

RUSH

Horse ridden by **B-western** film star Lash LaRue.

RUSSELL, CHARLES MARION
(1864–1926)

Born in St. Louis, Missouri, Charles M. Russell grew up wanting to go west. His family tried to dissuade him by dispatching him to military school and art school, but to no avail. He realized his dream and headed west to Montana in 1880. (Coincidentally, Frederic **Remington** made his first journey west that same year.) Russell worked at a variety of jobs, including hunting, trapping, and cowboying. He also worked at his art, rendering the scenes around him, usually in watercolor, as he worked as a cowboy. During winter layoffs, he sometimes exchanged a painting for food or lodging in town. He also modeled small clay figures, which presaged his later sculptures in bronze.

Russell sometimes drew sketches on letters, some of which have been preserved. In 1886 a Helena, Montana, cattleman asked him for a spring stock report. The horrendous winter had decimated herds on the northern ranges. Russell replied with a sketch he titled "Waiting for a Chinook." The picture (also called "Last of the 5,000") shows a single, gaunt steer with coyotes circling ominously in the background. In 1929 his wife Nancy Russell published a volume of Russell's illustrated letters titled *Good Medicine.*

In his late twenties, Russell concentrated on committing scenes of Montana range life to canvas. By the late 1880s, major eastern magazines were publishing his illustrations. In 1896 Russell met and married 17-year-old Nancy Cooper. He was 39. Thanks to her encouragement, he established a studio in Great Falls, Montana. Nancy's prodding gradually persuaded Russell to spend more time painting and less time drinking. Thanks to the growing eastern fascination with the Old West, Russell successfully sold paintings and illustrations. With Nancy handling finances, his work began fetching higher prices.

Russell traveled a bit but returned to his Great Falls studio, where he spent the remainder of his life. Except for his three-day stint at an art school as a teenager, Russell had no formal training. His flair for the dramatic and the fundamental honesty and realism of his work overshadowed any technical shortcomings.

Russell's paintings and sculpture may be viewed at many major western museums, including the Gilcrease, Stark, Whitney, and Amon Carter. All told, he created more than 2,600 works. Because he knew and lived cowboy life and rendered it with drama, **humor,** and authenticity, Russell became the working cowboy's favorite artist. (McCracken 1957; Russell 1927, 1929; Thrapp 1988)

See also Art of the Cowboy; Appendix B.

Self-portrait of Charles Marion Russell (1899)

RUSTLING

The terms *rustling* and *rustler* had several uses in the Old West. Cowmen referred to cattle and horses that foraged well as rustlers. This meant the animals could graze (rustle up some nourishment) on marginal land. A horse **wrangler** or camp cook might also be called a rustler, but the most widespread and notorious use of the word referred to a cattle thief.

Livestock theft is as old as herding itself, and it occurred on all cattle ranges. In Argentina a rustler was known as a *changador.* In the United States he might be known as a "brand artist" or someone who "threw a big loop." On the vast open ranges of a century ago, rustling could be a serious problem. Rustlers might drive stolen animals a great distance before a rancher even learned he had animals missing.

Gray areas developed as conditions changed on the range. Originally, cowmen accepted the practice of "mavericking," branding and taking ownership of unmarked, motherless calves. An unscrupulous few, however, thought up inventive ways to create **mavericks** at the expense of an honest rancher.

Rustlers or "brand artists" could blot or alter brands. They could also find unscrupulous cattle buyers. Some rustlers simply killed steers, buried the hides, and sold the beef. The vast distances to town (and hence law enforcement) often prompted ranchers to mete out justice themselves. Like horse thieves, rustlers might hang without benefit of trial or jury. (See Violence.)

Most of the cattle grazing was done on open ranges that were federal property. When sheep

Some rustlers wore shoes with horseshoes attached to the bottoms so their footprints could not be tracked.

ranchers began moving in and competing for water and grassland, range wars of great ferocity developed between cattle ranchers and sheep ranchers. Conflict over grazing lands also emerged when barbed wire was introduced and the open range began to be closed off. In Texas the transition was marred by the Fence Cutters' War of 1883 and other lesser outbreaks for about a decade, until the open range was virtually gone.

Court convictions for rustling could be difficult because of the animosity of small ranchers and settlers toward big cattle outfits. As a result, vigilante "justice" handled some accused rustlers. Mob action could be brutal. The *Cheyenne Daily Leader* (13 December 1878) reported the demise of two accused rustlers in Nebraska. The two men were

taken from the sheriff of Custer county and his posse by a mob of armed men, who tied them to a tree and burned them both to death. The mob was composed of twenty-five men nearly all herders and masked.

Cattle barons sometimes organized private protective associations. They also hired stock detectives like Tom **Horn** to hunt down rustlers and others considered a threat. Some ranchers offered drifting cowhands a few meals and a bunk during winter months. They hoped that this charitable practice would keep unemployed cowboys from killing "slow elk" (ranch cattle) in order to survive.

Rustling did not disappear with the open range. In the vastness of today's West, modern rustlers sometimes drive off with a large tractor trailer load of another person's cattle. New electronic and branding technology helps track animals, but there remain dishonest people who want to profit from selling cattle without the bother of raising them. (Hollon 1974; Lamar 1977; McGrath 1984; Slatta 1990; Westermeier 1955)

RYAN, TOM
(1922–)

Artist. See Art of the Cowboy.

SADDLE

The saddle is a concave leather seat held on a horse's back by one or more girths (cinches), straps that run under the animal's belly. The saddle developed over a period of more than 2,500 years. We know it today as the indispensable tool of the working cowboy. While fashion and personal preference certainly entered into saddle design, two main determinants shaped the cowboy's saddle: how he used his lasso and the type of climate and terrain in which he worked.

Asian and European Origins

Experts believe that nomads of the Eurasian steppe, Scythians, built the first saddles in about 700 B.C. The earliest material evidence of a rigid saddle, however, comes from the Han dynasty in China (206 B.C.–220 A.D.).

Early saddles lacked stirrups entirely. The first crude stirrups, which appeared in India late in the second century B.C., held only the big toe. The Chinese engineered the first full-foot stirrup around the fifth century A.D.

The Moors brought stirrups to Europe in about the eighth century, when they conquered the Iberian Peninsula. During the Middle Ages, stirrups led to a new form of warfare: shock combat between two mounted, armored soldiers who charged at each other with long spears (lances). Stirrups enabled these combatants to remain upright in the saddle. Modern stirrups differ very little from their medieval counterparts.

With stirrups a rider could be completely braced by the feet. This leverage freed the arms to wield weapons and increased the force behind a thrown spear. Stirrups enabled a rider to keep his seat on a horse while charging an opponent, throwing a weapon, or shooting an arrow.

Europeans developed several varieties of saddles. The English saddles used progressively lighter construction and materials adapted for specialized functions. Riders still use ultra-lightweight saddles for sporting events such as racing or jumping.

What we know as the western stock saddle developed from a type used in medieval Spain. It has a deep seat and substantial girths to hold it

securely in place while the rider ropes cattle. A sturdy horn provides an anchor for the lasso.

United States and Canada

The construction of saddles, lariats, and other riding gear varied across North and South America. Cowboys everywhere adapted their equipment to the terrain, climate, and tasks at hand. Spanish styles greatly influenced saddles in the United States and Canada.

Many Latin American cowboys could make part or all of their riding tack from rawhide. Artist Frederic S. **Remington** noted that "vaqueros make their own saddles and reatas; only the iron saddle-rings, the rifles, and the knives come from the patron, and where he gets them God alone knows, and the puncher never cares" (*Pony Tracks,* 1895).

Few cowboys in the more industrialized United States and Canada developed these advanced leather-working skills. They depended on specialists in saddle and **tack** making to construct their equipment. Historian Philip Ashton Rollins, in *The Cowboy* (1922), observed that "the American ranchmen's saddles were built by professional manufacturers and not, as commonly in Mexico, by the cowboys themselves."

Cattle roping and other such ranch chores required cowboys to have secure yet maneuverable seats. In stock-seat riding the rider sits erect with legs extending almost straight down. Both reins are held in one hand above the high saddle horn of the heavy western stock saddle.

Saddle makers in the United States gradually made changes in the original Mexican saddles. The western stock saddle went through decades of evolution and variation. The Mother Hubbard, for example, appeared during the late 1860s. It was a style in which a removable cloth covered the saddle; the cantle at the back and pommel at the front projected through holes in this covering.

The placement and number of cinches varied on western saddles. "Single-fire" rigs with just one central cinch traced their lineage most directly to the **vaquero** saddle. This type of saddle is also called a center-fire, California, or single-barreled rig. The Montana or three-quarter rig moves the cinch forward of the center-fire position.

Cowboy Jim Redfern described the types of saddles he saw on a trail drive from Oregon to Wyoming in 1885:

All but one of the saddles I noticed were rim-fire rigs, that is, having both front and rear cinches, as is true of Texas, Montana, and Wyoming rigs. One, however, was a center-fire or so-called Spanish rig, being a single cinch with the cinch well in the middle of the saddle. This rig was common in Oregon and California (Rollinson 1948).

Theodore Dodge *(Harper's Magazine,* July 1891) described the varieties of North American saddles that had developed in a few decades. The cowboy

rides what is well known as the cowboy's saddle, or Brazos tree. It is adapted from the old Spanish saddle.... The line of its seat from cantle to horn, viewed sidewise, is a semicircle; there is no flat place to sit on. This shape gives the cowboy, seen from the side, all but as perpendicular a seat in the saddle as the old knight in armour. There are, of course, other saddles in use. The Texas saddle has a much flatter seat than the Brazos tree; the Cheyenne saddle a still flatter one with a high cantle and a different cut of pommel arch and bearing.

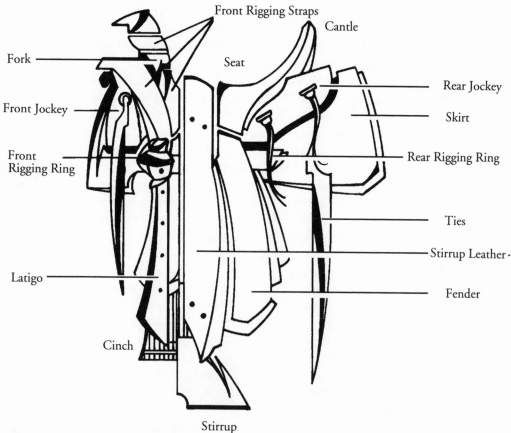

The construction of a cowboy's saddle

Bert Sheppard *(Canadian Cattlemen,* March 1949) of Longview, Alberta, recalled the old double-rigged saddles used by Canadian cowboys during the late nineteenth century. Many old-time saddles were built on "White River trees:"

The cantle boards of these trees were fairly high and sloped back with the top of the cantle beveled back. The bars were thinner than those in the present-day saddles. Occasionally a tree would break across the bars. The forks were fairly high and sloped

This leather saddle, on display at the Colorado State Museum in Denver, is typical of the indispensable saddle of the western plains. It has a deep seat, a high sturdy horn, stirrups, and a woven girth.

ahead a little. Also, the horn was high enough so that the hand could hook around it solidly when climbing on a bronc. The old saddles had very little leather in the seat and were built to tip a rider into the middle of the saddle.

Mexico and Hawaii

New Spain (Mexico) evolved two riding traditions and thus two main types of saddles. The *charro* tradition of the rich elite and the **vaquero** tradition of the poor working cowhand developed side by side.

Wealthy riders used *la silla charra* (charro saddle), heavy and richly ornamented. Finely tooled leather and rich silver trim embellished these imposing equestrian works of art. Scalloped silver rosettes (*conchas*, anglicized to conchos) held in place the many leather tie strings used to attach things to the saddle. Silver chains and coins decorated the breastband that kept the saddle from slipping backwards. Ostentation, power, and status radiated from the charro saddle.

The rider nestled deeply into the saddle between a high *lomillo* (cantle) and large horn. Elaborate charro saddles might also have fenders *(rosaderos* or *sudaderos)*, a broad piece of leather that fit between the inside of the rider's legs and the horse's sides.

La silla vaquera, the early vaquero saddle, consisted of a rather crude, light, rawhide-covered wooden tree. It featured a small horn and large wooden stirrups. The whole affair was lashed together with leather thongs and held in place by a single cinch. Leather straps called *latigos* (anglicized to larigos) held the saddle rigging to the cinch.

Over time, the vaquero saddle became larger and sturdier because vaqueros used the saddle horn to anchor a **rope.** Vaqueros were "dally men," meaning they wound the rope around the horn in winch-like fashion, using the horn to lever the rope and letting out slack as needed to play an animal. The term *dally* is a corrupted form of the Spanish phrase *dar la vuelta*, meaning to take a turn around the horn.

Frederic Remington *(Pony Tracks*, 1895) criticized the vaquero saddle and riding **tack:**

The Mexican punchers all use the 'ring bit,' and it is a fearful contrivance. Their saddle-trees are very short, and straight and quite as shapeless as a 'sawbuck pack-saddle.' The horn is as big as a dinner plate, and taken altogether it is inferior to the California tree. It is very hard on horses' backs, and not at all comfortable for a rider who is not accustomed to it.

Simple, functional vaquero equipment lacked rich design and materials. Over time, vaqueros developed a more comfortable, serviceable platform by adding a leather covering with built-in saddlebags, the *mochila* saddle. It provided greater comfort than the traditional thin, hard, rawhide model.

During the brief days of the Pony Express (1860–1862), riders used this rig. The mochila, filled with mail, could be moved quickly from the saddle of one mount to the next. The Pony Express mochila had three locked pockets. A fourth, the way pocket, could be accessed at any station.

For work in the thorny brush country, vaqueros added leather coverings that protected the feet by hanging over and below the stirrups. Mexican riders called these shields *tapaderas*, or in Spanish California, *tapaderos*. "Taps" also prevented the foot from sliding all the way through the stirrup. A vaquero riding with tapaderas could not get his foot hung in the stirrup and be dragged by his horse. Shapes and sizes varied. The monkey nose tap, for example, had a short, turned-up front.

Hawaii's cowboys inherited the vaquero saddle but put their own special stamp on it. Vaqueros brought the mochila saddle with them to the islands from Spanish California in the 1830s. Hawaiians, like **llaneros,** kept their saddle *(noho lio)* very light. Both had to ride and work in rainy, tropical climates. Although relatively lightweight, the paniolo saddle had a substantial, strong horn. Like his vaquero teacher, the paniolo was a dally man, so he needed a good saddle horn.

Hawaiians added a distinctive island touch to the mochila, which they called the *lala*. They tooled the leather covering with richly embellished floral designs. The paniolo saddle also retained the Mexican tapaderas. Short, bucket-shaped "bull-dog taps" offered protection when working in rough brush country. "Mule-ear taps," 8 to 12 inches long, more closely resembled the original Mexican model. These large taps protected the rider's legs and gave the saddle an eye-catching flourish.

Argentina, Uruguay, and Chile

Gauchos of the Río de la Plata used a flat saddle *(recado)* that consisted of seven or more different layers. The saddle was comfortable and well adapted to the flat **pampas**. British traveler William MacCann *(Two Thousand Miles' Ride through the Argentine Provinces,* 1853) well described the gaucho's multilayered saddle:

First a large sheepskin placed on the horse, then a woollen rug neatly folded, which serves the rider for a blanket; on this was laid a covering of untanned dry hide for the purpose of keeping off the rain; next came a woollen quilt made for such purposes in Yorkshire, with long tassels hanging from the corners: this was carefully folded, and on it was laid a piece of leather, sufficiently large to protect the whole from damp or rain, its end and sides were neatly stamped with an ornamental border: these coverings answer to the English saddle cloth. Then came what may be termed the saddle-tree, from which the stirrups are suspended, and made of strong leather and wood, forming the basis of a flat seat, although curved a little to suit the back of the horse. The entire of this furniture was secured by a large girth of raw hide, twelve or fourteen inches wide. The saddle is covered, for the sake of ease and comfort, also to serve for a pillow at night, with a sheep-skin, having the wool on....

Upon this is placed a flat covering, somewhat similar to the fringed woollen mats laid at drawingroom doors in England, and over that a piece of thin soft leather, forming the seat of the rider; the whole is again secured to the horse by an ornamental leather girth.

Gauchos used tiny round wooden stirrups. Usually riding barefoot or wearing open-toed soft boots, they inserted only the big toe into the stirrups. Years of riding in this fashion enlarged and deformed the big toes into talon-like claws. Bowlegged, with deformed toes, the gaucho found walking difficult as well as distasteful.

Chilean *huasos* used similar voluminous, multilayered saddles. Riders in both Chile and Argentina wore large **spurs**, made of silver for the rich and of iron for the poor. The huaso used very large stirrups in place of the small wooden toe rings favored by the gaucho.

Sir Francis Bond Head *(Rough Notes,* 1826) rode across the pampas several times in the 1820s. He contrasted equipment used by huasos and gauchos: "The spurs of the peons [in Chile] were bad, and their stirrups the most heavy, awkward things imaginable. They were cut out of solid wood, and were altogether different from the neat little triangle which just holds the great toe of the gaucho of the Pampas."

Venezuela and Colombia

The llanero's ultralight saddle was well suited to tropical heat and rain. It often had no horn to anchor a rope. Instead the llanero might tie the lariat to his horse's tail.

Like gauchos, llaneros used toe stirrups so they could dismount quickly in case a horse stumbled. In place of the flat, plump gaucho saddle, however, the llanero favored a high-backed, wedge-shaped seat. Scottish writer Robert B. Cunninghame Graham *(José Antonio Páez,* 1929), always an expert witness on matters of horsemanship, described the llanero saddle as

a sort of compromise between the Argentine 'recao' and the high peaked, high cantled saddle of the Mexicans. That is to say it has a horn, usually made of brass, but more for ornament than use. The cantle is almost as high as the cantle of the Western cowboy's saddle. The stirrups are small, and made to be used either bare-footed, or with the alpargatas [sandals] that the Llaneros all affect. Underneath the stirrups is a wedge-shaped prolongation to make it hang more steadily.

(Ahlhorn 1980; Beatie 1982; Carmichael 1949; Martin 1987; Rollinson 1948; Rossi 1966; Slatta 1990, 1992; Ward 1987)

See also Bit; Tack.

SADDLE BLANKET

Blanket placed on a horse's back as protection against the **saddle**.

SADDLE BRONC RIDING

See Rodeo Events.

SADDLE SLICKER

Also saddle stiff, saddle warmer—terms for cowboy.

SAGEBRUSH MEN

Cowboys working in the arid portions of Montana, Colorado, and Wyoming.

SAINT ELMO'S FIRE

Also known as fox fire, Saint Elmo's fire is an electrical discharge that produces an eerie, luminous blue light. This odd phenomenon most often occurs during weather disturbances, such as storms that include thunder, dust, or snow.

Fox fire has been seen during stormy nights playing off church steeples, ship masts, airplane wing tips, and even on mounted cowboys and cattle horns. Sailors in the Mediterranean deemed the light a sign of protection sent by Saint Elmo, their patron saint. Religious tradition identifies the figure with Spanish Dominican Saint Peter González (circa 1190–1246).

Cowboys most often saw Saint Elmo's fire when trailing cattle at night. Several hands who cowboyed at the Chapman-Barnard Ranch in Oklahoma during the 1940s remembered an odd light show. Raisins Rhoads saw the awesome beauty of the luminous blue lights on night drive:

> We was getting in a whole bunch of **King Ranch** Brahmers. And we was just starting to leave, and [we saw] all of that lightning playing across them horns. I never seen it but once or twice in my life, but that was the prettiest thing I ever seen in my life. And the most scariest. They try to make that happen in the movies, you know, show across there. It don't look right.

(Microsoft *Encarta* 1994; Ronda and Slatta 1993)

SALADERO

See Beef Cattle Industry; *Vaquería*.

SALOONS

Many Americans north and south drank great quantities of liquor during the eighteenth and nineteenth centuries. North American colonists favored rum and homemade whiskey. Drinking likely increased in the nineteenth century. Saloons and their main product, alcohol, became main targets of religiously motivated social reformers.

American West

Like sailors home from the sea, cowboys engaged in spree drinking when they got the infrequent opportunity. The completion of a long **trail drive** or **roundup** and branding season provided opportunities. Cowboys' drinking bouts were separated by long dry periods, however. Liquor was often unavailable outside of towns, and some ranchers insisted on sobriety on the ranch.

American social critics identified vagrancy, idleness, and tavern-going as vices associated with the "unworthy" poor. While spree drinking was pardoned, if not entirely condoned, no working cowboy or **vaquero** could afford (in monetary or social terms) to idle away very much time at the cantina.

In the American West, cowboys favored whiskey—bourbon, rye, or corn—which they generically termed "bitters." (Beer enjoyed great popularity toward the end of the nineteenth century as breweries moved into the West.) Texas cowboys referred to whiskey as "Kansas sheep-dip" in honor of the cow towns where they quaffed drinks at the end of a trail drive. Cowboys called very strong whiskey a "Brigham Young cocktail." As the saying went, "One sip and you're a confirmed polygamist." Other colloquial names for liquor included tornado juice, coffin varnish, mountain dew, redeye, red ink, snake poison, and tanglefoot.

Some cattle-country saloons became infamous. Violence at the original Bucket of Blood Saloon, owned by Shorty Young in Havre, Montana, led cowboys to apply the term to any tough whiskey mill. A Canadian cowboy, T. H. Whitney, visiting Havre in 1906 watched two cowboys ride their horses into the Dew Drop Inn; they "claimed they thought it was a modern feed barn" (Canadian Cattlemen, June 1939). At "hurdy-gurdy" houses, lonesome cowboys could spend time with the house women for a dollar per dance.

Much of the negative imagery of the cowboy as a drunken hell-raiser came from the cow towns of Kansas. After months of hard work on a trail drive without liquor, women, or entertainment, many trail hands did go "on a tear." Cattle towns obliged the hands by providing a wide range of entertainment to separate the cowboy from his pay. Letting off steam at the end of a long cattle drive, cowboys could cause quite a commotion.

Western saloons segregated customers by both class and race, a circumstance not unique to the cattle frontier. Racial segregation excluded Chinese, discriminated against Hispanics, and isolated blacks in separate establishments. The same class and racial divisions that cut through society in general also occurred in western whiskey mills.

Prices charged for beverages effectively segregated western saloons by social class. Denver saloons charged from five to 25 cents for a mug of beer. Cattlemen, buyers, and other businessmen gathered at fancier bars in hotels. Cowboys and others with little money gathered at the cheap saloons.

Latin America

Spanish culture condemned excessive drinking. To hurl the epithet "drunkard" was to lodge an extreme insult. Spanish American culture, however, permitted ritualized drunkenness during special festivals. According to one observer, Nathaniel Holmes Bishop, in The Pampas and the Andes (1883), "Feast days are strictly kept by the gauchos in their own peculiar way," which meant accompanied by much drinking.

Llaneros of Venezuela and Colombia favored aguardiente, a fiery rum, but the tropical llanos yielded a range of alcoholic beverages, including guarapo, made from sugarcane. Palm wine and chicha, a beverage fermented from maize like the pulque of Mexico, could also be found. The remoteness of the llanos meant that imported drink was less common than in either the American West or Argentina.

European travelers on the Argentine pampas formed unflattering portraits of the gauchos. Foreigners sometimes assumed that all gauchos did was lounge, drink, gamble, and fight at pulperías. These hybrid general stores and taverns dotted the plains and occupied many street corners in town. Similar small establishments operated all over Latin America.

Police records are rife with charges of knife fights and other violence at pulperías. In his fine gaucho novel, Don Segundo Sombra (1926), Argentine author Ricardo Güiraldes described a typical country tavern of the pampas:

It was a single building, rectangular-shaped; the taproom was an open room on the right with benches where we sat side by side like swallows on a wire. The store-keeper handed out the drinks through a heavy iron grating that caged him in with tiers of brightly labeled bottles, flasks, and jugs of every kind. Skin sacks of mate leaf, demijohns of liquor, different-shaped barrels, saddles, blankets, horse pads, lassos, covered the floor.

Gauchos in Argentina drank *caña* (a rum distilled from sugarcane juice) or gin at the pulpería. *Pulperos* (owners of pulperías) also sold other beverages. Scottish writer Robert B. Cunninghame Graham *(South American Sketches,* 1978) recalled a pulpería where "vermouth, absinthe, squarefaced gin, Carlon, and *vino seco* stand in a row, with a barrel of Brazilian caña, on the top of which the pulpero ostentatiously parades his pistol and his knife."

Mexico produced a variety of spirits, many of which crossed the border into the United States. Vaqueros visiting a cantina would imbibe tequila or *mezcal* (anglicized to mescal or mascal). Mexicans have long distilled both of these potent liquors from the agave or century plant. (Tequila is redistilled mescal.)

The use of alcohol remains a concern for Mexican traditionalists who participate in *charreada,* Mexican **rodeo.** Alcohol is served at rodeos, and prominent breweries and distilleries sponsor competitions. In her excellent study entitled *Charrería Mexicana* (1993), Kathleen Mullen Sands explains the basis for the concern:

> Drunkenness by a **charro** violates the gentlemanly code of behavior of charrería. A charro, or for that matter a charra (female competitor), who appears drunk in costume, whether at a competition or a social event, may be the subject of association sanctions.

Viewing cowboys at saloons, rather than at work in the saddle, caused many observers to draw unjustly negative conclusions about their character and way of life. For most cowhands, idling and drinking at saloons represented only a tiny, if highly visible, part of their lives. Like many elements of cowboy life, the amount of time spent "hellin' 'round town" became exaggerated and romanticized.   (Abbott

and Smith 1955; Erdoes 1969; Noel 1982; Slatta 1990)

SALT HORSE

Colloquial term for corned beef.

SAND

Colloquial term for grit, courage.

SANDALS

See *Bota de Potro;* Huaraches.

SANDOZ, MARI
(1896–1966)

Historian, novelist, and author of *The Cattlemen* (1958). See Historiography of the Cowboy.

SANTEE, ROSS
(1889–1965)

Born in Thornburg, Iowa, of Swedish parents, writer/artist Ross Santee showed an early aptitude for art. In his late teens he enrolled at the Chicago Art Institute, where he studied for four years. He left the institute in 1910 and spent five years trying to make a living as a cartoonist in New York. His efforts yielded little in the way of income or satisfaction. In 1915 he headed west to work on his uncle's ranch in Globe, Arizona, beginning at the bottom as a horse **wrangler.**

Santee continued to sketch, using his Arizona surroundings for models. He sold some to the *St. Louis Post-Dispatch* in 1917. During World War I, he served a one-year hitch in the army in Texas. After being discharged, he sold some sketches to magazines in New York. One editor asked him to write a short story to accompany the sketches. This first story, "Horse Trading," marked the beginning of his long, successful writing career. His first book, *Men and Horses,* appeared in 1926. Santee later wrote more than a dozen books and provided illustrations for 60 more written by other authors.

Santee's writing provides an accurate portrayal of cowboy life-style and language in the early twentieth century, after the end of the open range. *Cowboy* appeared in 1928, and folklorist J. Frank **Dobie** found much to admire in the book, which he termed "the best story of the making of a cowboy yet written."

In *Cowboy* Santee conveyed much about cowboy life, including cuisine. "The meals never varied much. We had steak an' eggs or salt pork for breakfast, hot bakin'-powder biscuits, frijole beans an' lick. Sometimes we had potatoes, an' there was always some kind of fruit—mostly dried peaches or apricots, for the outfit was burnt out on prunes."

Santee often told his short stories from the point of view of characters who were experienced hands. In many books, the veterans tell their tales to Santee, an inexperienced wrangler, who serves as a peripheral character.

Santee continued to work as a wrangler for several years. He also served as editor for the Arizona branch of the Federal Writers Program of the Works Progress Administration (WPA) from 1936 to 1941.

Santee rendered the great bulk of his art in black-and-white sketches. He continued to evolve as an artist, however, selling his first oil painting after he had turned 70. Santee died in the town where he had lived much of his life, Globe, Arizona. (Santee 1953, 1977; Thrapp 1988)

—*Nils E. Mikkelsen*

SARMIENTO, DOMINGO FAUSTINO
(1811–1888)

A liberal Argentine intellectual, writer Domingo F. Sarmiento gained political prominence after being exiled in 1840 by dictator Juan Manuel de Rosas. Living in Chile, he wrote anti-Rosas tracts. In 1845 he published his most famous book, *Facundo*. Mary Mann, wife of educator Horace Mann, translated the book into English as *Life in the Argentine Republic in the Days of the Tyrants; or Civilization and Barbarism* (1868).

Sarmiento divided Argentina into two camps based on geographical and racial differences. He represented the white, urban European sector seeking to bring civilization and modernity to the nation. On the other hand, Rosas, Facundo Quiroga, and other caudillos (military

strongmen), along with their **gaucho** hordes, represented nonwhite, rural barbarism. This powerful dichotomy shaped the Argentine self-image. It also influenced many Latin American leaders to promote and exalt European immigration and culture in order to uplift what they perceived to be the ignorant nonwhite rural masses.

Sarmiento considered the gaucho a force of reaction and barbarism. In 1861 he instructed one of his generals: "Do not try to spare the blood of gauchos. It is a contribution that the country needs. Blood is the only thing they have in common with human beings."

Despite his low opinion of the gaucho, Sarmiento devoted some of *Facundo* to describing their special skills. In chapter two he describes the skills of the tracker *(rastreador)*, guide *(baqueano)*, and minstrel *(payador)*. He also includes a fourth gaucho type, however, the outlaw *(matrero)*.

Sarmiento aided in the fight that overthrew Rosas in 1852. He himself entered politics and won the presidency in 1868. Sarmiento worked hard on behalf of public education and the promotion of European immigration. Ultimately, however, the Europeanist agenda of Sarmiento and his fellow liberals failed to bring the hoped-for social regeneration. Twentieth-century Argentina descended into horrific political and social divisions, and this time national leaders could not blame the gaucho, for he had already been effectively t amed and marginalized. (Sarmiento 1971; Slatta 1992)

See also Gauchesco.

SAVAGE, WILLIAM W., JR.

Historian. See Historiography of the Cowboy.

SAVAGE

Colloquial term for a cowboy who works at a **dude ranch.**

SAVVY

Corruption of the Spanish word *sabe,* meaning to know or understand. Anglo cowboys appropriated this and many other Spanish words. "Do you savvy?" means "Do you understand?"

SCAB HERDER

Derogatory term for sheepherder.

SCAMPER JUICE

Colloquial term for whiskey.

SCHAEFER, JACK WARNER

(1907–1991)

Born in Cleveland, Ohio, novelist Jack W. Schaefer grew up with his parents' appreciation for books. He graduated from Oberlin College in 1929 with a concentration in the classics and creative writing. He went on to Columbia University for graduate study but left after a year to pursue a career in journalism. Starting as a reporter for United Press in 1931, he later worked as editor or associate editor for several major newspapers. In 1949 Schaefer left journalism for a career as a free-lance writer.

Journalism's loss quickly became western literature's gain. Schaefer's first book, *Shane* (1949), established him as a first-rate western author. He based the novel on one of his previous short stories. Both the book and the Paramount film (1953) have become American classics.

Schaefer had never been west of Toledo, Ohio, when he wrote *Shane,* but he moved to Santa Fe, New Mexico, in 1953. That same year he published a collection of short stories, *The Big Range,* and his second novel, *The Canyon,* about a Cheyenne warrior's spiritual quest. Five more Schaefer stories became films, but the 1957 screenplay *Trooper Hook* marked his last formal involvement with Hollywood. His fine 1963 novel, *Monte Walsh,* became a motion picture starring Lee Marvin, without Schaefer's direct participation.

Schaefer set many of his early works in Wyoming Territory, but moved later plots to his adopted state of residence, New Mexico. While Schaefer enjoyed critical success and a popular following, he did not write a best-seller. His later stories reflect a stronger concern for historical accuracy, often depicting the tension between legality and justice. (Tuska and Piekarski 1983, 1984)

See also Films, Cowboy.

—*Stephen C. Keadey*

SCHOONOVER, FRANK

(1877–1972)

Artist. See Art of the Cowboy.

SCHREYVOGEL, CHARLES

(1861–1912)

Artist. See Art of the Cowboy.

SCORCHER

Colloquial term for branding iron or hot day.

SCOTT, ALEXANDER LESLIE

(1893–1974)

Novelist who wrote formula westerns under various names.

SCOTT, RANDOLPH

(1903–1987)

B-western film actor.

SCOUT

Tonto's horse in "The Lone Ranger."

SCRATCH

Colloquial term for spurring a horse. See Rodeo Events.

SCULPTURE

See Art of the Cowboy.

SEAGO

From Spanish *soga,* a loosely twisted hemp **rope**.

THE SEARCHERS

Film (1956). See Wayne, John.

SEEMANN, CHARLIE

Folklorist. See Music; Musicology.

SEGUNDO

Straw boss or second-in-command, as on a **trail drive**.

SELTZER, CHARLES ALDEN

(1875–1942)

Wisconsin-born author of formula westerns.

SELTZER, OLAF CARL

(1877–1957)

Painter. See Art of the Cowboy.

SERAPE

Also sarape; a **poncho**, shawl-like blanket, or mantle worn by **vaqueros.**

SERTÃO

Dry **plains** of northeastern Brazilian. See *Vaqueiro.*

SHANE

Novel (1949) by Jack W. **Schaefer** and film (1953) starring Alan Ladd. See Films, Best Cowboy.

SHANK

Extension on the back of a **spur** to hold the rowel.

SHAVETAIL

Horse whose tail has been cut, often used to indicate a broken mount.

SHAWNEE TRAIL

See Trail Drive.

SHEEPHERDER'S DELIGHT

Colloquial term for cheap whiskey.

SHIRREFFS, GORDON DONALD

(1914–)

Chicago-born author of western novels.

SHOOTIN' IRON

Colloquial term for six-gun. See Firearms.

THE SHOOTIST

Film (1976). See Wayne, John.

SHOP-MADES

See Boots.

SHORT, LUKE

Pseudonym for Frederick Dilley **Glidden.** See Pulp Novels.

SHORT HORSE

Another term for the American **quarter horse.**

SHORTHORN CATTLE

See Cattle Breeds.

SHOTGUN CHAPS

See Chaps.

SHOVE IN THE STEEL

Colloquial term meaning to **spur** a horse.

SILK

Colloquial term for barbed wire. See Fencing.

SILVER, NICHOLAS

One of the pseudonyms used by Frederick **Faust.**

SILVER

Name of movie horses ridden by Buck Jones and the Lone Ranger.

SILVER KING

Famous horse ridden by silent movie star Fred Thomson.

SILVERHEELS, JAY

Native American actor who played the character Tonto on "The Lone Ranger." See Television.

SING

The hissing noise made by a thrown **rope**.

SINGIN' TO 'EM
Riding night guard on a herd. See Music.

SINGLE STEER TYING
See Rodeo Events.

SINGLE-FIRE RIG
Also single-barreled saddle. See Saddle.

SINKER
Colloquial term for biscuit.

SIOUX
See Indians as Cowboys.

SIRINGO, CHARLES ANGELO
(1855–1928)
Born in a settlement of a dozen or so houses in Matagordo County, Texas, author Charles Siringo spent nearly his entire life on the frontier. He became a cowboy at age 11 and remained one until he was 26. He punched cattle for Abel Head ("Shanghai") Pierce at the Rancho Grande during the spring of 1871.

In 1874 the young cowboy helped push a herd north up the Chisholm Trail. He traveled throughout the Southwest, gaining the experiences that would fuel his writing. Siringo then served in the Pinkerton National Detective Agency for 22 years, and these experiences also provided material for his later writings.

Siringo published the first cowboy autobiography, *A Texas Cow-boy or Fifteen Years on the Hurricane Deck of a Spanish Pony*, in 1885. His memoirs, which accurately reflect real incidents of real cowboy life, rang true. The book became very popular with the public and was reprinted several times. Siringo's pioneering memoirs spawned a host of imitators, some good, but many very bad. He went on to publish several more books, many based on his adventures as a cowboy or detective.

Siringo is considered to be among the most honest of the cowboy writers. His books are largely autobiographical and his love of the frontier suffuses them. He painted a vivid picture of the cowboy life he loved. Siringo's works focused on cowboys and bad men, two groups with whom he had contact and empathy. Siringo set much of his life to print. According to folklorist J. Frank **Dobie,** "No other cowboy ever talked about himself so much in print; few had so much to talk about."

Siringo earned a reputation as being brave, cool-headed, and resourceful, traits useful to a cowboy or a detective. After leaving the Pinkerton Agency he spent the remainder of his life in New Mexico and California. He died in Hollywood. His other books include *A Cowboy Detective* (1912), *A Lone Star Cowboy* (1919), and *Riata and Spurs* (1927). (Dobie 1952; Pingenot 1989; Sawey 1981; Siringo 1979)

See also Autobiographies by Cowboys.
—*Nils E. Mikkelsen*

SIX-GUN
Also six-shooter—a six-shot revolver. See Colt Firearms; Firearms.

SIX-SHOOTER COFFEE
Colloquial term for strong cow camp **coffee.**

SKIM-MILK COWBOY
Duded-up tenderfoot.

SKIN STRING
Colloquial for a rawhide **rope,** or reata.

SKUNK EGGS
Descriptive colloquialism for onions.

"SKY KING"
See Television.

SLICK WESTERNS
Popular westerns printed on smooth paper. While the paper was superior to that used for pulp fiction, the literary quality was often the same. See Pulp Novels.

SLICKER
The cowboy's yellow oilskin raincoat, which he calls a "fish."

SLOW ELK
Also big antelope—colloquial terms for cattle poached by hungry, unemployed cowboys.

SLYE, LEONARD FRANKLIN
See Rogers, Roy.

SMITH, GIBBS M.
(1940–)
Gibbs M. Smith is a leading and very creative publisher of books about cowboy culture. His Peregrine Smith Books catalog is a wonderful sampler of today's cowboy culture. You will find beautifully produced, interesting books, book/audiotape combinations, notecards, and more.

"Our publishing tastes," says Smith, "are varied and eclectic. We care deeply about the books we publish; they are extensions of ourselves and our interests." Smith's interests include oil painting, horseback riding, and enjoying and preserving nature. Smith's fall 1993 catalog includes works on Southwest art, architecture, Indian blankets, nature, ecology, travel, and cookbooks. You will also find **poetry, music, humor,** furniture, and, of course, cowboy culture.

"We are especially pleased," says Smith, "to publish these books that celebrate and expand the western style." Smith publishes about 30 titles per year. He considers his operation "an alternative to the New York scene for authors of high quality books."

Smith is an author as well as a publisher. His first book, *Joe Hill,* appeared in 1970. Smith had completed his undergraduate education at the University of Utah and did graduate work at the University of California, Santa Barbara. He founded his publishing company in California in 1969. Four years later, he moved the operation to Layton, Utah. Appropriate to his interests and individualism, Smith's company operates from a remodeled barn built in 1916.

In 1985 Smith published *Cowboy Poetry: A Gathering.* The sampler, edited by Hal Cannon, covers cowboy poetry, old and new. The compact book fits nicely into the pocket of a pair of jeans or a jacket, and the small size makes it accessible anytime, anywhere.

The Hal Cannon/Gibbs Smith collaboration is natural. Both play important roles in the Western Folklife Center, which hosts the Elko Cowboy Poetry Gatherings. Smith has also published several other volumes of cowboy poetry and song.

Among these is *Old-Time Cowboy Songs* (1988), a creative songbook/audiotape combination. The book features music and words to about 50 traditional songs, while the audiotape includes ten foot-tapping renditions by the Bunkhouse Orchestra. Hal Cannon plays and sings with the group. He also edited the book, which, like the poetry volumes, is small enough to tuck into a pocket.

Each book has a unique twist. One, *Cowboy Poetry Cookbook* (1992), mixes delicious range recipes, delightful poems, and captivating illustrations. Smith published a well-illustrated, highly informative book about the popular group **Riders in the Sky** (1992). It includes songs, cartoons, black-and-white and color photographs, and a hearty dose of the cowboy humor that makes Too Slim, Ranger Doug, and Woody Paul so popular.

Many of Smith's publications examine cowboy material culture. *Cowboy High Style* (1992), by Elizabeth Clair Flood, is a beautifully produced hardcover book full of color photographs. The first portion of the book surveys the distinctive western furniture made by Thomas Molesworth (1890–1977) of Cody, Wyoming. Later chapters show the styles of many contemporary makers of furniture and accessories. Whether you are furnishing a dream log cabin or just want to "window shop," you'll spend many contented hours browsing through this book.

The Cowboy Boot Book (1992) features a lively, informative text by Tyler Beard. Jim Arndt's attractive colorful photographs illustrate the volume, which includes **boot** history, fitting, factories, boot makers, collectors, and more. Beard followed up in 1993 with *One Hundred*

Years of Western Wear, again with photographs by Jim Arndt.

Not to overlook cowboy **film** and music, Smith's 1993 list also included *Silver Screen Cowboys* and *Hollywood Cowboy Heroes,* both by Robert Phillips. The latter is an oversized book that includes eight color movie posters. *The Insider's Country Music Handbook* (written by Country Joe Flint and Judy Nelson) is a valuable 550-page compendium of useful facts about country singing stars.

Smith "believes that the very best forces of culture are propagated through the sharing of books."

Address: P.O. Box 667, Layton, Utah 84041; tel. 801-544-9800; toll-free orders, 800-421-8714.

SMITH, HELENA HUNTINGTON

See Autobiographies by Cowboys.

SMOKE POLE

Also smoke wagon; colloquial terms for a six-gun.

SNAFFLE BIT

See Bit.

SNAKE-HEAD WHISKEY

Also snake poison or snake water—cheap, crude liquor such as might have been sold to Indians.

SNAPPIN' BRONCS

Colloquial term for breaking wild horses. See Bronc Buster.

SNOW, CHARLES HORACE
(1877–1967)

Novelist who wrote formula westerns, especially popular in Great Britain.

SODBUSTER

Derogatory term for farmer.

SOFT-HORN

A tenderfoot, someone new to the West.

SOILED DOVE

Colloquialism for prostitute.

SOMBRERO

Wide-brimmed Spanish or Mexican **hat.**

SONGS

See Music.

SON-OF-A-BITCH STEW

Also son-of-a-gun stew. See Food.

SONS OF THE PIONEERS

See Rogers, Roy.

SOOGAN

Also sougan and sugan—a heavy, tightly woven blanket.

SORTIJA

See Equestrian Games.

SOURDOUGH

Colloquial term meaning a cook or a bachelor.

SPADE BIT

See Bit.

SPAGHETTI WESTERNS

See Eastwood, Clint.

SPANISH BIT

Also Spanish spade bit. See Bit.

SPANISH FEVER

Also Texas fever. See Stockmen's Association.

SPANISH PONY

See Horses.

SPANISH RIG

See Saddle.

SPANISH-AMERICAN WAR

See Roosevelt, Theodore.

SPAULDING, DON
(1926–)

Artist. See Art of the Cowboy.

SPENCER, TIM

Singer in Sons of the Pioneers. See Rogers, Roy.

SPINNER

A bucking horse that turns in tight circles. See Rodeo Events.

SPLIT-EAR BRIDLE

See Tack.

SPURS

The Chinese probably first invented spurs several thousand years ago. In western culture, horsemen have used spurs since at least the days of the Greek general Xenophon (430–355 B.C.) and possibly as long ago as 700 B.C. Spurs gained greater significance during the Middle Ages. After proving his mettle and worth, a brave, chivalrous knight "won his spurs," golden ones at that.

In *Western Words* (1968), Ramon F. Adams gives us some idea of the varieties of spurs by listing numerous synonyms. Cowboys might call their spurs can openers, grapplin' irons, gut hooks, gut lancers, gut wrenches, hellrousers, hooks, petmakers, or rib wrenches. Cowboys always rode and usually walked with some type of spurs in place.

Vaqueros would call their spurs *espuelas.* Many terms describing types of spurs *(mariscos, marineros, lloronas)* reflect the importance of the Spanish heritage in the development of spurs.

Many people hold the misconception that cowboys use spurs to brutally dig into the sides of horses. Nothing could be farther from the truth. The competent rider needs only to gently nudge the horse's side to achieve the desired result. In fact, in order to prevent injury to their horses, many cowboys file down the rowels on new spurs. No skilled cowboy wants a "buzz saw," a spur with long, sharp points.

Old-time Latin American cowboys, working with only partially tamed horses, might draw blood with their spurs. Horses were cheap and expendable, so **bronc busters** used brute force, not finesse. As horses became more expensive, Latin American riders adopted gentler taming methods.

The spur consists of three main parts: the knob (also called the chap hook), the shank, and the rowel. In addition, the spur button and the heel band keep the main parts attached to the boot. The shank is a solid shaft extending out from the heel of the boot. The rowel is the rotating part of the spur attached to the end of the shank. Knobs along the shank serve to prevent clothing from becoming entangled in the rowel.

Spurs vary both by the type of shank and the rowel. Shanks can extend straight back from the heel or bend up or down. The term *drop* refers to the amount of bend down in the shank. Some spurs, such as the "gal leg" and the "gooseneck," got their names from the shape of their shanks. California drag rowels received their name because the drop in the shank caused the rowel to drag in the dirt when the wearer walked.

The wheel or rowel has as many or more variations than the shanks. It can have many or few points, and the length of the points depends upon the wearer's preferences. Generally, the larger the number of points, the less likely the rowel would injure the horse.

Chihuahuas and Kelly's represent two better known types of spurs. The original Chihuahuas, named for the north Mexican state, possessed elaborate silver inlays and designs. Pascal Moreland Kelly (1886–1976) worked to address the complaints about earlier spurs. Kelly's became synonymous with superior spurs. Certainly Kelly never produced any "tin-bellies" (cheap, inferior spurs).

Many cowboys liked to attach jinglebobs (danglers) to their spurs. These small pendants did no more than make a noise that riders found pleasing. Heel chains often served the same purpose. Locked spurs helped keep the rider in the saddle under almost any circumstances. This procedure involved immobilizing the rowel so it could not turn, which allowed the rider to dig in and hold on. Of course, any man that cared about his horse tangled the spurs in something other than the horse's flesh.

Jane Pattie traced the variety and craftsmanship of spur making. Her book, *Cowboy Spurs and Their Makers* (1991), covers the history and techniques of spur making and describes many spur makers. Pattie interviewed many old-time spur makers between 1969 and 1988. The bulk of the text consists of five- to ten-page biographies of these people. Like many western art forms, spur making seems in danger of dying out. All of the spur makers that Pattie interviewed had died by the time the book was released.

Other workers also wear special **boots,** unusual **hats,** and other distinctive garb. Only horsemen wear spurs, and the cowboy is the quintessential horseman. As magazine ads for "Marlboro Mediums" cigarettes attest, spurs and other "horse jewelry" remain powerful (and marketable) American icons. (Adams 1968; Pattie 1991; Ward 1958)

—*Mark Mayer*

SQUEEZE THE BISCUIT

Also squeezin' Lizzie—phrases meaning to grab the **saddle** horn.

STAGECOACH

Film (1939). See Films, Best Cowboy.

STANDARD BREED

See Horses.

STANDARD EVENT

See Rodeo Events.

STAR ROWEL SPURS

Spurs with five or six sharp pointed rowels, capable of cutting a horse badly.

STARGAZER

A **horse** that carries its head high in the air.

STARRETT, CHARLES
(1903–1986)

B-western film actor known as the Durango Kid.

STEAGALL, RED

Singer and poet. See Music.

STEEL

"The horse the stars loved to ride," a sorrel quarter horse that appeared unbilled in many films during the 1940s and 1950s. Clark Gable, Ben **Johnson, Jr.,** Joel McCrea, Randolph Scott, and Robert Taylor all used the stallion in some of their films.

STEEL

Colloquial term for spurs.

STEELE, BOB
(1907–1988)

B-western film actor known as the Fightin' Kid.

STEER WRESTLING

Also steer rassling or bulldogging. See Rodeo; Rodeo Events.

STEGNER, WALLACE
(1909–1993)

Wallace Stegner was a prolific western writer and teacher whose works blend literary finesse with historical awareness. Born in Lake Mills, Iowa, he spent his formative years in Saskatchewan and Salt Lake City. His father was a rough, resourceful, violent man who spent his life wandering from place to place in search of the main chance. His mother was strong-willed, pious, and principled.

Stegner earned a B.A. at the University of Utah in 1930 and started graduate work in English at the University of Iowa. He left school in 1933 to nurse his mother through the last stages of cancer, then returned to school in 1934 and married Mary Stuart Page, also a graduate student.

He took his first teaching position at Augustana College in Rock Island, Illinois. The following year he finished his doctoral dissertation and returned to Utah to teach at his alma mater. By the end of 1937 Stegner had published his first fictional work *(Remembering Laughter),* witnessed the birth of a son, and taken a new job at the University of Wisconsin. He met Robert Frost, Bernard DeVoto, and other prominent writers at the Broadloaf writers' conference in Vermont in 1939.

In 1940 Stegner accepted an invitation to teach creative writing at Harvard. Family tragedy, however, tempered the joys of his quick professional advancement: It was the year his father committed suicide.

Stegner stayed at Harvard for four years. During this time he published short stories, novels, and a semiautobiographical family history, *The Big Rock Candy Mountain* (1943), a book that established him as a major literary figure. In 1945 Stegner returned to the West, this time to found and direct the creative writing program at Stanford University. He taught and wrote there until his retirement in 1971, the same year that he published his Pulitzer Prize winner, *Angle of Repose.*

Stegner wrote prolifically. He produced novels, short stories, and histories that reflect a lifelong quest for identity. Even the title of *Wolf Willow: A History, a Story, and a Memory of the Last Plains Frontier* (1962) reflects his desire to understand his own past. Two of its stories, "Genesis" and "Carrion Spring," mark the only time Stegner focused his attention directly on the cowboy.

Stegner's writing also reflects a distrust of formulaic solutions to the world's ills. He communicated the rich variety and complexity of human experience. Independent, principled, and outspoken, in 1992 Stegner refused to meet President George Bush to accept a National Endowment for the Arts award. His refusal served as a protest against the Reagan-Bush administration's politicization of the agency. Stegner also voiced opposition to Reagan-Bush policies that were detrimental to the environment.

Stegner died tragically in Sante Fe, New Mexico, following an automobile accident. The many tributes following his death included special essays published in the autumn 1993 issue of *Montana, the Magazine of Western History.* (Arthur 1982; Stegner 1955; Stegner and Etulain 1990; Tuska and Piekarski 1983, 1984)

—*Stephen C. Keadey*

STEPHENS, HARRY
Cowboy, songwriter. See Music.

STETSON, JOHN B.
(1830–1906)
See Hat.

STIRRUPS
See Saddle.

STOCK SADDLE
See Saddle.

STOCKMEN'S ASSOCIATION
A stockmen's association is a type of organization formed by ranchers that is variously known as a livestock association, stock growers' association, cattlemen's association, or stock grazers' association.

Ranchers in both North and South America banded together to promote their economic interests. In many parts of the West, stockmen's associations effectively ruled territories and states. Strong figures such as Charles **Goodnight** ruled their ranches and the surrounding ranges with paternalism and autocracy. As the population of the West increased, so did the likelihood of conflict over control and use of the land and its resources. Stockmen's associations codified, organized, and generalized rules of the range. They directed some of the new rules and actions against working cowboys. In some instances, cowhands responded to the associations by going on **strike.**

Colorado stockmen organized in 1867. As in other areas of the economy, the largest ranches dominated the proceedings and set policy. The associations governed all areas of ranching: **roundups,** grazing on public and Indian lands, and brand registration. The groups also served as the ranchers' political voice, lobbying strenuously and often successfully to promote their interests over those of farmers and sheep ranchers.

Cattlemen in Wyoming first organized in 1871. By the 1880s their group controlled roundups around the territory. The association did permit nonmembers to participate in association roundups.

Rich ranchers distrusted smaller ranchers just as much as sheepmen or farmers. The big outfits believed, with some justification, that small, independent outfits crossed the line in claiming too many **maverick** cattle. This animosity gave rise to violent class conflict, such as the Johnson County War of 1892. Wyoming ranchers later hired stock detective Tom **Horn,** who worked for their association until convicted and hanged for murdering Willie Nickell in 1903.

Ranchers on the northern ranges used their political clout to fight against Texas fever, a disease (also called red water fever, cattle tick fever, or Spanish fever) that was transmitted by Texas **longhorns** . This tick-born disease, which attacks the liver, spleen, and red corpuscles, proved deadly to northern cattle, while longhorns rarely died from it. Stockmen's associations succeeded in getting quarantine laws passed—laws that stifled free movement on the range and helped contribute to the end of open-range ranching and the **trail drives** from Texas.

Eastern and foreign capital poured into the western beef bonanza during the early 1880s. This heavy outside investment made some associations appear to be mouthpieces for foreign "cattle barons." The large corporate ranches that formed were precursors of the powerful agribusiness interests that came to dominate twentieth-century farm policy.

Cattlemen recognized that they needed national as well as regional political influence.

Some 1,300 ranchers from 34 states and territories gathered in St. Louis in November 1884 for the First National Convention of Cattlemen. The group fired off resolutions to the nation's capital urging the creation of a National Cattle Trail, demanding long-term grazing leases on federal lands, and urging government protection from Indian rustlers.

Cattlemen suffered a sharp decline in their national influence in the mid–1880s. Two successive hard winters brought death to the overstocked ranges and financial disaster to many cattle consortia. As the **beef cattle industry** modernized, however, stockmen's associations reasserted their power. Such organizations remain vocal and politically powerful in many western states. They continue to influence state and federal land and water use legislation through the present day. (Atherton 1961; Lamar 1977; Tractman 1974; Weston 1985)

STOCKMEN'S MEMORIAL FOUNDATION

Established in May 1980, this Canadian charitable foundation has the following objectives:

a) to identify, honour and remember the builders of the Alberta livestock industry;
b) to provide historical and business information relating to the Alberta livestock industry;
c) to familiarize the public with the lore of the livestock industry; and
d) to encourage a general appreciation of the sociological and economic significance of the livestock industry.

The foundation grew out of a meeting of interested members of the Western Stock Growers Association. The group operates a museum, western **art** gallery, and research library in Calgary. A membership lounge permits stock growers to meet, socialize, and discuss current business concerns. Members pay annual dues, and the foundation is working toward building a permanent home for its activities.

Address: 2116 27th Avenue NE, Calgary, Alberta, Canada T2E 7A6; tel. 403-230-3338.

STOGIES

Colloquial term for cheap, secondhand **boots**.

STOMACH PUMP

A spade bit. See Bit.

STOMP

Colloquial term for a dance.

STORY-TELLING

See Humor.

STOVE UP

Also stove in—descriptive term for a cowboy who is too old and/or injured to ride.

STRAIGHT BIT

See Bit.

STRAIT, GEORGE

Country singer. See Hat Acts.

STRAUSS, LEVI
(1829–1902)

See Levi's.

STRAWBERRY ROAN

Sorrel (reddish-brown) horse, immortalized in a poem of the same name by Curly Fletcher.

STRAY MAN

Another term for rep or outside man. See Roundup.

STRETCHIN' THE BLANKET

Colloquial term for telling a tall tale. See Humor.

STRIKES

Rodeo riders succeeded in banding together to form "the Union" in the mid–1930s. Ranch hands, however, never developed a strong labor union or pulled off a successful strike. On a few occasions, working cowboys did join together to improve their lot. During the 1880s Knights of Labor organizers worked among cowboys, as they did with other poorly paid western workers.

The *Denver Republican* of 27 March 1883 reported ominously on one cowboy strike:

> An extensive strike among the cowboys in the Panhandle of Texas is progressing, and trouble is apprehended. They demand an advance from $30, the present wage, to $50 per month, which the stockmen refuse to pay. The cowboys threaten **violence** to new men, if brought into the ranges.

Elmer **Kelton** used this strike by Canadian River cowboys as the basis for his excellent work of historical fiction, *The Day the Cowboys Quit* (1971). Unfortunately, Kelton's unrealistically rosy ending strays away from the bleak economic realities of cowboy life of the time. The ranchers broke the strike and blacklisted the participating cowboys.

Another cowboy strike occurred in 1886 when 80 cowboys banded together to form the Northern New Mexico Small Cattlemen and Cowboys' Union. Among the group's resolutions was that "the working season of the average cowboy is only about five months, and we think it nothing but justice that the cowmen should give us living wages the year around." The union also established a wage scale, based upon experience.

Cowboys also struck in Wyoming in 1886. These and other attempts at cowboy unionizing failed, however. Well-organized and powerful **stockmen's associations** responded by blacklisting cowboys who were active in union movements and by using strikebreakers. Union organizers differed little from rustlers in the eyes of the wealthy stockman. Both threatened his power and his wealth.

Literature scholar Jack Weston is one of the few authors to look into cowboy protests and efforts to improve his lot. According to Weston, "there are lots of references to slowdowns, threats, intimidating behavior, and collective defiance among cowboys displeased with their pay, bosses, or work conditions." Weston also uncovered some evidence of a variety of strike tactics—"organized, wildcats, slowdowns, walkouts (or rideouts if the strikers had their own horses), and sit-downs."

Cowboy unionization failed for the same reasons that cowboy wages remained low: ranchers generally enjoyed a labor surplus, and striking hands could easily be replaced. The political climate of the late nineteenth century was militantly antiworker. Both rural and urban workers often found themselves victims of government-condoned strikebreakers and violence. In addition, the dispersed and migratory nature of the ranch labor force made meeting and organizing difficult. With power, wealth, the law, and replacement workers, stockmen could face down the challenge of striking hands.

For many hands, however, cowboying remained a way of life, not just a job. They focused their attention on tending animals, with little concern for economic advancement. Many cowboys exhibited an independent, self-reliant streak that militated against collective action. It may well be that loyal cowboys willing to "ride for the brand" outnumbered those willing to strike for better pay and conditions. (Lopez 1977; Weston 1985)

STRING
Colloquial term meaning a **rope**, also a herd of mounts.

SUDADERO
See Saddle.

SUICIDE GUN
Colloquial term for a .32-caliber revolver, which gunmen considered too weak to be effective. See Firearms.

SUITCASE RANCHER
Colloquial term for absentee ranch owner.

SUNBURST
Also sunset rowel; a **spur** made with many closely spaced points on the rowel.

SUNFISHER
A bucking horse that rears up and twists its abdomen sharply from side to side. A sunfisher can mean a good score for a bronc rider at **rodeo,** if he can stay on.

SUNSET ROWEL
See Sunburst.

SUPPER
The cowboy's hearty evening meal—what city slickers might call dinner. See Food.

SWAMP SEED
Colloquial term for rice.

SWAMPERS
Wild cattle hunted on the east Texas Gulf Coast. See *Vaquerías.*

SWARTHOUT, GLENDON
(1918–1992)
Glendon (Fred) Swarthout was the author of *The Shootist* (1975). See Wayne, John.

SWING MAN
Also swing rider. See Trail Drive.

TABA

Gaucho game. See Gambling.

TACK

Staying on a horse does little good if you have no control of its motions. Riders need more than a **saddle.** A variety of additional equipment, tack, allows cowboys to get horses to go when and where they want 'em to go.

The headstall forms the basis of the control methods. It is simply the headgear of the horse. The exact components vary somewhat with the type of gear used. One type is the bridle. It consists of the crownpiece (a strap passing over the horse's head), browband (front part of the gear), throatlatch (straps fastening the bridle under the neck), and cheekpieces on the sides.

In conjunction with the bridle, the rider uses a **bit,** a metal bar that fits in the mouth of the horse. Some very cruel and painful bits exist, but no one who loves horses will use these.

Attached to the bit are the reins, leather straps consisting of either one or two pieces. The latter type can be tied together. If tied, the rider can use a romal, a flexible riding whip that remains attached to the reins. If he prefers not to have the whip attached he can use a **quirt,** a leather riding whip.

If the rider does not wish to use a bit, the hackamore can be used. The term and its variant hackamer come from the Spanish word *jáquima.* With a headstall similar to the bridle, the hackamore incorporates a bosal (a ring made of leather, metal, or rawhide) in place of a bit. The hackamore also has a browband that can be lowered over the horse's eyes. With this arrangement, you might also see a *fiador* (corrupted to theodore), a looped cord running from the front of the bosal over the horse's head. While a horse is being trained to use a bit, a hackamore can be used in conjunction with the bridle.

Another way to break a bronco is by using the bosalea. Very similar to the hackamore, this device places a piece of metal on the front of the nose band. Pulling on the reins then causes the metal to press against the horse's head. As the area becomes sore, the horse becomes more obedient. These devices can cut the horse's flesh, which makes them unacceptable to most riders.

When stopping for the night, a rider wants to allow his horse to graze but not go too far away. Hobbles filled both conditions. Generally, a hobble is anything that connects the forelegs of the horse to each other. (According to Jules Verne Allen, "hopples" connected the two back legs.) Hobbles used by old-time cowboys could be leather cuffs buckled on the forelegs with a short chain connecting them. They also could be as simple as rawhide straps—cowboys learned that rawhide could be made into just about anything necessary.

For those cowboys who wanted to decorate their gear, *conchas* (anglicized to conchos, from the Spanish for shell) were the way to go. Sometimes made of silver, conchas could have elaborate or simple designs. Cowboys took pride in their horse jewelry, so conchas appeared on old-style bridles, **chaps, spurs,** and other equipment. Today riding tack from the past has become much sought-after collectibles. (Adams 1968; Allen 1933; Mora 1973; Ward 1958)

—*Mark Mayer*

TAILER

Also tail rider—a cowboy who rides drag (behind a trail herd). See Trail Drives.

TAILING

See Equestrian Games.

TALIAFERRO, HAL
(b. 1895)

B-western film actor.

TALK LIKE A TEXAN

To boast, a propensity some folks attribute to Texans.

TALL TALES

See Humor.

TALL-GRASS COUNTRY

See Plains.

TALLOW

Fat, whether on humans or animals. See Beef Cattle Industry; *Vaquería*.

TALLOW FACTORY

See *Vaquería*.

TALLY MAN

The hand who counts (tallies) the number of calves branded during **roundup.**

TANGLELEG

Colloquial term for crude whiskey.

TAOS LIGHTNING

Colloquial term for cheap liquor.

TAPADERAS

Also *tapaderos*. See Saddle.

TARANTULA JUICE

Colloquial term for cheap whiskey.

TARZAN

Ken Maynard's famous movie horse.

TASAJO

Also *charqui, charque, carne seca,* all of which mean jerky (dried beef).

TAVERN

See Saloons.

TAYLOR, WILLIAM LEVI
(1857–1924)

The original "King of the Cowboys," Texas-born "Buck" Taylor grew up a cowboy. He rode north to Nebraska and worked at Buffalo Bill **Cody**'s ranch. In 1884 Cody hired Taylor for his Wild West show and gave him star billing. Thanks to Cody and Taylor, the term *cowboy* left behind much of its negative connotation and became a term evoking heroism, courage, and strength. The Wild West program lauded Taylor's "remarkable dexterity" and "genial qualities" and assured viewers that he was as "amiable as a

child." Taylor's riding tricks, such as snatching his hat and bandanna from the ground at full gallop, thrilled audiences. He also portrayed General Custer in the reenactment of the Battle of the Little Big Horn.

Along with Cody, Taylor captured the imagination of eastern writers eager to cash in on cowboy **mythology**. In 1887 Cody's friend and promoter Prentiss Ingraham published *Buck Taylor, King of the Cowboys; or, The Raiders and the Rangers: A Story of the Wild and Thrilling Life of William L. Taylor.* This work in Beadle's Half-Dime Library spawned many other **pulp novels** that built Taylor to legendary proportions. In some ways the pulp writers did not have to exaggerate. The handsome, mustachioed Taylor, standing 6 feet 5 inches tall, really looked like a bigger-than-life cowboy hero.

Unfortunately Taylor broke a leg during an 1887 performance in London. The ever-generous Cody continued to support his friend by giving him a **gambling** concession. He ranched in Wyoming for a time and organized his own show, which failed in 1894. Taylor lived to see the cowboy hero's transition from Wild West shows and pulps to the silver screen, but he did not participate in the new medium. (Russell 1960, 1970)

TEAM ROPING

Also tied team roping. See Rodeo Events.

TELEVISION

David Sarnoff of RCA demonstrated the world's first television at the 1939 World's Fair in New York. RCA based its technology on the research of Vladimir Kosma Zworykin, a Soviet immigrant. Corporate fights, contested frequencies, World War II, and the chilling effects of McCarthyism hampered television's evolution, but by the early 1950s, the three major commercial networks—NBC, CBS, and ABC—had established a range of programs.

In an appendix to *Shooting Stars* (McDonald 1987), Gary A. Yoggy lists 173 westerns that appeared on television from 1948 through 1985. The rise of television in the early 1950s helped doom B-western movies, although rising production costs played a larger role in the demise. Many western films stars, including Roy **Rogers,** Gene **Autry,** Hopalong Cassidy, and the Lone Ranger, made very successful transitions from **B westerns** and **radio** westerns to the new medium.

Clayton Moore and Jay Silverheels, for example, continued the famous radio characters, the Lone Ranger and Tonto. "The William Tell Overture" and "Hi-yo Silver, Away!" reached eager audiences from 1949 through 1957 and, in syndication, long thereafter.

Children's programs joined the television western lineup. Kirby Grant starred as "Sky King" (1953–1954 on CBS). This modern western had the hero in an airplane ("Songbird") as often as on horseback.

Like "The Lone Ranger," "Death Valley Days" moved successfully from radio to television. It dated back to 1930 as a radio program. The long-running series, sponsored by Twenty Mule Team Borax, ran from 1952 through the mid-1970s. Stanley Andrews, billed as the "Old Ranger," hosted for the first dozen years. Subsequently, Ronald **Reagan,** Robert Taylor, and Merle Haggard served as hosts.

The year 1955 brought "adult westerns" to join the juvenile fare. That year gave birth to new mythical western places, such as the Dodge City of "Gunsmoke." "Cheyenne," "Tales of the Texas Rangers," and "The Life and Times of Wyatt Earp" also appeared.

By 1957, 17 westerns aired weekly, ten of them on ABC. Offerings included "Maverick," "Tales of Wells Fargo," "Sugarfoot," "Wagon Train," "Zorro," and "Have Gun Will Travel."

CBS's "Gunsmoke" became the longest running series on commercial television, airing from 1955 to 1975. James Arness (Matt Dillon), Milburn Stone (Doc Adams), Dennis Weaver (Chester), and Amanda Blake (Miss Kitty Russell) became staples of Saturday night television (switching to Monday night in the late 1960s). Dillon's firmness, fairness, and ability to get his man fit well with traditional western film

values. CBS wanted John **Wayne** for the lead, but the Duke, unwilling to take on a full-time television commitment, recommended another tall actor, James Arness.

"Bonanza" ran for 14 seasons (1959–1973) Sunday nights on NBC. The original cast, Lorne Greene, Michael Landon, Dan Blocker, and Pernell Roberts, ran for six seasons. They made the Ponderosa Ranch in Nevada a familiar place to millions of viewers. Like Arness, Greene served as a stern but caring father figure. Unlike "Gunsmoke," however, "Bonanza" included no female characters among the permanent cast. Even the cook was a Chinese male (played by Victor Sen Yung). Originally, the Ponderosa existed only on Hollywood sound stages. Outdoor credits appeared over scenic views of the northeastern shore of Lake Tahoe. The program's success prompted Bill Anderson to build a ranch house. Anderson opened his Ponderosa at Incline Village, Nevada, to tourists in 1967. Visitors can still munch a Hossburger, ride horses, and even get married in the Church of the Ponderosa.

Perennial bad guy Richard Boone starred as the black-clad avenger Paladin, whose business card gave his series its name—"Have Gun, Will Travel." The series ran from 1957 to 1962 on CBS. Rough-featured Boone deftly played his complex character, a gunfighter, epicure, and intellectual.

James Garner played Bret Maverick, a tricky, likable gambler with great panache, in the series "Maverick" (1957–1961, ABC). Big Clint Walker played the scout named Cheyenne Bodie for eight seasons in "Cheyenne" (1955–1962, ABC).

The rash of spin-offs that followed these programs gave rise to some memorable acting careers. From "Wanted: Dead or Alive" (1958–1960, CBS) came Steve McQueen as bounty hunter Josh Randal. From "Rawhide" (1959–1965, CBS) came Clint **Eastwood** as Rowdy Yates, cattle drive ramrod.

Chuck Connors became widely known for his role as Lucas McCain in "The Rifleman" (1958–1963, ABC). Johnny Crawford played his son Mark. Dennis Hopper appeared in the series pilot, written by Sam Peckinpah. The trademark character, toting a custom 1873 **Winchester** with an oversized ring lever, earned Connors, who died at age 70 in November 1992, a place among performers honored by the **National Cowboy Hall of Fame** the preceding year. Connors used three rifles in his television series. One is on display at the Gene Autry Museum in Los Angeles. William Simon, who served in Richard Nixon's cabinet, owns another. The third was sold in Florida by sealed bid auction in 1994.

"The Virginian," based on the Owen **Wister** novel, debuted in 1960 on NBC. James Drury, Doug McClure, Lee J. Cobb, and Pippa Scott starred in the series. "The Virginian" was the first television western to run for 90 minutes. In 1971, with the addition of Lee Majors and Stewart Granger, the program became "The Men of Shiloh."

Although popular with audiences, TV westerns did not lack their critics. Federal Communications Commission (FCC) chairman Newton Minow sharply criticized "the vast wasteland" of TV in 1961. He complained about the high level of TV **violence,** "sadism, murder, western badmen, western good men, private eyes, gangsters, more violence, and cartoons." Three decades later, many critics remain concerned about television's excessive violence, low cultural level, and lack of educational content.

Popular interest in westerns rises and falls over time. By the early 1970s, most western series had folded; only "Bonanza" and "Gunsmoke" remained. The '80s saw few successful television westerns other than reruns. "The Young Riders," based on the Pony Express, lasted longer than the original institution. It continued in syndicated form into the 1990s.

After more than a decade in the doldrums, westerns stormed back in the late 1980s and early 1990s. *Lonesome Dove* (1989), a TV miniseries based on the novel by Larry **McMurtry,** proved one of the finest cowboy films of the eighties. Viewers got an unvarnished, unsentimental look at the hardships of ranch and trail life, with powerful, convincing characters played by

Tommy Lee Jones, Robert Duvall, Danny Glover, Anjelica Huston, and other fine actors. A sequel *(Return to Lonesome Dove,* 1993) starring Jon Voight proved less popular.

In February 1994 TNT television brought back the Cisco Kid (Jimmy Smits) and Pancho (comedian Cheech Marin) for a feature television movie, "The Cisco Kid." The characters, created nearly a century earlier by O. Henry, had already enjoyed several incarnations in B movies and television. Duncan Renaldo and Gilbert Roland starred as Cisco in several B westerns. Renaldo returned to the role for a television series in the 1950s, accompanied by Leo Carillo as Pancho. These earlier depictions suffered from unfortunate racial stereotypes and questionable **humor** that many Hispanics found offensive. The 1994 film shed the stereotypes but kept the dash and humor of Cisco and Pancho.

During the early 1990s, westerns returned en masse to television. In the fall 1992 season, "Dr. Quinn, Medicine Woman" became a big winner for CBS at the tough 8:00 P.M. Saturday slot. In the series, Jane Seymour stars as an eastern physician who goes to the frontier, along with her children. The show appeals to a wide age range and generally has a politically correct message of environmentalism or the like. Joe Lando stars as a young, handsome mountain man who helps Seymour out of difficulties.

Dr. Quinn's popularity spawned rampant "me-tooism" among other networks. A spate of westerns hit during the fall 1993 season. Bill Wittliff created "Ned Blessing: The Story of My Life and Times." Brad Johnson stars as Blessing, the sheriff of Plum Creek, who is surrounded by a cast of weird characters and caricatures. The nicely filmed program offers a gritty view of the West. The strangeness of the characters, however, give it a "Northern Exposure" rides south atmosphere.

More successful is Fox network's "The Adventures of Brisco County, Jr.," which blends humor, authentic-looking sets, and some supernatural touches. The plots usually have humorous elements, but people get shot and die. Brisco County (Bruce Campbell) runs into various types of trouble looking for his father's murderers. Campbell visibly enjoys the show. "This is an actor's dream, to mount a horse, kiss a girl, spin a gun, vanquish the bad guys and ride off into the dusty sunset," he says. In one scene, he explains that he does not ride on his father's reputation as the greatest lawman the West ever knew. "The important thing is that I can out shoot, out ride, out spit, out fight, and out think John Bly or anyone in his gang." Like the **film** *Silverado* (1985), "Brisco County, Jr." deftly blends campy humor and strong cowboy action.

The evening soap operas of the late 1970s, such as "Dallas," are gone. They seem, however, to be the inspiration for shortlived "Angel Falls" (1993). A western in location only, the cast included the usual soapy collection of the stupid, venal, cheating, and conniving.

A better addition to the new crop of westerns is "Harts of the West." As in the hit movie *City Slickers* (1991), the star (Beau Bridges as Dan Hart) hopes to find happiness and renewal in the West. After suffering a "coronary episode" at age 41, the lingerie salesman moves his family to Nevada. Harley Kozard plays his long-suffering wife Alison. Beau's real-life father Lloyd Bridges rounds out the lead roles as a crusty old-time cowboy.

The proliferation of cable television networks offers more access for syndicated reruns of old programs. In all likelihood, the Cartwrights, Matt Dillon, and a host of other television westerners will ride the range well into the next century. (Aylesworth 1986; Brown 1992; McDonald 1987; Miller 1979)

See also Films, Documentary.

"TEN COMMANDMENTS OF THE COWBOY"
See Autry, Gene; Mythology; Rogers, Roy.

TENDERFOOT
Derogatory term for someone newly arrived from the East and/or lacking in knowledge of ranch life.

TEN-GALLON HAT
See Hat.

TENNESSEE WALKER
See Horses.

TEQUILA
See Saloons.

TEXAS BUTTER
Colloquial term for gravy made with flour, hot water, and fried steak grease. See Food.

TEXAS FEVER
Also Spanish fever. See Stockmen's Association.

TEXAS HAT
See Hat.

TEXAS LEG
Close-fitting shotgun **chaps** that cover the entire leg.

TEXAS LONGHORN
See Longhorn Cattle.

TEXAS PLAYBOYS
See Music.

TEXAS RANGERS
See Discrimination.

TEXAS TIE
See Rope.

TEXAS TREE
Also Texas saddle. See Saddle.

TEXAS WING CHAPS
See Chaps.

THEODORE
Corruption of the Spanish *fiador*. See Tack.

THIRTY AND FOUND
Thirty dollars a month wages plus board.

THOMPSON, THOMAS
(1913–)
California-born author of formula western novels and short stories.

THREE-QUARTER RIG
See Saddle.

THUMB BUSTER
Colloquial term for a single-action six-gun that required cocking. See Firearms.

TIE STRINGS
Also tie straps. See Saddle.

TIED HOLSTER
A holster tied to the leg to facilitate a quicker draw. See Fast Draw.

TIE-HARD MAN
Also tie-hard-and-fast-man. See Rope.

TILGHMAN, WILLIAM MATTHEW, JR.
(1854–1924)
Peace officer. See Cow Towns.

TIN-BELLY
Colloquial term for cheap, poorly made spurs.

TINKER, EDWARD LAROQUE
(1881–1968)
Historian, collector. See Historiography of the Cowboy.

TINSLEY, JIM BOB
See Musicology.

TOBACCO
Cowboys throughout the Americas enjoyed one of the most profitable native crops, tobacco. South American cowboys most often smoked small, hand-rolled cigars made from dark tobacco. Gauchos of Argentina would trade hides or rhea feathers for tobacco at small country stores (pulperías.)

Cowboys in the United States enjoyed several types of tobacco products. "Chaw" or chewing tobacco has long been popular. The outline of a round tin of Copenhagen, the most popular brand, often marks the pocket of a cowboy's jeans or shirt. Other old-time brands included Star Navy and Brown Mule. Other later brands include Levi Garrett, Beechnut, Skoal, and Red Man.

While some hands preferred a plug of tobacco to a tin, others would pull out a "Bible" (also "prayer book" or "dream book"—a little packet of papers), and roll themselves a "quirly" (hand-rolled cigarette). Old-timers preferred carrying "fixins" (or "makins") to roll their own cigarettes long after machine-rolled brands became available. Cowboys also called their cigarettes "brain tablets," perhaps because they would light up when they took time to think through a problem.

Recognizing the strong association between the cowboy and tobacco, Philip Morris trotted out the Marlboro Man in the 1950s. The image of a strong, nameless cowboy puffing on a Marlboro became a worldwide icon. Darrell Winfield, the original Marlboro Man, remained relatively anonymous but paradoxically instantly recognizable (see Pitchmen).

Growing health concerns have sharply dampened the nation's longstanding love affair with tobacco. Around bunkhouses and behind rodeo chutes, however, the telltale outline of a tin of chaw is still visible in shirt or jeans pockets. (Blevins 1993; Watts 1977)

TOMBSTONE, ARIZONA
A famous town of the West, Old Tombstone has been the location of many western films.

TONGUE OIL
Colloquial term for strong liquor. See Saloons.

TONGUE SPLITTER
See Maverick.

TONSIL PAINT
Also tonsil varnish—colloquial terms for whiskey.

TONTO

See Television.

TONY, THE WONDER HORSE

Silent film star Tom Mix's famous chestnut mount that he rode beginning in 1918.

TOP HAND

Also top waddy or top waddie—a highly skilled cowboy.

TOPEO

Huaso game of pushing another's horse along a rail. See Equestrian Games.

TOPPER

Famous movie horse ridden by William Boyd (Hopalong Cassidy).

TORNADO JUICE

Colloquial term for whiskey.

TOTIN' STARS ON HIS DUDS

Real Texans seldom try to hide their roots in the Lone Star State. On the contrary, they proclaim their "Texanness" to anyone who will listen. Texas pride goes back a long way, even with regard to **fashion.** Texas cowboys wanted and got a wide range of clothing (duds) and equipment embellished with stars. An old western saying goes: "For a Texas puncher not to be totin' stars on his duds is most as bad as votin' the Republican ticket." Well, some things do change, even in Texas. (Adams 1968)

TRABUCO

Blunderbuss used by **llaneros.**

TRAIL BOSS

The man in charge of a **trail drive.** His word is the law.

TRAIL BROKE

Also road broke—accustomed to moving peacefully down the trail (referring to cattle).

TRAIL DRIVES

The trail drive or cattle drive is probably the most storied event in popular cowboy culture. We mark the classic era of the cowboy as the time of the great drives north from Texas from the mid-1860s through the mid-1880s. Edward Charles ("Teddy Blue") Abbott titled his cowboy memoir *We Pointed Them North* (1939). Countless movies, from *Red River* (1948) to *Lonesome Dove* (1991), have used drives as their central motif. Novelist Ralph Compton is authoring an entire "Trail Drive Series" commemorating cowboy life on the great drives.

Cattleman Edward Piper made what may have been the first northern drive when he moved a herd from Texas to Ohio in 1846. Beginning in 1866 and 1867, trail crews moved hundreds of thousands of cattle northward to the Kansas railheads. During the Civil War, Texans left to fight for the Confederacy. Their untended cattle multiplied in their absence, and the war cut Texas off from market access. Thus in 1865 Texas ranchers faced a dilemma: Overstocked ranges and low cattle prices. The solution: Move the animals out of Texas to northern ranges and markets at Kansas railheads.

Trail bosses used much the same system from the Río Grande to the Canadian border. Sources vary as to how many men were needed on a cattle drive. Most of the discrepancy is due to the nature and size of the herd. Wild Texas **longhorns** required more men than tamer, less formidable breeds. Figures range from eight to 20 hands to trail a herd of 2,000 to 3,000 cattle. Philip Ashton Rollins *(The Cowboy,* 1922) estimated one man per 250 to 350 head. All crews included a trail boss and cook, and some added an assistant foreman (segundo). A horse **wrangler** (generally a young boy) handled the six to eight mounts needed for each man.

If we visualize the herd as having a head (point) and feet (drag), then swing men watched the "shoulders" of the herd and flank men watched the "hips." Riders bringing up the drag got the full benefit of the herd's dust. Alkali flats made riding drag especially memorable and unpleasant. Under such conditions, a drag rider might keep a "wipe" (bandanna) tied across his face the entire day.

Drives from Texas began in early spring, when new grass had pushed up but before heavy runoff had swollen rivers. On northern ranges, drives had to be completed before autumn snowfalls. Crews did well to move a herd 12 to 16 miles a day. At a slower pace, say 10 to 12 miles per day, animals could graze and put on some weight en route. The drive cost the owner of the herd about $500 per month, however, so there was no dawdling. Cowboys on a drive supplied their own gear and earned $25 to $40 per month.

Cowboys trailed the animals north over several different routes. The Shawnee Trail, opened in the 1840s, ran from Brownsville, Texas, north through Dallas. After crossing Indian Territory (Oklahoma) into southeastern Kansas, the trail branched to Missouri railheads at Kansas City, Sedalia, and St. Louis.

Quarantines against Texas cattle carrying ticks and the interruptions of the Civil War closed the Shawnee.

After the war, the Chisholm Trail became the main cattle route, carrying about half the animals moved out of Texas. It ran north from San Antonio, Texas, through Fort Worth, and up through Oklahoma, terminating at Abilene, Kansas. The Chisholm was 600 miles long as the crow flies from San Antonio to Abilene. Cattle, however, never walked in a simple straight line.

The Eastern Trail ran to the east of the Chisholm, running through Wichita and Newton, Kansas, en route to Abilene. The Western Trail crossed the Oklahoma Panhandle into western Kansas and on to Dodge City, Kansas. Drovers moved cattle even farther northward into the Dakotas, Montana, and Wyoming on other trails, including the Bozeman, Northern, and Jones and Plummer.

The Stampede, *painted by Frederic Remington in 1909, portrays a dangerous stampede prompted by thundershowers—an occupational hazard for cowboys on trail drives.*

Charles **Goodnight** and Oliver Loving blazed a trail through west Texas Comanche country in 1866. They moved their herds northwestward out of Palo Pinto County, Texas, entering southeastern New Mexico at Pope's Crossing and continuing north to Fort Sumner and Fort Bascom. Goodnight branched to the northwest at Fort Sumner, blazing a trail through Raton Pass all the way to Denver. He also moved his herd along a more easterly route to John Wesley Iliff's ranch on the South Platte River in northeastern Colorado.

Cowboys pushed some 600,000 to 700,000 animals north from Texas during 1871 alone. The quarantine against Texas cattle enacted by Kansas in 1884 checked the large northern drives, however. In addition the northern **plains** were reasonably well stocked by then. The final blow to the trail drives came when railroads pushed trunk lines southward. Drives continued on a reduced basis until about 1895.

Latin American Drives

Long drives also had to be made on Latin American ranges. Descriptions of trail drives in Argentina sound much like those of the American West. Two **gauchos** rode point, while others guided the flanks and brought up the rear. An orderly herd might cover ten to twelve miles during the first four to five hours of the morning. Gauchos worried less about animal weight loss on the trail than the American cowboy. Until the late nineteenth century, Argentine ranchers marketed their animals for dried meat and hides, not beef. Weight loss did not matter until the advent of the chilled beef industry in the late nineteenth century.

Before noon, riders changed mounts and let the cattle rest and graze for an hour. Resuming the drive, the trail boss would try to find well-watered pasture a few hours before sunset. Generally, each thousand head of wild cattle required five riders. Drovers could handle tame herds with fewer men. Two other hands wrangled the spare mounts.

The vast distances of the **pampas** dictated many long drives. The drover (*tropero* or *resero*)

possessed specialized skills and commanded higher wages. In Argentina and in neighboring Uruguay, some drovers acted as buying agents for meat processing plants. They then trailed the animals to market. Ranchers earned lower prices for their cattle when selling to a middleman (the tropero). On the other hand, they avoided the expense and hazards of driving the animals themselves.

Llaneros in Venezuela and Colombia faced major trail drives at least twice a year. They also faced extremely difficult driving conditions since, on the llanos, floods alternate with droughts in six-month cycles. During the dry season, riders herded animals from the high northern llanos south to graze along the Apure River. The animals had to be moved back north by May or June before the onset of wet season flooding.

Llaneros had to navigate animals through the many watercourses of the vast tropical plain. Unlike most cowboys in the United States and elsewhere, llaneros had to be excellent swimmers and boatmen. They often used brute force to push cattle into the water. The herd instinct prompted the remainder to follow. Dangers abounded. If cattle began milling in the water, many animals and riders could drown. The tropical rivers also held electric eels, alligators, piranha, and other dangerous fish and reptiles. (Adams 1964; Gard 1954; Lamar 1977; Loomis 1962; MacEwan 1975; Rollinson 1948; Slatta 1990, 1992)

TRAIL TOWN
See Cow Towns.

TRAVIS, RANDY
(1959–)
Country singer. See Hat Acts.

TREE
See Saddle.

TRES MARÍAS
See *Bolas*.

TRIGGER

Roy **Rogers**'s famous golden palomino movie horse. Originally named Golden Cloud, Trigger was billed as "The Smartest Horse in the Movies." Rogers rode him from 1938 until 1957. Trigger died in 1965, and Rogers had him stuffed and mounted.

TRIGUEÑO

Brown, as a brown horse. The term is also used in Latin America to denote brown human skin color.

TRITT, TRAVIS
(1963–)

Country singer. See Hat Acts.

TROPERO

See Trail Drive.

TROPILLA

Gaucho's herd of remounts (extra horses needed for **ranch work** or on **trail drives**).

TRUCO

Gaucho card game. See Gambling.

TUBB, ERNEST
(1914–1984)

"The Texas Troubadour." See Music.

TUCSON BED

Where the down-and-out cowboy sleeps; you lie down on your stomach and cover yourself with your back. See Wages.

"TUMBLING TUMBLEWEEDS"

Song (1932); also the name of a movie. See Rogers, Roy.

TURTLE

Member of the Cowboy Turtle Association. See Rodeo.

TUTTLE, WILBUR COLEMAN
(1883–1969)

Montana-born author of humorous western short stories and novels.

TWISTHORN

Another name for **longhorn** cattle. The breed's very long horns could twist into very odd shapes, hence the term.

TWISTING DOWN

The part of **rodeo** bulldogging when the steer wrestler twists a steer's head and forces the animal to the ground. See Rodeo Events.

TWO GUNS AND A BADGE

Film (1954) generally cited as the last **B western**.

TYSON, IAN
(1933–)

Canadian Ian Tyson is probably the working hand's favorite singer, and also the favorite of fellow performer Michael Martin **Murphey**. Tyson's cassettes grace bunkhouses and pickup trucks throughout the American and Canadian West.

"I'm writing about the modern West, the contemporary West," Tyson told journalist Ian McCallum (*Scene Magazine,* February 1993):

> My music is rooted in the West and it really doesn't have anything to do with what they do in Nashville. My music is a regional thing you know. It comes from the slopes of the Rockies and that's pretty well where the inspiration originates.

Tyson's musical career began with the 1960s folk music revival as half of the group Ian and Sylvia (Fricker). They married in 1964 and recorded more than a dozen albums, mostly on the Vanguard label. Both also displayed a talent for songwriting: Tyson wrote "Four Strong Winds" and "Someday Soon," while Fricker wrote the folk hit, "You Were on My Mind." The duo formed a country rock band, Great Speckled Bird, and in the 1970s cohosted "Nashville North," a weekly Canadian TV series. Ian and Sylvia divorced and continued separate musical careers. "Nashville North" became "The Ian Tyson Show."

Along with his music, Tyson worked on his riding, cutting, and cowboying skills. He now raises cutting horses on his ranch, nestled in the foothills of the Rockies near Longview, Alberta. As of the early 1990s, Docs Summer Wages stood at stud. Tyson and his cutting horse Randy perform well in competitions throughout the West, although a broken arm in 1992 put a crimp in the guitar playing and riding for a time.

During the 1970s, Tyson turned from folk and country to western music. In fact, he learned to play the guitar while recovering from a **rodeo** accident. He played and sang in **saloons** but then gave up his music for a time. Tyson's second wife, Twylla, and others encouraged him to take up his guitar again. In 1983 he released *Old Corrals and Sagebrush,* the album that began his highly successful cowboy music odyssey.

In 1989 the Canadian Country Musical Hall of Fame (located in Swift Current, Saskatchewan) inducted Tyson as a member. In the early 1990s, fans enjoyed a steady output of great tunes on *Cowboyography, And Stood There Amazed, I Outgrew the Wagon, Eighteen Inches of Rain,* and other albums. Tyson and his talented Chinook Arch Riders continue to draw sell-out crowds.

In 1990 Shirlie Defoe founded the Ian Tyson Fan Roundup. She still heads the group. Members pay a $15 initiation fee and $5 per year thereafter.

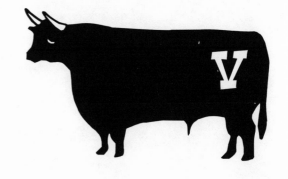

VACA

Spanish term for cow.

VALLEY TAN

Colloquial term for liquor. See Saloons.

VAMOOSE

Leave quickly, from the Spanish *vamos*.

VAN SHELTON, RICKY
(1952–)

Country singer. See Hat Acts.

VAQUEIRO

The *vaqueiro* is the cowboy of the *sertão*, the dry inland plains of northeastern Brazil. Settlement of the coastal plain on Brazil's "hump" did not begin until several decades after Portuguese explorer Juan Cabral bumped into it in 1500. The earlier Treaty of Tordesillas (1494), based on geographical ignorance, gave Portugal legal claim to the region jutting out into the Atlantic.

In 1532 Martim Afonso de Souza brought settlers and sugarcane to his settlement at São Vicente, near Santos. He also introduced cattle to Brazil. Other coastal sugar plantations sprang up along the tropical coast, which provided a good climate for a range of crops, including cotton, sugar, and tobacco. Planters imported large numbers of African slaves to labor in their fields.

Coastal plantation development stimulated a market for livestock, needed for beasts of burden and meat. Ranching grew along with plantation agriculture, but the expansion of plantations pushed ranching inland into the plains of the northeastern hump. In addition, the Dutch occupation of the northeast from 1624 until 1654 also pushed Portuguese ranchers toward the interior.

Vaqueiros herded hardy cattle capable of surviving in the desert austerity. Originally poor Portuguese worked as cowboys. Over time, however, miscegenation created a multiethnic society. By the eighteenth century, most vaqueiros were mestizos, Indians, or blacks.

The region's aridity made the São Francisco River valley an inviting location for herds. Historian Rollie E. Poppino, in *Brazil: The Land and the People* (1968), attributes great significance to the inland push led by the vaqueiro: "The effective incorporation into Portugal's American empires of these formerly untamed lands and peoples east of the line of Tordesillas was primarily the work of the *vaqueiro*."

Owing to a labor shortage, cowboys of the early colonial era enjoyed the unusual possibility of upward mobility. In exchange for their labor on **roundups,** vaqueiros received a share of the calves born on large ranches. Some cowboys used these animals to establish herds of their own. Northeastern ranches marketed both meat on the hoof and dried beef. Plantation slaves provided a local market for the latter product.

Like ranchers everywhere, those in the Brazilian northeast faced many problems. Rustlers, runaway slaves, bandits, and drought posed threats to cowboys and herds. Despite the problems, by the early eighteenth century the state of Bahia held an estimated 500,000 cattle and Pernambuco held about 800,000. This marked the high point of vaqueiro life.

During the eighteenth century, the economy, population, and political power in Brazil shifted south toward Rio de Janeiro. This shift left the northeast politically and economically marginalized and contributed to a decline in the northern livestock industry toward the end of the eighteenth century. Minas Gerais, a mining center, also became Brazil's new livestock center. Still farther south, *gaúchos* (Brazilian **gauchos**) herded cattle in Rio Grande do Sul.

Some Brazilian intellectuals conceived of the sertão, their northeastern cattle frontier, as a place of racial and social democracy. João Capistrano de Abreu was among the first Brazilians to take up the frontier theme. The grim historical reality of cowboy life in the desolate northeast was far less heroic than latter-day mythmakers would have us belief.

Both the vaqueiro and the gaúcho remained regional figures in Brazilian culture. Instead of the cowboy, it was the *bandeirante*—an explorer and slave hunter of São Paulo—who became Brazil's mythical frontiersman.   (Prado, Jr. 1971)

VAQUERÍA

Cassell's Spanish Dictionary gives the modern meaning of *vaquería* as a herd of cattle or a dairy. Historically, however, it meant a wild-cattle hunting expedition in the Río de la Plata region of South America. Hides and tallow represented the first marketable exports from the New World's livestock industry. Wild-cattle hunting expeditions continued as the main means of livestock exploitation into the eighteenth century. In 1609 the *cabildo,* or town council, of Buenos Aires began granting licenses *(acciónes)* to round up wild or escaped cattle. **Gauchos** chased and killed wild cattle (legally and illegally) and sold their hides for export.

Anglo cowboys in east Texas hunted wild cattle during the 1830s and 1840s in much the same fashion as their Latin American counterparts. Illegality tinged the Texas cattle hunts as it did those in South America. Many Anglo cowboys exhibited a ready indifference to the legal ownership of the cattle they hunted. Anglo cowboys raided Mexican stock, which they then drove to markets in Louisiana. Some Anglos exchanged arms for livestock with Indians in Texas. They also scoured the coastal plain for semiwild cattle, or "swampers," during annual roundup and branding season. Some crude hide-and-tallow factories operated along the Texas Gulf Coast.

Anglo cowboys were following in the footsteps of **vaqueros,** who had driven cattle illegally from Texas to Louisiana for generations. Throughout the eighteenth century, Spanish ranchers drove cattle to French Louisiana. In 1750 the Spanish governor proposed to no avail that the heavy traffic be licensed and regulated. Spain acquired Louisiana in 1763, thereby removing the stigma of illegality. After the United States acquired the Louisiana Territory in 1803, however, cattle movements east from Texas continued—again illegally.

As **Richard Henry Dana** vividly described, the hides-and-tallow trade also played a major economic role in Spanish California. As elsewhere, the process began with chasing and killing wild cattle and ended with the curing and export of hides. The Spanish term *matanza* referred both to the act of slaughtering the animals and the place where the killing occurred.

When the hide is taken from the bullock, holes are cut round it, near the edge, by which it is staked out to dry. In this manner it dries without shrinking. After the hides are thus dried in the sun, and doubled with the skin out, they are received by the vessels at the different ports on the coast, and brought down to the depot at San Diego. The vessels land them, and leave them in large piles near the houses. Then begins the hide curer's duty.

After soaking in seawater for two days, the hides were cured another two days in vats of brine. Workers again spread and staked the hides, taking time to cut out any bad spots of meat or fat that would rot the hides. "Then, having been salted, scraped, cleaned, dried, and beaten, they are stowed away in the house." Finally larger sailing vessels carried the hides to New England, where factories turned them into boots, shoes, and other leather goods.

Exhaustion of the wild-cattle herds and changing market needs ended the vaquerías in both North and South America. (Dana 1964; Dary 1981; Jackson 1986; Nichols 1968; Slatta 1992)

VAQUERO

The vaquero was the working cowboy of Mexico's missions and ranches. He suffered the same stigmas of race and class as his South American counterparts, the **gaucho** and **llanero.** Spaniards and creoles attached racial stereotypes to mestizos and other nonwhites. Mestizos (persons of mixed Indian and Spanish ancestry) were considered untrustworthy, criminal, and ignorant by birth. The Spanish had originally barred nonwhites from riding horses. The equestrian life was reserved for "decent people." It was too dangerous and democratic to let nonwhites rise up from the ground to mount a horse. The growing demands of ranching, coupled with the Spanish elite's aversion to manual labor, opened riding to Indians, blacks, and mestizos.

Missionaries played a leading role in establishing ranching in Arizona, New Mexico,

Frederic Remington portrayed the vaquero for the March 1894 edition of Harper's Monthly. *The vaquero's equipment and attire are very similar to his North American counterpart's.*

and California. In 1687 an Italian Jesuit, Father Eusebio Francisco Kino, established the mission of Nuestra Señora de las Dolores in Sonora, Mexico. Subsequent missions spread livestock throughout the Pimería Alta region (today southern Arizona and northern Sonora, Mexico). During his active missionary career (he died in 1711), Father Kino established stock ranches in at least 20 locations in the Santa Cruz Valley of Arizona.

Beginning with the establishment of San Diego in 1769, Father Junipero Serra's string of Franciscan missions spread along the California coast. As in Mexico, Indian vaqueros tended the livestock. Mission Indians quickly became skilled at all aspects of ranch work. They made and threw lariats, herded, and branded. Unfortunately for the Spanish, hostile Indians, especially the Apaches of the Southwest, also became excellent horsemen and formidable enemies.

Juan Bautista de Anza brought settlers and trailed livestock from Arizona to Monterey and then on to San Francisco. This route fulfilled one of Kino's ambitions—to supply California with livestock from Arizona.

Missions in Texas, as elsewhere, served as focal points for early ranching efforts. Franciscans founded a number of missions in the area of San Antonio de Bexar. These included the missions of San Antonio de Valero, established in 1718, and San José, built two years later. Indian depredations in east Texas forced the relocation in 1731 of three more missions: Concepción, San Juan Capistrano, and Espada. All three sat along the San Antonio River.

During the eighteenth century ranches and missions in Spanish Texas suffered from disease, drought, and Indian raids. Ranchers also lacked legal market outlets. Cattle smugglers moved herds surreptitiously into French Louisiana. Legal trade expanded in the 1770s, but smugglers continued operations to avoid paying an export tax of two reales per head. By the late eighteenth century, some 15,000 to 20,000 head moved eastward to Louisiana each year.

By the early 1800s illegal horse and mule trade joined the contraband cattle drives. The movement of Anglo settlers into the Mississippi Valley opened another market for livestock. Meanwhile, problems plagued the economic and religious activities at the missions. Unable to convert the hostile Indians, priests abandoned the missions in east Texas. The livestock, however, remained.

Regrettably, Anglo-American racism tinges most descriptions of the vaquero from the nineteenth and early twentieth centuries. Untrustworthy, lazy, drunken, and debauched are among the adjectives generally applied to vaqueros by Anglos. In *Ranch Life and the Hunting Trail* (1888), the observations of Theodore Roosevelt, who was deeply concerned with maintaining Anglo-Saxon superiority, are typical: "Some of the cowboys are Mexicans, who generally do the actual work well enough, but are not trustworthy; moreover, they are always regarded with extreme disfavor by the Texans in an outfit, among whom the intolerant caste spirit is very strong. Southern-born whites will never work under them, and look down upon all colored or half-caste races."

Folklorist J. Frank **Dobie** recognized and tried to correct the Anglo biases that colored the image of the vaquero. In 1931 he recorded a more accurate portrait of the Mexican cowboy. Dobie found the vaquero superstitious, a bit cruel to animals, close to nature, faithful, and hospitable.

He is full of stories about buried treasures, which priests and *gachupines* [Spaniards] are usually somehow connected with and which are guarded by white *bultos* [ghosts], clanking chains, eerie lights and other mysteries. If he does not know a witch, he knows of one. If he does not fear the evil eye, he respects it. If he or any of his family become very ill, he wants a doctor, but at the same time he yearns for a *curandero* [folk healer] (a kind of quack that a whole essay would be required to picture forth). He is familiar with the habits of every creature of his soil. For him every hill and hollow has a personality and a name. He regards the stars; he watches the phases of the moon. He knows the name and virtue of every bush and herb. He is a child of nature; he is truly *un hombre de campo* [a man of the land].

Either despite or because of his nearness to nature, he is as insensible to the sufferings of nature's progeny as nature is herself. He will run his horse into thorns and then have no thought of pulling the thorns out; he will ride a thirsty horse within fifty yards of a water hole and unless he himself is thirsty will not turn aside. He will rub sand into the eyes of a wild cow that he has roped, though in this he is no more cruel than the average old-time cowpuncher. He will sit all day in the shade of his *jacal* [hut] and never offer to carry a bucket of water for his over-worked wife.

For all that, the *vaquero* is kind to his family, sets no limit to his hospitality, and probably goes beyond the average human being in faithfulness. He will divide his last *tortilla* with any stranger who happens by. He will take the side of his *amo* [master], if he likes him, against any Mexican that tries to do his *amo* an injustice. The reputation he has somehow acquired in literature for being treacherous is, I believe, altogether undeserved.

Folk sources reveal the vaquero's pride, machismo, and vanity. "The Ballad of Manuel Rodríguez," supposedly based on a true incident at the **King Ranch** in Texas, depicts these characteristics. In the ballad, an especially bad horse threw Rodríguez in front of his fellow riders. An excellent **bronc buster,** the humiliated Rodríguez quit the ranch and vowed to go pick cotton—to the cowboy a particularly demeaning type of footwork. Like his equestrian fellows elsewhere, the vaquero looked upon the lowly farmer (as well as those who herded goats and sheep) with mixed pity and contempt.

Vaqueros admired their fellows who were long-suffering, patient, uncomplaining, and persevering, just as Anglo cowboys esteemed men who worked in bad weather or with pain, went without food, or tracked down stray animals at all costs. Like other cowboys, vaqueros valued courage. Virtuous actions would not bring praise, but failing to measure up to the vaquero standard could bring criticism, censure, or ridicule.

The vaqueros' virtues remained constant, but their dress varied with the terrain they rode. Many wore a **poncho,** called a serape in Mexico. They wore a broad-brimmed sombrero whose design influenced cowboy **hats** in the United States Theodore Dodge described the vaquero dress of northern Mexico in 1891: "Our Chihuahua vaquero wears white cotton clothes, and goat-skin chaperajos [chaps] with the hair left on, naked feet, and huarachos [*huaraches*], or sandals, and big jingling spurs. A gourd, lashed to his cantle, does the duty of canteen ... and his saddle is loaded down with an abundance of cheap plunder."

F. Warner Robinson left a slightly more detailed description *(Scribner's Magazine,* February 1912).

[His dress] consists of a short jacket made of some cheap coarse material, usually in colors, and tight-fitting pantaloons belled out at the bottom just enough to permit easy foot action. Down the outside seam of his trousers runs a broad strip of brilliant cloth. Instead of a belt he wears a *faja* (sash) which is wrapped around his body several times with the ends tucked in. It is always of some bright color, usually red or blue. His sombrero, of course, is an object of almost universal conjecture, often having a three-foot expanse of brim, which is dipped at a rakish angle, with a conical-shaped crown. It is made of braided straw and is invariably decorated with bands of brilliant colors.

On the range he always has about him somewhere his beloved *serape,* which seems indestructible. He wears it thrown over his shoulder like a shawl, and how he keeps it on, in the thick of a round-up, always puzzles the American cowboy. He also uses it as his bed at night; and when it rains, one will see him stoically sitting his horse (he rides a horse on the plain but not in the mountains), enjoying the full glory of it like an Indian chief on dress parade. His foot-gear is almost laughable, for instead of the high-heeled graceful boot worn by American cowboys, he wears the *charro shoe,* which is low-heeled, thin-soled, and very pointed at the toe, resembling, in every respect but the toe, the old-style congress shoe. It is usually of russett leather of very soft texture. As a rule, he wears no kerchief round his neck, and his chaps fit tight and flare at the bottom like his trousers.

Jo Mora was among the leading historians of the *californio,* the vaquero of Spanish California. He ably described the essentials of vaquero dress:

A kerchief was bound about his head, atop which, at a very rakish, arrogant angle, sat a trail-worn weather-beaten hat, wide of brim, low of crown, held in place by a *barbiquejo* (chin strap) that extended just below the lower lip. His unkempt black beard scraggled over his jowls, and his long black hair dangled down his back to a little below the line of his shoulders. His ample colonial shirt was soiled and torn, and a flash of brown shoulder could usually be seen through a recent tear. The typical wide, red Spanish sash encircled his lean midriff. His short pants, reaching to his knees, buttoned up the sides, and were open for six inches or so at the bottom. Long drawers (which were once white) showed wrinkles at the knees and were folded into wrapped leather *botas* (leggings). He wore a rough pair of buckskin shoes with leather soles and low heels, to which were strapped a pair of large and rusty iron spurs. This costume was finished off by a *tirador* (a heavy, wide-at-the-hips belt) that helped him to snub with the *reata* (rawhide rope) when lassoing on foot. The ever-present long knife in its scabbard was thrust inside the garter on his right leg.

In the deserts of Baja California and northwestern Mexico, vaqueros of the colonial era rigged their saddles with *armas*—large, stiff leather skirts hanging off the saddle. The leather protected riders from thorns and cacti. Later riders attached smaller skirts (called *armitas* or *polainas)* to their legs. These leather protectors were of course the forerunners of the vaquero's *chaparreras* and the **chaps** used by American cowboys. Leather comprised practically the entire outfit and equipment of the rider in Baja California. He wore a leather hat *(vaqueteada)* and a long, leather wrap-around coat *(cuera).* His stirrup coverings *(tapaderas),* **saddle** bags *(cojinillos),* and lariat (reata) were also made of leather.

Vaqueros considered **firearms** unmanly. They looked disdainfully at the gun-toting Anglo who could not protect himself like a real man. Vaquero folklore emphasized the value of outwitting an adversary, rather than confronting him with a gun. The vaquero relied on his knife and his **rope,** which served as both tool and formidable weapon.

Economic Position

Mexican vaqueros often found themselves in debt. In New Mexico, for example, debt peonage was already common by 1800. It persisted through the nineteenth century in Mexico. Frederic **Remington** noted that vaqueros "are mostly *peoned,* or in hopeless debt to their *patrons,* who go after any man who deserts the range and bring him back by force." Through the early twentieth century, vaqueros earned the equivalent of $8 to $12 per month. Vaqueros in Texas faced wage discrimination from Anglo ranchers. The Scott and Byler outfit, for example, paid their Anglo hands $20 per month, but reduced the wage to $10 to $12 for vaqueros. Only the highly skilled vaquero bronco buster could aspire to higher wages. He might earn $20 per month.

Political conflict repeatedly disrupted the Mexican ranching industry. Wars often moved vaqueros from ranch work to cavalry service. During the 1860s fighting between the liberal forces of Benito Juárez and the occupying French armies of Emperor Maximilian destroyed the huge estate of the Sánchez Navarros in Coahuila. By 1864 the ranch was a battlefield. Both sides looted and pillaged livestock and grain. Carlos Sánchez Navarro, a conservative, sided with the imperialist cause of Maximilian. This decision sealed the family's economic doom. Juárez exacted revenge on the family and jailed Sánchez Navarro after defeating and executing Maximilian in 1867.

Even peace in the countryside did not ensure a better life for the Mexican vaquero and peasant. The long dictatorship of Porfirio Díaz (1884–1910) greatly impoverished the rural masses. Díaz offered generous land concessions to foreigners, broke any attempted strikes, and generally reduced rural Mexicans to peon status.

The situation became increasingly dire in the early twentieth century. Farm wages fell 17 percent between 1895 and 1910. Ninety-eight percent of rural Mexicans were landless by 1910. Many labored as migrants to survive. Skilled cowhands did not suffer as drastic a wage decline as farmhands, but many vaqueros only found seasonal work on the great estates that dominated northern Mexico. For some, banditry became an alternative form of employment. Bandit leaders, such as Jesús Arriaga ("Chucho el Roto") and Heraclio Bernal, "the Thunderbolt of Sinaloa," became popular symbols of opposition to the dictatorship.

The violence and disorder of the Mexican Revolution broke forth in 1910. Armies proliferated under Emiliano Zapata, Francisco ("Pancho") Villa, Alvaro Obregón, Pascual Orozco, Pablo González, Venustiano Carranza, and other revolutionary chieftains. Orozco stole cattle from northern Mexican estates and sold them in the United States to purchase arms. All of the armies needed mounts, draft animals, and meat. They also needed vaqueros to tend the animals and to fight. Through forced and voluntary donations of livestock, ranchers lost their herds as armies swept through in advance or retreat. Some owners tried to ship cattle to the United States to avoid seizure.

The revolution largely destroyed Mexico's livestock industry. In 1902 an estimated 396,000 cattle roamed the state of Chihuahua. Pillage and disruption cut the number by about 75 percent by 1923. Sonora suffered a similar decline in that period from some 261,000 head to 69,000. Durango experienced the greatest loss, from 233,000 to 23,000. Overall, the number of cattle in Mexico dropped 67 percent between 1902 and 1923.

A new revolutionary elite emerged during the 1920s. The vaquero and other poor rural Mexicans found they had gained little from the revolution. The livestock industry gradually recovered, but vaqueros remained exploited, poorly paid, and landless. The revolution failed to overturn the stratified hacienda social order, with powerful landed elites at the top and poor cowhands and peasants at the bottom.

Because vaqueros were illiterate, they left few personal records. Some vaquero folklore passed into Mexican *corridos.* These folk songs have eight-syllable lines, with the second and fourth lines rhymed. Regional variations are legion. For example, the Huasteca variant often includes cowboy yells (*gritos de vaquero*).

Many corridos celebrate famous **horses** and horse races, important elements of vaquero culture. Vaqueros of the King Ranch in Texas sang "El Toro Moro" to eulogize a particularly fierce bull. One song, "Gallo de Cielo," even celebrates a famous fighting cock. Other songs dealt with the realities of ranch life. "Mi Caballo Bayo" recalls a vaquero who loved his cutting horse too much to sell him at any price.

Like **gaucho** folk songs, many corridos include political and social commentary. Some, such as ballads about Gregorio Cortés and Joaquín Murieta, celebrate the daring deeds of outlaw heroes. Other corridos recall the feats of the bandit Heraclio Bernal. Bernal attained Robin Hood status among the Mexican poor for defying the officials of Porfirio Díaz's dictatorship. Vaqueros and the rest of Mexico's rural poor commemorated those who rose above their humble origins to challenge and flaunt authority.

Mexico's vaquero remains identified with the great northern Mexican haciendas and with Spanish California. He did not establish the same national presence as the cowboy in the United States or the gaucho in Argentina. Mexico did honor a horseman, the elitist *charro*, with a monument constructed in 1926. (Dodge 1891; Dobie 1927, 1931, 1981; Mora 1949; Ramírez 1979; Rojas 1964; Slatta 1990)

VIGILANCE COMMITTEE
See Violence.

VIGILANTE
See Violence.

VIOLENCE
American West
Charles Marion **Russell** painted a number of canvases depicting arguments being settled by gunfire. In *Smoke of a .45*, mounted gunmen fire from the street back into a **saloon**. The street is littered with playing cards and a whiskey bottle. *Death of a Gambler* shows a very similar scene, with one gambler lying dead on the street amidst a pile of playing cards. A second gambler has just been shot and crumples against the wall of the saloon. *When Guns Speak, Death Settles Disputes* offers a wide-angle view of the same scene. In *The Long Horn*, two horsemen ride away, firing into the saloon as they flee. A third rider has been shot, has his foot caught in the stirrup, and is being pulled along in the dirt by his horse.

Saloons earned their reputations as places of fighting and death. The lethal combination of **gambling** and alcohol fueled many fights. Rousing, furniture-smashing fistfights ("dog fights") were largely creations of the western movies. Most cowboys disdained fisticuffs. As one old-timer remarked, "If the Lord had intended me to fight like a dog, He'd a-give me longer teeth and claws." Cowboys did not hesitate to fight with a knife and "manstopper" (gun).

Violence is a powerful part of the **mythology** and reality of the Old West. Frontier regions, often beyond the reach of police and judicial institutions, provided ample opportunity for violence. In a land with far more guns than lawmen, "death settles disputes," as Russell put it in the name of one of his paintings.

When citizens perceived a lack of law and order, they often organized into vigilante groups. Stockmen sometimes organized such groups to stem horse and cattle losses to rustlers. Montana ranchers executed at least 35 suspected rustlers in 1884 without benefit of trial, judge, or jury. Prominent rancher and politician Granville Stuart played a leading role. *The Democratic Leader* (Cheyenne, Wyoming, 10 August 1884) reported the vigilante actions:

> It becoming evident that it was a horse thieves' rendezvous, the cowboys congregated and ... crawled up close to the house and attacked it. Fourteen horse thieves were about the premises at the time. Nine were killed and five escaped. The cabin was set on fire and burned.
>
> There never was a period in the history of this or any other Territory when so much horse thieving was going on. The citizens are determined to effectually stop it. Fully thirty thieves were hanged or shot in the past month.

In some cases, mobs acted on impulse, without benefit of prior organization or leadership. In 1864 a bandit by the name of Joe Pizanthia met his end at Bannack, Montana, at the hands of an enraged crowd. A mob cornered the outlaw in a cabin, then opened fire on the building with a small howitzer. The wounded Pizanthia survived the fusillade, only to be shot and then lynched. The vigilantes fired more than a hundred shots into the hanging body. Still not satisfied, they set fire to the cabin and tossed the corpse into the flames. Western vigilantes killed at least 700 suspected criminals during the nineteenth century.

Long distances and short tempers often militated against due process in the West. The *Albuquerque Morning Journal* (15 October 1882) reported one of many cases of summary "justice:"

The western cowboy may suffer, forgive and forget, but there is one thing he will not condone—a horsethief and his work. An Indian horsethief was lassoed and dragged to death at Lewiston, Idaho, by white cowboys, for attempting to sell them stolen horses.

"Necktie parties" (lynchings) were the more common punishment meted out to accused horse or cattle thieves. Vigilantes often needed

Cowboys inflicted their own brand of justice, often resulting in "necktie parties." Pictured here in this circa 1882 photograph by H. R. Farr is the lynching of a man by the name of Frank McManus.

only a few minutes, a rope, and a tree to impose their brand of justice.

Gunfights quickly became a staple of penny dreadfuls (**pulp novels**) and **B-western** movies. The most famous conflict was the gunfight at the O. K. corral, which occurred on 26 October 1881. Virgil, Morgan, and Wyatt Earp along with Doc Holliday took on Billy Clanton, Ike Clanton, and Frank and Tom McLaury. A feud had brewed for months. Within a few seconds, the McLaurys and Clantons lay dying. Holliday and two of the Earps had been wounded. Rehashed in countless pulps, histories, and films, the short but vicious battle remains an icon of western conflict.

Famous outlaw gangs, their exploits magnified in the penny press, also contributed to the West's reputation for violence. Frank and Jesse James; Butch Cassidy; Cole, Bob, and Jim Younger; Emmett, Gratton, and Bob Dalton—these outlaws gained great notoriety throughout the country. Stories in the "respectable press" often read like the breathless, sensational pulp novels and plays that sometimes depicted the outlaw gangs as folk heroes. Bank, train, and stagecoach heists became staples of western iconography. Twentieth-century filmmakers further embellished the imagery, beginning with the 1903 movie, *The Great Train Robbery.*

While the frequency of gunfights in the Old West has been inflated by pulp novels and B movies, Anglo cowboys often did carry sidearms. Canadian cowboys carried guns far less often than American cowboys. Alberta cowman Henry Caven recalled that in Canada "there was none of the Wild West gunman stuff that the movies portray about early American west days."

Cattle towns had no monopoly on frontier violence. The mining frontier apparently rivaled the cattle frontier for boisterous behavior. Elliott West found high levels of homicide in saloons located in Rocky Mountain mining towns.

The reality was, of course, that far more cowboys died of work injuries than "lead poisoning." Hands faced the dangers of **ranch work,** omnipresent and often lethal, daily. A fall or kick from a horse could end a man's life. A charging **longhorn** bull could kill a horse and his rider. Far from medical attention, cowboys might die of relatively minor injuries or infection. Mythology, however, has fastened on violent forms of death.

Latin America

Like saloons of the Old West, Argentine *pulperías* became justifiably famous for fights. Some men went looking for trouble, and drink only heightened the likelihood of conflict. **Gauchos** skillfully wielded deadly *facónes,* or swordlike knives, which they preferred long after **firearms** had reached Argentina. With a degree of Freudian hyperbole, Argentine philosopher Ezequiel Martínez Estrada explained the significance of the facón in *X-Ray of the Pampa* (1971). The knife, he wrote, is "not part of the costume but part of the body itself. It pertains more to the man than to his apparel, more to his character than to his social status. He who shows his knife when there is no need for it commits an indecent act."

Like other Latin American horsemen (except the **llanero**), the gaucho disdained firearms. Real men fought with knives. Superstitious gauchos believed that some men could not be wounded with firearms. They called such invincible men *retobados* (literally, wily or cunning). **Vaqueros** also rejected guns as unmanly.

Argentine gauchos engaged in knife duels for manly sport, not necessity. While the supposed goal of such contests was only to mark or scar an opponent's face, many combatants died of knife wounds. An Argentine rancher suggested in 1856 (with some exaggeration) that 99 percent of homicides, injuries, and disorders occurred at pulperías. Police and justice of the peace records are full of cases in which knife duels ended in wounding or death. The perpetrator usually fled to other, more remote areas of the frontier.

During the bloody political conflicts of the early nineteenth century, throat-slitting in Argentina reached the status of a folk art. In 1833, Charles Darwin wrote from Argentina to his sister Caroline that "a more throat-cutting

Frank and Jesse James, pictured here proudly wielding their guns, are representative of the unbridled violence that pervaded the West and was capitalized by the penny press and movie makers.

gentry do not exist than these Gauchos on the face of the world."

Pulperías in Chile gained similar reputations as havens for drunkenness and violence. Colonial authorities in the early seventeenth century declared the humble taverns to be "dens of drunkenness, where Indians, Negroes and other castes exchange stolen goods for liquor." In 1635 Governor Francisco Laso de la Vega decreed a 30-peso fine for any "pulpero audacious enough to sell wine to any Indian, Negro or mulatto, male or female." Tavern owners were forbidden to purchase chickens, food, and small game because Indians "destroyed and robbed the farms and ranches and cattle of all types and took them to sell to said pulperos."

The problem of pulperías did not go away, however. More than a century later, in 1748, a Chilean bishop complained that men sold their horses, **spurs,** and even the clothes off their backs to purchase liquor. Even allowing for the racial and class biases adhering in such elite views, it is clear that pulperías maintained an active clientele from the colonial period forward.

William Taylor found the same volatile mix of machismo, drink, and violence in taverns of colonial Mexico frequented by the lower classes. Arguments and contests of dominance often spawned fights. In 1798, 45 percent of all arrests in Mexico City were alcohol-related. In both the Mexican countryside and the capital, refusal of a drink could be taken as a serious affront to manly honor and precipitate a fight.

Violence and lack of accountability for one's actions are part of a set of "time-out" norms when social conventions are suspended. In the case of the saloon culture, the time-out norms represent the values and behaviors of an exaggerated machismo. The killing of a gaucho in a drunken duel was considered to be a *desgracia*—unfortunate accident. In the eyes of his peers, the killer deserved sympathy, not blame. (Gard 1949; Hollon 1974; Pereira Salas 1947; Slatta 1987; Tractman 1974; West 1979)

See also Canada, Violence; Cow Towns; Fast Draw; Firearms.

THE VIRGINIAN
Novel by Owen **Wister** and a 1929 film starring Gary Cooper.

VON SCHMIDT, HAROLD
(1893–1982)
Artist. See Art of the Cowboy.

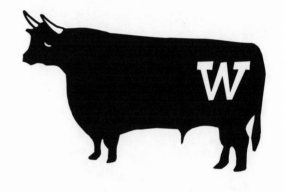

WADDIE

Also waddy—one of many terms for a cowboy. The word is of unknown origin, although speculation abounds. Like the term *cowboy,* *waddie* originally carried a negative connotation of a drifter or even a rustler. Over time, however, the word lost its negative associations.

WAGES

Ranchers in the United States and Canada generally enjoyed labor surpluses. As a result wages remained low, and the possibility of striking for better terms proved nearly impossible. Cowboy **strikes** and other protests against low wages have been recorded, but none of them was effective.

Records for the Spur Ranch in Texas indicate that the manager only once had difficulty securing enough hands between 1885 and 1909. The same records show a marked seasonality of cowboy employment. During the late nineteenth century, only one-third to one-half as many hands worked from December through March as from April to November. Nearly two-thirds worked only one season or just part of a season at the ranch. The *Kansas Cowboy* (25 July 1885) estimated that "the boys only get work three or four months in the year" on the northern ranges of Montana.

Those without work survived on handouts, hunting, and odd jobs. The prudent passed the winter living frugally off their meager savings. The diary of cowboy James C. Shaw reveals how a cowboy might cope with winter layoffs. He worked for six weeks in Wyoming during fall **roundup** in 1879. Laid off on Christmas day, he received permission from the rancher to hunt wild game until spring. When springtime came, Shaw found work on the Laramie River for $30 per month.

Canadian cowboys faced a bleak winter. Cattleman John R. Craig noted that after the fall roundup "there was not employment for them [the hands] until the following spring, and although they had been in recent good wages—$45 to $50 a month and board for the summer—they are 'broke.'" Men in these

circumstances did odd jobs, "rode the grub line" taking handouts at different ranches, or existed on wild game and "slow elk" (poached beef).

A new hand in the United States earned little more in 1904 than he had 30 years earlier. Special skills and more experience brought higher wages, however. Cowboy H. B. C. Benton earned top wages of $75 per month in 1882 to break horses for the Sand Creek Land and Cattle Company in Idaho. Cooks also commanded higher wages, earning from $70 to $90 per month during the 1880s, compared with $30 for a beginning hand. Daily wages from the 1860s through 1885 ranged from about $1.50 to $2. Wages also varied depending on whether the ranch provided "keep" (room and board).

Twentieth-century cowboys fared no better. Ranch work continued to hold its appeal as a way of life, but ranch wages lagged far behind those in other sectors of the economy. Writing in the *Wall Street Journal* of 10 June 1981, journalist William E. Blundell noted that "the days of the cowboy are marked by danger, drudgery, and low pay." Cowboy wages averaged $500 per month without room and board. Not much had changed in a century. (Craig 1971; Dary 1981; Frantz and Choate 1955; Slatta 1990; Weston 1985)

Sample Ranch Wages, United States, 1870–1909

Year(s)	Cowboy	Foreman	State/Territory
	(U.S. $ per month)		
1870s	25	—	Kansas
1872	20	—	Texas
1879	35	—	Wyoming
1880	30–75	—	Wyoming
1881	35–75	75	Wyoming
1882	30–75	—	Wyoming
1883	30–75	—	Wyoming
1884	30–50	—	Wyoming
1885	25–50	125	Texas, Wyoming
1886	25–50	—	Wyoming
1887	30–40	—	Wyoming
1888	30–40	—	Wyoming
1889	35–40	—	Wyoming
1890	30–45	125–150	Texas

Year(s)	Cowboy	Foreman	State/Territory
	(U.S. $ per month)		
1891	25–40	—	Wyoming
1892	25–30	—	Wyoming
1893	30	—	Wyoming
1904	30	—	Texas
1909	37	—	Texas

(Holden 1970; McCoy 1874, 1976; Rollins 1979; Rollinson 1948; Slatta 1990)

Sample Ranch Wages,
Alberta, Canada, 1881–1915

Year	Cowboy (Canadian $ per month)
1881	20
1883	45–110
1885	40–50
1887	40
1891–92	30–100
1904	20–30
1905	20–35
1906	25–40
1910	30–40
1912	35
1914	70
1915	70

(Breen 1975, 1983; Brado 1984)

WAGON BOSS

Person in charge of a **roundup.**

WAGON-SPOKE ROWEL

A long-shanked **spur** with rowels spaced out to resemble wagon wheel spokes.

WALKER, JAMES
(1881–1946)

Artist. See Art of the Cowboy.

WALKER PISTOL

Also Walker Colt. See Colt Firearms.

WAR BAG

Also war sack, wallet—a sack for personal belongings, usually tied behind the **saddle.** Also called a yannigan bag.

WAR BONNET

Colloquial term for **hat.**

WARTING

Scaly raised scar on an animal caused by poor branding done too deeply.

WASP NEST

Colloquial term for light bread.

WATER

See Windmill.

WATSON, ELLA

See Women.

WATTLE

Ranchers used many means to mark ownership of their cattle. Some cattlemen used a wattle, a mark on a cow's neck or jaw. A cowboy would cut a slit in a pinch of skin, and when the cut healed it left an identifiable flap of skin. Earmarks and branding on the hide, however, were the most commonly used methods of marking cattle.

WATTS, PETER CHRISTOPHER
(1919–)

London-born novelist who has written formula westerns under various names.

WAY POCKET

Also way pouch. See Saddle.

WAYNE, JOHN
(1907–1979)

More than any other figure, John Wayne came to epitomize the cinema cowboy. Most fans refer to him as "the Duke." His walk, talk, looks, and spirit dominated the finest days of A westerns from the late 1940s through the 1960s. Wayne appeared in some 250 films. His friend, director John Ford, gave Wayne his big break in *Stagecoach* (1939). The Duke also performed in many other Ford films, including *She Wore a Yellow Ribbon* (1949) and *The*

Searchers (1956). Howard Hawks directed Wayne in equally memorable roles in *Red River* (1948) and *Rio Bravo* (1959).

Wayne was born Marion Michael Morrison in Winterset, Iowa. The tall (6'4"), handsome, young Morrison caught Hollywood's eye in 1926. A freshman football player at the University of Southern California, he took a summer job at Fox Studios, earning $35 per week to move props. He soon began appearing onscreen as an extra.

After several years of bit parts, Morrison got a big break in 1930. On John Ford's recommendation, Raoul Walsh cast him in the lead role of *The Big Trail*. His salary, however, only rose to $75 per week. Walsh gave the 23-year-old Michael Morrison his stage name—John Wayne—but the film flopped. A bad script, technical difficulties, and Wayne's inexperienced, unconvincing performance all detracted from the movie. Viewed more than sixty years later, however, the film holds up remarkably well.

The Duke went back to marginal **B-western** roles. He even took a shot at being one of the screen's first singing cowboys (with dubbed songs), appearing as "Singing Sandy" in *Riders of Destiny* (1933). His singing character did not impress viewers, so Gene **Autry** and others took over as the singing stars.

In the mid-1930s, Monogram and Mascot, two producers of low-budget westerns, merged to form Republic Pictures. The fortunes of John Wayne, Gene Autry, and many other cowboy stars rose under the tutelage of the new production company. Wayne played in *Westward Ho* and two more Republic westerns in 1935. The following year Republic produced seven Wayne westerns. In 1938 he began to star as Stony Brooke in the "Three Mesquiteers" series. The cowboy trio, Ray ("Crash") Corrigan, Max Terhune, and Wayne, proved very popular.

Fortunately for Wayne, John Ford returned to westerns in 1939. Ford's faith in Wayne paid off handsomely for both men. As the Ringo Kid in *Stagecoach,* Wayne proved that he had learned to

act in the decade since *The Big Trail,* and Ford showed himself master of the medium.

As he rose to stardom, Wayne's personal life came under greater public scrutiny. Over the next several decades, he survived many public relations disasters. He persevered through three stormy marriages and divorces with Latin women. His hard drinking and stridently conservative politics alienated some fans and critics. In his drinking prime, he put away a quart of booze, often tequila, a day. "The great thing is that you never get hung over with tequila. But ya gotta watch your back, 'cause ya sure as hell fall over a lot."

Many film cowboys gave equal billing to their smart **horses.** Not Wayne. He considered the horse a tool of the trade, not a costar. His approach to horses resembled his no-nonsense attitude toward life in general. "Listen up, horse. You're gonna do what I tell ya, when I tell ya, or you're gonna regret it."

Wayne's own personal heroes attest to the power of cowboy **mythology.** Wayne named two other celluloid cowboys, Harry Carey and Hoot Gibson, among his heroes: myth begets myth. He admired the swashbuckling bravado of Douglas Fairbanks, Sr., and copied Jack Dempsey's fighting style in developing his own barroom brawl technique for the camera. Actor Paul Fix (Harry Carey's father-in-law) coached the Duke on his famous rolling gait.

Friend, actor, and stuntman Yakima Canutt (1895–1986) also played an important role in shaping the Duke's career. He doubled for the Duke, although the athletic Wayne often insisted on performing his own stunts. "I've learned as much about ridin', stuntin' and makin' pictures from Yakima Canutt as any man I've every known." Yak and Duke together perfected the "near miss" technique that added realism to fistfights.

Doing one's own stunts can prove hazardous. Wayne suffered several injuries making films. An unscripted horsefall in *The Defeated* (1969) broke three of the Duke's ribs. He barely escaped being burned to death while filming *Circus World* (1964). He also suffered many other miscellaneous bumps, bruises, and breaks.

Wayne's films often carried a message. His characters showed that one courageous man willing to take the lead, acting righteously, could ensure that right triumphed over wrong. Wayne believed in heroes and liked to depict them for the public. Beginning in the 1940s, his politics became intertwined with his art. In 1948 Wayne took over as president of the Motion Picture Alliance for the Preservation of American Ideals; he had helped found the zealously anticommunist group in 1944. An unquestioning patriot, Wayne expressed concern about "the infiltration of Communists and fellow-travelers into the picture business."

It was difficult to establish where the film John Wayne ended and the man began. He projected his ultra-conservative politics and patriotism on and off screen. Wayne directed, funded, and acted in *The Alamo* (1960) and *The Green Berets* (1968). Both are short on historical reality and long on hero worship. Film critic Brian Garfield calls *The Alamo* "childish and boring," "nearly a classic for students of awful movies." *The Green Berets* also met a well-deserved barrage of criticism. Nevertheless Wayne fans packed theaters to see the Duke take on the Commies. Wayne depicted the complexities of Southeast Asia in terms that most Americans preferred—good cowboys fighting off bad Indians.

Despite the flaws of these works, Wayne left a more impressive corpus of westerns than any other actor. Hollywood rather grudgingly recognized his film contributions in 1969. He finally won an Academy Award for his role as Rooster Cogburn, the crusty, old cowboy in *True Grit* (1969). His final role as J. B. Brooks in *The Shootist* (1976) took on added poignancy. The aging gunfighter he played was dying of cancer. Two years later the Duke underwent heart surgery, and shortly thereafter, physicians diagnosed spreading stomach cancer. The "Big C," which he had licked once in the 1960s, claimed his life in 1979.

The Duke dominated western film for half a century. Critic Jon Tuska (*Views and Reviews,* February 1974) well summarized his importance:

Duke Wayne is the last of the great traditionalists. When he passes from the scene, I do not think there will be another Western hero to replace him. As he mounts his horse straight of body as Tom Mix mounted Tony when Duke was a prop boy at Fox; when in *The Searchers* (Warner's, 1956) John Ford has Duke imitate a gesture characteristic of Harry Carey; when Duke's weathered face is photographed with lines of granite resolve reminiscent of Buck Jones, with whom Duke worked when they were both at Columbia—there you have the embodiment of almost half a century of Western filmmaking.

Wayne embodied the nation's concept of the cowboy hero more than any other person. The Duke never backed down; he talked straight, shot straight, righted wrongs, and punished the guilty. Unwavering in his belief in the rightness of his cause, he saw life with a clarity that many Americans admire. "They tell me everything isn't black and white," he said. "Well, I say why the hell not?" (Boswell and David 1979; Eyles 1979; Garfield 1982; Zolotow 1974)

See also Films, Best Cowboy; Films, Cowboy.

WE POINTED THEM NORTH

Book by "Teddy Blue" **Abbott.** See Autobiographies by Cowboys.

WEARING THE BUSTLE WRONG

Humorous term describing a pregnant woman.

WEDDING RING

See Rope.

WELLMAN, PAUL ISELIN
(1898–1966)

Oklahoma-born novelist and historian, author of *The Trampling Herd* (1939).

WESTERMEIER, CLIFFORD P.
(1910–1986))
Historian. See Historiography of the Cowboy.

WESTERN FOLKLIFE CENTER
See Poetry.

WESTERN HISTORICAL QUARTERLY
See Western History Association.

WESTERN HISTORY ASSOCIATION
The Western History Association (WHA) serves as the main gathering point for professional historians who study the West. The WHA sponsors an annual conference each October where members gather to present scholarly papers. The association began as the brainchild of Jack Carroll and Don Cutter. After discussions in 1959, they pushed ahead to organize professional western historians, a daunting task given the rugged individualism of the region. Interested scholars met at Detroit and Santa Fe in 1961. Ray Billington served as the first president of the WHA, which organized officially at a meeting in Denver of 1962. Joe Frantz (Texas), Walter Prescott Webb (Texas), Bob Athearn (Colorado), Gene Hollon (Oklahoma), and others helped with the initial organizing.

WHA membership is open to "anyone interested in the history and culture of the American West." Membership in the WHA is a genuine bargain. For dues of $30 per calendar year and up, members receive a newsletter and two quarterly publications, *Montana, the Magazine of Western History* (see Appendix C) and *Western Historical Quarterly (WHQ)*. Both journals publish articles by well-known western scholars. The difference is audience and format—*Montana* is a glossy, generously illustrated magazine that can be read and appreciated by a general audience.

As a professional journal, the *WHQ* includes more specialized articles of interest to scholars of the West. It also reviews books and lists recent articles dealing with western history. The *WHQ* is published at Utah State University in Logan, Utah.

The WHA originally consisted mostly of white males studying dead white males. Frontier scholars, many disciplines of Frederick Jackson Turner, predominated. The association has broadened and matured remarkably over the past three decades. Issues of gender, class, and ethnicity receive regular analysis. Women and ethnic minorities have given the organization a greater diversity of viewpoints. The WHA, like any other gathering of historians, includes its share of squabbling, but its publications and meetings continue to provide a hospitable focus for the wonderfully diverse and exciting world of western history.

For WHA membership information, contact Paul Hutton, History Department, University of New Mexico, Albuquerque, NM 87131.

WESTERN TRAIL
See Trail Drive.

WESTERN WRITERS OF AMERICA, INC.
Founded in 1953, the Western Writers of America (WWA) "is an organization of professionals dedicated to the spirit and reality of the West, past and present." According to its membership brochure, "WWA provides a unique fellowship for those using the written word or film to examine or celebrate the heritage of the West and its future."

The WWA membership includes novelists, poets, journalists, and scriptwriters. The group meets annually to present Spur Awards in many literary categories. Members receive *The Roundup Quarterly* and a monthly newsletter.

WWA has two membership categories. Authors of three or more books, at least one dealing with the American West, qualify as active members. Associate members must have published at least one book or five western articles or short stories, or one screenplay or three teleplays.

Address: P.O. Box 823, Sheridan, WY 82801; tel. 307-672-2079.

THE WESTERNER
Film (1940).

THE WESTERNERS INTERNATIONAL

An international organization "dedicated to the proposition that it would be a good thing if more people around our old world knew more about the Frontier Concept—especially the westerning movement in the Americas." Westerners International (WI) grew out of Friends of the Middle Border, founded by Leland D. Case in the late 1930s. In March 1944 Case, Franklin Meine, Elmo Scott Watson, and 20 other "founding fathers" met in Chicago and formed the first WI corral (chapter).

Each corral has a sheriff and elected posse to arrange monthly meetings to "chomp, chat and listen." Corral members eat together, socialize, present papers, and discuss all matter of things western. Deputy sheriffs, a roundup foreman, chuck wrangler, trail boss, and registrar of marks and brands joined the list of officers. Corrals also publish occasional "Brand Books" of papers related to western history and literature.

New corrals appeared in Denver (1945), St. Louis and Los Angeles (1946), New York (1952), and Tucson, Laramie, and the Black Hills (1953). The New York corral early provoked traditionalists by admitting "sage-hens" (women).

The Westerners went international with new corrals in England in 1954 and France in 1955. The group officially added "International" to its name in 1969. The organization maintained headquarters in Tucson until 1989, when it moved to Oklahoma City. By 1994 the group had some 90 corrals in 11 countries.

Founded for and by western buffs and amateurs, WI now includes professional historians. Many WI members figured among the historians who organized the **Western**

History Association (WHA) in 1961. Frontier historian Ray Allen Billington served as president of both the WHA and WI. Today volunteer "Wranglers" at the WI "Home Ranch" publish a quarterly *Buckskin Bulletin* and tend to organizational business. The **National Cowboy Hall of Fame** donates space for the headquarters.

Address: WI c/o National Cowboy Hall of Fame, 1700 NE 63d St., Oklahoma City, OK 73111; tel. 800-5341-4650.

WESTON, DICK
The Texas Troubadour. See Rogers, Roy.

WET STOCK
Livestock brought illegally across the Rio Grande from Mexico.

WHALE LINE
Colloquial term for **rope** or lariat.

WHEN THE LEGENDS DIE
Film. See Rodeo.

WHIP
See Quirt.

WHISKEY
See Saloons.

WHISTLE BERRIES
Humorous term for beans. See Food.

WHITE FLASH
Tex Ritter's movie horse.

WHITE-COLLAR RANCHER
Absentee ranch owner.

WHITNEY GALLERY
See Buffalo Bill Historical Center.

WHITTLER
Colloquial term for a good cutting horse.

"THE WHOREHOUSE BELLS WERE RINGING"

Bawdy song. See Humor.

WICHITA, KANSAS

See Cow Towns.

WIDOW-MAKER

Colloquial term for a very bad or "outlaw" horse.

WIEGHORST, OLAF
(1899–1988)

Artist. See Art of the Cowboy.

THE WILD BUNCH

Film (1969). See Films, Cowboy.

WILD COW MILKING

See Rodeo Events.

WILD HORSE RACE

See Rodeo Events.

WILD MARE'S MILK

Colloquial term for whiskey.

THE WILD WEST

Film (1975).

WILD WEST SHOWS

See Cody, William Frederick ("Buffalo Bill");
Lillie, Gordon William ("Pawnee Bill");
Miller Brothers 101 Ranch Wild West Show.

WILD WEST WEEKLY

See Pulp Novels.

WILD, WOOLLY, AND FULL O' FLEAS

Description of a genuine cowboy.

WILLIAMS, HANK
(1923–1953)

See Music.

WILLIAMSON, FRED
(1938–)

See African-American Cowboys.

WILLS, BOB
(1905–1975)

See Music.

WINCHESTER FIREARMS

The slogan of the Winchester Firearms Company is "The gun that won the West." While this is something of an overstatement, Winchester repeating rifles did hold a prominent position among firearms in the Old West. Two of the company's more famous patrons, Buffalo Bill Cody and Teddy Roosevelt, used Winchesters for everything from Wild West sideshows to big-game hunting.

Winchester repeating rifles developed from the Volitional Repeater and Volcanic arms. T hese earlier weapons benefited from improved ammunition but still had problems that kept them from becoming popular. Oliver Winchester invested in the Volcanic Repeating Arms Company. When it went bankrupt, he reformed it under the name New Haven Arms Company. In 1867 Winchester put the operation under his own name.

B. Tyler Henry developed a .44 caliber rim-fire metallic cartridge, and in 1860 he patented his Henry rifle. The New Haven Arms Company produced the rifle, which represented a great advance over early repeating arms. The Henry incorporated a tubular magazine, located under the barrel of the rifle, that held 15 cartridges. The lever action simultaneously ejected the old casing and loaded a new round.

The Winchester 1866 model improved on lever action technology. Also known as the Improved Henry, the weapon gained some acceptance, but the company manufactured relatively few of them. The 1866 would quickly be overshadowed by its famous successor.

The Winchester Model 1873 became one of the most important firearms of the Old West. More than 700,000 of these rifles sold. This rifle used center-fire ammunition (primarily 44-40) with a stronger casing and higher powder charge than earlier models. One of the greatest benefits of the Winchester 44-40 ammunition was its ability to use the same cartridges as the popular **Colt** Frontier revolver. Using these two weapons, frontiersmen had to buy only one type of round.

Buffalo Bill Cody wrote the company from Fort McPherson, Nebraska, with a personal testimonial. The 1875 Winchester catalog reprinted his letter:

> I have been using and have thoroughly tested your latest improved rifle. Allow me to say that I have tried and used nearly every kind of gun made in the United States, and for general hunting, or Indian fighting, I pronounce your improved Winchester the boss.
>
> An Indian will give more for one of your guns than any other gun he can get.
>
> While in the Black Hills this late summer, I crippled a bear, and Mr. Bear made for me, and I am certain had I not been armed with one of your repeating rifles I would now be in the happy hunting grounds. The bear was not thirty feet from me when he charged, but before he could reach me I had eleven bullets in him, which was a little more lead than he could comfortably digest.
>
> Believe me, that you have the most complete rifle now made.

The quest for a higher-powered rifle led to the Winchester Model 1876. Manufactured in a variety of calibers, this weapon never matched the popularity of the Model 1873.

For most types of shooting done in the West, the Winchester possessed the virtues of reliability, accuracy, and, most importantly, large magazine capacity. Chuck Connors made a modified Model '73 famous in his popular **television** program, "The Rifleman." Like other firearms of the Old West, Winchesters remain sought-after collectibles.   (Butler 1970; McDowell 1985)

—*Mark Mayer*

WINDIES

Colloquial term for tall tales. See Humor.

WINDMILL

The use of wind to pump water goes back thousands of years. The widespread use of windmills in the West came only after the development of the self-governing windmill. The vastness of the Great Plains and their high, frequent winds dictated that a windmill had to function largely unattended, except for repairs. The self-governing design kept the windmill from spinning itself to destruction in high winds. (Pumping mechanisms using sails would self-destruct unless an operator provided constant attention.)

Daniel Halladay of Vermont received the first patent for a self-governing windmill in 1854. His design incorporated numerous hinges so the blades could change pitch as the wind increased. The changed pitch slowed the revolutions of the wheel to which they were attached. The U.S. Wind Engine and Pump Company purchased Halladay's enterprise in 1863 and took it West, where it enjoyed great consumer demand among ranchers.

Other companies soon joined in the manufacture of windmills, competing fiercely and often using much different designs. The Eclipse, created by Leonard Wheeler in 1867, became one of the most popular of all designs. It utilized a hinged vane mounted behind the blades. The vane turned the wheel away from the main direction of the wind as wind speed increased. Other designs used a fixed-side vane capable of turning the blades away from the wind. They required counterweights to pull the wheel back into the wind as velocity decreased.

The primary use of windmills on ranches was to pump water up from wells to tanks or troughs for the livestock. In the arid regions of the Southwest, ranchers could seldom afford to depend on rivers for the maintenance of their herds. In order for the weight of cattle to be kept at a maximum, water had to be close to the herd. In practical terms, this meant that windmills needed to be numerous.

Less important to the rancher, but critical to others, was the windmill's task of pumping water for steam locomotives. Without those venerable constructs, transportation in the West would have been much more difficult. (Baker 1985; Torrey 1976)

—*Mark Mayer*

WINFIELD, DARRELL
(ca. 1929–)

The cigarette-puffing model who appeared in countless photographic advertisements as the Marlboro Man. See Pitchmen.

WINGED CHAPS

See Chaps.

WIPE

Colloquial term for bandanna or neckerchief.

WISTER, OWEN
(1860–1938)

Novelist Owen Wister was born to an intellectual family in Germantown, Pennsylvania. He received a good education in Europe and the United States. Early in life he exhibited considerable musical talent; he majored in music at Harvard and graduated in 1882. Teddy **Roosevelt** figured among Wister's undergraduate acquaintances. Wister studied music for two more years in Europe, which apparently tried his father's patience. The elder Wister ordered his musical son home, where he took work as a clerk.

In 1885 Wister traveled to Wyoming to aid his recovery after a nervous breakdown. The West captivated him, and subsequently he spent many summers in Wyoming. From this custom came the inspiration for Wister's writings.

Wister turned the cowboy into a figure acceptable to the eastern cultural establishment. He performed this feat with his sole western novel *The Virginian* (1902). The novel made the cowboy into a folk hero, spawned countless imitators, and gave us the famous phrase "When you say that, smile."

The Virginian exerted a strong influence on western literature. It is, however, justly criticized for its romanticized, inaccurate portrayal of cowboy life. Wister viewed the cowboy as a modern medieval knight. He appealed to eastern readers by layering artificial, proper, eastern values on his western subjects. Like many easterners, Wister saw what he wanted to see in the West, not what really existed.

Wister's short stories did a better job of accurately depicting western life. *Red Men and White* (1896), *Lin McLean* (1898), *The Jimmyjohn Boss* (1900), and *When the West Was West* (1928) offer less stylized images than *The Virginian*. Wister based many stories on events he had actually witnessed or been told about, which gave the stories added impact. Regrettably, his writings reflect a disdain for Native Americans typical of his times. Wister's writings on the American West earned him praise from his friend Theodore Roosevelt. Rudyard Kipling also appreciated his work. Indeed, Wister has been described as America's Kipling.

Within a decade after publishing *The Virginian*, however, Wister became disillusioned with the West and quit going there. Western realities failed to live up to his romantic notions. He continued his writing career but wrote far less about the West. His later stories exhibit a cynicism and nostalgia about the West. He died in North Kingston, Rhode Island, in 1938. A mountain in the Teton Range of Wyoming was named for him the following year. (Milton 1980; Payne 1985; Tuska and Piekarski 1983, 1984; White 1968)

—*Nils E. Mikkelsen*

WITCH'S BRIDLE

Colloquial term for tangles in a horse's mane.

WOMEN

Mention women in the West and images of Annie **Oakley**, the outlaw Belle Star, the accused rustler "Cattle Kate" Watson, and the outrageous Calamity Jane come to mind. What these women have in common is that they exist more as legends than as historical figures. Calamity Jane (born Martha Jane Canary) played a major role in creating her own **mythology.** She dressed

Martha Jane Canary, known as Calamity Jane, made herself a legend by acting and dressing like a man and telling stories of her adventures.

and drank like a man and told many a tall tale about her adventures. She claimed to have been Wild Bill Hickok's lover, a Pony Express rider, and a scout for Custer.

As the past generation of historical scholarship has established, real historical women populated the Old West. The region was not the sole domain of white males riding on horseback. Sarah Deutsch, Glenda Riley, Teresa Jordan, Sandra L. Myres, Judith Austin, Cheryl J. Foote, Anne M. Butler, Paula Petrik, Lillian Schlissel, Susan H. Armitage, Julie Roy Jeffrey, Joan M. Jensen, Carolyn Sacks, Sylvia Van Kirk, and many other scholars have revealed evidence of women at work and play throughout the West.

Cowboying, however, was a strictly gendered occupation. Nineteenth-century ranchers hired only men. The gender constructs of the time did not permit cowgirls to exist. Women could not tend cattle from horseback for a wage unless they passed as men (and a few did). Women lived on ranches and performed labors that we identify as part of cowboying, but they did so within a family, not as salaried workers.

Gender expectations and stereotypes kept women out of ranch wage labor. So did other socioeconomic factors. While gender discrimination often crumbles in the face of labor and economic pressures, ranchers rarely faced labor shortages and did not have to confront the issue of hiring women to do "man's work."

Women, of course, lived on the ranching frontier, even if they did not work as hired hands. Ranch wives, daughters, and widows worked in the saddle. We have memoirs and diaries from many ranch women. Other women worked at cowboy haunts in town, including stores, **saloons,** and brothels. They were not, however, the exact counterparts of working cowboys.

In popular usage the term *cowgirl* has little precision. It may refer to almost any woman in the West. *The Women* (1978) in the Time-Life Old West series, devotes eight of its 232 pages to cowgirls. The text mentions Lucille Mulhall and other **rodeo** performers, and Sadie Austin, a Nebraska rancher's daughter, but it offers only a single example of a female cowhand. "One independent-minded cowgirl rode with 500 cowboys in a roundup in the Washington Territory in 1885." Five hundred to one; that's probably a reasonable demographic estimate.

Likewise *Women of the West* (1982), by Cathy Luchetti and Carol Olwell, has little to say about women on ranches. Only five of the book's 148 illustrations show women on horseback or doing cowboy work. Three photographs show mounted Indian women. Another shows two white "women horseback riding on a *farm*" (emphasis added). The one bona fide shot of ranch work shows the two Becker sisters branding cattle in a Colorado corral in 1894. In sum, these and other photographic collections offer little evidence of women performing cowhand chores.

Scholarly treatments likewise have little to say about women cowhands. *The Women's West* (1987), edited by Susan Armitage and Elizabeth Jameson, is a collection of 21 essays. The index includes no references to cowgirls, cattle, **horses,** or ranch life. We do find an essay by Corlann Gee Bush titled "The Way We Weren't: Images of Women and Men in Cowboy Art."

In its spring 1991 issue, *Montana, the Magazine of Western History* published four articles under the topic "Contributions and Challenges of Women's History." The essays wisely stress the importance of avoiding a homogeneous view of "western women." As with society at large, class, race, and ethnicity created a varied western population of both men and women. None of these essays, however, takes up the question of women on the cattle frontier. In short, neither popular nor scholarly literature so far reveals much about nineteenth-century women working with cattle and horses.

Teresa Jordan's *Cowgirls: Women in the American West* (1982) specifically sought to address this void in the literature. Recognizing that very few cowgirls (strictly defined) really existed, Jordan broadens the term to encompass "women who work outside, on ranches or in the rodeo, on a regular basis." Jordan notes that, even with her expanded definition, "cowboys were always much more numerous than cowgirls, to be sure."

Jordan's definitional difficulties reveal several problems faced by anyone studying the social complexities of the West. We may well accept her view that both women living on ranches and

Although nineteenth-century women were not recognized as ranch-working "cowboys," they still played the part, dressing in cowgirl garb and performing in rodeo events.

rodeo performers have connections to "cowboy culture." She further dilutes the term *cowgirl,* however, by including women who "are more farmers than cowgirls." Her annotated bibliography includes the memoirs of women who lived on sheep ranches. We would not lump male farmers, cowmen, and sheep ranchers into a single social category. Why should we do so with women? These are different occupations with distinctly different values and cultures.

By casting too big a loop, Jordan overlooks the importance of class on the frontier. Ranchers and ranch widows owned land and animals. Property ownership set them far apart and above the working cowhand who usually owned very little. Further class distinctions often set large cattle outfits at odds with small, independent operators. Sacrificing important class differences to examine gender is a questionable tradeoff.

Finally, Jordan excludes outlaws, prostitutes, and ranch women who stayed indoors or who didn't like ranch life. These somewhat arbitrary exclusions further strip the term *cowgirl* of any substantive meaning as a social grouping. Prostitutes probably constituted the social group of women best known by cowboys. Most towns of any size included someone "blacksmithing" (pimping) the services of women to cowboys, miners, farmers, and other men. In terms of human relations, prostitutes might be considered much closer to cowboy culture than were farm wives.

Both the historical reality of cowboy life and the popular culture that it spawned are overwhelmingly male. If we wish to examine women's roles in the Old West, we must turn, as Jordan did, to people other than working cowhands. The recent studies of women in many areas of western life serve as much needed historiographical corrections, but the revisionism possible in the area of cowboy life is sharply limited by the demographic realities of the ranching frontier.

Things changed a bit in the twentieth century. June Cotton Martin Finn grew up on an Oklahoma ranch in the 1930s. As a teenager, she could do anything the boys could, including break horses. She married cowboy Glenn Finn, who worked on the Chapman-Barnard Ranch. "I talked 'em into letting me have my own string of horses," she recalled, "and I worked on the ranch just like a cowboy. I did everything the cowboys did."

Nevada poet Georgie Connell Sicking worked as a salaried cowhand most of her adult life. Many of her poems draw upon memories of her work on the range. If we throw in rodeo performers, we can find lots of "cowgirls," as shown in Mary Lou LeCompte's recent book, *Cowgirls of the Rodeo* (1993).

From military and fur-trading posts to ranch houses, mining camps, and brothels, women played active roles in western society. Gender has joined race and class as a major variable for analyzing western history. Ignoring women or gender distorts historical reality. Similarly, ignoring the gendered practice of cowboy work distorts the reality of nineteenth-century ranch work. (Armitage and Jameson 1987; Gilchriest 1993; Jordan 1982; Luccetti and Olwell 1982; Wood-Clark 1991)

WOMEN IN WESTERN FILM

Western film is traditionally a male genre. Woman are usually absent or appear only in cameo, stereotypical roles—we see a prostitute with a heart of gold or find ranch widows in need of male protection from the bad guys. Women are almost always secondary figures, along with sidekicks, villains, and, yes, horses. In film, women exist principally to be saved by cowboy heroes.

As Jon Tuska points out, the roles assigned to women in formula westerns changed very little over time. Even some of the A-western directors left women in marginal, minimal roles. In the **B westerns,** the heroine is often emotionally stunted. She frequently does not realize she loves the hero until well after the audience figures it out. She may even prefer the villain to the hero for a time.

To be sure, B westerns had their heroines: Marie Winsor, Vera Ralston, Linda Stirling, Gail Davies, Julie Adams, Peggy Stewart, Barbara Britton, Dorothy Gulliver, and Dale Evans. We can name dozens and dozens of male stars, however, for every actress from the B westerns.

Great actresses sometimes took memorable roles in westerns, but they did not specialize in the humble genre. Maureen O'Hara performed powerfully with John **Wayne** in several Ford pictures. We also remember Joan Crawford as a strong-willed **saloon** keeper in *Johnny Guitar* (1954). She is pitted against Mercedes McCambridge, an equally strong but vicious ranch woman, in the strange, heavily symbolic Nicholas Ray film.

Barbara Stanwyck played many tough, independent characters in her long, distinguished career. She starred in the 1935 film *Annie Oakley,* directed by George Stevens. Feisty Little Sure Shot falls in love with fellow shooter Preston Foster in the film. (In the 1950s, Gail Davis, a real-life **rodeo** performer, starred in a **television** series based on Oakley.) Stanwyck starred as a brave ranch woman in *The Cattle Queen of Montana* (1954) and other films. In *The Maverick Queen* (1956) she is a quick-shooting saloon keeper and friend to the outlaw Hole in the Wall Gang.

Other actresses also stepped outside the passive, stereotyped roles of B westerns. Marlene Dietrich plays the tough, sexy Frenchy in *Destry Rides Again* (1939). In Fritz Lang's *Rancho Notorious* (1952), Dietrich haughtily presides over a den of thieves that looks more like a supper club than a bandit hideout.

Mae West provides a comic caricature of the strong, sexual woman in *My Little Chickadee* (1940). Critic Brian Garfield terms *Lady from Cheyenne* (1941) "possibly the first women's lib oater." The film stars Loretta Young in a rather traditional role as a schoolmarm. Her character, however, is a suffragist, not a shrinking violet. She battles for women's right to vote in Wyoming.

Ella Raines played opposite John Wayne in *Tall in the Saddle* (1944). Raines played a rancher, scripted as a very strong character. Wayne's sidekick Gabby Hayes described her as "meaner'n a skilletful of rattlesnakes." Wayne, of course, overcame his cowboy shyness and fell in love with the tough beauty.

Women in western film, like men, came in two types—good and bad. *High Noon* (1952) offers excellent examples of both. Good women are bearers of civilization and goodness, like the schoolmarm. Bad woman, like outlaws, are an unfortunate but ubiquitous feature of frontier society.

Long a mainstay of all types of movies, sex appeal also surfaced in some westerns. Jane Russell's revealing role in *The Outlaw* (1943) is perhaps the most notorious example. Producer-director Howard Hughes even improved on nature by fitting Russell with a special cantilevered brassiere. Although the film raised eyebrows at the time, its sexuality now looks rather restrained and low key. Russell, however, is raped and abused in the film. The position and status of women becomes clear when Billy the Kid and Doc Holliday choose a **strawberry roan** over Russell as the stakes in a poker game.

In *The Outlaw,* Russell caressed and nursed Billy the Kid back to health. In 1952 she appeared as the outlaw in *Montana Belle.* In contrast to the earlier film, which emphasized her bust, *Montana Belle* has Russell disguised as a boy.

Movie cowboys often display an ambivalence toward women. Women represent a family and settling down—something that cowboys professed to avoid. We find outright misogynist statements in many films. A character in *Under Montana Skies* (1930) says, "Where there's women, there's trouble." In *Gun Fury,* a 1953 movie with Donna Reed and Rock Hudson, a cowboy says that "all women are alike. They just got different faces so you can tell them apart."

Indeed, there are more famous B-western horses than actresses. Who can imagine Roy **Rogers** or Ken Maynard without their golden palominos Trigger and Tarzan? Could Gene **Autry** have captured the bad guys without help from Champion? No way. Dale Evans was about

the only cowgirl to rate a horse costar, her beloved Buttermilk.

The excessive machismo of western movies, especially the B westerns, should come as no surprise. B-western filmmakers targeted a male, mostly juvenile audience. Many actors and directors, such as John Wayne and John Ford, lived, indeed reveled in, macho values and activities.

Film companies still target the large juvenile audience for some types of westerns. Universal Pictures delayed the release of *Cowboy Way,* an adolescent comedy, from March until June 1994 so the target audience—schoolchildren—would be on vacation.

The vision of women in westerns, then, is shaped by men making movies for an audience of boys and men. Little wonder that accuracy and subtlety take a beating. Brian Garfield reminds us, however, that the relative lack of women in western film is not completely ahistorical. "It simply reflects the dominate attitudes of the real West, in which men outnumbered women by about ten to one."

The nature of western film changed after the 1950s, but the roles for women remained much the same. Jane Fonda, for example, played a schoolteacher turned outlaw in the satirical *Cat Ballou* (1965). Costar Lee Marvin won an Academy Award for his dual roles, but Fonda's good girl/bad girl character hearkens back to B-western stereotypes.

Raquel Welch played a different, rather strange role in *Hannie Caulder* (1972). She appeared as a female version of Clint **Eastwood**'s spaghetti western avenger. After she is raped and her husband murdered, Welch seeks revenge. She wields a deadly six-gun from under a very revealing **poncho.** Caulder's philosophical commentary on sex relations in the West: "There aren't any hard women; only soft men."

More recently, Hollywood has released women in westerns from the old stereotypes. In 1994, Uma Thurman and Lorraine Bracco starred as decidedly liberated western women in *Even Cowgirls Get the Blues.* The film is a screen version of the Tom Robbins novel. In *The Quick and the Dead* (1994), Sharon Stone plays a gunslinger. *Bad Girls* (1994) features a female gang of cattle rustlers. Perhaps a new day is finally dawning for women in westerns. (Coburn 1994; Foote 1983; Garfield 1982; Tuska 1985)

WOMEN'S PROFESSIONAL RODEO ASSOCIATION

See Rodeo.

WOOD

Colloquial term for **saddle.**

WOOLLIES

Colloquial term for sheep.

WOOLSEY

Colloquial term for a cheap **hat,** usually made of wool.

WORCESTERSHIRE

Colloquial term for a **Winchester** rifle.

WRANGLE

To care for, herd, and drive a *remuda* (a herd of **horses**).

WRANGLER

Cowhand, often a boy or old man, who tends an outfit's herd of **horses.** Like many other terms, this one comes from Mexico. According to Ramon Adams, the word is a corruption of the Spanish term *caballerango,* which became caverango and then wrangler. (Adams 1968; Blevins 1993)

WYETH, NEWELL CONVERS
(1882–1935)

Artist. See Art of the Cowboy.

WYNNE, BRIAN

Pseudonym for writer Brian Garfield, who was also known as Frank Wynne.

YAKS

Colloquial term for Mexican cattle on a **trail drive.** Ramon Adams *(Western Words,* 1968) says the term stems from the cattle's origin in Mexican Yaqui Indian country.

YANNIGAN BAG

A bag in which the cowboy carried personal items; also known as a war bag.

YATES, ROWDY

Character played by Clint **Eastwood** on "Rawhide." See Television.

YEGUA

Spanish term for mare. Until the twentieth century, most Latin American cowboys refused to ride mares.

YELLOW BELLY

Also Yellow Boy—a **Winchester** Model 1866 rifle, nicknamed because of its bright brass color.

YIERRA

Also *hierra,* a term used in Argentina to mean the **roundup** and branding season.

YOAKAM, DWIGHT
(1956–)
Country singer. See Hat Acts.

"YOUNG RIDERS"

Television program of the 1980s based on the shortlived Pony Express. The show lasted longer than the real thing.

ZEBRA DUN

Striped, dull brown horse, immortalized in an anonymous poem by the same name.

ZEBU

See Cattle Breeds.

APPENDIX A

FILM AND VIDEOTAPE SOURCES

Many old western films appear in the action or western section of your local video store. For fans who want to own some of the classics, here are a few mail-order outlets and catalogs that feature western films or old television series on videotape.

Captain Bijou P.O. Box 87, Toney, AL 35773-0087. Tel. 205-852-0198.

Complete Guide to Special Interest Videos A mammoth catalog by James R. Spencer of 9,000 videos that sells for $19.95. James Robert Publishing, 3535 East Inland Empire Boulevard., Ontario, CA 91764.

Critics Choice Video P.O. Box 749, Itasca, IL 60143-0749. Publishes a small catalog called "The Movie Book." Classic westerns run from $10 to $25. Tel. 800-367-6675.

Facets Video 1517 West Fullerton, Chicago, IL 60614. A specialist in noncommercial, non-Hollywood films. Check here for documentaries and independent films, but not B westerns. Catalog is $7.95 plus $2 shipping. Tel. 800-331-6197.

Front Row Entertainment P.O. Box 5891, Edison, NJ 08818-5891. Front Row distributes many westerns, including spaghetti westerns. Their tapes sell for $5 to $15.

Fusion Video 100 Fusion Way, Country Club Hills, IL 60478. Stocks documentaries, westerns, and other classics. Tel. 800-959-0061.

Home Film Festival P.O. Box 2032, Scranton, PA 18501-9952. You can rent videos for a three-day period by mail ($6 for one, $11 for

two, $16 for three, plus shipping). Tel. 800-258-3456.

Meadow Tree 3716 Effingham Place, Los Angeles, CA 90027-1428. Sells how-to videos on training, caring for, and riding horses, both English and western styles. Tel. 800-223-6678.

Metro Golden Memories 5425 West Addison Street, Chicago, IL 60641. Specializes in rare movies as well as tapes of old television shows. Tel. 312-736-4133.

Movie Marketplace P.O. Box 429, Evanston, IL 60204. To subscribe to their catalog send $9.97 for 6 issues to P.O. Box 401, Mt. Morris, IL 61054-7782. Tel. 800-827-0821.

Movies Unlimited 6736 Castor Avenue, Philadelphia, PA 19149. Publishes a giant catalog, nearly 700 pages, for $7.95 plus $3 shipping. Telephone orders: 800-523-0823; fax orders: 215-725-3683; customer service: 215-722-8398.

Time-Warner Viewer's Edge P.O. Box 3925, Milford, CT 06460. Tel. 800-228-5440.

The Video Catalog P.O. Box 64267, St. Paul, MN 55164-0428. Tel. 800-733-2232.

Video Yesteryear (also Radio Yesteryear) Box C, Sandy Hook CT, 06482. Tel. 800-243-0987.

APPENDIX B

MUSEUMS

The following list of cowboy museums cannot pretend to be exhaustive. I have highlighted a few sites where cowboy art, material culture, and history can be enjoyed. The museums are listed alphabetically. Each western state has additional major state history and art museums.

American Quarter Horse Heritage Center and Museum Amarillo, TX. (See Quarter Horse entry.)

Amon Carter Museum of Western Art 3501 Camp Bowie Boulevard, Fort Worth, TX 76113; tel. 817-738-1933. This museum opened in 1961 thanks to a bequest by a Fort Worth newspaper publisher. Over the years, the collection has expanded remarkably beyond the original Remington/Russell focus. In addition to the artworks, the museum houses photographic and print archives and microfilm of nineteenth-century North American newspapers and periodicals.

Barbed Wire Museum 614 Main Street, La Crosse, KS 67548; tel. 913-222-3116. Devoted to the cowboy's nemesis, this collection highlights the history and varieties of "bob wire." This invention made modern ranching possible, but few old-time cowboys had anything good to say about it.

Boot Hill Museum Front Street, Dodge City, KS 67801; tel. 316-227-8188. Relive the wild and woolly cow town days.

Buffalo Bill Cody Museum See separate entry.

Buffalo Bill Historical Center See separate entry.

C. M. Russell Museum Complex 400 13th Street North, Great Falls, MT 59401; tel. 406-727-8787. This impressive complex includes Charles Russell's home and log cabin studio as well as a large museum with seven galleries and a library. Russell painted and sculpted more than 4,000 works in his busy lifetime. The collection at Great Falls is the most complete anywhere. Many other fine western painters are represented among the museum's 7,500 permanent works.

Cattleman's Museum 1301 West Seventh, Ft. Worth, TX 76102-2660; tel. 817-332-7064. Dedicated to the history of ranching and the cattle industry, this museum includes artifacts, artwork, and interactive exhibits. Leonard Stiles of Kingsville, Texas, for example, donated a collection of more than 1,000 branding irons to the museum. Waggoner Library has 3,000 reference works about the cattle industry as well as 25,000 photographs, including those of Erwin E. Smith.

Cowboy Artists of America Museum See separate entry.

Cowboys Then and Now Museum 729 N.E. Oregon Street, Suite 190, Portland, OR 97232 (about three blocks from the Lloyd Center); tel. 503-731-3200. Funded with seed money from the Oregon Beef Council and sponsored by the Cattlemen's Heritage Foundation of Oregon, this museum opened in the fall of 1991. It includes a tack room, an authentically restored chuck wagon, art and photographs, and a 600-plus-volume library. Mike Hanley, author of *Owyee Trails* and *Sagebrush and Axle Grease,* assisted with the project.

Gene Autry Western Heritage Museum 4700 Western Heritage Way, Griffith Park, Los Angeles, CA 90027-1462; tel. 213-667-2000. Created by Autry with assistance from Walt Disney Imagineering, this museum features seven permanent galleries. Called "The Spirits," they trace the history of the West forward from prehistoric times. The museum covers all areas of western history and culture, including imagery from films, television, and advertising.

Gilcrease Museum 1400 Gilcrease Museum Road, Tulsa, OK 74127; tel. 918-582-3122. Poised atop the Osage Hills near Tulsa, the Gilcrease houses more than 10,000 paintings and sculptures. Indian cultures are represented by paintings and more than 50,000 artifacts. The museum collection originated from the estate of Phillip Gillett Cole. His widow sold his huge, quality collection to Tulsa oilman (William) Thomas Gilcrease. In the 1940s, Gilcrease established an art museum on the grounds of his estate, and in 1958 he deeded the museum, grounds, and collection to the city of Tulsa.

Glenbow Museum and Archives 130-9th Avenue, SE, Calgary, Alberta, T2G 0P3 Canada; tel. 403-264-8300. The Glenbow Museum and Archives, western Canada's largest, covers all aspects of the region's development. Native peoples, the Mounted Police, ranching, farming, and oil industries all get attention. The Glenbow's holdings number 800,000 images. The archives boast a highly professional staff. Researchers may consult a wide range of primary and secondary historical sources, including photographs.

Institute of Texan Cultures 801 South Bowie Street at Durango Boulevard, San Antonio, TX 78294; tel. 512-226-7651. Administered by the University of Texas at San Antonio and housed at HemisFair Plaza, the institute depicts the rich ethnic mix of Texas.

Joe Gish's Old West Museum 502 North Milam, Fredericksburg, TX 78624; tel. 512-997-2794. Make this a stop on your trip to the delightful Texas Hill Country. A springtime visit will reward you with a bounty of bluebonnets and other colorful wildflowers.

Joslyn Art Museum 2200 Dodge Street, Omaha, Nebraska 68102; tel. 402-342-3300. From humble beginnings in 1931, the Joslyn has grown to encompass a wide range of the world's art. The museum began with the collection of George and Sarah Joslyn. It is rich in many genres, notably in depictions of prairie life. The museum acquired two major collections in 1962. The large Maximilian-Bodmer Collection includes some 400 sketches and watercolors by Karl Bodmer. This skilled draftsman provided glorious views of Native American life of the 1830s. The Stewart-Miller collection features 113 of Alfred Jacob Miller's field sketches from 1837. The Joslyn initially included a broader spectrum of western art, but in 1986 the museum sold a major portion of its western collection to Gene Autry. Those artworks now form a part of his museum in Los Angeles.

Judah L. Magnes Museum and Jewish-American Hall of Fame 2911 Russell Street, Berkeley CA 94705; tel. 510-549-6932. Founded in 1962, the Magnes is sometimes called the Jewish Museum of the West. Among those included in the Jewish-American Hall of Fame is, of course, Levi Strauss, who gave the West denim blue jeans. The museum's archival collection includes 78 items on Strauss and his descendants. Another well-known western figure, Broncho Billy Anderson, was also Jewish. Born Max Aronson, Anderson became the silver screen's first big cowboy hero of the silent era.

A special Commission for the Preservation of Jewish Cemeteries and Landmarks, established in 1963, maintains and restores six cemetery sites in California. Wyatt Earp, legendary lawman, is buried at a Jewish cemetery at Colma, south of San Francisco. The cemetery is maintained by Temple Sherith Israel. Earp's wife Josephine was Jewish, so she arranged for their burial plot. "Wyatt's family were almost all gone," she wrote, "and we had no children. My only home was where my parents rest. So I took Wyatt's ashes to San Francisco."

Museum of the Western Prairie 1100 North Hightower, Altus, OK 73521; tel. 405-482-1044.

Museum of Western Art 1727 Tremont Plaza, Denver, CO 80202; tel. 303-296-1880.

National Cowboy Hall of Fame and Western Heritage Center See separate entry.

National Cowgirl Hall of Fame and Western Heritage Center This museum has recently relocated from Hereford, Texas, to Fort Worth, Texas. It memorializes rodeo cowgirls and ranch women.

National Ranching Heritage Center Texas Tech University, sponsored by the American Cowboy Culture Association, P.O. Box 43201, Lubbock, TX 79409, tel. 806-742-2498. (See American Cowboy Culture Association entry.)

North Fort Worth Historical Society 131 E. Exchange Avenue, Suite 112, Ft. Worth, TX 76106; tel. 817-625-5082.

Norton Art Gallery 4747 Creswell Avenue, Shreveport, LA 71106-1899; tel. 318-865-4201. Holdings include one of the world's three largest collections of works by Frederic Remington and Charles Russell.

Prorodeo Hall of Fame and Museum of the American Cowboy See separate entry.

Remington Art Museum 303 Washington Street, Ogdensburg, NY 13669; tel. 315-393-2425. This museum specializes in the works of Frederic Remington.

Rex Allen Arizona Cowboy Museum P.O. Box 995, Wilcox, AZ 85644; tel. 602-384-3059.

Rockwell Museum 111 Cedar Street, Baron Steuben Place, Corning, NY 14830; tel. 607-937-5386. This museum houses an extensive western art and artifact collection gathered by Robert F. Rockwell. It makes accessible to easterners original works by Remington, Russell, and more than 100 other western artists.

Rodeo Hall of Fame
See National Cowboy Hall of Fame entry.

Roy Rogers and Dale Evans Museum
See Rogers, Roy, entry.

Stark Museum of Art P.O. Box 1897, 712 Green Avenue, Orange, TX 77630; tel. 409-883-6661. This museum's collection features western art collected by H. J. Lutcher Stark and her mother, Mariam Lutcher Stark. In the early 1970s Mrs. Nelda C. Stark initiated plans to build a museum to house the family collection. The museum opened in 1976. The Western Collection includes works by 68 artists Julie Schilmmel's handsome catalog, *Stark Museum of Art: The Western Collection 1978* provides a good overview of holdings. Of particular interest are works by George Catlin *(Pa-ris-ka-roo-pa)*, Alfred Jacob Miller *(Shoshone Caressing His Horse* and *Hunting Buffalo)*, bronzes and paintings by Remington and Russell, and several works by William Herbert Dunton. In 1990 the museum mounted a major exhibit titled "The American West: Creation of the American Identity."

Stradling Museum of the Horse
350 McKeown Avenue, Patagonia, AZ 85624; tel. 602-394-2264.

Texas Ranger Hall of Fame and Museum
Ft. Fisher Park, Rt. 135 and Brazona River, Waco, TX 76702; tel. 817-754-1433.

Tom Mix Museum   721 North Delaware, Dewey, OK 74029; tel. 918-534-1555.

Tucson Rodeo Parade Museum   4825 South Sixth Avenue, Tucson, AZ 85702; tel. 602-294-1280.

William S. Hart County Park   24151 San Fernando Road, Santa Clarita, CA 91350; tel. 805-259-0855. Famed silent film star William S. Hart lived at this ranch and home until his death in 1946. He also shot many of his films here between 1914 and 1925. The house contains many personal possessions, photographs, and other western art and artifacts. The site is administered by the Los Angeles County Department of Parks and Recreation.

APPENDIX C

PERIODICALS

Fans of cowboy culture enjoy a wide range of periodicals. As of 1994, most of the following publications targeted readers with interests in cowboy history and culture. This list includes brief descriptions of publications related to aspects of the West or horsemanship. For magazines and newsletters published by museums see Appendix B.

American Cowboy   P.O. Box 12830, Wichita, KS 67277-9924; tel. 800-369-0196. *American Cowboy,* a bimonthly begun in 1994, covers the full gamut of today's cowboy culture. It includes many short takes on current events, personalities, and news relating to ranch life. The August 1994 issue includes well illustrated destination pieces on the Calgary Stampede, Cody, Wyoming, and Michael Martin Murphey's Copper Mountain (Colorado) WestFest.

American Cowboy Poet   P.O. Box 326, Eagle, ID 83616. *American Cowboy Poet* previews and reviews regional cowboy poetry gatherings. It also provides a forum for original works.

American West   Box 3733, Escondido, CA 92055. *American West* is a glossy publication that has shifted its focus over time. During its early decades, the Western History Association helped underwrite the publication. From the 1960s through the late 1980s, the magazine included excellent historical articles penned by prominent scholars. Aimed at the lay audience, the articles generally featured historical photographs and maps. In the late 1980s, however, the magazine "went commercial," dropping serious history and going after buffs interested in western art and collectibles. In response to the lowered quality and new focus, the Western History

Association dropped its sponsorship and began supporting *Montana, the Magazine of Western History.* Owing to weak authors and editors, *American West* became a lightweight publication. It is now of little use for historical research. Older issues, however, are worth researching.

Arizona Highways   P.O. Box 6018, Phoenix, AZ 85005-9916; tel. 800-543-5432. *Arizona Highways,* the once staid bastion of landscape photography, has livened up its content and format. Recognizing the appeal of western culture as well as landscape, the magazine now includes much more than simply photo essays and destination pieces. In short, one can now enjoy reading the magazine, not just looking at the pretty pictures. The November 1993 issue featured a 14-page cover story entitled "A Regular Cowboy." Sam Negri wrote the text and Ken Akers shot the fine color photos of Eric DeWitt, a 33-year-old cowboy. "The cowboy's life is one Eric has chosen, preferring solitude and the challenge of relying on his own skills to solve whatever problems arise in a landscape so difficult to traverse that a helping hand might be hours away." The January 1994 issue included ten "great chili recipes." Travel tips, bits of folklore, and great color photography remain important parts of the magazine, published by the Arizona Department of Transportation.

Art of the West   15612 Highway 7, Suite 235, Minnetonka, MN 55345; tel. 612-935-5850. *Art of the West.* Western art has risen in stature, price, and desirability in recent decades. This bimonthly publication provides art appreciators and collectors with useful information on living western artists, shows, and more.

Boots   P.O. Box 766, Challis, ID 83226; tel. 208-879-4475. *Boots,* launched during the fall of 1990, "speaks for the cowboy artisan; it matters not the medium—words, leather, paint, song, or carving materials." Ethie Corrigan publishes and edits the black-and-white magazine. Cowboy poetry is the magazine's long suit. It really serves as an unofficial publication of the Cowboy Poets of Idaho. The Fall 1993 issue, which paid tribute to storytellers, included the names and addresses of the organization's 59 members. The premier issue featured many original cowboy poems as well as sketches of saddle maker Cary Schwarz and sculptor Charley Smith. Each issue also includes works by Idaho photographer David Stoecklein. Published twice yearly in Idaho, the magazine has a north plains and Alberta focus and flavor.

Cowboy Magazine   P.O. Box 126, LaVeta, CO 81055; tel. 719-742-5250. *Cowboy Magazine* began publication in the summer of 1990. Veteran cowboy actor Richard Farnsworth provided a "Welcome" to the magazine. After acknowledging that the cowboy and ranching had declined in economic importance over the past century, he added these thoughts:

> Still, much of the West is unsettled, and the land is best suited for cattle grazing. The cowboy is still out there turning grass into beef. With America now in the age of space technology, and only ten years away from the 21st century, the cowboy still endures. *Cowboy Magazine* is being published because the world still loves the cowboy.

Published by Darrell Arnold and edited by Jeannie McCabe, the magazine features interviews and profiles of westerners. Arnold explains the philosophy and goals of the publication:

> *Cowboy Magazine* is the voice of the cowboy—working cowboys, ranchers, rodeo cowboys, outfitters, horse trainers, team ropers, trail riders, singing cowboys, cowboy poets, movie cowboys, weekend cowboys, armchair cowboys, and people who are only cowboys in their fondest dreams.
>
> Above all, *Cowboy Magazine* strives to uphold the mythical image of the cowboy, the ideal cowboy whose word is truth and who tries to live by high standards of honesty, hard work, and respect for mankind and the earth.

The magazine has color covers but mostly black-and-white photography inside. Brief articles cover the full spectrum of topics, from rodeo to cowboy music, poetry, and material culture.

Cowboys & Indians   1800 Wyatt Drive, Suite 10, Santa Clara, CA 95054; tel. 408-562-1983. *Cowboys & Indians* appeared in 1993. Publisher Robert Hartman targeted a broad audience of readers interested in cowboy or American Indian culture and history. Of the current crop of popular magazines, this one pays the most attention to substantive, historical topics. Publisher Hartman and editor Charlotte Berney keep the articles lively and diverse. Splendid color photography by Jim Arndt and others appears in each issue. The magazine holds special appeal to readers interested in collectibles and history. The Winter 1993/94 issue covered a wide range of topics—memorabilia from the Miller Brothers 101 Ranch, Tlingit baskets, chaps, the history of dude ranches, a profile of the singing trio Sons of the San Joaquin, and a look at the Hawaiian cowboy or paniolo. Many western buffs enjoy elements of both traditional cowboy and Indian history and culture, and this magazine gives readers plenty of both.

Frontier Times
See *True West* below.

Horse & Rider P.O. Box 529, Mount Morris, IL 61054-7862; tel. 800-435-9610. *Horse & Rider* is a great monthly magazine for those who ride horses. This Cowles Media Company publication covers all aspects of western horse training, riding, and competing. Many articles provide nuts-and-bolts advice on everything from buying a horse trailer to treating animal wounds and creating "horse-show hairdos." The publication is illustrated with quality color photography.

Hunter's Frontier Times
See *True West* below.

Journal of the West Box 1009, Manhattan, KS 66502-4228; tel. 913-532-6733. *Journal of the West* is edited and published by the Kansas State University Department of History. The quarterly issues are usually devoted to single themes. Most articles are written by historians and other experts in western culture. Like *Montana, the Magazine of Western History,* this journal, which dates back to 1962, includes many historical photographs. Topics covered in past issues range widely from "Western Films: A Brief History" (very useful), to "Veterinary Medicine in the West," "Photography in the West," "Oil," and "Spanish and Mexican Land Grants and the Law."

The Journal: Official Publication of the Western Outlaw-Lawman History Association P.O. Box 853, Hamilton, MT 59840. *The Journal: Official Publication of the Western Outlaw-Lawman History Association* (WOLA) appeared in the spring of 1991. Jim Dullenty edits the publication that covers the history and legends surrounding outlaws, lawmen, and gunmen of the Old West. The publication is sent to members of the WOLA.

Montana, the Magazine of Western History P.O. Box 201201, Helena, MT 59620-1201; tel. 406-444-4708. *Montana, the Magazine of Western History* began publication in 1951 with a focus on its namesake state. In the late 1980s, however, the Western History Association began

sponsoring the publication after dropping its affiliation with *American West.* Since then, *Montana* has become a premiere outlet for serious but readable western history. Under editor Chuck Rankin, it has become a model of what a popular history magazine should be. Specialists and general readers alike will find plenty of good reading in this well-illustrated and attractively produced magazine. The best way to get this quarterly (as well as the *Western Historical Quarterly*) is to join the Western History Association (annual dues are $30 and up).

Old West
See *True West* below.

Persimmon Hill
See National Cowboy Hall of Fame entry.

Rope Burns P.O. Box 35, Gene Autry, OK 73436; tel. 405-389-5350. *Rope Burns* is "for folks who are tired of reading about real cowboys and want to get in on the fun and see some." It is "dedicated to the working cowboy and his lifestyle."

Rope Burns provides good coverage of poetry gatherings, songfests, chuck wagon cookoffs, collectibles shows and auctions, ranch rodeos, and similar cowboy events. Each 24-page newsprint issue reviews several such events and includes a comprehensive calendar.

Song of the West 136 Pearl Street, Fort Collins, CO 80521; tel. 303-484-3209. *Song of the West,* like *American Cowboy Poet,* focuses on a single aspect of cowboy culture, music. It calls itself, accurately enough, "the Magazine of Cowboy and Western Music." Bill Jacobson and Mary Rogers edit and publish the quarterly black-and-white magazine begun in 1989. Articles provide much better depth than the tiny blurbs all too common in so-called entertainment publishing. Interviews with songwriters and singers are long enough to explore issues. Historical articles bring back memories of some of the great pioneers of western music. Album and performance reviews go beyond merely regurgitating PR releases.

Anyone who listens to or researches cowboy and western music will enjoy the magazine.

Southwest Art P.O. Box 53186, Boulder, CO 80321-3186. *Southwest Art* is a glossy, full-color monthly from CHB Publishing, Inc. Established in 1971, it covers all aspects of historical and contemporary western painting and sculpture. Most issues include at least one article highlighting a cowboy artist. For example, the October 1992 issue carries a fine article written by Brian Dippie about the illustrations that Charlie Russell included on many of his letters. Donald J. Hagerty profiles Maynard Dixon in the April 1993 issue. *Southwest Art* also publishes an annual price index of contemporary artists, a useful service for collectors. Articles are meaty, running several pages, and are very well illustrated. In addition, they are placed on consecutive pages, a commendable practice.

That's Country P.O. Box 4000, Sisters, OR 97759-9901; tel. 800-858-6800, fax 800-432-9576. *That's Country,* a full-color glossy publication, premiered in 1993. Editor-in-chief Christopher Burkhardt is trying to capture a broad audience interested in southern-based country or western music and life-style. He explained his thinking in a special preview issue: "Once referred to as 'Country & Western,' country and its music has evolved into a rich and varied lifestyle that celebrates the best of both country and Western."

This magazine is meant to be the ultimate sourcebook for people who want to keep up with the latest in country style. In these pages you'll find the inside story on country fashion, music, dance, rodeo, travel, and furnishings as well as some of the best cowboy poetry ever penned.

Today's Old West Traveler Box 2928, Costa Mesa, CA 92628; tel. 800-755-WEST. *Today's Old West Traveler* is "dedicated to keeping the spirit of the Old West alive." Readers looking for an outdoor western travel adventure will find information on dude ranches, pack trips, trail drives, and other types of fun. A special magazine service promises "We'll find the right Old West trip for you."

True West P.O. Box 2107, Stillwater, OK 74076; tel. 800-749-3369; 405-743-3370. *True West,* like *Wild West* (see below), carries mostly stories about old-time gunmen—outlaws and lawmen. Cavalrymen, right down to the buglers (November 1993 issue) also get their due. Most articles are amply illustrated with black-and-white drawings and old photographs. Joe ("Hosstail") Small founded the magazine in 1953 and served as its longtime publisher. Steven K. Gragert is the current publisher and John Joerscke is editor.

The publisher, Western Publications, bills itself as "America's largest source of true stories of the Old West." In addition to *True West,* the company offers two companion publications—the monthly *Hunter's Frontier Times* and the quarterly *Old West.* The former reproduces magazines originally published beginning in 1923 by J. Marvin Hunter in Bandera, Texas. The latter includes "exciting tales of settlers, miners, Indians, explorers, gunslingers—and the lawmen who tracked 'em down." Western Publications also published the now defunct *Frontier Times* beginning in 1953. An index is available covering articles published in all three magazines through 1979. Many back issues of all the magazines are available from the publisher.

Western Historical Quarterly
See Western History Association entry.

Western Horse Magazine P.O. Box 2019, Waxahachie, TX 75165; tel. 214-937-7666. *Western Horse Magazine,* like *Western Horseman* below, is aimed at readers who enjoy riding western style. Much of the commentary below applies equally to both magazines

Western Horseman P.O. Box 7980, Colorado Springs, CO 80933-7980; tel. 719-633-5524, 800-877-5278. *Western Horseman* bills itself as the "World's Leading Horse Magazine Since

1936." Edited in Colorado Springs, the hometown of the Prorodeo Hall of Fame, the magazine naturally gives extensive coverage to rodeo. It also includes service articles about training, riding, and caring for horses. Articles also cover reining and quarter horse competitions and ranch life. An advertisement for the magazine invites people to "read all about cowboys and cowgirls, rodeos and horse shows, trail rides and pack trips, hard work and great fun, cattle ranches and dude ranches, fantastic vacations, fashions and tack, and much, much more."

Although horses and horsemanship today provides the publication's focus, it does include an occasional piece on cowboy history and culture. The April 1960 issue, for example, included articles on the Pony Express and the origins of the quarter horse. The November 1993 issue highlighted the filming (in Montana) of the television film *Return to Lonesome Dove.*

Western Styles   P.O. Box 369, Mount Morris, IL 61054-7737. *Western Styles* premiered in the spring of 1993 as the nation's first glossy fashion and life-style magazine targeted mainly at cowgirls and would-be cowgirls. A model dressed in cowgirl style adorns each cover. A publication of Cowles Magazines, it is expensively produced in rich, full color. The magazine is the brainchild of Harry Myers, general manager at Cowles. In the premiere issue, Myers explained something of the publication's coverage and target readership:

> Intuition told us a growing number of Americans exist with a real and abiding interest in our country's unique heritage called Western. We speculated this interest encompassed travel, history, art, music, and most important, fashions and lifestyles.
>
> As it turns out, 31 percent of the entire adult population qualify as Western Enthusiasts—nearly 58 million Americans who are deeply attentive to and involved with a variety of 'things western.'

Western fashion for women and men provides the magazine's focus. Meaty and historical articles are few and far between. While relatively lightweight, the publication does profile interesting westerners. Rodeo and related topics of interest to horse people also get their due.

The Westerner   Old West Shop Publishing, Box 5232-11, Vienna, WV 26105; tel. 304-295-3143. *The Westerner* is a quarterly magazine published and edited since 1986 by Roger M. Crowley. An eclectic publication, it includes a smattering of western Americana from B westerns to little-known incidents in history. Issue number 12 (August 1989), for example, included short articles on then-recently deceased actor Victor French, vigilantism, Arbuckle's coffee, and C. M. Russell. The publication also emanates from an unusual part of the West— West Virginia.

Wild West   P.O. Box 385, Mount Morris, IL 61054-7943. *Wild West* is a glossier competitor of *True West* magazine. Its focus is the gun-toting Old West—lawmen, the cavalry, outlaws, and gunfighters, as well as Native American chiefs and warriors. Each issue usually contains an article or two on other topics in frontier history. The December 1992 issue carried a profile of famed boatman Mike Fink, "half horse and half alligator." Don Holloway described the conquest of Mexico by Hernán Cortés in the August 1992 issue. John F. Murphy, Jr., summarized the 150-year history of the Hudson Bay Company in the February 1992 issue. Guns and the men who used them, however, remain the publication's franchise.

Yippy-Yi-Yea Magazine   8393 East Holly Road, Holly, MI 48442. *Yippy-Yi-Yea Magazine* is a *Western Styles* clone. Long on glossy photos and short on substance, it is aimed at people concerned with shopping for western furnishings and clothing.

APPENDIX D

WESTERN CULTURAL HAPPENINGS

The list below is a sampler of some of the delightful western cultural happenings that feature music and/or poetry. Such gatherings sometimes include other types of popular events, such as ranch rodeos, chuck-wagon cookoffs, collectibles shows, and more. Remember that things do change (including telephone numbers), so check ahead before you saddle up.

January

Cowboy Poetry Gathering Arvada, Colorado; tel. 303-431-3080, ext. 3470.

Cowboy Poetry Gathering Elko, Nevada; tel. 702-738-7508.

February

Bluestem Prairie Cowboy Poetry Gathering Augusta, Kansas; tel. 316-733-9447.

March

Texas Cowboy Poetry Gathering Alpine, Texas; tel. 915-837-8191.

National Festival of the West Scottsdale, Arizona; tel. 602-996-4387.

Cowboys in the Wild West Salina, Kansas; tel. 913-826-7410.

Radford Wrangler Roundup El Paso, Texas; tel. 915-565-2737.

Celebration of the American West Fargo, North Dakota; tel. 615-329-4487.

April

Cowboy Songs and Range Ballads Cody, Wyoming; tel. 307-587-4771.

Oklahoma Cowboy Poetry Gathering Oklahoma City, Oklahoma; tel. 405-478-2250.

Visalia Spring Roundup Visalia, California; tel. 209-738-3289.

Grand Junction Cowboy Poetry Gathering Grand Junction, Colorado; tel. 303-434-9814.

Voices W.E.S.T. Salt Lake City, Utah; tel. 800-748-4466.

May

Western Heritage Classic Abilene, Texas; tel. 915-677-4376.

Dakota Cowboy Poetry Gathering Medora, North Dakota; tel. 701-623-4828.

Cowboy Roundup USA, Amarillo, Texas; tel. 806-373-5926.

Cowboy Chuckwagon Gathering Oklahoma City; tel. 405-478-2250.

Old West Days Jackson Hole, Wyoming; tel. 307-733-3316.

June

Cowboy Music Gathering   Elko, Nevada; tel. 800-748-4466.

Chisholm Trail Festival   Yukon, Oklahoma; tel. 405-354-0600.

Old Wyoming Cowman's Song and Poetry Gathering   Newcastle, Wyoming; tel. 307-746-4231.

Northwest Cowboy Poets Roundup   Pendleton, Oregon; tel. 503-276-2321.

Alberta Cowboy Poetry Association Gathering   Pincher Creek, Alberta; tel. 403-329-0206.

July

Rendezvous at Prairie Song   Dewey, Oklahoma; tel. 918-241-1515.

Cowboy Poetry Review   Calgary, Alberta, Canada; tel. 403-261-9316.

New Mexico Cowboy Poetry Roundup   Roswell, New Mexico; tel. 505-622-8333.

Utah's Festival of the American West   Logan, Utah; tel. 800-225-FEST.

Michael Martin Murphey's Wild West Weekend   Grand Targhee Lodge at Alta, Wyoming; tel. 800-TARGHEE.

Swing Ding   Townsend, Montana; tel. 800-242-MUSIC.

August

Arizona Cowboy Poetry Gathering   Prescott, Arizona; tel. 602-445-3122.

Idaho State Cowboy Poetry Gathering   Nampa, Idaho; tel. 208-888-9838.

Great Pike's Peak Cowboy Poetry Gathering   Colorado Springs, Colorado; tel. 719-531-6333, ext. 1150.

Montana Cowboy Poetry Gathering   Lewistown, Montana; tel. 406-538-5436.

September

Michael Martin Murphey's WestFest   Copper Mountain, Colorado; tel. 800-458-8386.

National Cowboy Symposium and Celebration   Lubbock, Texas; tel. 806-742-2498.

Cowboy Poetry Gathering   Maple Creek, Saskatchewan; tel. 306-558-4414.

Texas Heritage Music Festival   Austin and Kerrville, Texas; tel. 210-845-4442.

Durango Cowboy Poetry Gathering   Durango, Colorado; tel. 303-259-1388.

October

Old Lincoln County Cowboy Symposium   Glencoe, New Mexico; tel. 505-378-4142.

Red Steagall Cowboy Poetry Gathering and Western Swing Festival   Ft. Worth, Texas; tel. 615-356-8176.

Wyoming Cowboy Poetry Roundup and Trapping Show   Riverton, Wyoming; tel. 307-856-7184.

November

Western Music Festival   Tucson, Arizona; tel. 602-323-3311.

December

Cowboy Classics   Phoenix, Arizona; tel. 602-258-8568.

BIBLIOGRAPHY

Abbott, Edward Charles ("Teddy Blue"), and Helena Huntington Smith. *We Pointed Them North: Recollections of a Cowpuncher.* Norman: University of Oklahoma Press, 1939, 1955.

Abernathy, Francis Edward, ed. *The Folklore of Texan Cultures.* Austin: Encino Press, 1974.

Ackerman, Joe A., Jr. *Florida Cowman: A History of Florida Cattle Raising.* Kissimmee: Florida Cattlemen's Association, 1976.

Adams, Andy. *The Log of the Cowboy: A Narrative of the Old Trail Days.* 1903. Reprint. Lincoln: University of Nebraska Press, 1964.

Adams, Les, and Buck Rainey. *Shoot 'em Ups: The Complete Reference Guide to Westerns of the Sound Era.* New Rochelle, NY: Arlington House, 1978.

Adams, Ramon Frederick. *Come an' Get It: The Story of the Old Cowboy Cook.* Norman: University of Oklahoma Press, 1952.

————. *The Cowman Says It Salty.* Tucson: University of Arizona Press, 1971.

————. *The Old-Time Cowhand.* Lincoln: University of Nebraska Press, 1961, 1989.

————. *The Rampaging Herd: A Bibliography of Books and Pamphlets on Men and Events in the Cattle Industry.* Norman: University of Oklahoma Press, 1959.

————. *Western Words: A Dictionary of the Range, Cowcamp, and Trail.* 1945. Reprint. Norman: University of Oklahoma Press, 1968.

Ahlborn, Richard E. "The Hispanic Horseman." *El Palacio* 89:2 (Summer 1983): 12–21.

————, ed. *Man Made Mobile: Early Saddles of Western North America.* Washington, DC: Smithsonian Institution Press, 1980.

Ainsworth, Edward Maddin. *The Cowboy in Art.* New York: Bonanza Books, 1968.

Alexander, Hartley B. "The Horse in American Culture" in *So Live the Works of Men: Essays in Honor of Edgar Lee Hewett.* Albuquerque: University of New Mexico Press, 1939.

Alexander, Kent. *Heroes of the Wild West.* New York: Mallard Press, 1992.

Allard, William A. *Vanishing Breed: Photographs of the Cowboy and the West.* Boston: Little, Brown, 1982.

Allen, Jules Verne. *Cowboy Lore.* San Antonio: Naylor, 1933.

Allmendinger, Blake. *The Cowboy: Representations of Labor in an American Work Culture.* New York: Oxford University Press, 1992.

Almaráz, Félix D., Jr. *The San Antonio Missions and Their System of Land Tenure.* Austin: University of Texas Press, 1989.

Alvarez de Villar, José. *Men and Horses of Mexico: History and Practice of Charrería.* Mexico City: Ediciones Lara, 1979.

Amaral, Anthony A. *Will James: The Last Cowboy Legend.* Reno: University of Nevada Press, 1980.

Anderson, Warren R. *Owning Western History.* Missoula, MT: Mountain Press Publishing, 1993.

Andrews, G. Reid. *The Afro-Argentines of Buenos Aires, 1800–1900.* Madison: University of Wisconsin Press, 1980.

Anon. *American Cowboy Songs.* New York: Robbins Music, 1936.

Anon. *La cocina del gaucho.* Buenos Aires: Ediciones Gastronómicas del Gato que Pesca, 1978.

Anon. *Children's Cowboy Songs.* New York: Treasure Chest Publications, 1946.

Appun, Karl Ferdinand. "Los llanos de El Baúl." Trans. Federica de Ritter. *Anales de la Universidad Central de Venezuela* 32 (January 1953): 155–242.

Argentine Republic, Embassy of the. *Martín Fierro en su centenario.* Buenos Aires: Francisco A. Colombo, 1973.

Armas, Julio de. *La ganadería en Venezuela: Ensayo histórico.* Caracas: Congreso de la República, 1974.

———. "Nacimiento de la ganadería venezolana." *Revista Shell* 3:11 (June 1954): 26–35.

Armas Chitty, José Antonio de. *Tucupido: Formación de un pueblo del llano.* Caracas: Universidad Central de Venezuela, 1961.

———. *Vocabulario del hato.* Caracas: Universidad Central de Venezuela, 1966.

Armitage, Susan, and Elizabeth Jameson, eds. *The Women's West.* Norman: University of Oklahoma Press, 1987.

Arnade, Charles. "Cattle Raising in Spanish Florida, 1513–1763." *Agricultural History* 35:3 (July 1961): 116–124.

Arthur, Anthony, ed. *Critical Essays on Wallace Stegner.* Boston: G. K. Hall, 1982.

Ashford, Gerald. *Spanish Texas: Yesterday and Today.* Austin: Jenkins Publishing, 1971.

Assunçao, Fernando. *El gaucho.* Montevideo: Imprenta Nacional, 1963.

———. *El gaucho: Estudio socio-cultural.* 2 vols. Montevideo: Dirección General de Extensión Universitaria, 1978–1979.

———. *Pilchas criollas: Usos y costumbres del gaucho.* Rev. ed. Montevideo: Master Fer, 1979.

Athearn, Robert G. *The Mythic West in Twentieth-Century America.* Lawrence: University Press of Kansas, 1986.

Atherton, Lewis E. *The Cattle Kings.* Bloomington: Indiana University Press, 1961.

Autry, Gene. *Back in the Saddle Again.* Garden City: Doubleday, 1978.

Axelrod, Alan, with Dan Fox. *Songs of the Wild West.* New York: Simon & Schuster, 1991.

Aylesworth, Thomas G. *Television in America: A Pictorial History.* New York: Exeter Books, 1986.

Azcuy Armeghino, Eduardo. *Artigas en la historia argentina.* Buenos Aires: Ediciones Corregidor, 1986.

Baigell, Matthew. *The Western Art of Frederic Remington.* New York: Ballantine Books, 1976, 1988.

Baker, T. Lindsay. *A Field Guide to American Windmills.* Norman: University of Oklahoma Press, 1985.

Baldwin, Gordon Curtis. *Games of the American Indian.* New York: Norton, 1969.

Ball, Charles E. *The Finishing Touch.* Amarillo: Texas Cattle Breeder's Association, 1993.

Ballesteros, José Ramón. *Orígen y evolución del charro mexicano.* Mexico City: Manuel Porrúa, 1972.

Bane, Michael. *The Outlaws: Revolution in Country Music.* Garden City, NY: CMM Press/Doubleday/Dalton, 1978.

Baretta, Silvio Duncan, and John Markoff. "Civilization and Barbarism: Cattle Frontiers in Latin America." *Comparative Studies in Society and History* 20 (October 1978): 587–620.

Barnes, William Croft. *Apaches and Longhorns.* Los Angeles: Ward Ritchie, 1941.

Barrán, José Pedro. "Uruguayan Rural History." *Hispanic American Historical Review* 64:4 (November 1984): 655–674.

Barrán, José Pedro, and Benjamín Nahum. *Historia rural del Uruguay moderno.* 7 vols. Montevideo: Ediciones de la Banda Oriental, 1967–1978.

Beard, Tyler. *The Cowboy Boot Book.* Salt Lake City: Peregrine Smith Books, 1992.

———. *100 Years of Western Wear.* Salt Lake City: Peregrine Smith Books, 1993.

Beatie, Russell H. *Saddles.* Norman: University of Oklahoma Press, 1982.

Becco, Horacio Jorge. "La poesía gauchesca en el Río de la Plata." *Inter-American Review of Bibliography* 24:2 (April 1974): 135–146.

———, ed. *Antología de la poesía gauchesca.* Madrid: Aguilar, 1972.

Bent, George. *Life of George Bent: Written from His Letters.* ed. George E. Hyde. Norman: University of Oklahoma Press, 1968.

Berney, Charlotte. "Hawaii's Paniolo Country." *Cowboys & Indians* 1: 3 (Winter 1993): 50–54.

Berthrong, Donald J. *The Cheyenne and Arapaho Ordeal: Reservation and Agency Life in the Indian Territory, 1875–1907.* Norman: University of Oklahoma Press, 1976.

———. *The Southern Cheyennes.* Norman: University of Oklahoma Press, 1963.

Berton, Pierre. *Hollywood's Canada: The Americanization of Our National Image.* Toronto: McClelland and Stewart, 1975.

Bieber, Ralph P., ed. *Exploring Southwestern Trails.* Glendale, CA: Arthur H. Clark, 1938.

Billard, Jules B., ed. *The World of the American Indian.* Rev. ed. Washington, DC: National Geographic Society, 1974, 1989.

Billington, Ray Allen. *Land of Savagery, Land of Promise: The European Image of the American Frontier in the Nineteenth Century.* Norman: University of Oklahoma Press, 1981.

———, ed. *The Frontier Thesis: Valid Interpretation of American History?* New York: Krieger, 1977.

Bishko, Charles J. "The Peninsular Background of Latin American Cattle Ranching." *Hispanic American Historical Review* 32:4 (November 1952): 491–515.

Black, Baxter. *Coyote Cowboy Poetry.* Brighton, CO: Coyote Cowboy Co., 1986.

Blackstone, Sarah J. *Buckskins, Bullets and Business: A History of Buffalo Bill's Wild West.* Westport, CT: Greenwood Press, 1986.

Blasingame, Ike. *Dakota Cowboy: My Life in the Old Days.* New York: Putnam, 1958.

Blevins, Winfred. *Dictionary of the American West.* New York: Facts on File, 1993.

Blouet, Brian W., and Merlin P. Lawson, eds. *Images of the Plains: The Role of Human Nature in Settlement.* Lincoln: University of Nebraska Press, 1975.

Bold, Christine. *Selling the Wild West: Popular Western Fiction, 1860–1960.* Bloomington: Indiana University Press, 1987.

Bolívar Coronado, Rafael (pseud. Daniel Mendoza). *El llanero: Estudio de sociología venezolana.* Caracas: Cultura Venezolana, 1922.

Bond, Johnny. *The Tex Ritter Story.* New York: Chappell Music, 1976.

Borges, Jorge Luis, and Adolfo Bioy Casares, eds. *Poesía gauchesca.* 2 vols. Mexico City: Fondo de Cultura Económica, 1955.

Borne, Lawrence R. *Dude Ranching: A Complete History.* Albuquerque: University of New Mexico Press, 1983.

———. *Welcome to My West: I. H. Larom: Dude Rancher, Conservationist, Collector.* Cody, WY: Buffalo Bill Historical Center, 1982.

Boswell, John, and Jay David. *Duke: The John Wayne Album.* New York: Ballantine Books, 1979.

Botkin, B. A., ed. *A Treasury of Western Folklore.* New York: Crown Publishers, 1951.

Bradley, James H. "Characteristics, Habits, and Customs of the Blackfeet Indians." *Contributions to the Historical Society of Montana* 9 (1923).

Brado, Edward. *Cattle Kingdom: Early Ranching in Alberta.* Vancouver and Toronto: Douglas and MacIntyre, 1984.

Bramlett, Jim. *Ride the High Points: The Real Story of Will James.* Missoula, MT: Mountain Press Publishing, 1987.

Branch, E. Douglas. *The Cowboy and His Interpreters.* 1926. Reprint. New York: D. Appleton, 1961.

Brand, Donald D. "The Early History of the Range Cattle Industry in Northern Mexico." *Agricultural History* 35:3 (July 1961): 132–139.

Breen, David H. *The Canadian Prairie West and the Ranching Frontier, 1874–1924.* Toronto: University of Toronto Press, 1983.

———. "The Ranching Frontier in Canada, 1875–1905," in Lewis G. Thomas, ed., *The Prairie West to 1905: A Canadian Sourcebook.* Toronto: Oxford University Press, 1975.

Brennan, Joseph. *Paniolo.* Honolulu: Topgallant, 1978.

Briceño, Tarcila. *La ganadería en los llanos centro-occidentales venezolanos, 1900–1935.* Caracas: Biblioteca de la Academia Nacional de la Historia, 1985.

Brimlow, George F. *Harney County, Oregon, and Its Range Land.* Portland: Binsford and Mort, 1951.

Brown, Bob, et al. *The South American Cook Book.* New York: Dover, 1939, 1971.

Brown, Les. *Les Brown's Encyclopedia of Television.* Detroit: Gale Research, 1992.

Burchan, L. T. "Cattle and Range Forage in California, 1770–1880." *Agricultural History* 35:3 (July 1961): 140–149.

Burroughs, John Rolfe. *Where the Old West Stayed Young.* New York: Morrow, 1962.

Busaniche, José Luis., ed. *Estampas del pasado: Lecturas de historia argentina.* 1959. Reprint. Buenos Aires: Solar-Hachette, 1971.

Butler, Anne E. *Daughters of Joy, Sisters of Misery: Prostitutes in the American West, 1865–90.* Urbana: University of Illinois Press, 1985.

Butler, David F. *Winchester '73 & '76: The First Repeating Centerfire Rifles.* New York: Winchester Press, 1970.

Byam, George. *Wanderings in Some of the Western Republics of America.* London: John W. Parker, 1850.

Byers, Chester. *Cowboy Roping and Rope Tricks.* New York: Dover, 1928, 1966.

Calzadilla Valdés, Fernando. *Por los llanos de Apure.* Santiago: Imprenta Universitaria, 1940.

Campion, Lynn. *Training and Showing the Cutting Horse.* New York: Prentice Hall, 1990.

Campo L., Carlos del, and Luis Durand. *Huasos chilenos: Folklore campesino.* Santiago: Leblanc, 1939.

Cannon, Hal, ed. *Cowboy Poetry: A Gathering.* Salt Lake City: Peregrine Smith Books, 1985.

————, ed. *New Cowboy Poetry: A Contemporary Gathering.* Salt Lake City: Peregrine Smith Books, 1990.

————, ed. *Old-Time Cowboy Songs.* Salt Lake City: Peregrine Smith Books, 1988.

Cannon, Hal, and Thomas West, eds. *Buckaroo: Visions and Voices of the American Cowboy.* New York: Simon & Schuster, 1993.

Cárcano, Miguel Angel. *Evolución histórica del régimen de la tierra pública, 1810–1916.* 1917. Reprint. Buenos Aires: EUDEBA, 1972.

Carmichael, Joe M. "Your Best Saddle is 1500 Years Old." *Cattleman* 36:4 (September 1949).

Carvallo, Gastón. *El hato venezolano, 1900–1980.* Caracas: Fondo Editorial Tropykos, 1985.

Cary, Diana Serra. *The Hollywood Posse: The Story of a Gallant Band of Horsemen Who Made Movie History.* Boston: Houghton Mifflin, 1975.

Catlin, George. *Episodes from Life among the Indians and Last Rambles.* Ed. Marvin C. Ross. Norman: University of Oklahoma Press, 1868, 1959.

Cawalti, John G. *The Six-Gun Mystique.* 2d ed. Bowling Green, KY: Bowling Green University Popular Press, 1984.

Chard, Thornton. "Did the First Spanish Horses Landed in Florida and Carolina Leave Progeny?" *American Anthropologist* 42 (1940): 90–106.

Chasteen, John C. "Twilight of the Lances: The Saravia Brothers and Their World." Ph. D. diss. University of North Carolina, 1988.

Chenevix Trench, Charles P. *A History of Horsemanship.* Garden City, NY: Doubleday, 1970.

Chevalier, François. *Land and Society in Colonial Mexico.* Trans. Alvin Eustis. Ed., Lesley Byrd Simpson. Berkeley: University of California Press, 1963.

Chrisman, Harry E. *The Ladder of Rivers: The Story of I. P. Olive.* Denver: Sage Books, 1962.

Christianson, C. J. *My Life on the Range.* Lethbridge, Alberta: Southern Publishing, 1968.

Cisneros, José. *Riders Across the Centuries: Horsemen of the Spanish Borderlands.* El Paso: Texas Western Press, 1984.

Clark, Kenneth S., ed. *The Cowboy Sings.* New York: Pauli-Pioneer Music, 1932.

Clark, LaVerne Harrell. *They Sang for Horses: The Impact of the Horse on Navajo and Apache Folklore.* Tucson: University of Arizona Press, 1966.

Clayton, Lawrence, and Kenneth W. Davis, eds. *Horsing Around: Contemporary Cowboy Humor.* Detroit: Wayne State University Press, 1991.

Cleaveland, Agnes Morley. *No Life for a Lady.* Lincoln: University of Nebraska Press, 1941, 1977.

Coburn, Marcia Froelke. "Guns and Gingham." *Chicago Tribune,* 25 January 1994.

Coel, Margaret. *Chief Left Hand, Southern Arapaho.* Norman: University of Oklahoma Press, 1981.

Collier, John. *The Indians of the Americas*. New York: Norton, 1947.

Collins, Michael L. *That Damned Cowboy: Theodore Roosevelt and the American West, 1883–1898*. New York: Peter Lang, 1989.

Coluccio, Félix. *Diccionario folklórico argentino*. 2 vols. Buenos Aires: Lasserre, 1964.

Cook, Michael L. *Dime Novel Roundup: Annotated Index, 1931–1981*. Bowling Green, KY: Bowling Green University Popular Press, 1983.

Coolidge, Dane. *Fighting Men of the West*. 1932. Reprint. Freeport, NY: Books for Libraries Press, 1968.

Coppock, Kenneth. "Another Came West." *Canadian Cattlemen* 1:4 (March 1939).

Cowan-Smith, Virginia, and Bonnie Domrose Stone. *Aloha Cowboy*. Honolulu: University of Hawaii Press, 1988.

Cozzens, Darin. "History and Louis L'Amour's Cowboy." *Purview Southwest* (1988): 61–94.

Craig, John R. *Ranching with Lords and Commons; or Twenty Years on the Range*. 1903. Reprint. New York: AMS Press, 1971.

Cray, Ed. *Levi's*. Boston: Houghton Mifflin, 1978.

Cross, Michael S., ed. *The Turner Thesis and the Canadas: The Debate on the Impact of the Canadian Environment*. Toronto: Copp Clark, 1970.

Cunningham, Eugene. *Triggernometry: A Gallery of Gunfighters*. Caldwell, ID: Caxton Printers, 1934, 1941, 1962.

Daireaux, Emilio. *Vida y costumbres en La Plata*. 2 vols. Buenos Aires: Lajouane, 1888.

Dale, Edward Everett. *Cow Country*. Norman: University of Oklahoma Press, 1965.

———. *The Range Cattle Industry: Ranching on the Great Plains from 1865 to 1925*. 1930. Reprint. Norman: University of Oklahoma Press, 1960.

Dana, Richard Henry. *Two Years before the Mast*. New York: New American Library, 1964.

Daniels, George G., ed. *The Spanish West*. Alexandria, VA: Time-Life Books, 1976.

Dary, David. *Cowboy Culture*. New York: Knopf, 1981.

Davis, Robert Murray. *Playing Cowboys: Low Culture and High Art in the Western*. Norman: University of Oklahoma Press, 1992.

DeArment, Robert K. *Knights of the Green Cloth: The Saga of the Frontier Gamblers*. Norman: University of Oklahoma Press, 1982.

DeLeon, Arnoldo. *They Called Them Greasers: Anglo Attitudes toward Mexicans in Texas, 1821–1900*. Austin: University of Texas Press, 1983.

Dellar, Fred, and Alan Cackett. *The Harmony Illustrated Encyclopedia of Country Music*. Rev. ed. New York: Harmony Books, 1977, 1986.

Dempsey, Hugh A. "Calgary's First Stampede." *Alberta Historical Review*, 3:3 (Summer 1955): 3–13.

Denhardt, Robert Moorman. "The Chilean Horse." *Agricultural History* 24:3 (July 1950): 161–165.

———. *The Horse of the Americas*. Rev. ed. Norman: University of Oklahoma Press, 1947, 1975.

———. *The King Ranch Quarter Horses, and Something of the Ranch and the Men that Bred Them*. Norman: University of Oklahoma Press, 1970.

Depons, Francisco. *Viaje a la parte oriental de Tierra Firme*. Trans. Enrique Planchart. 2 vols. Caracas: Tipografía Americana, 1806, 1930.

Díaz, José Antonio. *El agricultor venezolano ó lecciones de agricultura práctica nacional.* 2 vols. Caracas: Rojas Brothers, 1877.

Dinan, John. "The Pulp Cowboy." *Persimmon Hill* 15:3 (Autumn 1987): 18–26.

Dinsmore, Wayne. *The Horses of the Americas.* Norman: University of Oklahoma Press, 1978.

Dippie, Brian W. *The Vanishing American: White Attitudes & U.S. Indian Policy.* Lawrence: University Press of Kansas, 1982.

Dobie, J. Frank. *Cow People.* Boston: Little, Brown, 1964.

———. *Guide to Life and Literature of the Southwest.* Rev. ed. Dallas: Southern Methodist University Press, 1952.

———. "Indian Horses and Horsemanship." *Southwest Review* 35 (Autumn 1950): 265–275.

———. *The Longhorns.* New York: Grosset and Dunlap, 1941.

———. "The Mexican Vaquero of the Texas Border." *Southwestern Political and Social Science Quarterly* 8:1 (June 1927): 1–12.

———. *The Mustangs.* Boston: Little, Brown, 1952.

———. "Ranch Mexicans." *Survey* 66 (1 May 1931): 167–170.

———. *Southwestern Lore.* 1931. Reprint. Hatboro, PA: Folklore Associates, 1965.

———. *A Vaquero of the Brush Country.* Austin: University of Texas Press, 1957, 1981.

Dodge, Theodore A. "Some American Riders." *Harper's Magazine* (July 1891).

Donahue, John. *Don Segundo Sombra y El Virginiano: Gaucho y cowboy.* Madrid: Editorial Pliegos, 1988.

Downs, James F. *Animal Husbandry in Navajo Society and Culture.* Berkeley: University of California Press, 1964.

———. *The Navajo.* New York: Holt, Rinehart, and Winston, 1972.

Driver, Harold Edison, ed. *The Americas on the Eve of Discovery.* Englewood Cliffs, NJ: Prentice-Hall, 1964.

Dunae, Patrick A. *Gentlemen Emigrants: From the British Public Schools to the Canadian Frontier.* Vancouver and Toronto: Douglas and McIntyre, 1981.

Dunning, John. *Tune in Yesterday: The Ultimate Encyclopedia of Old-Time Radio.* Englewood Cliffs, NJ: Prentice Hall, 1976.

Durham, Philip, and Everett L. Jones. *The Negro Cowboys.* Lincoln: University of Nebraska Press, 1965, 1983.

Dusard, Jay. *The North American Cowboy: A Portrait.* Prescott, AZ: Consortium, 1983.

Dusenberry, William H. *The Mexican Mesta.* Urbana: University of Illinois Press, 1963.

Dyal, Donald H. *Sun, Sod, and Wind: A Bibliography of Ranch House Architecture.* Monticello, IL: Vance Bibliographies, 1982.

Dykstra, Robert R. *The Cattle Towns.* New York: Atheneum, 1976.

Echaiz, René León. *Interpretación histórica del huaso chileno.* Santiago: Editorial Universitaria, 1955.

Edwards, Don. *Songs of the Cowboys.* Weatherford, TX: Sevenshoux Publishing, 1986.

Edwards, Elwyn Hartley. *Horses: Their Role in the History of Man.* London: Willow Books, 1987.

Ellison, Glenn R. *Cowboys under the Mogollon Rim.* Tucson: University of Arizona Press, 1968.

———. *More Tales from Slim Ellison.* Tucson: University of Arizona Press, 1981.

Emrich, Duncan. *Folklore on the American Land.* Boston: Little, Brown, 1972.

Encyclopedia of Latin American History. 4 vols. New York: Charles Scribner's Sons, 1995.

Erdoes, Richard. *Saloons of the Old West.* New York: Knopf, 1969.

Erickson, John R. *The Modern Cowboy.* Lincoln: University of Nebraska Press, 1981.

———. *Panhandle Cowboy.* Lincoln: University of Nebraska Press, 1980.

Esman, Milton J. *Landlessness and Near-Landlessness in Developing Countries.* Ithaca: Cornell University Center for International Studies, 1978.

Etulain, Richard W. "Changing Images: The Cowboy in Western Films." *Colorado Heritage* 1 (1981): 36–55.

———, ed. "Western Films: A Brief History." *Journal of the West* 22:4 (October 1983).

Evans, Simon M. "The Passing of a Frontier: Ranching in the Canadian West, 1882–1912." Ph. D. diss., University of Calgary, 1976.

Everson, William K. *The Hollywood Western.* New York: Citadel Press, 1992.

———. *A Pictorial History of the Western Film.* New York: Citadel Press, 1969.

Ewers, John Canfield. *The Horse in Blackfoot Indian Culture, with Comparative Material from other Western Tribes.* Washington, DC: U.S. Government Printing Office, 1955.

Ewing, Sherm. *The Range.* Missoula, MT: Mountain Press Publishing, 1990.

Eyles, Allen. *John Wayne.* South Brunswick, NJ: A. S. Barnes, 1979.

———. *The Western.* South Brunswick, NJ: A. S. Barnes, 1975.

Faulk, Odie B. "Ranching in Spanish Texas." *Hispanic American Historical Review* 45:2 (May 1965): 257–266.

Felton, Harold W. *Cowboy Jamboree: Western Songs & Lore.* New York: Alfred A. Knopf, 1951.

Fife, Austin E., and Alta S. Fife, eds. *Cowboys and Western Songs.* New York: Clarkson N. Potter, 1969.

Findlay, John M. *People of Chance: Gambling in American Society from Jamestown to Las Vegas.* New York: Oxford University Press, 1986.

Fishwick, Marshall W. "The Cowboy: America's Contribution to the World's Mythology." *Western Folklore* 11:2 (April 1952): 77–92.

Fletcher, Carmen William ("Curly"). *Songs of the Sage: The Poetry of Curly Fletcher.* Salt Lake City: Peregrine Smith Books, 1986.

Flint, Country Joe, and Judy Nelson. *The Insider's Country Music Handbook.* Salt Lake City: Peregrine Smith Books, 1993.

Flood, Elizabeth Clair. "Dude Ranches: Where East Meets West." *Cowboys & Indians* 1:3 (Winter 1993): 36–40.

Folsom, James K. *The American Western Novel.* New Haven: Yale University Press, 1966.

———, ed. *The Western: A Collection of Critical Essays.* Englewood Cliffs, NJ: Prentice-Hall, 1979.

Foote, Cheryl J. "Changing Images of Women in the Western Film." *Journal of the West* 22:4 (1983): 64–71.

Forbes, Jack D. *Apache, Navajo, and Spaniard.* Norman: University of Oklahoma Press, 1960.

Forbis, William H. *The Cowboys.* Rev. ed. Alexandria, VA: Time-Life Books, 1978.

Foster-Harris, William. *The Look of the Old West.* New York: Bonanza Books, 1955.

Francis, R. Douglas. "Changing Images of the West." *Journal of Canadian Studies* 17:5–19 (Fall 1982).

——. *Images of the West: Responses to the Canadian Prairies.* Saskatoon, Saskatchewan: Western Producer Prairie Books, 1989.

——. "From Wasteland to Utopia: Changing Images of the Canadian West in the Nineteenth Century." *Great Plains Quarterly* 7:3 (Summer 1987): 178–194.

Frantz, Joe B., and Julian E. Choate, Jr. *The American Cowboy: The Myth and the Reality.* Norman: University of Oklahoma Press, 1955.

Fredriksson, Kristine. *American Rodeo: From Buffalo Bill to Big Business.* College Station: Texas A&M University Press, 1984.

Freedman, Russell. *Cowboys of the Wild West.* New York: Clarion Books, 1985.

French, Giles. *Cattle Country of Peter French.* Portland: Binsford and Mort, 1964.

Frey, Hugo, ed. *American Cowboy Songs.* New York: Robbins Music, 1936.

Friedman, Michael. *Cowboy Culture: The Last Frontier of American Antiques.* West Chester, PA: Schiffer Publishing, 1992.

Friend, John B. *Cattle of the World.* Poole, England: Blandford Press, 1978.

Frink, Maurice, W. Turrentine Jackson, and Agnes Wright Spring. *When Grass Was King.* Boulder: University of Colorado Press, 1956.

Fritz, Henry E. "The Cattlemen's Frontier in the Trans-Mississippi West: An Annotated Bibliography." *Arizona and the West* 14:1 & 2 (Spring, Summer 1972): 45–70, 169–190.

Fritze, Ronald H. *Legend and Lore of the New World before 1492.* Santa Barbara, CA: ABC-CLIO, 1993.

Frost, Dick. *The King Ranch Papers: An Unauthorized and Irreverent History of the World's Largest Landholders, the Kleberg Family.* Chicago: Aquarius Rising Press, 1985.

Fugate, Francis L. "Origins of the Range Cattle Era in South Texas." *Agricultural History* 35:3 (July 1961): 155–158.

Furlong, Charles Wellington. *Let 'er Buck: A Story of the Passing of the Old West.* 3d ed. New York: G. P. Putnam's Sons, 1923.

Furt, Jorge M. *Cancionero popular rioplatense.* 2 vols. Buenos Aires: Roldán, 1923.

Gale, Robert L. *Richard Henry Dana, Jr.* New York: Twayne Publishers, 1969.

Gallegos, Rómulo. *Doña Bárbara.* 1929. Trans. Robert Malloy. New York: Peter Smith, 1948.

Garavaglia, Louis, and Charles G. Worman. *Firearms of the American West, 1803–1865.* Albuquerque: University of New Mexico Press, 1984.

Gard, Wayne. *The Chisholm Trail.* Norman: University of Oklahoma Press, 1954.

——. *Frontier Justice.* Norman: University of Oklahoma Press, 1949.

Gardiner, Allen Francis. *A Visit to the Indians on the Frontiers of Chili.* London: Seeley and Burnside, 1841.

Garfield, Brian. *Western Films: A Complete Guide.* New York: Da Capo, 1982.

Garganigo, John F. *Javier de Viana.* New York: Twayne, 1972.

Garry, Jim. *This Ol' Drought Ain't Broke Us Yet (But We're All Bent Pretty Bad): Stories of the American West.* New York: Orion Books, 1992.

Getty, Harry T. *The San Carlos Indian Cattle Industry.* Tucson: University of Arizona Press, 1963.

Giberti, Horacio. *Historia económica de la ganadería argentina.* Buenos Aires: Solar-Hachette, 1954, 1970.

Gilchriest, Gail. *The Cowgirl Companion.* New York: Hyperion, 1993.

Gill, Sam D., and Irene F. Sullivan. *Dictionary of Native American Mythology.* Santa Barbara, CA: ABC-CLIO, 1992.

Gipson, Fred. *Fabulous Empire: Colonel Zack Miller's Story.* Boston: Houghton Mifflin, 1946.

Goldman, Marion S. *Gold Diggers and Silver Miners: Prostitution and Social Life on the Comstock Lode.* Ann Arbor: University of Michigan Press, 1981.

Goldstein, Kenneth S. "Bowdlerization and Expurgation: Academic and Folk." *Journal of American Folklore* 80 (1967): 374–386.

Góngora, Mario. *Vagabundaje y sociedad fronteriza en Chile, siglos XVII a XIX.* Santiago: Universidad de Chile, 1966.

Goodrich, Samuel Griswold. *The Manners, Customs, and Antiquities of the Indians of North and South America.* Boston: Bradbury, Soden, 1844.

Gori, Gastón. *Vagos y mal entretenidos: Aporte al tema hernandiano.* 2d ed. Santa Fe, Argentina: Colmegna, 1965.

Gould, Ed. *Ranching: Ranching in Western Canada.* Saanichton, British Columbia: Hancock House, 1978.

Graham, Don. *Cowboys and Cadillacs: How Hollywood Looks at Texas.* Austin: Texas Monthly Press, 1983.

Graham, Robert Bontine Cunninghame. *The Horses of the Conquest.* Ed. Robert M. Denhardt.

1930. Reprint. Norman: University of Oklahoma Press, 1949.

———. *José Antonio Páez.* London: Heinemann, 1929.

———. *Rodeo: A Collection of Tales and Sketches.* Edited by A. F. Tschiffely. Garden City, NY: Doubleday, Doran and Co., 1936.

———. *The South American Sketches of Robert B. Cunninghame Graham.* Ed. John Walker. Norman: University of Oklahoma Press, 1978.

Grant, Bruce. *The Cowboy Encyclopedia: The Old and the New West from the Open Range to the Dude Ranch.* Chicago: Rand McNally, 1951.

Grant, Ted, and Andy Russell. *Men in the Saddle: Working Cowboys of Canada.* Toronto and New York: Van Nostrand Reinhold, 1978.

Griffith, James S. "The Cowboy Poetry of Everett Brisendine: A Response to Cultural Change." *Western Folklore* 42:1 (1983): 38–45.

Grinnell, George Bird. *The Cheyenne Indians: Their History and Way of Life.* Lincoln: University of Nebraska Press, 1972.

Gruber, Frank. *Zane Grey, A Biography.* New York: World Publications, 1970.

Guarda, Gabriel. *La sociedad en Chile astral antes de la colonización alemana, 1645–1845.* Santiago: Andres Bello, 1979.

Guice, John D. W. "Cattle Raisers of the Old Southwest: A Reinterpretation." *Western Historical Quarterly* 8:2 (April 1977): 167–187.

Guichard du Plessis, Jean, and Jo Mora. *Cowboys et gauchos des Amériques.* Paris: André Bonne, 1968.

Güiraldes, Ricardo. *Don Segundo Sombra: Shadows on the Pampas.* Trans. Harriet de Onís. 1926, 1935. Reprint. New York: Signet, 1966.

Guy, Donna J. *Sex and Danger in Buenos Aires: Prostitution, Family, and Nation in Argentina.* Lincoln: University of Nebraska Press, 1991.

Hadley-Garcia, George. *Hispanic Hollywood: The Latins in Motion Pictures.* New York: Citadel Press, 1990.

Haigh, Roger M. *Martín Güemes: Tyrant or Tool?* Fort Worth: Texas Christian University Press, 1968.

Haines, Francis D. *Horses in America.* New York: Crowell, 1971.

————. "How Did the Indians Get Their Horses?" *American Anthropologist* 40:1 (1938): 112–117.

————. "The Northward Spread of Horses among the Plains Indians." *American Anthropologist* 40:1 (1938): 429–437.

Haley, J. Evetts. *Charles Goodnight.* Norman: University of Oklahoma Press, 1949.

————. *The XIT Ranch of Texas and the Early Days of the Llano Estacado.* Norman: University of Oklahoma Press, 1953, 1967.

Hall, Thomas D. *Social Change in the Southwest, 1350–1880.* Lawrence: University Press of Kansas, 1989.

Hanes, Bailey C. *Bill Pickett, Bulldogger: The Biography of a Black Cowboy.* Norman: University of Oklahoma Press, 1977.

Harris, Charles H. III. *A Mexican Family Empire: The Latifundio of the Sánchez Navarro Family, 1765–1867.* Austin: University of Texas Press, 1975.

Harris, Charles W., and Buck Rainey, eds. *The Cowboy: Six-shooters, Songs, and Sex.* Norman: University of Oklahoma Press, 1976.

Harrod, Howard L. *Renewing the World: Plains Indian Religion and Morality.* Tucson: University of Arizona, 1987.

Hassrick, Royal B. *History of Western American Art.* New York: Exeter Press, 1987.

Hatch, Alden. *Remington Arms in American History.* New York: Holt, Rinehart, 1956.

Havinghurst, Walter. *Annie Oakley of the Wild West.* Reprint. Lincoln: University of Nebraska Press, 1954, 1992.

Hayes, M. Horace. *Points of the Horse: A Treatise on the Conformation, Movements, and Evolution of the Horse.* New York: Scribner's, 1969.

Heide, Robert, and John Gilman. *Box Office Buckaroos: The Cowboy Hero from the Wild West Show to the Silver Screen.* New York: Abbeville Press, 1982.

Hendrix, John. *If I Can Do It Horseback: A Cow-country Sketchbook.* Austin: University of Texas Press, 1964.

Hennessy, Alistair. *The Frontier in Latin American History.* Albuquerque: University of New Mexico Press, 1978.

Hernández, José. *The Gaucho Martín Fierro.* Trans. Walter Owen. 1935. Reprint. Buenos Aires: Pampa, 1960.

Hilzheimer, Max. "The Evolution of the Domestic Horse." *Antiquity* 9 (1935): 133–139.

Hinton, Harwood P., Jr. "John Simpson Chisum, 1877–84." *New Mexico Historical Review* 31:3 (July 1956): 177–205; 31:4 (October 1956): 310–337; 32:1 (January 1957): 53–65.

Hodge, William. *A Bibliography of Contemporary North American Indians.* New York: Interland Publishing, 1976.

Hoebel, E. Adamson. *The Cheyennes: Indians of the Great Plains.* New York: Holt, 1960.

Hoig, Stan. *The Humor of the American Cowboy.* Lincoln: University of Nebraska Press, 1958, 1970.

Holden, William C. *The Espuela Land and Cattle Company: A Study of a Foreign-Owned Ranch in Texas.* 1934. Reprint. Austin: Texas State Historical Association, 1970.

Holder, Preston. *The Hoe and the Horse on the Plains.* Lincoln: University of Nebraska Press, 1970.

Hollon, W(illiam) Eugene. *Frontier Violence: Another Look.* New York: Oxford University Press, 1974.

———. *The Great American Desert Then and Now.* New York: Oxford University Press, 1966.

Horn, Tom. *Life of Tom Horn, Government Scout and Interpreter.* Norman: University of Oklahoma Press, 1964.

Hornung, Clarence P. *The Way It Was in the West.* New York: Smithmark, 1978.

Hough, Emerson. *Getting a Wrong Start: A Truthful Autobiography.* New York: Macmillan, 1915.

———. *North of 36.* New York: D. Appleton, 1923.

———. *The Story of the Cowboy.* New York: D. Appleton, 1897.

Howey, M. Oldfield. *The Horse in Magic and Myth.* London: Rider and Son, 1923.

Hoy, Jim. "Rodeo in American Film." *Heritage of the Great Plains* 23:2 (1990): 26–32.

Hughes, Stella. *Chuck Wagon Cookin'.* Tucson: University of Arizona Press, 1974.

———. *Hashknife Cowboy: Recollections of Mack Hughes.* Tucson: University of Arizona Press, 1984.

Humboldt, Alexander von, and Aimé Bonpland. *Personal Narrative of Travels to the Equinoctial Regions of the New Continent, during the Years 1799–1804.* Trans. Helen María Williams.

London: Longman, Hurst, Rees, Orme, Brown and Green, 1825.

Hunt, Frazier. *Horses and Heroes: The Story of the Horse in America for 450 Years.* New York: Scribner's Sons, 1949.

Hutchinson, William H. *The Life and Personal Writings of Eugene Manlove Rhodes, a Bar Cross Man.* Norman: University of Oklahoma Press, 1956.

Ings, Frederick W. *Before the Fences: Tales from the Midway Ranch.* Calgary: McAra Printing, 1980.

Iverson, Peter. *When Indians Became Cowboys.* Norman: University of Oklahoma Press, 1994.

Izard, Miguel. "Mi coronel, hasta aquí le llegaron las matemáticas: Los llaneros del Apure." In Izard, comp. *Marginados, fronterizos, rebeldes y oprimidos.* 2 vols. Barcelona: Ediciones del Serbal, 1985.

———. "Ni cuatreros ni montoneros: Llaneros." *Boletín Americanista* 31 (1981): 83–142.

———. "Oligarcas temblad, viva la libertad: Los llaneros de Apure y la Guerra Federal." *Boletín Americanista* 32 (1982): 227–277.

———. "Sin domicilio fijo, senda segura, ni destino conocido: Los llaneros del Apure a finales del período colonial." *Boletín Americanista* 33 (1983): 13–83.

Jablow, Joseph. *The Cheyenne in Plains Indian Trade Relations, 1795–1840.* Seattle: University of Washington Press, 1950.

Jackson, Carlton. *Zane Grey.* Boston: Twayne, 1989.

Jackson, Jack. *Los Mesteños: Spanish Ranching in Texas, 1721–1821.* College Station: Texas A&M University Press, 1986.

James, Garry. "The Ten Best Western Movies." *Cowboys & Indians* 1:2; 1:3 (Summer, Winter 1993).

James, Will. *Cow Country.* New York: Scribner's, 1927.

————. *Cowboys North and South.* Reprint. New York: Arno Press, 1924, 1975.

————. *Lone Cowboy: My Life Story.* New York: Scribner's Sons, 1930.

————. *Will James: The Spirit of the Cowboy.* Ed. J. M. Neil. Casper, WY: Nicolaysen Art Museum, 1985.

Jameson, Sheilagh. *Ranches, Cowboys, and Characters: The Birth of Alberta's Western Heritage.* Calgary: Glenbow Museum, 1987.

Jaques, Mary J. *Texan Ranch Life: With Three Months through Mexico in a Prairie Schooner.* 1896. Reprint. College Station: Texas A&M University Press, 1989.

Johnston, Moira. *Ranch: Portrait of a Surviving Dream.* Garden City, NY: Doubleday, 1983.

Johnstone, Iain. *Clint Eastwood: The Man With No Name.* New York: Quill/William Morrow, 1981, 1988.

Jones, J. Philip. *Gambling Yesterday and Today: A Complete History.* Newton Abbot, England: David and Charles, 1973.

Jordan, Roy A., and Tim R. Miller. "The Politics of a Cowboy Culture." *Annals of Wyoming* 52:1 (Spring 1980): 40–45.

Jordan, Teresa. *Cowgirls: Women of the American West.* New York: Anchor Books, 1982.

Jordan, Terry G. *Trails to Texas: Southern Roots of Western Cattle Ranching.* Lincoln: University of Nebraska Press, 1981.

————. *North American Cattle-Ranching Frontiers: Origins, Diffusion, and Differentiation.*

Albuquerque: University of New Mexico Press, 1993.

Karr, Charles Lee, Jr., and Carol Robbins Karr. *Remington Handguns.* New York: Bonanza Books, 1960.

Katz, William Loren. *Black People Who Made the Old West.* New York: Crowell, 1977.

————. *The Black West.* Garden City, NY: Doubleday, 1971.

Kauffman, Sandra. *The Cowboy Catalog.* New York: Crown, 1980.

Kelly, Leroy Victor. *The Range Men: The Story of the Ranchers and Indians of Alberta.* 1913. Reprint. New York: Argonaut Press, 1965.

Kelton, Elmer. *The Day the Cowboys Quit.* New York: Bantam, 1971, 1992.

Kent, Rosemary, ed. *The Genuine Texas Handbook.* New York: Workman Publishing, 1981.

Ketchum, William C., Jr. *Western Memorabilia: Collectibles of the Old West.* Maplewood, NJ: Rutledge Books, 1980.

Kiskaddon, Bruce. *Rhymes of the Ranges.* Ed. Hal Cannon. Salt Lake City: Peregrine Smith Books, 1987.

Klein, Barry T. *Reference Encyclopedia of the American Indian.* 7th ed. Santa Barbara, CA: ABC-CLIO, 1995.

Kroeber, Alfred L. *The Arapaho.* Lincoln: University of Nebraska Press, 1983.

Lago, Tomás. *El huaso.* Santiago: Universidad de Chile, 1953.

Lamar, Howard R. "Much To Celebrate: The Western History Association's Twenty-Fifth Birthday." *Western Historical Quarterly* 17:4 (October 1986): 397–416.

————, comp. *The Reader's Encyclopedia of the American West.* New York: Harper and Row, 1977.

Lamb, Gene. *Rodeo: Back of the Chutes.* Denver: Bell Press, 1956.

L'Amour, Louis. "The Cowboy: Reflections of a Western Writer." *Colorado Heritage* 1 (1981): 1–6.

Langman, Larry. *A Guide to Silent Westerns.* Westport, CT: Greenland Press, 1992.

Larkin, Margaret. *Singing Cowboy: A Book of Western Songs.* 1931. Reprint. New York: Da Capo Press, 1979.

Larson, T. A., comp. *Bill Nye's Western Humor.* Lincoln: University of Nebraska Press, 1968.

Laune, Paul. *America's Quarter Horses.* Garden City, NY: Doubleday, 1973.

Lavington, H. *Dude. Nine Lives of a Cowboy.* Victoria, British Columbia: Sono Nis Press, 1982.

Lawrence, Elizabeth Atwood. *Hoofbeats and Society: Studies of Human-Horse Interactions.* Bloomington: Indiana University Press, 1985.

————. *Rodeo: An Anthropologist Looks at the Wild and Tame.* Chicago: University of Chicago Press, 1984.

Laxalt, Robert. "The Gauchos: Last of a Breed." *National Geographic* 158:4 (October 1980): 478–501.

Lea, Tom. *The King Ranch.* Boston: Little, Brown, 1957.

LeCompte, Mary Lou. *Cowgirls of the Rodeo: Pioneer Professional Athletes.* Bloomington: Indiana University Press, 1993.

————. "The Hispanic Influence on the History of Rodeo, 1823–1922." *Journal of Sport History* 12:1 (Spring 1985): 21–38.

LeCompte, Mary Lou, and William H. Beezley. "Any Sunday in April: The Rise of Sport in San Antonio and the Hispanic Borderlands." *Journal of Sport History* 13:2 (Summer 1986): 128–146.

Lee, Katie. *Ten Thousand Goddam Cattle: A History of the American Cowboy in Song, Story and Verse.* Rev. ed. Jerome, Arizona: Katydid Books & Records, 1976, 1985.

Lee, Lawrence B. *Reclaiming the American West: A Historiography and Guide.* Santa Barbara, CA: ABC-CLIO, 1980.

Lenihan, John H. *Showdown: Confronting Modern America in the Western Film.* Urbana: University of Illinois Press, 1980.

Lichtblau, Myron I. *The Argentine Novel in the Nineteenth Century.* New York: Hispanic Institute in the United States, 1959.

Limerick, Patricia Nelson. *The Legacy of Conquest: The Unbroken Past of the American West.* New York: W. W. Norton, 1987.

Limerick, Patricia Nelson, Clyde A. Milner II, and Charles E. Rankin, eds. *Trails: Toward a New Western History.* Lawrence: University Press of Kansas, 1991.

Lincoln, John. *Rich Grass and Sweet Water: Ranch Life with the Koch Matador Cattle Company.* College Station: Texas A&M University Press, 1989.

Lingenfelter, Richard E., Richard A. Dwyer, and David Cohen. *Songs of the American West.* Berkeley: University of California Press, 1968.

Liscano, Juan. *Rómulo Gallegos.* 2d ed. Mexico: Novano, 1970.

Logsdon, Guy. "Cowboy Poets." In *Hoein' the Short Roes.* Edited by Francis Edward Abernethy. Fort Worth: South Methodist University Press, 1988.

———. *"The Whorehouse Bells Were Ringing" and Other Songs Cowboys Sing.* Urbana: University of Illinois Press, 1989.

Lomax, John Avery. *Songs of the Cattle Trail and Cow Camp.* London: T. F. Unwin, 1920.

Lomax, John Avery, and Alan Lomax, comps. *Cowboy Songs and Other Frontier Ballads.* New York: Macmillan, 1938.

Long, Philip Sheridan. *The Great Canadian Range.* Toronto: Ryerson Press, 1963.

Loomis, Noel M. "Early Cattle Trails in Southern Arizona." *Arizoniana* 3:4 (1962): 18–24.

Lopez, David E. "Cowboy Strikes and Unions." *Labor History* 18:3 (Summer 1977): 325–340.

Loveman, Brian. *Chile: The Legacy of Hispanic Capitalism.* 2d ed. New York: Oxford University Press, 1988.

———. *Struggle in the Countryside: Politics and Rural Labor in Chile, 1919–1973.* Bloomington: Indiana University Press, 1976.

Loy, Jane M. "Horsemen of the Tropics: A Comparative View of the Llaneros in the History of Venezuela and Colombia." *Boletín Americanista* 31 (1981): 159–171.

Luccetti, Cathy, and Carol Olwell. *Women of the West.* New York: Orion Books, 1982.

Lugones, Leopoldo. *El payador.* 4th ed. Buenos Aires: Huemul, 1916, 1972.

Lupton, Austin A. "Cattle Ranching in Alberta, 1874–1910: Its Evolution and Migration." *Albertan Geographer* 3 (1966): 48–58.

McCall, Michael. *Country Music U.S.A. from Nashville to Branson.* Lincolnwood, IL: Publications International, 1993.

McCallum, Henry D., and Frances McCallum. *The Wire That Fenced the West.* Norman: University of Oklahoma Press, 1965, 1985.

McCarthy, Cormac. *All the Pretty Horses.* New York: Alfred A. Knopf, 1993.

McCoy, Joseph G. *Cattle Trade of the West and Southwest.* 1874. Reprint. Readex Microprint, 1966.

McCracken, Harold. *The Charles M. Russell Book.* Garden City, NY: Doubleday, 1957.

———. *Frederic Remington, Artist of the Old West.* Philadelphia: J. B. Lippincott, 1947.

———. *The Frederic Remington Book: A Pictorial History of the West.* Garden City, NY: Doubleday, 1966.

———. *Great Painters and Illustrators of the Old West.* New York: Dover, 1952, 1988.

McDonald, Archie P., ed. *Shooting Stars: Heroes and Heroines of Western Film.* Bloomington: Indiana University Press, 1987.

McDowell, Bart. *The American Cowboy in Life and Legend.* Washington, DC: National Geographic Society, 1972.

McDowell, R. Bruce. *Evolution of the Winchester.* Tacoma, WA: Armory Publications, 1985.

MacEwan, John Walter Grant. *Blazing the Old Cattle Trail.* 1952. Reprint. Saskatoon, Saskatchewan: Western Producer Prairie Books, 1975.

———. *John Ware's Cattle Country.* Saskatoon, Saskatchewan: Western Producer Prairie Books, 1974.

McGrath, Roger D. *Gunfighters, Highwaymen, and Vigilantes: Violence on the Frontier.* Berkeley: University of California Press, 1984.

Machado, Manuel A., Jr. *The North Mexican Cattle Industry, 1910–1975: Ideology, Conflict, and Change.* College Station: Texas A&M University Press, 1981.

Mackay-Smith, Alexander. *The Colonial Quarter Race Horse.* Middleburg, VA: H. K. Groves, 1983.

Mackin, Bill. *Cowboy and Gunfighter Collectibles: A Photographic Encyclopedia with Price Guide and Markers Index.* Missoula, MT: Mountain Press Publishing, 1989.

McLoughlin, Denis. *Wild and Woolly: An Encyclopedia of the Old West.* Garden City, NY: Doubleday, 1975.

McMullen, Cyd, and Anne Wallace. *Cowboy Poetry Cookbook: Menus and Verse for Western Celebrations.* Salt Lake City: Peregrine Smith Books, 1992.

McMurtry, Larry. *Lonesome Dove.* New York: Simon and Schuster, 1985.

Macoun, John, ed. *Manitoba and the Great North West.* Guelph, Ontario: World Publishing, 1882.

McRae, Wallace. *Cowboy Curmudgeon and Other Poems.* Salt Lake City: Peregrine Smith Books, 1992.

Mails, Thomas E. *The Mystic Warriors of the Plains.* Garden City, NY: Doubleday, 1972.

Malone, Bill C. *Country Music, U.S.A.: A Fifty-Year History.* Rev. ed. Austin: University of Texas Press, 1985.

———. *Singing Cowboys and Musical Mountaineers: Southern Culture and the Roots of Country Music.* Athens: University of Georgia Press, 1993.

Malone, Michael P., ed. *Historians and the American West.* Lincoln: University of Nebraska Press, 1983.

Manson, Michael, ed. *The Country Music Book.* New York: Charles Scribner's Sons, 1985.

Mantilla Trejos, Eduardo. *Sobre los llanos.* Caracas: Fotomecánica Industrial, 1988.

Marks, Paula Mitchell. *Turn Your Eyes toward Texas: Pioneers Sam and Mary Maverick.* College Station: Texas A&M University Press, 1989.

Markus, Kurt. *Buckaroo: Images from the Sagebrush Basin.* Boston: Little, Brown, 1987.

Marrin, Albert. *Cowboys, Indians, and Gunfighters: The Story of the Cattle Kingdom.* New York: Atheneum, 1993.

Marriott, Alice Lee. *Hell on Horses and Women.* Norman: University of Oklahoma Press, 1953.

Marshall, Howard W., and Richard E. Ahlborn. *Buckaroos in Paradise: Cowboy Life in Northern Nevada.* Lincoln: University of Nebraska Press, 1981.

Martin, Lynn J., ed. *Nā Paniolo o Hawai'i.* Honolulu: Honolulu Academy of Arts, 1987.

Martin, Phil, comp. *Coolin' Down: An Anthology of Contemporary Cowboy Poetry.* Tulsa, OK: Guy Logsdon Books, 1992.

Martin, Russell. *Cowboy: The Enduring Myth of the Wild West.* New York: Stewart, Tabori and Chang, 1983.

Martínez Estrada, Ezequiel. *Muerte y transfiguración de Martín Fierro.* 2 vols. Mexico City: Fonda de Cultura Económica, 1948.

———. *X-Ray of the Pampa.* Trans. Alain Swietlicki. Austin: University of Texas Press, 1971.

Mason, Michael, ed. *The Country Music Book.* New York: Scribner's, 1985.

Matthews, Robert Paul. *Violencia rural en Venezuela, 1840–1858: Antecedentes socioeconómicas de la Guerra Federal.* Caracas: Monte Avila, 1977.

Mayer, John. "El llanero." *Atlantic Monthly* 3 (February 1859): 174–188.

Medicine Crow, Joseph. *From the Heart of the Crow Country: The Crow Indians' Own Stories.* New York: Orion Books, 1992.

Mellen, Joan. *Big Bad Wolves: Masculinity in the American Film.* New York: Pantheon, 1977.

Metzger, Linda. ed. *Contemporary Authors: New Revision Series,* volume 19. Detroit: Gale Research Company, 1987.

Miller, Leo O. *The Great Cowboy Stars of Movies & Television.* Westport, CT: Arlington House, 1979.

Miller, Nathan. *TR: A Life.* New York: William Morrow, 1992.

Miller, Robert Henry. *Reflections of a Black Cowboy.* Englewood Cliffs, NJ: Silver Burdett Press, 1991.

Milton, John R. *The Novel of the American West.* Lincoln: University of Nebraska Press, 1980.

Molinari, Ricardo Luis. *Biografía de la pampa: Cuatro siglos de historia del campo argentino.* Buenos Aires: Arte Gaglianone, 1988.

Monaghan, Jay, ed. *The Book of the American West.* New York: Bonanza Books, 1963.

Moody, Michael. "La fiesta huasa." *Américas* 38:1 (January 1986): 20–24, 46.

———. "Rodeo in Mexico: Charros and Charreadas." *Persimmon Hill* 17:1 (Spring 1989): 46–55.

———. "Rodeo is Hot—in Chile." *Persimmon Hill* 15:3 (Autumn 1987): 5–17.

Moon, Dolly M. *My Very First Book of Cowboy Songs.* New York: Dover, 1982.

Moore, Daniel G. *Log of a Twentieth Century Cowboy.* Tucson: University of Arizona Press, 1965.

Moore, Ethel, and Chauncey O. Moore. *Ballads and Folk Songs of the Southwest: More than 600 Titles, Melodies, and Texts Collected in Oklahoma.* Norman: University of Oklahoma Press, 1964.

Mora, Carl J. *Mexican Cinema: Reflections of a Society, 1896–1980.* Berkeley: University of California Press, 1982.

Mora, Joseph J. *Californios: The Saga of the Hard-Riding Vaqueros, America's First Cowboys.* Garden City, NY: Doubleday, 1949.

———. *Trail Dust and Saddle Leather.* Lincoln: University of Nebraska Press, 1946, 1973.

Morris, Michele. *The Cowboy Life: A Saddlebag Guide for Dudes, Tenderfeet, and Cowpunchers Everywhere.* New York: Simon & Schuster, 1993.

Morrisey, Richard J. "The Early Range Cattle Industry in Arizona." *Agricultural History* 24:3 (July 1950): 151–156.

———. "The Northward Expansion of Cattle Raising in New Spain, 1550–1600." *Agricultural History* 25:3 (July 1951): 115–121.

Motolinia, Toribio. *History of the Indians of New Spain.* Washington, DC: Academy of American Franciscan History, 1951.

Mueller, Ellen Crago. *Calamity Jane.* Laramie: Jelm Mountain Press Publishing, 1981.

Murphey, Michael Martin. "How I Became a Singing Cowboy." *Cowboys & Indians* 2:1 (Spring 1994): 77–78.

———, comp. *Cowboys Songs.* Secaucus, NJ: Warner Brothers, 1991.

Myres, Sandra L. *The Ranch in Spanish Texas, 1691–1800.* El Paso: Texas Western Press, 1969.

———. "The Spanish Cattle Kingdom in the Province of Texas." *Texana* 4:3 (Fall 1966): 233–246.

Nagler, Barney. *The American Horse.* New York: Macmillan, 1966.

Nash, Gerald D. *Creating the West: Historical Interpretations, 1890–1990.* Albuquerque: University of New Mexico Press, 1991.

Nichols, Madaline Wallis. *The Gaucho: Cattle Hunter, Cavalryman, Ideal of Romance.* 1942. Reprint. New York: Gordian Press, 1968.

———. "The Spanish Horse of the Pampas." *American Anthropologist* 41 (1939): 119–129.

Noel, Thomas J. *The City and the Saloon: Denver, 1858–1916.* Lincoln: University of Nebraska Press, 1982.

Nolan, Frederick. *The Lincoln County War: A Documentary History.* Norman: University of Oklahoma Press, 1992.

Nolan, Walter Frederick. *Max Brand, Western Giant: The Life and Times of Frederick Schiller Faust.* Bowling Green, KY: Bowling Green State University Popular Press, 1985.

Nordyke, Lewis. *Cattle Empire: The Fabulous Story of the 3,000,000 Acre XIT.* New York: Morrow, 1949.

———. *Great Roundup: the Story of Texas and Southwestern Cowmen.* New York: Morrow, 1955.

Norman, James. *Charro: Mexican Horseman.* New York: Putnam's, 1969.

Null, Gary. *Black Hollywood: The Negro in Motion Pictures.* New York: Carol Publishing Group, 1975, 1990.

Nunis, Doyce B., Jr. *The Life of Tom Horn Revisited.* Arcadia, CA: The Westerners Los Angeles Corral, 1992.

Nye, Nelson C. *The Complete Book of the Quarter Horse: A Breeder's Guide.* New York: Arco, 1964, 1978.

Ogden, Adele. "New England Traders in Spanish and Mexican California" in *Greater America: Essays in Honor of Herbert Eugene Bolton.* Berkeley: University of California Press, 1945.

Ohrlin, Glenn. *The Hell-Bound Train: A Cowboy Songbook.* Urbana: University of Illinois Press, 1973, 1989.

Oliphant, J. Orin. *On the Cattle Ranges of the Oregon Country.* Seattle: University of Washington Press, 1968.

O'Neal, Bill. *Encyclopedia of Western Gunfighters.* Norman: University of Oklahoma Press, 1979.

O'Neil, Paul. *The End and the Myth.* Alexandria, VA: Time-Life Books, 1979.

Osborne, Walter D. *The Quarter Horse.* New York: Grosset and Dunlap, 1977.

Ovalles, Victor Manuel. *El llanero: Estudio sobre su vida, sus costumbres, su carácter y su poesía.* Caracas: Herrera Irigoyen, 1905.

Pady, Donald Stuart. *Horses and Horsemanship: Selected Books and Periodicals in the Iowa State University Library: An Annotated Bibliography.* Ames: Iowa State University Library, 1973.

Páez, Ramón. *Wild Scenes in South America, or Life in the Llanos of Venezuela.* London: Sampson Low, 1863.

Pages Larraya, Antonio. *Prosas de Martín Fierro.* Buenos Aires: Raigal, 1952.

Paladino Giménez, José M. *El gaucho: Reseña fotográfica, 1860–1930.* Buenos Aires: Palsa, 1971.

Paredes, Américo. *Folktales of Mexico.* Chicago: University of Chicago Press, 1970.

———, ed. *A Texas-Mexican Cancionero: Folksongs of the Lower Border.* Urbana: University of Illinois Press, 1976, printed music.

Pattie, Jane. *Cowboy Spurs and Their Makers.* College Station: Texas A&M University Press, 1991.

Paul, Rodman W. *The Far West and the Great Plains in Transition.* New York: Harper and Row, 1988.

Paullada, Stephen. *Rawhide and Song: A Comparative Study of the Cattle Cultures of the Argentinian Pampa and North American Great Plains.* New York: Vantage Press, 1963.

Payne, Darwin. *Owen Wister: Chronicler of the West, Gentleman of the East.* Dallas: Southern Methodist University Press, 1985.

Peavy, Charles D. *Larry McMurtry.* New York: Twayne, 1977.

Pereira Salas, Eugenio. *Juegos y alegrías coloniales en Chile.* Santiago: Zig-Zag, 1947.

Pérez Amuchástegui, Antonio Jorge. *Mentalidades argentinas, 1860–1930.* 2d ed. Buenos Aires: EUDEBA, 1970.

Perkins, David, and Norman Tanis. *Native Americans of North America: A Bibliography.* Metuchen, NJ: Scarecrow Press, 1975.

Perry, Kenneth D., and Luanne Cullen. "The Cowboy: Balancing Fact and Fantasy in a Museum Project." *Curator* 25:3 (1982): 213–222.

Petersen, Gwen. "Git Along Li'l Doggerels: Cowboys and Poetry." *Persimmon Hill* 16:1 (Spring 1988): 28–37.

Pevoto, Charlotte Wren. *Cattle Barons and the Mansions They Built in Texas, 1870–1905.* Monticello, NY: Vance Bibliographies, 1984.

Phippen, George. *The Life of a Cowboy, Told Through the Drawings, Paintings, and Bronzes of George Phippen, as selected by Louise Phippen.* Tucson: University of Arizona Press, 1969.

Pingenot, Ben E. *Siringo: The True Story of Charles A. Siringo.* College Station: Texas A&M University Press, 1989.

Pinto, Luis C. *El gaucho rioplatense, frente a los malos historiadores.* Buenos Aires: Ciordia y Rodríguez, 1944.

————. *El gaucho y sus detractores: Defensa de las tradiciones argentina; reivindicación del gaucho.* Buenos Aires: Ateneo, 1943.

Place, J. A. *The Western Films of John Ford.* Secaucus, NJ: Citadel Press, 1974.

Pointer, Larry. *Rodeo Champions: Eight Memorable Moments of Riding, Wrestling, and Roping.* Albuquerque: University of New Mexico Press, 1985.

Porter, Robert Ker. *Sir Robert Ker Porter's Caracas Diary, 1825–1842: A British Diplomat in a Newborn Nation.* Ed. Walter Dupuoy. Caracas: Dupuoy, 1966.

Powers, Bob. *Cowboy Country.* Glendale, CA: Arthur H. Clark, 1987.

Prado, Caio, Jr. *The Colonial Background of Modern Brazil.* Trans. Suzette Macedo. Berkeley: University of California Press, 1967, 1971.

Prado P., Uldaricio. *El caballo chileno, 1541 a 1914: Estudio zootécnico e histórico hípico.* Santiago: Imprenta Santiago, 1914.

Prassel, Frank Richard. *The Great American Outlaw.* Norman: University of Oklahoma Press, 1993.

Rainbolt, Jo. *The Last Cowboy: Twilight Era of the Horseback Cowhand, 1900–1940.* Helena, MT: America and World Geographic Publications, 1992.

Raine, William. *Famous Sheriffs and Western Outlaws.* Garden City, NY: Garden City Publishing, 1929.

Ramírez, Nora E. "The Vaquero and Ranching in the Southwestern United States, 1600–1970." Ph.D. diss., Indiana University, 1979.

Randolph, Edmond. *Beef, Leather, and Grass.* Norman: University of Oklahoma Press, 1981.

Randolph, J. Ralph. *British Travelers among the Southern Indians, 1660–1763.* Norman: University of Oklahoma Press, 1973.

Rapoport, Mario, comp. *Economía e historia: Contribuciones a la historia económica argentina.* Buenos Aires: Editorial Tesis, 1988.

Rattenbury, Richard. *Packing Iron: Gunleather of the Frontier West.* Springfield, OH: Zon International Publishing, 1993.

Rausch, Jane M. *The Llanos Frontier in Colombian History, 1830–1930.* Albuquerque: University of New Mexico Press, 1993.

———. *A Tropical Plains Frontier: The Llanos of Colombia, 1531–1831.* Albuquerque: University of New Mexico Press, 1984.

Reagan, Ronald. *An American Life.* New York: Simon & Schuster, 1991.

Rector, Ray. *Cowboy Life on the Texas Plains: The Photographs of Ray Rector.* Ed. Margaret L. Rector. College Station: Texas A&M University Press, 1982.

Reese, William S. *Six Score: The 120 Best Books on the Range Cattle Industry.* Austin: Jenkins Publishing, 1976.

Reid, Jan. *The Improbable Rise of Redneck Rock.* New York: Da Capo, 1974.

Reiter, Joan Swallow. *The Women.* Alexandria, VA: Time-Life Books, 1978.

Remington, Frederic. *Frederic Remington's Own West.* Ed. Harold McCracken. New York: Dial Press, 1960.

———. *Pony Tracks.* 1895. Reprint. Norman: University of Oklahoma Press, 1961.

Remley, David. *Bell Ranch: Cattle Ranching in the Southwest, 1824–1947.* Albuquerque: University of New Mexico Press, 1993.

Reynolds, James. *A World of Horses.* New York: Creative Age Press, 1947.

Rhodes, Eugene Manlove. *Pasó Por Aquí.* Norman: University of Oklahoma Press, 1973.

———. *The Rhodes Reader: Stories of Virgins, Villains, and Varmints.* 2d ed. Selected by W. H. Hutchinson. Norman: University of Oklahoma Press, 1957, 1975.

Rincón Gallardo, Carlos. *El libro del charro mexicano.* 3d ed. Mexico City: Porrúa, 1960.

Rivas Sosa, Alejandro. *Nuestro ganado vacuno: La ganadería como fuente potencial de requeza nacional.* Caracas: Elite, 1938.

Roach, Joyce Gibson. *The Cowgirls.* 2d rev. ed. Denton: University of North Texas Press, 1990.

Robb, John Donald, ed. *Hispanic Folk Music of New Mexico and the Southwest.* Norman: University of Oklahoma, 1980. 891 pages of printed music.

Rodríguez Molas, Ricardo. *Historia social del gaucho.* Buenos Aires: Marú, 1968.

Roe, Frank Gilbert. *The Indian and the Horse.* Norman: University of Oklahoma Press, 1955.

———. "Remittance Men." *Alberta Historical Review* 2:1 (January 1954).

Rogers, Will. *The Autobiography of Will Rogers.* Ed. Donald Day. Boston: Houghton Mifflin, 1949.

———. *The Illiterate Digest.* New York: A. L. Burt, 1924.

———. *Rogers-isms: The Cowboy Philosopher at the Peace Conference.* New York: Harper and Brothers, 1919.

Rogin, Michael P. *Ronald Reagan, the Movie and Other Episodes in Political Demonology.* Berkeley: University of California Press, 1987.

Rojas, Arnold R. *The Vaquero.* Charlotte, NC: McNally and Loftin, 1964.

Rojas, Ricardo. *Historia de la literatura argentina: Ensayo filosófico sobre la evolución de la cultura en el Plata.* 4 vols. Buenos Aires: Coni, 1917–1922.

Rollins, Peter C. *Hollywood as Historian: American Film in a Cultural Context.* Lexington: University Press of Kentucky, 1983.

———. *Will Rogers, A Bio-bibliography.* Westport, CT: Greenwood Press, 1984.

Rollins, Philip Ashton. *The Cowboy: An Unconventional History of Civilization on the Old-Time Range.* 1922. Reprint. Albuquerque: University of New Mexico Press, 1979.

———. *Jinglebob: A True Story of a Real Cowboy.* New York: Grosset & Dunlap, 1927.

Rollinson, John K. *Wyoming Cattle Trails: History of the Migration of Oregon-Raised Herds to Mid-Western Markets.* Caldwell: Caxton Printers, 1948.

Ronald, Ann. *The New West of Edward Abbey.* Albuquerque: University of New Mexico Press, 1982.

Ronda, Jeanne, and Richard W. Slatta. "Cowboying at the Chapman-Barnard Ranch" *Persimmon Hill* 21:1 (Spring 1993): 36–41.

Roosevelt, Theodore. *Ranch Life and the Hunting-Trail.* 1888. Reprint. Ann Arbor, MI: University Microfilms, 1966.

Rosa, Joseph G. *The Gunfighter: Man or Myth?* Norman: University of Oklahoma Press, 1969.

Rosa, Joseph G., and Robin May Rosa. *Buffalo Bill and His Wild West: A Pictorial Biography.* Lawrence: University Press of Kansas, 1989.

Rosenberg, Bruce A. *The Code of the West.* Bloomington: Indiana University Press, 1982.

Rossi, Paul A. "The Western Stock Saddle." *American West* 3:3 (1966).

Rosti, Pál. *Memorias de un viaje por América.* 1861. Trans. Judith Sarosi. Caracas: Universidad Central de Venezuela, 1968.

Rothel, David. *The Great Cowboy Sidekicks.* Metuchen, NJ: Scarecrow Press, 1984.

———. *The Roy Rogers Book.* Madison, NC: Empire Publishing, 1987.

———. *The Singing Cowboys.* South Brunswick, NJ: A. S. Barnes, 1978.

Rouse, John E. *World Cattle.* Norman: University of Oklahoma Press, 1970.

Russell, Charles Marion. *Good Medicine: The Illustrated Letters of Charles M. Russell.* Garden City, NY: Doubleday, 1929.

———. *Trails Plowed Under.* Garden City, NY: Doubleday, 1927.

Russell, Don. *The Lives and Legends of Buffalo Bill.* Norman: University of Oklahoma Press, 1960.

———. *The Wild West: A History of the Wild West Shows.* Ft. Worth, TX: Amon Carter Museum, 1970.

Ruth, Kent. *Landmarks of the West: A Guide to Historic Sites.* Lincoln: University of Nebraska Press, 1963, 1986.

Rutherford, Michael. *The American Cowboy: Tribute to a Vanishing Breed.* New York: Gallery Books, 1990.

Ryan, Kathleen Jo. *Ranching Traditions: Legacy of the American West.* New York: Abbeville Press, 1990.

Ryden. Hope. *America's Last Wild Horses.* New York: Dutton, 1970.

Sachs, Karl. *De los llanos: Descripción de un viaje de ciencias naturales a Venezuela.* 1878. Trans. José Izquierdo. Caracas and Madrid: Edime, 1955.

Sackett, Samuel John. *Cowboys and the Songs They Sang.* New York: William R. Scott, 1967.

Sáenz Quesada, María. *Los estancieros.* Buenos Aires: Belgrano, 1980.

St. John, Bob. *On Down the Road: The World of the Rodeo Cowboy.* Englewood Cliffs, NJ: Prentice-Hall, 1977.

Sambrano Urdaneta, Oscar. *El llanero: Un problema de crítica literaria.* Caracas: Cuadernos Literarios, 1952.

Samper, José María. *Ensayo sobre las revoluciones políticas y la condición social de las repúblicas colombianos.* Paris: Thurnot, 1861.

Samuels, Peggy, and Harold Samuels. *Frederic Remington: A Biography.* Garden City, NY: Doubleday, 1982.

San Diego Museum of Art. *The Cowboy.* San Diego, 1981.

Sandoz, Mari. *The Cattlemen from the Rio Grande across the Far Marias.* Lincoln: University of Nebraska Press, 1958, 1978.

———. *Old Jules.* Boston: Little, Brown, 1935.

Sands, Kathleen M. *Charrería Mexicana: An Equestrian Folk Tradition.* Tucson: University of Arizona Press, 1993.

Santee, Ross. *Cowboy.* Lincoln: University of Nebraska Press, 1928, 1977.

———. *Lost Pony Tracks.* New York: Scribner's, 1953.

———. *Men and Horses.* Lincoln: University of Nebraska Press, 1926, 1977.

Sarmiento, Domingo F. *Life in the Argentine Republic in the Days of the Tyrants; or Civilization and Barbarism.* Trans. Mrs. Horace (Mary) Mann. 1845, 1868. Reprint. New York: Hafner, 1971.

Saubidet, Tito. *Vocabulario y refranero criollo.* 7th ed. Buenos Aires: Rafael Palumbo, 1975.

Savage, W. Sherman. *Blacks in the West.* Westport, CT: Greenwood Press, 1976.

Savage, William W., Jr. *The Cowboy Hero: His Image in American History and Culture.* Norman: University of Oklahoma Press, 1979.

———, ed. *Cowboy Life: Reconstructing an American Myth.* Norman: University of Oklahoma Press, 1975.

Savitt, Sam. *Rodeo: Cowboys, Bulls, and Broncs.* Garden City, NY: Doubleday, 1963.

Sawey, Orlan. *Charles A. Siringo.* Boston: Twayne Publishers, 1981.

Seemann, Charlie, producer. *Back in the Saddle Again.* New York: New World Records, 1983. LP record set.

Seidman, Laurence Ivan. *Once in the Saddle: The Cowboy's Frontier, 1866–1896.* New York: Knopf, 1973.

Sell, Henry Blackman, and Victory Weybright. *Buffalo Bill and the Wild West.* New York: Oxford University Press, 1955.

Serven, James E. *Colt Firearms Since 1836.* Harrisburg. PA: Stackpole Books, 1979.

———. *Conquering the Frontiers: Stories of American Pioneers and the Guns Which Helped Them Establish a New Life.* La Habra, CA: Foundation Press, 1974.

———. *200 Years of American Firearms.* Chicago: Follett Publishing, 1975.

Sharp, Paul F. "The American Farmer and the 'Last Best West.'" *Agricultural History* 21:2 (April 1947): 65–75.

———. *Whoop-Up Country: The Canadian-American West, 1865–1885.* Helena, MT: Historical Society of Montana, 1962.

Sherwin, Sterling. *American Cowboy Songs Old and New.* London: Francis, Day and Hunter, 1939.

———. *Singin' in the Saddle.* Boston: Boston Music, 1944.

Shestack, Melvin. *The Country Music Encyclopedia.* New York: Crowell, 1974.

Shirley, Glen. *Pawnee Bill: A Biography of Major Gordon W. Lillie.* Albuquerque: University of New Mexico, 1958.

Simons, Helen, and Cathryn A. Hoyt, eds. *Hispanic Texas: A Historical Guide.* Austin: University of Texas Press, 1992.

Sires, Ina. *Songs of the Open Range.* Boston: C. C. Birchard, 1928.

Siringo, Charles A. *A Texas Cowboy: or, Fifteen Years on the Hurricane Deck of a Spanish Pony, Taken from Real Life.* 1885. Reprint. Lincoln: University of Nebraska Press, 1979.

Slatta, Richard W. "'Civilization' Battles 'Barbarism': Argentine Frontier Strategies, 1516–1880." *Inter-American Review of Bibliography* 39:2 (1989): 177–194.

———. *Cowboys of the Americas.* New Haven: Yale University Press, 1990. Paperback edition 1994.

———. "The Demise of the Gaucho and the Rise of Equestrian Sport in Argentina." *Journal of Sport History* 13:2 (Summer 1986): 97–110.

———. *Gauchos and the Vanishing Frontier.* Rev. ed. Lincoln: University of Nebraska Press, 1983, 1992.

———. "Historical Frontier Imagery in the Americas," in Paula Covington, ed. *Latin American Frontiers, Borders, and Hinterlands.* Albuquerque: SALALM Secretariat, 1990: 5–25.

———, ed. *Bandidos: The Varieties of Latin American Banditry.* Westport, CT: Greenwood Press, 1987.

Slatta, Richard W., and Arturo Alvarez d'Armas. "El llanero y el hato venezolano: Aportes bibliográficos." *South Eastern Latin Americanist* 29:2–3 (September 1985): 33–41.

Slotkin, Richard. *The Fatal Environment: The Myth of the Frontier in the Age of Industrialization, 1800–1890.* New York: Atheneum, 1985.

Smith, Dwight L., ed. *The American and Canadian West: A Bibliography.* Santa Barbara, CA: ABC-CLIO Press, 1979.

Smith, Erwin Evans. *Life on the Texas Range.* Austin: University of Texas Press, 1952.

Solberg, Carl E. "A Discriminatory Frontier Land Policy: Chile, 1870–1914." *The Americas* 26:2 (October 1969): 115–133.

———. *Immigration and Nationalism: Argentina and Chile, 1890–1914.* Austin: University of Texas Press, 1970.

———. *The Pampas and the Prairies: Agrarian Policy in Canada and Argentina, 1880–1930.* Stanford: Stanford University Press, 1987.

Somora, Julian, Joe Bernal, and Albert Peña. *Gunpowder Justice: A Reassessment of the Texas Rangers.* Notre Dame, IN: University of Notre Dame Press, 1979.

Sonnichsen, C. L. *From Hopalong to Hud: Thoughts on Western Fiction.* College Station: Texas A&M University Press, 1978.

Stambler, Irwin, and Grelun Landon. *The Encyclopedia of Folk, Country, and Western Music.* New York: St. Martin's Press, 1983.

Stands in Timber, John. *Cheyenne Memories.* New Haven: Yale University Press, 1967.

Stanley, Clark. *The Life and Adventures of the American Cowboy: Life in the Far West, by Clark*

Stanley, Better Known as the Rattlesnake King. Providence, RI: C. Stanley, 1897.

Starlog Press. *Hollywood Cowboy Heroes.* Vol. 4 of *Screen Greats.* New York: Starlog Press, 1981.

Steffen, Jerome O., ed. *The American West: New Perspectives, New Dimensions.* Norman: University of Oklahoma Press, 1981.

Stegner, Wallace. *Wolf Willow: A History, a Story, and a Memory of the Last Plains Frontier.* 1955. Reprint. Toronto: Macmillan, 1977.

Stegner, Wallace, and Richard W. Etulain. *Conversations with Wallace Stegner on Western History and Literature.* Salt Lake City: University of Utah Press, 1990.

Steinberg, Cobbett. *TV Facts.* New York: Facts on File, 1980.

Stewart, Elinore Pruitt. *Letters of a Woman Homesteader.* Boston: Houghton Mifflin, 1942, 1982.

Stewart, Janet Ann. *Arizona Ranch Houses: Southern Territorial Styles, 1867–1900.* Tucson: University of Arizona Press, Arizona Historical Society, 1974; 1987.

Stoeltje, Beverly J. "Rodeo: From Custom to Ritual." *Western Folklore* 48:3 (1989): 244–255.

Stong, Philip Duffield. *Horses and Americans.* New York: Frederick A. Stokes, 1939.

Stuart, Granville. *Forty Years on the Frontier, Volume 2, Pioneering in Montana: the Making of a State, 1864–1887.* Lincoln: University of Nebraska Press, 1925, 1977.

Sullivan, Tom R. *Cowboys and Caudillos: Frontier Ideology of the Americas.* Bowling Green, KY: Bowling Green State University Popular Press, 1990.

Taft, Robert. *Artists and Illustrators of the Old West, 1850–1900.* 1953. Reprint. Princeton: Princeton University Press, 1982.

Tanner, Ogden. *The Ranchers.* Alexandria, VA: Time-Life Books, 1977.

Taylor, Lonn, and Ingrid Maar. *The American Cowboy.* New York: Harper and Row, 1983.

Taylor, Louis. *Harper's Encyclopedia for Horsemen: The Complete Book of the Horse.* New York: Harper and Row, 1973.

———. *The Horse America Made: The Story of the American Saddle Horse.* New York: Harper, 1961.

Texas Cowboy Artists Association. *The Texas Cowboy.* Fort Worth: Texas Christian University Press, 1986.

Thomas, Gregory E. G. "The British Columbia Ranching Frontier, 1858–1896." M. A. thesis, University of British Columbia, 1976.

Thomas, Lewis G., ed. *The Prairie West to 1905: A Canadian Sourcebook.* Toronto: Oxford University Press, 1975.

Thomas, Lewis H., ed. *Essays on Western History in Honour of Lewis Gwynne Thomas.* Edmonton: University of Alberta Press, 1976.

Thomas, Tony. *The West That Never Was.* New York: Citadel Press, 1989.

Thorp, N(athan) Howard (Jack), comp. *Pardner of the Wind: Story of the Southwestern Cowboy.* Lincoln: University of Nebraska Press, 1972.

———. *Songs of the Cowboys.* 1908. Reprint. Lincoln: University of Nebraska Press, 1984.

Thrapp, Dan L., ed. *Encyclopedia of Frontier Biography.* 3 vols. Lincoln: University of Nebraska Press, 1988.

Timmons, William. *Twilight on the Range: Recollections of a Latterday Cowboy.* Austin: University of Texas Press, 1962.

Tinkelman, Murray. *Little Britches Rodeo.* New York: Greenwillow Books, 1985.

Tinker, Edward Larocque. *The Horsemen of the Americas and the Literature They Inspired*. Rev. ed. Austin: University of Texas Press, 1967.

Tinsley, Jim Bob. *For a Cowboy Has to Sing*. Orlando: University of Central Florida Press, 1991.

———. *He Was Singin' This Song*. Orlando: University Presses of Florida, 1981.

Too Slim, Ranger Doug, and Woody Paul. *Riders in the Sky*. Salt Lake City: Peregrine Smith Books, 1992.

Torrey, Volta. *Windcatchers*. Brattleboro, VT: Stephen Greene Press, 1976.

Tosches, Nick. *Country: Living Legends and Dying Metaphors in America's Biggest Music*. Rev. ed. New York: Scribner's, 1985.

Towne, Charles W., and Edward N. Wentworth. *Cattle and Men*. Norman: University of Oklahoma Press, 1955.

Townsend, Charles R. *San Antonio Rose: The Life and Music of Bob Wills*. Urbana: University of Illinois Press, 1976.

Tozer, Basil. *The Horse in History*. London: Methuen, 1908.

Tractman, Paul. *The Gunfighters*. 1974. Rev. ed. New York: Time-Life Books, 1977.

Turney-High, Harry. "The Diffusion of the Horse to the Flatheads." *Man* 35 (December 1935): 183–185.

Tuska, Jon. *The American West in Film: Critical Approaches to the Western*. Westport, CT: Greenwood, 1985.

———. *The Filming of the West*. Garden City, NY: Doubleday, 1976.

———. *A Variable Harvest: Essays and Reviews of Film and Literature*. Jefferson, NC: McFarland, 1990.

Tuska, Jon, and Vicki Piekarski. *The Frontier Experience: A Reader's Guide to the Life and Literature of the American West*. Jefferson, NC: McFarland, 1984, 1990.

———, eds. *Encyclopedia of Frontier and Western Fiction*. New York: McGraw-Hill, 1983.

Tyler, Ronnie C. *American Frontier Life: Early Western Painting and Prints*. Fort Worth, TX: Amon Carter Museum, 1987.

Urbaneja Achelpohl, Luis Manuel. *El gaucho y el llanero*. Caracas: Elite, 1926.

Utley, Robert M. "The Range Cattle Industry in the Big Bend of Texas." *Southwestern Historical Quarterly* 69 (1965): 419–441.

Vallenilla Lanz, Laureano. *Disgregación e integración: Ensayo sobre la formación de la nacionalidad venezolana*. 2 vols. Caracas: Tipografía Universal, 1930.

Van Deventer, M. J. "Chaps: From Batwings to Woolies." *Cowboys & Indians* 1:3 (Winter 1993): 18–22.

———. "The Cowboy Hat." *Cowboys & Indians* 2:1 (Spring 1994): 10–16.

———. "The Story of Wrangler." *Cowboys & Indians* 2:1 (Spring 1994): 56–62.

Vannoy-Rhoades, Cynthia. *Seasons on a Ranch*. Boulder, CO: Pruett, 1986.

Vernam, Glenn R. *Man on Horseback: The Story of the Mounted Man from the Scythians to the American Cowboy*. Lincoln: University of Nebraska Press, 1964.

———. *The Rawhide Years: A History of the Cattlemen and the Cattle Country*. Garden City, NY: Doubleday, 1976.

Vila, Pablo. *Visiones geohistóricas de Venezuela*. Caracas: Ministerio de Educación, 1969.

Vonada, Damaine. "Annie Oakley Was More Than 'A Crack Shot in Petticoats.'" *Smithsonian* 21:6 (1990): 131–148.

Wagner, James. "Cowboy: Origin and Early Use of the Term." *West Texas Historical Association Year Book* 63 (1987): 91–100.

Wagoner, Junior Jean. *History of the Cattle Industry in Southern Arizona, 1540–1940.* Tucson: University of Arizona Press, 1952.

Walker, Don D., ed. *Clio's Cowboys: Studies in the Historiography of the Cattle Trade.* Lincoln: University of Nebraska Press, 1981.

Wallace, Ernest. *The Comanches: Lords of the South Plains.* Norman: University of Oklahoma Press, 1952.

Walters, Thomas N. *Seeing in the Dark.* Durham, NC: Moore Publishing, 1972.

Ward, Fay E. *The Cowboy at Work.* Norman: University of Oklahoma Press, 1958, 1987.

Watts, Cedric, and Laurence Davies. *Cunninghame Graham: A Critical Biography.* New York: Cambridge University Press, 1979.

Watts, Peter. *A Dictionary of the Old West, 1850–1900.* New York: Alfred A. Knopf, 1977.

Webb, Walter Prescott. "The American West: Perpetual Mirage." *Harper's Magazine,* May 1957.

———. *The Great Frontier.* Austin: University of Texas Press, 1951.

———. *The Texas Rangers.* Austin: University of Texas Press, 1965.

Weber, David J. *The Mexican Frontier, 1821–1846: The American Southwest Under Mexico.* Albuquerque: University of New Mexico Press, 1982.

———. "Mexico's Far Northern Frontier, 1821–1854: Historiography Askew." *Western Historical Quarterly* 7:3 (July 1976): 279–293.

———. *The Spanish Frontier in North America.* New Haven: Yale University Press, 1992, 1994.

Weinberg, Robert. *The Louis L'Amour Companion.* Kansas City: Andrews and McMeel, 1992.

Weir, Thomas R. *Ranching in the Southern Interior Plateau of British Columbia.* Ottawa: Queen's Printer, 1964.

Weissman, Dick. "Cowboy Songs: From the Open Range to the Radio." *Colorado Heritage* 1 (1981): 56–67.

Welsch, Roger L., ed. *Mister, You Got Yourself a Horse: Tales of Old-Time Horse Trading.* Lincoln: University of Nebraska Press, 1981, 1987.

West, Elliott. *The Saloon of the Rocky Mountain Mining Frontier.* Lincoln: University of Nebraska Press, 1979.

West, John O. *Cowboy Folk Humor: Life and Laughter in the American West.* Little Rock: August House, 1990.

Westermeier, Clifford P., ed. *Trailing the Cowboy: His Life and Lore as Told by Frontier Journalists.* Caldwell, ID: Caxton Printers, 1955.

Weston, Jack. *The Real American Cowboy.* New York: Schocken, 1985.

White, G. Edward. *The Eastern Establishment and the Western Experience: The West of Frederic Remington, Theodore Roosevelt, and Owen Wister.* New Haven: Yale University Press, 1968.

White, John I. *Git Along, Little Dogies: Songs and Songmakers of the American West.* Urbana: University of Illinois Press, 1975, 1989.

———. "A Montana Cowboy Poet." *Journal of American Folklore* 80 (July 1967): 113–29.

White, Richard. *"It's Your Misfortune and None of My Own": A New History of the American West.* Norman: University of Oklahoma Press, 1991.

Wilkinson, Andy. "Buck Ramsey: A Spirit Riding Wild and Free." *Persimmon Hill* 21:1 (Spring 1993): 50–54.

Williams, Roger M. *Sing a Sad Song: The Life of Hank Williams.* Urbana: University of Illinois Press, 1970.

Williams Alzaga, Enrique. *La pampa en la novela Argentina.* Buenos Aires: Estrada Editores, 1955.

Wissler, Clark. "The Influence of the Horse in the Development of Plains Culture." *American Anthropologist* 16:1 (1914): 1–25.

———. "The Riding Gear of the North American Indians." *Anthropological Papers of the American Museum of Natural History* 17 (1911): 1–38.

Witney, Dudley. *Ranch: Portrait of a Surviving Dream.* Garden City, NY: Doubleday, 1983.

Wittliff, William D. *Vaquero: Genesis of the Texas Cowboy.* San Antonio: Institute of Texan Cultures, 1972.

Wood-Clark, Sarah. *Women of the Wild West Shows: Beautiful, Daring Western Girls.* Cody, WY: Buffalo Bill Historical Center, 1991.

Woods, Lawrence M. *British Gentlemen in the Wild West: The Era of the Intensely English Cowboy.* New York: Free Press, 1989.

Worcester, Don. "Spanish Horses among the Plains Tribes." *Pacific Historical Review* 14 (1945): 409–417.

———. *The Spanish Mustang: From the Plains of Andalusia to the Prairies of Texas.* El Paso: Texas Western Press, 1986.

———. "The Spread of Spanish Horses in the Southwest." *New Mexico Historical Review* 19 (1944): 225–232.

Wright, Will. *Sixguns and Society: A Structural Study of the Western.* Berkeley: University of California Press, 1977.

Wunder, John R., ed. *At Home on the Range: Essays on the History of Western Social and Domestic Life.* Westport, CT: Greenwood Press, 1985.

Wylder, Delbert E. *Emerson Hough.* Boston: Twayne, 1981.

Wyman, Walker D. *The Wild Horse of the West.* Caldwell, ID: Caxton Printers, 1945.

Young, James Albert. *Cattle in the Cold Desert.* Logan: Utah State University Press, 1985.

Young, Mary. "The West and American Cultural Identity: Old Themes and New Variations." *Western Historical Quarterly* 1:2 (April 1970): 137–160.

Zolotow, Maurice. *Shooting Star: A Biography of John Wayne.* New York: Simon and Schuster, 1974.

Note: For information on archival and electronic resources consulted, please see the Acknowledgments. For information on periodicals, see Appendix C.

ILLUSTRATION CREDITS

7 The Denver Public Library, Western History Department

9 Library of Congress

13 National Museum of American Art, Washington, DC/Art Resource, NY; Lent by the U.S. Department of the Interior, Office of the Secretary

25 Library of Congress

28 The Denver Public Library, Western History Department

32 Glenbow Archives, Calgary

48 Photograph by Bjornson, n.d.; Montana Historical Society, Helena, MT

54 The Denver Public Library, Western History Department

65 The Denver Public Library, Western History Department

73 The Denver Public Library, Western History Department

98 The Denver Public Library, Western History Department

111 Library of Congress

122 Solomon D. Butcher Collection, Nebraska State Historical Society, Lincoln, NE

137 Courtesy Buffalo Bill Historical Center, Cody, WY

140 C. Matthew Ward, Denver, CO

141 The Denver Public Library, Western History Department

142 The Denver Public Library, Western History Department

150 Library of Congress

157 Courtesy Archivo General de la Nación, Buenos Aires, Argentina

163 The Denver Public Library, Western History Department

167 The Erwin E. Smith Collection of the Library of Congress on deposit at the Amon Carter Museum, Fort Worth, TX

172 The Denver Public Library, Western History Department

185 American Heritage Center, University of Wyoming, Laramie, WY

191 From George Byam, *Wanderings in Some of the Western Republics of America* (London, 1850)

193 The Erwin E. Smith Collection of the Library of Congress on deposit at the Amon Carter Museum, Fort Worth, TX

202 Woodward County Collection of the Western History Collections, University of Oklahoma, Norman, OK

237 Library of Congress

253 Courtesy Museum of New Mexico, Santa Fe, NM, neg. 30769

265 The Denver Public Library, Western History Department

267 Courtesy Buffalo Bill Historical Center, Cody, WY

272 Library of Congress

279 Library of Congress

290 Watercolor, gouache and graphite on paper, ca. 1898. Amon Carter Museum, Fort Worth, TX

293 The Denver Public Library, Western History Department

304 The Erwin E. Smith Collection of the Library of Congress on deposit at the Amon Carter Museum, Fort Worth, TX

309 The Kansas State Historical Society, Topeka, KS

311 From *Picturesque Illustration of Buenos Ayres and Montevideo* (London, 1829); Courtesy Edward E. Ayer Collection, The Newberry Library, Chicago, IL

317 Carnegie Branch Library for Local History, Boulder Historical Society Collection, Boulder, CO

321 Carnegie Branch Library for Local History, Boulder Historical Society Collection, Boulder, CO

326 Library of Congress

332 Montana Historical Society, Helena, MT

337 Courtesy R. W. Norton Art Gallery, Shreveport, LA

338 Wyoming State Museum, Cheyenne, WY

344 C. Matthew Ward, Denver, CO

345 Courtesy Colorado Historical Society

372 From the Collection of the Gilcrease Museum, Tulsa, OK

381 Courtesy Yale University Library

387 Minnesota Historical Society, St. Paul, MN

389 Denver Public Library, Western History Department

402 Library of Congress

404 Courtesy Colorado Historical Society

INDEX

Abbey, Edward, 3–4, 125, 132, 226, 294
Abbott, Edward C. ("Teddy Blue"), 4, 19, 289–291
Abilene, Kansas, 79, 80, 231, 291
Acción, 4, 38
Acevedo Díaz, Eduardo, 153
Adams, Andy, 4, 18
Adams, Clifton, 4
Adams, Ramon Frederick, 4–5, 51, 75, 194, 320, 357, 411
Advertising, 282–285
African-American cowboys, 5–8, 85
    buffalo soldiers, 53
    in Canada, 99
    cowboy historiography, 180
    discrimination against, 104, 253
    documentaries on, 136
    in film, 6–8, 132
    in rodeo, 134, 278–280, 322
    in South America, 102
    and unbranded (maverick) cattle, 235
    in Zane Grey novels, 166
Aftosa, 8–10, 40
Aguardiente, 10, 349
Ainsworth, Edward Maddin, 282
Airin' the lungs, 10
Airin' the paunch, 10
Alberta. See Canada, cowboys and ranching
Alcoholic drinks, 10, 348–350
    colloquial terms for, 47, 60, 97, 138, 145, 238, 325, 370, 379
    See also Saloon; Whisky
Alfalfa desperado, 10
Alkali grass, 10
Allard, William Albert, 281
Allen, Henry Wilson, 10
Allen, Jules Verne, 243, 250
Allen, Prairie Lillie, 316
Allen, Rex, 130, 188, 214, 245, 248

Allmendinger, Blake, 181
Alpargatas, 10
Alvin and the Chipmunks, 175
American Cowboy Culture Association, 10, 252
American Indian. See Native Americans
American Indian Rodeo Cowboy Association, 204
American National Cattlemen's Association, 31
Anderson, Broncho Billy, 11
Angoras, 11, 64
Angus-buffalo hybrid, 163
Animal rights, 253, 319
Apache, 200, 202, 203, 204
Appaloosa, 186, 187
Apple, 11
Arapaho, 11–12, 68–69
Araucanians, 99–100, 190
Arepa, 12, 143
Argentina
    beef cattle industry in, 38–40, 158, 227
    cowboys. See Gaucho
    indigenous peoples of, 99–102
    latifundia, 219
    literature of, 152–154
    pampas of. See Pampas
Armas, 12, 96, 384
Army model guns, 138, 309
Arness, James, 12
Arnold, Ben, 19
Arnold, Eddie, 245
Art (artists), 12–16, 236–237, 308–309, 336–337, 350–351
    cattle depictions in, 228
    gauchos in, 195
    illustrating difficulties of cowboy life, 95
    museums and collections, 52, 53, 81, 210, 259, 337, 360
    scenes of violence in, 386
    See also specific artists

Artigas, José Gervasio, 155
Asado, 144
Ascasubi, Hilario, 152–153
Association saddle, 16
Austin, Sadie, 403
Australian cowboy movies, 131
Autobiographies, 16–21
Autry, Gene, 21–22, 26, 64, 84, 130, 188, 245, 253, 303, 317

B western movies, 21, 25–26, 120
    horses in, 188
    poems about, 133
    women in, 405
    See also Films
Baby swapping, 194
Bagual, 26
Baile, 26
Ballard, Todhunter, 26
Bandana, 26
Bangtail, 26
Baquiano, 27
Bar dog, 27
Barbed wire, 121, 339
    collections, 123, 259
    colloquial terms for, 43, 353
Barde, Frederick S., 18
Bareback bronc riding, 320
Barker, Squire Omar, 27
Baxter, George Owen, 27
Bayetón, 27
Beadle's Half-Dime Library, 29
Bean, Judge Roy, 130
Bean eater, 29
Bean master, 29
Bears, 113–114, 253
Beckstead, James H., 281
Bedroll, 139, 188
Beef cattle industry, 29–40. *See also* Cattle
Beef in cowboy diets, 142–143
Beef jerky, 65, 143, 144, 160, 209, 366
Beery, Noah, Jr., 40
Belly wash, 40
Berninghaus, Oscar Edmund, 81
Berton, Pierre, 84
Bible, 40
Bickham, Jack Miles, 40
Bierstadt, Albert, 13, 52
Big augur, 40
Big house, 40

Billy the Kid, 19, 70, 136, 232
Biographical documentaries, 134
Biscuit roller, 40
Bison (buffalo), 11, 200, 201, 204, 221
    cattle hybrids, 163
    L'Amour on, 217
Bits, 40–41, 361, 365
Black, Baxter, 41, 133, 194–195, 254, 287
Black cowboys. *See* African-American cowboys
Black Jack, 41
Black-eyed susan, 41
Blancett, Dell, 316
Blandengue, 42–43, 100, 155
Blasingame, Ike, 20
Blocker, John, 330
Blowout, 43
Blue roan, 43
Blue stem, 43
Bobtail guard, 43
Bodega, 43
Bodmer, Karl, 12
Boggy top, 43
Bolas, 43–44, 101, 114, 155, 190, 273
Boleada, 44–45, 114
Bolton, Herbert Eugene, 182
Bombachas, 159
Bombilla, 45
"Bonanza," 367
Bonney, William H. *See* Billy the Kid
Boogered up, 45
Boone, Richard, 45, 367
Boots, 45–46, 86, 355
    advertising of, 284
    charro, 67
    colloquial terms for, 210, 361
    gaucho, 46, 155, 159
    huaso, 190
    practical jokes involving, 194
    and rodeo fashions, 119
Boren, James, 81
Borne, Lawrence R., 105
Bota de potro, 46, 155
Bower, Bertha Muzzy, 46, 294
Bowman, (Lewis) Edward, 322
Boyd, Bill, 245
Boyd, William, 47, 131, 188, 303, 371
Bramlett, Jim, 239
Branch, E. Douglas, 47
Brand, Max, 17, 120–121, 294

Branding, 47, 331, 334, 335
   rustling techniques, 47, 338
The Brave Cowboy, 3, 125, 132, 226
Brazilian beef industry, 227
Brazilian gaúchos, 160–161
Brazilian vaqueiro, 379–380
Brennan, Walter, 124
Bridle, 365
Bronc busters, 6, 47–51, 78, 96, 156, 357
Bronc riding, 320–321
   saddle for, 89
Broncho Billy, 128
Bronco Billy, 51, 132
Brooks, Garth, 51, 173, 247
Brooks, Leon Eric ("Kix"), 173
Broomtail, 51
Brown, Dee, 136
Brown, Johnny Mack, 51, 130, 188, 306
Brown gargle, 51
Brush popper, 51–52, 64, 313
Buckaroo, 52
Buckaroo Coffee, 75
Bucket of blood, 52, 349
Buckle bunnies, 52, 136
Buffalo. *See* Bison
Buffalo Bill. *See* Cody, William Frederick
Buffalo Bill Historical Center, 15, 52–53, 75, 106
Buffalo Bill Memorial Museum, 53, 75
Buffalo Bill's Wild West show, 74, 232, 252, 265
Buffalo Girls, 232
Buffalo soldier, 53
Buford, 53
Build a loop, 53
Bull hides, 53
Bull riding, 67, 112–113, 321
Bull tailing, 67, 112–113, 333–334
Bull whip. *See* Whips
Bulldogging, 54, 278, 322, 374
Bunkhouse, 54
Buntline, Ned, 17, 55, 72, 138, 266, 292
Burnette, Smiley, 188, 313
Butch Cassidy and the Sundance Kid, 125
Butter, 79
Buttermilk, 55, 188, 324, 406
Button, 55
Buttram, Pat, 26
Butts, Tonya, 318

Cabeza del fuste, 59
Cactus, 59, 188

Calaboose, 59
Calamity Jane, 59, 62, 232, 401–403
Calf fries. *See* Mountain oysters
Calf roping, 321–322
Calf slobbers, 59
Calgary, 34, 59–60
Calgary Stampede, 59–60, 84, 317
California drag rowels, 60
Californian vaqueros. *See* Vaquero
Camarillo, Leo, 289
Campanyero, 60
Campbell, Bob, 248
Caña, 60
Canada, cowboys, and ranching, 81–85
   beef cattle, 33–38
   bronc busters, 50–51
   discrimination, 97–99
   fencing, 123
   film depictions of, 84–85
   frontier imagery of, 60–61
   gambling and drinking, 151
   historiography, 181
   prostitution in, 291
   roping techniques, 330
   violence, 61–62
Canary, Martha Jane. *See* Calamity Jane
Canned cow, 62
Cannon, Hal, 62, 289, 355
Cantina, 62. *See also* Saloon
Cantle, 62
Canutt, Yakima, 129, 395
Capataz, 62
Caporal, 62
Carbine, 137
Carey, Harry, 62, 124, 129
Carillo, Leo, 368
Carne seco, 62
Carson, Sunset, 59, 188
Cartwright, Ben, 62, 165
Cassidy, Hopalong, 62, 131, 188, 283, 303, 371
Cat wagon, 62
Catch pen, 62
Catgut, 62
Catlin, George, 12, 52, 62, 273
Cattle, 29–40, 304–305
   advertising and, 283
   in Argentina, 38–40, 158, 227, 273
   in art, 16, 228
   Brazilian beef industry, 227
   breeds, 30, 62–64, 163, 214, 226–228, 267

Cattle *(continued)*
    in Canada, 33–38
    colloquial terms for, 53, 89, 238
    Colombian llanos, 226
    die-up, 97
    diseases, 8, 360
    grass feed, 285
    Hawaiian cowboys and, 275
    herd, 176
    historiography sources, 177, 180
    Judas steer, 210
    McCoy and, 231
    one-horned or hornless, 240
    querencia, 300
    rustling, 64, 158, 184, 338–339, 386
    singing to, 243–244
    slaughtering, 32
    snow and, 95
    Spanish terms for, 267, 268, 379
    stockmen's association, 31, 334, 359–360
    swampers, 362
    twisthorn, 374
    unbranded (maverick), 105, 235, 267–268, 338, 360
    wattle mark, 394
    wet stock, 398
    yaks, 411
    See also Ranching and ranch life
Cattle drives. *See* Trail drives
Cavallard, 64
Caylor, Harvey Wallace, 228
Cemetery, 45
Cepo, 64
Champion, 64, 188
Chandler, Lane, 130
Changador, 64
Chaps, 11, 12, 64–65, 82, 171, 190, 369, 384
    of bull hides, 53
    colloquial terms for, 70, 219
Charango, 65
Charolais, 63
Charque, 65, 144, 160, 209, 366
Charreada, 66–68, 314, 334, 350
Charro, 66–68
    alcohol use, 350
    documentary films, 134
    hats, 171
    historiography, 181
    horseback games, 110–111
    rodeo and, 314
    saddles, 346

Cheating, 151
Cherokees, 298
Chestnutt, Mark, 173
Cheyenne Frontier Days, 315
Cheyenne Indians, 11–12, 68–69, 72
Cheyenne roll, 69
Chickasaw, 298
Chicken race, 79, 114
Chicken saddle, 69
Chifle, 69
Chile
    cowboys. *See* Huasos
    indigenous peoples of, 99–100
    and latifundia system, 218
Chinks, 70
Chiripá, 70
Chisholm, Jesse, 70, 71
Chisholm Trail, 71, 79, 272, 231
Chisum, John Simpson, 30, 70–71, 162, 209, 219, 232
Chivalry, 83–84, 87
Choke the horn, 71
Chopper, 71
Chow, 71
Chuck, 71
Chuck-line rider, 71
Chuck-wagon, 139–141, 162
Cielo, 71
Cinch, 71, 93, 162
Cinchada, 71, 111
Cisco Kid, 97, 130, 188, 288, 368
Clancy, Frederick ("Foghorn"), 319
Clark, (Charles) Badger, Jr., 71, 243, 250
Clark, Walter Van Tilburg, 71
Cleaveland, Agnes Morley, 20
Clothing and ornamentation, 86
    advertising, 284–285
    brush poppers, 51–52
    California pants, 60
    Canadian cowboys, 82
    charro, 66–67
    conchas, 65, 78, 171, 346, 365
    country-western musicians, 245
    fashions, 119–120
    fish (oilskin jacket), 138
    gaucho, 70, 88, 155, 159
    Hawaiian cowboys, 275
    huaso, 190
    leggings. *See* Chaps
    Levi's, 220, 284

llanero, 222
poncho, 27, 190, 223, 288, 336, 383
totin' stars on, 371
vaquero, 383–384
See also Boots; Hats
Clowns, 320, 321
Clymer, John, 15
Cobija, 72
Coburn, Walt, 72
Cochrane, William F., 99
Cocinero, 72
Cockfights, 151–152, 253
Cody, William Frederick ("Buffalo Bill"), 43, 52, 55,
    72–75, 127, 133, 220, 252, 266, 366, 399, 400
    burial site, 53, 75
Cody Firearms Museum, 52
Coe, David Allan, 173–174
Coffee, 75–77, 139, 141, 223
    colloquial terms for, 51, 209, 354
Cohen, Davis, 250
Cola, 67
Colear, 112, 333–334
Collins, Bill, 312
Colombian cowboys. *See* Llanero
Colt firearms, 77–78, 138, 309, 400
Comanche, 200–203
Compadre, 78
Conchas, 65, 78, 171, 346, 365
Connors, Chuck, 367–368
Cook, James Henry, 19, 78
Cook, Will, 78
Cooks, 104
    colloquial terms, 72, 79, 105, 167, 171, 266, 288,
    356, 393
"Cool Water," 78
Coolidge, Dane, 78, 292, 294
Cooper, Gary, 78, 124, 130, 286
Coosie, 79
Corral dust, 79
Correr el gallo, 79, 114
Corridos, 385
Corriente breed, 63
Country-western music. *See* Music
Cow grease, 79
Cow towns, 79–81, 85, 286, 289
Cowboy Artists of America Museum, 81
Cowboy Hall of Fame. *See* National Cowboy Hall of
    Fame
Cowboys, 85–89
    Autry's Ten Commandments of, 21, 253

in Canada, 81–85
colloquial terms for, 52, 209, 282, 294, 305, 348,
    371, 393
dangers for, 94–97
genuine, 399
Indians as, 204–205
Cowboys for Christ (CFC), 308
"The Cowboy's Prayer," 71
Cowboy's Turtle Association, 316
Cowchips, 89
Cowgirls 403. *See also* Women
Cowhand, 89
Cowjuice, 89
Crabbe, Larry ("Buster"), 89
Crackerbox, 89
Crawford, Lewis F., 19
Crosby, Bob ("Wild Horse"), 319
Cross hobble, 89
Crow hop, 89
Crow Indians, 68, 201, 203–205
Crupper tricks, 89
Crying room, 90
Curtis, Ken, 245
Custer, George Armstrong, 69
Cutting horse, 90
Cyrus, Billy Ray, 174

D ring, 93
Dale, Edward Everett, 93
Dally, 93, 329–330, 346
Dana, Richard Henry, Jr., 93–94, 103, 380
Dances, 71, 119, 183, 361
Dangers of cowboy life, 94–97. *See also* Violence
Dart, Isom, 6, 8
Darwin, Charles, 44, 156, 273, 388–389
Dary, David, 97
Davis, Alvin, 252
Dead man's hand, 123
Deadwood Dick, 6, 292
Dean, Eddie, 130, 188
"Death Valley Days," 97, 367
Debo, Angie, 259
Debt peonage, 102, 384
Del Campo, Estanislao, 153
DeMille, Cecil B., 128
Denhardt, Robert, 97
Denim, 220
Derringer, 120, 137, 138
Desjarretadera, 97
Destry Rides Again, 120

DeVoto, Bernard, 15
Diablo, 97, 188
Dietrich, Marlene, 405
Die-up, 97
Digger Indians, 94
Dillon, Matt, 97
Dinner, 97
Discrimination, 180, 253
 against blacks, 104
 in Canada, 97–99
 Hispanics and, 103–104
 in myth and legend, 177
 saloons and, 349
 in South America, 99–102
 against women, 104
 See also African-Americans; Racism; Vaquero
Dixon, Billy, 18
Dixon, Maynard, 14
Doan's Crossing, 104
Dobie, James Frank, 16, 17–18, 20, 49, 51, 105, 178, 235, 350–351, 354, 382
"Dr. Quinn, Medicine Woman," 368
Documentary films, 6, 133–136, 242, 336
Dodge City, 80, 266, 289
Dofunnies, 105
Dogie, 105
Domador, 105, 156
Don Segundo Sombra (Güiraldes), 47, 154, 168, 332, 349
Doña Bárbara (Gallegos), 149, 182, 192, 223–225
"Don't Fence Me In," 105
Drago, Harry Sinclair, 105, 259
Dried beef, 39, 62, 65, 143, 144, 160, 366
Drover, 105
Drury, James, 105
Dude ranches, 105–106, 331, 351
Dunn, Ronnie Gene, 173
Dunton, William Herbert, 14
Durango Kid, 303, 358
Dwyer, Richard A., 250

Earmarks, 209, 267
Eastwood, Clint, 109–110, 119, 127, 132, 367, 411
Eatin' Irons, 110
Echeverría, 153
Edson, John Thomas, 110
Edwards, Don, 246
Eggenhofer, Nick, 16, 81
"El Paso," 110

Elliott, Ramblin' Jack, 246
Elliott, William ("Wild Bill"), 110
Ellis, Annie Laurie, 249
Ellison, Glen R. ("Slim"), 20
Ellsworth, Kansas, 80
Ellzey, Bill, 281
Encomienda, 66, 218
Equestrian games, 71, 79, 110–114, 276–277, 299
 bull tailing, 67, 112–113, 333–334
 crupper tricks, 90
 gambling on, 150
 Mexican charreada, 66–68
 See also Rodeo; *specific games*
Erickson, John R., 281
Estancias, 44, 102, 114–115, 158, 160
Estrada, Ezequiel Martínez, 273, 388
Evans, Dale, 115, 188, 251, 259, 323, 406
Evans, Evan, 115
Even Cowgirls Get the Blues, 406
Ewing, Sherm, 239

Facón, 101, 119, 155, 388
Facundo, 119, 149, 351
Fandango, 119
Farmers, colloquial terms for, 71, 165, 176, 260, 356
Farr, Carl, 119
Farr, Hugh, 119
Fashions, 119–120. *See also* Clothing
Fast draw, 120, 183
Faust, Frederick Schiller, 27, 115, 120–121, 234, 294, 353
Fausto, 153
Feed bag, 238
Feeder, 121
Feedlots, 31, 121
Fellowship of Christian Cowboys, 308
Feminist criticism, 125, 126
Fence Cutter's War of 1883, 286, 339
Fencing, 80, 95, 121–123, 213, 221, 304, 339
 in Brazil, 161
 public lands, 30
Ferber, Edna, 123
Fife, Alta S., 250
Fife, Austin E., 250
Films, 109–110, 210, 323, 356, 394–396
 African-Americans in, 6–8, 136
 Canadian cowboys in, 84–85
 Canadian frontier in, 62
 colloquial term for, 265
 cow towns in, 80

documentaries, 6, 133–136, 241–242, 336
history of, 127–128
horses in, 41, 59, 64, 97, 129, 188, 214, 266, 303, 313, 336, 353, 358, 366, 371, 374, 398, 406
John Ford era of, 131
modern westerns, 131–132
National Cowboy Hall of Fame, 259
poem about, 133
prostitutes in, 291
racial-ethnic biases in, 131
rodeo in, 234, 318
silent era of, 128–129
singing cowboys in, 130, 245, 395
talkies, 129–130
ten best, 123–127
Tom Horn depicted in, 184–185
violence in, 120
women in, 126, 135, 136, 405–407
See also Autry, Gene; Rogers, Roy; *specific actors, directors*
Finn, June Cotton Martin, 50–51, 404–405
Fire on the Mountain, 3
Firearms, 77–78, 88, 136–138, 183, 309–310, 399–400
Canadian Mounted Police and, 62
colloquial terms for, 41, 43, 110, 205, 271, 356, 362, 407
fast draw, 120
five beans in the wheel, 139
gauchos and, 101
llanero trabuco (blunderbuss), 371
museums and, 52
Native Americans and, 202, 203
notcher, 138, 260
vaqueros and, 384
See also Violence
Fish, 138, 354
Flaccus, David P., 238
Fletcher, Baylis John, 19
Fletcher, Curly, 286
Fonda, Henry, 123, 131, 259
Food, 139–144
arepa, 12, 143
Argentine asado, 16
beef, 142–143
chuck-wagon, 139–141, 162
colloquial terms for, 59, 62, 71, 79, 105, 139, 145, 167, 185, 213, 220, 221, 228, 268, 322, 350, 354, 362, 369, 394, 398
cowboy-related advertising, 282–283

dinner, 97
dried beef (jerky), 39, 62, 65, 143, 144, 160, 366
gaucho tea (mate), 45, 75, 76, 144, 158, 159, 235, 454
huaso preferences, 333
Latin American preferences, 143
llanero preferences, 223
milk, 76–77, 89
mountain oysters, 41, 59, 143, 238, 288
prairie cuisine, 285
supper, 362
See also Coffee; Cooks
Foot-and-mouth disease, 8, 40, 184
Footwear. *See* Boots; Sandals
Foran, Dick, 245
Forbis, William H., 282
Ford, John, 128, 129, 395
Foreman, 145
Foreman, Leonard London, 145
Fox, Norman Arnold, 145
Fox fire, 145, 348
Franciscans, 382
Frantz, Joe Bertram, 145
Fremont, John, 94
Frigorífico, 145
Fritz, 26, 145, 188
Frost, Lane, 319
Fundo, 145–146, 191, 218
Furniture, 119, 355
Fuste, 145

Gable, Clark, 358
Gaff, 149
Gallegos, Rómulo, 149, 182, 193, 223–225
Gambling, 149–152, 291
dead man's hand, 123
games and terms, 59, 60, 119, 236
gaucho games, 158
llanero games, 224
Gardner, Gail, 250
Garfield, Brian, 152, 407
Garner, James, 367
Garrett, Pat, 70
Gaucho, 38–39, 114, 154–159, 219, 271, 274
attitudes towards strangers, 192
bad reputation of, 158
bolas, 43–44, 155
in Brazil, 160–161, 379
caricaturist, 195
cepo punishment, 64

Gaucho *(continued)*
  clothing, 70, 155, 159
  cooking style (asado), 16
  drinking habits, 349–350
  equestrian games, 110–114, 276–277
  estancias and, 114
  ethnicity and racial biases, 102
  facón (knife), 101, 119, 155, 388
  folkdances, 71
  food preferences, 144
  footwear, 10, 46, 88
  gambling games, 149–150, 374
  Graham and, 164
  guides (baquiano), 27
  historians of, 182, 260, 322
  horses and, 46, 47, 100, 105, 156, 187, 188, 282,
    374
  indigenous people and, 99–100, 155, 159
  leg protection, 96
  literature (gauchesco), 152–154, 234, 278
  military units (blandengue), 42–43, 100, 101,
    155, 159, 167–168
  musical entertainment, 65, 102, 235, 277–278
  as national symbol, 282
  ostrich hunts, 43–44, 114, 156–158, 259, 273,
    310
  outlaws, 235
  religion and, 307
  riding whips, 300
  roping styles, 329
  roundup (hierra), 176, 332
  saddles, 306, 347
  Sarmiento and, 351
  spurs, 226
  tobacco use, 370
  toe stirrups, 347
  trail drivers, 310, 373
  U.S. exhibits, 259
  violence, 388–390
  wild cattle hunting and, 380
  women and, 289, 291
Gaucho tea (mate), 45, 75, 76, 144, 158, 159, 235
Gauderio, 161
Gene Autry Western Heritage Museum, 22, 135
George, Tammy, 318
Ghost Dance of 1890, 204
Gibson, Hoot, 84, 129, 130, 161, 188
Gilley, Mickey, 161
Girth, 161
Glidden, Frederick Dilley, 162, 292

Goat meat, 162
Good News, 3
Goodnight, Charles, 5, 30, 70, 139, 162–164, 219,
    232, 359, 372
Goodnighting, 162
Graham, Robert Bontine Cunninghame, 43,
    164–165, 182, 222–223, 225, 271, 347, 350
The Great Train Robbery, 123, 127, 128, 165, 388
Green, Ben K., 165
Green, Douglas, 312–313
Greene, Lorne, 62, 131, 165, 367
Greenhorn, 165
Grey, Zane, 14, 15, 17, 165–167, 292
Griffith, D. W., 128
Griffith, Nancy, 175
Gringo, 167
Güemes, Martín, 158, 167–168
Güiraldes, Ricardo, 47, 154, 168, 182, 192, 332, 349
Gunfight at the O.K. Corral, 388
Guns. *See* Firearms
"Gunsmoke," 367
Gutiérrez, Eduardo, 154

Haas, Benjamin Leopold, 171
Hacendado, 171
Hacienda, 171
Hackamore, 40, 50, 365
Hair case, 171
Hair pants, 171
Hair rope, 171, 231
Hale, Monte, 188, 245
Half-breeds, 35
Handle, 171
Hannah, Jack, 247
Harris, Frank, 18
Harris, Joel Chandler, 266
Hart, William S., 26, 84, 128–129, 145, 171, 188
Hasher, 171
Hat acts, 119, 173–176
Hato, 176
Hats, 86, 171–173
  Canadian cowboy, 82
  colloquial terms for, 209, 394, 407
  Hawaiian cowboy, 220, 275
  vaquero, 383, 384
"Have Gun, Will Travel," 367
Hawaii Rodeo Association, 316
Hawaiian cowboys, 96, 181–182, 220, 275–277,
    329–330, 346–347
Hawaiian ranches, 136, 275

Hawks, Howard, 130
Haycox, Ernest, 176
Hayes, George ("Gabby"), 21
Hayseed, 176
Hazer, 176
Heel, 176
Henderson, Prairie Rose, 316
Henry, O., 288, 368
Henry rifle, 137, 399
Herd, 176
Hereford, 63
Hernández, José, 153, 176, 234, 278
Heroines, 405
Hiatt, Tom, 248
Hickock, James Butler ("Wild Bill"), 79, 220, 231
Hidalgo, Bartolomé, 152
Hierra, 176
High Noon, 124, 176, 245, 406
High tail, 176
Highbinder, 176
Hill, Thomas, 13
Hinajosa, Tish, 175
Historiography of the cowboy, 177–179
    ethnicity and gender, 179–181
    western associations, 397–398
    See also Museums
Hobble, 89, 365
Hocking blade, 97
Hoe-down, 183
Hogan, Ray, 183, 313
Holliday, Doc, 137
Holloway, Winona Johnson, 20–21
Holmes, Llewellyn Perry, 183
Holmes, Ray, 21, 183
Holster, 120, 183, 370
Hombre, 183
Hombre del campo, 183
Home range, 183
Homesteaders, 31
Hoof-and-mouth disease, 8, 40, 184
Hooker, Henry Clay, 184
Hoolihan, 330
Hoosegow, 184
Hopkins, Monica, 20
Horn, Tom, 6, 184–185, 360
Horsemanship, comparative studies, 182
Horses, 185–188, 252, 297–300
    blue roan, 43
    breeds, 186–187
    Canadian cowboys and, 82

colloquial terms for, 51, 176, 188, 353, 358, 399
competition
cutting horse, 90
famous, rodeo, 289, 320–321
in film, 26, 41, 55, 59, 64, 97, 123, 129, 145, 188, 214, 266, 303, 313, 336, 353, 358, 366, 371, 374, 398, 406
gauchos and, 46, 100, 105, 156, 187, 188, 282, 374
grazing, 285
Hawaiian cowboys and, 275
huasos and, 190
humor and folklore, 193–194
Indian broke, 199
Indian side, 199, 265
John Wayne and, 395
in music, 242
Native Americans and, 68, 186, 187, 200, 265, 274, 298
quarter horse, 186, 353
remuda, 310
shavetail, 353
short-stirupped riding style (jinetea), 209
Spanish terms, 64, 268, 411
sunfisher, 362
taming, 47–51, 78, 96, 105, 156, 161, 278, 356
vaqueros and, 93, 383, 385
widow-maker, 399
women and, 406
    See also Bronc busters; Equestrian games; Rodeo; Saddle; Tack
Hot rock, 188
Hot roll, 188
Hough, Emerson, 15, 189
Hoxie, Jack, 129, 130
Huaraches, 189, 266
Huaso, 145, 182, 189–192
    food preferences, 333
    footwear, 266, 347
    gambling, 150
    horseback games, 110–111, 276–277, 371
    latifundia and, 218
    mate drinking, 76
    roundups, 332–333
    saddles, 347
Humane Methods Slaughter Act, 31
Humor, 192–195, 253, 325
    cowboy poetry, 233

Humor *(continued)*
    in films, 131
    in music, 242
Hung up, 195
Hunter, J. Marvin, 18
Hurricane deck, 195
Huston, John, 236
Hutchinson, William Henry, 312

Ikard, Bose, 5–6
Indian broke horse, 199
Indian side of a horse, 199, 265
Indian wars, 100–102, 203–204. *See also* Native
    Americans
Individualism, 254
Ingraham, Prentiss, 17, 72, 205, 366
Iron, 205

Jackeroo, 209
Jackson, Alan, 174, 209
Jackson, Harry, 15, 209
Jackson, Jack, 209
James, Jessie, 136
James, W. S., 17
James, William Roderick ("Will"), 15, 17,
    209, 239
Jáquima, 209
Jeans. *See* Levi's
Jeffries, Herb, 6, 136, 209
Jennings, Waylon, 135, 136, 209, 247
Jerky, 65, 143, 144, 160, 209, 366
Jesuits, 160, 382
Jinete, 209
Jinetea, 209
Jinglebob, 209, 357
John B., 209
Johnson, Ben, Jr., 135, 209–210, 259, 289, 358
Johnson, Frank Tenney, 14, 210
Johnson County War, 286, 360
Johnston, Moira, 281
Jones, Buck, 130, 210, 235
Jones, Stan, 246
Jordan, Teresa, 403–404
Joslyn Art Museum, 210
Jousting, 112
Jowers, Fletcher, 248
Juan Moreira, 154
Judas steer, 210
Judson, Edward Z. C., 210
Juniper, 210

Justins (boots), 45, 210
Juzgado, 184

Kansas City, 150
Kansas City fish, 213
Kapernick, Bertha, 316
Kelton, Elmer, 213, 259, 287, 361
Ketch rope, 213
Ketchum, Philip, 213
Kettle, 213
King, Pee Wee, 245
King, Richard, 30, 213
King Ranch, 30, 63, 103, 213–214, 219, 299
Kiowa, 68, 201
Kiskaddon, Bruce, 286
Kleberg, Robert J., Jr., 299
Knibbs, Henry H., 15, 214
Knight, Pete, 319
Knives, 223, 384, 388
    gaucho facón, 101, 119, 155, 388
Ko-Ko, 188
Koerner, W. H. D. ("Big Bill"), 15
Koko, 214
Kuczynski, Frank. *See* King, Pee Wee
Kyne, Peter B., 128

"La Cautiva," 153
Labour, Fred ("Too Slim"), 217, 312
Ladd, Alan, 124–125
Lamb licker, 217
L'Amour, Louis, 217–218, 253, 259, 294, 306
Lane, Allan ("Rocky"), 41, 218
Lang, k. d., 176, 248
Lariat, 218, 329. *See also* Rope and roping
Larkin, Margaret, 249
LaRue, Lash, 188, 336
Lasso. *See* Rope and roping
Latifundia, 218–219
Látigo, 219, 346
Lawrence, Elizabeth Atwood, 319
Lawyer roundup, 284
Lea, Tom, 16, 219
LeCompte, Mary Lou, 316, 405
LeDoux, Chris, 247
Lee, Johnny, 247
Lee, Katie, 249–250
Lei, 220, 275
Leone, Sergio, 109, 220
Levi's, 220, 284
Lewis, Anne, 316

Liberty, Margot, 220
Libraries, 53, 81, 260
Lick, 220
Lightnin', 188
Lillie, Gordon William ("Pawnee Bill"), 74, 220, 316
Limerick, Patricia Nelson, 255
Lincoln County War, 70
Line camp, 221
Line riders, 95
Lingenfelter, Richard E., 250
Lining his flue, 221
Little Bighorn, 69
Little Britches Rodeo, 316
Lizzy, 221
Llanero(s), 51, 96, 221–224
    blunderbuss (trabuco), 371
    clothing and appearance of, 27, 222
    cultural significance of, 224
    food and drink, 75, 76, 143–144, 349
    historiography, 182
    horses and, 49, 188
    literature, 149
    racial biases, 100, 102
    ramada, 303
    religion and, 307
    roping styles, 328
    saddles, 347–348
    trail drives, 373
Llanos, 219, 224–226, 274. *See also* Llanero
Lloronas, 226
Logsdon, Guy, 213, 226, 249, 251, 287
Lomax, John Avery, 226, 249
Lone Ranger, 26, 188, 283, 236, 303, 367
Lonely Are the Brave, 3, 125, 132, 226
Lonesome Dove, 5, 96, 368
Long rider, 226
Longhorn cattle, 63, 162, 213, 226–228, 252, 283, 285, 334, 360, 374
Loomis, Noel Miller, 228
Love, Nat, 6
Love apples, 228
Loving, Oliver, 5, 162, 228, 232, 373
The Lusty Men, 124, 228, 318
Lutz, Giles alfred, 228
Lynch, Benito, 154
Lynchings, 386–388

Maar, Ingrid, 281
MacCann, William, 44
McCarthy, Cormac, 294

McCarty, 231, 329
McClure, Jake, 231, 322
McCoy, Joseph G., 77, 79, 87, 96, 231
McCoy, Tim, 130, 188, 231
McCrea, Joel, 125, 134, 358
MacDonald, William Colt, 231
McDowell, Bart, 281
MacEwan, Grant, 232
Machetes, 223
Mackin, Bill, 239
McMurtry, Larry, 96, 164, 232–233, 281, 294, 368
McRae, Wallace D. ("Wally"), 133, 135, 195, 233–234, 254, 281, 287
McSpadden, Clem, 319
Maggot, 234
Maguey, 234
Mahan, Larry, 289, 319
Major Domor, 234
Mangana, 234
Manila hemp, 330
Manning, David, 234
Manzana, 234
Mariachi, 171
Marin, Cheech, 368
Marketing and advertising, 282–285
Marlboro Man, 283–284, 370, 401
Martin, Phil, 287
Martin, Russell, 281
Martín Fierro, 153, 234, 278
Marvin, Lee, 126
Massacre, 234
Masterson, Wiliam Barclay ("Bat"), 79
Matadero, 40, 234
Matambre, 144
Matanza, 380
Mate, 45, 75, 76, 144, 158, 159, 235
Matrero, 235
Matthews, Willie, 16
Maverick, Samuel A., 235
Maverick (film), 173
"Maverick" (television), 367
Maverick brand, 235
Maverick cattle, 235, 338, 360
Maynard, Ken, 26, 84, 130, 188, 245, 366
Mecate, 329
Meigs, John, 282
Mellen, Joan, 125, 126
Mesta, 218, 334
Mestizos, 35, 99, 103, 274, 380. *See also* Native Americans; Vaquero

Métis, 35
Mexican cowboys. *See* Charro; Vaquero
Mexican latifundia, 218, 219
Michener, James, 259
Midnight, 188
Midnight Cowboy, 132
Milk, 76–77, 89
Miller, Alfred Jacob, 13, 52
Miller Brothers' 101 Ranch Wild West Show, 235,
    280, 315, 322
Milonga, 235
The Misfits, 236
Missions, 160, 222, 381–382
Mitchell, Waddie, 10, 41, 135, 195, 236, 286, 287
Mitchum, Robert, 124, 228
Mix, Tom, 26, 84, 129, 235, 236, 266, 283, 303, 371
Molasses, 220
Molina Campos, Florencio, 195
Monkey nose, 236
Montana, Patsy, 199, 236, 246
Monte, 236
Monte Walsh, 126, 236, 352
Moore, Clayton, 236, 367. *See also* Lone Ranger
Moore, Daniel G., 20
Moran, Thomas, 13, 52, 237
Morgan, Mark, 238
Morgan horse, 186
Morland, Peter Henry, 238
Mormon Tea, 238
Morral, 238
Morrison, Marion Michael. *See* Wayne, John
Morton, Gary, 16
Moses, Anne. *See* Oakley, Annie
Moss head, 238
Mother Hubbard loop, 238
Mountain oysters (prairie oysters), 41, 59, 143, 238,
    288
Mountain Press Publishing Company, 238–239
Mounted Police. *See* Royal Canadian Mounted Police
Mules, 39
Muley, 240
Muley saddle, 240
Mulhall, Lucille, 316, 403
Murphey, Michael Martin, 75, 134, 173, 236,
    240–242, 243, 246, 254, 288, 374
Murray, Ty, 319
Museum of the American Cowboy, 289
Museums, 22, 52–53, 75, 81, 123, 210, 242,
    259–260, 281, 289, 300, 324, 337, 360
Music, 240–249, 286, 312–313, 323, 355, 374–375

documentary films, 135
female performers, 175–176
gatherings, 287–288
gaucho, 65, 235, 277–278
hat acts, 173–176
Hawaiian cowboys and, 276
Hispanic, 251
profanity in, 244–245, 251
singing cowboys, 21, 130, 245, 303
singing to cattle, 243–244
vaqueros and, 385
See also Autry, Gene; Rogers, Roy; *specific artists*
Musicology, 249–252, 286
Mustang, 49, 186, 199, 252, 267, 275
Mutt, 188
Mutton-puncher, 252
Muzzie Braun and the Boys, 248
My Darling Clementine, 123–124, 131
Myers, Harry, 252
Myrah, Newman, 15
Mythology, 252–255

National Association for the Advancement of Colored
    People (NAACP), 105
National Black Cowboys Association, 6
National Cowboy Hall of Fame, 10, 135, 213, 241,
    246, 259–260, 280, 292, 313, 321, 368, 398
Native Americans, 11–12, 68–69
    artisitic depictions of, 12, 52, 81, 308
    as cowboys, 204–205
    Dana and, 94
    discrimination against, 99–102
    documentaries on, 135
    dude ranches and, 106
    film depictions of, 131
    gauchos and, 42–43, 159
    half-breeds of, 35
    horses and, 68, 186, 187, 199–205, 265, 274, 298
    huasos and, 190
    L'Amour on, 217
    museum exhibits on, 52–53
    of the pampas, 155
    religious beliefs of, 203
    South American wars and, 100–102
    violence and, 202–203
    in Zane Grey novels, 166
    See also specific groups
Navajo, 75, 199
Navy model guns, 138, 309
Necktie party, 260

Nelson, Willie, 247, 260
Newton, Dwight Bennett, 260
Nez Perce, 186, 187
Nichols, Madaline Wallis, 260
Night hawk, 260
No time, 260
Nolan Bob, 260
Norbury, Rosamond, 238–239
Normand, Mabel, 235
Notcher, 138, 260
Nye, Edgar Wilson ("Bill"), 192, 261
Nye, Nelson Coral, 261

Oakley, Annie, 74, 127, 133, 265
O'Brian, Frank, 265
Obscenity. See Profanity
Off-side of a horse, 265
Ohrlin, Glenn, 250
Ojotas, 190, 266
O.K. Corral, 388
Old blue, 266
Old Glory Blowout, 43, 73, 314
Old woman, 266
Olive, Print (Isom Prentice), 266
O'Malley, D.J., 286
Omohundro, John Burwell, Jr. ("Texas Jack"),
        55, 266–267
Orejano, 267–268
Osgood, Ernest S., 268
Ostrich (rhea) hunt, 44, 114, 156–158, 259,
        273, 310
Otero, 268
Outlaw music, 175, 247
Outlaws, 386–390
        colloquial term for, 226
        documentary on, 136
        gauchos as, 235
Outriders, 221
Overholser, Wayne D., 237, 268, 313
Overo, 268
Oxbows, 268
Oxen, 39

Pack iron, 271
Páez, Ramón, 223–224
Palance, Jack, 126
Palomino, 187
Pampas, 38, 271–274
        Graham on, 164
        indigenous peoples of, 99–102, 155

latifundia on the, 219
        See also Gaucho
Pampas ostriches, 44, 114, 156–158, 259, 273, 310
Panela, 274
Paniolo, 96, 181–182, 220, 275–277, 329–330,
        346–347
Paredes, Americo, 251
Parker Ranch, 136, 275
Paso de la muerte, 67
Pato, 114, 276–277
Patrón, 277
Patten, Lewis Byford, 277
Patterson, Paul, 286–287
Paul, Woody, 312
Pawnee Bill. See Lillie, Gordon William
Payador, 102, 277–278
Pechando, 111–112
Peckinpah, Sam, 125, 132, 134, 368
Pecos Bill, 193
Pecos Rodeo, 314
Pecos War, 70
Pendleton rodeo, 315
Peon, 102, 278
Peregrine Smith Books, 233, 287, 355
Perrin, Jack, 130
Perryman, Lloyd, 278
Photojournalism, 238–239, 280–282
Pickens, Slim, 278
Pickett, Willie M. (Bill), 6, 8, 235, 259, 278–280, 322
Picking up contests, 112
Pigging string, 282
Pilgrim, 282
Pima, 202
Pingo. See Gaucho, horses and
Pinkerton National Detective Agency, 184, 354
Pistol, 282. See also Firearms
Pitchmen, 282–285
Pitz, Henry C., 282
Plains, 285–286. See also Llanos; Pampas
The Plainsman, 286
Plunder, 286
Poetry and poets, 41, 71, 233–234, 236, 240, 243,
        250, 286–287, 310, 355
        cowboy films and, 133
        gatherings, 287–288
        humor, 194–195
        See also Music
Poker, 151. See also Gambling
Poncho, 27, 190, 223, 288, 336, 383
Pony Express, 346, 411

Porter, Edwin S., 123
Porter, William Sydney, 288, 368
Portis, Charles McColl, 288
Postage stamps, 280
Practical jokes, 194
Prairie oysters. *See* Mountain oysters
Prairie wool, 288
Preacher, 78
Proddy, 289
Profanity, 194, 244–245, 251
Professional Rodeo Cowboys Association, 119, 316, 319, 320
Prorodeo Hall of Champions, 289, 319
Prostitution, 136, 289–291, 404
    colloquial terms, 42, 62, 161, 184, 356
    in literature, 19–20
Pull leather, 291
Pulp magazine, 29
Pulp novels, 17, 55, 72, 120–121, 217–218, 266, 292–294, 366
    Argentine gauchesco, 154
    B western plots, 25
    slick westerns, 354
    White Anglo biases, 253
    See also specific authors
Pulperías, 294, 349, 388–390
Pummill, Robert, 81
Punchy, 294

Quarantines, 360, 372, 373
Quarter horse, 186, 353
Querencia, 300
Quirt, 300, 334, 365

Racism, 97–104, 231, 253, 298–299
    in film, 131
    L'Amour and, 217
    Roosevelt and, 327
    in TV westerns, 368
    vaqueros and, 382
    See also Discrimination
Radio programs, 21, 245, 303, 312
Raider, 188, 303
Railheads, 303. *See also* Cowtowns
Raine, William Macleod, 303
Ramada, 303
Ramsey, Buck, 248
Ranching and ranch life, 29–40, 88, 303–305
    bunkhouses and, 54
    Chilean fundos and, 145–146, 191

cowboy historiography and, 180
documentaries on, 134–135, 241–242
dude ranches, 105–106, 331, 351
estancias, 44, 102, 114, 158, 160
fencing and, 30, 80, 95, 121–123, 161, 213, 221, 304, 339
haciendas, 171
Hawaiian, 136, 275
latifundia, 218–219
missions and, 382
spanish term for, 62
Venezuelan llanos, 149
wages in, 83, 393–394
windmills and, 121, 214, 400–401
women and, 403
    See also Cattle; Roundups; Trail drives
Ranching Heritage Association, 10
Range boss, 305
Range wars, 70, 286, 339, 360
Ranny, 305
Reagan, Ronald Wilson, 305–306, 367
Reata, 306
Reaugh, Frank, 228
Rebel, 188, 306
Rebenque, 300
Recado, 306, 347
Rector, Ray, 280
Red eye, 307
Red River, 124, 307, 395
"Reincarnation," 195, 233–234
Religion, 307–308
    colloquial term, 78
    Native Americans and, 68, 203
Religious missions, 160, 222, 381–382
Reloading outfit, 308
Remington, Frederic S., 13, 14, 52, 81, 228, 259, 282, 308–309, 327, 333, 336–337, 346, 384
Remington firearms, 137, 309–310
Remittance man, 36, 84, 310
Remuda, 310
Renaldo, Duncan, 368
Rep, 310, 334
Resero, 310
Rheas, 44, 114, 156–158, 259, 273, 310
Rhodes, Eugene Manlove, 15, 310–312
Richter, Conrad, 312
Ride for the brand, 97, 312
Ride the High Country, 125, 312
Riders in the Sky (group), 135, 246, 312–313, 355
"Riders in the Sky" (song), 246

"The Rifleman," 367–368
Ring Eye, 188, 313
Ringold, Clay, 313
Ringy, 313
Ritter, Maurice Woodward ("Tex"), 130, 188, 245, 259, 398
Roach, Ruth, 316
Robbins, Marty, 110, 245–246
Roberts, Wayne, 313
Roca, Julio A., 100–101
Rock hopper, 313
Rocky Mountain oysters. *See* Mountain oysters
Rodeo, 313–320
    African-American cowboys in, 6, 278–280, 322
    Autry and, 21–22
    blowing a stirrup, 43
    boots for, 46
    Calgary Stampede, 59–60
    cowboy unions and, 361–362
    crying room, 90
    documentary films, 134
    events, 315, 320–322, 331
    fashions, 119
    in film, 124, 234, 318
    groupies (buckle bunnies), 52
    in Hawaii, 275
    Mexican charreada, 66–68, 180, 334, 350
    Native Americans and, 204
    no time score in, 260
    photojournalism and, 239
    in poetry, 41, 287
    popular culture and, 318–319
    Prorodeo Hall of Champions and, 289
    saddle for, 16, 320
    women in, 22, 180–181, 316–318, 320, 403
Rodeo clown, 320, 321
Rodeo Hall of Fame, 259
Rodeo performers, 209–210
Rodgers, Jimmy, 245–246, 276
Rodman, Charmayne James, 317–318
Rodríguez, Molas Ricardo, 322
Rogers, Roy, 22, 78, 84, 130, 188, 245, 246, 251, 259, 283, 303, 318, 322–324, 374
Rogers, Will, 21, 192, 324–325
Rojas, Arnold, 325
Rollins, Philip Ashton, 325
Roosevelt, Buddy, 130
Roosevelt, Theodore, 14, 17, 77, 189, 252, 306, 308, 325–328, 382, 399, 401
Rope and roping, 53, 88, 93, 96, 218, 328–330

charro styles of, 67
Chilean styles of, 333
colloquial terms for, 62, 71, 77, 168, 213, 330, 362, 398
forefooting (mangana), 234
Hawaiian cowboys and, 276
heel, 176
home end, 183
horse hair, 171, 231, 329
Mother Hubbard loop, 238
rodeo events, 321–322
Spanish terms for, 219, 234, 306, 352
vaquero, 384
Rosas, Juan Manuel de, 102, 113, 153, 351
Rough neck, 331
Rough riders, 328
Roundups, 85, 304, 331–336
    and advertising, 284
    Brazilian vaqueiros and, 379
    in Canada, 34, 335–336
    chopper, 71
    documentaries on, 336
    gauchos and, 176
    huasos and, 190
    in Latin America, 331–334
    rodeo and, 313
    rules of etiquette and, 332
    Spanish terms for, 411
    tally man and, 366
    wagon boss and, 394
Rowel, 60, 336, 358, 394. *See also* Spurs
Roy Rogers and Dale Evans Museum, 324
Royal, 59, 61–62, 99
Royal Canadian Mounted Police, 36, 37
Ruana, 336
Ruckstull, Frederic, 308
Rush, 188, 336
Russell, Charles M., 13–14, 52, 81, 95, 126, 228, 259, 282, 336–337, 386
Russell, Jane, 406
Rustling, 64, 158, 184, 338–339, 386
Rutherford, Michael, 281
Ryan, Tom, 15, 81, 339

Saddle, 16, 343–348
    Cheyenne roll, 69
    choking the horn, 71
    collections, 259
    colloquial terms, 69, 89, 105, 195, 221, 261, 274, 282, 313, 407

Saddle *(continued)*
  full-rigged, 145
  gaucho, 306, 347
  Hawaiian, 346–347
  hornless, 240
  huaso, 347
  llaneros, 328, 347–348
  market trends, 119
  Plains Indian, 200
  for rodeo, 320
  Spanish terms for, 59, 145, 146, 234
  vaquero, 94, 343–344, 346
  for women, 163
  See also Tack
Saddle blanket, 348
Saddle bronc riding, 320
Saddle slicker, 348
Saint Elmo's fire, 145, 348
Saloons, 348–350, 386
  colloquial terms for, 41, 52
  gambling in, 150
  prostitution and, 289, 291
  pulperías, 294, 349, 388–390
  Spanish terms for, 62
Salsbury, Nate, 74
Salt horse, 350
Samper, José María, 224
Sand, 350
Sand Creek massacre, 69
Sandals, 10, 189, 266
Sandoz, Mari, 350
Santa Fe style, 119
Santa Gertrudis, 63, 214
Santee, Ross, 350–351
Sarmiento, Domingo Faustino, 27, 119, 149, 154,
    274, 278, 351
Saunders, George W., 19
Savage, 351
Savvy, 352
Scab herder, 352
Schaefer, Jack Warner, 294, 352, 353
Schreyvogel, Charles, 14
Scorcher, 352
Scott, Alexander Leslie, 352
Scott, Fred, 188
Scout, 26, 188, 352
Seago, 330, 352
The Searchers, 352, 395
Segundo, 353
Seltzer, Charles Alden, 353

Seltzer, Olaf Carl, 353
Serape, 383–384
Shane, 124–125, 352, 353
Shank, 353
Sharp, Joseph Henry, 81
Sharps rifle, 137
Shavetail, 353
Shawnee Trail, 372
Sheep, 39, 234, 407
Sheepherders, uncomplimentary terms for, 217,
    252, 352
Shelton, Ricky Van, 174
Shirreffs, Gordon Donald, 353
Short, Luke, 292, 353
Short Horse, 353
Shorthorn cattle, 30, 62
Shotgun, 137
Sicking, Georgie Connell, 255, 405
Sidekicks, 26
Silk, 353
Silver, 26, 188, 353
Silver, Nicholas, 353
Silver Bullet, 188
Silver King, 26, 188
Silverado, 126
Silverheels, Jay, 188, 353, 367
Singing cowboys, 21, 130, 245, 303, 395. *See also*
    Autry, Gene; Rogers, Roy
Single-action guns, 138
Sioux, 72, 204
Siringo, Charles Angelo, 16–17, 21, 314,
    354
Sitting Bull, 204, 265
Slatta, Richard, 259
Slaughtering, 32
Slavery, 160–161
Slick westerns, 354
Slicker, 354
Slow elk, 355
Slye, Len, 323
Smith, Gibbs M., 355
Smith and Wesson revolver, 138
Smoke pole, 356
Snappin' broncs, 356
Snow, Charles Horace, 356
Sodbuster, 356
Soft-horn, 356
Sombrero, 86, 171, 383
Son-of-a-bitch stew, 142, 356
Sons of the Pioneers, 245, 260, 323, 357

Sons of the San Joaquin, 247
Soogan, 356
Sourdough, 356
South African cowboy movies, 131
Spaghetti westerns, 109
Spanish horses, 186
Spencer, Tim, 357
Spurs, 60, 336, 353, 357–358
    charro, 67
    colloquial terms for, 97, 149, 161, 164, 165, 168,
        176, 312, 370
    gaucho, 155, 226, 347
    huaso, 190, 347
    jinglebobs on, 209, 357
    Spanish terms for, 114
    star rowel, 358
    sunburst, 362
    vaquero, 94
    wagon-spoke rowel, 394
Squeeze the biscuit, 358
Stabler, Ed, 248
Stagecoach, 123, 131, 358
Stanley, Clark, 249
Stanwyck, Barbara, 405
Star, Belle, 136
Star rowel spurs, 358
Stargazer, 358
Starrett, Charles, 188, 303, 358
Steagall, Red, 246–247
Steel, 358
Steele, Bob, 26, 130, 358
Steer wrestling, 322, 358
Stegner, Wallace, 61, 82, 95, 181, 239, 306, 358–359
Stern, Jane, 281
Stetson hats, 171–173
Stirrups, 43, 343
    colloquial term for, 268
    gauchos, 347
    llaneros, 348
    Spanish terms for, 114
Stockmen's association, 31, 334, 359–360
Stockmen's Memorial Foundation, 84–85, 360
Stogies, 361
Stove up, 361
Strait, George, 174
Strauss, Levi, 220
Strawberry roan, 361
Stray man, 361
Strikes, 359, 361–362, 393
String, 362

Stuart, Granville, 17
Stunt work, 129
Suicide gun, 362
Suitcase rancher, 362
Sunburst, 362
Sunfisher, 362
Superstitions, 223–224, 382
Supper, 362
Swamp seed, 362
Swampers, 362
Swarthout, Glendon, 362

Taba, 150, 365
Tack, 365
    bit, 40–41, 361, 365
    Californian vaqueros, 94
    cinch, 71, 93, 162
    collections, 259
    D-ring, 93
    market trends, 119
    Plains Indians, 200
    Spanish terms, 114, 123
    See also Saddle
Tailer, 365
Taliaferro, Hal, 365
Tall tales, 193–194, 361, 400
Tallow, 366
Tally man, 366
Taos Society of Artists, 81
Tapadero, 236
Tarzan, 26, 188, 366
Tasajo, 366
Taylor, Lonn, 281
Taylor, William Levi ("Buck"), 252, 366
Team roping, 67, 93, 322
Television, 131, 232, 323–324, 366–369, 411
    African-Americans in, 8
    cowboy-related advertising in, 284
    documentaries, 135
    and Zane Grey Western Theater, 166
Ten Commandments of the Cowboy, 21, 253
Ten gallon hat, 172
Tenderfoot, 369
Tennessee walking horse, 187
Texas butter, 369
Texas fever, 360, 369
Texas Jack's Wild West Show, 324
Texas leg, 369
Texas pride, 79, 371
Texas Rangers, 77, 103, 104

Thirty and found, 369
Thompson, Thomas, 370
Thomson, Fred, 26, 130, 188
Thorp, N. Howard (Jack), 249, 286
Tibbs, Casey, 289, 319
Tilghman, William Matthew, Jr., 79, 370
Tinker, Edward Larocque, 182, 370
Tinsley, Jim Bob, 251
Tirar al gallo, 111
Tobacco, 370
    colloquial terms for, 47, 139, 234, 288
Tomatoes, 228
Tombstone, Arizona, 370
Tonto, 26, 188, 209, 352, 353
Tony, 26, 129, 188, 371
Top hand, 371
Topeo, 371
Topper, 188, 371
Trabuco, 371
Trail boss, 371
Trail broke, 371
Trail drives, 29, 30, 80, 88–89, 162, 231, 286, 314,
        371–373
    autobiographical descriptions of, 18
    in cowboy art, 13
    documentaries on, 134
    in film, 124, 232
    gauchos and, 310, 373
    in music, 242
    primary sources, 177
    from Uruguay, 160
Travis, Randy, 174, 248
Trigger, 188, 324, 374
Trigueño, 374
Tritt, George Travis, 174–175
Tropero, 374
Truco, 149–150, 374
Tubb, Ernest, 245, 374
Tucson Bed, 374
Turner, Frederick Jackson, 103
Turtle, 374
Tuttle, Wilbur Coleman, 374
Twisthorn, 374
Twisting down, 374
Tyler, Tom, 130
Tyson, Ian, 82, 84, 135, 152, 234, 239, 243, 254,
        336, 374–375

Unforgiven, 109, 119, 127
Unionization, 361–362. See also Strikes

Urban Cowboy, 247
Uruguayan literature, 153
Utley, Robert, 259

Vaca, 379
Vamoose, 379
Vaqueiro (Brazilian cowboy), 161, 379–380
Vaquería, 38, 332, 380
Vaquero, 177, 254, 380–386
    advertising and, 283
    in art, 14
    attitudes towards strangers, 192
    bronc busters, 49
    Buffalo Bill's Wild West shows, 74
    chaps, 64, 96
    clothing and appearance, 383–384
    coffee preferences, 76
    Dana's description of, 93–94
    discrimination against, 103–104, 253
    documentary films about, 133, 134
    food preferences, 143
    footwear, 189
    gambling, 152
    Graham on, 165
    in Hawaii, 275
    historiography, 180, 181, 325
    horses and horsemanship, 94, 110–111, 114, 187,
        190, 385
    King Ranch and, 213, 219
    musical entertainment, 385
    in National Cowboy Hall of Fame, 259
    photographs of, 281
    ramada, 303
    regional employment patterns of, 5
    religion and, 307
    riding gear, 94
    rodeo and, 314
    roping styles, 329
    roundups, 333
    saddles, 343–344, 346
    spurs, 60, 357
    superstitions, 382
    wages, 384
    See also Paniolo
Venezuelan cowboys. See Llanero
Viana, Javier de, 153
Vigilantes, 339, 386
Villains, 26
Violence, 386–390
    in Canadian frontier, 61–62

Chisum and, 70
colloquial terms for, 105
equestrian games and, 112
fast draw, 120
in films, 132, 324
gauchos and, 388–390
Native Americans and, 202
notcher, 138, 260
plains regions, 286
in pulp novels, 292
racial, 104
saloons and, 349
in TV westerns, 368
vigilante, 339
See also Films; Firearms
The Virginian, 86, 130, 194, 368, 390, 401
Von Schmidt, Harold, 15

Waddie, 393
Wages, 83, 89, 393–394
for bronc busters, 49
thirty and found, 369
for vaqueros, 384
Wagon boss, 394
Wagon-spoke rowel, 394
Wagoner, Robert, 248
Wah-Maker, 119, 285
Wakely, Jimmy, 130, 245
Wales, Wally, 130
Walker, James, 14
Walters, Tom, 133
War bag, 394
War bonnet, 394
Ware, John, 99
Warren, Melvin, 81
Warting, 394
Wasp nest, 394
Watchtower, 236
Water hazards, 96
Watt, James G., 306
Wattle, 394
Watts, Peter Christopher, 394
Wayne, John, 109, 123, 124, 130, 131, 134, 217,
    259, 288, 394–396, 405–406
Wearing the bustle wrong, 396
Webb, Walter Prescott, 286
Wellman, Paul Iselin, 396
West, Mae, 405
Westermeier, Clifford P., 397
Western Heritage Research Library, 260

Western History Association, 397
Western music. *See* Music
Western Writers of America, Inc., 397–398
Westerners International, 398
WestFest, 241, 249
Weston, Dick, 398
Weston, Jack, 361–362
Wet stock, 398
Whale line, 398
Wheeler, Edward L., 6
Whips, 300, 334, 365
Whiskey, 348, 349
    colloquial terms for, 47, 53, 54, 77, 81, 168, 199,
        260, 271, 288, 307, 352, 353, 356, 366, 370,
        371, 399
    See also Alcoholic drinks
Whistle berries, 398
White, John Irwin, 250, 303
White Dust, 188
White Flash, 188, 398
White-collar rancher, 398
Wichita, Kansas, 80, 201
Widow-maker, 399
Wieghorst, Olaf, 15
Wild Bunch, 132, 399
Wild cattle hunting, 4, 38, 332, 380. *See also* Gaucho
Wild horse races, 322
Wild West shows, 40, 74, 133, 220–221, 235, 252,
    265, 266, 278, 315, 324, 366, 399
Wild, woolly, and full of fleas, 399
Williams, Hank, 245
Williams, Hank, Jr., 245
Wilson, Fox, 316
Wilson, Whip, 188
Winchester rifles, 136–137, 310, 399–400, 407, 411
Windies, 400
Windmills, 121, 214, 400–401
Winfield, Darrell, 401
Wipe, 401
Wister, Owen, 86, 194, 308, 368, 390, 401
Witch's bridle, 401
Witney, Dudley, 281
Wittliff, William D., 281
Wolf, Bernard, 281
Women, 253, 255, 401–405
    autobiographies of, 20
    Autry and, 21
    bronc busters, 50–51
    buckle bunnies, 52
    Californian, 93

Women *(continued)*
    Canadian cowboys and, 83–84
    in charreadas, 68
    country-western music performers, 175–176, 246,
        248
    cowboy chivalry, 83–84, 87
    cowboy historiography, 178, 180–181
    cowboy marriages, 89
    cowgirls as marketing icons, 283
    discrimination against, 103, 104
    documentary films on, 135, 136
    in film, 126, 405–407
    horses and, 193, 406
    Plains Indians, horses, and, 201
    pulp novels and, 294
    rodeo and, 22, 52, 180–181, 316–318, 320, 403
    side saddle for, 163
    in TV westerns, 368
    wearing the bustle wrong, 396
    See also Prostitution; *specific persons*

Woolsey, 407
Worcestershire, 407
Wrangler, 64, 407
Wyeth, Newell Convers, 15
Wynne, Brian, 407

Yaks, 411
Yannigan bag, 411
Yegua, 411
Yellow belly, 411
Yierra, 411
Yoakam, Dwight, 175
"Young Riders," 411
Youren, Jan, 318

Zane Grey Western Theater, 166
Zapata, Emiliano, 66, 385
Zebra dun, 411
Zebu, 62, 63